THE COMMUNITY LAND TRUST READER

THE COMMUNITY LAND TRUST READER

Edited by

John Emmeus Davis

LINCOLN INSTITUTE
OF LAND POLICY

Cambridge, Massachusetts

Library of Congress Cataloging-in-Publication Data

The community land trust reader / edited by John Emmeus Davis.
    p. cm.
 Includes bibliographical references and index.
 ISBN 978-1-55844-205-4
 1. Land trusts–United States.   2. Land trusts.   3. Land use, Urban–United States.
4. Community development–United States.   5. Housing development–United States.
I. Davis, John Emmeus, 1949–   II. Lincoln Institute of Land Policy.
 HD257.C65 2010
 333.2–dc22   2009034436

Designed by Peter Holm, Sterling Hill Productions
Cover and interior illustrations by Bonnie Acker. Used by permission.

Every effort has been made to locate copyright holders of all copyrighted materials and to
secure the necessary permission to reproduce them.

Composed in Adobe Garamond by Westchester Book Group in Danbury, Connecticut.
Printed by Puritan Press, Inc., in Hollis, New Hampshire. Bound by ACME Bookbinding
in Charlestown, Massachusetts. The paper is Rolland Enviro100, an acid-free, 100 percent
recycled sheet.

MANUFACTURED IN THE UNITED STATES OF AMERICA

CONTENTS

PART THREE   Definitions & Purposes

PART FOUR   Affordable Housing

PART FIVE   Beyond Housing

PREFACE

The community land trust (CLT) arrived quietly on the American scene in the late 1960s, an outgrowth of the civil rights movement in the Deep South. It was slow to spread. The cost of acquiring land was a formidable obstacle, as was the CLT model's novelty. In those early years, it was difficult to find funders or families who were comfortable with the notion of building and buying homes on land that was leased from a nonprofit organization controlled by a community larger than the leaseholders. Only half a dozen rural CLTs got started in the 1970s. Another 20, including the first urban CLTs, were organized in the 1980s. Then began a period of steady growth. By 1995, there were 100 CLTs in the United States. By 2005, there were over 200, with a dozen new ones being organized every year. Today, CLTs are operating in 45 states and the District of Columbia. They have begun appearing in other countries, as well; CLTs are underway or under development in Canada, England, Scotland, Australia, and Kenya. Once described as a "tentative, experimental model" with no assurance of survival,[1] CLTs are now firmly established and widely distributed. The model has become a movement.

Rapid growth has brought many newcomers to the CLT. They staff CLTs. They serve on CLT governing boards. They finance projects. They administer the programs of public agencies or private lenders that make possible the below-market pricing, affordable financing, and equitable taxation of CLT homes. Many of these new recruits are more technically proficient than the generation that preceded them. They bring with them an abundance of financial expertise, administrative skill, and development experience that was often in short supply among the social visionaries and community organizers who created the first CLTs.

What the newcomers generally lack, however, is a deeper understanding of the origins and evolution of the model to which they are so committed. Too few of them have heard of Henry George, Ebenezer Howard, Arthur Morgan, Ralph Borsodi, or Bob Swann (who also wrote as Robert Swann), whose ideas of property and community sowed the seeds for the modern-day CLT. Too few of them appreciate the intellectual debt that is owed to the founders of similar movements in other countries, where the long-term leasing of community-owned land was pioneered: the Garden City Movement in England, the Moshav Movement in Israel, and the Gramdan Movement in India. Fewer still are familiar with the lasting contributions of community organizers like Slater King, Charles Sherrod, Lucy Poulin, Marie Cirillo, and Chuck Matthei, who imbued the CLT with a passionate priority for serving people who had been excluded from the political and economic mainstream.

Does it really matter whether the present generation of CLT practitioners has little familiarity with individuals, innovations, and ideas that seeded the movement of which they are a part? I believe it does. As the number, size, and diversity of CLTs grow greater, the model is being pushed beyond the ideological, organizational, and operational boundaries that once defined it. The CLT is being adapted to a new set of problems. It is being carried to new places. It is being touted and supported by new champions, including a far-sighted vanguard of public officials who are asking CLTs to serve as the long-term steward for affordable housing, community facilities, and social enterprises established through the investment of public dollars or the exercise of public powers like inclusionary zoning.

With so many newcomers and so much variability, the former consensus on what it means to be a "community land trust" has become less certain. By cultivating a shared understanding of the model's origins, however, including the ideas and values underlying its many variations, we make it easier for distant CLTs to find a common identity; we make it easier for disparate CLTs to pursue a common agenda and for dispersed practitioners to find common cause in bringing this movement to scale.

At a time when much of the growth in the movement is being spurred by local government, it is especially important to be reminded of the model's core principles. When municipalities take the lead in starting a CLT, they are often tempted to sample selectively from organizational features of the "classic" CLT, preferring those that fit neatly into a municipality's existing programs. Some of the model's more participatory components, like inclusive membership and popular election of the governing board, may be stripped away. A wider knowledge of where this model came from—and *why* it was structured the way it was—may help CLT organizers to hold the line when well-meaning backers say, "We like this approach to landownership, we like this idea of retaining subsidies and preserving affordability, but do you really need to have leaseholders on the board? Do you really need a voting membership? Does a CLT have to include community?"

Conversely, a wider knowledge of the model's origins may help us to let go of features that no longer serve the model's purposes or constituencies. There will always be well-meaning advocates who warn against any deviation from the model they have known, forgetting that the CLT has been a malleable model from the beginning. Many CLT features that are considered classic today were once cheeky variations on a standard theme inherited from a previous generation. The CLT has been reinvented repeatedly over the years, adapting to new audiences, conditions, and applications. Such flexibility has been a perennial source of renewal and vigor, helping the CLT to spread far and wide. A deeper appreciation for the model's evolution may encourage today's practitioners to continue the experimentation that gave rise to the model in the first place. Understanding the CLT's past may help in securing its future.

The materials collected in this volume are not only about the past, however. They are also about a modern-day model of private, nonmarket ownership that is fighting for acceptance on a national stage where better-known tenures historically favored by the market and state are the featured players. These materials are about a contemporary movement that is still finding its way, both here and abroad. Thus, while there is lots of history to be found in *The Community Land Trust Reader*, including retrospective portraits of thinkers, prophets, and pioneers who shaped the CLT, there are just as many snapshots of current and coming events.

Much of the *Reader* is made up of reflections on the present state of the CLT. Described in the sections entitled "Affordable Housing" and "Beyond Housing" are various ways the model is now being applied—or could be applied—to promote economic equality, enhance residential security, and improve the quality of life in both urban and rural communities. Described in the section entitled "Beyond the United States" are various ways the model is now being adapted—or could be adapted—to conditions in other parts of the world. In England, for example, a robust CLT movement is already underway, with some two dozen CLTs up and running. In Australia, by contrast, the country's first CLTs are just getting started. Meanwhile, in Scotland, Mexico, and several other countries with large-scale land reform movements, there is fertile ground for CLT development, even if the seeds have yet to be planted. Most of these foreign adaptations of the CLT are in their infancy and some may never mature, but all are worth watching. Every time the CLT has spread to another region of the United States, there has been a burst of new ideas and new techniques that have enriched the movement as a whole. The same is sure to happen as the CLT spreads to other countries.

The *Reader*'s final section is entitled "Beyond the Horizon." Described here are trends, challenges, and opportunities that are likely to have a significant impact on limiting or expanding the CLT movement in the years ahead. Only the essay that examines the trajectory of municipal support, "The City–CLT Partnership," is focused directly on the model. The rest take a broader perspective, showcasing current debates about promoting homeownership, mandating stewardship, and capturing land gains for the common good. These issues are not unique to the CLT, although they have special relevance for the everyday practice of CLTs. They stake out the expansive intellectual and political space within which the movement as a whole may find room to grow.

The origins of this book can be traced to the National Community Land Trust Academy. Founded in 2006 as a joint venture of the National CLT Network and the Lincoln Institute of Land Policy, the Academy provides comprehensive training on theories and practices unique to CLTs. Many of the essays and excerpts contained in this collection have been regularly assigned as required readings in Academy courses. Until now, they have been distributed piecemeal as hard-copy handouts or as digital downloads. By bringing them together in a single volume, these materials can be made more accessible for classroom use. They can also be made more available for practitioners, public officials, and community activists who may never have the chance to attend an Academy training in person.

Because the CLT remains a work in progress, any collection like this one must necessarily be seen as a work in progress as well. Included in this volume are seminal texts by the movement's founders that will forever be essential reading for anyone interested in the CLT, but there are also a number of contemporary essays, some prepared expressly for this volume, that contain conclusions and predictions that may be far less enduring. They may be outstripped by a movement that is growing in diversity and gaining in strength. One measure of the CLT's future success, in fact, may be the speed with which much of this *Reader* goes out of date. If the best days for the CLT still lie ahead, the best writing about the CLT is still to be done.

NOTE

1. International Independence Institute. *The Community Land Trust: A Guide to a New Model for Land Tenure in America*. Cambridge, MA: Center for Community Economic Development, 1972.

ACKNOWLEDGMENTS

This collection of writings about community land trusts would not have been possible without the early encouragement and unwavering support of Roz Greenstein, former chair of the Economic and Community Development Department at the Lincoln Institute of Land Policy. Credit is also due to the Lincoln Institute's Emily McKeigue, who expertly and patiently managed the process of getting an unruly stack of paper ready for publication, and to Courtney Knapp, who doggedly pursued an elusive gaggle of authors and publishers for permission to include the many essays and excerpts that appear herein, some of which have long been out of print. Lastly, I must thank my colleagues at Burlington Associates in Community Development for challenging my comfortable assumptions about CLTs, for improving my professional practice, and for tolerating my frequent lapses in billing.

This book is dedicated to Acadia Worth Davis, who reminds me every day that the best things in life are perpetually affordable.

PART ONE

PRECURSORS

Origins and Evolution of the Community Land Trust in the United States

John Emmeus Davis
(2010)

The community land trust (CLT), both the model and the movement, was a long time coming. The organization generally credited with being the first attempt to create a CLT, New Communities, Inc., was founded in 1969. Ten years later, only a handful of CLTs were operational in the United States, all of them in remote rural areas. Another 20 years passed before the number, variety, and dispersion of CLTs reached the point where it was fair to speak of a CLT "movement," although the model's proponents had been brazenly using that term since the early 1980s. Today, there are over 240 CLTs in 45 states and the District of Columbia, and the model has begun spreading to other countries.

As long as it took for the model to become a movement, it took even longer for the CLT itself to become the model we know today. New Communities, Inc., did not suddenly sprout newly green and fully formed from the red clay of southwest Georgia without antecedent. It was deeply rooted in a fertile seedbed of theoretical ideas, political movements, and social experiments that had been laid down over a span of many decades. Even after the appearance of New Communities, moreover, this fragile shoot still required years of cultivation and hybridization before it was ready for wider adoption.

When laying out the story of the model's origins and evolution, it is convenient to group the distinguishing features of the CLT by ownership, organization, and operation—three clusters of characteristics that appeared at different times, each shaped by a different set of influences. The reality was much messier, of course, with ideas often leapfrogging the narrative boundaries between eras. History seldom unfolds as neatly in the living as it does in the telling.

Ownership: In Land We Trust

In the history of the community land trust, ownership came first. The CLT's unique form of tenure appeared in theory and practice long before "community" was grafted onto the model's organizational stem and long before "trust" was given the operational

---

This chapter was written for this volume.

meaning it has today. The search for the model's origins must begin, therefore, with its unusual approach to the ownership of land and buildings.

A CLT structures ownership in several distinctive ways:

- Land is treated as a common heritage, not as an individual possession. Title to multiple parcels is held by a single nonprofit owner that manages these lands on behalf of a particular community, present and future.
- Land is removed permanently from the market, never resold by the nonprofit owner. Land is put to use, however, by leasing out individual parcels for the construction of housing, the production of food, the development of commercial enterprises, or the promotion of other activities that support individual livelihood or community life.
- All structural improvements are owned separately from the land, with title to these buildings held by individual homeowners, business owners, housing cooperatives, or the owners of any other buildings located on leased land.
- A ground lease lasting many years gives the owners of these structural improvements the exclusive use of the land beneath their buildings, securing their individual interests while protecting the interests of the larger community.

This is hardly the way real estate is typically owned and managed in the United States. Instead of seeing land as part of a shared human heritage that should be shepherded and used for the common good, land is typically treated as individual property, chopped up into parcels that are bought and sold to the highest bidder. It is deemed to be our god-given right to accumulate as much of it as we can. If we're lucky and shrewd, we can beat everybody to prime parcels that are most likely to rise in value as a town expands, as a school is built, as a factory is sited, as a road or subway is extended. So rampant, so accepted, so deeply embedded in our national culture has been this notion of the individual's inalienable right to gather to himself all the land he can grab, enriching himself in the process, that Thorstein Veblen, a nineteenth-century economist, suggested that speculation, not baseball, should be seen as our true national pastime. He dubbed land speculation the "Great American Game."[1]

Side by side with this ethic of speculation, however, there has persisted another tradition in the United States—less obvious, less dominant, but just as old. This is an ethic of stewardship, in which land is treated as a common heritage: encouraging ownership only by those who are willing to live on the land and to use the land, not accumulating more than they need; emphasizing right use and smart development; capturing socially created gains in the value of land for the common good. This tradition of stewardship is precolonial, extending back to Native American attitudes and the New England custom of the town commons. It also survived in the thinking of people like Thomas Paine, Thomas Jefferson, and Abraham Lincoln.[2]

The American writer and politician who took this alternative conception of land the farthest was Henry George. Since the intellectual origins of the CLT begin with

George, it is useful to linger here a moment, heeding his condemnation of the ethic and evils of speculation.

The Georgist Critique

During his lifetime, Henry George was one of the most popular and influential public figures in the United States. He was also well known outside the United States. The only living Americans more famous than George in the rest of world at the time were Mark Twain and Thomas Edison, especially in those countries once parochially known as the "English-speaking world." But fame can be fleeting, especially for someone like George, who proposed to change radically the rules of the Great American Game. Not many people have even heard of Henry George today.

His was a classic rags-to-riches American success story. Born in Philadelphia in 1839, George went to work as an office boy at 13 years of age and ran away to sea at the age of 16. He eventually landed in San Francisco, where he found employment at a local newspaper. He worked his way up from printer to reporter, to editor, and, eventually, to becoming the newspaper's owner. He was entirely self educated. Reading widely, he encountered the work of the English political theorist John Stuart Mill. He was taken, in particular, with Mill's concept of the "social increment," an economic theory that asserts that most of the appreciating value of land is created not by the investment or labor of individual landowners, but by the growth and development of the surrounding society.

George asked himself a provocative question: Why is there immense poverty amid so much wealth, poverty that occurs despite social and technological progress? The answer he proposed, in a book published in 1879, entitled *Progress and Poverty,* was very different from the one provided by Karl Marx, who had wrestled with a similar question in *Das Kapital,* published 12 years earlier. Marx's answer had been that poverty of the masses is caused by ownership of the means of production by a small cadre of capitalists who are able to capture for themselves most of the value created by labor. George, by contrast, saw poverty as resulting from the ownership of land by a small cadre of landowners who are able to capture for themselves the appreciating value of land—i.e., real estate values that are created, as John Stuart Mill suggested, by the growth and development of society.

Landlords, in George's eyes, are little more than parasites, feeding off the productivity of others. Whenever there is economic progress—new technologies, higher wages, higher profits—landowners simply raise their rents or the selling price of their real estate holdings. This is, in George's words, "an invisible tax on enterprise," collected by those who contribute nothing themselves to increased productivity. Landlordism is a bane for capital and labor alike.

An obvious remedy for this sorry state of affairs would be for government to nationalize the land. But George was too much of a political realist—and too much an admirer of the Jeffersonian ideal of small-scale landholding—to propose such a radical solution. Instead, he proposed a single tax: Have government tax away the social increment, collecting for the benefit of the larger public all of the land gains that society itself has created. By George's calculation, this tax on the appreciating value of land would be sufficient to cover all of a government's costs of providing infrastructure, schools, and other public services. This would allow the elimination of all other taxes on profits, wages, and structural improvements. A single tax would do it all.[3]

Progress and Poverty sold over three million copies during George's lifetime, an astronomical figure for his day. It was followed by a steady stream of books and pamphlets in which George repeated and refined the ideas introduced in his 1879 book. His published works and public speeches brought him wide fame and a large following, spawning an international "single-tax movement." Single-tax clubs sprang up across the United States and throughout Europe, dedicated to promoting George's ideas.

George's fame was spread abroad not only through the publication and translation of *Progress and Poverty* and other works, but also by the presence of George himself. He made six trips outside the United States between 1881 and 1890. On his first trip across the Atlantic, soon after disembarking in Ireland, he made an inflammatory speech about land reform and was thrown into jail. This turned out to be wonderful publicity for his next stop, which was London. He filled lecture halls. George Bernard Shaw was among the London notables attending an early lecture by Henry George, and he became an instant convert. So did a quiet young man named Ebenezer Howard, who was to propose a new solution for the Georgist critique.

Planned Communities on Leased Land

Like George, Ebenezer Howard had little formal schooling. Instead of running away to sea, Howard had pursued an equally audacious adventure. At the age of 21, he had sailed from England to America with two friends, planning to become a homesteader in Nebraska. He soon discovered that he had no talent for farming, however, and moved to Chicago. He spent five years there, earning his living as a court reporter. He was also employed on occasion as a newspaper reporter.

Howard returned to England in 1876 and joined a firm producing parliamentary reports. This was bread labor, however. His real work, his true vocation, was studying and thinking about the dreadful condition of England's cities. Like George, he was a self learner, reading everything he could find. One of the books that made the greatest impression on him was *Progress and Poverty*, an influence that was reinforced when he heard George lecture in London.

In 1898, Howard published *To-Morrow: A Peaceful Path to Real Reform*, a book that was later reissued and retitled *Garden Cities of To-Morrow*.[4] The sweeping solution that Howard proposed for the crowding and chaos of urban areas was the creation of planned communities of 32,000 people ringing major cities and combining the best features of town and country. Inspired by George, he proposed that these Garden Cities be developed on land that was leased from a municipal corporation, where "men of probity" would serve as the "trustees" for this municipally owned land. Like

George, he wanted to capture the social increment for public improvement, not private enrichment. Unlike George, his mechanism was not the single tax but municipal ownership. Eventually, 32 Garden Cities were developed in England, starting with Letchworth in 1903 and Welwyn in 1909.

Meanwhile, back in the United States, other followers of Henry George were busy developing Garden Cities of their own. Structured similarly to Letchworth and Welwyn, these so-called single-tax colonies were based on community ownership of the land and individual ownership of the improvements. Two of the earliest of these colonies were created in Arden, Delaware, and Fairhope, Alabama on the Gulf Coast. Founded in the early 1900s, these leased-land communities have survived to today.

A whole new crop of intentional communities sprang up in the 1930s and 1940s, inspired by another follower of Henry George, Ralph Borsodi. It was Borsodi who first described these leased-land communities as "land trusts." Borsodi was born in 1886, the son of a New York City publisher who was an ardent follower of Henry George. Borsodi was home-schooled by his father, an education supplemented by his own extensive readings. He never attended college, although the University of New Hampshire later awarded him an honorary doctorate, recognizing the accomplishments of a self-educated social theorist who produced 13 books and 10 research studies during a long, productive life. In 1928, Borsodi published his first book, in which he decried land speculation and landlordism along lines similar to George's. He went further than George, however, in saying that land should never be individually owned. Only structural improvements should be treated as property. Land should be treated as a "trust." Indeed, throughout his varied career as a writer, teacher, homesteader, and social philosopher, Borsodi insisted on calling land "trusterty," not property.[5]

In 1936, amid the Great Depression, Borsodi moved to Suffern, New York, 36 miles north of New York City, and founded a community that he named the School of Living. Eventually, 30 families settled there, occupying separate homesteads around a folk school where workshops on adult education, gardening, and home production were held on a continual basis. Borsodi initiated a group title for the land, with individual homesteaders paying an annual lease fee for the use of their parcels.

Borsodi's writings and the example of the School of Living inspired a number of other experiments in community landholding. For the next 10 years, a steady stream of educators, authors, and back-to-the-landers beat a well-worn path to Suffern to learn about rural homesteading and land leasing.[6] One of the most successful of the leased-land communities modeled on Borsodi's blueprint was Bryn Gweled, started by a group of Quakers in 1940 after visiting the School of Living.[7] This "intentionally diverse community," as it describes itself today, was located on a 240-acre tract a few miles outside of Philadelphia. Ownership of the land was vested in a nonprofit corporation. Over 80 leaseholds were plotted, on which families could build houses, to which they held individual title. Bryn Gweled's ground lease was later included in the first book about community land trusts, published in 1972.

Two other influential experiments in community landholding were established during the period before World War II, one in Tennessee and the other in North Carolina. Arthur E. Morgan was the godfather of both. Morgan was born in 1878 near Cincinnati, but his family moved soon after his birth to St. Cloud, Minnesota, where Morgan was raised. His father was a self-taught engineer. Upon graduating from high school, Morgan found employment cutting timber in Colorado. Later, while working in a series of Colorado mines, he developed an interest in hydraulic engineering. Returning to Minnesota in 1900 to work with his father, he learned engineering from the ground up. He developed a special interest in dams and eventually traveled to Europe to investigate dam construction techniques on the other side of the Atlantic. He was in England soon after the first Garden City was founded, at Letchworth. He may have encountered Howard's ideas during this trip; there is no way of knowing for sure. Morgan never acknowledged his intellectual debt to Howard, even though many of the latter's proposals for the municipal ownership of land, cooperative ownership of community enterprises, and the development of planned communities through individual leaseholds were later incorporated into both of the leased-land communities that Morgan initiated in the 1930s.

In 1913, Morgan was hired by Dayton, Ohio, to build five dams after a flood had devastated the city. Winning local fame as a man of action and ideas who was also an able administrator, he came to the attention of Antioch College, a dying institution located 18 miles east of Dayton.[8] Elected to the board of trustees, he was later appointed president of the college. During his 15-year presidency, Morgan instituted what came to be famously known as the Antioch Plan, according to which the college's students were required to do four hours of local work for every four hours spent in the classroom.[9] He also published numerous articles about progressive education, community development, and new towns in popular periodicals like *The Atlantic Monthly*.

Morgan came to the attention of President Franklin Roosevelt, who was looking for someone to lead the newly created Tennessee Valley Authority (TVA). In 1933, he was appointed by Roosevelt as one of TVA's three cochairmen, but his tenure in that position was stormy and short-lived. After three years, he was dismissed by FDR. While still at the helm of TVA, however, Morgan seized the opportunity to realize his vision of the ideal community. He oversaw the construction of Norris, Tennessee, a planned community to house the workers who were building TVA's first dam, to control flooding and generate electricity. The land at Norris was owned by TVA and leased for residential and commercial development. No worker paid more than 25 percent of his salary for housing. The town's businesses were operated as nonprofit cooperatives located on land that was leased from TVA.[10]

Soon after his tenure at TVA, Morgan made a second effort to establish a planned community on leased land. He had been approached by a wealthy textile manufacturer from Chicago who offered to bankroll one or more of Morgan's utopian ideas for social improvement. In 1938, Morgan sent his son, Griscom, to western North

Carolina to look for land. Using money from the Chicago donor, he was able to purchase 1,200 acres in a mountain valley about 40 miles north of Asheville. Recruiting several other "men of probity," as Ebenezer Howard had called them, to serve on the board of directors, Morgan formed a nonprofit corporation to develop a leased-land community that he named Celo. In addition to houses and farming and a few cooperative enterprises, Celo developed a boarding school based on Morgan's ideas of progressive education. Both the community and the school exist today, still organized along lines laid down by Morgan 70 years ago.

Outside of the United States, land leasing gained a significant foothold in another country during the first half of the twentieth century.[11] Inspired by the theories of Henry George, the Jewish National Fund (JNF) began acquiring land in Palestine in 1901. The JNF executed 99-year leases for the use of its land. Its principal beneficiaries were cooperative agricultural communities, kibbutzim and moshim, developed on lands that were leased from the JNF. In 1967, when civil rights activists in the American South began exploring options for creating the first CLT in the United States, they looked to these agricultural communities for practical lessons, traveling to Israel to learn more about the mechanics of mixed ownership and long-term land leasing.

Organization: Putting the "C" in CLT

In all of these leasehold communities, including the Garden Cities in England, the single-tax communities in the United States, the agricultural cooperatives in Palestine, and the intentional communities at the School of Living and Bryn Gweled, there was common ownership of land, individual ownership of the buildings, and a long-term ground lease tying the interests of the parties together. These were planned communities on leased land. They were land trusts. They were not *community* land trusts, however, as that term is understood today.

Bryn Gweled was typical in this regard. All of the houses at Bryn Gweled were located on land that was leased from a nonprofit corporation. The nonprofit was governed by homeowners living on the corporation's land, but no one living outside of the community had a voice in running Bryn Gweled. There was neither a larger membership nor outside directors. It was an intentional community, an enclave of like-minded people. It was not a "community land trust," lacking as it did (and still does) most of the organizational and operational elements that define the contemporary CLT.[12]

What are the organizational characteristics that allow us to call a leased-land arrangement a community land trust? There are three:

- The landowner is a private, nonprofit corporation with a corporate membership that is open to anyone living within the CLT's geographically defined "community."[13]

- A majority of the governing board is elected by the CLT's membership.
- There is a balance of interests on the governing board, where seats are allocated equally among directors representing the CLT's leaseholders, directors representing residents from the CLT's service area who are not CLT leaseholders, and directors representing the public interest.

The person most responsible for putting the "C" in CLT was Bob Swann. It was Swann, working in partnership with Slater King, a cousin of Martin Luther King Jr., who was to modify the model pioneered by Ralph Borsodi and Arthur Morgan, adding organizational components that eventually made community a defining feature of the CLT. What the models of Borsodi and Morgan had lacked, according to Swann, was "broad participation by the town or community." Swann supplied this missing piece. In his words, "The practice I added was open membership in the corporation bylaws to all people living in the region. This was my major contribution."[14] This was, in truth, not his only contribution to the model's evolution, but it was the only one he ever claimed for himself.

Education of a CLT Pioneer

As a young man, Swann came under the influence of Bayard Rustin, then serving as youth secretary for the Fellowship of Reconciliation. Guided by Rustin and inspired by the published writings and personal example of Mahatma Gandhi, Swann made a fateful decision while an undergraduate at the University of Ohio. He would resist induction into the armed forces. This was just before America's entry into World War II. He was sentenced to five years in prison and, in 1942, entered the federal penitentiary in Ashland, Kentucky. He was soon joined there by his mentor, Bayard Rustin, along with 40 other conscientious objectors.[15]

As Susan Witt, Swann's second wife, was later to say in Swann's obituary, prison was Bob's "university and his monastery."[16] He was introduced there to many of the ideas that shaped the rest of his life. He was exposed for the first time to the writings of Lewis Mumford, Jane Jacobs, and Ralph Borsodi. All proved influential in his later thinking. But the book that impressed him the most he discovered in a correspondence course on community development that he and the other conscientious objectors took while serving out their time in the Ashland penitentiary. The book was *The Small Community*. It had been written by Arthur E. Morgan, the same man who had designed the course.

After leaving the Tennessee Valley Authority, Morgan had returned to Yellow Springs, Ohio. Two years later, in 1940, he founded Community Service, Inc., (CSI) as a vehicle for spreading his ideas about community development and small-scale, locally controlled enterprises. Among many other initiatives, CSI developed the correspondence course on the small community that reached Swann in prison. Beginning in 1943, CSI also published a nationally distributed newsletter that was mostly a showcase for Morgan's essays and experiments promoting small-scale community enterprise. It later featured many articles about CLTs.[17]

Swann was so impressed by Morgan's ideas that he wrote to him while still in prison, asking for work. Morgan offered him a job with Community Service, Inc. Released from Ashville in 1944, Swann moved his family to Yellow Springs. His wife, Marjorie Swann, a civil rights activist who had been actively involved with the Congress of Racial Equality (CORE) in Chicago, also found work at CSI. Soon after their move to Yellow Springs, she resumed her involvement with civil rights.

Bob Swann quickly realized that the job promised by Morgan was office work, which he was not interested in doing. He resigned from CSI and began building houses, the start of many years earning his living as an itinerant carpenter and house designer. After only a year in Yellow Springs, he and Marjorie moved with their three daughters to Kalamazoo and then to Chicago. This was followed by yet another move to the Philadelphia area, where Bob was employed by Stanley Millgram, building houses in racially integrated communities. During this period, the Swann family resided near Bryn Gweled and had several friends who lived there.[18]

In 1960, the family finally settled in Voluntown, Connecticut, where Swann and his wife worked full time as leaders and organizers for the Committee on Nonviolent Action (CNVA). They focused in the beginning on issues of war and peace: organizing teach-ins, marches, and direct action protesting the arms race with Russia, the quarantine of Cuba, and the escalating war in Vietnam. They were also drawn into doing support work for the southern civil rights movement.

The Southern Crucible

Bob Swann went south for the first time in 1963 to help rebuild black churches that had been firebombed by southern racists. His carpentry skills, honed over many years of building, designing, and supervising the construction of houses, large and small, were put to good use. He was to earn credibility and make connections among African American activists in the southern civil rights movement, not by making speeches but by pounding nails.

Soon after coming south, Swann was introduced to Slater King. Out of their partnership was to emerge the prototype for a new model of land tenure, known today as the community land trust. There were other influences on Swann's conception of the CLT, as well, including his previous exposure to the leased-land experiments at Bryn Gweled and Celo, his developing interest in the Gramdan Movement in India, and his close relationship with Ralph Borsodi and Clarence Jordan, the founder of Koinonia Farm. None of these influences did as much to affect Swann's thinking about the place of community in alternative institutions of property, however, as his association with the southern civil rights movement in general and with Slater King in particular.

Slater King was the owner of a successful real estate and insurance brokerage firm in Albany, Georgia. His brother, C. B. King, was a local attorney. Like their cousin,

Martin Luther King, both brothers were deeply involved in the civil rights struggle. They had helped to found the Albany Movement in 1961. Slater had served as the organization's first vice president and was elected its president one year later.

The Albany Movement was the first mass movement in the modern civil rights era to have as its goal the desegregation of an entire community. The white city council of Albany vowed that would never happen. Repeated attempts by the city's African American community to desegregate the bus station, the library, city parks, and other public facilities were stubbornly resisted. This was sometimes done quietly: The public library was closed rather than allow blacks to check out books; nets were cut off the tennis courts in the public parks rather than allow integrated teams to play. More often, the white establishment's resistance was strident and brutal. Protest marches organized by the Albany Movement resulted in mass jailings. On the orders of the city council, the police force of Sheriff Laurie Pritchard arrested every protester in sight, including Martin Luther King and Ralph Abernathy, who had been invited to town by MLK's cousins. Both men were jailed there three times in 1961 and 1962, along with more than a thousand other African Americans. When Albany's jails overflowed, hundreds of the protesters were sent to jails in the surrounding counties, where racist rural deputies were more likely to abuse black inmates. Slater King's own wife, Marion, was slapped, knocked to the ground, and kicked in the stomach by two policemen when she brought food and supplies to civil rights protesters in the Mitchell County jail. She was six months pregnant at the time. She lost the child.[19]

Martin Luther King came to consider the Albany Movement a failure because segregation had not been overturned by the time he moved on to Birmingham at the end of 1962. Albany's African American leaders disagreed. The Albany Movement, under Slater King's leadership, continued its efforts to register black voters and to integrate public schools. The Student Nonviolent Coordinating Committee (SNCC) and the Southwest Georgia Project, under the leadership of Charles Sherrod, continued to organize protest actions in Albany and in nearby Americus and Moultrie.

Slater King and Bob Swann met by accident. Before coming south in 1963, Swann had helped to organize the Quebec-Washington-Guantanamo Walk for Peace. This 1,000-mile peace march reached Georgia at the same time that Swann was in Mississippi rebuilding one of the state's firebombed churches. As the peace march moved farther south, feeder walks swelled its ranks, adding civil rights concerns to the march's original antiwar focus. When the march reached Albany, the city council refused to allow the integrated group to march on the main street. On their second attempt to walk through the downtown, Bradford Lyttle, Barbara Deming, and 20 other protesters were arrested by Sheriff Pritchard, the old nemesis of the Albany Movement. The protesters stayed in jail for nearly two months.

Bob Swann traveled to Albany during this period to organize support for his jailed friends. Since the Albany jail now held demonstrators from the Quebec-Washington-Guantanamo Walk for Peace, as well as local civil rights activists from southwest Georgia who had joined the march en route, Swann went to see C. B. King, the town's most experienced civil rights attorney, to ask what might be done to help the activists who were languishing in jail.[20] Soon after that meeting, Swann was introduced to King's brother, Slater.

Aside from a mutual desire to get their associates out of jail, Slater King and Bob Swann discovered they had much in common. Both men had spent several years organizing nonviolent protests, Swann as a peace activist, King as a civil rights activist. By the time of their initial meeting in 1964, both had begun to shift the focus of their thinking and activism, asking themselves, "What comes next?" Both were looking for ways to move beyond the "protest movement" to what Gandhi had called the "constructive movement." They had both reached the point in their lives where they were grappling with questions like "how are the gains of struggle to be secured? how is a new society to be built within the shell of the old?"

A meeting of minds was not the only basis for the unlikely alliance that was quickly forged between this white pacifist from the far North and this black civil rights activist from the Deep South, for this was not the first time that the paths of the Swann and King families had intersected. Twenty years before, while living in Yellow Springs, Swann's wife had been actively involved with a local affiliate of CORE. Marjorie Swann had befriended another civil rights activist, an Antioch student who was majoring in music and education. The two women became lifelong friends. On occasion, when the Swanns wanted a night off, they hired Marjorie's young friend as a babysitter for their three daughters. The babysitter's name was Coretta Scott. She later married a young reverend from Atlanta whose zeal for the civil rights struggle matched her own: Martin Luther King Jr.

A Vision of Constructive Change: Koinonia and Gramdan

As Bob Swann and Slater King were beginning what became a five-year conversation about land reform and economic self-sufficiency for African Americans, there was a place only 30 miles from Albany where a "constructive" program was already underway: Koinonia Farm. Founded in 1942 by Clarence Jordan, Koinonia was one of the few communities in the Deep South where black families and white families were actively living, working, and praying together, modeling the integrated society they wanted to see. Because of the racial mixing at Koinonia and because of Jordan's publicly declared views on racial equality, he and Koinonia's other residents had been excommunicated from the Rehoboth Baptist Church in 1950. Six years later, when Koinonia established an interracial summer camp, racist storeowners, wholesalers, and processors refused to do business with Koinonia and began boycotting Koinonia's agricultural products. This boycott continued into the late 1960s. The Ku Klux Klan pursued a more violent path, firing guns into Koinonia's buildings and threatening increased violence unless Jordan agreed to sell the farm. He refused.

Bob and Marjorie Swann visited Koinonia a number of times between 1964 and 1967. Dorothy Day, Wally and Juanita Nelson, and other noted American pacifists and civil rights activists were frequent visitors, as well. After personally witnessing the sustained economic pressure and scattered violence the community was forced to endure, several of these visitors established Friends of Koinonia. This national support network raised money for Koinonia and organized the sale of the farm's pecans and other agricultural products outside of the South in the face of the ongoing boycott by local businesses. Bob Swann served as the national chairman of Friends of Koinonia until 1968.

Koinonia provided Swann with a compelling vision of a cooperative agricultural community that was created, in part, to promote economic self-sufficiency for lower-income people, a community supported by a larger network of sympathizers and supporters. Koinonia was clearly a source of inspiration for New Communities, as Swann and Slater King began laying plans for an agricultural community on leased land. Incidentally, during one of his visits to Koinonia, Swann was apparently on hand when Clarence Jordan and Millard Fuller began discussing the possibility of creating a self-help housing program for low-income people.[21] Koinonia Partners was founded by Fuller as a separate nonprofit to undertake this project, an organization that eventually evolved into Habitat for Humanity.[22]

Swann formed another important partnership during this period. In 1966, a mutual friend introduced him to Ralph Borsodi, who had just returned to the United States after four years abroad, teaching economics in India. Swann was familiar with Borsodi's writings, which he had read in prison, and he had often visited Bryn Gweled, the leased-land community inspired by Borsodi's School of Living. When Swann and Borsodi finally met, they formed an immediate attachment.

One of the things they had in common was a keen interest in the work of Vinoba Bhave, who was doing something similar to what Borsodi had tried to achieve at the School of Living and that Swann had seen in practice at Bryn Gweled. But Vinoba Bhave was doing it on a massive scale and adding organizational elements that had been missing in Borsodi's model.

After Gandhi was assassinated in 1948, political leadership of his movement fell to Jawaharlal Nehru. Spiritual leadership fell to Vinoba Bhave. Gandhi's "constructive program" had envisioned a decentralized society based on autonomous, self-reliant villages. His concept of "trusteeship" asserted that land and other assets should be held in trust for the poor. Vinoba Bhave inherited Gandhi's concern for the plight of the rural poor, especially the so-called untouchables. He began walking across India, asking rich landowners to donate a portion of their land to the poor. To his surprise, hundreds of landowners generously responded. The "Land Gift" movement—the Boodan Movement—was born. At its height, Bhave and his followers were collecting 1,000–3,000 acres a day. By 1954, 3 million acres had been distributed to the poor, and Bhave was being hailed as the "Walking Saint of India."

But poor peasants had a hard time hanging on to the small plots they were given. Much of their land was quickly lost to moneylenders and speculators. Seeing this, Vinoba Bhave transformed the Land Gift program into a "Village Gift" program; the *Boodan* Movement became the *Gramdan* Movement. Bhave now insisted that any gifts of land must be donated to entire villages, not to impoverished individuals. The land would be held in trust by a village council—and leased—to local farmers.

By the time Borsodi left India, more than 160,000 Gramdan villages had been established. He was enormously impressed by these local experiments in land reform, discovering in the Gramdan Movement an affirmation and an audience for his own ideas about rebuilding rural economies on the basis of self-sufficient villages on leased land. Returning to the United States, Borsodi settled in Exeter, New Hampshire, and in 1967 formed a new organization to provide training and technical assistance for people who were interested in promoting rural development along the lines he had witnessed and supported in India. The name of this new organization was the International Independence Institute. Borsodi became chairman of the board and executive director. Bob Swann, who continued living at Voluntown after meeting Borsodi, was named the Institute's field director. Erick Hansch, a friend of Borsodi's from Portland, Oregon, was named assistant field director for Latin America.

In October of that same year, Borsodi and Swann traveled together to Luxembourg and London. In Luxembourg they incorporated yet another organization to complement the work of the Exeter-based International Independence Institute. According to its charter, the purpose of this new organization, named the International Foundation for Independence, was "to promote a world-wide social reformation to be based upon the theory that priority must be given . . . to the development of agriculture, local arts, local crafts, local enterprises, and local industries, and that the development of these basic social institutions should not be sacrificed to promote urbanism and industrialism." In Borsodi's expansive vision, the foundation would raise capital by issuing "notes and other instruments of indebtedness" and then loan these funds on reasonable terms to agricultural projects and rural villages in India, Latin America, and undeveloped regions in the United States, like the rural South.

Over the next 20 years, the International Independence Institute regularly changed its location and, eventually, its name. In 1971 it moved its corporate offices from Exeter, New Hampshire, to Ashby, Massachusetts. The next year, it moved again to Cambridge, Massachusetts, and changed its name to the Institute for Community Economics (ICE).[23]

New Communities, Inc.

Even as he was helping Ralph Borsodi to establish the institute in Exeter and the foundation in Luxembourg, Swann had kept in touch with Slater King. If the leased-land model that Borsodi had pioneered in 1936 could be combined with the sort of village trusts that had been developed on such a large scale in India, Swann and King believed they might have the makings of a land reform program capable of easing the residential and economic plight of African Americans living in the rural South.

Slater King had been talking to the National Sharecroppers Fund about buying land for black farmers being forced off the land, due to either the mechanization of agriculture or retaliation for their involvement in the civil rights movement. The executive director of this advocacy organization was Faye Bennett. She was a seasoned veteran of many struggles for social justice in the South and a personal friend of Eleanor Roosevelt.[24] Bennett was intrigued by the idea of creating leased-land agricultural cooperatives for black farmers. The National Sharecroppers Fund came up with the money to send a delegation to Israel to learn more about the kibbutz and moshav models of agricultural communities, both of which had been developed on lands that were leased from the Jewish National Fund. The delegation from the United States wanted to see how ground leasing worked.

Eight people made the trip to Israel in June 1968. In addition to King, Swann, and Faye Bennett, the delegation included Slater King's wife, Marion; Lewis Black, a board member of the Southwest Alabama Farmers' Cooperative Association; and Leonard Smith, a colleague of Faye Bennett's at the National Sharecroppers Fund. The final two members of this delegation to Israel were Albert Turner, field director for the Southern Christian Leadership Conference in Alabama, and Charles Sherrod.

Sherrod had come to Albany in 1961 as an organizer for SNCC, the Student Nonviolent Coordinating Committee. Earlier, while still a student at Virginia Union University, he had joined the first sit-ins of segregated department stores in Richmond. Soon after moving to Albany, he became part of the Albany Movement. Within that organization, he and his SNCC comrade, Cordell Reagon, were young, firebrand, grassroots organizers, nipping at the heels of the more cautious black leadership. Long after Martin Luther King left town and the Albany Movement began to ebb, Sherrod stayed on, continuing to organize against segregated schools and other vestiges of Jim Crow. He also turned his efforts toward promoting better housing for the area's African American population. When invited by Slater King to join the trip to Israel, he quickly signed on.

After a month in Israel, these eight activists, six blacks and two whites, returned to the United States, convinced that something like a network of agricultural cooperatives, developed on lands leased from a community-based nonprofit, might be a powerful model for the rural South.[25] They introduced this idea at a July 1968 meeting in Atlanta to which they invited representatives of nearly every civil rights organization in the South with an interest in addressing the land problems of African Americans. A planning committee was formed to explore the feasibility of developing a leasehold model of rural development for black farmers.[26]

In mid-1969, bylaws drafted by C. B. King were approved by the planning committee. The name adopted by the committee was New Communities, Inc., described in the Articles of Incorporation as "a nonprofit organization to hold land in perpetual trust for the permanent use of rural communities."[27]

Three of the officers for this new corporation had accompanied Swann to Israel. Slater King was elected president. Faye Bennett was elected secretary. Leonard Smith, Bennett's colleague at the National Sharecroppers Fund, was elected treasurer. The corporation's vice president was an African American priest from Louisiana, Albert J. McKnight. Father McKnight, along with Charles Prejean, had represented the

Southern Cooperative Development Program and the Federation of Southern Cooperatives on the planning committee. At the time of New Communities' founding, Father McKnight already had a long history of helping to develop rural cooperatives and credit unions. It was hardly a reach for him to embrace the notion of a cooperatively managed farm and planned residential community to be located on land that was leased from a community-controlled nonprofit.[28]

The board of New Communities, under Slater King's leadership, began immediately looking for land. They took an option on 5,735 acres located in Leesburg, about 30 miles north of Albany, using a $50,000 grant provided by the National Sharecroppers Fund. That left over $1 million they still had to raise before their six-month option expired. The whole process was almost derailed one month later, when Slater King was killed in an automobile accident. Despite this tragedy, the board decided to press on. Charles Sherrod was asked to assume the presidency of New Communities, a position he retained for many years.[29]

New Communities, Inc., managed to close on the land on January 9, 1970, coming into possession of 3,000 acres of farmland and over 2,000 acres of woodland. It had to borrow most of the $1,080,000 purchase price. This meant that, for the next 20 years, most of New Communities' profits from raising and selling its agricultural products—corn, peanuts, soybeans, watermelons, hay, and beef—went into servicing the debt on its land. Although several families moved into buildings that already existed on the land prior to its purchase by New Communities, no funds were ever secured from governmental agencies or accumulated from the farm's profits to build new housing or to develop the planned community envisioned by the organization's founders. Furthermore, New Communities faced the same resistance as Koinonia had experienced from the county's white-owned businesses and white farmers. As Charles Sherrod later recalled, "There was a time when [the white establishment] opposed us. They'd burn, and they'd fire at us; they threw one or two of us in jail."[30] By 1982, things had settled down. There was grudging acceptance by New Communities' white neighbors. But the economic risks of farming and the crushing debt on their land forced New Communities to sell 1,300 acres in the early 1980s. Five years later, they were forced to sell the rest.[31]

Guide to a New Model for Land Tenure

But the loss of New Communities was still many years away when Bob Swann and three of his colleagues at the International Independence Institute, Shimon Gottschalk, Erick Hansch, and Ted Webster, began writing a book meant to describe the "new model for land tenure" being tried at New Communities. Swann, Hansch, and Gottschalk provided the content. Webster served as the book's overall editor with the assistance of Marjorie Swann.

The Community Land Trust, published in 1972, was built around Swann's experience working with New Communities, but it also drew practical lessons from older leased-land communities in the United States and Israel. It included, for example, the complete text of the Bryn Gweled ground lease. The authors admitted that the new model they were proposing existed "only in prototype," yet they managed to describe many of the key components of ownership and organization that characterize the CLT of today.[32]

In particular, both the membership and board of the nonprofit landowner were opened up for the first time to people from the surrounding community and beyond who neither leased nor lived on the nonprofit's land. This was a direct legacy of Swann's involvement with Koinonia Farm and New Communities. He had helped to mobilize national support for a beleaguered Koinonia when it was attacked and boycotted by southern racists. He had worked beside Slater King and other civil rights activists in seeking representation from "almost every Southern organization concerned with the land problem of blacks" in planning and establishing New Communities.[33] These activists understood that such a radical experiment in racial advancement could survive in the hostile environment of southeast Georgia only through the continuing participation of sympathetic outsiders who might never live at New Communities themselves. When Swann and his colleagues got around to suggesting an organizational structure for their new model, they saw the merit of involving a larger, supportive community in guiding and governing the CLT. They proposed that "a majority of the board membership should consist of people somewhat removed from the resident community,"[34] although they did not specify a particular board configuration. It was only later, several years after their book was published, that the staff of ICE happened upon the three-part structure that eventually became a distinguishing feature of the CLT's board.[35]

Incidentally, it was Ted Webster who coined the name for this new model of tenure. After reading a rough draft of the manuscript that Swann and his colleagues had produced, he pointed out that they needed some way to differentiate their model from the intentional communities that had come before and from the conservation land trusts that were springing up across the United States. Webster innocently asked whether it might make sense to call the model a *community* land trust, in effect emphasizing the new organizational elements being grafted onto Borsodi's model.[36] Swann, Gottschalk, and Hansch liked the idea. From that point on, they began calling their prototype a community land trust.

Operation: From Trusterty to Trusteeship

With publication of the 1972 book, two of the three elements of the modern-day CLT were firmly in place, at least in theory. There was an ownership structure that established a new relationship between individuals and the land beneath their feet. There was an organizational structure that redefined the relationship between people living on the CLT's land and those residing in the surrounding community, a regional constituency both larger and more inclusive than the leaseholders who had populated and governed the land trusts created or inspired by Ralph Borsodi.

In practice, however, most of the CLTs formed in the decade that followed the incorporation of New Communities and publication of the first book about this new model for land tenure were organized on behalf of small groups of like-minded people. These homesteaders moved onto land that was leased from a nonprofit corporation to live in community with others who shared their social and political values.[37] Although they called themselves community land trusts, they were closer to being intentional communities—or, as Swann later called them, "enclaves." They did not embrace the open membership and balanced board of the model that Swann and his coauthors had envisioned.

It was not until 1978 that two organizations appeared that were to incorporate both the leased-land structure of ownership and the community-based structure of organization that Swann and his colleagues at ICE had envisioned. Both of these CLTs were located in rural areas, one in East Tennessee and one on the coast of northern Maine. Significantly, even as they fully embraced the model portrayed in the 1972 book, they pointed the way toward operational features that were to nudge the model in a new direction.

A Preferential Option for the Poor

The first of these CLTs was the Woodland Community Land Trust (WCLT). It was founded in 1978 by a former nun, Marie Cirillo, who had been doing community development work in the Appalachian Mountains of East Tennessee since 1967. While she was still a Glenmary Home Sister, a member of Marie's religious community had gone to Boston for a year of study and had heard Bob Swann talk about community land trusts. When she returned to East Tennessee, she told Marie and the other sisters about this new model of land tenure, suggesting that it might hold potential for their work with impoverished people in Appalachia. The sisters pooled their funds and paid for Swann to visit East Tennessee sometime in 1973.

Although the sisters were immediately convinced of the worth of Swann's ideas, it would take another five years before local residents of Rose's Creek, where Marie had settled, were willing to try a CLT. Many of these mountain people were already living on leased land, since most of the land and nearly all of the mineral rights in their Appalachian county were in the hands of absentee corporate owners, either land companies or coal companies. These companies were willing to lease land to the locals, but they never sold it. And the terms of the leases were always heavily biased in favor of the landowner, with little security or protection for the lessee. Having experienced the dark side of land leasing, the Appalachian natives of Rose's Creek were understandably cautious about starting a CLT.

Even after incorporating the Woodland Community Land Trust in 1978, another five years went by before the first houses were built on a 17-acre site owned by WCLT.[38]

When those houses were finished, WCLT's directors took a significant departure from the model that had been laid out in the 1972 book. They imposed resale controls on the houses. Drawing on the religious tradition of tithing, something quite familiar to the Southern Baptists who populated the hills and hollows around Rose's Creek, the Woodland CLT decided that homeowners would get 90 percent of the appraised value of their houses when they moved, leaving the other 10 percent in the house as a price reduction for future homebuyers.

Meanwhile, in northern Maine, another woman was leading the effort to establish a rural CLT. Sister Lucy Poulin and several other Carmelite nuns had come to Hancock County in 1968, settling in the town of Orland. They had supported themselves by sewing shoes for a Bangor shoe company. When the company closed in 1970, over 30 local women, including the nuns, were thrown out of work. The sisters responded by helping to form a sewing cooperative, where the women could work at home, making crafts that were sold through a storefront they opened on U.S. Route 1. HOME was the name they gave to their cooperative. The nuns later established a school and a daycare center for the co-op's members. They also organized Project Woodstove to deliver firewood to the elderly. Eventually, over 1,500 people were connected in one way or another to HOME Co-op.

Their next project was the construction of new housing. Sister Lucy took the lead in helping to start Self Help Family Farms in 1978. The aim of this organization was to settle low-income families in newly built homes on 10-acre leaseholds, where each family could enjoy a degree of self-sufficiency. The Covenant Community Land Trust was formed that same year to serve as the landholder, leasing out the land under these homesteads.[39]

From the beginning, Sister Lucy, like Marie Cirillo, regarded the CLT as a vehicle for helping and empowering low-income people who had been excluded from the economic and political mainstream. To express it in terms of her Catholic theology, there was a "preferential option for the poor." The CLT was not simply building houses; it was building a community of the dispossessed.

Development Without Displacement

That philosophy of empowerment was shared by Chuck Matthei, a friend of Sister Lucy's who had come to her aid in helping to establish the Covenant CLT. Over the next 30 years, Matthei was to do more than any other person to weave into the institutional fabric of the CLT the preferential option for the poor that Marie Cirillo and Lucy Poulin had espoused for their own CLTs. By doing that, he gave new operational meaning to the "T" in CLT.

Matthei was the movement's Johnny Appleseed, traveling back and forth across the United States over the course of many years in a string of beat-up, secondhand vehicles, speaking to any audience he could find about the community land trust. He helped to convince hundreds of people to stop talking about CLTs and to go out and start one. As Marjorie Swann later observed, when reflecting on the surprising growth of the movement her former husband had helped to spawn, the theoretical genius of a Ralph Borsodi or a Bob Swann was not sufficient to move CLTs into the mainstream. It took the motivational eloquence and political savvy of a Chuck Matthei to make the movement a reality.[40]

Matthei grew up in an affluent suburb of Chicago. A brilliant student, he was accepted to Harvard University. But he got sidetracked along the way. While still in high school, he had been regularly reading a newsletter published by a group of antiwar activists in Cincinnati known as the Peacemakers. This was the period right before Martin Luther King was assassinated, when King's philosophy of nonviolence had led him increasingly to combine his struggle against segregation with advocacy for the poor and opposition to the Vietnam War. This heady blend of civil rights, economic justice, and antiwar activism was precisely what the Peacemakers had been preaching since 1948, a moral concoction that Matthei found quite intoxicating. Graduating from high school in the summer of 1966, he hopped on his motorbike and headed to Cincinnati to meet in person the Peacemakers he had been reading about: Earnest and Marion Bromley, Wally and Juanita Nelson, and Maurice McCrackin.

To the fury of his father, Matthei never made it to Harvard. Instead, following in the footsteps of the Bromleys, the Nelsons, and McCrackin, Matthei became a life-long tax resister and social activist. He also became a close friend of Dorothy Day's, spending much time at the Catholic Worker house in New York City. Through the Peacemakers, he met Bob and Marjorie Swann. While on the staff of the Clamshell Alliance in New England, Matthei was befriended by Sister Lucy Poulin and helped her to start the Covenant CLT. That same year, in 1978, he was invited by Bob and Marjorie Swann to join the board of ICE, then headquartered in Boston.

One year later, ICE imploded. Mounting problems of personnel and finances precipitated the resignation of the entire staff and most of the board. When the dust settled, Chuck Matthei was made executive director, for a princely salary of $300 per month.[41] Matthei moved ICE to Greenfield, Massachusetts, and began gradually replenishing its coffers and rebuilding its staff. By 1988, ICE was employing 21 people, operating a multimillion-dollar revolving loan fund for CLTs, publishing a nationally distributed periodical called *Community Economics,* and providing technical assistance to a growing number of CLTs across the country.

One of the first CLTs to receive financial and technical assistance from ICE, after Matthei was named executive director, was the Community Land Cooperative of Cincinnati (CLCC). This inner-city CLT was started by the West End Alliance of Churches and Ministries in 1980, with Matthei's help. One of its leaders was Matthei's old friend Maurice McCrackin, a Presbyterian minister whose church lay in the heart of the West End, Cincinnati's oldest and most impoverished African American community.

The CLCC was unlike all previous CLTs in applying the model for the first time to an urban environment. This was new territory. Up until that point, CLTs had been successfully seeded only in rural settings.[42] Despite its urban surroundings, however, the CLCC bore a striking resemblance to the CLTs that had been established by

Marie Cirillo and Lucy Poulin. Like the Woodland CLT and the Covenant CLT, it served a population that had been excluded from the economic and political mainstream. It was a product of grassroots organizing and a vehicle for community empowerment: a means for controlling the development and fate of an impoverished inner-city neighborhood while involving the neighborhood's residents in the CLT's activities and governance.

It was also a vehicle for controlling the resale prices of any homes developed through the CLT. The CLCC was created, in part, to serve as a bulwark against gentrification. Its founders believed that simply removing land from the speculative market would not do enough to preserve the affordability of CLCC's homes or to prevent the displacement of the neighborhood's lower-income residents. Earlier land trusts, including the single-tax communities, Bryn Gweled, and the residential enclaves inspired by the CLT book of 1972, had not imposed long-term contractual controls over the resale of buildings located on leased land. The 1972 book had not contemplated permanent affordability being one of the purposes of this new model of land tenure. It was mostly silent on the subject of how a CLT's homes were to be transferred from one owner to another, saying only that "fair procedures can be worked out for the sale of this immoveable property when the owner decides to sell."[43] Rejecting this open-ended approach as too weak and uncertain to stem the tide of gentrification, the CLCC imposed permanent contractual controls over the pricing and conveyance of any homes developed on the CLT's lands.

The Community Land Trust Handbook

The founders of the Community Land Cooperative of Cincinnati, like many of the people who were attracted to the fledgling CLT movement in the 1980s—and whom Matthei was recruiting to staff a resurgent ICE—brought with them a new set of sensibilities. They shared many of the same values and heroes that had proved so influential for Bob Swann. They had come of age during the civil rights movement and protested the Vietnam War. Gandhi and Martin Luther King were two of their moral touchstones. But there were other influences, as well. People now working with local CLTs or joining ICE were more likely to have ties to the Catholic Worker or to faith-based organizations like community churches, religious orders, and ministerial alliances. Many more of them had experience as community organizers. A growing number of them came to a CLT or to ICE with prior experience working in urban neighborhoods or providing affordable housing for lower-income people. This influx of newcomers was to affect the ways and places the model was applied. It was also to alter, in time, what it meant to be a CLT, as new operational features like resale controls were added to the model's makeup.

By the 1980s, a new generation of community land trusts—and a new generation of CLT activists—were in need of a better blueprint for creating a CLT. Chuck Matthei pulled together a team of people to write and illustrate a book that would update and, in some cases, revise the model that Swann and his colleagues had proposed a decade before. Eight of the book's twelve contributors had a background in community organizing. Six had experience with housing or city planning. Two had worked for faith-based organizations.[44]

The Community Land Trust Handbook was published by Rodale Press in 1982. It drew on the experience of newer CLTs like those in Cincinnati, Maine, and East Tennessee, while paying homage to the ongoing experiment at New Communities. Although building on the foundation of the earlier book, the *CLT Handbook* introduced several organizational and operational refinements to the model:

- There was a new emphasis on urban problems, especially the preservation of affordable housing and the revitalization of residential neighborhoods.
- There was a new emphasis on building the social and political base for a new CLT through grassroots organizing.
- There was a higher priority on serving disadvantaged individuals and communities, accompanied by a "moral responsibility" for helping lower-income leaseholders to succeed as first-time homeowners.
- The open membership that Bob Swann and Slater King had brought to New Communities was defined more specifically in terms of two distinct voting blocks—leaseholder members and community members—who were each assigned responsibility for electing one-third of the governing board.
- The permanent affordability of owner-occupied housing (and other structures), enforced through a preemptive option and resale formula embedded in the ground lease, was made a defining feature of the CLT.[45]

The *CLT Handbook* also assumed an assertive moral and political stance in suggesting that some forms of property are better than others: more virtuous, more responsible, more just. The best forms of property were declared to be those in which the "legitimate" interests of individuals and their communities are durably secured and equitably balanced. The book of 1972 had been concerned, first and foremost, with reforming the relationship between people and land. The overriding concern of the *Handbook* of 1982, by contrast, was reforming the relationship between individual and community—finding an equitable and sustainable balance between private interests and public interests that regularly collide in the ownership and use of real property. The challenge, as the *Handbook* readily admitted, was how to reach agreement on what those legitimate interests should be and on how they should be limited by one another. The property interests that the *Handbook*'s authors were most comfortable calling "legitimate" were security, equity, and legacy. There was an individual dimension and a community dimension to each. A "satisfactory property arrangement" was described, accordingly, as one in which security, equity, and legacy were ensured for individuals who own homes and make use of land, without compromising a complementary set of community interests that are equally legitimate—public goods that must not be sacrificed to the single-minded pursuit of individual gains.

The CLT was extolled as a vehicle for securing this balance. In the CLT's structure of *ownership,* the rights and responsibilities of individual homeowners were balanced against those of the landowner. In its structure of *organization,* the powers of governance were balanced between people living on the CLT's land and people residing in the surrounding community. In its *operation,* the financial rewards from reselling a home were fairly allocated, balanced between a CLT's commitment to building wealth for the present generation of lower-income homeowners and its commitment to preserving affordability for future generations.

The bright moral thread running through all of the discussions was the programmatic priority that a CLT should give to solving the problems of low-income communities. In the vocabulary of the liberation theology of that period, there should be a "preferential option for the poor." Such a preference, using different words, was espoused repeatedly in *The Community Land Trust Handbook,* imbuing the "T" in CLT with new meaning.

The authors of the previous book on CLTs, in naming their "new model for land tenure," had explained their choice of the word *trust* by a "desire to emphasize Ralph Borsodi's idea of trusterty." Like Borsodi, they had argued that god-given resources like land, lakes, seas, and air, not being products of human labor, cannot be morally owned by individuals. These resources must be held in trust for the long-range welfare of all people. There was no suggestion, however, that some people might have greater needs than others or should be granted preferential access to the land trust's resources because of need.

Ten years later, the *Handbook* put forth a very different proposition. It was not only land that a CLT was to hold in trust, but the public's investment in developing the land, as well as the "unearned" increment in the appreciating value of houses and other improvements. It was not enough, moreover, for the CLT simply to act as the watchful steward for these resources. It had an affirmative obligation to use and develop its assets for the primary benefit of individuals who were socially and economically disadvantaged. It also had a moral responsibility to stand behind these individuals after they leased land and purchased homes through the CLT, helping them to maintain and retain their newly acquired property.[46]

Persons excluded from the economic and political mainstream were now assumed to have the first claim over a CLT's resources. Sister Lucy Poulin of the Covenant CLT, in an interview included in the *Handbook,* said it best: "We're talking about people who have never been accepted or had value in the community. And we're prejudiced in favor of these people—that's the community of people that we want as our community."[47] This was a notion of trust much closer to Gandhi's idea of "trusteeship" than to Borsodi's idea of trusterty.[48]

To be fair, it cannot be said that the model's potential for helping disadvantaged populations had been entirely ignored by the authors of the first CLT book. With New Communities as its centerpiece, an experiment that Swann and King had viewed as the harbinger of a homegrown Gramdan Movement to ease the plight of impoverished African Americans, the book's argument for a new model for land tenure spoke to some of the same social concerns later given such prominence in *The Community Land Trust Handbook*. In the earlier book's concluding chapter, entitled a "Mandate for Action," four possible paths were identified for creating "relatively large-scale, significant community land trusts." One of these options was described as establishing "new rural or urban communities for the primary benefit of poor and minority groups."[49]

Nevertheless, it was possible to read the 1972 text as purely a treatise on the "land question," a call to homesteaders, communards, and back-to-the-land idealists to structure the ownership of land in their intentional communities in a different way. The Gandhian grace notes were easily missed in the Borsodian score. In fact, many of the people who were moved to action by the book read it in precisely that way. Overlooking both the organizational prescription for an open membership and the operational preference for promoting economic equality, they created land trusts that bore little resemblance to Swann and King's vision of a Gramdan Movement in America.

The tilt toward the disadvantaged was much harder to miss in the *Handbook* of 1982. Highlighted there was the CLT's potential for aiding lower-income people and for empowering lower-income communities. Indeed, six of the nine case studies included in the book featured stories of CLTs emerging out of grassroots struggles to prevent the displacement, improve the housing, and promote the interests of persons of limited means whose communities were being buffeted by disinvestment or gentrification. In each of these places, a CLT had been established to secure property and power for people with too little of either.

With publication of *The Community Land Trust Handbook,* all the pieces of the model known today as the "classic" community land trust were finally in place. There was a two-party structure of ownership, with a nonprofit corporation holding land and leasing it out to the owners of any buildings. There was an inclusive structure of organization, with a two-part membership and a three-part board. There was an operational commitment to the stewardship of any housing constructed on the CLT's land, with priority access for persons too poor to acquire a home on their own. The main duty of stewardship was to ensure the permanent affordability of these homes, achieved through the CLT's management and enforcement of resale controls embedded in the ground lease. Beyond this contractual obligation, moreover, the CLT was charged with responsibility for helping its leaseholders to hang on to their homes and to keep them in good repair. In the *Handbook*'s words, "It is not enough to provide low-income people with land and financing for homes and then leave them to their own resources." A good steward does not expect people of limited means to go it alone. The CLT was durably, dependably there to help them succeed.

Conditions of Growth: From Model to Movement

This reworking of the CLT was to have both practical and political advantages for a model that aspired to become a movement. By prioritizing populations, places, and activities recognized as "charitable" under Section 501(c)(3) of the federal tax code, CLTs gained access to financial resources from public agencies and private foundations that were not available to organizations that lacked this exemption.[50] By prioritizing problems recognized as harmful for constituencies and communities of limited means—including the declining affordability of housing, the deterioration of inner-city neighborhoods, and the displacement of lower-income persons uprooted by market forces or public policies—CLTs gained relevance and acceptance among policy makers and community activists who were struggling to respond to the federal retreat from housing and community development in the 1980s. As new resources and constituencies were drawn to the model, the number of CLTs began to grow.

Urban CLTs formed the leading edge of this expansion. Three years after the founding of the first urban CLT in Cincinnati, community land trusts were started in Syracuse, New York, and Burlington, Vermont. By 1990, others had appeared in Durham, North Carolina; Youngstown, Ohio; Albany and Schenectady, New York; Worcester, Massachusetts; and Washington, DC.

One of the most significant CLT start-ups during this period was Boston's Dudley Neighbors, Inc., (DNI). DNI was established in 1989 as a corporate subsidiary of the Dudley Street Neighborhood Initiative (DSNI) for the purpose of acquiring, holding, and developing land for the revitalization of a multiracial residential neighborhood in the heart of Roxbury. Despite its subsidiary structure and the lavish funding it eventually received from private foundations and public agencies, DSNI/DNI was typical of many of the urban CLTs founded in the 1980s and early 1990s in espousing a dual commitment to community empowerment and community development. Its service area was a single, well-defined neighborhood with a historic sociopolitical identity. Its impetus came from the neighborhood's opposition to a top-down plan for the redevelopment of Roxbury that had been put forward by the City of Boston and local foundations.[51] When DSNI/DNI later proposed its own comprehensive plan for the neighborhood's redevelopment, it was the result of a participatory process of organizing and planning that engaged hundreds of community residents over many months. DSNI/DNI, like many emerging CLTs in other cities, viewed affordable housing as only one component of community development, a subset of the CLT's overall mission of transforming the physical, economic, and political life of its place-based community.[52] When DSNI exhorted the residents of Roxbury to "Take a Stand, Own the Land," it was not only so its CLT could secure buildable sites for affordable housing. It was also so a local community, through DNI's long-term control over land and improvements, could control its own destiny.

As CLTs were sprouting up in a number of cities, new CLTs were also appearing in rural areas of Massachusetts, Maine, Vermont, New Hampshire, and Washington state. Notably, many of the rural CLTs started during the 1980s staked out a service area much larger than the territory served by their urban counterparts.[53] They conceived of their "community" as being an entire county, region, or, in the case of the first CLTs in Washington state, an entire island.[54] One of the first of these rural CLTs to be established, soon after the pioneering efforts of Marie Cirillo and Lucy Poulin, was the CLT in the Southern Berkshires. It was founded in 1980 by Bob Swann and Susan Witt, the year after they left ICE. They also created a companion organization, the E. F. Schumacher Society, which, among many other programs, offered assistance to rural communities in creating CLTs of their own.

The Community Land Trust Handbook had spoken rather grandly of a CLT *movement*. In truth, only a handful of community land trusts actually existed in 1982, the year of the book's publication. Declaring these few CLTs a movement was like calling the first green shoots to appear in a muddy field a bumper crop. What was wishful thinking in the early 1980s, however, was becoming a reality by the middle of the 1990s. With a hundred CLTs scattered across the United States, the model was showing signs of actually becoming a movement.

How did this happen? How did a hothouse flower with unusual characteristics of ownership, organization, and operation become widely established, spreading from a few experimental garden plots in the Southeast and Northeast in the 1970s to more than 240 urban, suburban, and rural communities in 45 states and the District of Columbia? Many things combined to nurture such growth, so it is difficult to say for certain why this fledgling movement was able to thrive, but a handful of factors were arguably the most important, including a timely change in the political and economic climate; the standardization of CLT definitions, documents, and practices; the cross-pollination of ideas and techniques among CLT practitioners; an increase in private and public investment, boosting the productivity of CLTs; and diversification in the model and movement, invigorating both.

Climate

With the presidential election of Ronald Reagan in 1980, the federal government beat a hasty retreat from the field of affordable housing, repudiating the national commitment to a "decent home and suitable living environment for every American family" that had been endorsed by both political parties since the Housing Act of 1949. The deterioration of affordable housing and other symptoms of disinvestment afflicted many residential neighborhoods. Gentrification hit many others. Homelessness, largely invisible since the Great Depression, reappeared with a vengeance. At the same time, affordability controls began expiring on thousands of units of publicly subsidized, privately owned rental housing built nearly two decades before under federal programs like 221(d)(3) and Section 8. These so-called expiring-use projects provoked a new awareness of the social cost of failing to require long-term affordability in housing produced with public funds.

The mid-1980s was also a time when the price of owner-occupied housing began a steady 20-year climb, even as household incomes stagnated for the bottom three quintiles of the population and mortgage interest rates rose to historic heights. A new phrase entered the lexicon of public policy, the "affordability gap," the widening chasm between housing prices and household incomes.

As affordability became the nation's predominant housing issue, affecting both rental housing and homeowner housing, the confidence placed in traditional tenures was somewhat shaken. They seemed increasingly to be incapable of protecting and preserving affordable housing, especially in markets that were very hot. The CLT, by contrast, was specifically designed and uniquely positioned to do what market-driven models could not. As Chuck Matthei argued at the National CLT Conference in Atlanta in 1987, "No program, public or private, is a true or adequate response to the housing crisis if it does not address the issue of long-term affordability. It's time to draw the line politically. This is a practical challenge that confronts policymakers; it's the practical challenge that confronts community activists; and, happily, it is a practical challenge that the community land trust model has an ability to meet."

For the first time, both policymakers and community activists were listening. Municipal officials, in particular, became increasingly receptive to the argument that government could not afford to put more and more resources into closing the affordability gap, if this investment was going to be quickly lost. Permanent affordability began to look like a prudent course of action, a policy more fiscally responsible and politically defensible than previous governmental practice. As preservation rose higher on the public agenda, particularly in places where market prices were soaring, the number of CLTs began to grow.

To the surprise of many observers, the same proved true when prices started to plummet. By the end of 2006, it was no longer the affordability crisis that was grabbing headlines in the United States, although an affordability gap persisted in many housing markets; it was the foreclosure crisis. This, too, caused the number and acceptance of CLTs to rise.

The reason was not hard to see. CLTs do not disappear after selling a resale-restricted home. They stand behind the deal: intervening in cases of mortgage default, preventing foreclosures, backstopping the homeownership opportunities they have worked so hard to create. Stewardship is what CLTs do best. True, they also acquire land, develop housing, sell homes, organize communities, and a dozen other things, but so do a lot of other nonprofit housing developers. What the CLT does better than any other organization—its specialized niche in a densely populated nonprofit environment—is to preserve affordability when economic times are good and protect its homes and homeowners when times are bad. In the scorched landscape of the national mortgage crisis, CLTs were almost alone in reporting few defaults and even fewer foreclosures.[55] Such a stunning performance in a time of crisis attracted wider notice and greater governmental support for this unconventional model of homeownership.[56] This helped the movement to grow.

Cultivation

The second factor contributing to the proliferation of CLTs in the United States was the dissemination of educational materials, organizational documents, and "best practices" employing a consistent conception of the CLT. Early on, the leading role in nudging CLTs toward more standardization in the way their stories were told, their organizations were structured, and their programs were managed was played by the Institute for Community Economics, formerly The International Independence Institute (III). Over time, other actors and organizations came to play a larger part, eventually eclipsing ICE.[57]

ICE produced the first books about CLTs: *The Community Land Trust: A Guide to a New Model for Land Tenure in America* and *The Community Land Trust Handbook.* ICE introduced the CLT to an even wider audience through *Common Ground,* a narrated slide show about the Community Land Cooperative of Cincinnati, completed in 1985, and *Homes and Hands: Community Land Trusts in Action,* a video featuring CLTs in Durham, North Carolina; Albuquerque, New Mexico; and Burlington, Vermont, completed in 1998. The images and stories presented in these productions were clearly designed to persuade an audience of the model's practicality and worth. They served another function besides. They were not only promotional; they were also educational, instructing the audience in the particular features and purposes of the model described in the 1982 *Handbook.* They created a consistent message and common understanding of what it meant to be a CLT.

ICE also turned its attention to producing technical materials for a very different audience: lawyers who were working with CLTs. Employing the same approach it had used in writing *The Community Land Trust Handbook,* ICE pulled together a team of attorneys and CLT practitioners to develop a set of "model" documents and standard procedures for incorporating CLTs, leasing land, designing resale formulas, and a dozen other legal and technical details pertaining to the organization and operation of a CLT. These materials were collected in *The Community Land Trust Legal Manual,* published in 1991. A second edition, revising and updating the original, was published in 2002.[58]

Critical, too, to inculcating a common conception of the model was the CLT definition that was incorporated into federal law in 1992. With passage of the National Affordable Housing Act (NAHA) in 1990, cities and states began using pass-through funds from the federal government to support the projects and operations of what NAHA called "Community Housing Development Organizations." CLTs not only had an interest in securing their eligibility for this funding, they also wanted to make sure that the way in which a CLT was defined in federal law was consistent with the way that most CLTs, after 1982, were defining themselves. Not trusting the federal bureaucracy to describe fully and accurately the essential elements of ownership, organization, and operation that had been laid out in *The Community Land Trust*

Handbook, a decision was made by a small group of CLT advocates to beat HUD to the punch. They asked Congressman Bernie Sanders, whose administration had initiated and supported the Burlington Community Land Trust when he was mayor of Burlington, Vermont, to insert their definition of a community land trust into the Housing and Community Development Act of 1992.[59] Sanders shepherded this amendment through Congress and saw it signed into law without modification.

The most significant contribution in recent years to the cultivation of common standards—and higher standards—for explaining, organizing, and operating CLTs has been made by the National Community Land Trust Academy. Founded in 2006 as a chartered program of the National Community Land Trust Network, the academy has two purposes: to provide comprehensive training on theories and practices unique to CLTs, setting a high standard for practitioner competence; and to support research and publication on the best practices emerging from the field.[60] The Academy has not only been concerned with the nuts and bolts of making a CLT work; it has also tried, in its courses and publications, to cultivate a common understanding of the history and values underlying the CLT, reminding proponents and practitioners of where the model came from and why it is structured as it is.

None of these efforts made every CLT look and act exactly the same. Increasing the clarity and consistency of the messages, materials, documents, and practices of the nation's CLTs did little to deter the movement's diversification. But it did provide public officials, private lenders, and community activists outside of the movement with a sharper picture of how a CLT was structured, how it was different from other models of tenure, and how its projects might best be funded and financed. It also provided practitioners inside the movement with a common vocabulary for exchanging information about what worked well—and what did not—in a model of tenure that was still very much a work in progress.

Cross-Pollination

Peer-to-peer exchanges were essential to turning an untested, experimental prototype into a practical model that was fully operational. The audacious pioneers who started dozens of CLTs in the 1980s and 1990s were, in many respects, making it up as they went along. They crafted legal documents, designed resale formulas, arranged mortgages, sold homes, and adopted policies and procedures for a form of tenure with virtually no track record. They learned by doing. And they learned from one another.

Some of their communication was indirect, information they gleaned about each other's programs and procedures by reading *Community Economics,* a newsletter published and distributed by ICE from 1983 to 1996.[61] The stated purpose of this publication was to "strengthen the connections between the theory and practice of community economics," but it also strengthened the connections among far-flung CLTs. In an average year, two or three issues would be mailed out to hundreds (and later thousands) of people across the United States, many of whom were in the early stages of planning, organizing, or operating a CLT. This was a model and movement in flux. As ICE observed in the newsletter's maiden issue, published in summer 1983, things were changing so rapidly that it was hard for anyone to keep abreast of the latest developments; hence the need for *Community Economics*:

> Since finishing work on *The Community Land Trust Handbook,* we at ICE have been concerned with the need for some regular, ongoing publication to carry news of CLTs and related developments in the area of community economics. The *Handbook* brought the record on CLTs more or less up to date as of Autumn 1982, but now there are new developments to report—new groups, new interest, and new issues being confronted by established CLTs as they expand their programs.

Many issues of *Community Economics* profiled a particular CLT. Every issue carried news of resources that local CLTs were discovering, projects they were developing, or programs they were designing, information with relevance for CLTs in other communities. For 14 years, this newsletter pollinated the movement with new ideas, helping one CLT to learn from the mistakes and successes of others.

Interorganizational learning among CLT practitioners also happened more directly at national conferences convened every few years by ICE. The first conference was held in 1987 in an African American church in Atlanta,[62] a fitting venue since the country's first CLT had been organized in southeast Georgia nearly 20 years before by veterans of the civil rights movement. One of those veterans, John Lewis, who had attended the early planning sessions for New Communities, was on hand to remind the conference's participants of the CLT's roots, while applauding how far the model had come. The main business of the Atlanta conference, however, like all that followed, was the face-to-face exchange of stories, ideas, and technical information among people who were trying to get organizations and projects off the ground. Everyone had something to learn, and, because the model itself was so new, anyone with more than a year of CLT experience had something to teach.

Every two or three years thereafter, ICE convened another national conference, drawing together hundreds of CLT practitioners from across the United States and, on occasion, from Canada, England, and Australia, as well.[63] The 2003 conference in Syracuse, New York, was ICE's last. By the start of the new millennium, ICE's star had begun to fade, even as other national and regional organizations were beginning to play a larger role in assisting and connecting local CLTs. When ICE abruptly canceled the conference that had been scheduled for Portland, Oregon in 2005, an ad hoc coalition of CLT executive directors, funders, and consultants stepped forward to fill the vacuum.[64] They revamped the costly conference that ICE had planned, transforming it into a grassroots gathering of CLT practitioners sharing information and best practices in a series of peer-to-peer workshops. They also set aside half a day for CLT leaders from around the country to confer about a possible future without

ICE, since it looked like this national organization, which had provided so much support for CLTs in the past, was winding down.

Beginning with the conference in Portland, the nation's CLTs in effect took control of their own movement. This meant not only assuming responsibility for organizing future conferences, where practitioners could continue to learn from one another. It also entailed creating a new corporate structure for ensuring regular communication and coordination among hundreds of organizations scattered across the United States. The foundation for this interorganizational structure was laid down in Portland with the election of a steering committee charged with the task of drafting bylaws for a national association of CLTs. One year later, in Boulder, Colorado, these bylaws were refined and ratified by representatives from 51 CLTs. The National Community Land Trust Network was formally incorporated in June 2006.[65]

This greatly intensified the interaction and communication among the country's CLT practitioners. Under the auspices of the National CLT Network, there was now an annual gathering of practitioners. These national conferences included day-long trainings and half-day seminars offered by the National CLT Academy, along with membership meetings, faculty meetings, and board meetings for the Network and the Academy.[66] The Network's contribution to facilitating the flow of information and ideas among CLT practitioners was not confined to these annual conferences, however. The boards and committees of the Network and the Academy, made up predominantly of staff members and board members of local CLTs, met frequently throughout the year. The Network's listserv and web site provided other ways for CLT practitioners, old and new, to ask questions, solve problems, and share techniques. The same function that *Community Economics* had once served through the infrequent distribution of a printed newsletter was now being fulfilled regularly and instantaneously via the Internet.

Outside of the network, cross-pollination occurred in other ways, as well. The E. F. Schumacher Society, founded by Bob Swann and Susan Witt in 1980, and Equity Trust, which Chuck Matthei had founded in 1990, maintained web sites and brokered connections among different groups of grassroots organizations. Most were not members of the National CLT Network, but many were either structured as CLTs or engaged in applying land leasing and other components of the CLT model to conserving open space, preserving farmland, or promoting community supported agriculture. Peer-to-peer communication among CLTs was also spurred by the rise of regional CLT networks in the Pacific Northwest, Minnesota, and Colorado. While maintaining close ties to the National CLT Network, these regional networks operated quite independently: forging connections among their members; advocating for changes in state policy; sharing information about organizational policies, procedures, and administrative systems; and raising the standard of practice for every CLT in their region.[67]

In the early years of the movement, no one had any real experience in starting or operating a CLT, except those intrepid souls who were actually doing it. Nearly every pioneer was learning something worth sharing with everyone else who was blazing a similar trail. Nobody was an "expert," so everybody was. That remained true, even as the movement matured. A cadre of consultants gradually arose, drawn mostly from the staff of ICE or from the ranks of CLTs, but that was never a substitute for CLT practitioners swapping information with one another, directly or indirectly. The real experts remained those who were governing or running a CLT day to day. Keeping them connected has been an essential ingredient in the movement's growth.

Fertilization

Every CLT requires an abundance of financial resources to acquire land, develop housing (and other buildings), create affordability for low-income people, and sustain the operations of a nonprofit organization with stewardship responsibilities lasting close to forever. The lack of money, both equity and debt, was an impediment to CLT growth in the early years. The greater availability of public grants and private loans supporting CLTs and their projects has been an inducement to growth in more recent years.

Unable to access capital from more conventional sources, many of the first CLTs were forced to resort to what *The Community Land Trust Handbook* once described as the "miracle theory" of finance:

> Appropriate financing relies upon prior financial planning to match particular types and sources of funds with particular needs and uses for funds. Miracle financing awaits the lucky arrival of adequate funds to meet immediate needs: like manna from heaven, such funds may be urgently needed and patiently awaited, but hardly expected or prepared for. The latter cannot, of course, be lightly dismissed. Considering the remarkable accomplishments of numerous grassroots groups operating on shoestring budgets with little hope of long-term financial support, the miracle theory of finance must be credited with many good works and substantial social progress. Miracles do happen.[68]

Very few of the first CLTs got started without an occasional dose of "miracle financing" from a wealthy individual, a local church, a national religious order, or a faith-based charity like the Campaign for Human Development.[69] At ICE, Chuck Matthei was quick to recognize how important such small infusions of cash could be in nurturing the growth of CLTs. Instead of attempting to assemble large pools of capital from private investors, as ICE had tried to do with little success in the 1970s, Matthei looked for a way that small loans, offered at low rates of interest by socially motivated individuals or institutions, could be mobilized to help CLTs get their first projects off the ground. In 1979, soon after becoming ICE's executive director, he established a revolving loan fund at ICE for the purpose of accepting no-interest and low-interest "social investments" that could be reloaned to local CLTs. The fund was modest in scale. By 1983, its assets totaled $643,590. It had made 45 loans to CLTs, limited-equity housing cooperatives, worker-owned businesses, and community ser-vice groups. The average loan size was only $14,302.[70] By the end of 1985, the fund's assets had doubled, but the size of an average ICE loan remained relatively small, only $26,065.

Despite their size, these loans often made a critical difference to start-up CLTs, helping them to acquire their first parcel of land or rehabilitate their first house while building their credibility with public funders and private lenders. Just as important, ICE's own experience in building and managing its in-house loan fund—and seeing the impact these timely loans could make on seeding and supporting local CLTs—persuaded Matthei to expand ICE's technical assistance program beyond CLTs. Using ICE's revolving loan fund as the model,[71] Matthei and other staff from ICE began working with coalitions of social investors and community activists to estab-lish a variety of community development loan funds, including funds in New Hamp-shire, Boston, and Philadelphia. In 1985, ICE convened a national conference on com-munity development loan funds, attended by representatives from 35 nonprofit lenders. Out of this conference emerged the National Association of Community Development Loan Funds, chaired by Matthei for its first five years.[72]

Community loan funds (as Matthei called them) and community land trusts de-veloped on parallel tracks, complementing and supporting each other. CLTs were never the only beneficiaries of these alternative financial institutions, but they got loans when they needed them, especially during the years when start-up CLTs were having difficulty obtaining funding from local governments, which they were often fighting, or obtaining financing from local bankers who were initially uncomfortable making loans for houses on leased land.

Two breakthroughs occurred in the early 1990s that somewhat eased both difficul-ties. The 1992 amendments to the National Affordable Housing Act did more than provide a standard definition of CLTs. They cracked open the door to federal fund-ing. After 1992, many more CLTs were able to receive designation as a Community Housing Development Organization (CHDO). Many more were able to receive funding from the federal HOME program for their operations and their projects.[73] Equally important, federally supported technical assistance was made available to CLTs for the first time.[74] In November 1994, the U.S. Department of Housing and Urban Development (HUD) awarded ICE a three-year $470,000 technical assis-tance grant. With these funds (and two later technical assistance grants from HUD), ICE seeded CLTs in several states where none had existed, nurtured dozens that were just getting started, and helped many existing CLTs to become more productive.[75]

Around 1992, as well, at the request of local CLTs and the urging of ICE, Fannie Mae began developing riders to be used in combination with CLT ground leases. This boosted confidence in the CLT among private lenders and made mortgage fi-nancing more widely available for resale-restricted homes on land leased from a CLT. Even when a banker did not use Fannie Mae's rider or take advantage of the special loan product that Fannie Mae later developed for CLTs, there was less resistance to backing a model that Fannie Mae had recognized as a reasonable and bankable approach to homeownership.[76]

As crucial as these changes at the federal level have been in nourishing the growth of CLTs, most of the action in boosting CLT productivity in recent years has come from policy changes and new sources of financial support at the municipal level. Local government, here and there, has become an enthusiastic partner. This was not always the case. Relations between cities and CLTs, for most of the CLTs' early history, were chilly, to say the least. As *The Community Land Trust Handbook* once described it, "Most interaction between CLTs and municipal officials has been marked by benign indifference, with neither party doing more than is minimally required to meet whatever legal obligations each might have with regard to the other." Their actual relationship was often stormy and strained. In many a neighborhood like the West End of Cincinnati, the main impetus for starting a CLT was to protect the community *against* municipal priorities, projects, or plans. The same people who played the lead role in organizing a CLT had spent years fighting city hall before the CLT appeared. Hostilities did not cease when the CLT came along.

Opposition to local government has remained a motivating factor in many low-income communities, especially in communities of color, where CLTs have continued to be erected as an institutional barrier against market pressures made worse by the actions or indifference of city hall. Over the last decade, however, a countertrend has emerged. There are now an increasing number of cities, counties, and towns where CLTs receive political support from municipal leaders, administrative support from municipal staff, and financial support from municipal coffers.[77] In these places, the CLT has become a partner of local government, an ally rather than an antagonist.

This signals a seismic shift in municipal policy. Instead of allowing homeownership subsidies to be pocketed by homeowners when reselling their assisted homes, a common practice in the past, many municipalities are now looking for ways to lock those subsidies in place. Instead of allowing the affordability of publicly assisted homes to lapse, many municipalities are now looking for ways to make affordability last. This has made the CLT, along with several other forms of resale-restricted, owner-occupied housing, a favored recipient of municipal largess and has helped CLTs to grow.

Hybrid Vigor

In plant breeding, when two species with very different characteristics are combined, engendering an increase in size, yield, and performance beyond either of the parents, that salubrious result is known as hybrid vigor. Something similar has happened in the development of CLTs. Both the model and the movement are hybrids. The model was created by selecting favorable characteristics of ownership, organization, and operation from different strains of social change and combining them to form a new breed of tenure. The movement has prospered by mixing uses and merging agendas, bringing together organizational characteristics and political interests that are usually separate and frequently at odds. Over time, hybridization has brought into dominance the most productive and sustainable characteristics of the CLT and helped it to thrive.[78]

Hybridization continues, altering the CLT in significant ways. These changes have been spurred by four developments: decentralization of the support structure for CLTs, diversification in the application of CLTs, municipalization in the formation of CLTs, and regionalization in the area served by CLTs.

Decentralization

Over a forty-year period, the Institute for Community Economics went from being the center of the CLT universe to being one star among many and, finally, to being broken into pieces and propelled into orbit around brighter bodies. By 2008, ICE's most important intellectual properties, including *The CLT Legal Manual* and the *Homes and Hands* video, had been conveyed to Equity Trust; its revolving loan fund had been transferred to the National Housing Trust; and its archives had been boxed and mailed to the E. F. Schumacher Society. ICE's preeminent role as promulgator of CLT standards, convener of CLT conferences, and national clearinghouse for news and research about CLTs had been taken over by the National CLT Network. Technical assistance for new and existing CLTs, moreover, once the exclusive purview of ICE, was now provided by a wide assortment of national intermediaries, regional coalitions, private consultants, and even a few of the larger CLTs. With so many actors now saying what a CLT is—and how it should be organized and operated—there was no longer one version of the model, but many.

Diversification

Although Swann and his coauthors in 1972 had envisioned multiple applications for their new model of land tenure, the CLT came to be used most widely for the development and stewardship of affordable housing. Single-family houses, in particular, predominated among the early CLTs, since a majority of them were located in rural areas. As the model moved into city and suburb, however, its applications and activities became more diverse. The CLT was applied to other types and tenures of housing, including multiunit condominiums, limited-equity cooperatives, nonprofit rentals, homeless shelters, and manufactured housing in resident-owned parks. It was used to acquire and lease land under mixed-use buildings, community gardens, commercial greenhouses, social enterprises, and social service facilities. Back in the countryside, the CLT was being applied in novel ways to farming, forestry, and conservation, mixing community supported agriculture with community ownership of land; mixing affordable housing with the preservation of farmland, wetlands, and open space. Since form follows function, these new applications have sometimes reshaped the CLT. Some CLTs, for example, have been doing rental projects in which the CLT owns and manages both the land and building. Conversely, some CLTs have become involved with residential (and commercial) condominiums where the CLT owns neither the land nor the building, holding instead an affordability covenant on units sprinkled throughout a larger residential complex. As the ways the CLT is applied have grown more diverse, so have the ways the CLT is structured, especially in the ownership and operation of real property.

Municipalization

As the level of support from local government for CLTs has increased, the role played by municipalities in the life of a CLT has changed. Instead of waiting passively for a CLT to form, municipal officials in a number of cities have taken the initiative in starting one. Involved from the outset in planning and designing the CLT, city hall has sometimes been reluctant to let go, unwilling to be relegated to minority status in choosing the board and guiding the organization after it is established. Municipal support in some cities has also changed the CLT's mission and role. Where a local government has backed a CLT primarily for the purpose of serving as the long-term steward for affordable homes created by the investment of municipal funds or the imposition of a municipal mandate like inclusionary zoning, the municipality may not want the CLT to diffuse its focus by doing community development, as well. It may not want the CLT to do the kind of grassroots organizing that can occasionally lead to a neighborhood's residents fighting the same local government that is funding the CLT. City–CLT partnerships have sometimes produced CLTs, in other words, that are operated and structured much differently than CLTs in the past.

Regionalization

Twenty years ago, the territory served by the typical CLT was a single inner-city neighborhood or, in more rural areas, a single valley, island, village, or town. Today, an increasing number of CLTs, old and new, are staking out a much larger service area. They acquire lands, develop projects, and draw members from an area encompassing an entire city, county, or region. A couple of CLTs have even organized themselves on a statewide basis, coordinating and supporting the development of local CLTs across an entire state.[79] As their territory expands, CLTs multiply their opportunities for acquiring land, building housing, and cultivating the kind of public and private partnerships that can help to bring the CLT to scale. At the same time, their connections to community get stretched and thin. Organizationally, the CLT may retain an inclusive membership and a popularly elected three-part board, structures designed to keep the CLT accountable to the constituency it serves. Operationally, however, a CLT whose membership is spread over a metropolitan area containing millions of people or over a three-county region covering hundreds of square miles is going to have a different relation with its "community" than a CLT that is focused on and accountable to a single neighborhood or town. Size matters, affecting what a CLT is and does.

Decentralization, diversification, municipalization, and regionalization have accelerated the process of experimentation that has been going on among CLTs since the beginning. Hybridization has improved their performance and raised their productivity.

Hybrid vigor has helped the CLT to spread. On the other hand, while it has clearly been a boon for the movement, there is also a risk that too much hybridization could become a bane for the model, diluting or extinguishing characteristics that have made the CLT unique. Three challenges loom the largest in this regard:

- Will there still be a place for community in the organizational structure of the CLT, or will the heightened influence of local government or the expanded territory served by a CLT remove or reduce the active voice of local residents in governing the CLT?
- Will land still matter in the ownership structure of the CLT, or will a focus on affordable housing, in general, and the stewardship of multiunit housing, in particular, cause CLTs to ignore other uses of land or to abandon land leasing altogether in favor of selling the land and using deed covenants to preserve affordability?[80]
- Will the CLT still espouse an operational preference for the disadvantaged—holding lands in trust, keeping homes affordable, and protecting security of tenure for people with limited resources—or will the Gandhian legacy of trusteeship be lost in a frenetic scramble to increase the scale and broaden the appeal of the CLT?

A contest for the soul of the community land trust is contained in these questions, a contest that decentralization, diversification, municipalization, and regionalization have made more acute. How they are answered in the years ahead will determine whether the CLT of tomorrow continues to resemble the model of today.

There are reasons to believe that it will. The roots of the CLT run deep. Tended by the first generation of CLT practitioners, many of whom are still alive, and preserved for the next generation by institutions like the CLT Academy, the E. F. Schumacher Society, and Equity Trust, the ideas and values that gave rise to the CLT continue to ground it and nourish it. They give resiliency to a model buffeted by change, allowing it to bend without uprooting its core commitments.

Not all of the changes swirling around the CLT compel it away from what it has been. Some coax it back, returning the model to its roots. The recent focus on stewardship is one example. The revival of interest in the CLT among communities of color is another. When a CLT is asked to serve as the long-term steward for land-based assets donated or subsidized by the public, the CLT returns to the job it was designed to do. Land and other socially created assets are removed from the market, placed in common ownership, and held in trust for future generations.[81] When a CLT is formed by residents of an African American or Hispanic American community to resist market forces and public policies that are fueling the loss of minority-owned lands and eroding the community's residential security and historic identity, the CLT returns to a cause that animated its earliest days. The CLT serves simultaneously as a bulwark against displacement, a tool for development, and a vehicle for the empowerment of communities defined, in part, by their relation to place.[82]

In sum, internal changes and external pressures are pushing the CLT toward a future in which the model may come to look very different than it does today. At the same time, deeply rooted principles and recently revived applications are pulling the CLT in the opposite direction, reinvigorating elements of ownership, organization, and operation that have historically characterized the "classic" CLT. The past is not dead, William Faulkner once wrote, it is not even past. That has remained mostly true for the CLT, until now. Across years of experimentation and evolution, the model has occasionally strayed from the vision and values of its founders, but it has usually found its way back. The past may not always be so influential, however. A long time coming, the CLT still has a long way to go.

NOTES

Several reviewers helped in checking facts and correcting mistakes in an earlier draft of this chapter. The author wishes to thank Julie Orvis, Bonnie Acker, Kirby White, Marjorie Swann, and Lisa Byers for casting critical eyes on a historical narrative that covers lots of ground in relatively few pages. Any errors that remain, including those of selection and interpretation, are the author's responsibility alone.

1. Thorstein Veblen, *Absentee Ownership and Business Enterprise in Recent Times: The Case of America* (New York: B. W. Huebsch, Inc., 1923).

2. Paine: "Man did not make the earth, and though he had a natural right to occupy it, he had no right to locate as his property in perpetuity on any part of it. . . . It is the value of the improvement only, and not the earth itself, that is individual property." Jefferson: "The earth is given as a common stock for men to labor and live on." Lincoln: "The land, the earth God gave man for his home, sustenance, and support, should never be the possession of any man, corporation, society, or unfriendly government, any more than the air or water."

3. Here, too, George proved to be a faithful student of John Stuart Mill, who had written, "The ordinary progress of a society which increases in wealth, is at all times tending to augment the incomes of landlords; to give them both a greater amount and a greater proportion of the wealth of the community, independently of any trouble or outlay incurred by themselves. They grow richer, as it were in their sleep, without working, risking, or economizing. What claim have they, on the general principle of social justice, to this accession of riches? In what would they have been wronged if society had, from the beginning, reserved the right of taxing the spontaneous increase of rent, to the highest amount required by financial exigencies?" ("On the General Principles of Taxation," in *Principles of Political Economy with Some of Their Applications to Social Philosophy*, 1848; repr., New York: Oxford University Press, 1994).

4. Howard's book became a seminal text in city planning, heavily influencing people like Lewis Mumford, Clarence Stein, Frederick Law Olmsted, and many other American pioneers of urban design.

5. In addition to the writings of Henry George, Borsodi's thinking about property was influenced the most by his reading of John Locke, in whose works moral title to property was seen as resting exclusively on an owner having put his own labor into the thing made. There is also an echo in Borsodi's work, though unacknowledged by him, of the distinction made by R. H. Tawney between "passive property" and "active property." See Tawney's "Property and Creative Work," in *The Acquisitive Society* (New York: Harcourt Brace Jovanovich, 1920).

6. In 1945, the other homeowners decided they wanted to gain individual title to the land beneath their feet. Borsodi moved the School of Living to Ohio, relocating to a farm that was owned by John and Mildred Loomis. Borsodi and Mildred Loomis began publishing a newsletter soon after, named *Green Revolution*. This periodical helped to spread Borsodi's ideas and other theories of what Loomis came to call "decentralism."

7. The impetus for this leased-land community is described on the Bryn Gweled web site (www.bryngweled.org) as follows: "Rampant real estate speculation was exacerbating poverty and disenfranchisement. Henry George's approach held hope of finding ways to stem this rising tide. A contemporary visionary was Ralph Borsodi, whose School of Living near Suffern, NY, attracted the attention of the group. Several people made an expedition to the School of Living and brought back enthusiasm and useful ideas about how small homesteads in a cooperative setting could enable a degree of self-sufficiency." Bryn Gweled means "hill of vision" in Welsh.

8. Antioch had been founded in 1852 by Horace Mann, a progressive educator. Antioch was the first college in the country to admit both women and African Americans.

9. Morgan drew inspiration from John Dewey's theories of progressive education and from his own professional career as someone who had learned engineering by doing engineering. He was also heavily influenced by the utopian ideas of Edward Bellamy, the author of *Looking Backward*.

10. After World War II, the land underlying Norris, Tennessee, was sold by TVA to private investors.

11. Another large-scale example of new town development on leased land began in Australia around the same time. When Henry George visited Australia and New Zealand in 1890, he found an appreciative audience for his ideas. Twenty years later, his followers shaped the development of the Australian Capital Territory. Established by parliament in the Seat of Government (Administration) Act of 1910, the Australian Capital Territory was created as a special governmental district for the country's new capital, Canberra. George's influence (and perhaps Howard's, as well) can be seen in the Act's stipulation that "no Crown lands in the territory shall be sold or disposed of for any estate of freehold." The land was to be owned forever by the commonwealth and leased, not sold, to the owners of any buildings constructed thereon. This was done to discourage speculation and to defray the expense of building Canberra, "allowing unearned increments in land value to be retained by the Commonwealth Government."

12. There was also no control over the resale price of Bryn Gweled's homes, an operational feature not added to the CLT until the 1980s. Compared to the affluent suburbs that surround it, Bryn Gweled is more racially and economically diverse. Indeed, it calls itself "an intentionally diverse community." But its houses have become quite expensive over time.

13. Although nearly all CLTs are nonprofit corporations—or subsidiaries of nonprofit corporations—not all CLTs are exempt from federal taxes under Section 501(c)(3). Either they have not sought such an exemption, or their purposes and activities do not qualify them for such an exemption.

14. Robert Swann, "The Community Land Trust: Borsodi and Vinoba Bhave," in *Peace, Civil Rights, and the Search for Community: An Autobiography*, chapter 18. Available online from the E. F. Schumacher Society, Great Barrington MA, www.smallisbeautiful.org/publications.html.

15. Rustin was to become one of the most influential leaders and strategists of the American civil right movement, although he was often forced to work behind the scenes because he was gay. He was a cofounder of the Congress on Racial Equality and a close advisor to Martin Luther King Jr. The 1963 March on Washington was Rustin's idea, and he served as its principal organizer.

16. Tom Long, "Robert Swann, 84, Peace Activist Who Sought Land Reform," obituary, *Boston Globe*, February 19, 2003.

17. Griscom Morgan became the director of Community Service, Inc., when his father retired in 1964. Griscom's wife, Jane, became director in 1970, holding that position until 1997. Both had an interest in intentional communities and CLTs, stemming in part from their personal involvement with an intentional community in Yellow Springs, called the Vale, which they helped to establish in the 1970s. The land underlying the Vale was conveyed to a local CLT in the mid-1980s, named the Community Service Land Trust.

18. At some point during this period they also visited the Celo community and contemplated living there. They decided not to do that, although one of their daughters later attended the Arthur Morgan School at Celo.

19. Taylor Branch, *Parting the Waters: America in the King Years, 1954–63* (New York: Simon & Schuster, 1988), 524–632.

20. The protesters were eventually released after staging a hunger strike that frightened the police into turning them loose. They immediately staged a celebratory parade, black and white activists dancing defiantly down Main Street.

21. Robert Swann, "Clarence Jordan and Koinonia Farm," in *Peace, Civil Rights, and the Search for Community*, chapter 17.

22. It is fair to say, in retrospect, that Koinonia Farm was the seedbed for two national movements. Both the community land trust and Habitat for Humanity can trace their origins to conversations at Koinonia in the mid-1960s. Until recently, these movements evolved along parallel tracks, with little interaction between them. By 2008, however, a pattern of local cooperation had become apparent to the national leaders of both movements, with over three dozen documented cases of local CLTs and local Habitat chapters joining forces to develop affordably priced housing for lower-income families. With their local affiliates pointing the way, the National CLT Network and Habitat for Humanity International signed a memorandum of understanding in 2009 to foster cross-training, technical support, and collaborative development between their constituencies.

23. ICE relocated again in 1980, moving west to Greenfield, Massachusetts. After ten years in Greenfield, it moved once more to Springfield, Massachusetts.

24. The National Sharecroppers Fund was a nonprofit advocacy organization created by the Southern Tenant Farmers' Union in 1937 to publicize the plight of sharecroppers and to push for legislation, social services, and economic opportunities to expand the rights and ease the lives of these impoverished farmers. Faye Bennett was executive director of the National Sharecroppers Fund from 1952 to 1974. She was 54 years old when Slater King came calling, asking for her support for the cooperative farm/leased-land community he had been discussing with Bob Swann.

25. The cooperative model they found most attractive was the *moshav shitufi*. This was different than a kibbutz, where farming is done collectively and profits are shared equally. In a moshav, purchasing and selling are done cooperatively, but each family has its own leasehold and owns its own home.

26. The team of people who had made the trip to Israel were joined on this planning committee by Father A. J. McKnight, James Mayes, Charles Prejean, James Wood, John Lewis, and William Peace. C. B. King provided legal advice throughout the planning process.

27. It was probably not a coincidence that chapter 8 in Arthur Morgan's book *The Small Community*, which had made such an impression on Swann in 1943 when he was in prison, was entitled "The Creation of New Communities."

28. A decade later, Father McKnight was appointed by President Jimmy Carter to the first board of directors of the National Cooperative Bank. He later served as vice president of the board, the same position he had held on the founding board of New Communities, Inc.

29. The story of the planning, founding, and first years of New Communities can be found in the following sources: *The Community Land Trust* (International Independence Institute, Cambridge, MA: Center for Community Economic Development, 1972), 16–25; Robert Swann, "New Communities: 5,000 Acres and $1,000,000," in *Peace, Civil Rights, and the Search for Community*, chapter 20; and an interview with Charles Sherrod, conducted by John Emmeus Davis in 1981, excerpts of which were published in *The Community Land Trust Handbook* (Emmaus, PA: Rodale Press, 1982), 39–47.

30. *The Community Land Trust Handbook*, 46.

31. New Communities provided an object lesson for later CLTs, among whom it became an article of faith that "Thou shall not encumber thy land with debt." Even though the land was lost, New Communities, Inc., (NCI) did not dissolve. The corporation remained in existence. When black farmers in the South won a $375 million settlement from the United States Department of Agriculture in 1999, resolving a class-action suit that had charged USDA with racial bias, NCI filed a claim, alleging that discriminatory lending at USDA in the 1970s and early 1980s had contributed to the failure of NCI's agricultural business and the loss of its land. In the summer of 2009, after a decade of being rebuffed by USDA, NCI was awarded $12 million. Its board began searching for farmland to buy in the Albany area, land that would be owned, this time around, debt free. The final chapter of NCI has yet to be written.

32. New Communities itself never managed to put in place most of the features of ownership and organization described in the book that was based on its story. In a valiant 15-year struggle to hold on to its land, the vision and plan put down on paper for this CLT "prototype" were never realized on the ground.

33. *The Community Land Trust*, 17.

34. Ibid., 38.

35. At a seminar sponsored by the Lincoln Institute of Land Policy in 2004, Terry Mollner, who had served on ICE's staff during the second half of the 1970s, tried to recall how ICE had arrived at the tripartite allocation of seats among leaseholders, nonleaseholder residents of the surrounding community, and representatives of the "public interest." He could not. He expressed mild amusement that what had "seemed like a good idea at the time" had proven its worth over the years and become a fixture of the CLT model.

36. In Webster's own words, "Bob would give me scribbled drafts and notes. I would have to organize them and polish them. He kept talking about 'land trust' this, 'land trust' that. I said we have to be able to distinguish it from other land trusts doing conservation. Why don't we call it a *community* land trust? He liked the suggestion. That was probably my only contribution to the CLT movement." Conversation with John Emmeus Davis, 2007.

37. Several rural land trusts were created in the early 1970s, most notably Earthbridge in Vermont and Sam Ely in Maine. The latter published a national newsletter, the *Maine Land Advocate*, for seven years (1973–1979).

38. To oversee this project, WCLT hired its first executive director, Mike Brown, with funds obtained by Marie Cirillo from the Catholic diocese in Nashville. Brown served as WCLT's director from 1980 to 1984. He later joined the staff of ICE and went on to become a partner in a national consulting cooperative, Burlington Associates in Community Development, providing technical assistance to dozens of CLTs.

39. One of the Covenant CLT's first leaseholders, incidentally, was Ellie Kastanopolous, who later became the executive director of Equity Trust. The story of the founding of the Covenant CLT is told in *The Community Land Trust Handbook*, 62–75.

40. In an interview conducted by John Emmeus Davis in 2008, Marjorie Swann attempted to describe the different abilities and contributions of Swann and Matthei in building the CLT movement: "Bob was very good at the theoretical stuff, at putting it into words. . . . He

was brilliant when it came to articulating the ideas and putting them into a whole plan. But he was not good at motivating people. Chuck's genius was in inspiring people to do it. After Chuck took over ICE, the land trusts multiplied."

41. For the next five years, as Matthei rebuilt ICE's staff, $300 was the monthly salary earned by all of ICE's employees.

42. Matthei had earlier joined with Mitch Snyder, Perk Perkins, and other members of the Center for Creative Nonviolence and Sojourners in trying to establish a CLT in Washington, DC. The Columbia Heights Community Ownership Project was incorporated in 1976. Soon after gaining control of several inner-city properties, however, it moved on to other issues, leaving its CLT agenda behind. The community organizers at Sojourners decided that forming a CLT had been premature. They turned their energies toward developing a neighborhood tenants union, which battled condo conversions and promoted resident-owned housing cooperatives. It is fair to call the Community Land Cooperative of Cincinnati, therefore, the first urban CLT.

43. *The Community Land Trust*, 64. The text goes on to say, however, that the main goal of such procedures should be to "ensure that community-generated value increments accrue to the community and not to the individual." Responsibility for calculating and allocating such value was to be assigned to "a committee either named by the community or operating as part of the board of trustees."

44. *The Community Land Trust Handbook* was authored by Marie Cirillo, John Davis, Rob Eshman, Charles Geisler, Harvey Jacobs, Andrea Lepcio, Chuck Matthei, Perk Perkins, and Kirby White. It was illustrated with drawings and prints produced by Bonnie Acker and photographs taken by Kerry Mackin and Bob O'Keefe.

45. "Typically, the CLT retains a first option to buy the improvements at the owner's original invested cost, often adjusted for inflation, depreciation, and damage during the ownership period. . . . Thus, the first leaseholder is guaranteed equity in the improvements, and the succeeding leaseholder is able to buy the improvements at a fair price. No seller will profit from unearned increases in market value, and no buyer will be priced out of the market by such increases." *The Community Land Trust Handbook*, 18.

46. "While the CLT expects responsibility and a positive commitment from leaseholders, it also has a moral responsibility to them above and beyond the lease agreement, and a practical need to help them use their leaseholds appropriately and well. This is particularly true with low-income leaseholders, who have only limited access to credit and services that may be needed for such things as emergency repairs to their buildings." *Community Land Trust Handbook*, 215–216.

47. *The Community Land Trust Handbook*, 74.

48. Gandhi's concept of trusteeship is captured well in the following quote: "What belongs to me is the right to an honourable livelihood, no better than that enjoyed by millions of others. The rest of my wealth belongs to the community and must be used for the welfare of the community." M. K. Gandhi, *Trusteeship* (Ahmedabad, India: Navajivan Trust, 1960).

49. The three other "paths for action" proposed in the 1972 book's "Mandate for Action" were (1) having government "play the dominant role in financing and setting up a land trust"; (2) advocating for the stewardship of scarce natural resources placed in a land trust; and (3) convincing existing communes and intentional communities to "place their land under a common trust umbrella" organized on a regional basis.

50. Slater King's brother, C. B. King, had advised the planners of the first CLT to incorporate New Communities as a nonprofit corporation, not as a real estate trust. This practice has continued among CLTs to the present day. Although nearly every CLT is a nonprofit corporation, not all CLTs have secured—or even sought—a 501(c)(3) tax exemption. Most of

the early land trusts did not seek 501(c)(3) status. One that did, the Sam Ely Trust in Maine, had it stripped away because it was not operated in ways recognized by the Internal Revenue Service as "charitable." The IRS objected specifically to the assistance Sam Ely was giving to farmers (i.e., private farm businesses). The revocation of its tax exemption precipitated the organization's collapse.

51. The City of Boston later became both a supporter and a partner. The most dramatic evidence of such municipal support was the 1988 decision to grant DNI the power of eminent domain in the Dudley Triangle, aiding in the assembly of small, fragmented parcels of land into larger, developable sites for the neighborhood's revitalization. See Peter Medoff and Holly Sklar, *Streets of Hope* (Boston: South End Press, 1994).

52. DNI was eventually to assemble, hold, and lease lands not only underneath limited-equity cooperatives, limited-equity condominiums, and rental housing, but also beneath urban parks, commercial greenhouses, a job training center, and a community center.

53. An earlier CLT had done so, as well. An extensive service area had been carved out by the Northern California CLT, cofounded in 1973 by Erick Hansch, who had moved west after six years on the staff of the International Independence Institute. It was not until the early 1990s that NCCLT reorganized to focus on housing and community development in the Bay Area, rather than purporting to serve all of northern California.

54. The San Juan Islands off the western coast of Washington proved to be an especially fertile area for the growth of CLTs. Lopez Island and Orcas Island gave rise to the Lopez CLT and OPAL (Of People and Land), both founded in 1989. In later years, CLTs were organized on San Juan Island, Waldron Island, and Lummi Island.

55. In March 2009, the National CLT Network reported the results of a national survey of its members, tallying the incidence of defaults and foreclosures in each CLT's portfolio of resale-restricted, owner-occupied housing. At a time when over 7 percent of all residential mortgages in the United States were in default and 3.3 percent of all mortgages were in foreclosure, CLT homeowners were posting a default rate of 1.4 percent and a foreclosure rate of 0.5 percent (www.cltnetwork.org).

56. The CLT's success in preventing foreclosures has attracted attention not only in the public sector, but in the business sector, as well, especially among private lenders who have seen default and foreclosure rates soar since 2006. Where the mortgaging of resale-restricted homes on leased land was once seen as an exotic and risky loan, many lenders now regard the CLT as a credit enhancement.

57. Several other organizations gradually got into the game, proposing "model" documents and "best practices" of their own. The E. F. Schumacher Society, founded by Bob Swann and Susan Witt, developed model documents that were somewhat different than ICE's, focusing on rural CLTs. In 1990, Chuck Matthei left ICE and founded Equity Trust. Its publications focused on the application of CLTs to agricultural lands, including partnerships between CLTs and CSA (community supported agriculture farms). Regional coalitions of CLTs emerged in the Pacific Northwest and in Minnesota in 1999 and 2003, respectively, each of them promoting standardized systems for operating a CLT and documenting its performance. In 2005, the Florida Housing Coalition established the Florida CLT Institute to promote CLT development in the Sunshine State. The next year, 2006, the National CLT Network established its own academy to research, develop, publish, and teach best practices for CLTs.

58. Although many attorneys lent their expertise to this project, David Abromowitz, a Boston attorney who had advised DSNI, served as the *Manual's* principal legal advisor. Abromowitz must be given most of the credit for the model ground lease's careful and equitable balancing of the interests of homeowner, landowner, and lender. The overall editor for both editions of the *CLT Legal Manual* was Kirby White.

59. Congressman Sanders had invited Tim McKenzie, director of the Burlington Community Land Trust (BCLT), to testify before his House Subcommittee in the spring of 1992. McKenzie's testimony about the BCLT's success in creating permanently affordable homes was well received, convincing Sanders that there might be an opening for some sort of federal legislation supportive of the CLT model, especially if it had no budgetary impact. When asked by Sanders for suggestions, McKenzie brought the City of Burlington's housing director, John E. Davis, into the conversation. After consulting ICE, McKenzie and Davis urged Sanders to propose a statutory definition of the CLT to make it easier for CLTs to receive federal funding and technical assistance under the HOME program. Sanders readily agreed but then discovered that he had only a few days to get something into the hopper. A one-page definition of the "community land trust" was drafted overnight by McKenzie and Davis, reviewed by ICE, and sent off to Sanders' office two days later. Their definition was inserted by Sanders into Section 212 of the Housing and Community Development Act of 1992 and approved by Congress with no changes (*Congressional Record–House*, October 5, 1992: H11966).

60. The CLT Academy was started as a joint venture of the National CLT Network and the Lincoln Institute of Land Policy. The cochairs of its founding board were Lisa Byers, the Network's president, and Roz Greenstein, representing the Lincoln Institute.

61. The editorial coordinators for *Community Economics*, over its entire 14-year run, were Kirby White and Lisa Berger.

62. An earlier conference had been hosted by ICE at Voluntown, Connecticut in 1983, but it could hardly be called a "national CLT conference" since only a few CLTs existed at the time and none was represented in Voluntown. This was more a gathering of community organizers, housing professionals, and ICE staff who were interested in starting CLTs. ICE always pointed to the 1987 conference in Atlanta, therefore, as the first national conference of CLTs.

63. ICE convened a total of nine national CLT conferences from 1997 to 2003. They were held in Atlanta (1987); Stony Point, New York (1988); Burlington, Vermont (1990); Cincinnati (1993); Washington, DC (1996); Durham, North Carolina (1997); Saint Paul, Minnesota (1999); Albuquerque (2000); and Syracuse (2003). The lead role in coordinating most of these conferences was played by Julie Orvis, who became the longest-serving member of ICE's staff (1987–2005).

64. Among the many white knights who rode to the rescue of the 2005 conference were Allison Handler and her staff at the Portland Community Land Trust, several leaders from the regional CLT coalitions that had started in the Pacific Northwest and Minnesota, several of the principals from Burlington Associates in Community Development, and Roz Greenstein from the Lincoln Institute of Land Policy. Drawing on Lincoln's resources, Greenstein provided critical financial and logistical support for the Portland conference. One year later, she helped to fund the National CLT Academy and then served for three years on the Academy's founding board.

65. The Network's board was drawn from every region of the United States. Regional representation was a factor in choosing the executive committee, as well. The Network's first president was Lisa Byers (OPAL CLT, Washington state); the vice president was Jim Mischler-Philbin (Northern Communities CLT, Minnesota); the secretary was Dannie Bolden (Gulf County CLT, Florida); and the treasurer was Dev Goetschius (Housing Land Trust of Sonoma County, California).

66. Following the Portland conference in 2005 and the Boulder conference in 2006, the first national conferences convened by the Network were held in Minneapolis (2007); Boston (2008); and Athens, Georgia (2009).

67. The Northwest CLT Coalition was established in 1999, the Minnesota CLT Coalition in 2000, and the Colorado CLT Coalition in 2008.

68. *The Community Land Trust Handbook,* 181.

69. Nearly all of the first CLTs counted pastors, priests, nuns, or former nuns among their founders and leaders. This certainly contributed to the faith that was regularly put in the miracle theory of financing. Perhaps it also accounted for the frequency with which such miracles seemed to occur.

70. *Community Economics,* no. 1 (Summer 1983): 3.

71. As ICE's revolving loan fund grew larger and more complex—and as ICE's technical assistance to community loan funds increased—staff other than Matthei played a larger and larger role. For over a dozen years, from 1981 to 1993, as ICE's revolving loan fund grew from $45,000 to $12 million, the fund's main manager was Sr. Louise Foisey. Other members of ICE who contributed the most to ICE's work with community investment over the years were Sr. Corinne Florek; Greg Ramm; Mary O'Hara; Raylene Clark-Gomes; and the former president of ICE's board, Michael Swack.

72. NACDLF joined with the National Federation of Community Development Credit Unions, several community development banks, and a number of other organizations in 1992 to create the Community Development Financial Institution Coalition, aimed at securing federal support for CDFIs. The coalition changed its name to the National Community Capital Association in 1996 and to the Opportunity Finance Network in 2006.

73. Toward the end of 1992, HUD's Department of Community Planning and Development distributed a circular (HUD 21B) to "All Regional Administrators, All Field Office Managers, All Regional Directors for CPD, All CPD Division Directors, All HOME Coordinators, and All HOME Participating Jurisdictions," declaring that "HOME funds may be used by CLTs. CLTs may also receive HOME funds for administrative and technical assistance for operating assistance and organizational support." The circular went on to say, "Community land trusts are, perhaps, one of the most effective means of ensuring permanent affordability of resident ownership simply because the trust maintains ownership of the land."

74. In addition to providing a definition of the CLT, Section 212 of the Housing and Community Development Act of 1992 bestowed three benefits on CLTs that were unavailable to other nonprofit housing developers. A CLT could receive CHDO designation and HOME funding even if it did not yet have a "demonstrated capacity for carrying out activities assisted with HOME funds" or was unable to "show one year of serving the community." Furthermore, it said, "Organizational support, technical assistance, education, training, and community support under this subsection may be available to . . . community groups for the establishment of community land trusts." This opened the door for federal assistance to CLTs that were just getting under way.

75. Some assistance was provided by ICE's own staff, principally Jeff Yegian, who was based in Boulder, Colorado. Most of the on-site technical assistance offered to CLTs from 1994 to 2004, however, under ICE's TA contracts with HUD, was provided by Burlington Associates in Community Development. After HUD—and ICE—withdrew from the field, the partners in this national consulting cooperative continued to assist new and mature CLTs. By 2010, over 90 CLTs had received some degree of direct TA from Burlington Associates. Many others had benefited indirectly by having access to educational documents and technical materials posted on the Burlington Associates web site and freely shared with the public under terms of the Creative Commons.

76. Fannie Mae released a model lease rider for CLTs in 2001. As part of the same package, Fannie Mae also published *Guidelines on the Valuation of a Property Subject to a Leasehold Interest and/or Community Land Trust.* This document provided assistance to lenders and appraisers in valuing CLT transactions.

77. John Emmeus Davis and Rick Jacobus have documented a diverse array of municipal support for CLTs, including seed money for planning a CLT; donations of city-owned property, grants of municipally controlled funds, and low-interest loans for developing CLT projects; capacity grants for sustaining CLT operations; and equitable assessments in valuing and taxing a CLT's resale-restricted homes. See Davis and Jacobus, *The City–CLT Partnership* (Cambridge, MA: Lincoln Institute of Land Policy, 2008).

78. This analogy is evocative but not exact, since a hybrid in the breeding of plants is a one-generation phenomenon. Hybrids cannot breed true. The mixing of traditions and agendas in the CLT, by contrast, has produced a model that can be reproduced across many generations.

79. These are the Diamond State CLT in Delaware and the Community Housing Land Trust of Rhode Island.

80. This was one of Bob Swann's abiding concerns about the movement he had helped to found: "Creating perpetually affordable housing is a good idea. The only thing is that there is a danger of losing track of the land itself." See the interview of Bob Swann conducted by Kirby White for *Community Economics*, no. 25 (Summer 1992): 3–5.

81. Davis and Jacobus offered a similar argument in *The City–CLT Partnership*: "The role of steward draws the CLT back to its original mission of shepherding resources that a community invests and of capturing values that a community creates. Making stewardship its principal activity brings the model full circle, refocusing the CLT on what it does best" (38).

82. It is not only in communities of color that CLTs are being organized to protect lands, promote development, and preserve the identity of place-based communities. It is there, however, that market forces and public policies tend to take the greatest toll, especially in African American communities proximate to an expanding downtown or situated on the shoreline of a river, lake, or ocean. Recognizing the special needs of these communities and responding to the rising demand for CLT assistance from African American communities in the South, the National CLT Network launched a Heritage Lands Initiative in 2008.

Toward a Property Ethic of Stewardship

A Religious Perspective

Peter W. Salsich, Jr.
(2000)

Recent public discussions of tax reform and urban sprawl, two apparently unrelated topics, are manifestations of a deeper concern about a widening gap between haves and have nots in America. Enactment of budget, tax, and welfare reform legislation, while sweeping in its own right, has set the stage for serious debate about more fundamental change.

An important economic and cultural tenet of our society is the belief in the value of private property. However, as the gap in housing affordability becomes larger, questions can and should be raised about tax and zoning policies that encourage acquisition of residential property for investment beyond what may be needed for shelter. Religious principles respecting private property can inform such a discussion. As scholars have noted, economic thought, religious beliefs, and law often interact in significant ways (Gerber 1997).

This essay will explore the Judeo-Christian principle of stewardship and its application to land ownership. Particular attention will be paid to the historical significance of stewardship within Catholic social teaching, and to its potential for resolving the American housing dilemma of inaccessibility and unaffordability. The religious concept of stewardship is derived from the belief that all material goods, including land, belong to God. The earth and everything in it was created by God. Humankind was created in the image and likeness of God and given dominion over material goods of the earth. Since all humans are created in God's likeness, all have a claim to the earth's bounty. Individuals may appropriate what they need for their own sustenance and development but only what they need. Civil title to land, while giving the holder substantial power to possess, use, and dispose of that land, is not absolute. With title comes a responsibility to care for the land and use it wisely for the betterment of the landowner, the landowner's community, and future generations. The landowner, as steward, will ultimately be asked to give an accounting of that use to God, the Master.

Scholars trace the stewardship principle to the story of creation in the Book of Genesis, and reflections on that story by David and Isaiah (Bartlett 1915:87). God created humankind "in his image" and gave them "dominion . . . over every living thing that moves upon the earth" (Genesis 1:27–28).[1] In Psalm 8, David sings of the "glory and honor" God gave human beings by giving them "dominion over the works of [his] hands" (Psalms 8:5–6). In Isaiah, the notions that God is the "Creator . . . of all things" and that humans hold their souls, bodies, and goods "in stewardship for God, and for his ends" are emphasized (Bartlett 1915:87: citing Isaiah 40 ff).

Middle Eastern societies of antiquity were agrarian in nature and dominated by "kinship roles such as ancestor, patron, child or client, brother and sister . . . or political roles such as chief, king, lord, subject, warrior, counselor, citizen" (Malina 1997:8). The perception of all but the "urban elite" was that "all the desired things in life . . . exist in finite, limited quantity and are always in short supply" (Malina 1997:11). As a result, some scholars have argued that the study of biblical documents is of little or no value to a modern American society that is "individualistic, competitive [and] based on the presumption that all goods are limitless (even if some are scarce)" (Malina 1997:15).

However, if the Judeo-Christian tradition of stewardship that was first articulated in the Old Testament is viewed as an ideal, it has relevance to policymakers as well as economists today. The "rational model of behavior," so important to modern economic theory, assumes that people will make "the optimal decision" if they have full information and freedom of choice. But since people rarely have full information and unfettered choice, the optimal decision is really an "ideal standard against which actual behavior can be found wanting. . . . [Thus] the notion of optimality asserts the primacy of what ought to be against the reality of what is" (Welch 1998 quoting Wolfe 1991:34–35).

This chapter traces the stewardship principle through the Old and New Testaments, early Christianity, the Middle Ages, the Protestant Reformation, and the Industrial Revolution. Stewardship was a guiding principle of the Church during the first few centuries of Christianity. Early church philosophers such as St. Clement, St. Basil, St. Ambrose, St. John Chrysostom, and St. Augustine argued that private ownership of property should not be thought of in the Roman sense of absolute individual ownership but rather in a communal sense of sharing the means of production (Avila 1983). The conversion to Christianity of Roman Emperor Constantine and the subsequent rise in influence of the Church in affairs of state pushed the stewardship principle into the background for centuries. It was revived in modified format by St. Thomas Aquinas (Bartlett 1915; Hobgood 1991) and utilized in part by Puritan supporters of capitalism "who branded all careless consumption as a sin" (Wood 1954:154). The excesses of the Industrial Revolution led ultimately to the publication of the first social encyclical, *Rerum Novarum*. In that and subsequent encyclicals, the stewardship principle was resurrected as a part of Catholic social teaching, although in a way that produced tension among three strands of social theory, organic, orthodox, and radical (Hobgood 1991).

The text further explores stewardship advocacy in American churches during the 1970s, 1980s, and 1990s. During this period, American churches became increasingly active in calling attention to social problems. Some advocated a stewardship approach to land ownership in resolving housing problems for lower-income persons. Others became involved in stewardship-based community economic development and farm-land ownership.

The final section of the chapter suggests a stewardship approach to future concerns about scarcity of affordable housing opportunities for low and moderate income families in the United States. Under this approach, the shelter aspect of land ownership would be separated from the investment aspect of such ownership when applying federal tax and state zoning laws to residential uses of land. Reducing the extent of the residential mortgage interest tax deduction to free more funds for lower-income housing, or shifting from the deduction to a refundable housing tax credit, would focus more tax resources on the housing needs of lower-income families. Emphasizing inclusionary land use policies instead of exclusionary large-lot, single-family zoning would make more land resources available for affordable housing. Both sets of policies emphasize the social aspect of property, which is at the heart of the stewardship principle.

Judeo-Christian Traditions of Stewardship

Recurring property rights debates reflect an important and very emotional clash of basic values, including deeply felt individual interests in the free use of private property and correspondingly deeply felt concerns that land is a finite resource that must be shared and used wisely for the benefit of present and future communities. Land and its possession have had special significance for humans since ancient times. Philosophers, scholars, and theologians have debated the proper relationship between humans and the earth they inhabit almost as long. Whether land should be held in common by large entities (the state) or small ones (clans or families), or should be subject to private ownership by individual persons, has been one of the great questions of civilization.

Recent scholarship has found evidence of a blend of private and communal ownership of land as far back as 3000 B.C. in the ancient civilizations of Mesopotamia, Egypt, and Israel. In their fascinating study of the land laws of those civilizations, Robert Ellickson and Charles Thorland (1995:408–9) discovered examples of "private ownership of homes, gardens and small arable land plots; communal or institutional ownership of arable and grazing lands where the arrangement was necessary to exploit efficiencies of scale or spread risks; and a network of open-access land."

Old Testament Israel
In the Old Testament (Hebrew Bible), property was an expression of the covenant between Yahweh and the Israelites. God made the world and "God saw that . . . it was very good." God made "humankind in his own image . . . [and gave them] dominion . . . over every living thing that walks the earth" (Genesis 1:27–31). But "the earth with all that is in it" belongs to God, the creator (Deuteronomy 10:14).

God's covenant with Abraham included the promise of "the land where you are now an alien, all the land of Canaan, for a perpetual holding" (Genesis 17:18). As David Novak notes in his book, *Jewish Social Ethics*, the Hebrew Bible presents God "as the true and faithful provider of the things we basically need, . . . as a matter of grace, not justice" (Novak 1992:208).[2]

Land was given to the Israelites to hold and possess, but not to own. "The land is not to be sold in perpetuity, for the land is mine; with me you are but aliens and tenants" (Leviticus 25:23). The sabbatical year (land was to lie fallow every seven years) and the year of the Jubilee (return to ancestral property every 50 years) emphasized that land was owned by God rather than by humans and that it was to be used wisely and not overexploited (Leviticus 25:2–7, 10–13).

As stewards, the Israelites were to "[s]et apart a tithe of all the yield of [their] seed that is brought in yearly from the field." Also, "[s]ince there will never cease to be some in need on the earth, . . . '[o]pen your hand to the poor and needy neighbor in your land.'" In addition, Israelites who had been allotted property in the land given them to possess by the Lord "must not move [their] neighbor's boundary marker, set up by former generations" (Deuteronomy 14:22, 15:11, 19:14; Ellickson & Thorland 1995:344).

An important qualification to these apparent strictures against ownership was the widespread practice of private ownership of family houses, garden plots, and farms (Ellickson & Thorland 1995). Abraham, in accordance with ancient practices, insisted on purchasing land to enable him to bury his wife, Sara, rather than simply receiving it as a gift from the Hittites (Genesis 23:16–18). In addition, the Covenant Code in Exodus, the earliest of several law codes in the Pentateuch (Torah), requires restitution to be made in several situations, such as overgrazing of land by another's livestock (Exodus 22:5), destruction by fire of grain in a field (Exodus 22:6), and injury or death of a borrowed animal (Exodus 22:14; Ellickson & Thorland 1995).

Walter Brueggemann reviewed the long history of confrontation between kings and prophets in the Old Testament. The story of Ahab, Jezebel, and Naboth, particularly Elijah's rebuke of Ahab and Jezebel for their actions in conspiring to kill Naboth and take his vineyard, provides Brueggemann with an example of two classic views of land competing for our attention, even today. Ahab's offer to trade or purchase Naboth's vineyard is an example of land viewed simply as a tradable commodity. Naboth's refusal to bargain is based on his view that the land is "the inheritance of my fathers." To Naboth, "the land is not owned in a way that permits its disposal. . . . [It is a gift from Yahweh and] is held in trust from generation to generation; . . . [L]and management is concerned with preservation and enhancement of the gift for coming generations" (Brueggemann 1977:93; 1 Kings 21:3).

Early Christianity

Early Christian concepts of property were characterized by a "primitive communism . . . that had been eloquent testimony to the equality of all people in the sight of God" (O'Brien & Shannon 1977:18). In the Acts of the Apostles we read:

> Now the whole group of those who believed were of one heart and soul, and no one claimed private ownership of any possessions, but everything they owned was held in common. . . . There was not a needy person among them, for as many as owned lands or houses sold them and brought the proceeds of what was sold. They laid it at the apostles' feet, and it was distributed to each as any had need. (Acts 4:32, 34–35)

But taken literally, the doctrine "could breed explosive social discontent," prompting St. Paul and later Church leaders to counsel "resignation for the poor, benevolence for the rich, and charity for all" (O'Brien & Shannon 1977:18). Because of sin, humankind was imperfect and needed a social order. The social order at the time of the early Church was characterized by great disparities of wealth and power. The early Christians were a part of the Roman Empire. Roman property law had evolved from a combination of individual homesteads and a public domain of communal fields to a system of absolute private ownership of property, including land, concentrated in a small number of wealthy families. The only things remaining in common were the air, the sea, and the seashore (Avila 1983).

As the early Christian community sought to define its role in the world, it faced tensions illustrated by the gospel story of the rich young man and the parable of the talents. Matthew, Mark, and Luke all recount an incident in which a young man of wealth asks Jesus Christ what he must do to have eternal life. Christ tells him to keep the commandments. The man says that he has. Christ then responds: "If you wish to be perfect, go, sell your possessions, and give the money to the poor, and you will have treasure in heaven; then come, follow me." In all three accounts, the man "went away grieving, for he had many possessions" (Matthew 19:16–22; Mark 10:17–22; Luke 18:18–23). However, Matthew and Luke also recount a parable in which Christ praises two servants who doubled the talents given them by the master while he was away, but criticized severely one servant who hid the money and did not invest it because he was afraid of his master (Matthew 25:14–30; Luke 19:11–26).

The concept of stewardship helped church leaders reconcile the apparent contradiction illustrated by these stories. David O'Brien and Thomas Shannon, in their book collecting Catholic documents on peace, justice, and liberation, comment that "[t]he notion of stewardship . . . provided a foundation for accommodation to existing economic arrangements without surrendering control over the moral life of the individual" (1977:26–27).

Charles Avila examined the writings of early Christian philosophers, called Fathers of the Church, who dealt with questions of ownership and related issues. Sts. Clement of Alexandria, Basil the Great, Ambrose of Milan, John Chrysostom, and Augustine of Hippo confronted the Roman notion of absolute ownership and found it wanting. Since God gave all things to humankind, the land and its abundance were good. But relative wealth, the appropriation of land and material goods beyond what was needed for self-sufficiency, was evil in their eyes. To Clement, "God has given us the authority to use our possessions, I admit, but only to the extent it is necessary: He wishes them to be in common" (Avila 1983:37 quoting Clement, the Paidagogos [educator], in Wood 1954). Basil argues "[i]f each one would take that which is sufficient for one's needs, leaving what is in excess to those in distress, no one would be rich, no one poor" (Avila 1983:49 quoting a sermon of Basil's in Ryan 1913:8–9). Ambrose cautions "[w]e lose the things that are common when we claim things as our own" (Avila 1983:72). John Chrysostom asks "[w]hy then, if it is common, have you so many acres of land, while your neighbor has not a portion of it?" (Avila 1983:94 quoting John Chrysostom in Schaff 1952:421). Augustine warns "[t]he one who uses his wealth badly possesses it wrongfully, and wrongful possession means that it is another's property" (Avila 1983:110).

The patristic philosophy excerpted briefly above drew heavily on the Stoic tradition that when humankind was innocent there was no need for private property, but that when evil entered the world and innocence was lost, private property became necessary to control the greedy appetites of individuals (Carlyle 1915). The patristic sense of ownership, while not employing the term "stewardship," recognized the emphasis that the concept places on use of property for God's purpose of fellowship with Him. Individuals may use property to achieve self-sufficiency, and they may share property ownership in common to achieve fellowship with one another and with God. Absolute ownership, in the Roman sense of appropriation of more than what is necessary for self-sufficiency, was contrary to God's plan.

The Holy Roman Empire and the Middle Ages

The conversion of Roman emperor Constantine to Christianity had profound implications for the Church. The creation of the Holy Roman Empire and the establishment of Christianity as the official religion of the West led the church into direct involvement with affairs of state. As it gained official stature, the revolutionary aspects of Christ's message created tensions that Church leaders and theologians attempted to reconcile. Christ's message that his kingdom was "not from this world" (John 18:36), and his admonition to "give to the emperor the things that are the emperor's and to God the things that are God's" (Matthew 22:21), together with the "sinful nature of mankind," provided a frame of reference for the development of a structure of rules governing society. These rules, worked out over several centuries, were premised on the notion that the "given social order [was] ordained by God" (O'Brien & Shannon 1977:18). But as a result of this attempted accommodation with the social order, the socialistic aspect of early Christian philosophy about ownership was "relegated to a world of incrucifiable generalities and highly spiritualized realities" (Avila 1983:153).

The recognition of private property as a liberating influence on the human spirit and as a necessary means of regulating the greed of individuals gained prominence as Christianity grew in stature in the Western world. However, accumulation of private property was not an end in itself, but rather a means to obtaining what one needs.

Thus, "maintenance of the needy [is] an act of justice, not of mercy: for it is justice to give to a man that which is his own, and the needy have a moral right to what they require" (Carlyle 1915:126). According to Gratian, the twelfth-century compiler of the Canon Law, "[b]y the law of nature, all things are common to all men . . . it is only by the law of custom or of institution that this is mine and that is another's" (Carlyle 1915:127).[3]

As society became ordered in a feudal manner, people became obligated to one another in a hierarchical structure of serf, vassal, lord, and king. In support of the social order, the Church, primarily through Thomas Aquinas, articulated a theory of social duties that regulated the feudal relationships. Serfs owed specific duties to their lords, and lords owed duties to their serfs (O'Brien & Shannon 1977). Aquinas, heavily influenced by Aristotle, believed that society existed "for the mutual exchange of services for the common good" (O'Brien & Shannon 1977:19), and that private property was necessary to encourage peace and social order (Aquinas Pt. II-II, Q. 66, Art. 2 in Welch 1998). Aquinas lived during the rise of capitalism and trade and generally supported the work of the middleman trader so long as the price set was a just one, and monopoly, fraud, and usury were avoided (Hobgood 1991).

But Aquinas distinguishes the right to acquire and distribute property, which he supports, from the right to hold property for one's own use, which he qualifies by the requirement to provide for those in need (Aquinas Pt. II-II, Q. 66, Art. 2 in Carlyle 1915). Aquinas wrote that "man ought to possess external things, not as his own, but as common, so that, . . . he is ready to communicate them to others in their need" (Aquinas Pt. II-II, Q. 66, Art. 2; Bigongiari 1953, 130; Pope Leo XIII 1891:36). The Thomistic division of property unto acquisition for purposes of distribution and use consistent with the needs of the community reflects the stewardship ideal. Anyone who has more property than he needs is a steward required to care for the surplus property, which belongs to humankind. Property that persons acquire to satisfy their needs should be used for that purpose and not wasted.

The Protestant Reformation

The expansion of the economy of Western Europe and the growing importance of trade caused new challenges to Christian concepts of private property. As O'Brien and Shannon (1977) note, the Church's status as the official religion of a growing capitalistic society led it into complex economic entanglements that produced serious conflicts with the teachings of its founder. While the Church's teaching regarding the limits of private property continued to stress the obligation to hold only what was necessary for self-sufficiency, and to share any surplus with the needy, Church institutions and officials amassed considerable wealth. In part, this was the result of the injunction to share. Wealthy individuals gave large tracts of land to support mendicant orders of monks and nuns. In part it was evidence of the religious idea that private property was a result of sin entering the world. Greedy individual church officials sanctioned excessive acquisition of land, blinded by the false notion that they were following the will of God, and made almost no effort to reconcile ownership and social responsibility as the stewardship principle required.

The authors of an economic history of Europe published in the 1950s note, for example, that the Church was heavily involved in a tug-of-war over interest-bearing loans between the thirteenth and sixteenth centuries. A pope allegedly threatened excommunication of an archbishop for refusing to pay usurious interest rates to some bankers, and a churchman later declared a saint held that a seller sometimes could charge as much as 50 percent over the fixed price. "Dante assigned the money lenders of Cahors a special place in hell, but a pope gave them the title of 'peculiar sons of the Church'" (Clough & Cole 1952:82). The inability to reconcile the conflicts resulting from the Church's economic activity contributed to the Protestant Reformation. For example, Martin Luther's 95 theses included a strong attack on the practice of generating wealth for the church by the sale of indulgences (Aland 1967).

The Reformation brought a clash between Catholic and Protestant churches on a wide variety of issues. Protestant reformers rejected many of the Church's methods of fulfilling the obligations to God, as well as practices considered venal and corrupt. But they accepted the principle of stewardship that while "the earth was provided by God for the use of humans . . . the fruits of labor were not one's own alone" (O'Brien & Shannon 1977:24). For example, John Calvin, in advocating a theology of edification that emphasized a discipline of work and patience with one's lot in life, argued that Scripture "regulates the use of earthly things . . . [which] were so given to us by the kindness of God, and so destined for our benefit, that they are, as it were, entrusted to us, and we must one day render account of them (Leith 1984:30–31).

Martin Luther explained the commandments against stealing and coveting, saying "[T]o steal is nothing else than to acquire another's property by unjust means. . . . God does not wish you to deprive your neighbor of anything that is his, letting him suffer loss while you gratify your greed, even though in the eyes of the world you might honorably retain the property." To Luther and his followers, "stewardship becomes a means to embody 'faith active in love' for the sake of the neighbors" (Bloomquist 1996:29–33).

As capitalism took hold and the mercantile economy expanded, many Catholic theologians and Protestant reformers endorsed private accumulation of property. But the stewardship ideal was not discarded. Both Catholic and Protestant leaders were guided by the "firm conviction that individuals were responsible to God for the use of their talents and wealth, and that the obligation could and should be given practical expression in the life of the Christian community" (O'Brien & Shannon 1977:26–27).

Even John Locke, regarded as the founder of modern property concepts through his labor theory of ownership, wrote from deeply religious motivations. In laying out his theory that government is based on the consent of the governed, Locke used his first treatise to refute the divine right of kings theory by close examination of the biblical story of creation. Adam was not monarch of the whole world. God gave Adam "not

Private Dominion over the Inferior Creatures, but right in common with all Mankind" (I Tr. 24; Laslett 1988:157). Peter Laslett, in his lengthy introduction to Locke's *Two Treatises on Government*, notes that Locke's famous labor theory of property "was confined originally to what a man and his family could consume or use, and must not be wasted, and that he recognized the community's claim to an individual's property through the laws of escheat (II Tr. 36, I Tr. 90; Laslett 1988).

Others argue that Locke was using his first treatise response to Sir Robert Filmer as a device for examining the Scriptures. Through this examination, Locke attempted to work out a theory of human revelation. The Bible story of "creation, domination, and fall" reflects the fundamentals of the created world in which humankind is "free to obey" the creator. "Man is far more in the position of the shepherd tending to the flock of another, for the world is God's and man's title to it is by no means one of right, but only one of gift and one of sufferance by the creating God" (Zuckert 1980:71–72). Locke disagrees with this interpretation, according to Zuckert (1980:73–74), and argues that because of human mortality, it is necessary for humankind to provide the necessities of life through human labor. The Lockean proviso that property can be acquired by labor "at least where there is enough, and as good left in common for others" (II Tr. 27; Laslett 1988:288) has a stewardship ring to it. But his emphasis on the right of individuals to be protected from an oppressive State led him, in the mind of critics, to lose sight of the "social aspects of property" (McDonald 1939:104).

The Industrial Revolution and the Christian Response

The overwhelming social and political upheavals of the Industrial Revolution posed enormous challenges to established religions. The vast technological changes in the way goods could be produced, the increasing control of the means of production by a relatively small number of people, the need for large numbers of workers to attend the new machines in urban factories, and the altered social patterns that resulted challenged Protestants and Catholics to respond to new classes of poor and suffering persons. A major response in the late nineteenth century and throughout the twentieth century was the emergence of social Christianity. The Catholic social encyclicals, the Protestant social gospel, liberation theology, and the Christian conservative tradition were all offsprings of this movement (Atherton 1994).

Both Catholic and Protestant responses to modern social problems have been informed by theories of capitalism and socialism and their variants. Property plays a central role in both theories. Acquisition and exchange of private property through the operation of a free market are essential to capitalism. Socialism views with suspicion the individualistic nature of private property and argues that the collective community should hold property resources. Adding to the complexity of the religious dilemma is the structural tradition, particularly in the Catholic Church, of the hierarchical model of society inherited from Roman and feudal times. Mary Hobgood (1991) argues that the Church's responses to modern social problems have been plagued with internal inconsistencies because of a failure to come to grips with these tensions. The stewardship principle offers a way to come to grips with the tensions, at least with respect to the role of private property in society, because it recognizes both the personal aspect of ownership and the communal setting in which individuals function.

The Social Encyclicals

Between 1891 and 1991, the Catholic Church issued six encyclicals focusing on social problems: *Rerum Novarum* (1891), *Quadragesimo Anno* (1931), *Mater et Magistra* (1961), *Populorum Progressio* (1967), *Sollicitudo Rei Socialis* (1987), and *Centesimus Annus* (1991), as well as *Gaudium et Spes* (1965), the Pastoral Constitution on the Church in the Modern World. All spoke to the question of private property, with the stewardship ideal playing an increasingly important role.

In *Rerum Novarum,* Pope Leo XIII accepted the argument that private property was part of the natural law. In speaking to the condition of workers at the end of the nineteenth century, Leo (1891:par. 20 cited in Mclaughlin 1932:10) stated that "the essential reason why those who engage in any gainful occupation or undertake labor . . . is to obtain property, and thereafter to hold it as his very own." Mary Hobgood (1991:100) argues that Leo XIII, because of the Church's opposition to socialism, actually went beyond the Thomistic idea of private property as a rational development of positive humanmade law and elevated it to a natural law precept. But stewardship remained a part of the equation. The special status of the poor was a reason for limiting the exercise of property rights so as "to serve the common interest of all" (Welch 1998:1613 quoting Pope Leo XIII).

Forty years after *Rerum Novarum*, Pope Pius XI in *Quadragesimo Anno* reaffirmed the natural law basis for private property and emphasized "the twofold aspect of ownership, which is individual or social according as it regards individuals or concerns the common good" (Pius XI 1931:20). Pope John XXIII, recalling Leo XIII's words 70 years later in *Mater et Magistra*, stressed not only the "natural right" to private property but also the "social aspect [of] private property. . . . Our predecessors have always taught that in the right of private property there is rooted a social responsibility" (1961:par. 19, 119). Stewardship was implicit in this notion of social responsibility. The goods of this world should be used, not only for the betterment of the property owner, but also "for the benefit of others" (Pope John XXIII 1961:par. 119 quoting Leo XIII).

In *Populorum Progressio*, Pope Paul VI (1967:par. 23) quotes St. Ambrose concerning the "proper attitude of persons who possess anything towards persons in need: 'The world is given to all, and not only to the rich.'" In *Sollicitudo Rei Socialis*, Pope John Paul II reviews the validity of private property and declares that it "is under a 'social mortgage' which means that it has an intrinsically social function based upon and justified precisely by the principle of the universal destination of goods" (1987:par. 42:86). God has placed a lien for the benefit of humankind on the enjoyment of the goods of the world. Owners of property will have to account for their stewardship of the land and its products. He returns to this theme in his 1991 encyclical, *Centesimus Annus*, emphasizing the origin of material goods as gifts from God "to the whole human race," and, while acknowledging that "the possession of know-how, technology and skill" has become as important, it is not more important than ownership of land (1991:par. 30–32).

In the Pastoral Constitution on the Church in the Modern World, *Gaudium et Spes*, the Second Vatican Council proclaimed in 1965 that since God intended the earth and its goods to be for the use of all persons, "a man should regard his lawful possessions not merely as his own but also as common property in the sense that they should accrue to the benefit of not only himself but of others. . . . By its very nature, private property has a social quality deriving from the law of the communal purpose of earthly goods" (O'Brien & Shannon 1977:249–51 quoting par. 69 & 71).

Stewardship Advocacy in American Churches

Since the 1970s, a number of religious organizations in the United States have issued statements addressed to a variety of social problems. Many of these have focused on land ownership imbalance and have adopted stewardship principles in framing recommendations for collective action.

In 1975 the National Conference of Catholic Bishops issued a major statement entitled "The Right to a Decent Home." That same year, Catholic bishops in the Appalachian area issued a statement endorsing stewardship of land, "This Land Is Home to Me" (Catholic Committee of Appalachia 1980). In 1980, Catholic bishops in 12 midwestern states issued "Strangers and Guests: Toward a Community in the Heartland," a statement "addressing land issues from a moral perspective," that endorsed the concept of stewardship (Catholic Bishops of the Heartland 1980). This was followed by the 1985 paper, "Housing: The Third Human Right," issued by the U.S. Catholic Conference's Campaign for Human Development. In the 1987 U.S. Bishops' pastoral letter, "Economic Justice for All," a number of values and principles were discussed that have clear implications for housing. "Homelessness and Housing," a 1988 statement of the Administrative Board of the U.S. Catholic Conference, called attention to the human tragedy and moral challenge of homelessness and unaffordable housing.

In analyzing local housing conditions in 1992, the Human Rights Commission of the Archdiocese of St. Louis identified five moral norms from these documents to guide an assessment of property and housing policies:

1. The "right to housing" is among the basic human rights necessary to preserve the dignity of each individual.
2. The notion of "stewardship" requires that the gifts of God's creation are for the benefit of all, not just some.
3. The concept of "participation" ensures that all people are able to shape their own destiny and meet their own basic needs by a broader participation in economic, civil, and social life.

4. The "preferential option for the poor" is a moral obligation urging us to evaluate social and economic activity from the perspective of the poor.

5. The "common good" tradition is seen as the sum of those conditions of social life that allow groups and their individual members relatively thorough and ready access to their own fulfillment. (1992:3–4)

These norms reaffirm the value of private property, but emphasize its communal character captured eloquently by Pope John Paul II with his "social mortgage" metaphor. As the new catechism of the Catholic Church teaches, "[p]rior to our natural right to own property . . . is the right of every person to have a share of material goods for needed subsistence" (Wuerl, Lawlor, and Lawlor 1995:301).

In a 1996 study prepared for deliberation on current social problems, the Division for Church in Society of the Evangelical Lutheran Church in America described stewardship as "our calling to care for the land, resources, people, other species and ecosystems, and the goods for which we bear responsibility. . . . We serve as trustees or caretakers for the sake of [God's] intentions" (Bloomquist 1996:32). The study asserts that the proper way to evaluate economic practices from the perspective of God's will is to embrace a "vision . . . of sufficient, sustainable livelihood for all." Stewardship plays an important role in this vision because, according to "Lutheran confessional writings . . . how we use the property we have is the moral basis for our right to own it" (Bloomquist 1996:43).

In addition to publishing statements and studies, religious organizations have become directly involved in community-based development projects founded on stewardship principles. For example, the Catholic Church's Campaign for Human Development has raised and dispensed millions of dollars in past decades to local and regional community development organizations. In 1989, the Lilly Endowment began an ecumenical support effort, the Religious Institutions as Partners in Community-Based Development Program. Grants and technical assistance were provided to 28 religious-community partnerships working to improve housing and economic development in urban, rural, and suburban settings. Their activities include community land banks and land trusts, community development credit unions, economic revitalization planning, home buyer counseling, private and rental housing, and mortgage guarantees (Scheie 1994:5–6, 55–63).

A Stewardship Approach to Housing

The heart of the stewardship concept is the responsibility to care for property belonging to another. In the Judeo-Christian tradition, the land belongs to God. It has been given to us as a gift. We are responsible to God for the way we use the land.

For most of this century, public policy has encouraged private ownership of residential property, primarily through favorable tax and land use laws. For a large portion of

American families, these policies have been successful. However, the growing gaps between rich and poor and between city and suburb raise stewardship questions. Coinciding with the increase in the minimum wage to $5.15/hour in September 1997, a report of the National Low Income Housing Coalition asserted that a family of four needed an income of double the minimum wage in order to afford a median-priced, two bedroom apartment in the United States without seriously neglecting other family needs. Using the benchmark allocation of 30 percent of income for housing, the study estimated that 44 percent of American households with three or four members would not find the median-priced unit affordable (NLIHC 1997).

At the same time, people are distancing themselves from one another in gated communities and through continued use of relatively large-lot, single-family zoning as the principal means of exclusionary land use control in exurban areas. Blakely and Snyder, in their book, *Fortress America: Gated Communities in the United States*, estimate that more than eight million Americans now live in gated communities. Large concentrations are found in major metropolitan cities, Chicago, Houston, Los Angeles, Miami, New York, and Phoenix, with the major growth occurring in middle and upper middle class markets. Both new suburban developments and older inner-city areas are moving in this direction (Blakely & Snyder 1997:7, 180). Despite impressively researched assertions that single-family zoning is no longer a defensible land use strategy (Babcock 1983; Ziegler 1983), many new cities and suburbs impose several-acre minimum lot requirements.[4]

For much of this century, American housing policy has been dominated by the belief that ownership of detached, single-family residences is the best way for the American family to secure shelter. Not only does such ownership offer basic shelter, it also enables families to maximize their privacy and to generate wealth through appreciation in land values as they repay loans used to acquire their homes. As a result, families who own their homes are believed to be more likely to put down roots and become productive members of their communities than renters or mobile home owners because the former are believed to be more stable and more responsible.

The single-family home ownership policy has been implemented primarily by two governmental activities, one an indirect federal subsidy and the other an exercise of the state police power. Since 1913, homeowners have had the ability to deduct from their federal income tax liability the amount of interest they pay on residential mortgages (see Internal Revenue Code 1995:§ 163). In 1926, the Supreme Court put its stamp of approval on the emerging land use regulatory technique of comprehensive zoning, giving single-family home ownership a particularly strong plug by characterizing apartment developments as "mere parasite(s)" on residential neighborhoods (*Euclid v. Ambler* 1926, 272 U.S. 365, 394).

The mortgage interest tax deduction and the use of zoning favoring large-lot, single-family home ownership cater to an individualistic ethic. The tax deduction encourages accumulation of wealth and control by individual homeowners, and large-lot single-family zoning encourages homeowners to separate themselves from persons who are not in their economic or social classes, especially in suburbs and "edge cities." Both policies become more valuable as persons ascend the economic ladder, and both encourage the production and consumption of larger houses than are necessary for basic or even comfortable shelter. Single-family home ownership is generally out of reach of persons in the lowest economic quartile without major subsidies. For the remaining quartiles, the bigger the mortgage, the bigger the mortgage interest tax deduction; as homes get larger, so do their tax shelters.[5]

Zoning also encourages larger homes because of the popularity of minimum lot size regulations. The economics of real estate development require a considerably larger house to be built on a 1-acre lot than would be built on a quarter-acre lot. Our land is finite and our tax resources have limits. Stewardship principles suggest that policies encouraging particular allocation of those resources should be directed toward public needs rather than public wants. In the housing context, this would mean a reallocation of homeowner tax preferences toward low and moderate income families, a reallocation of land use policies toward smaller lots in the inner portions of metropolitan areas, and the encouragement of integrated communities by race and class.

Techniques to accomplish these goals include federal legislation to expand the reach of the present cap on the mortgage interest tax deduction by reducing the amount triggering the cap from $1 million to $2–3 hundred thousand, or to shift from a tax deduction to a progressive tax credit. Examples of land use policies that implement the stewardship ideal include state legislation mandating the establishment of inclusionary housing plans as a condition of local zoning powers, establishing a presumption in favor of affordable housing proposals that are consistent with inclusionary housing plans, and limiting the expenditure of state funds for public works and capital improvements in metropolitan areas to urban service/primary growth areas as established by a collaborative state, regional, and local planning process.

Conclusion

This brief review of Judeo-Christian religious teachings reveals a consistent acceptance of the concept of private land ownership, coupled with an ideal of stewardship whose influence has waxed and waned over the years. While individuals, church leaders, and congregations may have failed to be good stewards of property entrusted to them, the ideal has survived through all the centuries of recorded Western religious thought. The fact that individuals and institutions have failed to live up to an ideal does not mean that the ideal is flawed.

Stewardship contemplates equitable distribution of land—take only what is necessary and use it wisely. Tax and zoning policies encouraging home ownership, if true to the stewardship ideal, will support the acquisition of affordable and decent shelter by all members of society, but leave the acquisition of wealth to private endeavor. Stewardship as an ideal is a consistent part of historical and current Judeo-Christian teachings. It is at the heart of the modern Catholic analysis of private property, explicitly in some encyclicals, implicitly in all of them. Private ownership of land, while supported as a means of reconciling humankind to the world and to humankind's sinful nature, has, in the words of Pope John Paul II, a "social mortgage" attached to it. This social mortgage, even if only an ideal, should encourage inclusionary policymakers to limit the scope of tax and zoning policies designed to encourage land ownership. So limited, these policies could help a wide range of families obtain decent housing rather than maximizing acquisition advantages for families who do not need governmental assistance to achieve their investment or shelter goals.

The book of Amos provides a final backdrop for this discussion. The prophet spoke at the height of Israel's national prosperity, achieved through military strength and inattention to social justice. Poor people were forced off their lands, and as they lost their ability to use clan lands, they lost their standing in the social order. Amos warned Israel about this practice:

> Therefore because you trample on the poor and take from them leaves of grain,
> you have built houses of hewn stone, but you shall not live in them. (Amos 5:11)

Can we hear echoes of that warning today in the plight of millions of working citizens who seek in vain to obtain decent housing for their families?

NOTES

Special thanks for valuable research assistance and consultation are extended to Carla J. Fletcher, Saint Louis University School of Law; Michael Hussey, Saint Louis University School of Law; Sr. Joy Jensen; Sandra H. Johnson, Saint Louis University School of Law; Thomas A. Shippey, Department of English, Saint Louis University; Patrick J. Welch, Department of Economics, Saint Louis University; and to colleagues who critiqued my presentations of this topic at the Arts and Sciences Endowed Chairs Lecture in 1997 and at the School of Law Faculty Development Colloquium in 1998.

1. This and all following biblical references come from the *New Oxford Annotated Bible,* New York: Oxford University Press, 1994.

2. Land ownership is recognized in a variety of forms in the Jewish law of property, as first compiled in Maimonides' Mishnah Torah in 1180 and more systematically presented in the *Encyclopedia Judaica* and a companion textbook, *Jewish Law Association Studies: Principles of Jewish Law* (Thomas 1996).

3. Many of the mendicant orders arose at this time in part as a protest against excessive accumulation of private property (O'Brien and Shannon 1977:22–24).

4. See, for example, the City of Wildwood Master Plan (1998:63). The East-West Gateway Coordinating Council reported in 1996 that more land is being developed for single-family residential use in the Saint Louis metropolitan area than new households are forming (East-West Gateway Coordinating Council 1996).

5. The key stewardship point in homeowner tax preference reform is to reemphasize the shelter aspect of home ownership over its investment aspect. Retaining the tax deduction with the current $1 million cap is not particularly useful to families making less than $40,000 or slightly less than the national median income for a family of four (Dreier

1997:9). However, retaining the deduction and capping it at a first-time homebuyer range could accomplish two goals: retaining the home ownership shelter incentive and releasing billions of dollars in currently forgone tax revenues that could be split between reducing the national deficit, if one exists, and seeding a low income housing trust fund to provide, for example, direct subsidies to organizations providing rental housing for persons coming off welfare who have entry level jobs but cannot yet afford home ownership. An alternative approach would scrap the mortgage interest tax deduction in favor of a progressive tax credit targeted primarily to moderate income families (Dreier 1997:18–19; Salsich 1997:65–69).

REFERENCES

Aland, K. (ed.) 1967. *Martin Luther's 95 Theses.* St. Louis: Concordia Publishing House.

Atherton, J. (ed.) 1994. *Christian Social Ethics.* Cleveland: Pilgrim Press.

Avila, C. 1983. *Ownership: Early Christian Teaching.* Maryknoll, NY: Orbis Books.

Babcock, R. 1983. The Egregious Invalidity of the Exclusive Single-Family Zone. *Land Use Law and Zoning Digest* 35:4–8.

Bartlett, V. 1915. *The Biblical and Early Christian Idea of Property.* In A. J. Carlyle, ed., *Property: Its Duties and Rights* 2nd. ed. London: Macmillan.

Bigongiari, D., ed. 1953. *The Political Ideas of St. Thomas Aquinas.* New York: Free Press.

Blakely, E. J., and M. G. Snyder. 1997. *Fortress America: Gated Communities in the United States.* Washington, DC, and Cambridge, MA: Brookings Institution Press and Lincoln Institute of Land Policy.

Bloomquist, K. 1996. *Give Us This Day Our Daily Bread: Sufficient, Sustainable Livelihood for All.* Chicago: Evangelical Lutheran Church in America.

Brueggemann, W. 1977. *The Land.* Philadelphia: Fortress Press.

Carlyle, A. J. 1915. *Property: Its Duties and Rights* 2d ed. London: Macmillan.

Catholic Bishops of the Heartland. 1980. *Strangers and Guests: Toward Community in the Heartland.* Sioux Falls, SD: Heartland Project.

Catholic Committee of Appalachia. 1980. *This Land Is Home to Me.* 5th anniversary ed. Prestonsberg, KY: Catholic Committee of Appalachia.

City of Wildwood. 1998 *Master Plan.* Wildwood, MO.

Clough, S. B., and C. W. Cole. 1952. *Economic History of Europe.* Boston: D. C. Heath.

Dreier, P. 1997. The New Politics of Housing. *Journal of the American Planning Association* 63:5–27.

East-West Gateway Coordinating Council. 1996. *Where We Stand.* St. Louis: East-West Gateway Coordinating Council.

Ellickson, R. C., and C. Thorland. 1995. Ancient Law: Mesopotamia, Egypt, Israel. *Chicago-Kent Law Review* 71:321–411.

Euclid v. Ambler, 1926. 272 U.S. 365.

Gerber, D. J. 1997. Law, Values and Economic Thought: Notes for a Research Agenda. *Forum for Social Economics* 26:43–51.

Hobgood, M. B. 1991. *Catholic Social Teaching and Economic Theory: Paradigms in Conflict.* Philadelphia: Temple University Press.

Human Rights Commission, Archdiocese of St. Louis. 1992. *Housing in St. Louis: A Challenge and an Opportunity.* St. Louis: Commission on Human Rights, Archdiocese of St. Louis.

Internal Revenue Code, 26 U.S.C.§163. 1995. Washington, DC: Government Printing Office.

Laslett, Peter, ed. 1988. "Introduction." In John Locke, *Two Treaties of Government.* Cambridge: Cambridge University Press.

Leith, J. H., ed. 1984. *John Calvin: The Christian Life.* San Francisco: Harper and Row.

Locke, J. 1988. Two Treatises. In Peter Laslett, ed., *Two Treatises on Government.* Student ed. Cambridge: Cambridge University Press.

Malina, B. J. 1997. Embedded Economics: The Irrelevance of Christian Fictive Domestic Economy. *Forum for Social Concerns* 26:1–20.

McDonald, W. J. 1939. *The Social Value of Property According to St. Thomas Aquinas.* Washington, DC: Catholic University of America Press.

McLaughlin, J. B. 1932. *The Immortal Encyclical.* London: Burns, Oates and Wasbourne Ltd.

Metzger, B. M., and R. E. Murphy, eds. 1994. *The New Oxford Annotated Bible.* New York: Oxford University Press.

National Conference of Catholic Bishops. 1975. *The Right to a Decent Home.* Washington, DC: United States Catholic Conference.

National Low Income Housing Coalitions. 1997. *Out of Reach: Rental Housing at What Cost?* Washington, DC: National Low Income Housing Coalition.

Novak, D. 1992. *Jewish Social Ethics.* New York: Oxford University Press.

O'Brien, D. J., and T. A. Shannon. 1977. *Renewing the Earth: Catholic Documents on Peace, Justice and Liberation.* Garden City, NY: Image Books.

Pope John Paul II. 1987. *Sollicitudo Rei Socialis.* Washington, DC: United States Catholic Conference.

———. 1991. *Centesimus Annus.* Washington, DC: United States Catholic Conference.

Pope John XXIII. 1961. *Mater et Magistra.* In D. J. O'Brien and T. A. Shannon, eds., *Renewing the Earth: Catholic Documents on Peace, Justice and Liberation.* Garden City, NY: Image Books.

Pope Leo XIII. 1891. *Rerum Novarum.* Washington, DC: National Catholic Welfare Conference.

Pope Paul VI. 1967. *Populorum Progressio.* In D. J. O'Brien and T. A. Shannon, eds., *Renewing the Earth: Catholic Documents on Peace, Justice and Liberation.* Garden City, NY: Image Books.

Pope Pius XI. 1931. *Quadragesimo Anno.* In D. J. O'Brien and T. A. Shannon, eds., *Renewing the Earth: Catholic Documents on Peace, Justice and Liberation.* Garden City, NY: Image Books.

Ryan, J. A. 1913. *Alleged Socialism of the Church Fathers.* St. Louis: Herder.

Salsich, P. W. 1997. Welfare Reform: Is Self Sufficiency Feasible without Affordable Housing? *Michigan Law and Policy Review* 2:43–70.

Schaff, P. 1952. *A Select Library of Nicene and Post Nicene Fathers of the Christian Church.* Grand Rapids, MI: W. B. Eerdmans.

Scheie, D. M. 1994. *Better Together: Religious Institutions as Partners in Community-Based Development.* Minneapolis: Rainbow Research Inc.

Second Vatican Council. 1965. *Gaudium et Spes.* In D. J. O'Brien and T. A. Shannon, eds., *Renewing the Earth: Catholic Documents on Peace, Justice and Liberation.* Garden City, NY: Image Books.

Thomas, D. 1996. Instructive Comparisons between Jewish and Anglo-American Land Use. In E. A. Goldman, ed., *Jewish Law Association Studies: Principles of Jewish Law,* vol. 7. Atlanta: Scholars Press.

Welch, P. J. 1998. The Encyclicals and Rights to Distributions in Contract-and-Status-Based Economies. *International Journal of Social Economics* 25:1608–17.

Wolfe, A. 1991. Market, State and Society as Codes of Moral Obligation. In M. Mendel and D. Salee, eds., *The Legacy of Karl Polanyi.* New York: St. Martin's Press.

Wood, S. P. 1954. *Clement of Alexandria.* New York: Fathers of the Church.

Wuerl, D. W., R. Lawlor, and T. C. Lawlor, eds. 1995. *The Teaching of Christ: A Catholic Catechism for Adults.* 4th ed. Huntington, IN: Our Sunday Visitor Publishing Division.

Ziegler, E. 1983. The Twilight of Single-Family Zoning. *UCLA Journal of Environmental Law and Policy* 3:161–217.

Zuckert, M. 1980. An Introduction to Locke's First Treatise. *Interpretation* 8:58–74.

FROM *Social Problems*

Henry George
(1886)

The First Great Reform

Do what we may, we can accomplish nothing real and lasting until we secure to all the first of those equal and unalienable rights with which, as our Declaration of Independence has it, man is endowed by his Creator—the equal and unalienable right to the use and benefit of natural opportunities.

There are people who are always trying to find some mean between right and wrong—people who, if they were to see a man about to be unjustly beheaded, might insist that the proper thing to do would be to chop off his feet. These are the people who, beginning to recognize the importance of the land question, propose in Ireland and England such measures as judicial valuations of rents and peasant proprietary, and in the United States, the reservation to actual settlers of what is left of the public lands, and the limitation of estates.

Nothing whatever can be accomplished by such timid, illogical measures. If we would cure social disease we must go to the root.

There is no use in talking of reserving what there may be left of our public domain to actual settlers. That would be merely a locking of the stable door after the horse had been stolen, and even if it were not, would avail nothing.

There is no use in talking about restricting the amount of land any one man may hold. That, even if it were practicable, were idle, and would not meet the difficulty. The ownership of an acre in a city may give more command of the labor of others than the ownership of a hundred thousand acres in a sparsely settled district, and it is utterly impossible by any legal device to prevent the concentration of property so long as the general causes which irresistibly tend to the concentration of property remain untouched. So long as the wages tend to the point of a bare living for the laborer we cannot stop the tendency of property of all kinds to concentration, and this must be the tendency of wages until equal rights in the soil of their country are secured to all. We can no more abolish industrial slavery by limiting the size of estates than we could abolish chattel slavery by putting a limit on the number of slaves a single slaveholder might own. In the one case as in the other, so far as such restrictions could be

---

This selection, originally written in 1883, first appeared as a chapter in *Social Problems* by Henry George (New York: Henry George, 1886), 275–296. Asterisked footnotes have been changed to numbered notes.

made operative they would only increase the difficulties of abolition by enlarging the class who would resist it.

There is no escape from it. If we would save the republic before social inequality and political demoralization have reached the point when no salvation is possible, we must assert the principle of the Declaration of Independence, acknowledge the equal and unalienable rights which inhere in man by endowment of the Creator, and make land common property.

If there seems anything strange in the idea that all men have equal and unalienable rights to the use of the earth, it is merely that habit can blind us to the most obvious truths. Slavery, polygamy, cannibalism, the flattening of children's heads, or the squeezing of their feet, seem perfectly natural to those brought up where such institutions or customs exist. But, as a matter of fact, nothing is more repugnant to the natural perceptions of men than that land should be treated as subject to individual ownership, like things produced by labor. It is only among an insignificant fraction of the people who have lived on the earth that the idea that the earth itself could be made private property has ever obtained; nor has it ever obtained save as the result of a long course of usurpation, tyranny and fraud. This idea reached development among the Romans, whom it corrupted and destroyed. It took many generations for it to make its way among our ancestors; and it did not, in fact, reach full recognition until two centuries ago, when, in the time of Charles II, the feudal dues were shaken off by a landholders' parliament. We accepted it as we have accepted the aristocratic organization of our army and navy, and many other things, in which we have servilely followed European custom. Land being plenty and population sparse, we did not realize what it would mean when in two or three cities we should have the population of the thirteen colonies. But it is time that we should begin to think of it now, when we see ourselves confronted, in spite of our free political institutions, with all the problems that menace Europe—when, though our virgin soil is not quite yet fenced in, we have a "working class," a "criminal class" and a "pauper class"; when there are already thousands of so-called *free* citizens of the republic who cannot by the hardest toil make a living for their families, and when we are, on the other hand, developing such monstrous fortunes as the world has not seen since great estates were eating out the heart of Rome.

What more preposterous than the treatment of land as individual property? In every essential land differs from those things which being the product of human labor are rightfully property. It is the creation of God; they are produced by man. It is fixed in quantity; they may be increased illimitably. It exists, though generations come and go; they in a little while decay and pass again into the elements. What more preposterous than that one tenant for a day of this rolling sphere should collect rent for it from his cotenants, or sell to them for a price what was here ages before him and will be here ages after him? What more preposterous than that we, living in New York city in this 1883, should be working for a lot of landlords who get the authority to live on our labor from some English king, dead and gone these centuries? What more preposterous than that we, the present population of the United States, should presume to grant to our own people or to foreign capitalists the right to strip of their earnings American citizens of the next generation? What more utterly preposterous than these titles to land? Although the whole people of the earth in one generation were to unite, they could no more sell title to land against the next generation than they could sell that generation. It is a self-evident truth, as Thomas Jefferson said, that the earth belongs in usufruct to the living.

Nor can any defense of private property in land be made on the ground of expediency. On the contrary, look where you will, and it is evident that the private ownership of land keeps land out of use; that the speculation it engenders crowds population where it ought to be more diffused, diffuses it where it ought to be closer together; compels those who wish to improve to pay away a large part of their capital, or mortgage their labor for years before they are permitted to improve; prevents men from going to work for themselves who would gladly do so, crowding them into deadly competition with each other for the wages of employers; and enormously restricts the production of wealth while causing the grossest inequality in its distribution.

No assumption can be more gratuitous than that constantly made that absolute ownership of land is necessary to the improvement and proper use of land. What is necessary to the best use of land is the security of improvements—the assurance that the labor and capital expended upon it shall enjoy their reward. This is a very different thing from the absolute ownership of land. Some of the finest buildings in New York are erected upon leased ground. Nearly the whole of London and other English cities, and great parts of Philadelphia and Baltimore, are so built. All sorts of mines are opened and operated on leases. In California and Nevada the most costly mining operations, involving the expenditure of immense amounts of capital, were undertaken upon no better security than the mining regulations, which gave no ownership of the land, but only guaranteed possession as long as the mines were worked.

If shafts can be sunk and tunnels can be run, and the most costly machinery can be put up on public land on mere security of possession, why could not improvements of all kinds be made on that security? If individuals will use and improve land belonging to other individuals, why would they not use and improve land belonging to the whole people? What is to prevent land owned by Trinity church, by the Sailors' Snug Harbor, by the Astors or Rheinlanders, or any other corporate or individual owners, from being as well improved and used as now, if the ground rents, instead of going to corporations or individuals, went into the public treasury?

In point of fact, if land were treated as the common property of the whole people, it would be far more readily improved than now, for then the improver would get the whole benefit of his improvements. Under the present system, the price that must be paid for land operates as a powerful deterrent to improvement. And when the improver has secured land either by purchase or by lease, he is taxed upon his improvements, and heavily taxed in various ways upon all that he uses. Were land treated as the property of the whole people, the ground rent accruing to the community would suffice for public purposes, and all other taxation might be dispensed with. The improver could more easily get land to improve, and would retain for himself the full benefit of his improvements exempt from taxation.

To secure to all citizens their equal right to the land on which they live, does not mean, as some of the ignorant seem to suppose, that every one must be given a farm, and city land be cut up into little pieces. It would be impossible to secure the equal rights of all in that way, even if such division were not in itself impossible. In a small and primitive community of simple industries and habits, such as that Moses legislated for, substantial equality may be secured by alloting to each family an equal share of the land and making it inalienable. Or, as among our rude ancestors in western Europe, or in such primitive society as the village communities of Russia and India, substantial equality may be secured by periodical allotment or cultivation in common. Or in sparse populations, such as the early New England colonies, substantial equality may be secured by giving to each family its town lot and its seed lot, holding the rest of the land as townland or common. But among a highly civilized and rapidly growing population, with changing centers, with great cities and minute division of industry, and a complex system of production and exchange, such rude devices become ineffective and impossible.

Must we therefore consent to inequality—must we therefore consent that some shall monopolize what is the common heritage of all? Not at all. If two men find a diamond, they do not march to a lapidary to have it cut in two. If three sons inherit a ship, they do not proceed to saw her into three pieces; nor yet do they agree that if this cannot be done equal division is impossible? Nor yet is there no other way to secure the rights of the owners of a railroad than by breaking up track, engines, cars and depots into as many separate bits as there are stockholders? And so it is not necessary, in order to secure equal rights to land, to make an equal division of land. All that it is necessary to do is to collect the ground rents for the common benefit.

Nor, to take ground rents for the common benefit, is it necessary that the State should actually take possession of the land and rent it out from year to year, or from term to term, as some ignorant people suppose. It can be done in a much more simple and easy manner by means of the existing machinery of taxation. All it is necessary to do is to abolish all other forms of taxation until the weight of taxation rests upon the value of land irrespective of improvements, and takes the ground rent for the public benefit.

In this simple way, without increasing governmental machinery, but, on the contrary, greatly simplifying it, we could make land common property. And in doing this we could abolish all other taxation, and still have a great and steadily increasing surplus—a growing common fund, in the benefits of which all might share, and in the management of which there would be such a direct and general interest as to afford the strongest guarantees against misappropriation or waste. Under this system no one could afford to hold land he was not using, and land not in use would be thrown open to those who wished to use it, at once relieving the labor market and giving an enormous stimulus to production and improvement, while land in use would be paid for according to its value, irrespective of the improvements the user might make. On these he would not be taxed. All that his labor could add to the common wealth, all that his prudence could save, would be his own, instead of, as now, subjecting him to fine. Thus would the sacred right of property be acknowledged by securing to each the reward of his exertion.

Practically, then, the greatest, the most fundamental of all reforms, the reform which will make all other reforms easier, and without which no other reform will avail, is to be reached by concentrating all taxation into a tax upon the value of land, and making that heavy enough to take as near as may be the whole ground rent for common purposes.

To those who have never studied the subject, it will seem ridiculous to propose as the greatest and most far-reaching of all reforms a mere fiscal change. But whoever has followed the train of thought through which in preceding chapters I have endeavored to lead, will see that in this simple proposition is involved the greatest of social revolutions—a revolution compared with that which destroyed ancient monarchy in France or that which destroyed chattel slavery in our southern states, were as nothing.

In a book such as this, intended for the casual reader, who lacks inclination to follow the close reasoning necessary to show the full relation of this seemingly simple reform to economic laws, I cannot exhibit its full force, but I may point to some of the more obvious of its effects.

To appropriate ground rent[1] to public uses by means of taxation would permit the abolition of all the taxation which now presses so heavily upon labor and capital. This would enormously increase the production of wealth by the removal of restrictions and by adding to the incentives to production.

It would at the same time enormously increase the production of wealth by throwing open natural opportunities. It would utterly destroy land monopoly by making the holding of land unprofitable to any but the user. There would be no temptation to any one to hold land in expectation of future increase in its value when that increase was certain to be demanded in taxes. No one could afford to hold valuable land idle when the taxes upon it would be as heavy as they would be were it put to the fullest use. Thus speculation in land would be utterly destroyed, and land not in use would become free to those who wished to use it.

The enormous increase in production which would result from thus throwing open the natural means and opportunities of production, while at the same time removing the taxation which now hampers, restricts and fines production, would enormously augment the annual fund from which all incomes are drawn. It would at the same time make the distribution of wealth much more equal. That great part of this fund which is now taken by the owners of land, not as a return for anything by which they add to production, but because they have appropriated as their own the natural means and opportunities of production, and which as material progress goes on, and the value of land rises, is constantly becoming larger and larger, would be virtually divided among all, by being utilized for common purposes. The removal of restrictions upon labor and the opening of natural opportunities to labor, would make labor free to employ itself. Labor, the producer of all wealth, could never become "a drug in the market" while desire for any form of wealth was unsatisfied. With the natural opportunities of employment thrown open to all, the spectacle of willing men seeking vainly for employment could not be witnessed; there could be no surplus of unemployed labor to beget that cut-throat competition of laborers for employment which crowds wages down to the cost of merely living. Instead of the one-sided competition of workmen to find employment, employers would compete with each other to obtain workmen. There would be no need of combinations to raise or maintain wages; for wages, instead of tending to the lowest point at which laborers can live, would tend to the highest point which employers could pay, and thus, instead of getting but a mere fraction of his earnings, the workman would get the full return of his labor, leaving to the skill, foresight and capital of the employer those additional earnings that are justly their due.

The equalization in the distribution of wealth that would thus result would effect immense economies and greatly add to productive power. The cost of the idleness, pauperism and crime that spring from poverty would be saved to the community; the increased mobility of labor, the increased intelligence of the masses, that would result from this equalized distribution of wealth, the greater incentive to invention and to the use of improved processes that would result from the increase in wages, would enormously increase production.

To abolish all taxes save a tax upon the value of land would at the same time greatly simplify the machinery and expenses of government, and greatly reduce government expenses. An army of customhouse officers, and internal revenue officials, and license collectors and assessors, clerks, accountants, spies, detectives, and government employés [*sic*] of every description, could be dispensed with. The corrupting effect of indirect taxation would be taken out of our politics. The rings and combinations now interested in keeping up taxation would cease to contribute money for the debauching of voters and to beset the law-making power with their lobbyists. We should get rid of the fraud and false swearing, of the bribery and subornation which now attend the collection of so much of our public revenues. We should get rid of the demoralization that proceeds from laws which prohibit actions in themselves harmless, punish men for crimes which the moral sense does not condemn, and offer a constant premium to evasion. "Land lies out of doors." It cannot be hid or carried off. Its value can be ascertained with greater ease and exactness than the value of anything else, and taxes upon that value can be collected with absolute certainty and at the minimum of expense. To rely upon land values for the whole public revenue would so simplify government, would so eliminate incentives to corruption, that we could safely assume as governmental functions the management of telegraphs and railroads, and safely apply the increasing surplus to securing such common benefits and providing such public conveniences as advancing civilization may call for.

And in thinking of what is possible in the way of the management of common concerns for the common benefit, not only is the great simplification of government which would result from the reform I have suggested to be considered, but the higher moral tone that would be given to social life by the equalization of conditions and the abolition of poverty. The greed of wealth, which makes it a business motto that every man is to be treated as though he were a rascal, and induces despair of getting in places of public trust men who will not abuse them for selfish ends, is but the reflection of the fear of want. Men trample over each other from the frantic dread of being trampled upon, and the admiration with which even the unscrupulous money-getter is regarded springs from habits of thought engendered by the fierce struggle for existence to which the most of us are obliged to give up our best energies. But when no one feared want, when every one felt assured of his ability to make an easy and independent living for himself and his family, that popular admiration which now spurs even the rich man still to add to his wealth would be given to other things than the getting of money. We should learn to regard the man who strove to get more than he could use, as a fool—as indeed he is.

He must have eyes only for the mean and vile, who has mixed with men without realizing that selfishness and greed and vice and crime are largely the result of social conditions which bring out the bad qualities of human nature and stunt the good; without realizing that there is even now among men patriotism and virtue enough to secure us the best possible management of public affairs if our social and political adjustments enabled us to utilize those qualities. Who has not known poor men who might safely be trusted with untold millions? Who has not met with rich men who retained the most ardent sympathy with their fellows, the warmest devotion to all that would benefit their kind? Look to-day at our charities, hopeless of permanent good though they may be! They at least show the existence of unselfish sympathies, capable, if rightly directed, of the largest results.

It is no mere fiscal reform that I propose; it is a conforming of the most important social adjustments to natural laws. To those who have never given thought to the matter, it may seem irreverently presumptuous to say that it is the evident intent of the Creator that land values should be the subject of taxation; that rent should be utilized for the benefit of the entire community. Yet to whoever does think of it, to say this will appear no more presumptuous than to say that the Creator has intended men to walk on their feet, and not on their hands. Man, in his social relations, is as much included in the creative scheme as man in his physical relations. Just as certainly as the fish was intended to swim in the water, and the bird to fly through the air, and monkeys to live in trees, and moles to burrow underground, was man intended to live with his fellows. He is by nature a social animal. And the creative scheme must embrace the life and development of society, as truly as it embraces the life and development of the individual. Our civilization cannot carry us beyond the domain of law. Railroads, telegraphs and labor-saving machinery are no more accidents than are flowers and trees.

Man is driven by his instincts and needs to form society. Society, thus formed, has certain needs and functions for which revenue is required. These needs and functions increase with social development, requiring a larger and larger revenue. Now, experience and analogy, if not the instinctive perceptions of the human mind, teach us that there is a natural way of satisfying every natural want. And if human society is included in nature, as it surely is, this must apply to social wants as well as to the wants of the individual, and there must be a natural or right method of taxation, as there is a natural or right method of walking.

We know, beyond peradventure, that the natural or right way for a man to walk is on his feet, and not on his hands. We know this of a surety—because the feet are adapted to walking, while the hands are not; because in walking on the feet all the other organs of the body are free to perform their proper functions, while in walking on the hands they are not; because a man can walk on his feet with ease, convenience and celerity, while no amount of training will enable him to walk on his hands save awkwardly, slowly and painfully. In the same way we may know that the natural or right way of raising the revenues which are required by the needs of society is by the taxation of land values. The value of land is in its nature and relations adapted to purposes of taxation, just as the feet in their nature and relations are adapted to the purposes of walking. The value of land[2] only arises as in the integration of society the need for some public or common revenue begins to be felt. It increases as the development of society goes on, and as larger and larger revenues are therefore required. Taxation upon land values does not lessen the individual incentive to production and accumulation, as do other methods of taxation; on the contrary, it leaves perfect freedom to productive forces, and prevents restrictions upon production from arising. It does not foster monopolies, and cause unjust inequalities in the distribution of wealth, as do other taxes; on the contrary, it has the effect of breaking down monopoly and equalizing the distribution of wealth. It can be collected with greater certainty and economy than any other tax; it does not beget the evasion, corruption and dishonesty that flow from other taxes. In short, it conforms to every economic and moral requirement. What can be more in accordance with justice than that the value of land, which is not created by individual effort, but arises from the existence and growth of society, should be taken by society for social needs? . . .

Man is more than an animal. And the more we consider the constitution of this world in which we find ourselves, the more clearly we see that its constitution is such as to develop more than animal life. If the purpose for which this world existed were merely to enable animal man to eat, drink and comfortably clothe and house himself for his little day, some such world as I have previously endeavored to imagine would be best. But the purpose of this world, so far at least as man is concerned, is evidently the development of moral and intellectual, even more than of animal, powers. Whether we consider man himself or his relations to nature external to him, the substantial truth of that bold declaration of the Hebrew scriptures, that man has been created in the image of God, forces itself upon the mind.

If all the material things needed by man could be produced equally well at all points on the earth's surface, it might seem more convenient for man the animal, but how would he have risen above the animal level? As we see in the history of social development, commerce has been and is the great civilizer and educator. The seemingly infinite diversities in the capacity of different parts of the earth's surface lead to that exchange of productions which is the most powerful agent in preventing isolation, in breaking down prejudice, in increasing knowledge and widening thought. These diversities of nature, which seemingly increase with our knowledge of nature's powers, like the diversities in the aptitudes of individuals and communities, which similarly increase with social development, call forth powers and give rise to pleasures which could never arise had man been placed, like an ox, in a boundless field of clover. The "international law of God" which we fight with our tariffs,—so short-sighted are the selfish prejudices of men—is the law which stimulates mental and moral progress; the law to which civilization is due.

And so, when we consider the phenomenon of rent, it reveals to us one of those beautiful and beneficent adaptations, in which more than in anything else the human mind recognizes evidences of Mind infinitely greater, and catches glimpses of the Master Workman.

This is the law of rent: As individuals come together in communities, and society grows, integrating more and more its individual members, and making general interests and general conditions of more and more relative importance, there arises, over and above the value which individuals can create for themselves, a value which is created by the community as a whole, and which, attaching to land, becomes tangible, definite and capable of computation and appropriation. As society grows, so grows this value, which springs from and represents in tangible form what society as a whole contributes to production, as distinguished from what is contributed by individual exertion. By virtue of natural law in those aspects which it is the purpose of the science we call political economy to discover, as it is the purpose of the sciences which we call chemistry and astronomy to discover other aspects of natural law,—all social advance necessarily contributes to the increase of this common value; to the growth of this common fund.

Here is a provision made by natural law for the increasing needs of social growth; here is an adaptation of nature by virtue of which the natural progress of society is a progress toward equality, not toward inequality; a centripetal force tending to unity, growing out of and ever balancing a centrifugal force tending to diversity. Here is a fund belonging to society as a whole from which, without the degradation of alms, private or public, provision can be made for the weak, the helpless, the aged; from which provision can be made for the common wants of all as a matter of common right to each, and by the utilization of which society, as it advances, may pass, by natural methods and easy stages from a rude association for purposes of defense and police, into a cooperative association, in which combined power guided by combined intelligence can give to each more than his own exertions multiplied many fold could produce.

By making land private property, by permitting individuals to appropriate this fund which nature plainly intended for the use of all, we throw the children's bread to the dogs of Greed and Lust; we produce a primary inequality which gives rise in every direction to other tendencies to inequality; and from this perversion of the good gifts of the Creator, from this ignoring and defying of his social laws, there arise in the very heart of our civilization those horrible and monstrous things that betoken social putrefaction.

NOTES

1. I use the term "ground rent" because the proper economic term, "rent," might not be understood by those who are in the habit of using it in its commonsense, which applies to the income from buildings and improvements, as well as land.

2. Value, it must always be remembered, is a totally different thing from utility. From the confounding of these two different ideas much error and confusion arise. No matter how useful it may be, nothing has a value until some one is willing to give labor or the produce of labor for it.

FROM *Garden Cities of To-Morrow*

Ebenezer Howard
(1902)

The Town-Country Magnet

I will not cease from mental strife,
  Nor shall my sword sleep in my hand,
Till we have built Jerusalem
  In England's green and pleasant land.

—BLAKE

Thorough sanitary and remedial action in the houses that we have; and then the building of more, strongly, beautifully, and in groups of limited extent, kept in proportion to their streams and walled round, so that there may be no festering and wretched suburb anywhere, but clean and busy street within and the open country without, with a belt of beautiful garden and orchard round the walls, so that from any part of the city perfectly fresh air and grass and sight of far horizon might be reachable in a few minutes' walk. This the final aim.

—JOHN RUSKIN, *Sesame and Lilies*

The reader is asked to imagine an estate embracing an area of 6,000 acres, which is at present purely agricultural, and has been obtained by purchase in the open market at a cost of £40[1] an acre, or £240,000. The purchase money is supposed to have been raised on mortgage debentures, bearing interest at an average rate not exceeding £4 percent.[2] The estate is legally vested in the names of four gentlemen of responsible position and of undoubted probity and honour, who hold it in trust, first, as a security for the debenture-holders, and, secondly, in trust for the people of Garden City, the Town-country magnet, which it is intended to build thereon. One essential feature of the plan is that all ground rents, which are to be based upon the annual value of the land, shall be paid to the trustees, who, after providing for interest and sinking fund, will hand the balance to the Central Council of the new municipality,[3] to be

These excerpts are from *Garden Cities of To-Morrow* by Ebenezer Howard, 50–59, 135–137. Copyright © 1965 Massachusetts Institute of Technology, by permission of The MIT Press. Howard's book was originally published in 1898 with the title *To-Morrow: A Peaceful Path to Real Reform*. It was reissued as *Garden Cities of To-Morrow* in 1902 with revisions made by Howard. The version in this volume is faithful to the 1902 version except that the original note and diagram numbers have been changed.

employed by such Council in the creation and maintenance of all necessary public works—roads, schools, parks, etc.

The objects of this land purchase may be stated in various ways, but it is sufficient here to say that some of the chief objects are these: To find for our industrial population work at wages of *higher purchasing power,* and to secure healthier surroundings and more regular employment. To enterprising manufacturers, cooperative societies, architects, engineers, builders, and mechanicians of all kinds, as well as to many engaged in various professions, it is intended to offer a means of securing new and better employment for their capital and talents, while to the agriculturists at present on the estate as well as to those who may migrate thither, it is designed to open a new market for their produce close to their doors. Its object is, in short, to raise the standard of health and comfort of all true workers of whatever grade— the means by which these objects are to be achieved being a healthy, natural, and economic combination of town and country life, and this on land owned by the municipality.

Garden City, which is to be built near the centre of the 6,000 acres, covers an area of 1,000 acres, or a sixth part of the 6,000 acres, and might be of circular form, 1,240 yards (or nearly three-quarters of a mile) from centre to circumference. (Diagram 1 is a ground plan of the whole municipal area, showing the town in the centre; and Diagram 2, which represents one section or ward of the town, will be useful in following

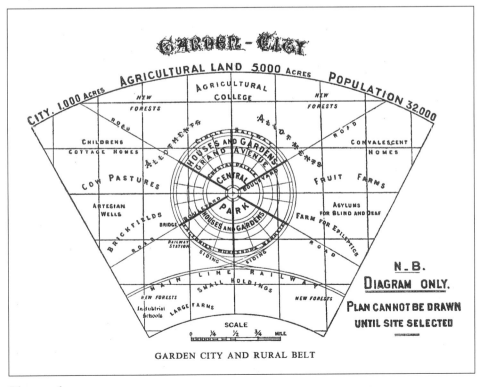

GARDEN CITY AND RURAL BELT

Diagram 1

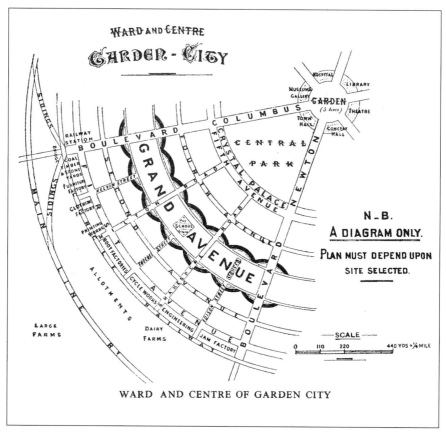

Diagram 2

the description of the town itself—*a description which is, however, merely suggestive, and will probably be much departed from.*)

Six magnificent boulevards—each 120 feet wide—traverse the city from centre to circumference, dividing it into six equal parts or wards. In the centre is a circular space containing about five and a half acres, laid out as a beautiful and well-watered garden; and, surrounding this garden, each standing in its own ample grounds, are the larger public buildings—town hall, principal concert and lecture hall, theatre, library, museum, picture-gallery, and hospital.

The rest of the large space encircled by the "Crystal Palace" is a public park, containing 145 acres, which includes ample recreation grounds within very easy access of all the people.

Running all round the Central Park (except where it is intersected by the boulevards) is a wide glass arcade called the "Crystal Palace," opening on to the park. This building is in wet weather one of the favourite resorts of the people, whilst the knowledge that its bright shelter is ever close at hand tempts people into Central Park, even in the most doubtful of weathers. Here manufactured goods are exposed for sale, and here most of that class of shopping which requires the joy of deliberation and selection is done. The space enclosed by the Crystal Palace is, however, a good deal larger than is required for these purposes, and a considerable part of it is used as a Winter Garden—the whole forming a permanent exhibition of a most attractive character, whilst its circular form brings it near to every dweller in the town—the furthest removed inhabitant being within 600 yards.

Passing out of the Crystal Palace on our way to the outer ring of the town, we cross Fifth Avenue—lined, as are all the roads of the town, with trees—fronting which, and looking on to the Crystal Palace, we find a ring of very excellently built houses, each standing in its own ample grounds; and, as we continue our walk, we observe that the houses are for the most part built either in concentric rings, facing the various avenues (as the circular roads are termed), or fronting the boulevards and roads which all converge to the centre of the town. Asking the friend who accompanies us on our journey what the population of this little city may be, we are told about 30,000 in the city itself, and about 2,000 in the agricultural estate, and that there are in the town 5,500 building lots of an *average* size of 20 feet × 130 feet—the minimum space allotted for the purpose being 20 × 100. Noticing the very varied architecture and design which the houses and groups of houses display—some having common gardens and cooperative kitchens—we learn that general observance of street line or harmonious departure from it are the chief points as to house building, over which the municipal authorities exercise control, for, though proper sanitary arrangements are strictly enforced, the fullest measure of individual taste and preference is encouraged.

Walking still toward the outskirts of the town, we come upon "Grand Avenue." This avenue is fully entitled to the name it bears, for it is 420 feet wide[4] and, forming a belt of green upwards of three miles long, divides that part of the town which lies outside Central Park into two belts. It really constitutes an additional park of 115 acres—a park which is within 240 yards of the furthest removed inhabitant. In this splendid avenue six sites, each of four acres, are occupied by public schools and their surrounding playgrounds and gardens, while other sites are reserved for churches, of such denominations as the religious beliefs of the people may determine, to be erected and maintained out of the funds of the worshippers and their friends. We observe that the houses fronting on Grand Avenue have departed (at least in one of the wards—that of which Diagram 2 is a representation)—from the general plan of concentric rings, and, in order to ensure a longer line of frontage on Grand Avenue, are arranged in crescents—thus also to the eye yet further enlarging the already splendid width of Grand Avenue.

On the outer ring of the town are factories, warehouses, dairies, markets, coal yards, timber yards, etc., all fronting on the circle railway, which encompasses the whole town, and which has sidings connecting it with a main line of railway which passes through the estate. This arrangement enables goods to be loaded direct into trucks from the warehouses and workshops, and so sent by railway to distant markets, or to be taken direct from the trucks into the warehouses or factories; thus not only effecting a very great saving in regard to packing and cartage, and reducing to a minimum loss from breakage, but also, by reducing the traffic on the roads of the town, lessening to a very marked extent the cost of their maintenance. The smoke fiend is kept well within bounds in Garden City; for all machinery is driven by electric energy, with the result that the cost of electricity for lighting and other purposes is greatly reduced.

The refuse of the town is utilized on the agricultural portions of the estate, which are held by various individuals in large farms, small holdings, allotments, cow pastures, etc.; the natural competition of these various methods of agriculture, tested by the willingness of occupiers to offer the highest rent to the municipality, tending to bring about the best system of husbandry, or, what is more probable, the best *systems* adapted for various purposes. Thus it is easily conceivable that it may prove advantageous to grow wheat in very large fields, involving united action under a capitalist farmer, or by a body of cooperators; while the cultivation of vegetables, fruits, and flowers, which requires closer and more personal care, and more of the artistic and inventive faculty, may possibly be best dealt with by individuals, or by small groups of individuals having a common belief in the efficacy and value of certain dressings, methods of culture, or artificial and natural surroundings.

This plan, or, if the reader be pleased to so term it, this absence of plan, avoids the dangers of stagnation or dead level, and, though encouraging individual initiative, permits of the fullest cooperation, while the increased rents which follow from this form of competition are common or municipal property, and by far the larger part of them are expended in permanent improvements.

While the town proper, with its population engaged in various trades, callings, and professions, and with a store or depot in each ward, offers the most natural market to the people engaged on the agricultural estate, inasmuch as to the extent to which the townspeople demand their produce they escape altogether any railway rates and charges; yet the farmers and others are not by any means limited to the town as their only market, but have the fullest right to dispose of their produce to whomsoever they please. Here, as in every feature of the experiment, it will be seen that it is not the area of rights which is contracted, but the area of choice which is enlarged.

This principle of freedom holds good with regard to manufacturers and others who have established themselves in the town. These manage their affairs in their own way, subject, of course, to the general law of the land, and subject to the provision of sufficient space for workmen and reasonable sanitary conditions. Even in regard to such matters as water, lighting, and telephonic communication—which a municipality, if efficient and honest, is certainly the best and most natural body to supply—no rigid or absolute monopoly is sought; and if any private corporation or any body of individuals proved itself capable of supplying on more advantageous terms, either the whole town or a section of it, with these or any commodities the supply of which was taken up by the corporation, this would be allowed. No really sound system of *action* is in more need of artificial support than is any sound system of *thought*. The area of municipal and corporate action is probably destined to become greatly enlarged; but, if it is to be so, it will be because the people possess faith in such action, and that faith can be best shown by a wide extension of the area of freedom.

Dotted about the estate are seen various charitable and philanthropic institutions. These are not under the control of the municipality, but are supported and managed by various public-spirited people who have been invited by the municipality to establish these institutions in an open healthy district, and on land let to them at a peppercorn rent, it occurring to the authorities that they can the better afford to be thus generous, as the spending power of these institutions greatly benefits the whole community. Besides, as those persons who migrate to the town are among its most energetic and resourceful members, it is but just and right that their more helpless brethren should be able to enjoy the benefits of an experiment which is designed for humanity at large.

The Revenue of Garden City, and How It Is Obtained—The Agricultural Estate

It is my object to put forward a theoretical outline of a community so circumstanced and so maintained by the exercise of its own free will, guided by scientific knowledge, that the perfection of sanitary results will be approached, if not actually realized, in the co-existence of the lowest possible general mortality with the highest possible individual longevity.

—Dr. B. W. Richardson, *Hygeia; or, a City of Health* (1876)

When drainage everywhere, with its double functions, restoring what it takes away, is accomplished, then, this being combined with the data of a new social economy, the products of the earth will be increased tenfold, and the problem of misery will be wonderfully diminished. Add the suppression of parasitism and it will be solved.

—Victor Hugo, *Les Misérables* (1862)[5]

Amongst the essential differences between Garden City and other municipalities, one of the chief is its method of raising its revenue. Its entire revenue is derived from rents; and one of the purposes of this work is to show that the rents which may very reasonably be expected from the various tenants on the estate will be amply sufficient, if paid into the coffers of Garden City, (a) to pay the interest on the money with which the estate is purchased, (b) to provide a sinking fund for the purpose of paying off the principal, (c) to construct and maintain all such works as are usually constructed and maintained by municipal and other local authorities out of rates compulsorily levied, and (d) (after redemption of debentures) to provide a large surplus for other purposes, such as old-age pensions or insurance against accident and sickness.

Perhaps no difference between town and country is more noticeable than the difference in the rent charged for the use of the soil. Thus, while in some parts of London the rent is equal to £30,000 an acre, £4 an acre is an extremely high rent for agricultural land.[6] This enormous difference of rental value is, of course, almost entirely due to the presence in the one case and the absence in the other of a large population; and, as it cannot be attributed to the action of any particular individuals, it is frequently spoken of as the "unearned increment," i.e. unearned by the landlord, though a more correct term would be "collectively earned increment."

The presence of a considerable population thus giving a greatly additional value to the soil, it is obvious that a migration of population on any considerable scale to any particular area will be certainly attended with a corresponding rise in the value of the land so settled upon, and it is also obvious that such increment of value may, with some foresight and prearrangement, become the property of the migrating people.

Such foresight and prearrangement, never before exercised in an effective manner, are displayed conspicuously in the case of Garden City, where the land, as we have seen, is vested in trustees, who hold it in trust (after payment of the debentures) for the whole community, so that the entire increment of value gradually created becomes the property of the municipality, with the effect that though rents may rise, and even rise considerably, such rise in rent will not become the property of private individuals, but will be applied in relief of rates. It is this arrangement which will be seen to give Garden City much of its magnetic power. . . .

The Path Followed Up

. . . There is, however, one form of material wealth which is most permanent and abiding; from the value and utility of which our most wonderful inventions can never detract one jot, but will serve only to make more clear, and to render more universal. The planet on which we live has lasted for millions of years, and the race is just emerging from its savagery. Those of us who believe that there is a grand purpose behind nature cannot believe that the career of this planet is likely to be speedily cut short now that better hopes are rising in the hearts of men, and that, having learned a few of its less obscure secrets, they are finding their way, through much toil and pain, to a more noble use of its infinite treasures. The earth for all practical purposes may be regarded as abiding for ever.

Now, as every form of wealth must rest on the earth as its foundation, and must be built up out of the constituents found at or near its surface, it follows (because foundations are ever of primary importance) that the reformer should first consider how best the earth may be used in the service of man. But here again our friends, the Socialists, miss the essential point. Their professed ideal is to make society the owner of land *and of all instruments of production*; but they have been so anxious to carry both points of their programme that they have been a little too slow to consider the special importance of the land question, and have thus missed the true path of reform.

There is, however, a type of reformers who push the land question very much to the front, though, as it appears to me, in a manner little likely to commend their views to society. Mr. Henry George, in his well-known work, *Progress and Poverty*, urges with much eloquence, if not with complete accuracy of reasoning, that our land laws are responsible for all the economic evils of society, and that as our landlords are little better than pirates and robbers, the sooner the State forcibly appropriates their rents the better, for when this is accomplished the problem of poverty will, he suggests, be entirely solved. But is not this attempt to throw the whole blame of and punishment for the present deplorable condition of society on to a single class of men a very great mistake? In what way are landlords as a class less honest than the average citizen? Give the average citizen the opportunity of becoming a landlord and of appropriating the land values created by his tenants, and he will embrace it to-morrow. If then, the average man is a potential landlord, to attack landlords as individuals is very like a nation drawing up an indictment against itself, and then making a scape-goat of a particular class.[7]

But to endeavour to change our land system is a very different matter from attacking those individuals who represent it. But how is this change to be effected? I reply: By the force of example, that is, by setting up a better system, and by a little skill in the grouping of forces and manipulation of ideas. It is quite true that the average man is a potential landlord, and as ready to appropriate the unearned increment as to cry out against its appropriation. But the average man has very little chance of ever becoming a landlord and of appropriating rent-values created by others; and he is, therefore, the better able to consider, quite dispassionately, whether such a proceeding is really honest, and whether it may not be possible to gradually establish a new and more equitable system under which, without enjoying the privilege of appropriating rent values created by others, he may himself be secured against expropriation of the rent-values which he is now constantly creating or maintaining. We have demonstrated how this may be done on a small scale; we have next to consider how the experiment may be carried out on a much wider scale. . . .

NOTES

The following quotation appeared at the head of this chapter in the edition of 1898. *Ed.*
"No scene is continuously and untiringly loved, but one rich by joyful human labour; smooth in field; fair in garden; full in orchard; trim, sweet and frequent in homestead; ringing with voices of vivid existence. No air is sweet that is silent; it is only sweet when full of low currents of under sound—triplets of birds, and murmur and chirp of insects, and deep-toned words of men, and wayward trebles of childhood. As the art of life is learned, it will be found at last that all lovely things are also necessary;—the wild flower by the

wayside, as well as the tended corn; and the wild birds and creatures of the forest, as well as the tended cattle; because man doth not live by bread only, but also by the desert manna; by every wondrous word and unknowable work of God."—John Ruskin, *Unto This Last* (1862).

1. This was the average price paid for agricultural land in 1898; and, though this estimate may prove far more than sufficient, it is hardly likely to be much exceeded.

2. The financial arrangements described in this book are likely to be departed from in form, but not in essential principle. And until a definite scheme has been agreed upon, I think it better to repeat them precisely as they appeared in *To-morrow*, the original title of this book—the book which led to the formation of the Garden City Association. (Footnote to 1902 edition. *Ed.*)

3. This word, "municipality," is not used in a technical sense.

4. Portland Place, London, is only 100 feet wide.

5. These and several other quotations, which appeared in the original edition of 1898, were omitted from later editions. *Ed.*

6. These and all other figures are given as in the original edition of the book in 1898. Money values in England have of course changed considerably since that date. *Ed.*

7. I hope it is not ungrateful in one who has derived much inspiration from *Progress and Poverty* to write thus.

FROM *Utopian England*

Community Experiments 1900–1945

Dennis Hardy
(2000)

Cities in the Sun

. . . The inauspicious early career of Ebenezer Howard gives little indication of his
subsequent renown as the founder of the Garden City Movement. Howard, born in
London in 1850, spent a short period as a clerk before seeking in vain to make his
fortune in the United States; on his return he gained employment as a shorthand reporter in the House of Commons. At all stages, however, with an inherent sense of
justice combined with a natural curiosity, he observed social conditions keenly, read
widely and attended lectures on a variety of topics. Progressively, as his own ideas crys-
tallized, he sought ways to improve the lot of ordinary people and to find better ways
to build cities than he had observed in his travels. He drew inspiration from various
figures who were prominent in London in the 1880s and 1890s, including visitors such
as the American proponent of land nationalization, Henry George. Another American
who influenced him was Edward Bellamy, author in 1888 of *Looking Backward*, the
vision of a socialist utopia; after reading that, Howard was "permanently convinced
that our present industrial order stands absolutely condemned and is tottering to its
fall, and that a new and brighter, because a juster, order must ere long take its place."[1]
Howard's skill, though, was in adapting ideas to an English setting, removing what he
saw as excesses of public intervention and interference. Thus, as well as acknowledging
a debt to the likes of George and Bellamy, he refers directly to earlier political idealists,
such as Thomas Spence, and through him to an even earlier period of dissent (reaching
back to the English Revolution) that appealed to Howard's own brand of radical non-
conformism. He is also influenced by various contemporaries, such as William Morris
and the municipal socialist, Sidney Webb (although the latter had little time for
Howard's own ideas). And in the course of attending meetings in London, he strikes
up an acquaintance with George Bernard Shaw, and the two remain in contact at various stages in the development of garden cities.

This excerpt from the chapter "Cities in the Sun" was originally published in *Utopian England: Community
Experiments 1900–1945* by Dennis Hardy (London/New York: Routledge, 2000), 61–75. Copyright ©
Dennis Hardy 2000. It is reproduced by permission of Taylor and Francis Books UK. Original note
numbers have been changed.

Inspired by various sources, Howard's unique blend of ideas gradually coalesced into what became known as the garden city, the settlement of the future. Although the focus of his efforts was limited to the scale of ideal settlements, Howard was convinced from the outset that this would be enough to unlock the whole complex of society's ills. Indeed, using the same analogy, he referred to his solution at one stage as The Master Key: "what I solemnly believe to be the key to the great social problem—how to enter upon a higher plane of being."[2] There is no doubt that Howard was consistent in seeing garden cities as a means to a wider end: "a golden opportunity for the reconstruction of the entire fabric of our civilisation. . . . New cities well planned and thought out because the needs of all will be considered and will displace the cities of today which are chaotic, disorderly, untidy, because founded in selfishness."[3]

During the 1890s, he not only refined his ideas but also removed what he saw as the more intrusive side of socialism, in the form of heavy state intervention. When, in 1892, he delivered a series of lectures entitled "Commonsense Socialism," he attracted the interest of socialists of various persuasion who were instrumental in the formation of an organization, the Cooperative Land Society, devoted to the promotion of home colonies on land in common ownership. Howard was less than comfortable with aspects of the new organization, and his subsequent rejection of the aim of municipalization of enterprise effectively brought it to an end. Some land had been identified in Essex but this came to nothing. Instead, he searched for what he repeatedly referred to as a middle course, and set about writing his own book to explain his ideas.

The outcome of his endeavours was the publication in 1898 of *To-morrow: a peaceful path to real reform*. Together with an amended version, *Garden Cities of To-morrow*, published in 1902, this represents the definitive exposition of the garden city utopia. Like most ideas which attract a following, the nature of the scheme was ingenious but simple; presentationally, it was carefully crafted to appeal to the widest possible readership. The very name "garden city" was one which could offend no-one, and even his book title was amended in its second edition to focus on his ideal settlements rather than the process of political change that he believed would result (but which might in the interim deter more timorous readers).

In the manner of a rhetorical preacher, Howard developed his argument in answer to the question, "The People: where will they go?" Presented with what he likened to three magnets—town, country and the garden city—the people would be drawn inexorably to garden cities. In this new environment "all the advantages of the most energetic and active town life, with all the beauty and delight of the country, may be secured in perfect combination."[4] Significantly, garden cities would serve as building blocks in the progressive reconstruction of society as a whole—the peaceful path to real reform referred to in the title of the first edition of his book. This was to be Howard's contribution, "however small it might be, in helping to bring a new civilisation into being."[5]

From the general to the particular, much of the book consists of detailed specifications, an archetypal blueprint for utopia. The garden city of the future would be built on a central core of 1000 acres, with a surrounding ring of 5000 acres of farmland (the latter to be reorganized into new farm units). 30,000 people would live in the city and a further 2000 in the agricultural belt. In contrast to the haphazard way in which most towns had grown, the garden city would be carefully planned. Circular in form, land use would be strictly zoned to keep apart incompatible uses and ensure that the distribution of functions was in the best interests of the community as a whole. Thus, the very centre of the settlement was reserved for civic uses: an ornamental garden surrounded by a spacious layout for the main civic buildings (town hall, concert hall, theatre, library, museum, art gallery and hospital) and beyond that an extensive park. This central complex would be bounded by a Crystal Palace, a wide glass arcade with shops and exhibitions. Tree-lined avenues and wide boulevards were proposed, not simply to provide access, but also to distinguish the different neighbourhoods, and to separate the housing from nonresidential areas.

All housing was to be built on ample plots (the minimum size being a frontage of twenty feet and a depth of one hundred feet), a city of gardens as well as a city within a garden. Factories (fuelled by electricity to keep the air clean), warehouses, dairies, markets, timber and coal yards, and other services would be confined to an outer ring, served by a circular railway which, in turn, would be connected to a main line into the centre of the settlement and outwards to other parts of the country's rail network. Beyond the circular railway the farmland would begin, a mixture of large farms, smallholdings and allotments; in a traditional balance of town and country, the land would be fertilized with sewage from the residential areas, and produce would be sold to the local market.

It was, in purely spatial terms, an attractive plan, but what distinguishes it from other model schemes is its unique treatment of land values and tenure arrangements. The land for the settlement as a whole would be purchased by a sponsoring trust at agricultural land values (then about £40 per acre), with a rate of return for trustees of not more than four percent. All occupants would pay a rent (referred to as a rate-rent as there was no separate general rate levy), and the income received in this way would be used for three purposes: to pay interest on the initial capital sum, to pay back the capital, and to pay for the general running costs and welfare of the garden city. Over a period the first two items of expenditure would decrease, and the municipality would be left with greater choice of what it could do to improve amenities for its population. Such a prospect was unknown in traditional settlements, where rising values would be enjoyed primarily as a source of profit for private landlords. The secret, claimed Howard, was to retain the land in common ownership and to plan the whole project systematically from the outset.

To maintain the balance of the scheme, a way had to be found to accommodate potential growth beyond the limits of the planned city. This was done through a plan for satellite cities (which Howard termed social cities), whereby growth would be channelled to new settlements beyond the agricultural belt. In time, a ring of such cities might result, each of a comparable population but with the subsequent emergence of a larger central city to provide higher level services. Thus, it would be possible to plan for a total population of a quarter of a million, in the form of a cluster of relatively small and largely self-contained settlements.

Such was the essence of Howard's plan for garden cities. Although he intended it as a practical manifesto, commentators at the time and since have referred to the plan, sometimes disparagingly, as utopian. Typically, following the publication of his book, one critic wrote that "Mr Howard is not content with half measures; like Sir Thomas More he builds a Utopia—a charming Garden City of 32,000 people. . . . the only difficulty is to create it; but that is a small matter to Utopians."[6] Howard himself was adamant that his ideas were not fanciful: "I am no Utopian for to me the building of a city is what I have long set my mind upon."[7] The idea of the garden city was far-reaching—"transformative" according to Lewis Mumford[8]—and communal ownership was the key to a radical change in society, but Howard saw the attachment of a utopian label as distinctly unhelpful to his cause. If he retained his vision of a rebirth of civilization it was not this aspect that was most prominent in his propaganda. Indeed, he went to great pains to detach the garden city idea from other schemes that represented a more direct challenge to society. No reader of his book, he claimed, would "confuse the experiment here advocated with any experiment in absolute Communism. Nor is the scheme to be regarded as a socialistic experiment. . . ."[9] Understandably, those from whom Howard tried to distance himself in turn poured scorn on his ideas. The Fabian Society, for instance, which saw the road to socialism through a working-class majority in Parliament, referred to "the unpalatable dough of his [Howard's] Utopian scheming. . . . We have got to make the best use of our existing cities, and proposals for building new ones are about as useful as would be arrangements for protection against visits from Mr Wells's Martians."[10]

The truth, as to whether or not the garden city idea was utopian, lies somewhere between allegation and denial. Seen as a means to transform the whole of society, there is undoubtedly a powerful utopian element. Mumford was prepared to acknowledge that "Howard's ideas have laid the foundation for a new cycle in urban civilization: one in which the means of life will be subservient to the purposes of living, and in which the pattern needed for biological survival and economic efficiency will likewise lead to social and personal fulfilment."[11] However, other than through inference, the detailed means by which the great transformation would take place—from garden city to a new civilization—was, in the manner of other utopias, barely touched upon by Howard. If anything, his scheme was a *quasi* utopia, concentrating on the fulfilment of the perfect city, initially at least in an imperfect world.

Utopian authenticity, however, depends less on the soundness of argument of how to reach the Promised Land than on the depth of the vision itself. Howard seems quite consciously to have designed building blocks for his new society, and then to have recognized that in order to get even one of these building blocks into place he would need to temper its impact. One of his biographers shows how Howard consciously moderated his presentation to maximize its appeal, even to the point of working through several drafts of the title before deciding on *garden city*, with its "beguilingly soft English attraction about it."[12] Much of his writing and propaganda emphasizes this moderation, a product in part of political pragmatism but also of his own inner belief that people instinctively shied away from extremes. Thus, Howard sought to chart a course between total individualism and total collectivism, "between the Scylla of anarchy and the Charybidis of despotism."[13] He was at pains to avoid any sense of coercion, stressing that his scheme should not be regarded as a strait-jacket into which all had to fit. He was undoubtedly right when he observed that past utopian schemes had often failed because they had asked too much of human nature.[14] His own preference was to seek to create a climate in which social experiment could flourish, but not to impose a single way of doing things. In the agricultural belt, for instance, he could imagine that the farms would be managed by a mixture of capitalist, cooperative and individual methods. "Here, as in every feature of the experiment, it will be seen that it is not the area of rights which is contracted, but the area of choice which is enlarged."[15]

In a similar way, Howard addressed the overall balance that should be struck between municipal and private enterprise. He contrasted the views of the socialist and the individualist, each of which favoured one form of enterprise rather than the other, and concluded that probably the true answer is to be found at neither extreme, is only to be gained by experiment, and will differ in different communities, and at different periods.[16] His own preference was to see an extension of municipal activity, but this would best come about gradually through the example of merit and should, in any case, never claim a "rigid monopoly."[17] Elsewhere, Howard described the approach as one of Social Individualism, where the association of individuals for the common good would be seen as a natural rather than as an imposed and artificial way of doing things.[18]

Even George Bernard Shaw, an admirer of Soviet Russia and normally with little time for compromise, could in this case see advantage in an ideological mix. "The economic future of the land is with collective farms and garden cities," he proclaimed boldly, only to concede that it would be "psychologically advisable to plan collective farms and garden cities in such a fashion that every house should have attached to it a private plot to play in or grow flowers and vegetables, or keep one's own cow or what not."[19]

Eschewing extremes (and the scorn of extremists), Howard appealed to capitalists and workers alike for their support. Rather like the utopian socialists of the early nineteenth century, he believed that vested interests and opposition would somehow fall away in the face of reasoned argument. Owners of capital, he maintained, had nothing to fear from a scheme that elsewhere he claimed would change the very nature of society.

> My proposal appeals not only to individuals but to co-operators, manufacturers, philanthropic societies, and others experienced in organisation, and with organisations under their control, to come and place themselves under conditions involving no new restraints but rather securing wider freedom.[20]

In his political naivety there is much that is recognizably utopian. He relied on the sheer logic of his case rather than on established doctrine or institutional support to achieve his ends. But his naivety was effective as well as appealing, and almost single-handed he set about the task of putting into place the first building block in his new society. Rather than await the intervention of the state or a wealthy benefactor, in 1899 he joined with others to form a new organization, the Garden City Association, charged with the object of building the first garden city.

Building Utopia

> *No more in sunless cities, grim and grey,*
> *Thro' brick-built conduits shall the nation pour*
> *Her dwindling life in torment . . .*
> *For you in league with sunshine and sweet air,*
> *With comfortable grass and healing flowers,*
> *Have sworn to bring man back his natural good,*
> *Have planned a Garden City, fresh and fair,*
> *When Work and Thought and Rest may ply their powers,*
> *And joy go hand in hand with Brotherhood.*[21]

The formation of the Garden City Association was a direct outcome of the recommendation in the penultimate chapter of Howard's book: "One small Garden City must be built as a working model, and then a group of cities. . . ."[22] If this could be done, he remained convinced that vested interests would fall away and that the reconstruction of London itself (which, with the dispersal of its people to garden cities, would by then have a much smaller population) would inevitably follow. In the event, Howard and what became known as the Garden City Movement were directly responsible for two experiments, Letchworth and Welwyn, and influenced a third, Wythenshawe, in England before the Second World War. Over a longer period and at an international level the evidence of building garden cities is considerably more extensive.[23]

But, as Howard anticipated, it all started in a small way, with Howard and twelve like-minded men (for indeed they were all men) meeting in 1899 in an accountant's office in the City of London. Six of this original group were already members of the Land Nationalisation Society, and one, J. Bruce Wallace, had formerly established a Brotherhood Church and was constantly searching for cooperative solutions to society's ills. What they shared in their new organization was a commitment to spread the ideas expounded in Howard's book and to take the first steps to build a garden city. At their inaugural public meeting an industrialist and Liberal member of the London County Council, Mr T. H. W. Idris, was elected as Chairman of the Association. Sidney Webb, the campaigning socialist, would have been especially scornful of Idris: the cooperative commonwealth could not be created overnight, he argued, but "through such pettifogging work as slowly and with infinite difficulty building up a Municipal Works Department under the London County Council."[24]

Undeterred either by critics or by the enormity of their task the Garden City Association set up sub-committees to investigate different aspects of the building of a garden city, and within a few months resolved to form a limited company to manage the process. Potential investors were less than impressed, however, and immediate plans were withdrawn in favour of a further period of propaganda. A full-time Secretary of the Association was appointed, Thomas Adams, and he soon made his mark by efficiently organizing two important conferences, at the model industrial settlements of Bournville and Port Sunlight. Howard was enthusiastic about the settings, believing that delegates would be inspired by the sight of earlier achievements: at Bournville he claimed that "a Garden Village has been built; a Garden City is but a step beyond."[25] Following the second of these conferences, in July 1902, the First Garden City Pioneer Company was registered, and this time there was no difficulty in raising the required capital to sponsor preparatory work. Apart from Howard, Board members were all wealthy industrialists (or, in the case of the Chairman, Charles Neville, an influential lawyer), a sign that capitalists had been convinced that this was no revolutionary plan. Such an alliance of interests, however, could not be gained without the associated risk of losing sources of support in the process.

So the search was on for an ideal site for the first garden city. If the vision was clear, the way of achieving it was not. C. B. Purdom, employed by the Pioneer Company as a junior clerk (and later to be a stalwart of the Garden City Movement) recalled how the company shared a crowded office with the Garden City Association, and "how there was nothing short of chaos. . . . the office floor was covered with maps and offers of sites, extending from fifty acres to large estates, sent from all over the country."[26] What was envisaged was a greenfield site of 6000 acres, and only at the eleventh hour was Letchworth chosen in favour of an estate at Chartley, near Stafford. What attracted the Company to Hertfordshire was its proximity to London, and the fact that the land (a sad product of years of agricultural depression) was practically deserted. It was smaller than hoped for (under 4000 acres), and an aggregate of fifteen separate parcels, but in other respects it seemed ideal. Contracts were signed in early 1903 at what proved to be a competitive price of about £40 per acre. Later that year, in September, First Garden City Ltd. was registered with an authorized capital of £300,000, and the first prospectus was issued, inviting subscriptions for £80,000 share capital. The Pioneer Company was duly wound up. Thus, on a firm legal and financial footing, and five years after the publication of his book, Howard's scheme was finally launched. Whether or not it had already lost its utopian intent can only be judged by what was actually built.

In fact, what took shape showed a mixture of conformity and change. There was much in the composition of Letchworth that was little different from the likes of Bournville and Port Sunlight, where the intention had been to provide industrial workers and their families with a decent environment in which to live and work and to promote social harmony. At Letchworth, two exceptional young architects, Raymond Unwin and Barry Parker, were commissioned to prepare the overall plan and to influence the design of individual buildings. Their own pedigree was impeccable for the task, steeped in an Arts and Crafts tradition and with strong sympathies for a very English brand of socialism; over Unwin's desk were portraits of Edward Carpenter and William Morris.

Most of the first garden city was in one sense quite conventional, yet in another sense marked a material improvement in the quality of the everyday environment of its inhabitants. Under the influence of Unwin and Parker, houses were designed in a picturesque, vernacular style, based on that of sixteenth- and seventeenth-century cottages. Typically, they would have steeply-sloping red tile roofs, with gables and dormer windows, and white or cream roughcast elevations; and grouped, often in terraces of four, along tree-lined avenues or around village greens. Important architects of the day were invited to design some of the larger houses (the aim being to attract residents from all classes), which tended to follow the style set by Unwin and Parker. Every dwelling had its own garden, and the architects were careful to ensure that as far as possible natural features in the landscape were preserved. As a result, visitors were invariably impressed by the verdant appearance of the town and by the profusion of flowers.

There was a conscious attempt to ensure that a reasonable proportion of new housing would be available at low prices. Unwin and Parker designed four-roomed cottages for as little as £132, and were less than enthusiastic for a commercially sponsored competition which invited architects to produce their own designs and to build demonstration cottages for less than £150. Although this exercise, the Cheap Cottages Competition and Exhibition, attracted considerable interest, the feeling was that it led to a dilution of the dominant style and that some cost-cutting was achieved only at the expense of a lowering of standards.

Separated from the housing, industrial development made good progress in the early years. Firms were attracted to locate at Letchworth, not necessarily by the radical principles that Howard first expounded (though some who moved, like the Idris Mineral Water Works, and the publisher, Dent, were more than sympathetic), but probably more often by the practical advantages of serviced sites with good communications and a ready supply of labour. Much to the dismay of those, not least of all women, who looked to Letchworth for a break from past conventions, the most prominent factory was that of the Spirella Corset Company.

Typically, however, it was less the evidence of solid achievement in creating a high quality environment with local employment that attracted most interest amongst observers, as opposed to that which was seen as quirky and eccentric. In spite of the acceptance of Howard's ideas by respectable businessmen, the garden city never lost its more challenging, utopian association in the minds of critics and supporters alike. And in its way this association became self-fulfilling, with those with a bent for alternative lifestyles finding their way to the pioneer settlement and encouraging others to join them. Letchworth thus became something of a crossroads for free-thinkers, on a perpetual journey to and from the various points on the utopian map of England: "for here a town was to be built that would, they thought, change the face of England."[27]

There had been many false dawns amongst the community experiments of the previous century, but Letchworth inspired new optimism, with the prospect of "a Utopia of clean, pure air, flowers and perpetual sunshine."[28] Tolstoyans, Ruskinian Socialists, and members of the Independent Labour Party were amongst those who made their home in the garden city. To outsiders they seemed an odd set, "a typical Garden citizen clad in knickerbockers and, of course, sandals, a vegetarian and member of the Theosophical Society who kept two tortoises which he polishes regularly with best Lucca oil. Over his mantelpiece was a large photo of Madame Blatavsky [sic] and on his library shelves were *Isis Unveiled* and the works of William Morris, H. G. Wells and Tolstoy."[29]

Jan Marsh has shown how a popular area for these free-thinkers was in the southwest of the town, in a cluster of more expensive cottages. She cites a contemporary view that those who found their way there were the "enthusiasts who had been looking forward for years to the founding of the town. They came to it in a spirit of adventure, they discovered it as if it were a new land."[30] Mervyn Miller, author of the seminal book on Letchworth, agrees that before 1914 there was something special about the place, "a Golden Age of Garden City life."[31] In that period it acquired a reputation for "smocks, sandals and, in the context of highly conventional moral standards of the day, scandals."[32] Miller is also careful to point out that, in spite of this reputation, the free-thinkers were always very much in a minority—"almost universally middle class, the successors of the Utopianists of earlier centuries"[33]—and most of the town got on with its business much as in any other place.

In spite of their minority status, the free-thinkers exercised a disproportionate influence on the cultural life of Letchworth in its early days, with a predictable diet of "improving" lectures, craft-making, revival of traditional music and dance, and educational experiments. High-minded pioneers supported a temperance policy, conviviality in the Skittles Inn was fuelled by cocoa and fruit cordials, and vegetarianism was strongly advocated. For those who wished to, there were opportunities for cooperative living, with its offer of a mixture of private accommodation and shared facilities, including kitchens, dining rooms and gardens. "Homesgarth," the first housing cooperative in Letchworth, was designed by the Fabian architect, J. Clapham Lander. It accommodated about thirty residents, who, in spite of the socialist provenance of the project, were largely limited to the middle class. Undeterred by its failure to attract a more representative sample of society, Howard enthused about the scheme's "happy people" and of his own "great ambition to carry out a similar scheme which will benefit the people of the working class."[34]

As in any utopian experiment, education attracted considerable interest, and various experiments were tried. Although the local board of education curbed some of the more radical proposals, its first school nevertheless contained elements that were certainly progressive by normal public standards: small classes, access for all classrooms to fresh air, the tending of garden plots, and country dancing. Additionally, a number of private, progressive schools were established, offering a healthy mixture of fresh air, vegetarian diets, manual work, and an appreciation of arts and crafts. Foremost in reputation amongst these schools was St. Christopher's, which, under its headmaster, Lyn Harris, was to emerge nationally as a leading progressive school. There was also the St. Christopher Fellowship, formed to support craft guilds, as "a contribution to the evolution of the Social-Industrial life of the New Age."[35]

Probably, though, the alternative activity which attracted most interest was that which centred on The Cloisters, a purpose-built residential college for disciples of the New Life. The project was sponsored by the daughter of a London ironmaster, Annie Jane Lawrence, who believed in "eternal reality" and the "perfect inviolable whole."[36] As Jan Marsh explains, fresh air and water were at the heart of Miss Lawrence's conception of the New Life, and with sleeping accommodation separated from the elements only by a sheet of canvas, this was reflected in the architecture of The Cloisters. Green marble columns were designed to symbolize upward growth and aspiration, and a flowing fountain represented the eternal stream of wisdom. Permanent members of the community were encouraged to grow their own food, although there seems to have been more interest in philosophizing about the meaning of life than in doing anything practical for its maintenance. Communards preferred to laze in hammocks and to sit around the marble swimming pool than to toil in the gardens, knowing in any case that Miss Lawrence's benevolence would ensure the provision of meals each day on a pink alabaster table.

Miss Lawrence also fell under the spell of one of the founder members of the Garden City Association, J. Bruce Wallace, who saw in her wealth the opportunity to pursue some of his more fanciful ideas. By then he was wedded to Theosophy and a new movement called the Alpha Union, and persuaded Miss Lawrence to let him use The Cloisters for summer schools and other residential courses. Many were attracted to spend a week or more in various quests for personal freedom, psychic growth, oneness with Nature, and a higher reality. They also joined with the permanent residents in practical activities, making sandals, weaving and carving wood. Wallace saw his summer students as potential disciples of his theories of Social Christianity and Land Work, his own role being to train those who shared his beliefs to go out in the world and "lift people to an adequate conception of what they really are."[37] Unfortunately for the fulfilment of this vision, Wallace's association with Miss Lawrence ended rather acrimoniously in 1912, and increasingly The Cloisters took on the less *avant garde* function of a community centre for the town, albeit with a continuing emphasis on some of its traditional activities, such as craft classes, folk-dancing and open-air bathing.

Even without the more exotic features of the new settlement, Letchworth was a pioneering project and attracted a regular stream of international as well as domestic visitors. In the summer of 1905, for instance, 60,000 people were attracted to the Cheap Cottages Exhibition. Recognizing the propagandist value of the new settlement as a model that others might be encouraged to emulate, the Garden City Association was active in arranging its own visits and publicising progress in other ways; its periodical, *Garden City,* for instance, carried monthly notes and articles on this.[38] Additionally (and largely as a result of the work of Thomas Adams) the Garden City Company played its own part in this process. Adams organized a diverse programme of visits, hosting such groups as adult education bodies, cyclists, women Liberals, vegetarians, the Christian Social Union, and MPs from all parties. By these means, Simpson has concluded that "Adams spread the word of Garden City and helped to integrate it into the mainstream of social reform."[39]

On balance, the response of visitors appears to have been favourable. Some grumbled about the mud, and the half-finished state of it all, but most saw beyond the short-term difficulties. After all, here—in contrast with the harsh reality of conventional urbanism—was evidence of well-designed housing in a healthy environment, with local employment, accessible to working people as well as being attractive for these and other reasons to middle-class residents. Whether or not it was, in a literal sense, utopian would have mattered little to those who personally experienced a dramatically improved environment. "You are going nowhere better," said one pioneer to those who passed the town by.[40] Even George Bernard Shaw, not one to give praise lightly, is in 1904 prepared to commend (in his play, *John Bull's Other Island*) the building of a garden city in Ireland, and a copy of Howard's book is handed on the stage from one actor to another; while in the following year, in *Major Barbara*, Letchworth is featured in the guise of Perivale St. Andrews, "a spotlessly clean and beautiful hillside town."[41] By 1914 some 10,000 people lived in the garden city, and this alone represented no mean achievement when compared with the many earlier schemes that had never progressed beyond the printed word.

In other respects, though, Letchworth fell short of utopian ideals. Conditions might have been improved for its workers, but the basic infrastructure of capitalist society remained untouched. Moreover, even on its own terms, the garden city on the ground had lost something of Howard's original ideals. In an internal memorandum, Adams pointed to differences between theory and practice in relation to methods of raising capital, administration, ownership of the sites and public services, land tenure, the size of the estate, the proportion reserved for agriculture, restrictions on growth, layout, and the system of distribution.[42] Some of the reasons for these differences were purely pragmatic (depending, for instance, on the extent and configuration of the estate) but Adams also noted a tendency to adopt a more commercial approach than had been originally intended. The fact is that Letchworth was, not surprisingly, a reformist rather than a revolutionary project, with its own strengths as well as weaknesses. This positioning was noted in an article in *The Race-Builder*.

> The revolutionist may regard it as a last ditch for the hard-pressed forces of capitalism, but the evolutionists should surely see it as an effort to find a way out of the competitive chaos towards a well-ordered society. If the scheme retains some old evils, it introduces new qualifying virtues.[43]

Similarly, Armytage notes how the loss of some of its idealistic elements widened its appeal: "The green banner of the garden city became respectable and the sharp Utopian outlines of Howard's sketches softened and blurred." [44]

Paradoxically, in spite of its obvious reformist qualities, there were at the same time those who condemned Letchworth for being fanciful, diversionary and irrelevant to the real needs of the country; in short, for being utopian. Such critics were less interested in the solid achievements of Letchworth and more in the extremism of a minority. They were quick to jeer at the "cranks" in the town, pouring scorn on the wearing of smocks and djibbahs, on the making of their own sandals, on the vegetarian and nonalcoholic régime, and on the long hair and beards. They found an easy butt for their ridicule in the fare of the Food Reform Restaurant and the prospects of a stay at the Simple Life Hotel. Some of the cartoons and press articles were merely humorous but sometimes they revealed a note of spite, if not fear of potentially subversive effects on society. In *Mr Standfast*, John Buchan sent his First World War hero, Richard Hannay, *incognito* to Bigglewick (Letchworth by another name) in search of dissidents. Our hero is quick to discover that most of them are pacifists, but apart from being "the rummiest birds you can imagine" generally harmless. At worst they were misguided: "about half were respectable citizens who came here for country air and low rates, but even these had a touch of queerness." [45] Some years later, George Orwell, in *The Road to Wigan Pier,* used the popular view of Letchworth to support his broadside on what he saw as the "cranky" side of socialism; in the garden city, he claimed, one could find "every fruit juice drinker, sandal wearer, sex-maniac, Quaker, nature cure quack, pacifist and feminist in England." [46]

Letchworth, disliked by some for not going far enough and by others for being too utopian, was caught in a cleft stick of criticism. But on the ground it continued to grow, and although Howard's rational path to a world of garden cities was not universally or quickly followed, the experience gained was nevertheless to have some consequential effects. . . .

NOTES

1. Beevers, R. *The Garden City Utopia* (London: Macmillan, 1988), 27.

2. Ibid., 35.

3. Ibid., 31–32.

4. Howard, E. (1898) *To-morrow: a peaceful path to real reform.* London: Swann Sonnenschein. Revised and republished in 1902 as *Garden Cities of To-morrow.* Swann Sonnenschein. Republished in 1946 with prefaces by F. J. Osborn and L. Mumford as *Garden Cities of Tomorrow.* London: Faber and Faber; and in 1965 with a new forward by F. J. Osborn.

5. Stanley Buder (1969) Ebenezer Howard: the genesis of a town planning movement. *Journal of the American Institute of Planners,* vol. 35, 391.

6. Review in *The Times,* following the publication of Howard (1898) in Beevers (1988), 1.

7. Beevers (1988), 1.

8. Mumford, L. *The City in History,* 1966 edition (Harmondsworth: Pelican, 1961), 590.

9. Howard (1902), 114.

10. *Fabian News,* December 1898, in Howard (1902), 11.

11. Mumford, Preface to 1946 edition of Howard (1902), 40.

12. Beevers (1988), 54.

13. Extract from *Daily Chronicle* article, quoted in Howard (1898) at the start of chapter 9.

14. Howard (1902), 113.

15. Howard (1898), 18.

16. Ibid., 64.

17. Ibid., 65.

18. This concept predates a fuller development of his thoughts on municipal activity, and is explained in a short essay [undated] in the Howard Papers, Folio 20, Hertfordshire County Record Office.

19. Shaw, G. B. *Everybody's Political What's What?* (London: Constable, 1944), 19.

20. Howard (1902), 116.

21. Rev. Canon Rawnsley (1905) The garden city. *Garden City,* vol. 1, no. 2, February, 9.

22. Howard (1946 edition), 48.

23. See, for instance, Ward, S. V. *The Garden City: Past, Present, and Future* (London: Spon, 1992).

24. Webb, quoted in Marshall, P. "A British Sensation," in Bowman, S. E., ed. *Edward Bellamy Abroad* (New York: Twayne Publishers, 1962), 106.

25. Howard in Simpson, M. *Thomas Adams and the Modern Planning Movement* (London: Mansell, 1985), 11.

26. Purdom, C. B. *Life Over Again* (London: Dent, 1951), 39.

27. Ibid., 4.

28. This view of an industrialist, Lewis Falk, in Armytage, W. H. *Heavens Below* (London: Routledge and Kegan Paul, 1961), 374.

29. Ibid., from a diary of Letchworth events.

30. Observation of C. B. Purdom in 1913, cited in Marsh, J. *Back to the Land* (London: Quartet, 1982.)

31. Miller, M. *Letchworth: the First Garden City* (Chichester: Phillimore, 1989), 88.

32. Ibid.

33. Ibid.

34. Howard, *Daily Mail,* 27 March 1913.

35. Cited in Marsh (1982), 243.

36. Ibid., pp. 238–241, for a helpful description of The Cloisters.

37. The vision of another of Wallace's sponsors, W. E. Swinton, in Armytage (1961), p. 375.

38. For a full account of the work of the Association, see Hardy, D. *From Garden Cities to New Towns* (London: E & FN Spon, 1991).

39. Simpson (1985), p. 22.

40. Bill Furmston, in Marsh (1982), p. 232.

41. Andrew Undershaft, describing the town in which his armaments factory is located, in *Major Barbara*, in Shaw, G. B. *Complete Plays of Bernard Shaw* (London: Odhams, 1905), p. 492.

42. Garden City Association: Memorandum by the Secretary, undated but probably 1903.

43. From *The Race Builder,* May 1906, in *Garden City,* vol. 1, August 1906, 159.

44. Armytage (1961), p. 381.

45. Buchan, J. *Mr. Steadfast* (Ware: Wordsworth Editions, 1919), 19.

46. Orwell, G. *The Road to Wigan Pier* (1989 Edition, Harmondsworth: Penguin, 1937), 161.

A Delaware Delight

The Oasis Called Arden

Henry Wiencek
(1992)

The name rings like a merry little bell for all who know their Shakespeare—"Arden." It was the name of the enchanted forest in *As You Like It*—the forest that resounded with music and song, the murmurs of lovers and the jests of Touchstone—where a jolly band of young gentlemen went willingly into exile with the banished duke, there to "fleet the time carelessly, as they did in the golden world." It is a joyous spot on literature's map, and in the early 1900s a merry band of American dreamers put an Arden on the map of Delaware. It is there today, tucked among the suburbs of Wilmington, an oasis of idiosyncrasy.

Its citizens have been people of ideas—poets, novelists, playwrights and actors; painters, sculptors, metal-smiths and potters; Socialists, Communists, pacifists and anarchists; promoters of Esperanto, advocates of free love, and in the words of one early resident, "conservatives who had no ideas at all." In their enchanted forest they built a forge and craft shops in order to earn their livings by making and selling useful and beautiful things; they built an intimate open-air theater for performances of the works of the Bard; they staged elaborate medieval pageants, in costumes of their own design, to re-create the spirit of a simpler age; in the twilight, they gathered by a bonfire to sing songs and tell stories, cherishing their sense of community. Valuing cooperation above competition, they strove to be happy rather than rich. Delawareans thought they were nuts.

I wish I could say that I discovered Arden in some appropriately romantic fashion—that my Land Rover was stopped by hooded archers in a bosky byway; that I was kidnapped by free-love agitators on a dark and stormy night; or that I tracked a fugitive Soviet coup meister to a secret Stalinist camp in the Delaware woods. Alas, I found it in a book. Browsing through the 1938 Works Progress Administration (WPA) guide to Delaware, I discovered a long description of Arden and decided to find out if this wonderful settlement could possibly have survived the intervening decades.

I found, first of all, that it is not easy to collect information about Arden in the usual ways. I called Directory Assistance to ask for the number of the Arden town hall.

"No listing."

"Office of the mayor or village supervisor?"

This selection was originally published in *Smithsonian* 23, 2 (May 1992): 124–142. It is reprinted by permission of the author.

"No listing."

"All right, the chamber of commerce, then?"

"No listing."

"Historical society? Rotary? Kiwanis? Elks?"

"No listing."

"Is there a listing of any kind for any town offices?"

"None. But there is an Arden Club."

"I'll take that."

A few phone calls later I was talking with the grand-daughter of Ella Reeve (Mother) Bloor, the famous Communist labor agitator, and she invited me to visit the next Sunday afternoon.

Arden had apparently not changed all that much: I was able to navigate through it quite well by the 54-year-old WPA map. The whole place had a relaxed and congenial atmosphere. The obsessive orderliness of the typical American suburb is absent here. Arden's houses seem to lounge haphazardly under their leafy canopy of trees. That lawn could use a trim; that house, a dose of paint. The street signs are not the standard-issue green rectangles with glow-in-the-dark white letters; they are wooden, with the names carved into them. Surrounding the village green are stuccoed cottages and half-timbered Tudor fantasies, one of them displaying the motto "Tomorrow is a New Day" in Gothic letters. That's Arden for you—the future in Gothic script.

Mother Bloor's granddaughter, Joan Ware Colgan, told me about children learning modern dance on the green from a member of Isadora Duncan's troupe; about Upton Sinclair living here for a while and losing his wife to some wandering poet; about a pacifist who went to jail during World War I and then went to Russia to teach the Communists how to drive a tractor. She talked about William Morris' idea that artists could live together and make the things they need, and about something called the single tax, which is not a special levy on the unmarried. Listening to Joan, I realized that, by some strange alchemy, the theories and philosophies and crazy hopes of a hundred years ago remain very much alive in this place.

Arden was founded in 1900 by a 40-year-old sculptor and businessman named Frank Stephens. He was slim and good-looking, with a rugged, chiseled face and short, sandy hair. By nature he was autocratic, and he could be hot-tempered in the defense of his beliefs. As an amateur Shakespearean actor, his favorite tragedy was *Julius Caesar,* in which he liked to play the title role, savoring the sweet pain of imagining himself the betrayed, misunderstood dictator. His character was a curious, contradictory mixture of idealism and practicality, of the progressive and the reactionary, of the puritan and the libertine—all of which, in time, would come to be a good description of Arden itself.

All across America there are dead utopias—Brook Farm, Oneida, Kaweah, Modern Times, Memnonia—places where dreamers pledged to plow and thresh together, to share equally in the sweat and fruits of labor, to yield their individuality or their spouses to the commune. Stephens made no such demands for socialist communality on his fellow citizens; indeed, Arden has always been a crazy quilt of ideologies and an arena of spectacular personality clashes. Stephens did, however, found the village upon a set of economic and social principles. For years he had been a foot soldier in a reformist crusade that is virtually forgotten today, but which fired the world with hope a century ago—the single-tax movement led by the maverick, self-taught economist Henry George. Arden is a living vestige of George's ideals.

The first 40 years of Henry George's life were like a Horatio Alger story without the payoff. Born in Philadelphia in 1839, he went to work at age 13 as an office boy; at 16 he went to sea on a freighter. Back in Philadelphia, and then in Boston and San Francisco, he worked hard at a variety of occupations, mainly journalism. But his efforts to start a news service ran smack dab into an unbreakable monopoly. Meanwhile he sank deeper into debt and degradation. Everywhere he looked he saw poverty growing worse and worse as America's wealth increased, and he wondered why. The answer, he decided, was land. At home in San Francisco, he poured his ideas into a book called *Progress and Poverty*, which for a time threatened to turn the country on its ear.

Henry George's ideas require something larger than a nutshell, but fundamentally he believed that it was a mistake to have private ownership of land. Landowners were nothing but parasites, feeding off the productivity of others through their extraction of rent and high selling prices for land. Whenever productivity improved, bringing increases in wages and business profits, landowners raised their rents or selling prices for the ground beneath homes, stores, businesses and factories, even though they themselves had contributed nothing to the increased productivity. "Rent," George reasoned, "is thus an invisible tax on enterprise . . . a tax on capital as well as on wages.

His remedy? Ideally, the federal government should nationalize the land, but that was not practical. *"It is not necessary to confiscate land,"* George wrote, *"it is only necessary to confiscate rent."* Taxing land at its full rental value would effectively turn all the profits of landholding to the common use. The revenue from such a tax would be so great that all other levies could be abolished, replaced by the single tax.

The idea captured the imagination of people from every social and economic class. *Progress and Poverty* sold two million copies in the United States and was translated into a dozen languages. Both George Bernard Shaw and Sun Yat-sen said their ideas were shaped by Henry George. John Dewey declared that George was one of the ten greatest philosophers since Plato. Leo Tolstoy wrote an introduction to a Russian edition of George's works and approached the Romanovs about converting Russia to the single tax. (Interestingly, Karl Marx hated *Progress and Poverty*, dismissing it as the "capitalists' last ditch.")

Throughout this country, enthusiasts joined single-tax clubs to discuss and promote George's ideas. Among the more fervent from the economist's hometown of Philadelphia was Frank Stephens. In the early 1890s Stephens went to New York to place himself at George's service, becoming one of his valued lieutenants. With other

Philadelphia single-taxers, Stephens plotted strategy for a blitzkrieg during the 1896 elections. They needed to capture an entire political entity where they could install the single-tax system and prove that it worked. They decided to take over Delaware.

In preparation for the campaign, scores of single-taxers went into training as public speakers. It is said that Demosthenes put pebbles in his mouth and orated to the waves; the single-taxers formed a Shakespeare Club and honed their skills on "Friends, Romans, countrymen!" Brown uniforms, emblazoned with a symbol of the Earth, were stitched up, and thus attired, the single-taxers commenced the invasion of Delaware to promote their slate of candidates.

But Delaware resisted being made the test tube for the millennium. Denounced in the press as "depraved and irresponsible vagabonds," the invaders were arrested one by one for violating the public-speaking and public-assembly regulations; Stephens was the second to be hauled in. In the face of diligent police work, the campaign was in danger of faltering, but Stephens believed he had a trump card. The master himself, Henry George, was monitoring the campaign with his chief strategists. If the authorities arrested him, there would be an immense public outcry. In high excitement, the single-taxers wired George: "Do you wish to personally test the law? Sentence for 30 days certain." But George drew the line at civil disobedience and refused to come. The single-tax slate was resoundingly defeated.

It was just as well that George stayed out of jail. Although he was only 58 years old, his health was failing rapidly. He suffered a fatal stroke in October 1897.

It would be difficult to exaggerate the scope of the grief felt at George's sudden death. An elderly abolitionist said that in his memory only Lincoln's assassination had touched the nation more deeply. George's son, touring Russia about a decade later, paid a call on Tolstoy, who offered to carry a personal message to George in the afterlife: "I shall see your father before you do. What shall I tell him?" "Tell him," said the son, "I kept the faith."

So did Frank Stephens. With another single-taxer from Philadelphia, an architect named Will Price, Stephens made plans for Arden. It would be right under the noses of his old enemies in Delaware. With his own money and some of Price's, and a loan from millionaire soap manufacturer Joseph Fels, who had a deep interest in the single-tax movement, Stephens purchased a 162-acre farm north of Wilmington.

Stephens drew up a deed of trust that established Arden as a single-tax enclave along the lines that George had proposed: there would be no private ownership of land; the land would be held in trust by three trustees, who would grant 99-year leases to residents. The trustees would determine the value of each parcel and set the land rent—the single tax—to be paid annually. (This duty was soon to be taken over by elected assessors.) No other local levies would be assessed. As time went on and land values rose, rents would increase—so the wealth created by the community, reflected in the rising value of the land, would be shared by the community. Residents could sell their houses but not the land. Upon the sale of a house, the land lease would be transferred to the new owner.

It was one thing to draw up a document governing a patch of empty acres; it was quite another to fill those acres with a living population. Turning to the ideas of the English reformers John Ruskin and William Morris, Stephens envisioned a community of artists and artisans who would support themselves in modest comfort, producing fine objects. In this village of tidy cottages and shops and forges, of genial fraternity and sorority, the true coin of the realm would be art. Accordingly, Stephens drew up a manifesto of principles: "The Arden craftsmen are a company of men and women who believe with the great English craftsman and prophet William Morris that 'all men should have work to do which shall be worth doing and be of itself pleasant to do' and which should be done under such conditions as would make it neither overwearisome nor overanxious. They believe also with Ruskin that men need not be baited into a shop like moths into a candle and that there are those who will buy what is useful without being ill-designed and dishonestly made even though its cost is more than that of factory goods."

The program required the proper setting. Will Price laid out the village, devoting nearly half of the land to greens, forests, paths and roads. He arranged house lots and roads to follow the contours of the land rather than the grid of a draftsman, and knitted the town together by a network of paths in an early example of separating vehicular and pedestrian traffic. Price's carefully groomed rustic setting and half-timbered cottages brought to life the medievalist spirit of William Morris. The spirit of Shakespeare hovered over the enterprise as well. One of the first communal building projects was an open-air theater for Shakespearean productions.

After a slow start, Arden took off. Some people were merely summer residents, living in tents; others, more permanent, commuted by rail to jobs in Philadelphia or Wilmington. But true to Stephens' vision, a cadre of stay-at-home artists and artisans went at their happy toil. The forest rang with the music of hammers. In the medieval fashion advocated by Morris, most of the artisans were organized into guilds. There were potters, stained-glass craftsmen, silversmiths, woodworkers, printers and furniture makers. The Weave Shop was begun with one employee who made wool and other sturdy fabrics. Eventually it had about 30 weavers who made fine linens. Stephens devoted his attention to the Arden Forge, which produced lamps, lanterns, door latches and hinges, fireplace tools, and other works of iron. Cash-poor Ardenites could not afford to buy their own products, so the guilds depended on the New York, Philadelphia and Wilmington carriage trade. Members of the du Pont family were occasional customers, and it is said that stage and screen stars Lillian and Dorothy Gish visited Arden to buy wool.

Stephens welcomed all comers; one did not have to declare allegiance to the thoughts of Henry George to take up residence. As a practical matter, putting down roots in Arden was cheap because you could *not* buy land. Most of the residents did their own construction and other work, a self-sufficiency that pleased Stephens.

Fred Whiteside, later well known in Delaware as the perennial Socialist candidate for governor and State Senator, inadvertently created one of the enduring myths about Arden when he built a tree house as a retreat for Sunday-morning reflection. The Delaware press expanded this single tree house into headlines and stories proclaiming that Ardenites lived in trees.

The tree house affair was nothing compared with the cyclone of publicity generated by the presence in Arden of America's most famous Socialist, Upton Sinclair. The muckraking author arrived in the spring of 1910, three years after Helicon Hall, his own experimental colony in New Jersey, had mysteriously gone up in flames. Although widely celebrated as author of *The Jungle*, Sinclair had an aversion to spending. Arden seemed a perfect place to live cheaply and write. He settled into a humble compound of three tents with his wife, Meta, their son, David, a secretary (with whom Will Price fell in love) and Mary Craig Kimbrough, who would become Sinclair's second wife. "How many of the so-called necessities can men dispense with when they have to!" he exulted in his autobiography. "I bathed every morning of that winter in Arden with water in a tin wash-basin and a newspaper spread upon a tent floor." In 1911, with funds from the sale of a novel, he hired Stephens to build him a two-story cottage, which still stands.

Into his Eden, Sinclair invited the serpent in the form of Harry Kemp, the "Tramp Poet," who traveled with hoboes and worked the Great Lakes ore boats. In his memoir *Tramping on Life*, Kemp describes finding "toy houses picturesquely set under trees that fringed the Common," occupied by "folk of every shade of radical opinion . . . who here strove to escape the galling mockeries of civilisation and win back again to pastoral simplicity." Simplicity included not washing the dishes—Sinclair and his family ate from wooden plates and tossed them into the fire at the end of a meal.

Kemp moved into a tent provided by Sinclair and quickly adapted to the rhythm of life in Arden. He was awakened by the birds, and spent his days writing and in literary conversations with Meta. He attended a "circus" in which all the animals were Ardenites in costume, and passed many a pleasant twilight at the communal sing-alongs in the woods: "the music softened our hearts and fused us into one harmony of feeling."

It would be gratifying to say that Arden enjoyed a long era of good feeling, but that was not the case. Stephens' open-door policy created problems because many of the settlers were Socialists (a few were anarchists) who regarded the single-taxers as politically suspect and had little use for their theories. In the summer of 1911, an anarchist shoemaker named George Brown, who thought the village was getting a bit too respectable, decided to stir things up: he used a public committee meeting as a forum for his theories of sexuality, prompting the committee to have him arrested for disrupting the proceedings. Noting that the committee members habitually played baseball on the town green on Sundays, Brown went into Wilmington to have *them* arrested for "gaming on the Sabbath" in violation of an ancient state law. Upton Sinclair was caught in this net, as he had played tennis on the Sunday in question, and spent a night in the county workhouse with the other violators. A crowd of reporters descended upon New Castle County to get the story, giving Sinclair the opportunity to denounce conditions in the jail to a national audience.

Sinclair soon made headlines again, in a scandal that helped create Arden's reputation as a free-love nest. The marriage of Upton to Meta had been unraveling before they got to Arden, and the arrival of Harry Kemp made for a triangle. During a chat with Meta, Kemp's eye had caught "the white gleam of one of her pretty legs where the elastic on one side of her bloomers had slipped up." Several weeks later Meta was slipping her bloomers completely off, as she and a naked Kemp played nymph and satyr, chasing each other through the Arden woods. One afternoon there was a moment of panic when they couldn't recall where they had stashed their clothes. Harry and Meta left Arden for New York, and Upton filed suit for divorce to the accompaniment of trumpet blasts of publicity.

Free love was not part of the single-tax program, but it might as well have been. The story is still told of a beautiful young model who fell in love, simultaneously, with two artists who were painting her. She told them to flip a coin to see who would claim fatherhood of her son, and they did. At some point in his life Stephens became a believer in free love. In the 1880s he had been married to Caroline Eakins, the youngest sister of the painter Thomas Eakins. She died in 1889, not long after giving birth to her third child. In a strange controversy that took place in 1886, Stephens had been the prime mover in the ouster of Eakins from his post as director of the Pennsylvania Academy of Fine Arts, supposedly because of liberties Eakins had taken with his female students. But in the 1890s Stephens was living in sin quite openly with a woman named Elenor Getty. She never liked the free-love arrangement and finally persuaded him to go through with the formality of marriage—to his dismay.

One of today's Ardenites whose memories stretch back to the early years is Amy Potter Cook. Ask her about the romantic scandals that swirled around Arden, and she responds, "Free love—we had that all over the place." But joshing an outsider, especially on the subject of sex, is an old Arden sport. As Amy relates, "Frank Stephens used to tell people, with a straight face, 'On very hot nights we take off our clothes and go into the creek to sleep.'"

Amy has vivid memories of Stephens working at his forge and of Will Price acting in Arden's Shakespeare productions. "Their whole idea," she says, "was to reenact Merrie Olde England." Her recollection is borne out by photographs of elaborate pageants, with knights and maidens (but no Godivas) riding through the town. Few onlookers appear because just about everyone in Arden was *in* these pageants. "The costumes were magnificent," Amy recalls. A brief memoir by Marjory Poinsett Jobson describes the Venetian Water Carnivals. During the day there were diving contests, races, games and music. When night fell, the revelers walked down a path illuminated by candles to the creek for a waterborne pageant: "a queen and her court . . . came floating downstream on a barge with torches glowing and music playing as the pretty girls in long flowing dresses smiled and threw flowers to the crowd."

With the coming of World War I, Arden and the whole single-tax movement were split on the issue of pacifism. Daniel Kiefer Sr., an Arden resident and pacifist, was removed from the chairmanship of the national single-tax organization. Stephens' son Donald spent nine months in jail for refusing to serve. He was nearly joined by his father.

In 1918 a certain Mabel P. Van Trump called upon Ardenites to buy Liberty Bonds. Stephens fell upon her like a tiger: "You are a murderer and everybody who sells Liberty Bonds!" he thundered. "You are sending our soldiers abroad to be murdered!" Van Trump duly reported this outburst to the authorities, and Stephens found himself in federal court, charged with "making a certain false statement with intent to interfere with the operation and success of the military and naval forces of the United States." A jury refused to believe that calling Mabel Van Trump a murderer in Arden put the doughboys in jeopardy in France. Stephens was acquitted. One of the jurors sent him the $9 he had received for sitting on the panel.

In 1922 the single-tax experiment expanded with the creation of Arden-town on 110 acres adjacent to Arden. A few years later, Stephens helped found Gilpin's Point, another single-tax community near Denton, Maryland. Visiting there with his two sons in 1935, he merrily organized an Arden-style campfire and, according to Donald, was "the life of the evening. He sang, recited and read Uncle Remus stories to us." The next day, Stephens, who had a history of heart trouble, was dead of a heart attack.

By that time Arden had been dealt heavy blows by the Depression, which wiped out much of the market for expensive, high-quality crafts and forced the closure of the Craft Shop. But the Ardenites hung on. Joan Colgan remembers that there was a lot of bartering during the Depression, and "a lot of cooperation." The townspeople grew their own food and had communal canning sessions at the Gild Hall. Arden managed to survive, but no one knows how. As Amy Potter Cook says, "Everybody in Arden always wondered about that themselves."

Then, in 1950, there was a further expansion. Donald Stephens was instrumental in the purchase of another section of adjacent land to form the town of Ardencroft. This time the planners reached out to one group that had previously been left out of the Arden experiment—African-Americans. Village leaders went into Wilmington to recruit them. The presence of these families brought Ardenites face-to-face with the question of integrating their grammar school. They did so, becoming the first locality in Delaware to integrate voluntarily.

In the early 1950s Arden was still a place apart, a forest surrounded by farms. Then came the suburbs. The growth of the du Pont company spawned huge housing developments around Wilmington. Arden was protected from unwanted development by its deed, which set aside the forests and other common lands as forever untouchable. Isolated within its bastion of greenery, with its private holidays and pageants and its peculiar history, Arden was viewed with wariness by the new neighbors. The old stories of free love, anarchism and Communism floated up again.

Alan and Maria Burslem, who grew up in Arden in the 1950s and '60s, recall the culture shock that occurred when Arden kids graduated from the town's grammar school and ventured into the regional junior high school. Maria says, "I had some friends in junior high who were not allowed to come to Arden. Their parents had heard rumors about that crazy little town, that it was a nudist camp."

Alan thinks that the outsiders' fears arose partly because Arden just looked so different: "We had trees and dense growth. Arden was a scary place to go into from the land of a thousand brand-new houses and no trees."

The Burslems and their two sons live in a house Maria's great-grandfather built as a summer place in 1919 (it has been greatly enlarged since then). She has the deed fixing the original annual rent of $10.65 for the land. Also on the property are Alan's pottery workshop and showroom. "It's a great place to be an artist," he says. "We wander around to each other's studios. I drag people into mine when I'm excited about new work."

Maria finds that the old Arden spirit is still alive: "There is a deep caring among those who live here. We treasure that closeness. You're in contact with all different generations. It's inspiring to see Rae Gerstine dancing away at the folk dance every Wednesday, at age 91 or whatever."

Rae can indeed be found at the regular Wednesday folk dancing at the Gild Hall, a meeting place that had been the barn of the farmer who sold the land to Frank Stephens. Under the lofty ceiling, people of all ages square dance to recorded music and a live caller. After a few numbers, the caller steps down from the stage, and a folk-dance instructor puts on recordings of Polish, Armenian, Israeli and other dances. When Rae finally decides to sit out, she talks animatedly of her life in Arden. "I was 93 last November, but I still function. I do so much I can't keep pace with everything. I dance and I go swimming." She is also one of the financial pillars of the town, serving as the secretary-treasurer of the Arden Building & Loan, which she operates out of her home to keep the overhead low. "We charge no points," she says proudly. "When someone asks for a loan, I tell them the fee is $5, payable in singles." The B & L takes two singles to cover processing costs (it makes loans only in the three Arden communities), and the appraisal committee gets the remainder.

Two beneficiaries of the Building & Loan's lending program are Susan and Edward Rohrbach, who are putting an addition on their house facing the Arden Green. Called Rest Cottage, the half-timbered house is one of the oldest in town. It was designed by Will Price himself. Both Rohrbachs are painters, and Edward is an architect as well. He is designing and building the addition himself, to harmonize with the original architecture. The interior is cozy, and crowded with books and artworks. A large wood-burning stove takes up a good part of the living room; there is no other heat. In the yard, the Rohrbach children, ages 10 and 13, have a ramshackle playhouse built of scraps, harmonizing with no particular style but entirely in the spirit of Arden.

Susan grew up near Arden and always yearned to get in, especially after she had children. "I wanted them to experience the freedom and involvement of living in a community like this. They can be themselves here, and they also feel a real responsibility to the town. It's like an extended family."

With a population of about 500, Arden still operates under the single-tax system, which has an unusual effect on homeowners, an effect that is not to everyone's liking. Because Arden collects taxes based on land alone, regardless of what stands upon it, a small house on a half-acre is taxed at the same rate as a large house on a half-acre. As Henry George intended, the single-tax system rewards someone who gets maximum economic use from the smallest amount of land.

In a film history of Arden, Mike Curtis, an Arden resident who is the director of the Henry George School in Philadelphia, defends the peculiar results of the single-tax system: "What is a man getting from the community? He's getting . . . land. Well, he should pay the community for that. Through his own efforts he's built a big house. Why should he owe other people money for that? Why should he pay a fine for his industry? To me, it makes all the sense in the world." (Single-tax fervor runs deep in Mike's family: at a raucous town meeting in 1954, his grandmother literally dropped dead arguing about someone trying to sell—sell!—land.)

Since 1967, when the village was incorporated, the controlling government body has been the Town Assembly, which meets four times a year. Budgets must be approved by a majority of eligible voters—age 18 or older—attending. The town's 1992 budget is about $220,000, which Arden collects from its citizens through land rent. Of that amount, roughly $150,000 will go to New Castle County for schools, police protection and property taxes (the town is *not* exempt from county property taxes). Arden pays for its own trash collection and road maintenance, and is covered by a nearby volunteer fire department.

The tax payment, or land rent, for a quarter-acre lot is about $720, subject to adjustments according to the desirability of a lot's location. No bureaucracy exists; indeed, there are only two paid employees, both part-time: the secretary and the treasurer. Well-organized committees staffed by volunteers do just about all of the work. In the words of one resident, "It's the purest democracy you can get."

With very little effort, Arden could have transformed itself into a tourist stop—a faux art colony with weekend studio tours and troubadours on the Green, or a Colonial Williamsburg of socialism and free love. But Ardenites have never aspired to make their community a living museum. Visitors who wander into it looking for entertainment will come away disappointed. It is quiet and picturesque, but there's no place to buy ice cream or HENRY GEORGE T-shirts. Nor is Arden an architectural theme park—mingling with the half-timbered cottages are ranch houses and split-levels. Despite the architectural impurities, Frank Stephens and Will Price would recognize much of their town if they stopped by today. They would also find the old spirit of Arden intact, a spirit described by a visitor in 1915: "Arden is the capital of the state of Uncritical Friendliness; it belongs to the federation of Mutual Helpfulness, under a constitution of Equal Opportunity. It is far removed from the world we know."

FROM *Gandhi Today*

A Report on Mahatma Gandhi's Successors

Mark Shepard
(1987)

The King of Kindness: Vinoba Bhave
and His Nonviolent Revolution

After Gandhi's assassination on January 30, 1948, many of Gandhi's followers looked to Vinoba for direction. Vinoba advised that, now that India had reached its goal of *Swaraj*—independence, or self-rule—the Gandhians' new goal should be a society dedicated to *Sarvodaya,* the "welfare of all."

The name stuck, and the movement of the Gandhians became known as the Sarvodaya Movement. A merger of constructive work agencies produced Sarva Seva Sangh—"The Society for the Service of All"—which became the core of the Sarvodaya Movement, as the main Gandhian organization working for broad social change along Gandhian lines.

Vinoba had no desire to be a leader, preferring a secluded ashram life. This preference, though, was overturned by events in 1951, following the yearly Sarvodaya conference in what is now the central Indian state of Andhra Pradesh. At the close of that conference, Vinoba announced his intention to journey through the nearby district of Telengana.

He couldn't have picked a more troubled spot.

Telengana was at that moment the scene of an armed insurrection. Communist students and some of the poorest villagers had united in a guerilla army. This army had tried to break the land monopoly of the rich landlords by driving them out or killing them and distributing their land.

At the height of the revolt, the guerrillas had controlled an area of 3,000 villages. But the Indian army had been sent in and had begun its own campaign of terror. Now, many villages were occupied by government troops during the day and by Communists at night. Each side would kill villagers they suspected of supporting the other side. So most villagers lived in terror of both sides.

The government had clearly shown it would win, but the conflict wasn't nearly over by the time of the Sarvodaya conference. Vinoba hoped to find a solution to the conflict and to the injustice that had spawned it. So, refusing police escort, he and a small company set off on foot.

This selection has been excerpted and adapted from *Gandhi Today: A Report on Mahatma Gandhi's Successors* by Mark Shepard (Arcata, CA: Simple Productions, 1987). Copyright © 1987, 1988 Mark Shepard. For more information, visit www.markshep.com/nonviolence.

On April 18, the third day of his walk, Vinoba stopped in the village of Pocham-palli, which had been an important Communist stronghold. Setting himself up in the courtyard of a Muslim prayer compound, he was soon receiving visitors from all the factions in the village.

Among the visitors was a group of 40 families of landless Harijans. (*Harijan* was Gandhi's name for the Untouchables, the outcasts from Hindu society. Literally, it means "child of God.") The Harijans told Vinoba they had no choice but to support the Communists, because only the Communists would give them land. They asked, Would Vinoba ask the government instead to give them land?

Vinoba replied, "What use is government help until we can help ourselves?" But he himself wasn't satisfied by the answer. He was deeply perplexed.

Late that afternoon, by a lake next to the village, Vinoba held a prayer meeting that drew thousands of villagers from the surrounding area. Near the beginning of the meeting, he presented the Harijans' problem to the assembly. Without really expecting a response, he said, "Brothers, is there anyone among you who can help these Harijan friends?"

A prominent farmer of the village stood up. "Sir, I am ready to give one hundred acres."

Vinoba could not believe his ears. Here, in the midst of a civil war over land mo-nopoly, was a farmer willing to part with 100 acres out of simple generosity. And Vinoba was just as astounded when the Harijans declared that they needed only 80 acres and wouldn't accept more!

Vinoba suddenly saw a solution to the region's turmoil. In fact, the incident seemed to him a sign from God. At the close of the prayer meeting, he announced he would walk all through the region to collect gifts of land for the landless.

So began the movement called Bhoodan—"land-gift." Over the next seven weeks, Vinoba asked for donations of land for the landless in 200 villages of Telengana. Cal-culating the amount of India's farmland needed to supply India's landless poor, he would tell the farmers and landlords in each village, "I am your fifth son. Give me my equal share of land." And in each village—to his continued amazement—the dona-tions poured in.

Who gave, and why?

At first most of the donors were farmers of moderate means, including some who themselves owned only an acre or two. To them, Vinoba was a holy man, a saint, the Mahatma's own son, who had come to give them God's message of kinship with their poorer neighbors. Vinoba's prayer meetings at times took on an almost evangelical fervor. As for Vinoba, he accepted gifts from even the poorest—though he sometimes returned these gifts to the donors—because his goal was as much to open hearts as to redistribute land.

Gradually, though, the richer landowners also began to give. Of course, many of their gifts were inspired by fear of the Communists and hopes of buying off the poor—as the Communists were quick to proclaim.

But not all the motives of the rich landowners were economic. Many of the rich hoped to gain "spiritual merit" through their gifts; or at least to uphold their prestige. After all, if poor farmers were willing to give sizeable portions of their land to Vinoba, could the rich be seen to do less? And perhaps a few of the rich were even truly touched by Vinoba's message.

In any case, as Vinoba's tour gained momentum, even the announced approach of the "god who gives away land" was enough to prepare the landlords to part with some of their acreage.

Soon Vinoba was collecting hundreds of acres a day. What's more, wherever Vinoba moved, he began to dispel the climate of tension and fear that had plagued the region. In places where people had been afraid to assemble, thousands gathered to hear him—including the Communists.

At the end of seven weeks, Vinoba had collected over 12,000 acres. After he left, Sarvodaya workers continuing to collect land in his name received another 100,000 acres.

The Telengana march became the launching point for a nationwide campaign that Vinoba hoped would eliminate the greatest single cause of India's poverty: land monopoly. He hoped as well that it might be the lever needed to start a "nonviolent revolution"—a complete transformation of Indian society by peaceful means.

The root of oppression, he reasoned, is greed. If people could be led to overcome their possessiveness, a climate would be created in which social division and exploitation could be eliminated. As he later put it, "We do not aim at doing mere acts of kindness, but at creating a Kingdom of Kindness."

Soon Vinoba and his colleagues were collecting 1,000 acres a day, then 2,000, then 3,000. Several hundred small teams of Sarvodaya workers and volunteers began trekking from village to village, all over India, collecting land in Vinoba's name. Vinoba himself—despite advanced age and poor health—marched continually, touring one state after another.

The pattern of Vinoba's day was daily the same. Vinoba and his company would rise by 3:00 a.m. and hold a prayer meeting for themselves. Then they would walk ten or twelve miles to the next village, Vinoba leading at a pace that left the others struggling breathlessly behind. With him were always a few close assistants, a bevy of young, idealistic volunteers—teenagers and young adults, male and some female, mostly from towns or cities—plus maybe some regular Sarvodaya workers, a landlord, a politician, or an interested Westerner.

At the host village they would be greeted by a brass band, a makeshift archway, garlands, formal welcomes by village leaders, and shouts of *"Sant Vinoba, Sant Vinoba!"* ("Saint Vinoba!")

After breakfast, the Bhoodan workers would fan out through the village, meeting the villagers, distributing literature, and taking pledges. Vinoba himself would be settled apart, meeting with visitors, reading newspapers, answering letters.

In late afternoon, there would be a prayer meeting, attended by hundreds or thousands of villagers from the area. After a period of reciting and chanting, Vinoba would speak to the crowd in his quiet, high-pitched voice. His talk would be completely improvised, full of rich images drawn from Hindu scripture or everyday life, exhorting the villagers to lives of love, kinship, sharing. At the close of the meeting, more pledges would be taken.

There were no free weekends on this itinerary, no holidays, no days off. The man who led this relentless crusade was 57 years old, suffered from chronic dysentery, chronic malaria, and an intestinal ulcer, and restricted himself, because of his ulcer, to a diet of honey, milk, and yogurt.

As the campaign gained momentum, friends and detractors alike watched in fascination. In the West, too, Vinoba's effort drew attention. In the United States, major articles on Vinoba appeared in the *New York Times,* the *New Yorker*—Vinoba even appeared on the cover of *Time.*

By the time of the 1954 Sarvodaya conference, the Gandhians had collected over 3 million acres nationwide. The total eventually reached over 4 million. Much of this land turned out to be useless, and in many cases landowners reneged on their pledges. Still, the Gandhians were able to distribute over 1 million acres to India's landless poor—far more than had been managed by the land reform programs of India's government. About half a million families benefited.

Meanwhile, Vinoba was shifting his efforts to a new gear—a higher one.

After 1954, Vinoba began asking for "donations" not so much of land but of whole villages. He named this new program Gramdan—"village-gift."

Gramdan was a far more radical program than Bhoodan. In a Gramdan village, all land was to be legally owned by the village as a whole, but parceled out for the use of individual families, according to need. Because the families could not themselves sell, rent, or mortgage the land, they could not be pressured off it during hard times—as normally happens when land reform programs bestow land title on poor individuals.

Village affairs were to be managed by a village council made up of all adult members of the village, making decisions by consensus—meaning the council could not adopt any decision until everyone accepted it. This was meant to ensure cooperation and make it much harder for one person or group to benefit at the expense of others.

While Bhoodan had been meant to prepare people for a nonviolent revolution, Vinoba saw Gramdan as the revolution itself.

Like Gandhi, Vinoba believed that the divisiveness of Indian society was a root cause of its degradation and stagnation. Before the villagers could begin to improve their lot, they needed to learn to work together. Gramdan, he felt, with its common land ownership and cooperative decision-making, could bring about the needed unity.

And once this was achieved, the "people's power" it would release would make anything possible.

Vinoba's Gramdan efforts progressed slowly until 1965, when an easing of Gramdan's requirements was joined to the launching of a "storm campaign." By 1970, the official figure for Gramdan villages was 160,000—almost one-third of all India's villages!

But it turned out that it was far easier to get a declaration of Gramdan than to set it up in practice. By early 1970, only a few thousand villages had transferred land title to a village council. In most of these, progress was at a standstill. What's more, most of these few thousand villages were small, single-caste, or tribal—not even typical Indian villages.

By 1971, Gramdan as a movement had collapsed under its own weight.

Still, the Gramdan movement left behind more than a hundred Gramdan "pockets"—some made up of hundreds of villages—where Gandhian workers settled in for long-term development efforts. These pockets today form the base of India's Gandhian movement. In these locales, the Gandhians are helping some of India's poorest by organizing Gandhian-style community development and nonviolent action campaigns against injustice.

As for Vinoba, he returned to his ashram for the final time in June 1970, after thirteen years of continual marching and five more of presiding over the "storm campaign."

During his final years, Vinoba continued to inspire new programs—for instance, Women's Power Awakening, a Gandhian version of women's liberation. He also launched an ongoing campaign against "cow slaughter" to try to halt the butchering of useful farm animals, a practice destructive of India's traditional agriculture.

In the mid-1970s, Vinoba and some close followers became estranged from Sarva Seva Sangh when he opposed the nationwide protest movement of fellow Gandhian Jayaprakash Narayan against the government of Prime Minister Indira Gandhi (no relation to the Mahatma). The "JP Movement" led to Indira Gandhi's infamous declaration of emergency and then indirectly to her temporary ouster from office. In the long run, the value of that movement's accomplishments proved open to question, and much of Vinoba's criticism of it was borne out.

Vinoba died on November 15, 1982. In his dying, as in his living, he was deliberate, instructive, and, in a way, lighthearted. After suffering a heart attack, Vinoba decided to "leave his body before his body left him." He therefore simply stopped eating until his body released him.

Another Great Soul had passed.

FROM *The Community Land Trust*

A Guide to a New Model for Land Tenure in America

International Independence Institute
(1972)

Experiments in Community Landholding

The examples of land trusts and related experiments described in this chapter are for the most part not remarkably significant as models of the community land trust in its pure form. What is important is that each illustrates one or more elements of the community land trust concept and proves that, in fact, it *can* be done, even within an alien legal and economic framework. (Where there have been failures—and there have been many—they are perhaps caused more by internal problems than by external pressures; establishing a community land trust depends mostly on ability and the will to make it happen. Keeping it going depends upon maintaining that internal momentum.)

To describe or even survey the many historical and contemporary experiments related to the land trust concept would fill a book in itself. Right now it would seem more useful to outline the general types of experiments or movements—both foreign and domestic—in the direction of alternate, or "ethical," land tenure, illustrating the broader concepts of common ownership, trusteeship, or tax enclaves, and in the latter part of the chapter briefly present several experiments in the United States that may be seen as particularly relevant to the model of the community land trust.

Foreign Models

Insofar as the community land trust concept applies to the problem of redistribution of land for the common welfare, the various efforts (mostly in other countries) in land reform are relevant. In these cases, new landholding patterns have been implemented in existing communities.

In the socialist countries, land is usually appropriated by the central government and allocated in what is judged to be the common national interest. When done within a framework of decentralized control, this might be considered in the spirit of

This piece was published as a chapter in *The Community Land Trust: A Guide to a New Model for Land Tenure in America* by the International Independence Institute (Cambridge, MA: Center for Community Economic Development, 1972), 7–15. It is reprinted by permission of E. F. Schumacher Society, 140 Jug End Road, Great Barrington, MA, 01230. www.smallisbeautiful.org. Original note numbers have been changed.

the community land trust concept. Probably the best example is Tanzania, as described below.

Ujamaa Vijijini

In the traditional societies of the African tribes of Tanzania, no individual owned land; instead each had the right to use what he needed to grow sufficient food. When a man wanted a plot of land, he went to the chief, elders, or clan leaders, and asked for an appropriate piece which would then be allocated to him. The shifting cultivation practiced at that time meant that the users of land were moving from place to place every few years as the nutrients in the soil became depleted. As soon as a field was abandoned, another person had the right to cultivate there or graze his cattle.

When the German and, later, British colonists came to what is now Tanzania in the late 1800s, they introduced the European concept of "ownership" of land. Land began to be bought and sold, perpetual deeds issued, and speculation started, particularly in and near the major towns.

Julius K. Nyerere, prime minister of Tanzania, in 1967 called for a return to the traditional landholding concept in his program of *Ujamaa Vijijini* ("familyhood in villages"):

> The African's right to land was (traditionally) simply the right to *use* it; he had no other right to it, nor did it occur to him to try to claim one. The foreigner introduced a completely different concept—the concept of land as a marketable commodity. According to this system, a person could claim a piece of land as his own private property *whether he intended to use it or not.* . . .
>
> The Tanganyikan African National Union government must go back to the traditional African custom of landholding. That is to say, a member of society will be entitled to a piece of land on condition that he uses it. Unconditional, or "freehold," ownership of land (which leads to speculation and parasitism) must be abolished.[1]

In 1967–68, when the Nyerere program was implemented, all land was nationalized and land speculation died. Land belonged to all the people but could be held only under the condition that it be used. Land left unused could be taken by any interested group or individual. Tanzania might therefore be considered a *national* land trust.

Ejido

One of the best examples of the gradualist, or nonrevolutionary, approach to land reform combined with local village trusteeship is the Mexican *ejido* ("village lands") system. According to Matthew Edel, a student of the village land system in Mexico, this form of community control of village lands is now practiced in more than 20,000 villages. Edel writes:

Community control, through the *ejido*, was replacing landlord rule. Community institutions were to bring about economic progress without the problems usually ascribed to industrialization. Communities controlling their own lands would liberate and preserve the village as an "organic, breathing entity." . . . The villagers themselves clearly wanted it, for they flocked to petition for their communal lands.

Under the agrarian code, land is redistributed only when a village asks for it. Within the community, those with less than a minimum amount of private property organize themselves into an assembly, sign a petition for land, and select an executive committee to represent their claim. They are entitled to receive either restitution of lands usurped from their village before the Revolution, or donation of any lands from farms of excess size within seven kilometers of the village. The land is taken from the former owner without compensation, leaving him only a medium sized family farm as his remaining property. The village also receives the new land as its *ejido* free, but only after complicated administrative proceedings. . . .

The recipient community normally divides the *ejido* into parcels for each family. . . . Each resident is supposed to cultivate his parcel every year personally. He may pass it on to his heirs, but he may not sell it. If he abandons his land, it reverts to the community, and the *ejido* committee reassigns the parcel. Legally, an *ejido* parcel is a very complex form of property, with the individual (land user), the *ejido* committee, and the state all in some sense possessed of partial property rights to it. In effect, though, the *ejido* committee is the most powerful "owner." This governing body is elected by the members, and charged with . . . supervising the division and use of the land, and collecting the members' annual dues to a communal fund for expenses and local public works.[2]

Gramdan

The Indian *Gramdan*,[3] or "village gift" movement, compares with the *ejido* as an example of a deep-reaching approach to land reform. *Gramdan* is often mentioned as significant, but there has been little in-depth study of it in the United States, and its dynamic leaders remain relatively unknown. An extension of the Gandhian movement, *Gramdan* is dedicated to the development of a new India on a decentralist, village basis. Originally a "land gift" (*Bhoodan*) approach was used, in which small farmers were given title to land on an individual, private basis. It soon became evident that this was no long-range cure (since many of these new owners succumbed to the first opportunity to sell the land when a good offer was made by some wealthy landowner—a fate shared by most government-induced land reform programs). In the *Gramdan* that evolved, the village served as trustee of the land on behalf of the whole community, granting individual use-rights to the land. The *Gramdan* movement now involves more than 18,000 villages in India.

Jewish National Fund

The Jewish National Fund[4] is perhaps the best example of an existing community land trust. It is a public but nongovernmental institution comprised of trustees who hold title to land in Israel. Land is leased to those who can use it in keeping with the long-range public interest. Much of the land is agricultural and is leased to collective ownership communities (*kibbutz* or *moshav shitufi*) or cooperative smallholders' settlements (*moshav ovdim*), although urban land has recently been acquired and is also being held in accordance with the land trust concept. The Fund observes the important principle of distinguishing between the land and natural resources, and man-made property externalities, granting leases on the land only.

The Jewish National Fund has been in existence since 1901, thereby offering experience over a period of several generations of working out problems of inheritance, handling disposition of immovable man-made property when users choose to move, working out leases and appraisals, and planning over a long period in which land values appreciate. It operates on a gradualist basis, purchasing land from titleholders at market value, and is quite large, now owning about 60 percent of the reclaimed and cultivated land in Israel. The Fund offers an example of the healthy impact on a national economy when this proportion of the land area has been removed from the private speculative market.

Many of the community land trust concepts are based on the development experience of Israel during the past 70 years. Through use of the leasehold system, Israel has been one of the few countries in the world to be successful in preventing the process of uprooting the poor tenant farmer from taking place. The leasehold system has brought security of land tenure to the small farmer and his family, and has prevented the control of land by absentee landlords, speculation in land, and exploitation of farmworkers by a landowning class.

American Experiments

Over the past one hundred years or more there have been in the United States numerous experiments in community that relate to what we define as the community land trust idea. These experiments—historical and contemporary—will be surveyed below. Each is significant in some way: as a precedent of the land trust model; as a living example of certain aspects of the model; as a potential physical component of some future regional land trust network. What is unfortunate is that their legacy does not include a large pool of land which might be incorporated into land trusts of significant scale. One hope for the land trust concept is that it can serve as a framework that will help isolated experiments achieve the kind of continuity required for long-range historic significance—but it must be recognized that a strong foundation or legal structure alone is no substitute for the internal dynamism or energy of the participants.

Intentional Communities

Throughout the nineteenth century in the United States there were a series of "utopian" community experiments. Some might be described as primarily philosophical, such as Fruitlands, the short-lived Transcendentalist experiment in Harvard, Massachusetts, led by Bronson Alcott and Ralph Waldo Emerson. Others were religious or industrial, such as the several Shaker communities, or Oneida, New York. These communities are described in detail in *Heavens on Earth*.[5] They are not, however, particularly significant to the land trust concept since they were not primarily concerned with landholding as an economic problem.

Akin to the idealistic experiments of the nineteenth century were the numerous "company towns" which flourished in that era, most notably those built by the large textile mills. These were some of the first true "planned" communities in this country, and were characterized by the absence of individual ownership and the presence of a trusteeship function (in the form of the company). Despite these similarities to the community land trust, and certain parallels with the utopian communities of the same period, these towns illustrate that the mechanisms alone do not necessarily ensure the development of humane community; the mechanisms can be considered essentially neutral, to be used for the common welfare or only for private gain.

Religious Communities

Contemporary religious or mystical communities might be considered to some degree instructive since a number of them continue to grow and flourish as islands of communal ownership in an economic sea of private ownership, demonstrating that there are no insurmountable legal, political, or economic barriers against communities based on a completely different system. The contrast is in the incentive: these groups are fueled primarily by the impulse toward spiritual salvation, the community land trust by that of economic salvation.

Among these religious groups are a number of energetic and growing rural communities, such as the Hutterites in the United States and Canada, and the Dukhobors in Canada. The Society of Brothers (Bruderhof) has rural communities in New York, Connecticut, and Pennsylvania, with a large part of their income derived from community manufacture of quality hardwood toys (Community Playthings). Koinonia, with 1,400 acres near Americus, Georgia, is now thriving after many years of boycott and harrassment because of its interracial character. A group of American Quakers established Monte Verde in the highlands of Costa Rica. Its dairy industry is doing well and the community seems to be surviving and growing.

Another group of communities, or communes, which might be considered religious, are those based on a mystical cult or individual personality. These, however, are probably less significant in terms of this guide since they have not yet had time to become permanently established (which may indeed never happen) and because, like the monastic religious communities, they do not generally have an internal economic basis but rely upon cash donations from the outside. The Brotherhood of the Spirit after several years shows signs of taking root in Warwick, Massachusetts, and continues to grow. The Mel Lyman Family has a well-established community atop Fort Hill in Boston, consisting of a group of adjacent houses, and has recently purchased 280 acres of farmland near Marysville, Kansas, and a $160,000 mansion in Los Angeles.

Tax Enclaves

Communities of "economic rent"[6] (land rent based on site value) or "tax enclaves" are based on the single tax principles of Henry George. Other aspects such as cooperative work and fellowship may be present but are normally considered as secondary. The keystone of Henry George's single tax principle is the concept of "site value":

> In order to make land available [to all], the accumulation of undeveloped land . . . could be made unprofitable by the government taxing the property to its full site value [its value derived from the community]. . . . The principles of the single tax enclave have been experimented with on some dozen enclaves in this country. These enclosures are corporations to which the landholders pay a ground rent on long term leases, generally for 99 years. All improvements and enterprise are untaxed. . . . Fairhope, off Mobile Bay, Alabama; Arden in Delaware near Wilmington; Free Acres near Summit, New Jersey; and Tahanto at Harvard, Massachusetts, are some of the notable single tax colonies. Tahanto, founded 25 years [ago], now grown to 784 acres with over 50 leaseholders, is a typical enclave.[7]

Site value taxation (also called land value taxation) is designed to shift the tax burden to the land, which is "valued in terms of its potential higher use if it were to be developed or redeveloped for such higher use." This tax principle is based on the fact that land values rise primarily because of population pressures and services (such as roads and sewers) made available by the municipality. Since the private landowner has not been responsible for this increase in the value of his land, "the gains should be taxed away for the benefit of the population whose growth caused the increase in values."[8] Carried to its extreme, there would be a 100 percent tax on the site value, and none on buildings or other improvements. This is the single tax advocated by Henry George.

The ideas of site value taxation and economic rent are commonly associated with the community land trust concept. Although land rents in a trust need not be based exclusively on the site value principle, the theory is instructive and relevant. It places emphasis on land as the source of wealth, and there is indication that either within a large tax enclave or as the basis for general tax reform it could lead to better utilization of land and more just placement of the land tax and rent burden.

Homesteader Communities (Single Tax Emphasis)

Ralph Borsodi, advocate of the idea of trusterty, is an activist as well as theorist and has pioneered several communities based on the single tax principles of Henry

George. The School of Living was founded and carried on by Borsodi at the new community in Suffern, New York. In 1945, the School moved to Brookville, Ohio, and since then has been guided largely by Mildred and the late John Loomis.

The School of Living has been advocating ethical land tenure and other concepts related to the community land trust for many years.[9] Mildred Loomis describes the formation of the Borsodi-related homestead communities as follows:

> In the 1930s Borsodi made an effort to rehabilitate the unemployed in Dayton, Ohio, by getting families onto small homesteads on a group purchase basis. Complicated by financial problems and government supervision, it had limited success. . . . However, the importance of the effort was widely discussed and the plan put into effect by homesteading communities formed by Borsodi in 1937–39 as an outgrowth of his new School of Living in Suffern, New York.
>
> Van Houton Fields Community (of 35 homesteads) and Bryn Gweled Homesteads (80 homesteads) near Philadelphia were formed and still flourish today. In each case a small group of families came together in a common effort to establish themselves on small homesteads. They pooled their funds, and engaged a lawyer to help them form an association and secure the land.
>
> Thus Homesteading Associations secured land and held it in the name of the "project" as a whole rather than cutting it up and deeding it to individual families. Land was leased by members, who were taxed according to their site value and not penalized for improvements, and who owned their own homes free and clear within ten years.[10]

Bryn Gweled Homesteads is a contemporary, functioning example of an effort to apply at least some aspects of the community land trust idea. On the surface, the community appears to be a typical, attractive suburban development; any "revolutionary" aspects are buried deep within the community structure.

New Community Trust

A Boston, Massachusetts, program that contains a number of elements of the community land trust concept has been initiated by Inter-seminarian, Inc., "Intersem" is a nonprofit corporation that sponsors several service programs, primarily for the youth community. The best-known of these programs is Project Place, a drop-in center and drug counseling service.

The Intersem community leased a large farm in New Hampshire as a retreat center and then initiated a program to acquire this and other properties through the New Community Trust. An offering of $20,000 in 6½ percent Subordinated Notes . . . was successful and permitted the purchase of the farm. Recently a second property, Healey House, was acquired in Somerville, Massachusetts. This urban center now houses ten Project Place volunteers and, with planned renovation, will house an additional six.

This effort, consisting of two scattered sites now with more anticipated in the future, is significant as an example of urban property placed under the umbrella of a trust which encompasses a larger area. It does not entirely conform to our model since the land is not separated from the man-made structures thereon.

Morningside Gardens

Another example of a model somewhat resembling the land trust concept but in the urban setting is a cooperative housing development such as Morningside Gardens (Morningside Heights, New York, N.Y.). This complex consists of six 20-story buildings between 121st and LaSalle Streets in upper Manhattan. It was built with federal financing under the sponsorship of an association of ten cultural and educational institutions in the Morningside Heights area (Riverside Church, Columbia University, Jewish Theological Seminary, among others).

In some respects it resembles the public, low-income housing project the property abuts; in other respects, it resembles a typical urban condominium development. But there are key differences that make Morningside Gardens a singularly important community: it is owned and operated by the people who live there within certain very important guidelines set up by the original founders. First, cost of the units is fixed and, regardless of rising rentals elsewhere in the city, cannot be raised on a speculative basis. No renting is permitted and if someone leaves he can receive only the amount he invested (around $2,500 for a typical unit). In other words, ownership and use cannot be separated.

Second, although tenant selection is implemented through a committee (elected by the owners), it is done so according to guidelines spelled out by the project organizers. The goal is to encourage continuity and provide a healthy mix of different races, income levels, and age levels. There are special programs for assisting the elderly. Twenty percent of the tenants must be nonwhite. Although there is a waiting list of several years for the project, former tenants always are at the top of the list.

Operating costs are collected from residents and are well below most other nonsubsidized housing in the city. Of the typical $125 per month charge, half is debt financing and the rest for common services. Owners may deduct that portion used for interest payment from their income tax the same way homeowners can. The investment cannot grow; there is no speculation. (Yet this does not deter demand, as illustrated by the waiting list.)

Morningside Gardens offers a unique feeling of "community." There are many programs and service activities: a shop and sewing area; child care on a cooperative basis; a chorus. The project is owned and controlled by the residents within the overall context spelled out by the founding institutions (which is the function of the trustees in the community land trust.) In the midst of serious urban decline, the project illustrates how a community can prosper when founded on sound economic principles.

New Communities, Inc.

As of this writing, New Communities, Inc., of Lee County, Georgia, is the largest, if not the purest, example of a community land trust in the United States. NCI consists of about 5,700 acres of good farmland and a number of buildings. Lack of funding has slowed development, but plans call for the settlement of up to 800 families on the land in several community clusters. Educational programs and commercial farming on a significant scale are now under way.

NCI plans to turn over all control and ownership of the community, except for the land itself, to the people who actually settle it. The land will remain in trust in perpetuity for its settlers—a concept similar to the land tenure system practiced by the Indians, the African custom of sharing land, and more recently, the *Gramdan* movement in India of land gifts to villages as common property.

Homestead and Commune Movements

One of the most heartening and realistic responses to the problems of today's industrial society is the literally thousands of people who in the last ten years have returned to the land to find alternatives to traditional lifestyle and economic patterns. The homesteader and rural communes they form are generally based on the same values, the same feeling for the land, as the community land trust, yet they have for the most part not thought beyond the idea of "common ownership" to that of "ownership for the common good." Reaction to the latter concept is almost always positive, which is not surprising since in addition to sharing the same values those establishing a homestead community are also faced with the problem of setting up a legal entity to accommodate their values. And, in some cases, the land trust as a public body dedicated to social ends holds forth the hope of obtaining access to land use without having to build up a personal financial stake.

The land trust idea can indeed speak to each of these concerns. In addition, it lends strength to the larger movement: aligning a group of individual communities under the umbrella of a trusteeship organization would lead to the creation of a *regional land trust*, which could provide both political force and economic strength to benefit all those involved. The regional trust could better perform the function of resource allocation within the broader geographic framework and, perhaps most important, would foster the continuity and growth of this movement. . . .

NOTES

1. *Seeds of Liberation* (a compendium of articles from the magazine), ed. Paul Goodman (New York: George Braziller, Inc., 1964).

2. Matthew Edel, "A Lesson for Community Control in the United States," *Cambridge Institute Occasional Bulletin*, No. 1 (Cambridge, Mass.: The Cambridge Institute, October 1969).

3. For a useful monograph on the *Gramdan* movement, see Erica Linton, *Gramdan— Revolution by Persuasion* (London: Friends Peace and International Relations Committee. Available from the American Friends Service Committee, 48 Inman St., Cambridge, Mass.)

4. There are several reasons why the Jewish National Fund is not being emphasized in this guide. First, it is such a large-scale land trust that the reader might forget the concept is one which is applicable to many types of decentralized, small experiments. The second problem, as far as this guide is concerned, is that the Fund is in a unique position as a recipient of vast amounts of money from the worldwide Zionist movement, a condition which of course cannot be duplicated elsewhere. Finally, it is unique in that it preceded the formation of the government of Israel, and therefore the legal system that developed had to accommodate the philosophy of the Jewish National Fund, rather than vice versa. Nevertheless, throughout this guide there will be frequent references to the Fund since within its experience lie the answers to many of the questions and reservations often raised in connection with the community land trust concept.

5. Mark Holloway, *Heavens on Earth* (New York: Library Publishers, 1951).

6. The definition of "economic rent" traditionally refers to payment made for the use of the land. What is paid for the use of improvements is not rent in the narrow sense but rather interest on the value of the improvements.

7. *Enclaves of Economic Rent for the Year 1933* (Being a Compendium of the Legal Documents Involved together with a Historical Description by Charles White Huntington) published by Fiske Warren, Harvard, Mass., 1934. Since the publication of the above text, several other communities have been established with this emphasis, including those at Suffern, N.Y.; Bryn Gweled Homesteads, Pa.; and Van Houton Fields, N.Y. In the case of some of the earlier tax enclaves, title to the land was held by trustees, as Tahanto was. Bryn Gweled and similar modern enclaves are nonprofit corporations with all residents voting as members.

8. Quotes on site value taxation are taken from *Property Taxation: Effects on Land Use and Local Government Revenues*. This booklet also contains a good survey of the American experience with land value taxation. An extensive evaluation of site value taxation can be found in Dick Netzer, *Economics of the Property Tax* (Washington, DC: Brookings Institution, 1966), pp. 197–212. For a rather brief but thorough description of economic rent and site value taxation, see Lord Douglas of Barioch, *Land-Value Rating* (London: Christopher Johnson Publishers, Ltd., 1961). The author is chairman of the British section of the International Research Committee on Real Estate Taxation.

9. *Green Revolution,* the newspaper published by the School of Living since 1943, is now published at the School, Heathcote Center, Rte 1, Freeland, Md. 21053.

10. This experiment is described in detail in Ralph Borsodi, *Flight from the City* (New York: Harper & Row, Harper Colophon paperback, 1972).

PART TWO

PROPHETS & PIONEERS

FROM *The Small Community*

Foundation of Democratic Life

Arthur E. Morgan
(1942)

The Place of the Community in Human Culture

The roots of human culture are not its fine arts, its technology, its political institutions. These are the flower and fruit. The roots of culture are the underlying drives, motives, incentives, manners, habits, and purposes. If these are socially sound and vitally alive in a good social soil, then the flowers and fruit will appear. If these underlying elements are unrefined, weak, and undisciplined, then the fine arts, the technology, and the complex organization of society cannot long endure.

Young human life is avid for example and instruction which it can accept and imitate. It takes to itself whatever is available in the culture of its environment, and makes that its own. It becomes fundamentally and intimately like the culture in which it grows. The characteristics of the existing culture are acquired during the very early years, and produce a set of personality which seldom is fundamentally altered. Probably the ages up to ten years are more compellingly formative than all the rest of life taken together. It is during those years that the individual's tastes, standards, and appreciations are largely determined.

The crowning inheritance of humanity is its basic culture of community habits, traits, and attitudes. Yet there is evidence that some of the finest of human cultures have almost disappeared. The preservation and dissemination of the best of these is a fundamental human need.

When we come to observe the exact processes by which the transfer of culture takes place, we see that it is chiefly through intimate personal contacts. It is the same process as that by which children acquire spoken language and inflection. It is a process of contagion, of imitation of others. First of all there is the family, and next there is the community surrounding the family. The permanent set of personality is determined in early life chiefly through those two relationships, always influenced, of course, by inborn native quality. Supplementary influences include church, school,

This selection originally appeared as two chapters in *The Small Community: Foundation of Democratic Life* by Arthur E. Morgan (Yellow Springs, OH: Community Services, Inc., 1942), 55–61, 99–106. They are reprinted by permission of The Arthur Morgan Institute for Community Solutions, formerly known as Community Services, Inc. www.communitysolution.org. Original note numbers have been changed.

government, etc., and more recently radio and movies, alike powerful in their characteristics of intimacy and penetration.

Influences appearing later in life overlie and modify fundamental sets of character, but seldom change the main traits of personality. Occasionally profound change does take place in later years, but only by great personal effort, and in a relatively small number of cases.

For the most promising development of great personalities the family must have the support of the nearby environment. Very generally the home is too small a part of the child's total environment to be conclusive. If playmates and neighbors tend to nullify the influence of parents, serious stresses and conflicts may be set up in the growing personalities. A great home needs to be supplemented by a great community, so that the cultural inheritance which a child receives at home is in harmony with that which comes to him from the community. When a young person from such a home is married, the peculiar character of that home is to some extent lost unless the mate also has inherited it.

As a rule great leadership occurs when exceptional intelligence and vigor project onto a larger scene of action the drives and purposes that were learned in the intimate associations of early years. It follows that society and government in their larger units will not be moved by any more refined motives, and will have no higher objectives, than do the families and the communities from which their leadership arises. The community is the mother of society. As the community is, so will society be.

The home and the community are not only the places of origin, but also the principal preservers, of the most intimate and sensitive values of our cultural inheritance, those elusive traits of good will, considerateness, courage, patience, and fellowship, which are the best and finest fruits of the long process of social evolution. Those finest and most distinctive traits originate where but a few persons are immediately involved, and where fine qualities can be sheltered and nourished during their infancy. In the family and the community the sympathy and understanding of a few will protect such traits from destruction until they are matured and tempered so that they can make their way in the larger and less hospitable world. Human cultures, like human beings, have periods of infancy during which they cannot survive without such shelter and nurture. The higher the animal or the higher the culture, the more surely is this true.

It follows that the family and its community environment are imperatively necessary for the creation and preservation of the finest cultural values. Yet, what have we in America done with the community? We have taken for granted intimate human culture, without realizing its need for an abiding place. As individual families have come to this country from Europe, torn loose from their cultural roots, we might by conscious design have worked with them to assemble and transplant the best elements of the cultural traditions, creating new communities with a synthesis of culture beyond anything the past has known. As a matter of fact, we have tended to keep these newcomers isolated from the best and most intimate elements of American life. We have prevented the preservation and extension of cultural traits which takes place through contagion and imitation. The elements of the new-world culture which have been most visible and accessible to immigrants have been those one meets on the street, in business, in the movies. Similarly, the finer traits which the immigrants brought with them tend to be dropped as part of their old-world habits.

For several reasons the small community has been the basic source of the underlying culture of a people. In the first place, the family by itself is not a large enough group to be an adequate cultural unit. Children overflow the immediate family environment, and are much affected by the neighborhood or community environment. Exceptionally good or exceptionally poor family environment goes far to set the character of children, but the larger environment tends strongly to improve the poorest and to debase the best, and to reduce all to an approximation to uniformity. Just as the human body supplies an almost ideal environment for each of its cells such as no individual one-celled animal could provide for itself, so the community may create a favorable milieu for the development of each of its members.

A second reason is stated as follows in the *Systematic Source Book in Rural Sociology*:

> Like water which flows naturally from a higher to a lower level, population generally flows naturally from rural to urban centers and from agriculture to industries and other urban occupations. Rural communities have been the centers of production of a surplus of human beings, and the urban communities the centers of their consumption. This . . . trait . . . practically speaking, has been permanent in the history of mankind.[1]

In this one-way movement of population from the small community to the large urban center or to its suburbs, the controlling basic culture of the small community carries over and provides the dominant incentives of the city. Since the small community is the controlling source of population of a country, the character of the small community becomes the character of the country.

Historically, the small community, we have seen, is the preserver of basic culture. In Greece, fine sculpture and architecture died because they were arts of the city and the aristocracy; but fine pottery and masonry lived because they were part of the life of common people in small communities. Religious liberalism was established and survived in England largely because Wyclif and his followers penetrated the small communities, where their movement became established. The culture which survives catastrophic changes generally is that of small communities.

Notwithstanding the profoundly important part which the community has taken and is taking in human history, it has been generally neglected in social planning. As a rule the small community has been robbed of its best population, economically exploited, despised, and left to shift for itself. Even public knowledge of the facts about American communities is fairly recent. Writing in 1926, Charles Luther Fry in his *American Villagers* stated:

. . . little is known about villages . . . for incorporated places having less than 2,500 inhabitants, the Census volumes furnish only a single figure—the total population. . . .

The principal sources of information about villages, aside from the Census, are a small number of first-hand studies made by individual investigators.[2]

In the United States there has been much study of the isolated farm and of agriculture on the one hand, and of cities on the other; but until the last two decades the small community has been generally overlooked, and it was not recognized as the reservoir of basic human culture. During the past fifteen years the situation has greatly changed, and now there are qualified men and a very substantial literature in that field.

Because of neglect of the small community in social planning, it has tended to be stagnant and uninspiring, and to pass on its weaknesses to the city. Partly as a result of the failure of society through the ages to recognize the significance of small communities as the sources of population and as the sources and conservators of culture, the long upward climb of society is constantly impeded and interrupted. There is a constant slipping back to the cultural level of the neglected small community.

Characteristic limitations of the small village, neighborhood, or hamlet have been socially enforced conformity of thought and action, narrowness of outlook, clannishness, jealousies, tendency to gossip, and lack of recreation facilities or of direction and counsel for young people.

Such limitations tend to exist in small groups whether they are true communities or simply ununified aggregations of people. In the latter case there may be little restraint and control of social action. Where there is a true community there may be very effective discipline to prevent or to control such faults. Stefansson, in his accounts of well-integrated Eskimo communities, states that the social offense most frowned upon is "trouble making," and that social controls to prevent such faults are very effective indeed.[3]

Just as individuals learn chiefly by imitating others, so communities on the whole, when they have endeavored to improve their designs, only rarely have undertaken original study and planning. For the most part they have imitated what was most obvious. For instance, practical management of American villages and cities by coordinated, business-like methods had been necessary for more than a century, but no one seemed creative enough to devise appropriate methods. Then the city-manager plan was initiated in a small city; and other communities, now having something to copy, imitated that example, until now there are hundreds of cities and villages with that type of government.

The creation of even one finely designed community, and the development there of a vital community spirit, probably would lead to that general type of social organization being imitated and reproduced many times. If skillful community leadership should grow up in such a community, it probably would be called on from many directions. It is not the size but the quality of a society which, in the long run, determines its influence. Greece and Palestine have had far greater influence on the world than have many vast empires. To work at creating a good community is not a retreat from national or world affairs, but may be the most vital way of contributing to them.

The Creation of New Communities

In a period of transition and flux like that of the present, when men are groping to find footholds for significant living, opportunities are as great as they were in pioneer America for the development of communities dominated by the aim to achieve the good proportion characteristic of a well-developed human body.

Throughout the course of history the successful planned creation of new communities has occurred more often than is generally realized. The Greeks definitely planned new colonies. Sometimes they had ideal legal codes developed by specialists and had the lands laid out by professional planners. The Hebrew nation was a colonist enterprise. Eastern Europe is dotted over with cities populated by people from other regions, chiefly Germans, who came as members of organized colonies. For centuries the Teutonic Knights followed the policy of extending German-Christian civilization through colonies. Millions of people in East European cities are descendants of these colonists. In the history of India and the East Indies the planning and creation of new colonies and communities sometimes was a major element of national policy, and some of these new settlements grew into great empires.

In the South Seas, when an island became fully populated it was customary to prepare large double canoes that would hold fifty to two hundred people, with food for two or three months and with seeds and animals for beginning new settlements. These, manned by young men and women, would start out into the unknown ocean, hoping to discover new lands before their supplies were exhausted. Sometimes they were fortunate enough to come to islands in the vast expanse of waters, and then they would begin as integrated communities, with continuing customs, traditions, and arts.

The planning and founding of new communities has been a common undertaking in America, as it has been the world over. Hundreds, and perhaps thousands, of American communities have been originated deliberately as new creations. There is an impression that planned communities in America generally have failed. Such is far from the case. Of the many American communities which were deliberately created, very many in large degree realized the picture of their founders. The most influential single element in the formation of American life, that of New England, began as premediated new communities, not as an unorganized movement of individuals. For some time in early Massachusetts, settlement was limited by law to those who lived within a mile of the community center. When that area was occupied the surplus inhabitants started other communities, which often retained the name of the original. Thus we have Newton, Newton Center, Newton Highlands, Newton Lower Falls, Newton Upper Falls, and West Newton, as reminders of the manner of early New England settlement.

The founding of Pennsylvania by the Quakers also made a deep impression on the national pattern. The Fenwick community in New Jersey, also a Quaker colony, had a similar successful career. Many semi-idealistic communities, such as Oneida, New York; Greeley, Colorado; Amana, Iowa; and Fairhope, Alabama, have lived for long periods. Some, built from an economic motive, like Gary, Indiana, and Pullman, Illinois, also have continued to grow. The original Mormon colonies have multiplied and increased to a population of three quarters of a million. Much of the quality of American culture has been the outgrowth of community efforts. In many cases, whether they originated with idealistic purposes, as did Oneida, or primarily with economic motives, as did Gary, there has been lacking a mature and well-proportioned concept of the community as a fundamental element of human culture.

But also there are scattered over our country the vestiges of many communities which were built by enthusiasts or by one-track minds. Even where these have taken root and have grown and prospered economically, which is true of many cases, there has resulted a narrowness of life and a provincial outlook which must be outgrown before a community can become a significant factor in cultural evolution. The difference between those emotional or naïvely inspirational developments and a soundly designed community undertaking is somewhat like the difference between the methods of "Darius Green and his flying machine," on the one hand, and the methodical and analytical work of the Wright brothers on the other.

Many American undertakings to create new communities have been tragedies because they lacked a spirit of inclusiveness and a sense of good proportion. Brook Farm had only dreams and transcendental theories. It had no economic roots. Its members lacked patience, steadiness of purpose, and self-discipline. Fairhope had little more than single-tax and a good climate. New Harmony depended unduly on a theory of social organization. A thousand vigorous Americans have created as many villages or cities with economic production as their principal interest. That is, they built mill towns, factory towns, and mining towns. Often these were dreary aggregations of families, housed in sordid shacks, assembled with no hint or vision of human dignity. Kingsport, Tennessee, was an effort to add to the quality of living by creating an industrial community with employees continuing to live on surrounding farms. Its chief shortcoming arises from its phenomenal success, which has led to overgrowth and to the consequent partial loss of some of the qualities aimed for. Sometimes industrial men built model towns, such as Kohler, Wisconsin, but often their ideas went little further than provision for physical conveniences and architectural design, and too often the creators of these paternalistic communities were made bitter by the ensuing "ingratitude."

Each of these industrialists embarked on the most interesting adventure he knew. Had such a man possessed a more lively imagination, had his cultural inheritance included more understanding of men, more respect and good will for them, more of friendly interest and neighborliness, a wider range of cultural appreciation, he would have sought for his community a diversity of satisfactions, including greater participation on the part of the community members in directing their own lives and that of the community. He would have broken through the prevailing industrial habits and interests of the day and would have seen that, by including the whole range of human values in his concern rather than financial profits or physical convenience alone, he would have had a more interesting life along the way, and would have left behind a greater residue of human values, and for his children better character and greater prospect for social and political security.

Fundamental to all living is a philosophy of life which gives it content, direction, and a sense of worth. Without it men are only educated animals. Communities in which this quality of life purpose was strong have survived much better than others. A common way of putting it is that communities with a religious purpose and motivation have maintained their original quality much better than those which lacked such purpose.

The limitations of American communities have not been primarily that they have not fulfilled the dreams of their founders, but that those dreams were commonplace. Adequate design is not spontaneous; it must be worked for and practiced for. It is because those pictures as a rule were rudimentary and lacking in imagination that American communities have no more character.

Community making sometimes is looked upon as an escape process for people who shrink from rough-and-tumble competition, but that is an inadequate view. The determination to build a favorable social environment would seem to be more reasonable than to create a great estate for one's children while leaving them in a social setting which does not stabilize or refine their characters. The creating of new communities always has been one of the ways by which men have tried to begin again to realize their hopes for a good society, and there is no reason to believe that the process will not be used in the future. The chance for like-minded men to work together in order to realize their common aims is too alluring to be abandoned. Such a course makes possible to an unusual degree the securing of unity of purpose in community life and work, and the achievement of new values. It may provide happier and more productive adventure than political or financial ambition.

From time to time in America opportunities or necessities occur to create new communities. The establishment of new industries, public need for reducing unemployment, or desire to create better social and economic conditions may provide the occasions. For such projects to be restricted to minimum housing and economic needs is a waste of opportunity, and as in the case of Pullman, Gary, and other industrial towns, may fail to result in best conditions for economic production. The writer has found in several cases in his work as engineer and administrator that even the special economic purposes of such communities can be better assured by looking beyond the immediate utilitarian requirements and making possible well-proportioned community life.

For persons determined to make such occasions yield their fullest possible economic and social values, they offer chances to create and develop new communities which, both in the people who compose them and in the concept of what a community might be, may provide opportunity for originating community types of widespread significance. Few contributions to our national culture would be more important than actual cases of communities in which all major human needs and interests were recognized and developed in good proportion. Few experiences would be more satisfying to the persons involved and to their children than participation in competently designed undertakings of that kind. Only rarely are people creative. Far more frequently they are ready to imitate whatever of excellence may appear. Wherever men of competence and creative intelligence are willing to pay the price in preparation and in the arduous, persistent effort which creation always involves, the designing and developing of new communities is a worthwhile field of effort.

One of the first difficulties encountered in undertaking to build a new community is that such an undertaking tends to attract persons who are misfits in society, or single-track minds searching for a panacea, as well as those who deliberately and competently seek to create an environment favorable to significant living. In this we see a repetition of the incentives which brought about the settlement of our country. Comparing the temper of life in an American community with that in most small European communities, one gets the impression that America to no small extent was settled by individuals who were ill-adjusted or discontented. In most cases, each man or family emigrating from Europe to America was so dissatisfied with home conditions as to be willing to pull up by the roots and remove to an alien land. Both the strength and weakness of America lie in that fact. With some who came, discontent was largely due to personal maladjustment, while the dream of a promised land was naïve and undisciplined. With others, the discontent sprang from mature imagination and disciplined purpose.

Just at present there is a great outburst of new community building in both Great Britain and America. In the United States the central government has been doing it, though often with tragic results due to bureaucratic and autocratic fumbling and interference. Some of the private undertakings are by persons or groups who have enthusiasm, but who lack the disciplined skill and the experience to make a success of any substantial undertaking. The failure of these projects—and many others will fail—does not condemn the process any more than the failure of nineteen out of twenty merchants is a reflection on the process of storekeeping. But such failure of ill-designed and poorly managed community projects wastes valuable human and material resources, leads to discouragement and disillusionment, and brings the process into disrepute.

A deliberately planned and created community has the best prospect for all-round success if it is a neighborhood of people who have in common enough of cultural life, social purpose, and capacity for mutual understanding to be good neighbors, and who have in common such discipline of life and refinement of purpose that children growing up in that community would find the cultural influence of the family supported by that of the neighborhood. In the development of such a community, or in the regeneration of those already existing, there should be effort to provide variety in economic undertakings and in cultural interests, so that young persons of differing tastes and abilities could find opportunities for their lives. There should be wholehearted commitment to a spirit of free inquiry and of critical open-mindedness, as a recognized quality of a good community. Otherwise some form of provincialism and atrophy will appear.

In such a community there should be range and variety of cultural contacts. Even where the occasion for the creation of the community is economic, as the development of a new industry, or educational, as in the case of a "college town," no one factor, such as economic self-support, or religious uniformity, or political or social views, should dominate, but rather there should be effort to recognize and to develop in reasonable proportion all the major interests of men and women. The analogy of the highly developed systems of stimuli and controls, of checks and balances in the human body, with the aim of maintaining good relations and good proportion in structure and in function, is especially applicable to a community. It is not any single kind of excellence, but diversity and balance and good proportion of excellence, which make a good community.

NOTES

1. Sorokin, P. A., Zimmerman, Carle C., and Galpin, Charles J. *A Systematic Source Book in Rural Sociology,* vol. 1, 230–231, by permission of the publisher, The University of Minnesota Press, Minneapolis, Minnesota.

2. Fry, Charles Luther. *American Villagers* (New York, Harper & Brothers, 1926), 22. Reprinted by permission of the publisher.

3. Vilhjalmur Stefansson (1879–1962) was a Canadian Arctic explorer and ethnologist. He spent the winter of 1906–1907 living in an Inuit village on the MacKenzie Delta in Canada, an experience he later described in several books and ethnographic papers.

The Possessional Problem

Ralph Borsodi
(1978)

For why? Because the good old
rule sufficeth them, the simple
plan that they should take who have
the power, and they should
keep who can.

—William Wordsworth
"Rob Roy's Grave"

Our need to find a right solution to the Possessional Problem has a terrible urgency at this time. If we could solve, in a moral and rational manner, the Possessional Problem, today's world-wide "energy crisis" precipitated by the oil-producing cartel, might be solved. Such a solution also might have enormous implications for the world population explosion, the Arab-Israeli conflict, the globally-crucial question "who owns the oceans?," Indian territorial rights and claims and even the endless struggle between capitalism and communism.

To identify the basic Possessional Problem, we must distinguish between those kinds of possessions which can be considered legally ownable and those which morally cannot. It is perfectly obvious that the air we breathe cannot be "owned" by anybody or any corporation or any government. Yet, the air is only one of the many different kinds of things, it seems to me, to which everyone must have access without having to pay a legally-declared "owner" for it.

To the pragmatist, any solution of the Possessional Problem which "works" is valid. However, the pragmatist's test of what is true and valid by itself is not nearly as justifiable as its proponents believe. Slavery certainly solved the labor problem! It provided the labor which built many of the awe-inspiring structures of earlier civilizations. Slavery also provided most of the hard labor which sustained mankind until just a few hundred years ago. But slavery was patently wrong.

For thousands of years slaves were declared legally ownable. They were still legally ownable a little over a hundred years ago here in the United States. But can one human being "own" another? He can legally; statutes can be passed. But where is one's

A version of this piece originally appeared in *Seventeen Problems of Man and Society* by Ralph Borsodi (Anand, India: Charotar Book Stall, 1968). It has been edited and revised with Borsodi's permission by Gordon Lameyer and Lydia Ratcliff, and published by *Green Revolution,* 1978. It is reprinted by permission of the School of Living, Julian, PA.

moral title of ownership? On the other hand, things which are made, created, or grown can be both legally and morally the property of the person or persons who produced them. An author or artist, for instance, has a moral title to his work; a farmer is morally entitled to the profits from his crops. But what about the "natural resources" provided to all of mankind by nature, resources such as coal or oil or land itself? Can these be morally ownable?

Back of all the confusion about the Possessional Problem is the failure of so-called social scientists and social reformers to make an adequate study of the nature of possessions. Instead of using the scientific method to determine what possessions really are, they have jumped to wrong conclusions about them. The classical economists who maintained everything should be treated as property were wrong, and so are the Marxist economists who said that nothing should be treated so.

If a wise and workable solution to the Possessional Problem is ever to be adopted, and if existing solutions are to be evaluated, seven concepts must be understood: (1) exploitation; (2) possession; (3) title; (4) tenure; (5) allocation; (6) property; and (7) trusterty.

Exploitation

Of the myriad forms which exploitation takes, this study will consider only two: *behavior exploitation*, and legal or, more correctly, *legalized exploitation*.

The term exploitation, as the concept will be used here, is defined by the dictionary as the act of basely or illegitimately using another person to one's own advantage or profit. By this definition exploitation, no matter how it takes place and no matter how it is rationalized, is always immoral. No matter how respectable those who practice it, no matter how acceptable by custom, no matter how completely sanctioned by law, it is a breach of morality. It is always either an individual or an institutional evil, and very often both.

Behavioral Exploitation

It was behavioral exploitation to which Robert Burns referred in his immortal words: "man's inhumanity to man makes countless thousands morn." Those engaged in behavioral exploitation are motivated by either the love of riches or the love of power.

No decent human being can excuse exploitation when it is practiced nakedly, shamelessly, and ruthlessly. But even very intelligent and decent human beings will accept and defend many subtle forms of exploitation when it is rationalized and when its real nature is hidden. When stripped of its disguises, every form of exploitation is ugly. But most people are so mis-educated on the nature of possession that millions indulge in exploitation without the slightest realization that what they are doing is morally indefensible.

It is difficult for members of labor unions who take advantage of the monopoly of labor they enjoy and who exact higher wages than they legitimately earn or who furnish less than an honest day's labor for an honest day's pay to realize that they are engaged in exploitation of the consumers who must absorb the resulting higher costs. What everybody around them is doing and what nobody seems to think wrong somehow does not *seem* to be wrong.

The officers and stockholders of an apparently respectable corporation may be deceiving and bamboozling the consuming public with its advertising; engaging in "restraint of trade" whenever it can get away with it; or polluting the air, the water, or the land in the operation of its factories. But it is equally difficult for those profiting from this exploitation to recognize that they are exploiting both present and future generations.

The principle of *caveat emptor* (let the buyer beware!) is morally indefensible. Nobody has the moral right to sell anything to another and take advantage of the other's ignorance when he does so. If this sort of business exploitation is acceptable, as Social Darwinists maintain in this dog-eat-dog world which they accept as inescapable, then stealing is equally acceptable.

Finally, a land-owner who takes advantage of the legal privilege which the existing system of land tenure confers upon him and pays less than its economic rent in taxes, or a land speculator who sells land he owns and pockets the "unearned increment" of land is also engaged in indirect exploitation. But this type of exploitation today is recognized only by the followers of Henry George.

Legalized Exploitation

Author-philosopher Albert Jay Nock is entitled to the credit for making a distinction between what he called the "political means" and the "economic means" of making money. What he calls the "political means" I would call the "legalized means"; what he calls the "economic means" I would prefer to call the "legitimate means" or "earning money honestly."

Legalized exploitation is made possible (1) by special privilege, conferred by law upon a certain person or persons which enables them to take advantage of those who do not possess this privilege, and (2) by monopolies or oligopolies.

Because what is declared legal is identified by most people with what is right, nearly everybody tends to believe in these legalized forms of exploitation and to take them for granted. Not only do states legalize exploitation in various ways; they also confer upon the exploiters the right to call upon the state to use police powers to force recalcitrant victims of the exploitation "to render unto Caesar" what the law says the exploiters are legally entitled to exact.

Over the years, most governments have "legalized" exploitation by private interests of many kinds of natural resources. A dramatic illustration of legalized exploitation took place in 1973 when the oil-producing countries of the Middle East, Africa, and South America formed a cartel called OPEC (Organization of Petroleum Exporting Countries). The victims of this cartel numbered in the hundreds of millions, including the populations of all the nations which were dependent upon Middle East oil: Japan, India, Pakistan, the Philippines, most of Europe, all of Africa, and all of South and North America, particularly the United States. In the summer of 1973 OPEC raised the price of oil from $3.12 a barrel to $11.65. That made oil so expensive that, in other countries, factories shut down, farmers could not buy fertilizers, automobiles and trucks stopped running, unemployment shot up, homes could not be heated, and millions of people in developing nations began to go hungry. Economic collapse of the whole West was threatened. However, none of the victims questioned OPEC's right, under existing law, to exploit those dependent on its oil. Were not the oil wells OPEC's property? Could not OPEC do with its own property what OPEC wanted? Could not those who owned the oil charge "all the traffic would bear"?

No form of legalized exploitation is less excusable than the special privilege represented by the creation of corporations for private profit. The law today ignores the distinction between natural persons and artificial persons, between human beings who live and breathe and corporations which have no hearts but only stomachs. The entire history of corporations, since corporations for private profit were first legalized in 1811, is one of shameless greed and chicanery. All efforts to control them and make them behave decently have failed. The claim that private corporations make possible economies of large-scale production may be true, but they do so largely because of the special privilege of limited liability, a privilege not conferred on partnerships or the former joint stock associations which existed before for-profit corporations were legalized. Limitation of liability encourages large outside investments, but it does not hold the officers of the corporation morally responsible for the debts that they incur for the corporation, thus allowing giant bankruptcies to occur in which the public investors and creditors are swindled. A good society, I believe, would demand the return to the legal situation which existed when the only corporations chartered were nonprofit or those which provided public utilities. If all corporations were owned cooperatively by those who used their services, corporate exploitation would be far more difficult.

So far as exploitation of labor is concerned, the take-over of the economy by corporations in the first half of the twentieth century has simply continued the exploitation in which private employers had previously indulged. Labor was exploited ruthlessly until labor unions became strong enough to stop it; but eventually the unions joined the employer in exploiting the consuming public. Private corporations added enormously to consumer exploitation, because they used lavish advertising to mislead consumers and because they restrained competition by merging, by forming "trusts" and by organizing cartels.

In addition, the legalization of corporations for private profit introduced an entirely new form of exploitation, the exploitation of the investors. For nearly two hundred years the organizers of corporations, the managements of corporations, and those who traded their securities have been fleecing investors. And yet, no matter how often they have been shorn, they continue like "lambs" to raise the wool for the "bulls and bears" to sheer again. Although it is capitalist heresy to say so, there is not a single, valid, moral reason for the existence of corporations.

Karl Marx held that profit-takers, all interest-takers, all rent-takers; all capitalists small or mighty who in any way retained what Marx called the "surplus value of production" were engaged in "capitalist expropriation." Economic exploitation, in my view, does exist, but it is quite different from what Marx referred to as "expropriation." Economic exploitation, for instance, would not occur in the form of profit-taking providing a genuine free market exists, and the profit is genuinely *earned*.

Economic exploitation occurs only when profit-taking is *abused*, as it is: (a) when it is made possible only by special legal permission granted by the government; (b) when it is the result of nonproductive speculation (what in Common Law used to be called regarding, forestalling, and engrossing); and (c) when it involves taking advantage of the scarcity created by a calamity of some kind.

The very concept of profit-taking, however, is a misnomer. It is actually profit-and-loss taking. In a free economy the excess of profits over losses amounts to not much more than what is earned from undertaking enterprises in which the entrepreneur's capital and labor is risked and employed. For their risks, entrepreneurs are entitled to a return which, in a genuinely free economy, is limited by competition, preventing the entrepreneurs from becoming exploitive.

If a genuinely free market ever existed or if such a market now existed, economic exploitation would not be possible. No person or class can exploit another "economically" unless it has been legally permitted to do so, as was the case when the "nobility" exploited those the law designated as "commoners" or "serfs." Such a situation was never a free economy, but rather a constrained economy and a servile state.

Exploitation takes place in every kind of society or state—capitalist or communist, open or closed, servile or free, partly or entirely corrupt. Although, in so-called "free economies," exploitation frequently has the appearance of expropriation, it consists, in fact, of a breach of morals and frequently as a breach of law. When there are no statutes which forbid a particular kind of exploitation, it is in fact a defect in the law, or indifference or corruption by public officials who should enforce the law. For instance, business is indulging in inexcusable exploitation of consumers today here in America by fooling the public with its deceptive and overblown advertising about the purity, the quality, and sometimes even the quantity of goods offered for sale. Examples can be seen in dairymen coloring butter, and corporations adulterating and selling toxic products like cosmetics, detergents, pesticides, chemical fertilizers, cigarettes, and many kinds of drugs. Exploitation, no matter what form it takes, is always harmful in terms of moral law. In common and statutary law, exploitation is what is called today a tort or delict. A tort is an offense for which the offender can be sued for redress and damages by his victim or victims. Perpetrators of torts are not subject to arrest and prosecution, as are other criminals. Although exploitation is considered a private, in contrast to a public, crime, exploiters, do in fact commit not only private crimes but in many cases public crimes as well.

Class actions, in which a group of individuals may sue an exploiter, not only for themselves but also to make the exploiter pay damages to every victim of the same kind of tort, is a much more terrible threat than an individual suit. But the legislators who are more interested in defending the interests which contribute to their election than in their constituents have discouraged legislation which would popularize class suits on the grounds that this might lead to the "harassment" of business. If it were easier to bring class suits, an army of lawyers would find it profitable to sue exploiters, which would serve as a powerful restraint on the temptation to exploit. The reluctance of legislatures and courts clearly goes back to the time when the law was interpreted primarily in the interest of the "haves" and not at all in the interest of the "have nots."

Debtors are natural subjects for exploitation. In the United States those who are most exploited are the installment buyers and users of certain credit cards. But many of the "victims" buy on credit when they should buy for cash, and therefore deserve no sympathy. In countries like India, however, the institutionalized system of land tenure enables the *zamindars,* the big land-owners, to exploit the hard-working land-less peasants who are at their mercy and also at the mercy of the money-lenders. Real land reform is the only way in which this exploitation can be corrected.

Possessions

Possessions can and always have been held in one of two ways: by title or *ownership* or by tenure or *trusteeship*. For years I have been calling this second basic category "trusterty." However the public has always treated both categories as legally ownable property.

The confusion about property vs. trusterty is at the root of the conflict between individualism and socialism. The individualist maintains that we should have a social system in which it is possible to say, "This store is my business; I own it." However, the socialist maintains that nobody should be able to make such a statement, that it should only be possible to say, "This is our business, we all own it."

If we use the words "my" and "his" or "hers," and "ours" and "theirs," we discover that possessions can be either tangible, like money, or intangible like integrity. It is possible to say "my money" or "his money," and "my integrity" or "his integrity." Possessions, we also discover, involve every kind of possessiveness from "my self" and "my house" to "my language" and "my country." They involve every kind of individuality and collectivity.

The magnitude of the confusion is apparent when a man refers to "my wife" or a woman refers to "my husband." Clearly, there are many kinds of possessions which cannot and should not be treated as property. If every trace of ownership is eliminated from them, they should be treated as a trust, as a responsibility, or as a sacred obligation. Such is the case when a man or woman says "my child" or when a child says "my father" or "my mother," and when anybody says "our town" or "our country" or "our Lord" or "my Lord and Savior," and even when we say "my moral values" or "our environment."

Title

There is an important distinction between a patent (or first title) and a title which has been acquired as the end-result of a chain of titles, going back to the original patent. A *patent* is an instrument, representing the grant by a "paramount grantor" (a government, a king, or a pope) or title to something either tangible (as in the case of land) or intangible (as in the case of a copyright) to an individual or individuals. A *title*, on the other hand, is an instrument issued by the owner of anything to another, giving the new owner the right: (a) to its exclusive possession; (b) to its occupation and holding; (c) to its use; (d) to its consumption and destruction; and (e) to its transfer to another by sale, by gift, or by bequest.

Existing law and existing political, economic, and popular beliefs ignore the fact that there are some things—like land—which cannot be morally or properly owned by anybody or by any power or authority and that every patent and every title to such a thing is tainted with the original immorality and impropriety of granting ownership to it. No matter how often a stolen automobile changes hands and no matter how many owners pay previous owners for it, the automobile remains stolen property. It still cannot be treated as honest property. It still belongs to its original owner.

First titles and patents come into existence in two ways which can be rationally and morally vindicated: (a) *title by manufacture,* as a tailor obtains when he makes clothes or as a farmer gets when he grows a crop; and (b) *title by creation*, as an author obtains for a book he has written, a musician for a song she has composed, or an inventor with a patent for the device he has invented.

By contrast, five additional categories can be vindicated only by might, by special privilege, or by arbitrary fiat: (c) *title by occupancy,* as in "Squatters" rights; (d) *title by appropriation*, as in finding something or appropriating something which nobody at the time is claiming; (e) *title by discovery*, as in the discovery of America, to which Columbus took title for the Crown of Spain; (f) *title by conquest,* as when the United States took California from Mexico, Mexico took it from Spain, and Spain took it from the Indians; and (g) *title by legal grant* of a special privilege like a saloon license, railroad rights to land, etc. by a government with enough power to enforce observance of its grants.

Finally, there is one category which I think of as (h) *title by sacred fiat,* such as Jehovah, through Moses, gave His chosen people, the Israelites, which was in effect a title to the land of Canaan, and such as centuries later the Pope gave when he divided the New World between the Crowns of Spain and Portugal.

The validity of title by manufacture—under which the manufactured item was produced with the individual's own labor—is almost self-evident. This is also true of title by creation and invention. Only when production involves a large number of workers does the problem of where title lies occur. However, this problem can be resolved by dividing what is produced according to the value of the labor contributed by each worker.

Tenure

Tenure is a right, usually evidenced by an instrument called a lease, to hold something—particularly real estate—in trust for a stated, sometimes an indefinite, period of time, in return for the payment of money or some other agreed-upon service or commodity. Under current practice the leaseholder or tenant has all the rights of an owner except one: the right to consume, destroy, or permanently alter what is entrusted to him. Owners and title-holders hold their possessions in what is legally referred to as "fee simple absolute"; tenants and leaseholders hold it in trust upon conditions agreed upon, enjoying only its use while maintaining it in its original condition and its original state of fertility.

Allocation and Allotment

No existing paramount grantor—none of the governments which now claim sovereignty over the earth—can vindicate in rational and moral terms the granting of patents and the issuance of title in "fee simple absolute"; therefore, we must face the problem of how land and other resources should be allocated.

I suggest that the authorities which now have authority to deal with this problem must be completely transformed or new ones created for the purpose. The existing authorities must be deprived of their power to permit exploitation of the earth and the continuance of the use of land for speculative purposes. Exploitation, such as that now being perpetrated by the nations belonging to the OPEC group, would then become impossible. No individual or nation could claim sub-soil rights just because a certain mineral resource of the world happened to surface on his or its soil. Who has the moral right to profit from the world's natural resources? Natural resources, such as oil, should be held *in trust* by an international organization, such as the U.N. for the benefit of future generations, and the per-barrel surcharge on oil should be collected by this organization.

We need area and regional authorities and, with regard to other vast and crucially important natural resources as the oceans, a global authority. The "Land of the Seas" conference, sponsored by the United Nations, has been struggling with this continuing international problem. These authorities should not only allot, apportion, and assign the land which has not already been preempted by land owners but both fix the conditions to be observed by everybody who uses any kind of trusterty and fix the payment to be made, the ground-rent or mineral-royalty, as the case may be, by the holders and users. Finally, if human morality is to be honored, each authority must use the revenue it obtains for the benefit of the whole population of each area, of each region, and of the planet itself.

Once the validity of these principles is accepted by the determining number of nations, the billions now being collected by the sheiks and shahs of Arabia for oil which they did not lift a finger to put into the earth and who therefore have no moral title to it would then become available to a world authority, such as the United Nations, to maintain global peace. However, before any nation would ever accept holding of oil reserves in trust, it would have to recognize the moral distinction between property and what I call "trusterty," those things which should be held in trust.

Property

All discussions of the Possessional Problem are absurd if we fail to recognize that there is not just one type of possession which lawyers call "property" and economists call "wealth," but at least ten kinds—seven of which are property and three trusterty. The law nowhere recognizes this distinction, and economists simply add to the confusion by failing to classify possessions systematically and scientifically.

Property is legally defined as the exclusive right to possess, enjoy, and dispose of things; but "things" are not defined. This absurdity is responsible for defining as property all sorts of things which actually are trusterty, things which at one time were legally ownable such as wives and children, slaves and serfs, which can no longer be considered property.

The seven categories of possession which can be considered property include:

(a) *consumption goods:* food, clothing, housing;

(b) *producer equipment* or capital equipment: factories, machines, barns, livestock, raw materials, and merchandise;

(c) *claims:* coins, paper money, notes, mortgages, bonds, accounts receivable;

(d) *creative assets:* intangible assets consisting of inventions, literary and musical compositions, formulas, good-will (created by satisfactory conduct of an enterprise or of a professional practice), and other assets of the same nature;

(e) *inherent assets:* the characteristics which human beings possess such as physical strength, intelligence, knowledge, skill, diligence, craftsmanship, artistic and professional ability, thrift, integrity, and wisdom;

(f) *inherent liabilities:* the characteristics which human beings possess such as ignorance, incompetence, unreliability, and dishonesty;

(g) *tangible liabilities:* debts.

Because these seven kinds of possessions came into existence only as a result of human labor or human creativity or lack of same, they are things to which it is possible to establish a valid original title. They are all things into which an individual's labor is, so-to-speak, "frozen," things to which an honest original title can be established. They can be properly treated as property, because they can come into existence only by producing them, as a farmer produces a crop which he therefore owns; by earning the money with which to buy them from those who originally produced them; by saving the money so earned and investing it and thereby becoming the owner of the claims which represent their earnings; by using one's own inherent assets to produce a commodity, render a service, or bring into existence a creation or invention. Finally, both tangible liabilities like debts which are acquired by the person who contracts them, and intangible liabilities like a person's competence, are in fact his "property."

Trusterty

The three categories of possession which should be called trusterty, as contrasted with property, are:

(a) *human beings*, such as wives and children which were considered property under ancient law not only in Rome but in most ancient civilizations, and such as serfs and slaves, who were treated all over the world as if they were two-legged cattle, to be bought and sold;

(b) *natural resources*, such as land, rivers, lakes, the seas, the air, natural forests, coal, oil, and minerals which are still in the earth;

(c) *legal grants*, both legitimate and illegitimate; they include titles to land, forests, mines and oil reserves, the right to use the atmosphere and the seas; grants of eminent domain—to railroads, power companies, telephone companies, and other public utilities; charters to corporations, banks, and insurance companies; licenses of all kinds; benefices, sinecures, monopolies, tariffs, import and export quotas and permits, permits for foreign exchange (permitting the operation of cartels and other monopolistic devices), and other special privileges.

These kinds of possessions all come into existence deliberately by the action or inaction of law. Those which are legitimate should be treated as trusts; those which are illegitimate, completely forbidden.

Few chapters in the history of mankind have described more shameless inhumanity to man than the history of lands acquired by "discovery" or by "conquest." Land which is owned today often is, in effect, stolen trusterty. Read the history of how the U.S. Government first acquired title to the land it is now granting to privileged people and corporations, land to which it obtained title only under the law of conquest. Even when the Indians signed treaties at the point of the white man's guns, they insisted that they had no right to "sell" the land. Land, they said, "cannot be sold; it is a gift of the Great Spirit to them and to their children to use, not to sell."

Solution to the Problem

Man has been confronted with the Possessional Problem from the moment the first person found something he wanted (nuts, fruit), caught or killed something (fish, animals), captured something (cattle, horses, prisoners), or made something (axes, baskets, pots, cloth) which other people also wanted.

If we classify systematically all the possible solutions of the Possessional Problem which have been practiced, proposed, and advocated, the same three basic types of solutions of *all* basic problems emerge: fideistic (relying on faith rather than reason), pragmatic, and philosophic. Many of these solutions have been rationalized and elaborated in ideologies which conflict with one another. A few make it apparent that the problem can be dealt with justly and intelligently only if the determining number of people are rightly educated with regard to them.

Fideistic Solutions

No religion has a definite dogma covering the Possessional Problem in all its ramifications. It is said in the Bible that Jehovah gave the land of Canaan to the Jews whom Moses led out of Egypt. Unfortunately, He granted land which was already occupied by the Canaanites. Thus, His chosen people had to fight for it, and they have been fighting ever since. Many of the higher religions tend merely to accept traditional or prevailing solutions—the status quo—in the culture in which they were first launched or to which they subsequently spread. That, plainly, is the reason why Marx condemned these religions and called religion the opiate of the masses. In the teachings of Jesus we find, "Render unto Caesar the things that are Caesar's and unto God the things that are God's"—without even asking the question of whether Caesar was rightly entitled to what he claimed as his.

The Judaic Doctrine of Land Possession

The Judaic approach to the Problem is suggested in the book of Leviticus: "The earth hath the Lord given to the children of men." It should not, however, be treated as a permanent possession in "fee simple absolute," as it is treated by the law today, because it is always the Lord's: "The land should not be sold forever; for the land is Mine; for ye are strangers and sojourners with Me." To ensure this idea, the Jews believed that the land should be redistributed every fifty years during the Year of Jubilee:

> And ye shall hallow the fiftieth year, and proclaim liberty throughout the land: it shall be a jubilee unto you, and ye shall return every man unto his possession [every man who sold or lost his allotment of land should have it returned] and ye shall return every man unto his family [every enslaved or bound servant should be freed]. Leviticus 25:9, 10

This injunction also deals, as you can see, with the problem of "possessing" serfs and slaves.

Title by Sacred Fiat

In spite of St. Francis' doctrine of holy poverty, Roman Catholicism, with its genius for accepting completely irreconcilable doctrines, developed a property doctrine which I think of as Sacred Fiat. In its heyday, it vested in the Pope the power of paramount grantor of the whole earth. The Reformation did not eliminate this contradiction. Protestantism permitted and actually encouraged the accumulation of property but at the same time and in varying degrees advocated in principle—but rarely in practice—the idea of stewardship. Recently in India this idea of stewardship has been revived in an entirely different context and called *sarvodaya*. However, unless teeth are put into the doctrine by law, property-owners in India will continue to do exactly what Protestant property-owners have done—namely, pay no attention to it. Only when the sanctity of private property is threatened by a change in positive law or by a threatened take-over by communism are property-owners much disturbed.

Pragmatic Solutions

Prevailing solutions of the Problem, both in the capitalist world and in the communist world, are all based upon the idea of creating titles by might. In his book, *The State,* Franz Oppenheimer claims that all states come into being through an act of conquest. Pragmatic solutions to the Possessional Problem are thereafter sanctioned by the law, and back of the law is the power of the state.

Hard-headed, practical, and materialistic modern man accepts this solution. It *works,* doesn't it? But the practical man is usually practical only in the short run and rarely in the long. Nor is he much interested in the ethical aspects of things which work. Back in 1890 Henry George said that if nothing were done about setting up an honest system of land tenure, the whole property system would be abolished by socialism. At the time he stirred up quite a following, but the number of practical people who were profiting from the existing system was simply too great for the acceptance generally of such an idea.

No matter how profitable to its beneficiaries, the trouble with the pragmatic solution to the Possessional Problem is that it cannot be justified either intellectually or morally. As Wordsworth put it, it can only be vindicated "Because the good old rule sufficeth them, the simple plan that they should take who have the power, and they should keep, who can."

The Capitalist Solution

The capitalist solution of the Possessional Problem is based not on the idea of private property but on the idea of private ownership of capital, of what Marx called "the means of production and distribution." Capitalism insists on private ownership of *all* capital and public ownership of none. It recognizes that a great deal of the wealth of a nation, such as the public domain and public buildings, and of what Ruskin called the "illth," such as armaments, battleships, and warplanes, must be publicly or governmentally owned. But it wants government ownership and operation limited to those areas which cannot be handled by private enterprise: the police; the judicial and penal systems to maintain "law and order"; the military establishment "to defend the realm"; the street and highway system; the public school system; the postal system and other necessary public services. Not all defenders of capitalism go even that far. Some would have private enterprise take over the schools and the post office and many other government activities which most capitalists are willing to leave to the public sector.

The capitalist solution to the problem of the possession of land is simple in the extreme. All land should be privately owned in fee simple absolute. Whatever land is left in the public domain—mineral land, forest land, grazing land—should be disposed of and patents granted for it to private owners. The only exception is land kept for such essential activities as oil reserves for military purposes.

The capitalist solution of the problem of the possession of labor is even more simplistic. The laborer, whether a wage laborer, a salary earner, a professional person working for fees or working for himself in a business of any kind owns himself; his labor and skill (or lack of it) is a possession of his; it is his own property, and he can either use it for himself or his family, as subsistence farmers and housewives do, or sell it to whomever he wishes on his own terms and conditions.

Since capitalism takes private ownership for granted, it ignores both the question of its moral validity and its economic utility. As I see it, capitalism is from beginning to end a rationalization. To justify having everything privately owned, including what should be held in trust—the airwaves for instance, or mineral resources—its proponents have to accept all sorts of qualifications of the doctrine and all sorts of government intervention and regulation of business operations.

The flaws which have developed in practice have been so outrageous that the solution is vulnerable to the most radical criticism. Greed is practiced generally by both labor and capital. "The invisible hand" of which Adam Smith spoke which was to transform the private pursuit of profit into the general welfare of all was dependent upon the maintainance of perfect competition, of a really free market, where there were no import tariffs, and of a really free system of enterprise, where no price-fixing was tolerated.

We live, however, not in a free economy but in what could be called a *constrained* economy where all kinds of exploitations by special interest groups are allowed. Our alodial system of land tenure involving full possession; our monetary system which is controlled by the government; our regulatory laws and regulatory agencies which give only lip service to preventing monopolies, oligopolies, and cartels; our labor unions which misuse their power, have all made the U.S. version of capitalism smell to high heaven.

Capitalism, particularly as it is practiced in the United States today, has only one real virtue. It does permit a large measure of freedom such as free speech, free assembly, and free press. By contrast, the fatal flaw which damns communism is the political necessity for making each nation a closed society; communism's inability to function in a free and open society is apparent in Russia, China, Eastern Europe, and Cuba.

The Communist Solution

The communist solution to the problem of possession of capital maintains that *all* "the means of production and distribution" and *all* the capital equipment must be owned by society as a collective whole; that this ownership should be vested for practical reasons in a sovereign centralized state, able to use its police power for the maintenance of its sole right to produce and distribute. Police power and even military power, both in theory and in practice, as the history of Russia demonstrates, had to be used first to seize all the farms and factories, all the means of transportation and distribution ("expropriate the expropriators"), and then to keep the property which has been "well seized" from those who had owned it and who might otherwise immediately begin to re-appropriate it. Communism permits one exception to this sweeping principle of possession: the private ownership of personal paraphernalia, of household appliances and other consumption goods purchased in state stores and used by a family to provide for its own private needs and desires.

The communist solution of the problem of the possession of land is like the capitalist solution, simple in the extreme: the land and all the other natural resources of the nation must be owned exclusively by the state, and none at all owned privately.

The communist solution of the problem of labor is that labor, from the lowest of what Marx called "the lumpen proletariat" to the most highly trained engineers and most highly educated professionals of all kinds, belongs to the State. Those who rule Soviet Russia never say that they have reduced the people of Russia to serfdom, but this is precisely what they have done. It took a man like Friedrich Hayek in his book, *The Read to Serfdom*, to tell us the truth about the communist proletariat.

In Soviet Russia the laborer is, in effect, attached to his job, just as nearly all the peasantry in the feudal social system were bound to the soil. No Russian may leave his job without permission; nobody may emigrate without permission. If for some reason a person is permitted to emigrate, he must repay the state for his education. If this is not serfdom, what is?

Ironically, communism substitutes a kind of "state slavery" for the wage slavery which communists condemn as intolerable in the capitalist world. Under the communist system the state becomes the owner of everything and everybody, including labor. Calling everybody a comrade sounds much better than calling people serfs or slaves, but it does not alter the facts. The state's planning commission has the sole right to employ people. It also has the sole right to determine what every worker will be paid and what the conditions will be under which workers will work; there are no unions and no strikes are permitted. Everybody is thus deprived of his/her exclusive right to own him or herself. The result is the transformation of human beings—the most important of all kinds of trusterty—into state-owned public property.

(It is ironic that servile labor is again being introduced into the United States as well. Only those states which have expressly enacted "right to work" laws recognize that compulsory unionism denies a laborer the right to own and freely dispose of his own labor. Compulsory unionism is reminiscent of indentured labor in the colonial period of America. Colonialists would "buy" labor from shipowners who brought men and women from the Old World. So desperate were they to get to America that they "sold" themselves for a period of years to pay for their passage. Such labor is now forbidden by statutes which prevent the importation of what is called "contract labor.")

The Socialist Solution

Swedish socialism has been widely viewed as the model of socialism. Like Capitalistic America, socialistic Sweden can boast of one of the highest scales of living in the world. The solution of the problem of the possession of capital in the Swedish-type socialist state, usually called a social democracy, is dualistic: there is a private sector in which capital can be owned as it is in capitalist states, and there is a public sector in which capital is owned by the state. There is no discernible theory as to which industries will be state-owned and which will be permitted to be owned and operated capitalistically. Public utilities are almost invariably state-owned; big industry, like steel, is usually, but not invariably, state-owned. The rule seems to be that whenever any of "the means of production and distribution" fail to please either those working for a particular industry or the public, it is taken over by the state. It is not, however, expropriated; compensation of the private owners is always made.

The socialistic solution of the problem of the possession of land is not very different from that of the capitalists. Land is publicly-owned whenever the state feels it should be, but land also can be privately-owned.

So far as the possession of labor is concerned, the socialist solution is identical with that prevailing in all free and open societies. Everyone owns him or herself; a person may join a union; may strike; may change from one employer to another and even go into business privately; a person may also emigrate. State regulation of the conditions of labor may be greater than in capitalistic societies, but the difference is a matter of degree, not of kind.

The Fascist Solution

As Fascism has been practiced, it differs from free and open societies by being dictatorial in nature and by claiming for the state the right to regulate and, if the government desires, to take over any industry or any land as well as to dictate the conditions of labor. Benito Mussolini, who was originally a communist, rationalized his leadership, as he called his dictatorship, by saying that socialism was his goal. For the same reason Adolf Hitler called his kind of fascism National Socialism.

Francisco Franco in Spain called his fascism and his fascist party "falangism," and Portugal's Salazar made no pretenses about setting up a socialist society. They both justified their dictatorships in terms of the need for orderly government. Such has also been the case with the many fascist military dictatorships which now exist and which existed in the past.

Aside from the fact that the dictatorships all dealt arbitrarily with the problem of possession, they differed little from capitalist or socialist states in the manner in which they dealt with the possession of capital, land and labor. In the short run, they worked, and sometimes—as Portugal illustrated—long outlasted the original dictator.

The Feudal Solution

The feudal states and nations which developed all over Europe after the breakdown of the Roman Empire dealt with the possessional problem in similar ways. Craftsmen produced goods in shops which they owned, and sold them directly to the people. Merchants, who also owned their own shops, dealt mainly in imported goods. Except for the guilds, in which membership was voluntarily accepted, there was no regulation of commerce by the state. Most of the population, however, consisted of farmers and peasants. The possession of land, capital, and labor was dealt with very differently from the way they were dealt with after the industrial revolution.

Aside from the simple equipment, the livestock, and the barns, the capital used by peasants and farmers consisted entirely of land. This capital was held "in fee," rather than owned outright by anybody. In theory, it was held by a hierarchy of people, beginning with a paramount grantor—perhaps a pope or an emperor—who enfeoffed counts and lords of the manor, who in turn enfeoffed their vassals and serfs.

The feudal solution of the problem of the possession of land is interesting in that, in principle, though unfortunately not in fact, enfeoffment was an embryonic form of alloting land by entrusting it to its users as opposed to selling it in fee simple absolute as we do in most of the Western world today.

The feudal approach to the problem of the allotment of land was based on a concept which is variously called fees, feuds, or fiefs; or hereditary estates which ranged in size from that of a freeman's small holding to that of a king's domain. The holder of a fee was a vassal and the grantor of the fee, his lord. The vassal was anything from a churl to a king. Churls could hold a fee but could have no vassals. Earls, thanes, and even kings received their fees from a superior lord. The only lord who had no superior, the paramount grantor, was in theory the Emperor of the earth. In Italy this idea led to a great historic struggle which lasted for generations between the Ghibellines, who maintained that the emperor was paramount, and the Guelphs, who maintained that the emperor was a vassal of the Pope whose paramountcy as grantor derived from the fact that he was the vicar of God on earth. No such issue arose in ancient Rome where the Pontifex Maximus knew his place nor in the Chinese Empire where the emperor himself was supposed to be the Son of God.

The feudal solution of the problem of labor denied, for the most part, the principle that a person owned him or herself. Yeomen or freeholders in the country and masters in the towns and cities were exceptions to the rule. The peasantry consisted mainly of vassals and serfs; most of the workers in the cities were apprentices and journeymen. Men owned their wives; children were often sold as apprentices; the commoners were always beholden to the nobility. Those who find it difficult to think of laborers as ownable should bear in mind that, over the course of history, slavery was not limited to the ownership of manual laborers. Slaves ranged all the way from ox-like farm workers to teachers and artists, mechanics and housekeepers, tutors and even intellectual giants like Epictetus.

Philosophic Solutions

Other solutions of the Possessional Problem are based on two important assumptions. The first is that capital—money which has actually been *saved* by those who have earned it legitimately, and which is needed to provide a good life for everybody—may and should be accumulated by private property owners who get it by starting an enterprise of their own—a farm, a shop, a store, a professional practice; or by investing in such enterprises as savings banks, policies of life insurance companies, a cooperative of some kind, or even the securities issued by a corporation which is not engaged in any kind of exploitive or predatory enterprise. Long experience has shown that no truly free society can exist if the state can arbitrarily take over the ownership of any enterprise or industry in the private sector, make it a state monopoly, and forbid private enterprise to compete with it. Competition is a good thing not only between private enterprises but between private enterprises and government enterprises. Obviously the denial of such free enterprise is a denial of freedom itself.

The second important assumption is that the only way to make possible a truly good life for mankind is to utterly abolish the principle of absolute ownership of land and other natural resources, and completely replace it with agreements of tenure in trust. No amount of legalization can provide an honest title to any portion of the earth.

Capitalist and Communist Solutions

Alodialism, or land which was held free of any feudal landlord's tenurial rights, introduced land preemption and speculation—economic evils so subtle in nature that to this day they are hardly recognized by either capitalist or communist economists. As a result, rationalization by law and by the courts popularized the idea that speculating in land was a right to which free men were entitled. In America speculating in land has become a way of life. Recent generations who have been brought up on the game Monopoly have learned the "virtues" of hoarding land for speculative reasons.

On the other hand, nationalization of the land, which communist idealism supposes will do away with the evils of outright land ownership, is in many respects worse. It permits the state to exploit the farming population, and to promote urbanization and industrialism. With absolute ownership, the evil is at least diluted if the land is held by many owners. But with state ownership a new species of serfdom is introduced in which the state plays the role which the feudal nobility played before the industrial revolution.

The American Indian's Solution

No primitives anywhere, including American Indians, ever dealt in "real estate." The idea of selling land was inconceivable in the Indian culture. They fought to hold the land against the invading white man; they felt they were holding it in trust for the future generations of their tribes. In all its stark simplicity, the Indian's possessional doctrine was that the land was to be used, not to be owned. Every treaty and every so-called sale of land was extracted from the Indians by the white man's bamboozling them with talk, trinkets, and whiskey. If these techniques did not work, the land was seized from them at gunpoint. When the first state was organized and boundaries first invented, primitive man's idyllic feeling for the land, the natural resources of the earth was replaced by "civilized" man's exclusive and exploitive feeling for them.

Henry George's Solution

Like his precursors, Mencius in China and Thomas Paine in America, Henry George accepted facts which primitive mankind had long taken for granted: that land was entrusted to mankind; that nobody had ever or could ever properly "own" it; that no person, no corporation, and not even the state itself could show an honest title to any of it. Certainly, God (or Nature), the Creator of the earth, issued no titles to any land to anybody.

In his book, *Progress and Poverty*, Henry George undoubtedly traced the evils of alodial ownership more searchingly than any other great social reformer. His unique contribution to the solution of the Possessional Problem was his ingenious proposal to shift from alodial title to land to equally-secure *tenure* of land—but with the land, in effect, entrusted by leasehold to the holder. Basing his proposal upon Ricardo's law of rent, he proposed that the full ground rent be collected from the existing *holders* of land in lieu of taxes on both the land and all the buildings and other improvements on it. By relieving those who were actually using the land from taxes on their improvements, this change would encourage improvements, and by taxing the speculative owners of land for the full ground rent, this provision would make it profitless to hold out of use land which a speculator hoped to obtain a profit from the land's rise in value. Without expropriating the existing owners but merely by shifting from the existing injustice of taxing users for the improvements on their land and failing to collect the full ground rent from the speculating owners of unimproved land, exploitation and appropriation of what George called the "unearned increment" would be ended.

Sarvodaya

This proposal comes from the followers of Gandhi. It would eliminate all exploitation, including exploitation of land, by a moral reformation. It calls for no legislation, no confiscation of property from present owners, no abnegation of their property by its owners. It asks merely for the voluntary substitution of trusteeship for ownership, with each owner at one and the same time both donor and trustee with the public and particularly with the propertyless who are the beneficiaries in the new regime.

Sarvodaya became a reality with Vinoba Bhave's (the "Walking Saint of India," and a disciple of Gandhi) great movement for *bhoodan* (voluntary surrender of surplus land to the landless) and with *gramdan* (voluntary pooling of all the land of a village by all the landowners, large and small). Gramdan was realized in many hundreds of villages in India; bhoodan in thousands. But both movements died down as Vinoba Bhave and his successor, Jayaprakash Narayan, became too old to provide inspiration for them. Mass conversions of this kind take place only so long as there are charismatic figures such a Vinoba Bhave—sages, saints, prophets, whatever they may be called—to inspire them. Nevertheless, the land trust movement has been felt in India. Narayan's home state of Bihar, a rural Northern state, is now three-quarters under gramdan.

Sarvodaya assumes in its approach to the Possessional Problem that human beings are not innately greedy; that existing teachings, customs, and statutes which stimulate greed should be eliminated and that everybody should be conditioned to get satisfaction in life from activities other than the accumulation of riches. To institutionalize the ideal of Sarvodaya, two basic reforms seem to me essential: an honest system of land tenure such as Henry George suggested, and an honest investiture system—a system of legal grants free from any kind of special privilege.

In the West, the concept of social trusteeship has been attributed to Edmund Burke. In a speech in 1783 in the House of Commons, he said that "all political power which is set over man . . . ought to be in some way or other exercised utimately for public benefit," and that "every species of political dominion and every commercial privilege . . . are all in the strictest sense trusts."

The Land Trust Movement

The first land trusts were set up by Georgists in the late 1890s: Free Acres in New Jersey, Arden in Delaware, and Freehope in Alabama. Later, during the Great Depression, one of my books about the Borsodi family's experience with country living led to a sort of "back to the land" movement for the unemployed. To make land available for such a movement at a time when it was almost impossible to get money for anything at all, I proposed setting up land trusts. To demonstrate the possibility of making the unemployed self-sufficient in this way, I set up a demonstration project in Dayton, Ohio, and another in Suffern, New York. I obtained the land and financed (through local banks) the building of what I called homesteads on the land. The demonstration worked; I had the pleasure of visiting two of the communities fifty years after they were started. But interest in the movement declined when the Second World War began and the whole nation suddenly found itself fully employed. The movement, however, did not die out entirely.

Communities whose land is held in trust have been proliferating in recent years from Florida to California and Maine to Mexico, and today a vigorous revival of the land trust movement is under way. Nonprofit organizations such as the Institute for Community Economics in Cambridge, Mass., have been actively promoting the idea. The movement has immense potential. It not only makes land accessible to those who cannot pay the speculative prices for the land they want to farm but it also protects the environment. And it leads to public recognition that property, such as land, should in fact be held as trusterty.

While homesteading land was freely available, Americans took pride in being independent, self-sufficient, and able to take care of themselves in what the immigrants called "the land of opportunity." If we want to recreate such a buoyant state, land must again be made accessible. The overwhelming majority of the people, I believe, should again live on homesteads of their own and not live in big megalopitan centers. This shift in habitation does not call for a return to the technology of the past; it does not assume that there was ever a Golden Age in the past to which we should return. It takes for granted that today we can do most things much better than we did them in the past. The vast majority can say "no" to the dictates of our corporate monstrosities, the dictates of labor union bosses and even to the bureaucrats and politicians—only if they have the option to obtain land where they can be in command of their own labor.

Like strength and intelligence, the capacity to perform labor is an inherent asset of every individual human being and therefore should be considered property. It is not possible to live a good life if human beings are treated as a means and not as an end. Kant's categorical imperative disposed of that question long ago. If the laborer is not a means, then he should not be treated as property. He must own himself. He should not be owned by a lord, a state, or any other entity. The laborer, like every human being, is and should be treated as trusterty. If he owns his own labor, then he is free to sell his labor, to give it away, to use it in his own home or in his own ship. But if he does not own his own labor, if he is in effect property, as were the slaves in pre–Civil War America and as are laborers in communist and fascist states today, then he is servile, not free.

John Locke based his argument for "life, liberty, and property" on the assumption that a moral title to property can be created in only one way: by producing or manufacturing the property. By putting his own labor into the thing made, the maker causes it to be his. Locke assumed, just as the classical economists later assumed, that it was possible to establish both what was produced by an individual worker, and also the output of a group of individuals producing "socially." The wages, the rent, the profits, and the interest paid represented what each of the participants had contributed to the value of what had been produced and also what each was entitled to. Locke based this argument upon what can be clearly seen in the creating of a farmer's title to his crops. If he had "hired" men to help him, this help had been paid wages and so had received what they were entitled to for their contribution to the production of the crops. If he had paid rent or interest, this represented the amount which land and capital had contributed. What was left was his, and to this part he was entitled for his labor and his enterprise.

Marx, on the other hand, based his solution of the Possessional Problem on the analysis of industrial—not agricultural—production. He was a child of the city; he knew nothing of country life. He was fascinated, when the factory system was in its infancy, with its possibilities and at the same time horrified by the exploitation of the factory workers by the factory owners. To him it was clearly impossible to trace title to what was produced by each individual worker on the theory of individual production. Therefore, in his terms, the owner of the factory could show no honest title either to the goods or to the profits produced by "his" factory. He ignored the fact that it was possible to do so in the case of self-employed craftsmen and workers in cottage industries. He considered irrelevant the fact that the individual weaver of a bolt of cloth knew perfectly well who had produced it. For Marx, the factory had rendered all individual small-scale production obsolete. He felt that everything in the future would be socially produced. Marx believed that everything produced by mankind belonged not to private owners but to the whole of society.

The doctrine of individual production as the basis of determining title to property will work justly, I suggest, only if the injustice of special privilege is abolished. The disparity between the exploiting rich and working masses has its source not in a possessional system which recognizes private title to property but in a political system which legalizes special privileges.

Both the doctrine of individual production, as capitalist economists developed it, and also the doctrine of social production, as communist economists developed it, failed to recognize the part which special privilege played in making exploitation possible. The legalization of the seizure of the commons in the villages of England by the landed nobility drove small farmers off the land; there followed the surplus of labor which made it possible to push down wages to a subsistence level. The later enactment of protective tariffs enabled the factory owners to exploit the consuming public by making foreign competition virtually impossible.

Most of the great fortunes have come into existence because of these inexcusable special privileges. Read Meyer's *History of Great American Fortunes.* True, some were made without benefit of special privileges (Henry Ford, Thomas A. Edison, Marshall Field, and John Wanamaker, for example). But most of the great American fortunes were made by ruthless buccaneers who took advantage of the special privileges politicians were delighted to dispense in return for help in attaining office and the perquisites office-holding provided. Most of the early great American fortunes in the North were made in land speculation and in the South both in land and slavery. Then came the tariff and railroad fortunes; the coal, oil, and mining fortunes; the public utility fortunes; the stock promotion and investment banking fortunes.

It is sad in the modern world, with all its institutions of learning, the relatively simple truth about the Possessional Problem is not taught. And it is not taught because the modern educational curriculum is not problem-centered. As a result, the existing methods of dealing with this Problem are never evaluated in terms of the basic problems to which they purport to be the solutions.

REFERENCES

Fideistic Solutions

Bhave, Vinoba, *Sarvodaya and Communism,* Sarva Seva Sangh, Benares; Bhoodan Yasna, Navajivan Press, Ahmedabad, India, [1957].

Narayan, Jayaprakash, *A Picture of Sarvodaya Social Order,* Sarvodaya Prachuralaya, Tanjore, 1961.

Tawney, R. H., *Religion and the Rise of Capitalism,* Harcourt, Brace and Co., N.Y., 1926.

Pragmatic Solutions

Agar, Herbert, *Who Owns America?,* Houghton Mifflin & Co., N.Y., 1936.

Berle, Adolf A., Jr., *The Modern Corporation and Private Property,* Macmillan, N.Y., 1932.

Brandeis, Louis, *Other People's Money and the Banker's Use of It,* Stokes Co., N.Y., 1933.

Burnham, James, *Suicide of the West, the Meaning of Liberalism,* John Day Co., N.Y., 1965.

Engels, Friedrich, *Origin of the Family, Private Property, and the State,* Lawrence & Wishart, Ltd., London, 1941.

Foreign Policy Association, *The Population Problem and World Depression,* N.Y., 1936.

Heaton, Herbert, *Economic History of Europe,* Harper, N.Y., 1936.

Prentice, E. Parmalee, *Hunger and History,* Harper, N.Y., 1939.

Taussig, F. W., *Principles of Economics,* Macmillan, N.Y., 1939.

Wolfe, Bertram D., *Marxism: One Hundred Years in the Life of a Doctrine,* Dial Press, N.Y., 1965.

Philosophic Solutions

Belloc, Hilaire, *An Essay on the Restoration of Property,* The Distributist League, London, 1936.

Chesterton, Gilbert, *The Common Man,* Sheed and Ward, London, 1950.

Corey, Lewis, *The Crisis of the Middle Class,* Covici, Firede, N.Y., 1935.

Gandhi, H. K., *Trusteeship,* Navajivan Pub. Co., Ahmedabad, India.

Geiger, George R., *The Theory of the Land Question,* Macmillan, N.Y., 1936.

George, Henry, *Progress and Poverty,* Garden City Pub. Co., N.Y., 1926.

Gesell, Silvio, *The Natural Economic Order,* Crusade Publishing Co., Denver, Co. 1895.

Hayek, F. H., *The Pure Theory of Capital,* Routledge and K. Paul, London, 1952.

Howe, Frederick C., *Denmark, the Cooperative Way,* Coward-McCann, N.Y., 1936.

Millay, Edna St. Vincent, *Aria do Capo,* Harper & Bros., N.Y., 1920.

Narayan, Jayaprakash, *Picture of Sarvodaya as a Social Order,* Sarva Seva Sangh, Benares, India: from *Socialism to Sarvodaya,* Sarva Seva Sangh, Benares, In.

Quesnay, Francois, *Oeuvres Economiques et Philosophiques,* Dr. J. Baer & Co., Frankfort, 1888.

Swann, Robert S., et al., *The Community Land Trust: A Guide to a New Model for Land Tenure in America,* Institute for Community Economics, Cambridge, Mass., 1972.

Plowboy Interview

Dr. Ralph Borsodi

Mother Earth News
(1974)

PLOWBOY: Dr. Borsodi, you've lived a rich and full life and your many achievements have been copiously documented by the press . . . yet, in at least one important area, you appear to be a man of mystery: No one seems to know just how old you are.

BORSODI: No, well I don't know myself. I think I was born in either 1886 or '87. The only documented evidence of age I have is my passport, which shows me to be 88 . . . upon the testimony of my older brother.

PLOWBOY: I understand you were born in New York City and grew up there, but that you were educated by your parents rather than enrolled in the city's public school system.

BORSODI: Well, my parents took me to Europe when I was four or five and I lived there several years under their tutelage. I remember, though—and you're asking me to recall things that took place a long time ago—that I did go to school in New York for at least a few months when we returned from Europe. I attended public school for just a short time, and I went to private schools from then on.

PLOWBOY: Is that where you got your training in economics?

BORSODI: No . . . well, let me explain something about my educational history before I answer that. Curiously enough, you see although I've been sporting both a Master of Arts and a doctorate in recent years—I've never had a Bachelor of Arts degree . . . which, of course, is supposed to come first. I did a lot of studying in my youth, but my formal education was very sketchy. I was introduced to economics by working for my father, who was a publisher and who had connections in the field of advertising. That was my first job—I was just a boy—and it opened my eyes in many ways. It was while I was there, too, that I became interested in the idea of homesteading. My father wrote the introduction to *A Little Land and a Living*. This was a book about farming for self-sufficiency written by Bolton Hall. He was a very distinguished author and the book played an important part in the back-to-the-land movement that took place during the banking panic of 1907. Now I'd been raised in the city and in these private schools and this was the first

---

time I was at all conscious of the fact that there was another way of living. My father had some land in Texas then and, compared to today, the state was a brand new country at that time. So, with an equally new awareness of what life could be, I moved out there in 1908 and began to spread my wings a little.

PLOWBOY: That must have been when you started to develop your theories about decentralist patterns of life.

BORSODI: Well, I guess it began about then . . . but I didn't really become conscious of the question of *patterns of living* until much later. I had come back to New York, you see, and I had a wife and two sons and I was working as an economic consultant for Macy's and some other marketing firms. Then, in 1920, there was a great housing shortage in the city and the home we were living in was sold right out from under us. So we left. I moved my family out of New York in 1920 in a deliberate effort to get away from urbanism.

PLOWBOY: You were launched upon your whole life's course, then, by a housing shortage.

BORSODI: Yes, yes . . . but I also left the past behind for another very good reason. My first wife was raised on a farm in Kansas and I knew that I could draw on her experience. With my wife's help I would be able to do things in the country that my city background would have made it extremely difficult for me to do alone. My theory was that it was possible to live more comfortably in the country than in the city. We wanted to experiment with building and making things for ourselves . . . to have some security independent of the fluctuations of the business world.

PLOWBOY: You were trying to become self-sufficient?

BORSODI: Yes, we put almost all our savings into the down payment on a little place—we called it Seven Acres—in Rockland County, an hour and three-quarters from New York City. I continued to work in the city and we made monthly payments out of my salary while we rebuilt an old barn on the property into a house. By the end of the second year we had a very comfortable and modern homestead.

PLOWBOY: And you were relishing this comfort when others were becoming desperate! I think you've written about that time in these words: ". . . in the depression of 1921, when millions were tramping the streets of our cities looking for work, we began to enjoy the feeling of plenty which the city dweller never experiences." You were, of course, referring in part to the fact that you had plenty of eggs, meat, milk, fruit and vegetables to eat while many others had none.

BORSODI: Yes.

PLOWBOY: Your experiment, then, was an immediate success.

BORSODI: It was. So much so that we soon outgrew our first homestead. In 1924 we bought 18 acres—which we named Dogwoods after the beautiful trees on the land—and developed it into an even more satisfying place to live. I built quite a formidable home and three other buildings there from the natural rocks we found on the property.

PLOWBOY: Did you do all that work yourself?

BORSODI: Oh no, that would have been impossible. After all, the main building was three stories high and 110 feet long and I was still busy in the city at the time. I had contractors do some of the work on the big house. But I also did a lot on that structure myself, particularly on the interior—and I did even more on the other houses we put up. We were using a modification of Ernest Flagg's method of building with stone, you know.

PLOWBOY: How did you acquire the necessary construction skills? Did you learn by doing?

BORSODI: That's right. Practice and reading and observation . . . one of the best of all ways of getting an education. We've forgotten, you see, that at one time most people obtained their training by apprenticeship. Even doctors and lawyers, before we had medical and law schools, learned those professions as an apprentice to an already established M.D. or attorney.

PLOWBOY: Well I must say that you certainly used your "learn by doing" philosophy to good advantage. Not only did you teach yourself—with or without the help of others—to build stone houses but, in the course of turning Dogwoods into a self-sufficient homestead, you learned to milk a cow, shear sheep, plow, churn butter, operate a millstone, weave on a loom and do many other things. You even documented all this activity in one of your books . . . a book that you typeset yourself in the basement of the Dogwoods house.

BORSODI: Yes, well I didn't particularly do that to prove a point or anything. It's just that I found the book a difficult one to write . . . so difficult that I finally put a linotype machine in my basement and set the copy myself as I wrote it.

PLOWBOY: While we're talking about your books, I'd like to mention *This Ugly Civilization*. It was published, I believe, in 1928 and also contained a great deal of information about your experiences at Seven Acres and Dogwoods. The book was so inspirational, in fact, that the Council of Social Agencies in Dayton, Ohio, used it as a guide in setting up a self-help program for the unemployed of that city during the depression.

BORSODI: Yes, that's right.

PLOWBOY: I understand that you eventually became involved with the project.

BORSODI: In 1932 the people who had started that program—and they were some of the most distinguished people in Dayton—came to Dogwoods and invited me to come and see what they were doing. It was a very interesting program but they were having trouble raising the money they needed. After all, one-third of Dayton's working force was unemployed during the depression . . . you can imagine what the conditions were like. So I told the Council, "I know Harry Hopkins, who is Franklin D. Roosevelt's right-hand man, and I think I can get some money from Washington."

PLOWBOY: So you went to Washington and . . .

BORSODI: So I went there and I did get $50,000 and it was the biggest mistake I ever made in my life. I brought back the money all right . . . but with it came the federal bureaucracy. Harry Ickes, the Secretary of the Interior, federalized the project in the spring of '34. From then on it was just agony trying to accomplish anything on the Dayton project. I finally got fed up with it all and decided to try to start a nonfederally sponsored movement—that would get people out of the cities and into the pattern of life which I call "homesteading."

PLOWBOY: I think I should point out for our readers that when you speak of "homesteading," you're actually talking about the founding of self-sufficient communities . . . rather than splendidly isolated little farms.

BORSODI: Yes. I'm certainly not an advocate of what happened almost only in the United States . . . and almost entirely only in the U.S. Mid and Far West. When that part of our country was settled, see, it was done under the original Homestead Act. This legislation allowed you to locate on 160 acres—a quarter section of land—and gain title to the property merely by sticking it out and living there for four years. So what this did, of course, was to, sprinkle our West with literally millions of people living on isolated homesteads. And back in those days, when you only had horses with which to travel, you might not see your neighbors for days. You went to town probably once a week if you went that often. Now this kind of living is just as unnatural as packing people like sardines into the boxes of New York City. Man is a gregarious animal. He's not supposed to live in isolation. He should actually live in a community, but a community does not necessarily have to be a city. There's all the evidence in the world that the building of cities is one of the worst mistakes that mankind has ever made: For both physical and mental health we've got to be close to Mother Earth.

PLOWBOY: So where does that leave us?

BORSODI: The normal way to live—and I've discussed this endlessly in my books—is in a community of what I call "optimum size." Not too large and not too small. A place where, when you walk down the road, everyone says, "Good morning" . . . because everyone knows you.

PLOWBOY: And that's the kind of community you decided to establish after you left Dayton.

BORSODI: Yes, and I immediately saw that the center of such a community should be a school where everyone—not just the children—could study the most enormously important subject of all: the philosophy of living. I think that philosophy, as it's taught in the academic world, is a *completely* meaningless discipline. Philosophy as a way of living, on the other hand, is just enormously important. Abraham Lincoln once said that the future of America depends upon teaching people how to make a good living from a small piece of land. Now this is the technology we must study . . . how to make a good living—not just a Spartan existence, but a good living—on a small piece of land.

PLOWBOY: I suppose you began your new community, then, with one of these schools.

BORSODI: Yes. I established a School of Living back in Rockland County, New York during the winter of 1934–'35. Before long about 20 families began coming out regularly from New York City to spend the weekends at this school. How they scraped up the money to get there I don't know. It was the middle of the depression, you see, and some of these people didn't have any source of income. I remember when we got ready to commence building our first community. I told them, "I'll begin if there are enough of you who will put up a little money with which to start." Do you know how much those 20 families could raise? Two hundred dollars. The whole batch of them. They laid the money on the table and I gave them receipts for it and that's all there was. It was up to me to go out and find a way to buy the land we needed.

PLOWBOY: How did you do it?

BORSODI: Well, I had a tract I wanted to use . . . about 40 acres I'd spotted near Suffern. It belonged to a Jewish delicatessen owner in New York City, a man by the name of Plotkin. I went to him and I said, "Mr. Plotkin, you've got 40 acres of land and you know that now, during the depression, it's almost worthless . . . and it'll be years and years before you can begin to get back what you've put into that property. Now I haven't got any money, but I'll sign a contract for your 40 acres . . . a contract that binds me to pay you for one-fortieth, or whatever part of the land I'm using, every time I build a house on it. And each time I start a new building, I'll go to the bank and raise enough to start construction and to pay you for that section of the property." After dozens of talks with Mr. Plotkin and his family, I got them to agree.

PLOWBOY: And this was the start of . . .

BORSODI: Of the Bayard Lane community. I should mention, too, that Mr. Plotkin kept five acres of land for himself and joined the experiment. He and his wife, in fact, were still farming there when I paid Bayard Lane an "anniversary visit" in 1973. So the idea worked out well for them.

PLOWBOY: Did all 20 of your original families also join?

BORSODI: No, only 16. And as I've mentioned, they didn't have much ready cash. So I said to them, "The lots here should cost you a little less than $1,000 but you're not going to have to buy those lots. All you'll have to scrape up is rent, including taxes, of about $5.00 a month. Then I started raising money, mostly by issuing certificates of indebtedness which could be paid off with those rent installments. What I had done, you see, was create a land trust . . . really an economic, banking and credit institution. We called it the Independence Foundation, Inc. It was a new and ethical way of holding land in trust . . . of making low-cost, cooperatively shared credit available to people who wanted to build homesteads in our community. This institution made it possible to provide people access to land without their having to pay cash for the property in the beginning.

PLOWBOY: Great! But how did you then finance the construction of homes?

BORSODI: Well, most of the families who joined Bayard Lane were unemployed, but a few did have jobs or a little money. So we just put the first group to building houses and raising gardens and doing other productive work, and the second furnished enough cash to cover the basic expenses. We followed pretty much this same course of action a little later, when we started Van Houten Fields . . . a second School of Living project in the Suffern, New York area.

PLOWBOY: What happened to these communities . . . and were others built?

BORSODI: The two communities, of course, are still there. They've changed somewhat over the years—only a few families still raise the big gardens—but they're still there. As for others . . . well, World War II with its priorities made building materials impossible to get. It also put so much fresh money into people's pockets that no one much wanted to think about self-sufficient homesteads for the next 20 years. What with one thing and another, I gave up the Independence Foundation during the war and Mildred Loomis took the School of Living to Ohio. She continued to operate it there with her husband, John, until his death in 1968. Mildred then moved the school to Freeland, Maryland where it's still teaching today's back-to-the-land people the basics of doing for themselves.

PLOWBOY: Dr. Borsodi, if the mail we receive at *Mother Earth News* is any indication, there are now hundreds of thousands—probably millions—of people in this country who feel that today's urbanized and industrialized society just doesn't work anymore . . . that the so-called "system" no longer satisfies basic human wants, needs and desires.

BORSODI: Well, the dissatisfaction with "modern" society in this country that you talk about is nothing new. We've had it again and again, especially during and after great depressions, since the nation was founded. The unrest usually spawns a "back to the land" movement that catches fire for a while . . . and then times get better and we repeat the cycle all over again.

PLOWBOY: Why?

BORSODI: Why? Because the whole Industrial Age—which began roughly 200 years ago when Adam Smith wrote *The Wealth of Nations*—is based on false premises. Smith, you see, eulogized the factory system of production as the way to end want in the world. He pointed out that if you make things on a large scale in a factory, you reduce the cost of producing those items . . . and this is perfectly true. But Adam Smith completely overlooked what factory production does to distribution costs. It pushes them up. Goods cannot be manufactured in a factory unless raw materials and fuel and workers and everything else are brought there. This is a distribution cost. And then, after you've put together whatever you're making in that plant, you've got to ship it out to the people who consume it. That can become expensive too. Now I've produced everything from tomato crops to suits of clothing which I've hand spun on my own homestead and I've kept very careful records of every expense that went into these experiments. And I think the evidence is pretty clear that probably half to two-thirds—and it's nearer two-thirds—of all the things we need for a good living can be produced most economically on a small scale . . . either in your own home or in the community where you live. The studies I made at Dogwoods—the "experiments in domestic production"—show conclusively that we have been misled by the doctrine of the division of labor. Of course there are some things—from my standpoint, a few things—that cannot be economically produced in a small community. You can't make electric wire or light bulbs, for example, very satisfactorily on a limited scale. Still, virtually two-thirds of all the things we consume are better off produced on a community basis.

PLOWBOY: What about quality?

BORSODI: Well, when you make things for your own use you try to produce the best you can. And when people produce items that are traded face to face, there's a certain human relationship and a pride of craftsmanship that keeps the quality high. But when you just set up machines and run them solely for the purpose of making a profit, you usually begin to exploit the consumer. That's what's happening right now and it's one of the reasons so many people feel cheated by our industrialized system.

PLOWBOY: But still the emphasis on factory production goes on.

BORSODI: Oh yes. They even apply it to farming now. They call it agribusiness. I see it right here in New Hampshire with the dairy farms. The School of Agriculture at the University of New Hampshire and other "experts" teach the little farmers that it doesn't pay them to have a cow or two to produce their own milk. And this is just not true. Let me call your attention to some curious facts about a cow: In the first place, to estimate the value of such an animal, the average person would say, "Well, let's figure out what its milk is worth." Now, you can put a dollar value on that milk, but you can't put just a dollar value on it. Because, when you produce your own, it's pure and fresh milk . . . unlike the bottled variety which is all processed and pasteurized and treated and, in my opinion, inferior. So you have the milk. But that cow also produces manure and, if you have enough manure, you don't need to buy any chemical fertilizer. Also, you've got to consider the value of the calf which that cow has each year. By the time you add up all the income a farmer can realize from a cow, you'll see that the return on his investment is quite substantial . . . provided that he and his family use the milk. If, on the other hand, the farmer sells the milk at wholesale prices to someone else, then he gets only a little return for it which he must spend at retail prices for the things he wants. The milk is worth the most to him, in other words, when he uses it. This is an example of the economic law that I discussed in my book *The Distribution Age*. It has to do with distribution costs. When you buy milk, you pay very little for the milk itself. Most of what you pay is for the distributing of the product. When you produce your own milk, however—or your own vegetables—you don't have such costs. This is the story which should be told in the schools of agriculture . . . instead of the miseducation that those institutions teach.

PLOWBOY: So. You say that—even though we've become dissatisfied time and again in this country with our increasingly industrialized society . . . and even though this dissatisfaction has repeatedly produced back-to-the-land movements— nothing has yet reversed our nation's trend to the prepackaged, energy-intensive, dehumanized existence . . . at least partly because our institutions teach people to value an industrialized over an agrarian society.

BORSODI: As long as the universities—particularly the schools of agriculture—extol the values of urbanism and industrialism, it's like trying to roll a stone uphill whenever you attempt to show people the virtues of the more nearly self-sufficient life. Every generation, you see, is taught to think of homesteading as something that is past and romantic and best forgotten. So the real battle is not in finding individuals who've got the hardihood, the stamina and the ingenuity to make it on their own . . . but in getting the educational establishment interested in showing these people how to go about it.

PLOWBOY: Is it just the educational establishment that's at fault?

BORSODI: Well, you must remember that we're educated—our tastes and ideas are determined—by far more than just schools and universities. The church used to teach us how to live, but the church has lost its influence. Schools then stepped into the breach and—as I've said—now often deal in misinformation but, as a matter of fact, it's no longer the schools that teach the American people what they want. We now have an even more persuasive educational institution ramming the goods that factories produce down the throats of our people . . . and that educational institution is called advertising. Now, very few individuals think of advertising as the real educator of the American populace, but, over and over again, it teaches us to want all sorts of things which are not good for us . . . but which make money for those who control the factories. The heart of economics, you see, is the satisfaction of wants. So it's just good business to create a want that only your factory can satisfy. But nature doesn't have factories, so it's obvious that the creation of such a demand is probably unnatural . . . wrong. And when you encourage people to want the wrong things, you're really creating a pattern of life—a way of living—that you shouldn't.

PLOWBOY: Still, despite your arguments with industry, you're not what anyone could call "antitechnology."

BORSODI: Oh no. I'm very interested in one kind of technology: the technology of decentralization and self-sufficiency and good living. Unfortunately, most of the rest of the modern world is concerned with the technology of centralization and mass production and money. Mostly money.

Do you know what the word "economics" really means? It comes from the Greek word *oeconomia* or housekeeping. The Greeks insisted that every recognized citizen had to have a homestead—or estate, as they called it—and the workers to support him so he could devote his time to public works and the defense of the state. So *oeconomia* was the study, the scientific study, of how to conduct a household.

It had nothing to do with making money. The Greeks had another word for that . . . *chrematistikes. Chrematistikes* meant "moneymaking" and they despised that. To make a living—a good life—was the work of a gentleman . . . to try to make money was the work of a menial who was looked down upon. We've turned this completely around. There are two kinds of income, see. There's what I call non-monetary—or imputed—income, and monetary income. On a homestead most of your income is imputed. You produce wealth in the form of goods and services but you don't get paid for it. Cook a meal at home and you're doing exactly what you'd do if you were hired to cook it for a restaurant . . . but in the one case you're producing imputed income and in the other, monetary income. And it's only the latter our world is interested in these days.

PLOWBOY: I believe you make a similar distinction when it comes to the ownership of property.

BORSODI: I very carefully divide the possessions of mankind into two categories: one I call "property" and the other "trusterty." Now property, by definition, is anything which can be owned . . . legally owned. But you know there are some things that can be legally—but not morally—owned. For instance, slaves used to be legally owned. The statutes of our states and the Constitution of the United States made it legal to own human beings . . . but no amount of legalizing made it moral. I feel the same way about the natural resources of the earth. When you make something with your own labor you have, so to speak, frozen your labor into that thing. This is the way in which you create a moral title to that thing, by producing it. You can sell it to somebody else and, in return for what he pays you, you can give him your moral title to whatever it is. But no man created the earth or its natural resources. And no man or government has a moral title to the earth's ownership. If it is to be used, and we have to use it in order to live, then it has to be treated as a trust. We have to hold the earth in trust. We can enjoy the fruit of the land or of a natural resource, but the land or the resource itself must be treated as a gift. A man who uses the land is a trustee of that land and he must take care of it so that future generations will find it just as good, just as rich, as when he took possession of it. A trustee is entitled to a return for administering his trust . . . but he must never destroy the trust itself. The moment you lay down this simple moral principle, of course, you make ducks and drakes of our existing method of treating the natural resources of the earth. The history of America is just one gigantic land exploitation . . . and very few people realize that this creates exactly the conditions which make individuals—in desperation—turn to socialism and communism. So long as land is available as the ultimate resource to which you can turn to support yourself, nobody can exploit you. It's only when all the land is expropriated by speculators or by people who are living on it that it's impossible to turn to the earth as the ultimate source of employment. Not everyone has to be a farmer, of course, but so long as land is available to those who want to work it we'll have none of the desperate unemployment that finally led Marx to propose communism as the solution to the problems that capitalism has created.

PLOWBOY: Then you would say that preserving the land and holding it in trust for the use of everyone, including generations yet unborn, is the only morally correct course of action . . . from the standpoint of both the earth and mankind.

BORSODI: Of course.

PLOWBOY: But we've never done that in this country. As a matter of fact, few—if any—cultures have.

BORSODI: No. Well, let me put it this way: The only worthwhile histories that have ever been written have been histories of civilizations. Histories of single nations are what Napoleon called a "lie agreed upon." National histories just aggrandize the story of a country. Histories of civilizations, though, are something different. Toynbee, you know, has written an account of 21 civilizations . . . and the interesting point about them is that every one of them died. As Toynbee explained it—and he does in historical terms—they were challenged by some problem, some crisis. Toynbee called these confrontations "times of troubles" . . . and if the civilization wasn't equal to the challenge, the whole thing simply collapsed. Now this is what we face. Have you ever heard of Spengler and his big book *The Decline of the West*? Well, it made a tremendous sensation when it appeared, because he predicted exactly what is taking place today. Spengler's thesis is that what every civilization seems to do is to pile up all the wealth and all the health in big cities . . . where they finally decay. And then there's a collapse and an overwhelming population decline and the people who are left are forced back to the land. Now, it seems tragic to me that we do not listen to men like Toynbee and Spengler. They've shown us what can happen. We now know . . . and, instead of waiting for a crash to drive us to a better way of living, we should use all the wits we've got—all the technology we've got—to develop that sort of living before the coming collapse takes place.

PLOWBOY: Is such a catastrophe inevitable?

BORSODI: Well, if we, as a culture, were thoughtful about it and asked ourselves what kind of civilization we needed to develop to accomplish these ends, we might ensure a good living for all our citizens and organize ourselves so that no calamity could take place. But we haven't done that. We haven't done that at all. We're on a collision course with destiny and the crash that's coming is going to make the last depression look like a joke.

PLOWBOY: Is there no hope at all of warding off the seemingly inevitable?

BORSODI: Well . . . maybe. Just maybe. The warning flags are up all around us. The energy crisis, you see, is interesting to me for this very reason. Because, for the *first* time, the public is getting a faint glimmer of the fact that we're living in the twilight of industrialism. The crunch is beginning. In another 20, 30 or 40 years all the oil will be gone at the rate we're using it. And that's not all, of course. There are other shortages. Nearly all the industries are experiencing shortages of minerals and materials. See, this is another point that Adam Smith completely overlooked when he wrote *The Wealth of Nations*: The factory system can only last as long as our irreplaceable resources are cheap and available. Well, those resources are never going to be cheap again and they're going to become increasingly unavailable. We're living in the twilight of industrialism and urbanism.

PLOWBOY: I think that many of *Mother*'s readers agree with you, but what can we do about it?

BORSODI: We must develop what a friend of mine calls a "biotechnology"—a *life* technology—to replace the inorganic technology that we've built. Instead of continuing to plunder our irreplaceable resources—which we won't be able to plunder much longer anyway—we must begin to explore the use of replaceable resources. Consider energy, for example. The oil is running out. Even the coal, which we still have a lot of, won't last forever. But the wind! You can use the wind to drive a motor and produce power and you can do so as much as you want. It doesn't lessen the quantity of wind in the world a particle and it doesn't pollute anything. We ought to have literally thousands of windmills all over this country. There's a whole new technology—in which we use wind, water and the sun—to be developed. All the money, all the research, now being put into an attempt to keep our existing inorganic technology alive is a colossal mistake.

PLOWBOY: Again, I'm sure that many of our readers agree with you. An increasing number of them, as you know, are already building biotechnic ways of living on an individual basis. They're setting up homesteads that are largely self-sufficient, supplying their energy requirements with wind plants and solar collectors, and otherwise trying to build satisfying life patterns that will allow the planet to endure.

BORSODI: Yes, of course, and those who are wise enough to build these little islands of security will—to a large extent—be able to withstand the horrors that lie ahead. But this may well be too little and too late. It may not be enough, you see, for a few hundred thousand—or even a few million—people to make this effort. I'm afraid we're going to have to change our society from top to bottom, and quite rapidly, if we're going to have a meaningful impact. Your magazine, *Mother Earth News*, prints marvelous articles about alternative energy sources and composting and so on. But that's not enough. You're just one small periodical. It's perfectly ludicrous that you should be trying so desperately to publish information that should be taught in every school in this country. See, I started the School of Living and you print a magazine, but it's not enough! Somehow, if we're really going to change the country—and do it in time—we've got to get the universities to teach the truth about this. The teachers in the colleges and universities have got the leverage we need. I've studied history . . . the history of social movements. And this thing we're engaged in is a social movement. Now, there's only one way of getting something like this accepted: institutionalize it in your educational establishment. Get the churches and the schools and the advertising industry, if you must have one, to make it the prevailing doctrine of your culture. Then you've got to start putting together the necessary support system . . . and let me illustrate what I mean by that. The automobile. I bought my first automobile in 1908 when I was in Texas. At that time there were no garages and you had to find your own machine shop or actually be a machinist if you had repairs to make. Or you had to send your vehicle to the factory. The roads weren't very good back then, either, and I had to buy gasoline at every country store I passed. There were no gas pumps or garages or anything that motorists take for granted nowadays. Today's low-slung automobiles, with their complicated parts and electronic ignitions wouldn't have lasted very long in 1908. Even if a few people had gotten together to design and build their own "vehicle of the future" back then and even if it had turned out to be exactly like a 1974 automobile, it wouldn't have had much impact. Not many individuals would have found it practical to operate such a car. The kind of roads it would have needed—the support systems—weren't available. Now, that's the situation we face today. It's not enough for a few of us to build our own windmills and solar-heated houses. We've got to come up with a technology that can keep equipment like this working for millions upon millions of people. We've got to develop the necessary support systems.

PLOWBOY: That sounds like a big job.

BORSODI: It is a big job. It involves changing every social and economic institution in the country. Many of the ills that bedevil mankind and the planet today, you know, stem from a statute passed by the New York State Legislature in 1811. That law, for the first time, authorized the formation of corporations for private profit. Up until then you could only organize a corporation for public, or quasipublic, purposes: The construction of a toll road or a bridge or something of that nature. In 1811, however, the New York statute granted corporations the status of artificial persons . . . with special privileges denied to natural people. And that was the start of the tremendous corporate exploitation from which we now suffer. There's a difference between classical capitalism and corporate capitalism, you see. If that 1811 statute hadn't been passed, we would live in a totally different world today.

PLOWBOY: So you'd change that law.

BORSODI: Well, you can't have a free economy once you've given virtually endless special privileges to various corporations. I would abolish those privileges. I would also introduce a rational system of land tenure and a rational system of money . . . money that couldn't be inflated at the whim of politicians.

PLOWBOY: And you'd establish Schools of Living in every community.

BORSODI: You'd have to if you expected to decentralize society and make people self-sufficient. Living in the country, you know, has been called "the simple life." This is not true. It's much more complex than city life. City life is the one that's simple. You get a job and earn money and you go to a store and buy what you want and can afford. The decentralist life in the country, on the other hand, is something else again. When you design your own things and make plans about what you're going to produce and really live in a self-sufficient manner, you've got to learn . . . you've got to master all sorts of crafts and activities that people in the city know nothing about. But there's more than just solving the how-to problems. I've often said that if we're going to have a real rural renaissance I'd just take the solving of the how-to problems for granted. The first thing I'd provide would be festivals.

PLOWBOY: Festivals?

BORSODI: If you study the lives of peasants and farmers the world over, you'll find that their seasons the year around have been a series of celebrations. Even when they were shamefully exploited by the nobility—as in the Middle Ages—they always had their festivals. Sometimes 150 a year. They always had, in other words, a satisfying and challenging cultural life. Active participation in such activities is, to a large extent, denied an individual in our society. We're supposed to get our culture in the form of prepackaged entertainment and distractions . . . secondhand, at that, from one media or another. That's why we introduced singing and music and folk dancing in our School of Living back in the 30's. We want bread and we want good bread . . . but man doesn't live by bread alone. Don't underestimate that fact. We've got to develop a way of living that is practical and successful. But it's got to be satisfactory in a cultural sense too. All work and nothing but work makes Jack a dull boy.

PLOWBOY: Dr. Borsodi, thank you.

BORSODI: And thank you.

Ralph Borsodi, 1886–1977

Prophet of Decentralism

Bob Swann
(1978)

Ralph Borsodi's life spanned close to one century (he was over 90 when he died). Within his lifetime he lived to see the nation and the world change from a primarily agrarian world to a primarily industrial world. This was not a change for the better in his view. He often commented on the "madness of industrialism" and much of his writing and work was aimed at trying to show the futility of subordinating agriculture to the voracious demands of industrialism. Long before the recent proliferation of books and articles about the "limits to growth" Ralph Borsodi (in the 1920s and 1930s) had been pointing out laws of economics such as "for almost every increase in the efficiency and scale of production there is an offsetting inefficiency and cost in distribution." He kept pointing out that practically all of conventional economic thinking of whatever variety was only concerned with the problem of production. In his magnum opus, *Seventeen Problems of Man and Society,* he defined at least five of the major problems as being part of the so-called "economic problem."

Economics and Ethics

Among these are: Wealth and Illth—the problem of economic values, in which he argued that economic values are not different from other values and must be viewed from a moral or ethical viewpoint. He eschewed the modern economists' notion that there is a purely "objective" way of looking at economic values. Rather, he championed a "normative" approach to values which includes making "moral judgements about economic proposals and economic activities." He insisted that no economist, except a charlatan, which he called John Maynard Keynes, could advocate an economic system which required the government to "embezzle" the savings of its citizens through planned inflation with government spending in order to "solve" the problem of employment. He correctly predicted in the 1940s when the International Monetary Fund was set up at Bretton Woods that not only *Inflation Is Coming* (title of his best selling book) but that eventually unemployment would get worse also. While his predictions of increasing inflation plus unemployment took more years to come than

This selection originally appeared in *The Catholic Worker* (January 1978). It is reprinted by permission of *The Catholic Worker.*

he had thought, no one today would dispute its reality. What emerges today as the reason for this "grace period" is that we have been able to avoid largely the economic consequences of government spending (inflation and unemployment) up to this point in history because we have exploited the earth's resources without regard to the physical ecological consequences. As E. F. Schumacher (who met Borsodi twice and with whom there was much agreement) put it, "We have been acting as if there were an unlimited supply of earth's capital available—an attitude which no businessman would ever consider regarding his own capital investment." But the charge which mother nature has put on this unheeding use of her capital now appears as increasing damage to the environment and to ourselves. Moreover, the illusion that we can spend our way out of the morass is beginning to be clear to the average person—even if not to the government or to the economists who advise the government. Looking at the Carter administration programs, it would appear that nothing has been learned— perhaps nothing can be learned by governments which are simply destined to repeat the mistakes of the past.

Borsodi, at least, had little hope or expectation from governments, and advocated taking the power of issuing money (through debt mechanisms) away from governments and establishing a nongovernmental money system. This could be done, he believed, by having nonprofit banks issue "honest money." By honest money, he meant money which could not inflate or deflate because it would always be measured by a broad commodity index and always be redeemable in commodities of the index. He spent much of his last years working to help establish such a nongovernmental bank and writing about how it could work (these writings are unpublished as are many of his later writings). He was convinced that, unless some such movement to take the issuance of money out of the hands of government could be successful, all present economic exchange (at least in the capitalist world) would be in deep trouble in the face of impending collapse (primarily through runaway inflation) of present monetary systems. In this he was not alone as increasingly more economic prophets have announced the impending collapse.

Property and Trusterty

The second problem of economics which Borsodi tackled is what he called the "Possessional Problem." Here he contributed a major new concept to economic thinking which he called *trusterty*. All possessions, he said, could be divided into two groups, those he called trusterty and the other *property*. Simply put, trusterty includes all of earth's treasures (land, water, sky, natural resources) which humankind must utilize to provide its needs and desires, but which can only be used and never really possessed. Property consists of all those things which are actually fashioned by a person or are purchased from another person (in this sense a corporation is also a "person") who has fashioned them and thus are truly "owned." All land and resources must properly be held in trust by each generation and passed on to the next generation in equally good condition. Even if we exploit the raw minerals from the earth we must find a way to ensure that future generations will not suffer from environmental degradation or loss of basic resources for survival needs. While such a principle can be simply stated and understood (even by children), it has revolutionary implications regarding most of our basic institutional arrangements—starting with the legal notion of "fee simple title" to land. Putting into practice such a simple but revolutionary concept is, of course, many times more difficult. But Borsodi was always a man of action. Once he was clear on the direction, nothing could prevent him from taking action.

So it happened that in the middle of the depression of the 1930s, without any money in his pocket, he went to Suffern, New York, to demonstrate in practice both the concept of trusteeship of land and also his "notions" about small scale homesteading which he had been practicing in his own home ever since leaving New York City (he had already written a book on this experience, *Flight from the City,* recently republished by Harper & Row, as the new move "back to the land" began in the early 1970s). Approaching a landowner of a piece of land in Suffern which seemed appropriate for his needs, he suggested buying the land with only a note which he would sign to give the owner. Surprisingly, the landowner agreed and the first modern example of a Community Land Trust and homestead project was born—eventually twenty homes were built on the land. Borsodi didn't call it a Community Land Trust, and today we would refer to it as an "enclave" of land ownership rather than a CLT, which, with Borsodi's agreement, we have defined as a corporate entity which includes a broad representation of the existing community (or region) rather than only the individuals who happen to live on the land held by the CLT. Nevertheless, the legal documents, which ensued from this development, and which were worked out with the help of several lawyers, most of whom contributed their time to this innovative work, have become the basis on which we (here at the Institute for Community Economics which Ralph Borsodi, myself, and a few others organized in 1966) have created the rapidly growing Community Land Trust movement.

A Matter of Justice

But land trusts, in Borsodi's view (and mine), are not to be considered merely an effort to "save the environment," not merely to "preserve nature" from degradation, but rather are also and primarily an effort to bring justice into the distribution of land. As Borsodi says in his chapter on the "Distribution Problem" (*The Seventeen Problems of Man and Society*):

> In a badly organized society (as ours is badly organized in this respect) the pre-emption of land deprives the masses of the population of any alternative

to the acceptance of employment on whatever terms employment is available. In such a society, those seeking work act under constraint whenever business conditions create what is miscalled a "surplus of labor." Only when business conditions are very good, and the so-called surplus of labor disappears is the worker freed from constraints of this kind.

It was, therefore, the usurpation of land first by a few individuals and later large corporations which first created the "proletariat" in Europe and then later in the United States. If access to land remained free in Europe and the United States, even Marx agreed, the "proletariat" would not have been created. Land reform, then, in the Henry George sense, is what land trusts are all about, because otherwise we have only two choices—a move towards fascism of the right or a move towards a totalitarian form of communism. People will give up freedom when they are starving but when they give up freedom they give up the sustenance of the spirit. The very last day I saw Borsodi (that night he had a stroke from which he never recovered), he said to me: "I have only one problem with the land trust movement—it isn't going fast enough." Patience was not a virtue for which Borsodi was known among his friends but, then, he saw further into the future than most of us and saw the consequences of our lack of appropriate action.

While a critic of Marxism and a bitter foe of communism, Borsodi called for a decentralized society and a fourth way which was neither capitalism, socialism, nor communism. He called for a world in which the key "determining number" (because "no matter how good the system, in the final analysis it is not the system but the controllers of the system that count") would be rightfully educated, or what the Buddhists call "understanding right livelihood." By this he meant that those who must carry—even in a decentralized world—more responsibility for apportioning capital resources must recognize their true profession as trustees who only act for the good of the larger society:

> A bad system will make it easier for bad men to take advantage of their fellow men: a good system will make it easier to deal with bad men, but no system will ever be able, in the final analysis, to guarantee that bad men, because of the system, will apportion justly.

"Right education," then, is ultimately and finally, and first and foremost, the primary problem of society. But for that education Borsodi did not propose a change in the public education system. He proposed rather that education for living should be embodied and institutionalized in the form of a "school for living" which should form the central focus of every small community school primarily for adults not based on academic subjects but on the needs, the aspirations, and the dreams of the people it serves. A school which would inspire, yet also be practical, which would be closer to the folk schools of Denmark than American schools. But a school which would above all place the search for excellence as its philosophic ideal and its highest teaching—not the "bitch-goddess Success" nor the struggle for Power.

A man like Borsodi (or a man like Gandhi) is hard to define or relegate to one of the pigeonholes of the mind. Was he a "conservative"? In the true sense of the word—yes. Was he a "radical"? In the true sense of the word—yes, because he went to the roots of problems. Was he an anarchist? No, because he advocated, not the absence of governments, but the diminution of government (like Jefferson), or what he referred to as "minarchy." Was he a Socialist? Definitely not when used with the capital *S*, and yet holding of land resources for "the common good" would sound socialistic to many people. Was he for democracy? Certainly he was for a greater democracy and participation than even conceived within our present system, but his notion of "the determining number" might be considered elitist by many people who believe in pure democracy.

What we can say of Borsodi for certain is what he said about himself. "I may not have the right answers, but I think I have asked the right questions, and asking the right questions is often more than half of the problem." Perhaps, more than any other man or woman before him, Borsodi asked more questions and tested those questions and his answers against the best questions and answers which had preceded, or against his own carefully examined experience. Those questions ranged over every aspect of the human "problem," from philosophy and metaphysics through every practical and scientific aspect. But, I suspect that his greatest contribution as measured by history will be that he sorted out the many problems relating to what we call "economics" so that, perhaps, for the first time in history, we have adequate "tools" for thinking about economics. Of the seventeen problems of "man and society" (in his last years he came to the conclusion there was probably one more problem, making eighteen total), the "economic" problem comprises five problems, plus a link with the political problem—at least in modern society. But this link with the political problem is what Borsodi wanted to change, separating politics from economics as much as possible.

Ralph Borsodi's Principles
for Homesteaders

Mildred Loomis
(1978)

Ralph Borsodi (1886–1977) was the author of 13 books and 10 research studies. He was also physically active, a productive homesteader and a real doer who practised what he preached. He experimented and implemented on many levels—from good nutrition, through building his own home and garden; weaving his clothes and furnishings; organizing experimental small communities, a School of Living for a new adult education, and developing new social institutions: the Community Land Trust and a noninflationary currency, which he called Constants.

No one of today's specialty-labels encompass Ralph Borsodi. I am pushed to use more general and abstract terms—decentralist, liberator and human benefactor. This article will concentrate on his efforts to implement the community-use of socially-created values in land as part of his plan to encourage people to leave cities for more rural living.

Ralph Borsodi was never in public school, infrequently in private schools, and did not attend college. (Yet St. Johns College of Annapolis later conferred on him a Masters, and the University of New Hampshire, a Doctorate.) He was educated mostly by wide readings in libraries, and by his father, a publisher in New York City. Borsodi Sr. wrote the introduction to Bolton Hall's *A Little Land and a Living*, which encouraged living on, and intensive production on, small plots of land, and the public collection of site-values.

Ralph Borsodi Jr. joined the Single Tax Party which grew out of popular enthusiasm for Henry George and his two campaigns for the mayoralty in New York in the 1880s. Borsodi mounted his soap box in Union Square to exhort people to vote for the land-value tax. The Party named Borsodi editor of *The Single Taxer*. In it he discussed the need for a school to teach economics as George presented it, placing land in a category separate from capital, showing how the law of rent determined the law of wages, and how private use of land values resulted in the disparity of wealth— poverty on the one hand and riches on the other.

When still a young man, in 1910, Borsodi was sent by his father to dispose of some Texas land holdings. What to do with several hundred acres of land in the Houston area? He knew that this land was part of a "great Savannah"—in the path of progress.

This selection was first published in *Land & Liberty Magazine* (November/December 1978) by The Henry George Foundation of Great Britain. It is reprinted by permission.

His errand brought him both conflict and guilt. As people would come to this area, the value of the Borsodi land would rise. What price should he ask for it? Should he accept money which he had not earned? "Don't be foolish, man," a local hotel-keeper advised him. "Hang on to that land and who knows you might become a millionaire!"

Troubled, Borsodi bought a small-town paper, *The Rice City Banner*, wrote editorials, printed news, and discussed the land problem. After a year, he made a decision. He would sell the land at a modest price to a realtor. But Borsodi would go on to find ways to "solve" the land problem. The realtor would not worry about unearned increment from the land, and doubtless went on to pocket a large sum.

Borsodi returned to the East with a mission. Now, 1911, he saw Megalopolis with new eyes. More than ever he was conscious of ground space. On Manhattan's 22 square miles, two million people were rushing to and fro, on, above and beneath its surface, needing space and giving to land its fabulous value.

At that time New York City represented 20 billions of dollars worth of wealth. Half of it was in land, most of the value concentrated in a small core at the centre. A few blocks away was an ocean of squalor, filth and poverty. Who had title to that land? Certainly not the two million people working there. Probably a few large holders with familiar names—Rockefeller, Astor, Vanderbilt. Land bought and sold for hundreds of thousands of dollars a front foot! Millions of tenants paid rent each month with barely enough left over to keep body and soul together. To Borsodi, New York was a devouring ugly monster.

His friendship deepened with Myrtle Mae Simpson, a Kansas farm girl. They married in 1912, and Borsodi's father assigned them to a job in Chicago. Chicago's Loop was even more concentrated, though with more over-all sprawl, destitution, slums and ugliness than in New York.

Borsodi contacted Louis Post, editor of *The Public*, a journal devoted to Henry George's principles. Borsodi used its columns to challenge Socialist and Marxist ideas.

Then Borsodis took other radical steps. Myrtle Mae's anemia, the children's coughs, and Borsodi's rheumatism led them to investigate natural therapies. They turned to whole foods. Explaining it as best they could to the two boys, Ralph and Myrtle Mae gathered up the loaves of white bread and boxes of white sugar and packaged cereals and chucked it all into the garbage pail. In 1920 they left the city and moved to 16 wooded acres in Rockland County. They built temporary shelters and settled down to modern "homesteading."

They used rock to build shelters for chickens, rabbits, goats and a pig; and for the first of a three-sectioned home for themselves. They added a craft section for looms and weaving; a breeze-way for pool and billiards. They planted, tilled, harvested and processed vegetables, and in a few years berries and fruit. They were 80 percent self-maintaining in food. They felled trees and cut wood for fireplaces and furnace. They built a swimming pool and tennis court, and installed a linotype in their basement—Borsodi had things to say about the modern crisis and what to do about it.

In 1928 Borsodi startled the world by publishing *This Ugly Civilization*, America's first documented critique of over-centralized industrialism, which was widely read during the ensuing Great Depression. Because of it Borsodi was invited to Dayton, Ohio, in 1932, to deal with their overwhelming unemployment. Borsodi saw this as a way to extend "homesteading" as a social movement, and a way to implement a trusteeship, rental-form of land-tenure.

He proposed that families should return to the land: "Ring Dayton with many small communities of from 30 to 50 families, each producing their food and shelter on 2 to 5 acre plots. Let a Homestead Association of families hold title to the land; let each family pay an annual rental fee to their association rather than pay an outright purchase price."

Persons involved agreed. Social agencies advanced money to buy 80 acres. Independence bonds were issued to provide loans to families for buildings and equipment. Families applied, plots were assigned, individuals instructed in gardening and building: construction was begun. Suddenly the funds were exhausted.

To obtain more financial support, the only alternative seemed to be: "Borrow from the Federal Government." Borsodi advised against it. "Government money usually means government supervision and control. Government is to protect persons and property from harm—not to build homes. Keep Government out of business." Borsodi concluded that if the homesteaders chose government aid, he would withdraw and return to his homestead.

The homesteaders chose government funds. Borsodi withdrew, saying: "If we in the U.S. are to get a proper balance between city and country, and learn the proper function of government, we will need a new education." Family and friends helped him plan and establish the School of Living in 1936, near Suffern, New York. On its four-acre homestead, the school was at the centre of 16 family homesteads, on a 40 acre plot called Bayard Lane Community. Here, too, Borsodi initiated the group-title to land, with member-families paying an annual rental rather than a fee for outright private ownership.

Affairs went well; sixteen lovely homesteads surrounding the School of Living, where gardening, home-production and workshops in adult education were continuous. Educators, authors, homesteaders, and social-changers attended, from 1936 to 1945. After college degrees and social work in Chicago's slums, I studied with, and assisted, the Borsodis for the year 1939–1940.

One Bayard Lane homesteader, H. M., had good results with his homestead flock of chickens. He envisioned a thriving business of 1,000 laying hens in a 3-storey chicken house. But his contract under group-title to land prevented this. He would change the land-tenure back to private ownership. He was determined and energetic. By a narrow margin of votes, these homesteaders rejected group-tenure and reverted to fee-simple.

Borsodi resorted to writing and travel. In 1939 he analyzed predatory economics in *Prosperity and Security*. He described and advocated modern homesteading in *Agriculture in Modern Life*. Reluctantly he sold the School of Living building to a homesteader, and in 1945 moved its library and activities to the Loomis homestead in Ohio. He travelled to Mexico and India, studying and lecturing at a Gandhian University in Ambala. There he examined the village-title to land, wrote *A Decentralist Manifesto*, and began his magnum opus, a curriculum for adult education—the definition and analysis of *Seventeen Major Problems of Living*, along with alternative (including decentralist) solutions.

Returned to the United States, now past 80 years, Borsodi had a new opportunity to achieve his two most cherished ideas of land and money reform. A younger friend, Robert Swann, was in Georgia—hoping to prevent the racial tension from erupting into violence. Swann was appalled by the poverty, the helplessness and the illiteracy of both blacks and whites. "What these people need is an economic base," he decided, and turned to Borsodi for guidance.

"What shall we do?" he asked.

"Get the families on the land!" Borsodi replied.

"But how?"

For weeks Borsodi and Swann worked on what in 1966 was registered in Luxembourg as The International Independence Institute (III)—to teach and help establish the trusteeship of land. III is a quasipublic cooperative corporation, in which individuals become members and in which they may invest funds. The III secures land, by purchase or gift, and then declares the land in trust, never to be sold again. The III is taking land, now, and making it available to users for an annual rental to the Trust. It does not wait until voters in a country, state or nation are persuaded to use the socially-created value of land for the community in lieu of taxes. It proceeds to secure land and turn it as a "gift to mankind" for users who contract to use it ecologically.

FROM *Peace, Civil Rights, and the Search for Community*

An Autobiography

Robert Swann
(2001)

A Gramdan (Community Land Trust) Movement for the United States

Having spent so much time in the South made me aware not only of the pervasive racial inequalities but also of the economic realities that blacks continued to face even after legal segregation ended. I was determined to work for a more equitable solution to land ownership and economic security. Part of the answer seemed to lie in a land-reform program that would restore at least some of the land that had been taken from blacks after the Civil War. I began to put Borsodi's model together with Vinoba Bhave's Gramdan or "village gift" program in India.

After Gandhi was murdered in 1948, the spiritual leadership of the nonviolent independence movement in India fell into the hands of Vinoba Bhave according to Gandhi's wishes. Vinoba was a scholarly man, who knew at least six languages. He had the reputation of a saint and was not active in the political wing of the independence movement as was J. P. Narayan. With Gandhi's death, violence broke out in several provinces or states of India, in part stimulated by the communists, who were agitating against landlords in these areas where landlords controlled all the land and the number of landless was increasing.

At the urging of his followers Vinoba decided to go to one of the places (I believe it was Kerala) where the situation was becoming serious. Although he didn't have any idea of how to prevent the violence, he went to one village and asked the villagers what the problem was. One villager stood up and said simply, "We need land." So Vinoba put a direct question to those assembled, not really expecting to get a positive reply. Pointing to the man who had just spoken, he said, "My brother here is without land. Who can give me some land for him?" To Vinoba's amazement, one man stood up and said he had some land he could give. Then another stood up and another until there was enough land for at least two or three landless farm families. What to do now? Vinoba said he would act as trustee for the land, and his followers worked out a

---

These excerpts are from an oral history by Robert Swann that was recorded and transcribed by the E. F. Schumacher Society and posted on its web site. They are printed by permission of E. F. Schumacher Society, 140 Jug End Road, Great Barrington, MA, 01230. www.smallisbeautiful.org.

plan for how to divide it among the landless. This was the beginning of the Boodan or "land gift" program.

Vinoba began a walk (a Padyatra) through the villages, stopping in each one to ask for gifts of land. Gifts of land continued to be made, but an unexpected problem developed. When the land was transferred, the landless were given deeds; the new owners, however, didn't have the means to buy tools, fertilizer, or seeds nor did they have credit to purchase any. All they had was the value of the land itself. What happened is typical of most land-reform programs: in desperation the landless sold the land, and after the money ran out they ended up back on the streets of Calcutta begging. Vinoba realized something must change, and thus began the Gramdan or village-gift movement, whereby, as I noted, the land is given to the village as a whole, which acts as trustee for the land. It is actually the village elders who are the trustees. They see to it that the land is fairly distributed among the landless, who hold a lease to use the land, and they help individual farmers to purchase seeds, fertilizer, etc. Most importantly, *the trustees cannot sell the land.* Vinoba continued to walk through the villages for over ten years, during which time thousands of acres of land were donated and 10,000 villagers benefited from the Gramdan movement. When I talked with Vinoba in 1978 at his ashram in India, he assured me that the Gramdan movement was alive and well.

The answer to how a land-reform movement could happen in the United States emerged from the next large-scale project that CNVA [Committee for Non-Violent Action] initiated in 1965 when we sponsored a long walk from Quebec to Guantanamo in Cuba. The walkers never made it to Cuba because the police chief in Albany, Georgia, arrested all thirty of them, but through this confrontation there appeared the man who could start the Community Land Trust movement in the South. He was Slater King, a cousin of Martin Luther King, Jr., and a key leader in the civil rights movement in Albany.

As one person put it, "If Slater had been white, he would have been the mayor of Albany." The police chief, known as the toughest chief in the South, arrested the marchers on grounds that they were violating a local law against "racial mixing." All thirty went on a fast in jail. Tough as the chief was, he let them out in thirty days. They proceeded to walk together through the streets of Albany, breaking down segregation there for the first time ever. The marchers won over the hearts of the black community. The joy at their release was felt everywhere. For Slater, this was the first victory he, as head of the Albany movement, had tasted, and it helped open him to the idea of a Gramdan movement in the South. Thus began my close working relationship with Slater.

As a first step, Faye Bennett (director of the National Sharecroppers Fund), Slater King, his brother C. B. King, and I decided to learn more about the land trust concept. With the help of the Jewish National Fund and the National Sharecroppers Fund, we were able to plan a trip to Israel, where a similar land reform movement had been in existence since the late 1800s. Members of the Zionist movement familiar with Henry George (author of *Progress and Poverty*) had established the Jewish National Fund around 1890 to purchase land from Arab land owners in Israel and lease it to Zionists who were coming to set up kibbutzim (cooperatives) and moshavim (villages) in Israel at that time. Their objective, following Henry George, was to prevent land speculation—with all the newcomers land prices were being driven up. They were successful in holding the price of land down until after Israel became an independent country in 1948. At that point the Jewish National Fund decided to raise the lease price and buy the land with money raised from private owners. This would prevent a relatively few land owners from becoming rich at the expense of the refugees arriving from Europe after the war. We arranged for a group of civil rights leaders to visit Israel in 1967 and spend a month with our host, the Jewish National Fund, studying the Israeli example. When we returned, Slater set out to locate a large tract of land for a model community land trust, which we called New Communities.

New Communities—5000 Acres and $1,000,000

Because Slater was a real estate agent, he was familiar with land availability in the Albany area. Eventually he located a 5000-acre former plantation outside of Albany called Featherfold Farm, at the price of approximately $1,000,000. On such a tract we could put several hundred homes and still have plenty of land for farming. In Israel this is called a Moschav Shitivi—a village with small homesteads of half an acre each clustered around a village center and large, cooperatively-farmed fields surrounding the village. This model was adopted by the civil rights leaders as the best way to relocate families on the land.

The main problem was how to raise $1,000,000. Faye Bennett and I (the only other white person on the trip to Israel) arranged a $50,000 one-year option with her organization. We set out to raise the money with the one-year deadline at our backs. Fortunately Slater had many friends from his work in the civil rights movement and from his years as a student at Oberlin College. One of these friends was Chester Carlson, the inventor of Xerox and a multimillionaire. He was very interested in the project and offered to give the money for the land on one condition—that Slater and I should first meet with the Fellows at the Center for the Study of Democratic Institutions. The Center had been established by Robert Hutchins, formerly President of the University of Chicago, where the Great Books method of education started. We agreed, of course, and flew out to Santa Barbara with great expectations. Here was the chance to dialogue with these distinguished Fellows. But most important was the million dollars.

At the Center W. H. ("Ping") Ferry acted as liaison for us. Hutchins arranged an evening meeting with ten or twelve of the Fellows around a large table. The dialogue went well, with several constructive suggestions offered to improve our proposal. But before the meeting began, Ping asked us to come into an adjoining room and relayed a message he had just received that our benefactor had died suddenly a few hours before! This was the first disappointment in our quest to raise the money, but not the last.

The next disappointment came when a promised grant from Lyndon Johnson's War on Poverty program failed to materialize. The story is that Robert Kennedy had managed to have a twenty-million-dollar fund set aside within the Office of Equal Opportunity (OEO) for programs to help poor people, primarily in the South. What was unique about this fund was that it was designed to prevent racist governors from blocking such grants for the South—as they had been doing by refusing to approve the grants. Bobby Kennedy's fund removed the requirement of approval.

With the help of friends inside and outside of government we managed to get a commitment from the OEO for $1,000,000 from the Kennedy Fund. The only provision was that within a year's time we do a feasibility study, for which we were given a $100,000 planning grant to be administered by McClaughry and Associates. We completed the study, and although the plan was approved, we never saw the million dollars. Slater King had been killed in a car accident, and without his leadership in Albany the OEO staff probably questioned the ability of other local leaders, in particular Reverend Charles Sherrod, to manage such a large project effectively.

We still had the option on the land, however, and we set out to raise the loan money from private sources. We had to patch it together with $20,000 here and $50,000 there, mostly from Church groups who were ready to "put their money where their hearts were." Out of this experience came the idea of a nonprofit Community Investment Fund for the purpose of investing in socially responsible businesses.

Altogether we had to borrow over half of the million dollars, including a first mortgage with Prudential Life Insurance. The background on this is interesting. The two brothers who were the sellers of the land had a mortgage of $400,000. Customarily, such a mortgage can readily be taken over by the buyers. In this case, however, Prudential at first refused to transfer the mortgage on the grounds that when they had given a mortgage to a church several years earlier, the church defaulted on the loan. Because the church was a religious, nonprofit organization, Prudential decided not to collect on the mortgage in order to avoid bad publicity. Therefore, the company adopted a policy of not lending to a nonprofit organization, which they considered New Communities to be. It would be willing, however, to give a mortgage if New Communities were a for-profit organization. Fortunately we found a sympathetic Wall Street lawyer, who arranged almost immediately a for-profit "shelf" corporation to take over the New Communities corporation and then lease the property back to New Communities—all very legal. Now as a for-profit corporation, we had the approval of Prudential—and not only approval, Prudential increased the mortgage!

While the first mortgage from Prudential went a long way toward our target of $1,000,000, at the end of the day before the option was due to run out, we were still $50,000 short of our goal. But we did have a promise from a black church group in North Carolina that they would loan the $50,000. C. B. King, Slater's brother and also a lawyer, Slater's wife, Marion, and I were still in the offices of our Wall Street lawyer in New York. He had just received a call from the group in North Carolina confirming that they would have a $50,000 check in C. B. King's office in Albany, Georgia, before the noon deadline the following day.

It was late in the afternoon when I called for reservations on a regular flight from New York to Atlanta and on to Albany. I was told that all seats were sold out from Atlanta to Albany. After two more calls I located a private airline that could accommodate us. So far so good, but when we got to Atlanta and found the private airline, the manager informed us that the plane could not take off because the rear door wouldn't close. I asked if he had some rope, and after getting a reluctant yes, I finally convinced him that I could hold the door shut with the rope all the way to Albany, which I did.

The next morning we arrived early at C. B. King's office. Everyone assembled had an interest in the project, including, of course, the two brothers who owned the property. They were nervous and clearly hoped the sale would not go through because apparently they had been threatened by some of their neighbors. As the hands of the clock moved to twelve noon and past, the two brothers jumped up and gleefully shook hands, saying "too bad." C. B. King, however, called their lawyer aside, and after a brief consultation with the two brothers their lawyer announced that his clients would extend the time for another twenty minutes. At that very moment a messenger arrived with the $50,000 check. Now it was time for our group to cheer. Everyone, of course, wanted to know what C. B. King had said to their lawyer, but he said only that he had certain information that their lawyer would not want reported.

Tragedy marked the history of New Communities. When Slater was killed in an auto accident just before we took the option on the land, there was serious discussion about whether to continue with the project. With trepidation but as a tribute to Slater, the vote was to go forward. Then, one night only a year or so after purchase of the land, came another accident—a truck with its lights off blocked the road on which six key workers from the farm were traveling. They were in the hospital for months, which set the project back immeasurably.

In spite of all these setbacks the many people involved managed to hold on to the land for over twenty years although few of the plans worked out under the OEO plan were ever realized. This was a great disappointment because New Communities could have been an exceptional model for integrating large- and small-scale farming enterprises and creating small industries to provide long-term employment. Perhaps these models would have prevented the mass exodus of blacks to northern cities, where property became tinderboxes for rioting, drugs, and gang warfare.

During the period we spent raising funds for New Communities we were able to do a lot of "spade work" with church groups, foundations, and other nonprofit groups that had considerable money invested in stocks and bonds. Most of these investments were in securities considered "safe or prudent," but they were often with companies that manufactured products harmful to health and the environment or socially destructive. Our appeal to these nonprofit groups was to use an investment "screen" to establish criteria for investment from a social perspective. "Put your money where your mouth is." This became known as "social investing." (Morris Milgram was one of the early proponents of this approach, which he used to raise funds for his work in creating integrated housing.) Most of the early social-investment funds used what we called negative criteria (no pollution, no segregation, no pesticides or insecticides, etc.) We, however, developed what I believe were the first positive criteria for social investing, and New Communities was the first example.

There was considerable resistance from board members of these nonprofit groups, many of whom were bankers. They thought their responsibility was only to make investments that would earn maximum profits. Moreover, they were convinced that "social investing" could not, by its nature, be as profitable as "regular" investments. This assumption has proven to be wrong, and gradually social investing has become respectable as well as profitable. But in the 1960s it was still a "hard sell." Today billions of dollars are in social investments.

FROM *The Community Land Trust*

A Guide to a New Model for Land Tenure in America

International Independence Institute
(1972)

One Experiment: Organizing New Communities, Inc.

One of the more common questions in connection with the land trust concept is: How do you get started? One way to answer this is to offer the general guidelines presented in Part Two of this guide. Another way is to present in some detail how a specific land trust was actually started, which is the purpose of this chapter.

The particular example of New Communities, Inc., is used for several reasons. First, it is an example of an application in the United States of some of the important principles used overseas by the Jewish National Fund. Second, the authors were intimately involved in getting it started and so can speak from first hand experience.

We should stress, however, that we are not trying to create the impression that this is the only model for a community land trust but instead to show how one group met certain key issues and problems.[1] The applications are, of course, much broader. As a community land trust NCI is a tentative, experimental model, with no assurance as of this writing that it can survive and grow into the community envisioned.

New Communities, Inc.—The Early Years

The story of New Communities, Inc., begins with a man who was born in Albany, Georgia, attended Oberlin College, returned to help his father run a small grocery store, started his own real estate business, and then became involved in the civil rights movement of the early 1960s. Slater King was one of the leaders of the 1962 "Albany Movement," when Martin Luther King brought Southern Christian Leadership Conference (SCLC) staff and workers to Albany to nonviolently challenge the iron grip of legally sanctioned racial segregation in this Southern community.

From a concern with civil rights, Slater King moved to issues of economic justice. In these efforts he was joined by Charles Sherrod, the director of the Southwest Georgia Project, the rural counterpart of the Albany Movement, in nine adjacent counties.

This selection was published as a chapter in *The Community Land Trust: A Guide to a New Model for Land Tenure in America* by the International Independence Institute (Cambridge, MA: Center for Community Economic Development, 1972), 16–25. It is reprinted by permission of E. F. Schumacher Society, 140 Jug End Road, Great Barrington, MA, 01230. www.smallisbeautiful.org. Original note numbers have been changed.

Sherrod, trained for the ministry, had moved to southwest Georgia in 1960, during the early days of the Student Nonviolent Coordinating Committee (SNCC), as a rural community organizer.

In June 1968, under the leadership of these two men and with the sponsorship of the International Independence Institute and the National Sharecroppers Fund, a group of eight civil rights leaders from the South (Charles Sherrod; Slater and Marion King; Faye Bennett, executive secretary of National Sharecroppers Fund; Robert Swann, International Independence Institute; Albert Turner, coordinator of SCLC in Selma; Lewis Black, a board member of the Southwest Alabama Farmers Cooperative Association; and Leonard Smith, regional director of National Sharecroppers Fund) traveled to Israel to study land tenure practices and learn about the solutions to problems of rural settlement that had been developed in that country.

These eight people had all known one another through work in the Southern civil rights movement. Except for Sherrod and King, they had worked with the National Sharecroppers Fund and all felt the need to deal with the problem of land, after which the issues of housing and economic justice could follow.

A family friend of King's, a philanthropist who believed in their community concept, offered financial support for the venture and on the basis of this King was able to get a New York foundation to put up the money for the trip. (Unfortunately, the death of the philanthropist two months after the return from Israel greatly dampened the financial hopes of carrying on and generating broader support for the movement.)

The participants returned in July, enthusiastic about experimenting in the South with a method of land tenure for landless sharecroppers and tenant farmers similar to the *moshav shitufi* type of settlement in Israel that provides small plots for individual farming as well as encourages cooperative farming. The *moshav* model was selected as a guide for the land tenure model rather than the *kibbutz*, since the group felt the importance of maintaining the integrity of the individual family.

A variation of the *moshav* that the organizers hoped to adapt to a new community in this country would permit individual families to cultivate small plots of land on their own and also farm large tracts of land on a cooperative basis, thus increasing efficiency through mechanization. Unlike the *kibbutz*, however, individual families would receive portions of the profit from the cooperatively farmed land on the basis of the hours they work. The remainder of the profit would go toward the development of the entire community.

The enthusiasm of the group was reinforced by W. H. Ferry, a friend of King's at the Center for the Study of Democratic Institutions in Santa Barbara, California, who arranged a conference at the Center in September on the ideas of alternate land tenure. The conference was successful and well-attended, and succeeded in its purpose by giving the concept more legitimacy (and exposure) and moving the idea ahead.

Exploring the Feasibility of a Land Trust Program

Invitations to a July meeting to share ideas were extended to every key leader, organizational affiliate, and interested individual, resulting in a good representation of almost every Southern organization concerned with the land problem of blacks. Among those attending, who later became members of the ongoing planning group, were: Father A. J. McKnight of the Southern Cooperative Development Program (later to become the Federation of Southern Cooperatives); James Mays of Mississippi, a field director for National Sharecroppers Fund and later a member of the permanent board of NCI; Charles Prejean of the Southern Cooperative Development Program; James Wood and John Lewis of the Southern Regional Council; William Peace of the Southern Rural Project; and Leonard Smith, Southern Regional Director of the National Sharecroppers Fund. The meeting was held in Atlanta at a hotel, to avoid either political or organizational bias.

Form of Ownership: The Leasehold Principle

The initial discussion on land ownership raised both questions and concern over the issue of control and of lease arrangements. The idea of the leasehold principle—and trusteeship—can be expected to be resisted by individuals who have never had the chance to own land. Members of minority groups who have been excluded from land ownership over the years see ownership as the only way to gain control of both land and their own lives; the demand for "local control" is thus understandable in reaction to generations of exclusion.

Convincing some of the more militant blacks that the leasehold system was not antithetical to black control and ownership and that such a system could—and, indeed, would—provide land tenure security presented a problem. The concept of land ownership and private property was and is strong (even though ownership is usually only nominal, with land often mortgaged by poor farmers and then lost to creditors). Although history has shown that the leasehold principle is needed to keep people from losing their land; to prevent land speculation, absentee ownership, and exploitation; and to assure land utilization for maximum usage, people would need time to learn to accept this form of land tenure.

It was agreed in the meeting that there would be no subleasing permitted and that the land should be used productively to earn a living. The leaseholder would only lose his lease if he did not use the land productively; he would not lose his equity in his house or other buildings and equipment, as would be the case under forfeiture of a conventional mortgage.

The meeting uncovered additional problems: many of the people farming Southern land are old and any new program, to be effective, would have to encourage younger people to stay on the land or return to it. Basic needs in the rural South are land, decent homes, and a means of making a living. These have to be provided immediately to attract future residents. Other necessary services would evolve after the people met their basic needs.

A further exploratory meeting on leasehold arrangements in September adopted the following four motions:

1. The leasehold principle is paramount and basic to the land trust in the rural South; there shall be a National Board of Trustees which will hold all acquired land in trust. The Board will include in its membership users of the land, including present land owners and nonowners and representatives of nonprofit organizations; and that the Board will select and hire the necessary experts, who will, in consultation with the users of the land, submit plans pertaining to the productive and economic use of the land. If conflict in selection of plans occurs, the will of the users of the land will prevail.
2. The local group (users of the land) shall have the final decision in all areas of consideration pertaining to their own livelihood, except for basic principles specified here and elsewhere.
3. The basic purpose of the leasehold agreement shall be for the purpose of developing communities. However, this does not preclude the possibility of leasing plots to individuals.
4. The land will be leased to each family in the community on an equitable basis; the size of the plot will depend on the productivity of the land; leased land must be used productively.

The motions listed above are considered major principles of the leasehold agreement and cannot ever be changed without destroying the hallowed principles embodied.

Preliminary Organizational Structure

The early structure of the board was casual and flexible, carried over from the civil rights movement. Everyone who participated was automatically a member of the board. This flexibility played a role in structuring the community and continues to affect its operation with both positive and negative effects. It created what might be ideal conditions for participatory democracy since everyone present at a meeting could vote, but it was difficult to arrive at a "legal" decision because members were not identifiable.

At the September meeting on leasehold arrangements a three-phase program was proposed that would provide a preliminary organizational structure and actually launch the land trust movement. The phases offered and adopted were:

Temporary Board (Pro-Tem). Everyone who is now participating, and wants to serve, would become a temporary board member. Committees would be selected from this board, which would serve until a permanent board could be selected (approximately 6 months), and land options would be sought during this period.

Permanent Board. A permanent and more representative board would be selected in approximately six months. This board would include local people.

Actual field work to organize groups of people would begin. Work on planning communities would begin.

Total Involvement. Potential users of the land would become involved in selecting plans and arriving at other arrangements which would affect their lives under the leasehold arrangement.

The following committees were selected and immediately became functional:

Legal. Purpose: to work with attorneys toward incorporation.

By-Laws. Purpose: to develop by-laws that will govern the conduct of the organization.

Land Acquisition. Purpose: to arrange options and catalogue possible available land for sale; to acquire land when offered for sale as funds permit.

Fund Raising. Purpose: to raise funds for land acquisition offered for sale or option.

Committee on Permanent Organizational Structure. Purpose: to conduct any and all necessary business in the interim period.

The Process of Incorporation

A large October meeting was held in Atlanta to discuss the process of incorporation, the issues of structure, tax exemption, and election of officers.

LEGAL TRUST VS. NONPROFIT CORPORATION

The choice between incorporating as a trust or as a nonprofit corporation was discussed at length. Some argued that the nonprofit corporation would be less restrictive than a legal trust. A trust might require getting court approval on every transaction, while a corporation would be legally empowered to borrow money and pay interest to acquire capital for land purchase. A motion was adopted to set up a nonprofit corporation and apply for federal tax exemption. Six or seven Southern states were selected to be investigated to determine the one with the most suitable statutes for incorporation.

An attorney from Albany explained the steps of the incorporation procedure in Georgia: a *de facto* corporation is approved by the court as soon as it has been determined that it does not duplicate another corporation—a process that might take six weeks—and then it may begin operation. And although IRS tax exemption itself might be obtained in six months, it often requires a great deal longer. Five incorporators are required, furthermore, two of whom must reside in the state.

It was agreed that individual families would lease the land and pay a modest rent that would be used to pay off the loans plus interest. Leases would be made directly from the landholding corporation to individual farmers or settlers who will be using the land. Any land used and held cooperatively would be leased to the cooperative.

The meeting unanimously adopted the name New Communities, Inc., as first choice of several names submitted for consideration. (A second and third choice of names was also made, in case a corporation with an identical name by chance already existed.) The following subtitle was also adopted: "A nonprofit organization to hold land in perpetual trust for the permanent use of rural communities."

ELECTION OF OFFICERS

A slate of temporary officers was chosen for the positions of chairman, treasurer, and secretary, and a temporary executive committee was established, made up of these officers plus the chairmen of all the standing committees. The group voted that all board members would be selected for their individual performances and not as representatives of organizations, and that the board should consist of not less than seven nor more than 25 people. Permanent offices would be president, vice-president, secretary, and treasurer. The decision on the final number of officers and their exact titles was left up to the attorneys.

The temporary treasurer was requested to prepare a six-month operating budget for which funds would be sought as soon as possible. In the meantime, the group decided that about $2,000 should be raised for immediate operating expenses.

BYLAWS DRAFTED

The interim board met in Albany on March 23, 1969, to draft the bylaws after they had been read and discussed section by section. Permanent officers were elected: Slater King, president; Father A. J. McKnight, vice president; Faye Bennett, secretary; and Leonard Smith, treasurer.

EXECUTIVE COMMITTEE SELECTED

On May 10, 1969, the board provided for an executive committee by adopting the following resolution:

> It being noted by the Board that the size of the Board of New Communities, Inc., is such that a smaller working group is necessary to carry on the work of New Communities, Inc., between Board meetings, it is hereby resolved that an acting Executive Committee be and hereby is created and the necessary power and authority is hereby delegated to the Executive Committee to act on behalf of the Board of New Communities, Inc., between Board meetings.
>
> A. The Committee members will consist of the officers of the board of New Communities, Inc., and the Chairmen of the standing committees of New Communities, Inc. A majority of the number of members will constitute a quorum.
>
> B. This acting Executive Committee will meet at least once between each Board meeting and at such other times as is deemed necessary by its chairman or on petition of four members of the Committee.

C. The Committee shall have the power to act and carry on the duties for New Communities, Inc., whenever necessary. All actions to be reported to the Board of Directors.

Location of the Office

At the meeting of the interim board on December 7, 1968, in Atlanta, a major portion of the discussion centered around the location of the office and the scale of the trust.[2] A narrow focus might obscure the fact that the land trust concept has an almost universal potential; if the office were located in Albany, the trust might appear too localized and limit the possibilities for being translated elsewhere on a larger scale. But from a practical standpoint it did not make sense to have it in Atlanta, 180 miles away, since Albany was the vortex of interest, especially after the land decision was made. Finally, because the core leaders—Sherrod and King—were from Albany, Albany was chosen for the office location and later became the home of New Communities, Inc.

Financing the Initial Land Purchase

The May 10 meeting decided that a file should be kept on all available land, even though there was not yet money to make purchases, and agreed to have the Land Acquisition Committee find out what government land might be available for purchase (or available some other way) for the use of poor people.

Buying a large tract of land for a black-oriented community development project can be difficult anywhere, but particularly in the deep South. The task had to be done quietly, since it was more than an ordinary business transaction. The NCI acquisition was thus considered something of a coup since it is doubtful the land would have been sold—at any price—if it had been known what kind of project was planned. The reason is obvious: land, especially in this agriculturally oriented area, means power, and since the project was to be run predominantly by and for blacks, it meant black power.

In the late spring of 1969, the board decided to take an option on a large farm— Featherfield Farm, an old plantation owned by two brothers—about 30 miles north of Albany, Georgia. The property contained 4,800 acres; 3,000 acres were good cultivated land and the rest wooded. There were a number of buildings in varying states of repair, including six houses. The president of the corporation negotiated a one-year option on the property at a total sale price of $1,080,000 for $50,000, which was put up by the National Sharecroppers Fund. At $225 per acre, the price seemed good. This left $1,030,000 to be raised within one year.[3]

The board hoped that federal funds might be secured through one of the farm or poverty agencies to finance at least a portion of the acquisition. The Office of Economic Opportunity made a planning grant in the amount of $98,000, under Title I-D. This could not be used to purchase property, but the funding opened up access to expert legal and financial contacts that proved extremely valuable.

The property was already mortgaged in the amount of $400,000 from a major insurance company which agreed to increase this to $500,000. But when a Texas businessman put up personal stock in the amount of $300,000 in securities as collateral, the insurance company extended its mortgage to $800,000. What amounted to an additional mortgage in the amount of $50,000 was secured from a special fund of a Protestant church denomination, guaranteed by the Georgia synod of a second denomination. A small number of private individuals were able to assemble the balance of $180,000 in cash on a loan basis, guaranteed through a note from an economic development corporation subsidiary of still another Protestant church denomination. This corporation in turn was given a second mortgage to the property.

The insurance company, however, had a policy that precluded mortgaging the property of a nonprofit corporation such as New Communities, Inc., based partially on the reasoning that from a public relations standpoint it would be undesirable to close on a nonprofit group. In response, a "shelf corporation"—a dummy corporation set up in advance for just this sort of purpose—was dusted off, the previous nominal board members replaced by members of the New Communities board, and this "for-profit" corporation, Benenden Corporation, proceeded to purchase the property and continues to hold title.

All the pieces were now dangling: the major piece—the first mortgage—was secured by the land; the critical links—the church loans—were not possible without collateral of some sort. The final key to putting the package together was the idea of subordinating all these loans with at least partial backup in the form of Texas business securities.

In spite of the complications, the financing was arranged by late 1969 and a closing date set for noon, January 9, 1970. However, while all this was going on, as might be expected, local pressure was being placed upon the sellers, and by the end of the year they were seeking ways to kill the transaction. In fact, it was not even known for sure that the purchase could be completed until the host of lawyers representing all the parties involved had assembled and the checks were laid on the table.

The checks to close the deal were New York-drawn and had to be certified through the local Albany bank to be satisfactory to the owners and the lawyers. A committee of eight—lawyers and others—worked in New York to process the checks the day before the closing. The only flight that would get them to Albany in time to certify the checks the next morning left at 1:00 a.m., but when they boarded the plane it was discovered that a defective door might force the flight to be scrubbed. Nevertheless, with some ingenuity the flight took off, the fate of the New Communities experiment virtually hanging on the rope the passengers used to hold the door shut during the flight!

As soon as the bank opened in the morning the group went into Albany to get the checks certified before meeting with the sellers for the closing. By noon, the deadline for the closing, one church check was still missing; the sellers, already under pressure (and minor harrassment) from local people, as tension mounted became even more leery and at noon started to walk out. What followed involved more legal maneuvering: the lawyers for the sellers worked also for the insurance company holding the first mortgage. Since this raised a possible conflict of interest, as was pointed out by the NCI attorney, the sellers were talked into waiting. Five minutes later the missing check arrived and the papers could be signed. At last, New Communities, Inc., (in the form of Benenden Corporation) received title to several thousand acres of rich farmland in Georgia.

Of course, the story of financing New Communities, Inc., is just the beginning. A good portion of the funds used to secure land is in the form of loan money, so there is a very high interest burden to be carried, not to mention development costs. As of this writing, the struggle continues to develop new funding methods to reduce the carrying costs and attract development money. Work is being done on several . . . methods including inflation-protected "social investment" bonds and establishing limited partnerships for production of housing and other improvements, with shareholders taking advantage of tax loss benefits.

The Reality: Building the Community

Community participation has been a cornerstone of the New Communities approach to developing its land. Not only is the story of NCI one of committee planning sessions, but in an effort to bring together potential participants, leadership, and resource people so they might learn from each other, a "charrette"—a type of extended encounter session first used in France as a planning tool—was held in Albany in the late winter of 1970. Over 100 attended, including 30 potential residents, students from black colleges, and those who had so far been involved with the project.

Out of this and other meetings what appeared to be an effective "farm committee" formed; however, during the critical first working summer of 1970, New Communities was again robbed of crucial human resources by an automobile accident. The farm committee, returning from a meeting at the farm, struck a truck parked in the middle of the road. All four occupants were seriously injured and by a miracle survived. But, for that season at least, farm supervision was almost completely wiped out.

In spite of this second tragedy, substantial progress was achieved in 1970. During this first crop year 1,200 acres were utilized for various crops, including corn, peanuts, soy beans, watermelons, and hay. All of the existing houses were repaired as needed and seven families moved onto the trust land. One house was remodeled for a day care center and two others for housing volunteer workers. During that year of the highly publicized "Venceremos Brigade" of Americans who worked in Cuba on the sugar harvest, a less publicized "Georgia Brigade"—mostly students, some from as far away as Los Angeles and Boston—traveled to Georgia to swell the labor force. By the end of that year an educational program was launched for teenagers, utilizing another of the existing buildings.

Besides farming and education, various forms of industry are also envisioned. These include a horticultural greenhouse operation, catfish farming (three streams run through the land), recreational facilities, and processing plants for locally grown produce. There is a plan to establish ties between the local welfare department and New Communities community development corporation so that welfare families can participate in the community as worker-owners of the farm.

Whether or not these plans can be implemented depends on the availability of two key ingredients: stable leadership and suitable long-range financing. These two elements may indeed determine the very survival of the New Communities experiment.

NOTES

1. In the following account of how New Communities, Inc., was organized and financed, we have attempted to be as specific as possible. Much of the following material has been extrapolated from accounts of meetings. Quoted material has been excerpted from meeting transcripts. For additional information on the founding of the community, see Gottschalk, Shimon and Swann, Robert S., "Planning a Rural Town in Southwest Georgia," *Arete* 2:1, Journal of the Graduate School of Social Work, University of South Carolina, Fall 1970.

2. One of the charter petitioners, an attorney, explained that the principal office is the place where records, legal documents, and legal papers can be served on someone officially connected with NCI. The main operating office might be located elsewhere to facilitate a wider spread organizational thrust at a later time.

3. A short time after the option was secured, the president, Slater King, was killed in an automobile accident. This tragedy robbed New Communities, Inc., of a man who had been a key figure in its inception and development. The loss did not cause the program to founder but certainly handicapped its subsequent development.

FROM *The Community Land Trust Handbook*

An Interview with Charles Sherrod
Conducted by John Emmeus Davis

Institute for Community Economics
(1982)

New Communities, Inc., Leesburg, Georgia

Incorporated in 1968, New Communities was the first American institution to be shaped by the CLT concept as it was being articulated in the 60s. Soon after its founding the organization acquired a single, very large tract of agricultural land near Albany in southwest Georgia—a total of 5,735 acres, for a price of $1,080,000. Most of this sum was borrowed. Since that time the organization has been forced to sell a portion of the land in order to reduce this very large debt and relieve the burden of annual interest payments; however, the remaining tract of 4,387 acres still makes New Communities by far the largest landholder among American CLTs.

Another significant way in which New Communities, at least in its origin, differed from most recent CLTs is that it was not created by a single, geographically limited community. In fact, New Communities was founded by a group of people—most of them widely involved in the southern civil rights movement—who were concerned with the land issue as it affected the security and opportunities of rural blacks throughout the South. As the name of the corporation suggests, the original ambition of these people was to acquire land and found new communities wherever they could throughout the region. In this ambition they were influenced by settlement policies in Israel, where a number of new communities have in fact been founded on land held in trust by the Jewish National Fund. However, the very large commitment that the group made to its single acquisition in southwest Georgia has effectively planted the organization in that one locality, so that today, as a practical matter, it can be viewed as an individual CLT.

. . . It is in some ways a very simple and direct application of the CLT concept: The founders simply acquired as much land as they could, to make it available to people and to use it as a base on which to develop economic opportunities for these people. From the beginning, the fate of the organization has been tied to the initial acquisition. It is a situation that continues to hold both important possibilities and serious limitations.

This interview was originally published as a chapter in *The Community Land Trust Handbook* by the Institute of Community Economics (Emmaus, PA: Rodale Press, 1982), 39–47. It is reprinted by permission of Equity Trust, Inc.

*The details of New Communities' early history have been published elsewhere (*The Community Land Trust, *International Independence Institute, 1972). The following interview with director Charles Sherrod concentrates on the founding of the organization and the opportunities and limitations that it faces today.*

QUESTION: You were associated with the early civil rights movement. Would you talk a little bit about the evolution of your thinking—of how you went from working for civil rights to this interest in land and the founding of New Communities?

CHARLES SHERROD: I guess the thing that prompted me to think in terms of self-sustaining capacity more than anything else was knocking on doors all over the country—whether it was in Mississippi, Alabama, Georgia, or in Virginia where I was born. I was hearing people say the same thing time and time again. "What you going to do if I'm kicked out of my house? You young people are talking a good talk—this is a good thing you're doing—but I live on this man's land, and what am I going to do if they take my job, take my house? What am I going to do with my children?"

This was when I was organizing in the field and that was a resounding echo in my mind for years and years, a question that I was never able to answer: Who shoulders responsibility when it happens? It wasn't as if it was a hollow question, because right there before my eyes every year were examples of people getting kicked out of their houses, people losing their jobs and all security, contracts dishonored, children not being able to eat. So what could I do? There they were. And there I was—with my commitment, but no power; my love, but no bread. And with all my tenacity and strength of mind, I couldn't employ nobody. So years of that—on dusty roads, thinking and talking, riding through and looking at people's homes on plantations, getting kicked off plantations myself, perilling other people's houses and sustenance myself, just being on their plantation. The only solution that one could come to would be that we have to own land ourselves.

Most of these people have gone to every known agency possible. FmHA [Farmers Home Administration] wasn't giving any housing loans—only for white people. The Federal Land Bank people weren't about to give any—they were controlled by the white farmers. The ASCS [Agricultural Stabilization Conservation Service] committees were all controlled by the white farmers, who were the same people who were part of the establishment which gave birth to the Ku Klux Klan. So we didn't look to the existing structures of government, or government programs. We didn't look to any of those programs for aid for our people to get land, or to reclaim land. Of course at the same time a lot of our people had land, but they had it heavily mortgaged. Knowing farming and knowing nothing else to do but farming, they continued to do what they knew—at the same time wondering why they were failing every year. Of course we all knew the reason was the structures that helped farmers stay farmers weren't geared to help *small* farmers to stay farmers, or to hold land, or to reclaim land.

Actually, during the same time, black *and* white farmers were losing their land. But my knowledge was of the black farmers, the small black farmers principally, losing their land. It wasn't just crop failure or a failure to get financing that was the cause—it was a calculated attempt to *take* land from these farmers. In many cases, we found people paying taxes on people's land and trying to gain land by adverse possession, and other methods: getting people that can't read and write to put their X here and there, and taking that land; getting people to become involved in some get-rich-quick scheme, and losing land *that* way. Through the years we have documented many of these instances where well-known figures have taken land from our people. Those instances are what led us to think in terms of how we could sustain ourselves, sustain people who were being kicked off their plantations. In our area there are large numbers of plantations. Absentee landlords in Michigan, New York, California; large companies that own large tracts of land; and now there's a big influx of foreign landownership.

QUESTION: Why were people kicked off the plantation?

CHARLES SHERROD: Well, technology for the most part. Large machines. Monster tractors come into our area and do 500 acres a day. So no need for small tractors and tractor-drivers to work. The big cultivators and pesticides and herbicides we have—there's no need for pulling weeds and that sort of hand cultivation.

Long-Range Goals and Present Needs

QUESTION: What were your plans when you founded New Communities? What were the founding principles of the organization?

CHARLES SHERROD: One, to hold land. Two, to become self-sustaining, to have this land as a base from which we can allow small farmers some stability of their market. For production. For information. For transportation facilities. The economics of buying together, for example, to bring down the price of seed, fertilizer, and these other things that people need to farm with. Utilization of a large tractor by a larger number of farmers to accelerate the efficiency of the farm unit. These kinds of ideas we had in mind.

QUESTION: Have these changed over the course of time?

CHARLES SHERROD: No, they're still here with us. Meanwhile, the overriding priority is holding on to this large piece of land. And nobody's come to our aid to help us to finance this land in such a way that we can put part of the money that we make into promotion and development of the land. We haven't been able to *do* any development. We haven't been able to pay any consultants to do any planning. We can't get the fellows in government to help us. We can't get grants—I don't know where we'd get the grants from now to do planning and development. We got the people, we got contacts all over south Georgia, people who'd be willing to live on this land, people who'd be willing to hook up with our kind of idea—'cause it's good economics to them. We got the facilities here that a good number of farmers could use. But we are pressured to talk about *survival* and holding on to the land. Maybe our children will be talking about how they want to develop or divide the land or how they want to lease it—this part for farming, that part for industry, that part for something else. That sort of thing may be done by our children. But unless someone comes out of the woodwork it looks like we're going to be dealing with holding on to it and paying for it.

QUESTION: If someone did come out of the woodwork—if you had the money— what kind of housing would you like to see built?

CHARLES SHERROD: We've always wanted to build a large number of houses all at once, not one at a time. Part of the reason for not building just one here and there is that we were scared we'd put the stuff in the wrong place. But if we have some feeling that we're going to put houses in the same general area and if we get a big grant from somewhere, or some big financing to do a wastewater facility, then we could do 15 or 20 houses. Those kinds of things are not easily financed by an organization like ours. We have to get some help on that.

QUESTION: But you're thinking now of trying to build a house or two every year?

CHARLES SHERROD: Yeah, we gradually build that up, then we'll go after a large lump of money to tie them all together with one water source, one line for sewage, and one line for wastewater. We have those kinds of things in mind. But we still want to go into a *planned* housing development. We don't want to have it be just out here, out there, and out there.

QUESTION: You've had to sell 1,348 of your original 5,735 acres. What forced you to sell it?

CHARLES SHERROD: We had to sell it to hold on to what we had. We had an annual debt service of $203,000 and we were making about $100,000 clear on our farming, which was our only income. We had to raise the rest of the money every year. Some years I'd have to raise the total million dollars to refinance. Now we have to raise a debt service of about $150,000.

QUESTION: Who did you sell the land to?

CHARLES SHERROD: Private buyers. We held off as long as we could. People who were financing us were understanding—they thought they had our interest at heart—but they were also forcing us to sell so that they could get part of their money. They saw a great business opportunity to sell for $600 an acre land that we bought for $250 an acre. But we weren't interested in making money off the land in that way. We wanted to hold on to it. What people could have done, they could have cleared 1,348 acres for us. We could have clear-cut it, given them all the money for the trees and so forth. On top of that, in the next four years, we could have brought the land in production up to a sufficient level to satisfy them.

The Community and the Farm

QUESTION: Are any people living on the land now?

CHARLES SHERROD: Just a few houses, five houses. The people aren't leasing, not legally. People who live on the land don't have to pay rent. They keep the houses up. The houses were already here.

QUESTION: And the people are also part of the labor force for New Communities?

CHARLES SHERROD: Yeah, for the most part. Everybody's not. Somebody's husband may be working and the wife not, or the wife may be working and the husband not. If you want to be part of New Communities, you can be. If you don't choose to be then you don't have to be, even though you're on the land.

QUESTION: Are you employing people from outside communities?

CHARLES SHERROD: Everywhere. There's no such thing as *outside* to us. We're not an *inside* community as such. We *are* a community, but we are not a concrete community.

QUESTION: How many people actually receive a wage from New Communities?

CHARLES SHERROD: About 14—that's full-time. In the summer we might have 25 or 30, kids, adults. When the grapes ripen there might be 20 or 30 people just at that.

QUESTION: How are your farm operations organized? How are decisions made on a day-by-day basis?

CHARLES SHERROD: It is a controversy among us as to whether or not we should have a farm manager with all the powers that a traditional farm manager has. So far, our creative approach has won out. We have a meeting with the farm committee and decide how many acres of this we're going to plant. Then the staff gets together as a team during the week, apart from the farm committee, and speaks to the specifics for the week. Then, on Monday, when you're ready to go at it, our team leader—that's Sam Young—has the last word; he'll tell you to do this and you to do that. It may be what we said in the meeting and it may not be because, for instance, if it rains and we forgot to say in the meeting that if it rains we'll do such and such a thing, it may be different.

QUESTION: With your need to get as much value out of the land as possible in order to retire the debt, have you been forced to do things to the land or do farming in a way that you'd prefer not to?

CHARLES SHERROD: Well, there's not many other ways we can do farming. It's true, though, we wouldn't be planting certain crops right behind one another. We *are* forced, for example, to plant soybeans behind soybeans over and over—just because we have to make as much money as we can. We can't rotate with corn because corn is just too expensive a crop. We don't plant any more corn than we have to to feed our hogs.

QUESTION: You have a pretty sophisticated farming operation going here—a couple of hundred head of cattle, a few hundred hogs, 800 acres of soybeans, corn, grapes. Where do you get the technical know-how to put it all together?

CHARLES SHERROD: When we started out I didn't even know the difference between grass and hay. But we've learned. We've had people come in that knew about farming and technology. But in the long run it's cheaper to home-grow technology. You know you're going to need expertise; you know you're going to need it from now on. If you are an organization that plans to exist from now on, then you need to home-grow that expertise as much as possible, not rely on people outside. They say you've got to get a surveyor; then your architect's got to come in and he says you got to do this. A lot of that is just bull-jive. You can't tell me that with all the blue-prints they've drawn up in this country, with all the kinds of buildings, you've got to pay somebody when all you've got to do is change this and add something here and put it up yourself. If you home-grow these guys, you can save that money a hundred times as you need that expertise again and again.

QUESTION: But it sounds like someone like Sam Young already had some skills when he came to you.

CHARLES SHERROD: He grew up on a farm. His father was a farmer and *his* father was a farmer. So he knows farming. And his whole family was in the movement. So he started working with us, all through the 1960s. He was on my staff, and when we went into the New Communities project he just worked with it. He also prints. He went to school in printing, two years. He's real smart.

Did I ever tell you about Boll Weevil? This guy was over in Calhoun County. I was invited over there to help with school desegregation. I kept hearing every day about Boll Weevil, Boll Weevil. He'd been working for this white lady, working on her farm. We hired him. We found out he'd never been to school, but he could fix diesel motors, special equipment motors, transmissions, alternators, anything. Boll Weevil! He's got about 36 or 35 children, got about 13 living with him now. I think the first house we're going to build is going to be for him. He's got a large family. He lives in that block house there now.

Then there's Marge. She's a midwife, she's a taxi driver, she cures our meat, she makes soap—all those old ways of doing things that people knew to make ends meet. She knows leaves for various teas. All the old ways. She drives for over an hour a day to come here. She's also got a job as a deputy sheriff.

QUESTION: It sounds as if most of the folks who actually live on the land are there because of their commitment—beyond just a paycheck.

CHARLES SHERROD: Yeah. They understand what we're working for. They understand that it's not just them that's going to prosper from the land. It's going to affect thousands of people if we're successful.

The Larger Community; The Future

QUESTION: What kind of training have you been able to do for people who either work here on the land trust or who are from the wider community?

CHARLES SHERROD: First of all, we had to learn a lot of things ourselves. The things that we have learned, we've put to use. And by demonstration we've shown people what we know, and what we don't. So based on that, at various times in the past 10 or 11 years we've had seminars, workshops. We've talked about the various kinds of cooperatives that could be developed if people would get together. We've shown and talked about various federal guidelines that were current. And we've helped people hold on to some of their equipment. We've made small loans to various farmers where we could help them. We have sent some young people to school—through our contacts, and we have given some money at various times.

QUESTION: Will these students come back and work at New Communities?

CHARLES SHERROD: That's what we ask. Not many of them have come back, to be quite honest. But it's not too late, you know. For example, one student in Albany is a lawyer. We sent him to college, and helped him some in grad school. When he came back he didn't come and work with us in the way that we had asked him to—a year or two for free—but at the same time, we still have him. He's here; he's in the area. We can go to him and ask him this and ask him that. He is accessible to the people. So, while he didn't come back to us as an organization, he *did* come back home. That's good enough as far as I'm concerned. And there are other people. In our society, when a woman marries she goes with her husband, so we can look at some of our students we've lost by that. But they are in community-related, upgrading projects, so although we don't have them at *our* disposal, they *are* at the disposal of other poor people somewhere in the country.

QUESTION: How does the white establishment in this area regard New Communities?

CHARLES SHERROD: They're not opposing us now. There *was* a time when they *did* oppose us. They'd burn, and they'd fire at us; they threw one or two of us in jail. But at this point, they have accepted us. They even ask for our judgment on certain things. The white farmers lease cropland from us, year by year. People come and fish on our land, for a minimum fee—white people.

QUESTION: If you had it to do over again, do you think you would start out with as much land as you did or do you think you'd start out with a little less?

CHARLES SHERROD: No, I'd start out with as much as I could start out with. See, I've heard those arguments too. But, well, I say it like this: How many groups in the country have as much land as we have? See? Chances are we wouldn't have had it either if we hadn't been lucky to have a certain group of people together at one time, a certain kind of people together at one time.

QUESTION: Other people around the South, other organizations haven't tried to organize community land trusts. Why?

CHARLES SHERROD: Land costs money. It's something our folk don't have. If they did have, they'd buy land for themselves. They'd buy a car for themselves; they'd build a house for themselves. So also there's got to be political commitment, a deep philosophical underpinning, to move toward these kinds of goals, given our upbringing. There's got to be a commitment to the movement, a broader movement for a better life in our country.

QUESTION: Have you talked with some of the black farmers in the area about putting *their* land into trust?

CHARLES SHERROD: Not really, not legally. That'll come later. I've talked with some farmers, some people who have land, about willing their land to us when they die—instead of letting it go to certain individuals who really have no interest in it but to sell it and move to New York. These happen to be their children, so it's a hard thing to get over to somebody. But there *are* some people who, when I've asked, find it easier to understand and identify with the idea.

QUESTION: Is there still resistance to the idea of *leasing,* rather than owning land?

CHARLES SHERROD: Not resistance—why should I resist if nobody's imposing it on me? But if you try to sell that idea—the idea of personal ownership is more intriguing because we've grown up in a kind of greedy society. So you've got to overcome 20, 30, or 40 years of that kind of indoctrination. That's why anybody making the kind of moves we're making has to be *committed* to another way of life. Because we are continually shown the glittering of the individual approach, individual ownership, individual rising from rags to riches. *That* is success in our society. We have to write a *new* way of success, new criteria for success in our society.

QUESTION: And this is what you're trying to do with New Communities?

CHARLES SHERROD: This is what I'm trying to do with my children and my other contacts and people who are part of New Communities.

Stories from an Appalachian Community

Marie Cirillo
(2000)

I am a member of the Federation of Communities in Service, founded in 1967 by women who work in the Appalachian region. In 1968 one of our members, Monica Appleby, spent a year at Harvard. In the course of that year she heard Bob Swann talk about community land trusts. When she came back, some of her friends met in Knoxville to welcome her home. She told us what she had heard about the concept of the community land trust and said she thought it was perfect for Appalachia. We were so enthused. We each chipped in enough money to pay Bob's plane fare for him to come to Tennessee. He accepted our invitation, and he spoke to ten or twelve of us about a way of having the community hold land in trust and lease it to people indefinitely to live on or to farm without having to buy the land. The lease fee pays for the land over a long period of time.

Excited by what I had heard, I went back to my home up Roses Creek Hollow in the Clearfork Valley and told people there about what I had learned, but I must not have gotten the idea across. A few years later I invited Bob to come back and talk to one of the local organizations, and they didn't quite get it then either. But by 1977 some people began to say yes to the idea of a community land trust. They said, "Aha! A community land trust might work. Maybe that makes sense." This was partly because every time a project was brought to the stage where it was ready for a place to be housed, the group involved couldn't find the land on which to build their needed facility. They had gone to the big companies, gone here and there, in search of land—with no success.

First I mobilized the Regional Land Trust for Appalachian Communities. Its main purpose was to spread the word about community land trusts into rural areas like the Clearfork Valley. The people there were landless because the land had been bought up in the late 1800s for the coal that was needed as the eastern part of our nation was being developed. This explains the large amount of absentee ownership.

I met many times with some local people before I asked if they would be interested in forming an organization and serving as its board members. They said yes, and in 1977 they found a forty-acre parcel of land for sale but had no money to purchase it. I approached the Regional Land Trust, and they knew how to mobilize funds and

find legal council. They purchased the forty acres for $20,000 and then negoti-
ated with our community land trust, which had incorporated as a nonprofit and
taken the name Community Land Trust Association. Forty acres, as opposed to the
40,000 acres in the Clearfork Valley owned by the American Association, a British
company.

Not having the cash to purchase the land outright, the Community Land Trust
Association knew that it could settle people on the land and collect land leases. The
members calculated how many they could reasonably settle each year and then presented a payment plan to the Regional Trust. The Trust had received $7000 of the
purchase price as a grant and offered to turn that into a grant to the local group if it
would speed up the repayments based on its projection of land-lease income. The incentive worked. Within seven years the group was free of its debt. By vote of the local
people its name was changed to Woodland Community Land Trust.

We soon had questions about how to proceed, so I went in search of answers,
thinking we could learn from other CLTs. And then I found out that there weren't
many of them at all! Somehow I had thought this was a movement I just hadn't happened to hear of yet. Probably if we had known we were one of only five or six in the
country, we would have been afraid to start. But we did, and I turned to Bob Swann
and Susan Witt [executive director of the Schumacher Society] quite often for their
thoughts and ideas. They have been real mentors for me. I must say that I can't understand why the concept of the community land trust doesn't catch on in Appalachia. It could be such a wonderful solution for the landless.

To help you understand what life in Appalachia is like for the rural poor, I'd like to
tell you a little bit about my life. I have spent fifty-one years with the Appalachian
people. And because my first nineteen years were spent in Brooklyn, I am always
asked how I got from Brooklyn to Appalachia. I could mention specific events that
took me there, but mainly it was fate, a fateful attraction to rural life. My whole experience has been a wonderful mix of rural and urban living that has shaped my
personality.

The deeper I go into Appalachia's history, the more I realize that the story of Appalachia's rural poor is different from the story of the black slaves in the cotton fields;
it is different from the labor abuses of the migrant farmer. Appalachia is clearly a
place where the area and the people have been sacrificed for the sake of energy, and I
think that's what fits in with the idea of cold evil, although the connection between
all the coal that has been mined as an energy resource and what has happened to our
community is not obvious.

One result of being exposed to poor rural communities was that I became aware of
all the handwork done there. Your whole personal development is affected when you
make by hand so much of what you depend on to live. It's such a contrast to buying
the commercialized products of cities and to the idea that you can't get anything if
you don't have the money to buy it. Another result of my exposure to Appalachia as it
relates to American history and my own family history has been a fascination with

migration patterns. The move of rural people to the cities from the Deep South, from Appalachia, and from the Midwest, along with my mother's move from Kentucky to New York and my father's move from a rural community in Italy to New York, all told a story I wanted to understand. What was this all about? I wondered that from my earliest days, and as I grew up I began to understand that what I had observed—both in terms of migration and the predominance of handwork—is clearly related to development policies and land ownership.

Whether it's a capitalist or a socialist system, the design of a political economy that supports an industrial country shapes society. I have a sense from my own experience that as politics and industry were influencing our urban society, religious and educational institutions quickly fell into working cooperatively with both.

I was born in Brooklyn in November of 1929, the month of the stock-market crash and the year the Depression began. I was twelve years old before my mother bought me my first commercially made dress. I can remember her sewing our clothes. She would always cut out a little piece of cloth for me to make a dress for my doll. Because my mother was from Kentucky and this was during the Depression years, she would take her four daughters there every summer. During those summers we would help tend the garden, preserve what came out of it, and help churn butter. We would enjoy the home-made ice cream. We would feed the chickens to get out of doing dishes. All of these activities were wonderful little experiences of producing what we needed. Grandfather would always help mother pack up the canned goods and ship them to our home in Brooklyn. So when this food arrived, I knew where it came from; I knew my grandfather had tended the garden and my grandmother had directed the canning. It was an important lesson in appreciating what we made ourselves, in developing survival skills, and recognizing our dependence on the land.

I remember coal being delivered to our house when I was a child. The furnace was in the basement, and I knew how it worked. I saw the way my mother fired it up in the morning and banked it at night. When we got up in the morning, we ran to the radiator so we could get dressed next to its warmth. I didn't know where coal came from, but I thought it must come from someplace special. Finding that place later gave me great satisfaction. Once again, I learned that something essential to our household came from the land. It took decades of living in Appalachia for me to understand the importance of the interconnection between urban and rural places.

By 1947 I was a big girl and wanted to get out of the city. The way to do that was to join a group of missionary sisters. They were called the Glenmary Home Mission Sisters of America, and I was going to join them in their work in rural communities and save the world. As part of my experience as a missionary, I remember giving food away, giving clothes away, giving baskets at Christmastime, providing health services, and teaching in Bible schools. But I also remember valuing the fact that people were growing their own food and finding their own firewood and going to the railroad tracks to pick up pieces of coal. They were making quilts from scraps and their children's clothes from feed sacks. I loved being with such people. I liked that identity. It connected me to my roots, to my deepest values. I also witnessed great generosity from the poorest of the poor. They, like the land, gave generously of what the Earth gave them. When I fell in love with Pond Creek in the southeastern corner of Ohio when I was sent there as a Glenmary Sister, I knew I would never leave rural America.

In 1967 I left this order of missionaries with forty-three other women who wanted to continue working with the Appalachian people but not within the institutional Church setting. We formed a nonprofit group and called it the Federation of Communities in Service (FOCIS). It was then that I moved from the immigrant neighborhood of uptown Chicago, where I had spent the past four years, to a place called the Clearfork Valley. I have been there ever since.

Ninety percent of the people from the Clearfork Valley had left since the 1950s. One of the things that attracted me to it was the fact that the 10 percent remaining were still part of those other societies of hunter-gatherers and of agriculture, even though they had also become part of today's industrial society. The Appalachian people I know live in all three worlds. What they understand as industrial society in their mountains are the corporate extractive fossil-fuel industries, whereas those who left for the cities have been exposed to factories, which are more typically understood as part of an industrial society. In any case, the real truth of the lived experience of people in the Clearfork Valley, as opposed to the stereotyping of backwoods mountain people, continues to fascinate me.

The Clearfork area is made up of twelve unincorporated communities located between the towns of Jellico, Tennessee, and Middlesboro, Kentucky. When I arrived there, the company towns had been dismantled, mainly because of the shift from deep mining to strip mining as new technology made that possible. Big machines now dug the coal. Production no long required people, so the companies tore down the miners' homes because they no longer had to provide housing. That was when people realized for the first time that over the years the companies had bought up most of the land.

Because the company towns had been dismantled and the county political system had little history of being involved with anything other than roads and schools, it was clear that change would come only if people were willing to make it happen themselves. My work since 1967 has been to help people organize their own community-based nonprofit organizations. Together we have organized for health clinics, small business enterprises such as craft production and industrial wood pallets, child-care centers, and other service programs. We did some organizing to address land issues, which at that time centered around coal production, taxes on coal, and environmental concerns about strip mining. In those days hardly anyone was aware of environmental matters. If Appalachian people spoke in public about the environment, it was as though they were talking to a brick wall. No one knew what it was all about. Even today, most people still don't make the connection between urban consumption, with the resulting environmental problems, and rural production, with its different but no less serious environmental problems.

I found it significant that 90 percent of the land was owned by absentee companies and about 90 percent of the population had fled. This made me think that the local people's plight must be related to the fact that they didn't own land. And I began to understand what we were going through as a leading industrial society. With three million blacks leaving the Deep South for the cities in the 1920s and 1930s and three million Appalachians leaving for the cities in the 1950s and 1960s, and who knows how many farmers leaving the Midwest for the cities, this country experienced the largest rural to urban migration in the history of the world. And we didn't even realize it! It took me a while to get smart and learn from my own experience. I came to appreciate my community as the most valuable classroom of all. I never got tired of being there because I was always learning something new that I had never learned from college textbooks.

E. F. Schumacher said that in order to turn potentiality into reality, the task of education must be first and foremost the transmission of ideas, of values. This impressed me. Popular books about Appalachians such as *Yesterday's People* suggested that anyone who had any get-up-and-go got up and went. But I found that the few who stayed had good reasons for staying. They might be cash poor, but those I met and began to work with were people who chose that life-style because of certain values they held. I was familiar with some of these values from my own childhood experiences and also from what had been transmitted to me by my mother, from whom I learned a love of beauty and the creative capacity of Earth, and my father, who instilled in me a love of music and history.

What drew me to the Glenmary Missionaries in 1947 was the call to convert the rural people who were moving to cities in huge numbers; if they could be brought into the Church before they moved, the urban churches would benefit greatly. The Catholic Church was basically an urban church, and Glenmary's founder felt that it was lacking something that rural people could provide. If Glenmary could give something to the mountain people, then when they moved to the city they, with their strong values, would give something back to the Church. Many years later I came to see this principle of giving to one another as the basis for the partnerships we developed in the Clearfork Valley between churches and community-based organizations, between colleges and community-based organizations.

My four years in Chicago, where I spent my last years as a Glenmary Sister from 1964 to 1967, brought a rude awakening. People did not welcome hillbillies into their community. They didn't even want them as part of their church. And as a matter of fact, many of the migrants didn't want to be in Chicago. They would often return home to try again, only to come back defeated. They had no choice but to get a job in the city, where neither church nor community welcomed those I had come to love.

When I left Glenmary and helped found FOCIS, we made a commitment to the people who had decided to stay in their rural place. Not that we were against those choosing to leave, but we cared about those who stayed, and we wanted to build our life with them. It was interesting that in the 1960s so many people were joining communes. I didn't feel I had to do that. Appalachians had their own ready-made communities. If they would just accept me into their way of living, I would find community. They did, and I did.

Though I didn't realize it when it was happening, a bonding experience took place between the FOCIS members and the Appalachians living in the area of the coal fields. I was one of over 103 of 120 Sisters to leave the order. Many left singly, whereas forty-four of us left to continue our work with the Appalachians through FOCIS. Like us, the Appalachians scattered as they left their rural home place. Some went on their own while others moved with their extended family to places such as Cincinnati, Detroit, and Chicago. And like us, they remained in touch with those they had left behind. Both groups had the experience of being disrupted by the system we were living in. I read in a recent United Nations publication that there are 23 million people experiencing internal displacement within their countries today. So the system is still promoting this kind of diaspora, still causing the breakdown of rural society and the loss of roots.

The personal growth I have experienced during my thirty-three years in the Clearfork Valley is very important to me. For the first ten years I was feeling my way around. What I did was help people organize to provide services. That was good; it empowered people. They learned how to work together to reach their goals, to sustain their work, and to stay within their financial limitations, having to do without. Then, in 1977, new ideas took shape in our collective mind. It was after the massive floods of that year, and even the few people who remained in the region were losing their homes to flood waters. Federal officials from Housing and Urban Development were shocked to find that there was no available land on which to resettle people in the emergency mobile units they were bringing in. The governor of West Virginia used his power of eminent domain to take corporate lands to house the homeless. It was time to start talking about community land trusts as a citizen approach to the problem. That was when we founded our own CLT.

Something else happened in 1977: a number of our women's groups (most of the nonprofits were run predominantly by women) formed a coalition called Mountain Women's Exchange, which was later incorporated. The question was raised: What is it that each of us needs but can't get on our own? The groups agreed on the answer: a college education. So we mobilized and were able to contract with a college to come in and offer the courses we thought we should take. That was also the year when we organized a five-county antistrip-mining group called Save Our Cumberland Mountains. These endeavors continue today, still with the same vision.

In the 1990s more groups and projects came into being. I'm sure they had been germinating in our heads for some time, but I credit their realization primarily to the community land trust. Once we acquired land, once we had a plan for its use, and once people settled on it who had a consistent ethic about land being held in trust, we began to care for it, to share it, and to distinguish between public and private land. This is what led to new developments.

One of the new groups is the Forest Visioning Circle, which we started partly because of Champion Paper coming in and buying 80 thousand acres to clear-cut for chip mills. Another group we called ABCDE, which stands for Appalachian-Based Community Development Education. We are a network of grassroots organizations from the Appalachian areas of Kentucky, Tennessee, Virginia, and West Virginia. We get together in Middlesboro, Kentucky, to plan our strategies, and we try to recruit college students to join us in the summertime to help. We also organized a women's group named Economics in the Clearfork Valley. We meet every Monday for lunch to discuss what is going on in the county court, the schools, and the county in general. This group came out of the Woodland Community Development Corporation (WCDC), which the land trust started in 1987 when it was seeking others to take on housing so it could continue to focus on the critical land-acquisition issue. We had been spending too much time trying to provide housing and mortgage financing.

WCDC had worked on housing issues for quite a while. It built commercial houses but soon realized that nobody could afford a commercial house, and no bank would give a loan for such a building, so it initiated a project with a group of seven people to work on what they called the Native Material House. They had observed how poor folks built a house. They cut the logs, they brought them to the sawmill, they built as much as they could. Then when they got more money, they added another window or put sheet rock in another room. So the Native Material House tried to combine these people's way of building with conventional housing construction.

WCDC offered two families a little bit of money to help with the materials they had to buy in return for coming and meeting with the group of seven every other week to explain what they did. WCDC wanted to find out how much they called on their family for help and how much work they traded, such as someone putting in the wiring in return for having a car repaired. These activities have given the community some clear messages about the real economy—one that doesn't have everything to do with money. It's been fun. Building does come to a standstill once in a while until a new impetus comes along to get things going again.

In addition, WCDC supports families in generating income, making use of the Grameen Bank model (the peer micro-lending program that originated in India) and one called the Individual Development Account. This is a new program introduced around the time welfare reform went into effect. People in leadership positions were telling the government that poor people cannot get out of poverty if they do not have assets. As a way to gain assets the program recommended establishing small savings groups of from five to ten people, who would meet every other week. They would bring in a little bit of money and put it in a savings account. Then when they were ready to take it out for a house, a small business start-up, or educational purposes, the sponsors of the program matched the savings two to one. Hence, instead of having $2000 to start their house they had $6000.

We also have a spin-off of local currency. We never succeeded in putting a full-scale currency in place; with little more than a general store in our area, everybody has to go to town to shop. We have neither the funds nor the talent (to our knowledge) to initiate this unfamiliar kind of service. But we did start something similar called a Community Investment Certificate. My concern was that if we teach people how to develop their personal assets through the Individual Development Account program, we also should promote the idea of *community* assets. People need help in finding ways to make their contribution to building up the assets of the community. An old school building in Eagan, which is approximately in the center of the Clearfork Valley, was given to Woodland Community Land Trust, but we didn't have money to renovate it. I tried to recruit volunteers, telling them they would be helping to build a community asset. This new group is being organized to manage the renovation for a community learning center. People will be given Community Investment Certificates for the volunteer hours they put in. Then, when the center opens, activities that cost money can be paid for with these certificates.

Those were the exciting things that emerged between 1977 and 1998, a period of development that had reached a new level beyond that of the previous ten years. As local people were taking these initiatives, land in the Clearfork Valley was changing hands as the use of natural resources was shifting. The 40,000 acres held since the 1880s by the American Association, Ltd., the British absentee land company whose interest was coal, was sold in the 1980s to the J. M. Huber Corporation of New Jersey, whose primary interest was timber. Now the land is being sold once again.

The present change of ownership being negotiated leaves citizens in the dark regarding their fate at the hands of yet another absentee landholder. Even though we know that the interest today is more in timber, we see that there is still some coal, gas, and oil being extracted locally—although the coal is almost gone. Compared to other Appalachian states Tennessee has only a small portion of the region's coal, and what remains is of poor quality. Better-grade coal is coming from the West, but we think someday when that runs out, the companies will come and take ours again until it too runs out. We continue on with the idea that we have nothing to lose by trying to stretch our minds. The new millennium has provided some added momentum for us to think boldly about the future. Change is coming. The cheap energy that built our industrial society is running out.

The American Association had flatly denied the requests from local organizations to sell or lease a bit of company land, refusing even to enter a lease agreement for a half acre that the Clearfork Clinic needed to build a facility. Nor would the company consider a request from the Model Valley Development Corporation (founded in 1970) for land or access to timber when it was trying to build an industrial wood pallet factory. The J. M. Huber Corp., on the other hand, donated twenty acres to Model Valley Development in addition to the Eagan school building with its twelve acres, which were then transferred to Woodland Community Land Trust. We regarded this as progress!

All of the old schools of the coal camps have been torn down except for the one in Eagan. When it was turned over to Woodland Community Land Trust in 1999, the school was pretty dilapidated. The roof had fallen in, the windows were all broken, the pipes were broken, and sheet rock had crumbled away. The Huber Corp., which owned almost all the land in the valley, wanted to get rid of this building. They either were going to tear it down or give it away. Woodland was the only group interested in it. The management tried to interest other groups because, as a for-profit land company, they did not want to donate the twelve acres and school building to what they thought the owners might perceive as another land company, even if ours was not for profit. At one point in the negotiations, Huber sent some of its people to see us. They listened and even seemed to understand our efforts and concerns. We were delighted to see them face to face after all these years of not knowing the major players in this community.

The Huber Corp. decided not to give the school to our CLT, but through quiet negotiation we arranged for the Model Valley Development Corporation to accept it as a gift and then turn it over to Woodland. Huber did ask for $5000 to cover legal and surveying costs. The land trust raised this amount and paid it to Model Valley in 1999.

We received the land and building just a year before the new millennium, which meant that our visioning included what a building like this could be used for. We spent a good bit of time thinking that through until it became apparent that what people wanted could be organized within a learning center. We came up with the idea of a Clearfork Community Institute, which would promote sustainable economics and community-based education. We also wanted to focus on spirit/culture—what do we value, what do we want for our families and our community?

Until now, Woodland CLT has been leasing land for housing—thirty acres out of the 200 it now holds in six separate parcels on Roses Creek. Some of the thirty is being used as common land for family gardens, play areas, or whatever is agreed upon by the residents. The remaining land is being managed as undeveloped forest. Now Woodland has a new facility that will be suitable as public space for the larger Clearfork Valley community. We will be able to manage land and buildings for the common good. But creating a public space in a community lacking local government and a local tax base brings with it both financial and governance challenges—challenges we are ready to meet.

Another opportunity the land trust took advantage of was the chance to purchase a 200-acre mountaintop in Eagan. This mountain had been strip-mined, deep-mined, and clear-cut. Now the owner, one of the more colorful local strip-miners, was ready to sell it for $50,000. There were two steps involved in raising the money:

1. We withdrew the $10,000 we had collected from partnerships established with churches over the years.
2. We were given a $50,000 line of credit with a local bank, thanks to the help of eight friends who purchased certificates of deposit to be held by the bank as collateral for three years. By the time the certificates matured, Woodland had

raised enough money through donations to repay the bank all that it had withdrawn, and the eight friends got their money back.

We bought that land with the idea of devoting ourselves to restoring it. There is no way for this area to revive itself as a rural community dependent on natural resources if we don't commit time to healing our place on Earth.

A special boost was given to the life of our region and our community by the Bonner Foundation. Mrs. Bonner, who is ninety-one years old and chairs the foundation board, was born in Eagan when it was the Blue Diamond Coal Camp. Her father worked as a miner for Blue Diamond. When she came to visit, she give us $50,000 to put a new roof on the old schoolhouse. With offices in Princeton, New Jersey, the foundation gives scholarships to college students, mostly to low-income youth in the South, including Appalachia. All students who receive a scholarship must agree to a certain amount of community service. Mrs. Bonner would love to have us develop a program for students to come and work with us. This would mean that the interaction between young people and the community has a future. Those working to establish the Clearfork Community Institute like to think of the Clearfork Valley as a community that has something to teach because of its rural life-style, its struggle to keep that alive, and its experience with urban migration.

There is an unfortunate disconnect in our nation between rural and urban life, and it is encouraged by our education system. Urban people like to go to the country, admire the scenery, take a walk in the woods, but that's not helping to keep a rural community and a rural life-style alive. It disturbs me that so little is being done to address this separation. I hope the service component of the Bonner Scholars Program will play an important role in whatever we do with the old school building in Eagan and will also help provide colleges with a meaningful curriculum linking the urban and the rural environment.

With these general areas of concern in mind, we started looking at the new initiatives to see if they fit in with our goals for an institute. Can we do enough? Can we generate enough income to keep the doors open? Right now we are at a standstill in that regard, but the hardest part was getting the vision in the first place.

Another important development resulting from activities among grassroots community-based groups is that over the years connections have been established. We created partnerships that established five-year commitments from both partners. We also linked with strong networks that emerged: one of them is called In Praise of Mountain Women. Every other year women from the region come together for a weekend. The main part of the agenda is to honor what we have accomplished and what we are struggling for. This might not seem like much, but it's important to gain faith in yourself when the rest of the world thinks you are just a poverty-stricken, backward person. There's also a Tennessee network called Women in Self-Sufficiency, whose members are primarily from low-income neighborhoods and are working in community to improve their lives. These women appreciate what our community land trust has accomplished, and we appreciate what they are doing. It's a good connection.

We are part of the National Congress of Neighborhood Women, made up of grass-roots groups from low-income urban neighborhoods and poor rural communities of the United States. We get together every year for a week-long institute. Don't ask what we eat or where we sleep, but we manage to get there. You have to spend the whole year saving your money in order to go to the institute for a week. And when you get there, you're exhausted from the preparations to leave home—finding someone to take care of the kids and preparing enough food to last while you're gone. The first day we always spend catching our breath. So it's not moving very quickly, but we are not going to give up. We've stayed together for twenty years because we have important work to do. We're hoping that enough good things will come together to spark a flame.

Because the National Congress of Neighborhood Women is an official nongovernmental organization (NGO) we've learned about activities at the United Nations and have gotten in touch with grassroots women in other parts of the world. Now we have a small but wonderful organization called GROOTS, which stands for Grass-Roots Organizations Operating Together in Sisterhood. Of course with the internet we are making even more connections that are helpful and extremely enlightening.

All these women's groups comprise my main connective system. There are other good ways of being connected, but I guess my own history of coming from a family with four daughters and joining a convent of 120 Sisters, forty-four of whom then organized FOCIS, determined the route I have traveled. I want to say that the support of our hopes and visions by women like Susan Witt has played an important role for grassroots women.

It hasn't all been fun, nor has it all been struggle. But it certainly has been a challenge to try to slow down the runaway system of outmigration, the loss of roots, the alienation of Americans from the land as prime resource, and the dwindling of skills that sustain a rural society. What keeps my feet to the fire are the wisdom and values of mountain people. Home is much more for them than the walls that provide shelter for the family. Home is the physical, geographic place in a natural setting where they and their friends become part of the larger living community. It is a microcosm of Earth. The place-based community is extremely important to us, and together we do what we can to resist the ways in which society tends to disconnect us from it. Unfortunately, industrial development has worked against many aspects of a rural community, and much wisdom has been lost in the process.

People's ability to hold on to values that sustain rural communities is at risk. The oppressive control over rural people by an urban mind-set has been hurtful to them and also dangerous for our country as a whole. When a society loses consciousness of its dependency on natural resources, it becomes wasteful of them. (I've heard said it would take three Earths for everyone to have as much as we in the United States have.) Often the people are wasted along with the resources taken from a place-based community such as ours. Then a nation loses its wealth and its soul, and the nation deteriorates. This is what challenges me to keep working to sustain rural communities for America.

The desire for change expressed in the popular vote has no effect on the Tennessee state government. Agencies like the federal Tennessee Valley Authority (TVA), created in 1933 to develop cheap electric power, and production systems like the nuclear conglomerate for atomic research in Oak Ridge can easily exert *their* influence on state government and Tennessee's universities. One of the hardest things for me to accept is that during my thirty-three years in the Clearfork Valley, in spite of all the efforts and struggles of the local people to accomplish something in their communities, the state Office of Community and Economic Development has not given us one penny—except on the few occasions when we had enough energy to mount a political fight. They just want us to move away to a city. They say it's not economically efficient for us to live there, and they find excuses to justify the government's lack of assistance to most rural communities of Tennessee.

In that context I want to say this hasn't been the case just during *my* years there; it has been a whole century of living with industrialization and urbanization that resulted in the Appalachian people's present struggle. During the first half of the twentieth century the federal government chose to sacrifice our region for the sake of expansion of the cities of New York and Boston. The East Coast was built with our timber and heated with our coal. There is no feeling of responsibility for what was taken from us, nor has there ever been. But we are still living with some of the consequences of being made to serve other areas so they could be developed efficiently. And when World War II came, what else was there except to win the war? Our government chose Oak Ridge as the place to conduct research to develop a new kind of bomb to do that. Who cared about our beautiful mountain region and the special people it gave birth to? We were chosen to be sacrificed. It's easy for people to forget now that it's over, but we still live with that memory. From an earlier perspective, many of the people are of Cherokee origin, and they still live with the pain of having lost their land.

Sometimes jokingly referred to as the secret society, TVA and Oak Ridge are part of that system Andrew Kimbrell associated with cold evil, a system that needed our coal to build the East Coast, to win World War II, to move us into the post-War era of fossil fuels and then nuclear power. The proliferation of cars and plastics made possible by fossil fuels caused industries and cities to grow beyond all predictions. Rural America lost in big ways: the Clearfork Valley lost its population, lost its coal, water, soil, trees, and wildlife. And yes, we almost lost our spirit. We have to deal with that cold evil. If we try to challenge these powerful institutions, we don't fare very well and are not treated very well. Those of you familiar with the history of Appalachia know that the army has been called in to stop union strikes. We have had our people disappear, but you never hear about that on the news. I have certainly lived with harassment and threats and burning as have many others. In the past year and a half our community land trust has lost seven of its seventeen buildings to arson. Our development efforts are not supported or viewed with favor by those with money and power.

Tennessee is a special part of Appalachia. It is unique because of TVA and Oak Ridge. But I am fighting on behalf of *all* of Appalachia in my work in the Clearfork Valley, where we have lost 90 percent of our population, where 90 percent of the land is owned by absentee landlords, and where our water has been polluted, our land ruined. I'm not letting anyone forget that. What place is going to be sacrificed next for the needs of the industrialized world for which America serves as the model?

It took us 40,000 years to move from a hunter-gatherer society to an agricultural one and 10,000 years to move from an agricultural society to an industrial one. In less than 1000 years our industrial society already seems to be falling apart. What comes next? Whose vision will move us forward? It is a changing world, and we have no clear answers, but I do think the interactions between the poor and the rich, between rural and urban, North and South, whites and people of color, male and female are very important. We need to keep connected as we try to find our new interactive relationship with Earth. Human relationships are only part of what needs improvement; Earth calls for a better and broader-based relationship with all that is—with all that sustains life.

It is an operating principle for me not to think in terms of either/or. It is not science/technology *or* indigenous knowledge. It's how you connect the two so you can have the proper balance. It's not capital *or* labor. It's not commercialism *or* do-it-yourself production. It's not poverty *or* wealth. It's not a rural life *or* an urban life. It's both/and.

We in the valley know we are a small place, and much of what Schumacher says in *Small Is Beautiful* makes sense to us even when it contradicts the thinking of the big corporate enterprises that overshadow our community efforts. People everywhere need to gain an appreciation for the fact that small and big both have their place. It is not an either/or. The fact is that both can be right or both can be wrong, according to the principles we choose to live by.

Two weeks ago I went to a workshop in Ohio sponsored by the Appalachian Regional Commission. When I heard representatives of big government talk about small business as the future of America, I thought for a few hours that perhaps our country was moving toward a better balance. The up-and-coming economic strategists told us that we're not going to have big corporations anymore; instead, our country's economy is now being built around small businesses. There were speakers who explained how the new system works: Venture capitalists buy into small businesses, and when $10 million has been generated in a specific region, the government will match the $10 million; the aim is to have $20 million in many venture-capital funds in many regions of the country as quickly as possible. I was telling this to one of my neighbors, and he said, "Oh yes, some businessmen invited me to Lexington to tell them about my business. They were playing around with the idea of how they might invest their money in it."

As we were being told how the new system works, there were questions from the audience: Is there any concern for labor? If you hire ten or twelve people, are they going to be protected? Is there any concern for environmental protection? The quick and decisive answer was that profit is the bottom line. So now we have the little guys doing exactly what the big guys have been doing all these years. This is entrepreneurship American-style. I could hardly believe what I was hearing. Recently I've heard about a curriculum on entrepreneurship for grades K–12. I've got to get my hands on this curriculum to see what our children are being taught. It's frightening.

I see these as my tasks:

1. I want to keep attention focused on the migration in and out of cities. Why? Because what happened in America is now happening globally. According to a United Nations report 23 million people are experiencing internal displacement within their countries today. In May of 1999 I had the privilege of going to the United Nations seventeenth session of the Commission on Human Settlements held in Nairobi. I was one of the official government people, so I got to sit in on the preparations for each day. GROOTS, the women's network, was participating as an NGO, and I would meet with them at night in addition to meeting with the government people during the day. The Commission determined that one of the major problems over the next twenty years will be massive migrations worldwide. It's estimated that in twenty years 70 percent of humanity will be living in cities. Two major related issues are the impact these migrations are having on governance and land tenure.

My most significant contribution during the government meetings was to say, "You know, this trend started in our country; maybe we should look back to see what we have learned and share our insights." People agreed, but I don't think they gave it another thought. I did find it confirming, though, that others, including our government, shared my concern over migration and recognized the land problems it is causing in both the cities and the rural areas.

2. I want to find allies. . . . Where can I find others who share our views? I read an interesting article in the newsletter published by Harvard Divinity School. A visiting professor, a city planner from Korea, was describing his vision of the future: ten or fifteen cities throughout the world will bear the highest impact of people and their urban life-style. Surrounding the city will be an agricultural circle and beyond that another circle with the hunter/gatherer or wilderness area. Each of these cities, comprised of all three elements, will be one nation. It sounds crazy, yet whoever starts visioning something new sounds crazy to some, but has a kernel of truth for others. In our search for a future way we should remember that there is a need to link those

three different modes in meaningful ways. I know that the many who have moved from Appalachia to cities are still connected to the mountain people.

Community land trusts are one way of making the connection. The land trust movement has been growing in urban centers. The Dudley Street Neighborhood Initiative in Boston is a marvelous example of how the appreciation for land can be expressed in the city. You are not just getting land for your house; you are getting enough land to live, to have a garden, to play, to have a small business, etc. When land is put into trust, it can have a central integrating impact in shaping a new community.

3. I want to help make Appalachia a place to learn in the new millennium. The Clearfork Valley is ready to identify itself that way. With our community-based organizations, our land and people, our rural values, our knowledge and skills, we have a community from which both rural and urban people can learn. We are presently holding a building and a mountain for this use, but we need supporters, and we need to raise money. We are hoping to form a partnership with urban counterparts to develop the Clearfork Community Institute as a regional center for creative action that will integrate our private and public lives into Earth life.

We are depending heavily on community-based organizations to be integral to the learning experience. Our newer groups—such as the Forest Visioning Circle, Earth Day Celebration Committee, the Native Material House, Appalachian-Based Community Development Education—and our connection to colleges with their service-learning and participatory research interests have shaped the vision. Both service learning and participatory research provide our community with an opportunity to take the lead. The students involved learn as well as teach, even as community people learn and teach. The community becomes a place of learning for both residents and students. The process of breaking down barriers based on differences of class and place while building up a sense of interrelatedness can begin.

We have friends in churches, in colleges, and in foundations. We have begun to approach local timber and energy-based corporations. We are seeking individuals and institutions to partner with us in developing the Clearfork Community Institute.

4. When asked by Vice President Gore what I would do if I were President, I said I would work for land reform. And what would land reform look like? I have learned from my international network of peers that forced land reform by governments generally doesn't work; it backfires on the poor. I think we in Appalachia need dialogue among community groups and corporate land owners to come to a better understanding of the both/and rather than the either/or attitude. Is there not room for all of us? Is there not value in doing land use planning together?

The community land trust model demonstrates how residents can empower themselves through a proper relationship with the land. The model adopted in Voi, Kenya, has been listed in UN literature as a Best Practice. Our Woodland CLT fulfills the needs of the landless poor. It is trying to do exactly what the United Nations says the agenda for every nation should be—to further adequate governance and expand land tenure. The answer cannot be one set of rules for the 30 percent left in rural area and another set of rules for the 70 percent in urban areas. The challenge for the new millennium is to make life whole. We must never forget that rural resources are essential to building cities and that it will take wise people to keep these resources healthy and productive.

If land-holding companies would turn over some of their land to a community land trust such as Woodland and work with us, together we could shape a local and global economy that would serve the best interests of present and future generations as well as the present and future needs of Earth. And if we could persuade government to put money into paying citizens to reclaim the lands that have been ruined in the twentieth century, it would then be up to the people who are Woodland partners (individuals and institutions who pledge to contribute to its land-purchase fund for five years) to work with local leaders in creating the Clearfork Community Institute, where sustainable economics, community education, and spirit/culture can be promoted.

If we ever receive federal funding to restore the land and empower the people of this community, we will need to have a strong enough foundation to prevent government from taking control of what our people are learning and to ensure that this learning gives them a role in the policy-making that affects their lives. Values having to do with community and sustainability must not be violated as local people are trained in ways to generate income. As land is restored by local labor and then developed, the people doing the work must be involved in deciding which of the restored lands are appropriate to allocate to homesteads and which to commerce, industry, agriculture, and hinterland. Eventually the circles of agriculture and hinterland (in our case, forestland) surrounding human settlements will be in better balance with urban interests. Located as it is in a rural area in a predominantly urban society, the institute can become a center for addressing the critical need for a better balance between rural and urban land use and development.

Community learning centers such as the Clearfork Community Institute can help urban as well as rural settlements see more clearly that they are part of one experience, one consciousness. Communities have the potential to unify the many accomplishments of a new social, economic, and political order. Land-tenure policies will have to change to accommodate the reshaping of rural and urban societies. There must be a consistent ethic to support a holistic vision for Earth that values the diversity of its parts. The attitudes of humans will change significantly during this time of transition from an industrial society to the yet unnamed society that will replace it. In conclusion I would like to say that Appalachia, with its land and its people, has the potential to make a significant contribution to our changing world. To do this the region needs to expand its network to connect with other already existing networks.

It is with this possibility in mind that I am grateful for the opportunity you have given me to share my story with you. Bob Swann and Susan Witt have been a great source of strength for me. I see you as their friends. Thank you Bob, Susan, the Schumacher Society, and all of you.

PART THREE

DEFINITIONS & PURPOSES

FROM *The Community Land Trust*

A Guide to a New Model for Land Tenure in America

International Independence Institute
(1972)

The Community Land Trust

Defining the Community Land Trust

The community land trust constitutes a social mechanism which has as its purpose the resolution of the fundamental questions of allocation, continuity, and exchange.

The community land trust is a legal entity, a quasipublic body, chartered to hold land in stewardship for all mankind present and future while protecting the legitimate use-rights of its residents.

The community land trust is *not* primarily concerned with *common ownership.* Rather, its concern is for *ownership for the common good,* which may or may not be combined with common ownership.

Precisely how the community land trust attempts to resolve the questions of allocation, continuity, and exchange is detailed throughout the guide. In this chapter, we will introduce only the most salient assumptions, definitions, and principles.

The Concept of Trust

The choice of the word "trust" is based upon our desire as authors to emphasize the notion of "trusteeship" or "stewardship." If land is limited, then its use in the face of steadily expanding human demands upon it must be regulated for the long-range welfare of all people.[1]

Our choice of the word "trust"[2] can be explained further by our desire to emphasize Ralph Borsodi's idea of "trusterty." Borsodi suggested that possessions should be classified as either "property" or "trusterty." Property is created by man through his labor. Trusterty includes land, the atmosphere, rivers, lakes, seas, natural forests, and mineral resources of the earth. Since these do not come into existence as a result of human labor, they cannot be morally owned; they can only be held in trust.[3]

Originally land was "free"; it had no price. But with time, as desirable land has become increasingly scarce, its price has increased. During the past century this

---

These excerpts are from several chapters in *The Community Land Trust: A Guide to a New Model for Land Tenure in America* by the International Independence Institute (Cambridge, MA: Center for Community Economic Development, 1972), 25–28, 38, 64. They are reprinted by permission of E. F. Schumacher Society, 140 Jug End Road, Great Barrington, MA, 01230. www.smallisbeautiful.org. Original note numbers have been changed.

increase has progressed at a rate that far exceeds the rise in the cost of living. (It may be reasoned that whenever men derive economic value from that which they have not produced, this becomes at least one factor behind inflation—and some economists go so far as to say it is the only factor.) *When land is exchanged as "property" (rather than as "trusterty"), the impact of such exchanges upon the total economy are in the long run dramatic, if not catastrophic.*

Land is held by the community land trust in perpetuity—probably never to be sold. Thus, the problems of exchange are virtually eliminated. The trust leases the land to the users with the expectation of preserving or enhancing its long-range resource value. The leases are long-term, restricted to the actual users of the land; absentee control and subleasing are specifically proscribed. The residents have secure use-rights to the land and are free to control and build their own community through cooperative organizations or individual homesteads.

Both in concept and in practical operation, the community land trust distinguishes between land with its natural resources and the human improvements thereon, often called externalities.[4] The land is held in trust, not the improvements. Homes, stores, and industrial enterprises created by the residents will be owned by them, either cooperatively or individually.

Community

We use the word "community" in the term community land trust fully conscious of the fact that it is an overused, imprecise, and confusing word. Throughout this guide we will try to be relatively specific in our usage. We will refer to the people actually living on the land trust as the "resident community." The larger "community" includes the resident community as well as those who intend to be residents, support the trust, or who otherwise identify with the trust. And although we have tried not to use it in this sense, we recognize the broader connotations of the concept of the community land trust: "community" in the largest sense, the community of all mankind, an idea that is essential to the concept of trusterty. . . .

Getting Started

. . .

The Issue of Control and Exercise of Trusteeship

Building on the experience of the various experiments in the United States and elsewhere, it becomes possible to isolate and define two issues that are basic to the community land trust concept: the issue of control and exercise of the trusteeship function. Crucial to the successful implementation of land trusteeship is the resolution of tension between two principles: the right of the individual user of land to control his life; and the need for a body somewhat removed from the day-to-day problems related to use of the land, that can perform the long-range allocation function and ensure that the goals of the trust, as spelled out in the charter, are preserved.

Hereafter, we will talk about *control* as the function of the land users (both individually and as a group) and *trusteeship* as a function of a separate group, though perhaps overlapping in membership with those who exercise control. We will use this distinction to consider the issue of rights of users in contrast to the rights of posterity or other nonusers. Our discussion has as its model the New Communities, Inc., experience. The NCI board (made up of civil rights and other leaders and specialists from many different states) can be conceptualized as exercising the trusteeship function, and the local population of southwest Georgia can be viewed as the main or potential users of the particular piece of land that NCI seeks to hold in trust.

Local Control Within the Community Land Trust Framework

Local control is primarily control by users who are accustomed to thinking in terms of individual ownership; their readiness to work in a community land trust framework is conditioned by this attitude. Moving to the concept of group ownership from individual ownership is therefore a difficult transition, made even more difficult if that ownership is not vested in the users alone but in a board that is not confined to people in the local community.

People who have never had a chance to own land—especially low-income persons, whether in rural or urban settings—may very well reject the idea of a trusteeship over the land they expect to use. Members of minority groups who have been typically excluded from land ownership and often view it as the only way to gain control of both land and their own destinies, may see such a trusteeship as merely another exclusion.

Yet, in fact, the land trust concept can be seen as the best way in which local control can be gained *and* maintained. A program of local education and orientation among potential users and a careful structuring of the trusteeship board's relation to the local control mechanism can help defuse this very difficult issue. But it must be recognized that the issue is never completely resolved. It is an illustration of the more general problem everyone faces—accommodating local needs to the needs of a larger community.

Establishing the Line Between Control and Trusteeship

As might be expected, there are differing views on where to establish the critical line between control and trusteeship. What is agreed is only that experience demonstrates the necessity of a more or less broadly based board distinct from the users of the land; the advantages justify the effort of grappling with the interface between the two.

It is important never to lose sight of the primary purpose of the community land trust: to acquire land and hold it in trusteeship. Thus, the trust should not be deeply involved in the development of the community, population selection, site planning, or institutional development. These concerns affect the interests of the trust only to the extent that the long-term value of the land and its resources are enhanced or depleted, or to the extent that the fundamental principles of its trusteeship charter are affected. The development functions should be performed primarily by the actual and potential users of the land through separate community-based organizations, such as a community development corporation.

On the other hand, early decisions of the trustees will have an important lasting impact on the nature of the land trust. In the United States, this impact will stem from the local constituency or community groups involved initially in the trust, identified as the "local sponsor."

In contrast, somewhat greater continuing control on the part of the trustees is exercised by the Jewish National Fund:

> It is essential that the trust itself—or bodies that are totally under its control—continue with the infrastructure of the first stages of development even after having assured ownership of the land. This is to ensure the necessary follow-up during the early stages of development and also to reduce the burden placed on the prospective individual land holder.
>
> Similarly, it will ensure the correct approach to the *utilization* of the land and guarantee that the intrinsic normative value of the land—which rises significantly with the initial planning and development—remains for utilization by the trust. It should be added, though, that the final development, such as building and construction work, etc., must be transferred from the trust to the landholders themselves or to their delegated authorities; this obviously, though, only for the permitted aims of the settlement. (There is a theory that the personality of a man is determined during his first two years of childhood. I fear that similarly during the first stages of land purchase by the trust and the initial development planning, the fate of the land is determined for at least one whole generation.)
>
> Although it is essential that [the fundamental assumptions concerning the utilization of the land] remain in the hands of the trust, it is preferable that either the trust sets up an advisory board of the people of the place concerned or that it co-opt to its own board (as advisors) some of the land holders. The inclusion of the local people is of democratic significance, though being close to the land in question arouses local interests, biases, and pressures which distort the overall position and general principles of the trust.[5]

It is in the final analysis the representational mix of the board of trustees that will determine the balance between local control and the trusteeship function. In the case of New Communities, Inc., strong demands for local control resulted in weighting the balance in the direction of the resident community. But we should emphasize here that this compromises the ideals behind the land trust idea. A major long-range goal of the land trust idea is to provide access to the land for all people, and particularly for those—the poor—who have been excluded from land in the past. It can be argued therefore that the majority of the board of trustees should consist *not* of those who have already received access to land through the land trust, but rather people who can identify with those *not* on the land. . . .

Internal Organizational Structure

. . .

Selection of the Board

Since the board, or the trustees, represents the ultimate authority over the land, the method of selection is critical. In keeping with the main thrust of the land trust concept . . . a majority of the board membership should consist of people somewhat removed from the resident community, serving on a relatively long-term basis.[6]

In general, the board should represent various groups in the larger "community." A certain proportion of members should be allocated to the resident community (in New Communities, Inc., two-fifths of the board members represent the potential or actual resident community); others should represent local organizations—groups operating within the land trust, such as farm co-ops or community development corporations, or groups in the larger local community acting as the local sponsor. In addition, "elder statesmen" might be selected—as individuals or representing certain key organizations so that the larger, public interest is represented on the board. They might be chosen because of special skills or resources in areas such as law, finance, planning, or ecology.

For various practical as well as symbolic reasons, the board of a regional land trust ought to include public appointees—chosen by the town, county, or state government. Depending on what proportion of the board is made up of public appointees, the land trust might approach the kind of public corporation that has been proposed to set up and administer conservation land banks and other public trust land in various states.

If the composition of the board is by organizational allocation, there is danger that changing circumstances could make the bylaws obsolete or unworkable. Organizations sometimes dissolve, or their interests change. New groups are formed. Perhaps a provision could be included that the organizational allocation be re-examined yearly and perhaps changed by a three-fourths majority of the board. Certain groups which will always be in existence and involved (such as the resident community and government organizations) might be excepted from reallocation.

The method by which each organization chooses its representatives should be left up to that organization, although there might be a provision to ensure some turnover without discontinuity. Terms of four or five years might be reasonable, with the expiration dates staggered. . . .

Utilizing the Land

. . .

Improvements on the Land
Transfer of Property Ownership

Whereas the land itself is held by the trust for the common good, the form of ownership of improvements (immovable property, such as dwellings, farm or factory buildings) is usually left to the choice of members of the community. Ownership may be individual, cooperative, or corporate. None of these arrangements, however, should restrict the mobility of land users nor dampen their interest in investing capital and labor on improvements. Fair procedures can be worked out for the sale of this immoveable property when the owner desires to move. *The main goal of any such procedures is to ensure that community-generated value increments accrue to the community and not to the individual.*[7]

When an individual wants to leave the community, he should notify the community and upon meeting all his financial obligations be released from his contract. Unless there are specific provisions in the lease contract to the contrary, he may reclaim and remove all the movable personal property that he wants. Immovable property (held by a departing individual or organization) will have to be transferred in either of two ways:

1. Property will be appraised by a committee either named by the community or operating as part of the board of trustees. It will then be purchased by the community or the land trust and turned over at an agreed price to a new tenant.
2. The departing owner may sell his property directly to the new land tenant, subject to the approval of the community or trust.

The former procedure is the more advantageous for both the old and new tenant since the community might be able to act as the financing intermediary. This, of course, would require some type of contractual agreement between the individual and the community that would perform the function of a mortgage but not *be* one. This arrangement also would prevent hidden land speculation from creeping in, as when charges for improvements actually represent appreciation in land values.

Sale of Property by Cooperatives or Corporations

Cooperatives and private corporations will be free to terminate their leases and sell the improvements to approved parties at any time, with due notice given. The land trust will exercise control over speculative increase in the value by establishing a high enough rent on the parcel used by the cooperative or corporation to prevent unearned profit. As with individual property, assessment will be made by a committee, and the property will be transferred to the trust, to the community, or to a new user group. The selling group will allocate the proceeds according to arrangements previously spelled out with its members in the cooperative or corporation bylaws.

Ambiguous Improvements

The lease principle rests on the concept of separating the land and natural resources which are not created by man, from man-made improvements. In most cases it is not hard to make this distinction: buildings, fences, and roadways are obviously in the latter category. However, an attempt should be made in the lease to define ambiguous or marginal improvements and spell out how they can be assessed and proceeds of sale allocated. In this category might be included improvement of the land for agriculture through labor and application of capital—draining or irrigating, building up the soil through use of fertilizers, care of timber and planting or care of orchards. Assessing soil values will perhaps be the most difficult measurement. When the bulk of the farming is carried on cooperatively on cooperative land, the problem of transfer of property ownership is greatly eased.

NOTES

1. A variety of modern thinkers have cried but for the restoration of the notion of trust in connection with land. The best known are such disparate souls as Marx and Gandhi. In the West, Henry George's *Progress and Poverty* (1880) became an instant worldwide bestseller; the reading public seemed hungry for new approaches to the "land problem." During the Depression, it was the social philosopher Ralph Borsodi, perhaps more than anyone else, who discovered a way to translate George's ideas (of land as a source of wealth) into the field of applied economics.

2. Hopefully, the community land trust will not be confused with an ordinary real estate trust which usually has individual, private beneficiaries and has as its purpose the protection of private profits.

3. The concept of "trusterty" includes more than natural resources; it includes also abstractions such as legal grants. It is more complex than it might first appear to be. For a full discussion of trusterty, see Ralph Borsodi, *Seventeen Problems of Man and Society* (Anand, India: Charotar Book Stall, 1968), especially pp. 333–372. The book is available from School of Living, Freeland, Md.

4. The leasing of land only, without structures, may seem to be a novel concept, but this is neither a new nor an uncommon idea. It is used in such dissimilar places as Canberra, Australia; Irvine, California; and part of Baltimore, Maryland. It is a standard way of handling commercial urban land; the corporate owners of many a skyscraper do not own, but only lease, the land upon which it stands.

5. Shimon Benshemesh, letter to Robert Swann, December 7, 1971. As mentioned by Mr. Benshemesh, certain initial decisions by the organizers of the trust will determine the "personality" of the trust for at least one whole generation. It is important, therefore, to proceed but to proceed with care and foresight, never losing sight of the fundamental beliefs on which the community land trust concept is based.

6. We recognize that in many cases the initial composition of the board will be self-defining; as mentioned above, it will consist of the organizing group. But to meet the organizational requirements of the state—and also to provide continuity as the effort becomes institutionalized in the future—it is essential to spell out carefully how the board is to be selected.

7. A secondary consideration, which could perhaps conflict, is that should an individual decide to resettle outside on private land, he will not be penalized by the undervaluation of his property in terms of the larger economy. In any case, though, he would probably *not* be compensated for the community-generated site value he leaves behind.

FROM *The Community Land Trust Handbook*

Institute for Community Economics
(1982)

Land and Property: Individuals and Communities

America once offered millions of people an opportunity they had never known before—access to land, and secure homes where they could enjoy the fruits of their labor. It offered them, also, an opportunity to shape and control communities.

Today much has changed. There is no longer a vast reserve of land waiting for settlement. Americans can no longer pull up roots, turn their backs on old problems, and make a new start on the frontier. The problems before American society today must be faced. And at the heart of many of these problems is the fact that an increasingly large number of Americans are being denied access to land and to the economic and social benefits of land.

Urban America

America is plagued increasingly by land speculation and absentee ownership of both land and buildings. Speculation often pushes the price of urban property far beyond the reach of the people most dependent on it—poor and moderate-income families in need of secure homes, small businesses in need of commercial and industrial sites, local residents in need of parks and open space for recreation and health. Absentee ownership has made matters even worse, particularly in neighborhoods with large concentrations of poor, minority, and working-class families. More than 75 percent of the land and housing may be owned by absentee landlords, leaving residents bereft of any meaningful control over local development or their personal futures. Frequently, all of the businesses and profitable property in an area are owned by people who live in other, more affluent communities, so that inner-city neighborhoods have little capital to reinvest in their own improvement. It is common to find row after row of abandoned buildings, left vacant by landlords who have taken all of the income tax deductions the law allows while deferring payments for property taxes and repairs. Until recently, when the problem was finally confronted by homeowner militancy and federal laws, banks often refused credit to certain "redlined" neighborhoods. Starved for financing for mortgages and home improvements, these neighborhoods deteriorated further each year.

This selection was originally published as chapters 2 and 3 in *The Community Land Trust Handbook* by the Institute of Community Economics (Emmaus, PA: Rodale Press, 1982), 1–35. It is reprinted by permission of Equity Trust, Inc.

Such scenes of disinvestment coexist in urban America with a new problem—gentrification. Inner-city neighborhoods of low-income and working-class people have begun to attract the interest of real estate brokers, luxury developers, and young, affluent professionals interested in moving back to the city. In neighborhoods long starved of capital, reinvestment of any kind is initially welcomed with open arms. But enclaves of new, affluent city-dwellers tend to expand—changing the social, racial, and class composition of the entire area, displacing the original population, and destroying the community that was previously there.

Whether due to disinvestment or reinvestment, displacement has become an ever-present possibility for people who neither own nor control the urban land that is under their feet or the roof that is over their heads. The poor, of course, face the greatest threat, but they are no longer alone. All people who rent, all people who cannot afford to own their homes, face the possibility of being ousted from their homes by the sale of the property, by its conversion to condominiums, or simply by increases in rent to unaffordable levels. Homeownership, however, is a dream that is receding further and further away for most Americans. So little affordable housing is being built and remaining available that in 1980 the president of the National Association of Home Builders was prompted to write:

> Unless current trends are reversed soon, a housing cost crisis of unknown proportion could engulf this nation—pitting one generation of Americans against another and pushing from the mainstream of American society those who are being denied decent, affordable shelter—the young, the elderly, and the poor.

Rural America

The land and housing problems of urban America are paralleled by the speculation, concentration of ownership, absentee ownership, and housing shortages of rural America. Gentrification has its counterpart in the resort, vacation, and second-home development that is rapidly spreading across the country, displacing traditional occupations and indigenous families from the land they depend upon. Redlining has its rural equivalent in the reluctance of banks and government agencies to finance basic affordable housing that meets the needs of local people but does not meet the banks' idea of what is "marketable."

There are also serious problems that relate directly to farmland and farming. The United States has been converting agricultural land to nonagricultural uses at the rate of about three million acres per year. For the land that remains in agriculture, ownership is increasingly concentrated. One percent of the farmland owners possess 30 percent of the farmland, and 5 percent of the owners own nearly half of the land. A third of the land is owned by nonfarming landlords. These trends—farmland conversion, concentration of ownership, and ownership by absentee landlords—have been spurred by the rapid appreciation in land prices. Since land prices in recent years have risen faster than the general inflation rate, farmland has become an attractive investment for farmers and nonfarmers alike. As investors try to outbid each other for the available land, it becomes more and more difficult for small farmers and other local residents to retain access to land in their own communities.

If these trends continue, farms will become still fewer and larger, barring entry to more and more young, would-be farmers. *The Summary Report on the Structure of Agriculture,* issued in 1981 by the USDA, warned that public officials must act to slow these trends. Failure to act, concludes the report,

> will amount to a decision to accept greater and greater separation among the business functions of farming—ownership, management, labor, and operation—and greater concentration of landownership among fewer and fewer people, violating a long-held American principle and relegating the concepts behind "the family farm" to the status of museum relics.

Nowhere are the problems of speculation, concentration, and absentee ownership more obvious and more destructive than in the resource-rich corporate fiefdoms of Appalachia. In 1974 the editors of a West Virginia newspaper, the *Herald-Advertiser and Herald-Dispatch,* commissioned an investigation into who owns West Virginia. They discovered that absentee landlords—primarily a few dozen giant fuel, transportation, and lumber companies—own or control at least two-thirds of the privately held land in West Virginia. Six years later, the Highlander Center in New Market, Tennessee, asked a similar question for all of Appalachia, and set out to study landownership in 80 rural Appalachian counties. The center discovered that all 15 of the largest landowners in these selected counties were corporations, and that corporations owned 40 percent of the land and 70 percent of the mineral rights, while 75 percent of the land and 80 percent of the mineral rights were held by individuals or groups from outside the counties themselves. The center also discovered that property taxes paid by these absentee owners were extraordinarily low.

Corporate landowners have drawn tremendous wealth from Appalachia in essentially the same way that colonial powers draw wealth from their colonies. The land and resources of the region have not enriched the people of the region. The process of removing wealth from the region has impoverished a major part of the population, leaving them without access to land in their own communities, without the land they need to continue traditional forms of subsistence, to develop new economic opportunities for themselves, or even to provide secure homes for themselves. As a result, tremendous numbers of families have been forced to leave Appalachia in search of greater opportunities elsewhere.

But most have not found opportunities elsewhere. Like the black families of the Deep South who have been forced off their land by similar economic forces, the people of Appalachia have gone to northern cities. There they have found the urban problems described earlier in this chapter.

It is time to ask what has gone wrong. Our land still holds tremendous opportunities for those who control it. If millions of Americans are being denied the most basic kinds of opportunities, it is time to look at the ways in which American land is being controlled and used, and to ask in whose interest this is being done.

Individuals, Communities, and Property

Land and Property

The problems do not spring from the land itself. They spring from the ways that the land is controlled, owned, and used. They are not land problems as such; they are *property* problems. The distinction between the words *land* and *property* is an important one, even though the words are often used as though they mean the same thing. People may speak of the same one-acre lot as either a "piece of land" or "a piece of property." When the lot is called "land" it is being described simply as an area of the earth's surface, something that exists independently of all human activity, all human laws and institutions; but when it is called "property" it is being described as a human possession, as something *owned* according to the laws of human society. Our concern here is with the arrangements whereby land is treated *as* property, and with the effects that these arrangements have on people.

Public and Private Property

For the most part, property is seen as falling into one or the other of these two categories. It is seen either as privately controlled by a private owner to serve the owner's "private interest," or as publicly controlled by one or another level of government in the "public interest." In fact, actual patterns of property ownership and control today are not nearly this easily categorized. Nevertheless, these are the terms—"public" or "private"—in which current property problems are normally discussed, and they are very much the terms of current political rhetoric. As such, they are often surrounded with a great deal of emotion, and a great deal of confusion. In effect, the words have become banners flapping over an increasingly complicated field of controversy. These banners—"public" and "private" waved aloft—do not tell us much about the subject of the controversy; nor do they tell us much about the real interests of the people who wave them. We will therefore set the words aside for the time being. At the end of this chapter we will examine the complicated property arrangements that lie behind these words today, but we will approach the subject here in more basic terms.

Individuals and Communities

The words we use to describe particular property arrangements are not as important as how these arrangements help or hinder people in getting the things they want and need from the land. These interests must be identified before the virtues and limitations of particular arrangements can be discussed.

People need and want certain things from the land as individuals, but they also need and want certain things as communities. The interests of individuals may be more obvious because they are more immediate. The interests of communities tend to be long-term interests, but in the long term they are no less important than individual interests. Though there are forces at work in our society that tend to undermine our *sense* of community, we do continue to live in communities and to depend on them in essential ways. Communities, in turn, depend on the land they occupy; if the community's interests in this land are ignored, the community will weaken until it can no longer provide those things that its individual members need from it.

The Legitimate Interests of Individuals

Security

Every person has a legitimate interest in having a secure home. In fact, the very idea of *home* calls necessarily for a degree of security. Home implies continuity and stability: it is the place we want to hang on to, the place we expect to come back to. It is also a *private* place; we think of it as our own whether we are technically homeowners or renters or squatters.

For many people this interest in security involves only the housing they occupy, but for others on homesteads or farms the interest extends to the land that they work and depend on for their livelihood. Here, too, continuity is essential. Those who work the soil want and need some assurance that they will be allowed to reap what they have sown.

Earned Equity

People have a legitimate interest in keeping whatever value they put into their homes, or into the land they occupy and use, when this value is derived directly from their personal efforts. If they improve their property either directly through their own labor or by spending on it what they have earned elsewhere, they have an obvious and legitimate interest in retaining as equity the value of these improvements.

A Reasonable Legacy

The development of a home, or of a farm or small business, is often a family effort extending over more than one generation. Families have a legitimate interest in protecting the continuity of such efforts—in seeing that members of a new generation can inherit the family homes, farms, or businesses in which they already have a stake.

The Legitimate Interests of Communities

Community Access

A community has a legitimate interest in maintaining continuing access to its land for all of its members. The land and natural resources of a community are the necessary base for its economic and social well-being. Land must be available for housing, jobs, and social services if the community is to be healthy and secure.

Community Equity

A community has a legitimate interest in retaining and utilizing for the common good whatever value it has created or nurtured. In other words, it has an interest in retaining value that accumulates not through the sort of individual efforts that create an individual's "fair earned equity," but through communal efforts that improve the community as a whole—whether these efforts involve obvious immediate accomplishments such as improvements in streets or parks or schools, or such long-term accomplishments as the nurturing of a stable and agreeable community character and a healthy local economy. It has an interest as well in retaining a reasonable share of that value that has not been earned by anyone but that derives from the community's natural resources or from the larger economic process in which it participates.

Community Legacy

A community has a legitimate interest in preserving its environment and guiding its own development in a way that will provide for the legitimate interests of future generations. Like individual families, communities exist over periods of time that span many generations. What is done to a community's environment by one generation will affect other generations far into the future.

Balancing Individual and Community Interests

As isolated propositions, these statements of individual and community interests are relatively simple. But when the effort is made to protect both the legitimate interests of all of the individuals within a community and the legitimate interests of the community itself—all within one consistent set of property arrangements—the problems that must be faced are not so simple. What one individual does to secure his or her interests may interfere with the interests of either other individuals or the community. And what the community does to secure its interests may interfere with the interests of individuals. A satisfactory property arrangement must not advance the interests of one individual or group at the expense of another.

Any effectively balanced arrangement requires that there be agreement not only on what the legitimate interests are but on how they are limited by each other. It also requires that there be effective means of enforcing these limitations so that one interest does not overrun another. This is a task that grows more difficult as American society feels increasing pressures on its traditional property arrangements.

As this chapter has shown, our present property arrangements are not working well enough. It makes sense to look for alternative approaches that are based on respect for the legitimate interests of both individuals and communities and that provide an effective means of balancing these interests. The community land trust is one such approach. . . . Though it offers a real alternative to current arrangements, the CLT model is not a completely new invention; it is a fresh adaptation of some very old ideas. In fact, the view of land and property that has shaped the CLT is much older than our modern notion of private property.

The Roots of a Two-Sided View of Land

Throughout most of the time that human beings have lived on the earth there was little concept of land as private property. Private property consisted of such things as clothes and tools, which were direct extensions of the individuals who made and used them. But no human being made the earth, and the idea of owning a piece of land made no more sense than the idea of owning a piece of sky. Communities of people might identify themselves with their territories—the large areas of land they knew and depended on for their survival—and they might be prepared to defend their territories against others. In this sense, community property can be said to have existed long before individual property, but these community lands were still not understood to be property in our modern legal sense. The association between a community and its territory derived from continuing occupancy and use rather than abstract legal claim.

These were originally the attitudes of more or less nomadic people, hunter-gathers who depended on access to large areas of land and on community cooperation in utilizing these large areas for survival. Our traditions of individual property can be traced to the emergence of agriculture. Though agriculture was practiced on a communal as well as an individual basis, it did raise new questions about individual interests. When people till the earth, they mix their labor with the land, and it becomes natural to think of them as having a special claim not only to the crops they produce but to the land they have improved with their labor. They also, of course, tend to establish permanent homes on or near the land they work, and in thus occupying a piece of land permanently they develop strong interests in it as individuals.

Yet as civilization has evolved away from the life of the nomadic hunter-gatherer, the sense of land as a common ground has not been completely left behind. No matter how preoccupied people may become with property—with their rights to specifically limited pieces of land—they continue to identify with larger areas as well. They continue to see the land around them not just as so many separate pieces of individual property but as the domain of their community, and, as we have noted, they continue to be dependent on this larger area as members of the community.

Thus our view of land has been two-sided from the very beginnings of civilization. This dual view is inherent not only in our social and legal institutions but in the Judeo-Christian tradition that underlies so much of our sense of what is right and what is wrong in the world.

The Old Testament has a good deal to say about both individual property interests and the ways in which these interests must be limited. The earth itself, we are told, belongs ultimately to God. It was given to humanity to use and to enjoy, but it was a gift with certain conditions attached to it. People must care for the land entrusted to them: they may not waste it, use it up, or trade it away permanently for short-term profits. The individual's right to take value from the land is clearly limited by the interests of the community and the interests of future generations. Many of these conditions are described in the Book of Leviticus—including the provision that after every period of 50 years all land must be returned to its original owners, so that its value can never be permanently lost to the community: "The land shall not be sold forever: for the land is mine; for ye are strangers and sojourners with me" (Lev. 25:23). If a traditional precedent is needed for the way in which a community land trust limits the rights of individuals to sell the land they use, it can be found in this passage.

Today the Old Testament's balanced approach to land and property is emphasized by many religious leaders. As Pope John Paul II has said, "There is a social mortgage on all private property."

Private Property in America

Since the first European settlers arrived in America, individual property has had a special importance in American society—as was noted by Alexis de Tocqueville, the shrewd French observer of nineteenth-century America.

> In no country in the world is the love of property more active and more anxious than in the United States; nowhere does the majority display less inclination for those principles which threaten to alter, in whatever manner, the laws of property.

This American "love of property" has been analyzed in various ways, but central to any explanation must be the fact that America offered the *opportunity* for individuals to own land—as many had been unable to do in Europe, where there was no abundance of land to begin with and where opportunities for acquiring land were severely limited by the feudal traditions that still affected much of European society. Settlers came to this country with a thirst for land, and they came with a profound dislike of these feudal traditions.

Feudalism was a system in which rights to land originated at the "top" of society, with monarchs and with powerful nobility, and were passed downward to those who actually used the land but who could not hold it in their own rights. Thus, feudal arrangements worked against the idea of private property except for a very few powerful individuals. By the time of American settlement, feudalism had been undermined in Western Europe by the increasing wealth and power of an urban "middle class," but opportunities for individual ownership of land, especially in rural areas, were still limited by traditional feudal arrangements.

Access to American land was not limited in this way, and the Americans who founded our nation had no intention of allowing it to become so. In America, property rights were to originate with individuals, not with kings. And the fact that there was an abundance of unsettled land made it possible for many people to acquire property. As de Tocqueville noted, the American love of property was not limited to a landed minority; it was a love felt by the majority of Americans, and it was a love that did not need to go unsatisfied as long as the vast "public domain" west of the Appalachians was being divided up and made available, year after year, to individual owners.

The conversion of this federally owned public domain to private ownership was an event unprecedented in human history. This is not the place for a thorough discussion of this long, variable, and often controversial process, but two large generalizations can be made. First, it is true that federal land policies were in some ways designed and manipulated to serve the interests of speculators who used their wealth and influence to acquire large tracts of land at low prices. As settlement proceeded and the value of this land increased, such people were able to sell it at great profit, often without having contributed anything to its improvement, and sometimes without even having seen it. Second, in spite of large-scale speculation in land, millions of people who had previously owned little or no property did acquire land in America. There were genuine opportunities for ownership for the people who actually settled and developed the land. Though there was risk and often failure, a great many people's basic interests in security, equity, and legacy were served by this land.

These generalizations suggest two distinct elements in the American love of property. On the one hand, private property has been valued as a source of profit. The best use of land has often been seen as the most profitable private use. On the other hand, we have continued to see private ownership of land as the basis of individual security, earned equity, and legacy. The idea of a secure place where one can enjoy the fruits of one's own labor continues to be a major element of the American Dream.

Community Property in America

In spite of the American emphasis on private property, not all of the public domain was turned over to individuals. America does have a tradition of community land, going back to earliest colonial times when New England villages transplanted the English tradition of the "common." Originally set aside as community pasture land, some of these commons, like Boston Common, exist today as public parks. The unsettled public domain also served frontier communities as a kind of common, where people shared access to fish and game and other natural products of the earth—until this land, too, was divided into private holdings and the frontier moved on.

Federal land-distribution policies themselves addressed the needs of communities. The public domain was surveyed into townships containing 36 "sections" of one square mile each. In each township one section was set aside to help the new town establish a community school. Either the section was sold and the proceeds turned over to the town, or the land itself was turned over to the town. In either case, the policy involved a clear recognition not only of the need for local political structures but of the idea that communities should be able to draw on the land they occupy to meet community needs. Also, as new states were formed in the West, tracts of land were turned over to them by the federal government to help them finance the services they would need to provide, such as roads and law enforcement. Additionally, the 1862 Morrill Act granted a total of 13 million acres to the states for the purpose of endowing land grant colleges, which have since become some of our major state universities.

In spite of provisions such as these, federal land policy was weighted in favor of individual rather than community interests. One major reason for this emphasis was, again, the abundance of the public domain itself. As long as there was so much public land waiting to be settled there was relatively little pressure to deal with the long-range interests of the communities that were being created. Even in the older cities, people could look to new opportunities in the West rather than address the immediate problems of overcrowded city neighborhoods. At least it could always be argued that those who really wanted to could make new lives for themselves in the West.

Private and Public Property Today

Now much has changed. Americans may still move restlessly from place to place, but there is no longer a great reserve of unsettled land offering new opportunities. In this century millions of rural people have been forced to leave their land and move to the cities, where they often remain as landless tenants, dependent on others for housing as well as for jobs and community services. The problems of both rural areas and cities continue to grow. We can no longer turn away from these problems—for if we do turn from one troubled community, we are likely to find the same problems in the next.

In trying to deal with these problems we have had to concern ourselves with the ownership and control of land in more complicated terms than applied in the nineteenth century when the central concern was that of converting the public domain to individual property. The meaning of "private" and "public" property has changed and is changing in America today.

Private Property—Corporate Property

To most people, *private* is a very attractive word. It is strongly associated with the privacy and security of the home. However, much private land in America is not owned by people who live on it. Most land today is concentrated in the hands of a relatively small part of the population (75 percent of the privately held land in America is owned by 5 percent of the private landholders). And absentee ownership is increasingly common.

Some absentee ownership is still relatively private. When the narrator of Robert Frost's poem says, "Whose woods these are I think I know. His house is in the village though," he is speaking of an individual member of his own community who probably owns a few acres of woodland, a few miles from home, as his private source of firewood. But most absentee ownership today is not of this sort. Today if you stop by a woods in Maine or Georgia or Oregon, or by any area of extensive woodland not owned by government, and ask whose woods these are, the answer is likely to be International Paper or Georgia Pacific or Weyerhaeuser or some other giant corporate landowner. If you then ask where his house is, the answer must be "anywhere and nowhere." He is not a private individual. He is not a member of any community. In this case, private ownership does not necessarily mean individual ownership.

Corporate ownership is not limited to forest land, of course. As indicated at the beginning of this chapter, large corporations own a major share of the country's most valuable land. They own large areas of agricultural land. They have vast mineral holdings, often in the form of mineral rights beneath the surface of land belonging to others. They own residential and commercial property (buildings and the land beneath them) as well as land that is held for its *potential* value as residential or commercial property.

But large corporations are not the only factor separating our popular notion of private property from the actual property arrangements that surround us. People tend to think of property as something indivisible—either you own it or you don't. Yet legally, property must be understood as a bundle of distinct rights which can be separated and distributed among a number of parties. Our woodlot owner, for instance, may sell the timber rights to his land, or the mineral rights, or water rights, or development rights, or any number of rights-of-way. He may sell (or donate) these rights to other private parties or to public bodies. It is therefore possible—and increasingly common—to have property in which private and public ownership are mixed.

Public Control of Private Property

Even more common than mixed ownership is the mixture of private and public *control* of property. Many Americans still cherish the idea that you can do whatever you want with your own property. In fact, this has never been entirely true. As has been noted, our view of property has always been two-sided. Even in America, community as well as individual interests in property have been protected. It was Benjamin Franklin, not some latter-day land reformer, who said, "Private property is a creature of society, and is subject to the calls of society, whenever its necessities shall require it." In the twentieth century, as these "necessities" of society have become more complex, the ways in which private property is "subject to the calls of society" have increased. Particularly since 1926, when the U.S. Supreme Court upheld the constitutionality of zoning laws, public control of private property has become more and more extensive.

Our woodlot owner may not have sold the timber rights to his land, but if the land is on a flood plain he may be prevented from cutting trees by a law designed to protect the community from the effects of flooding and erosion. He may retain mineral rights but still be prevented from engaging in certain kinds of mining operations that would endanger the community or its environment. He may retain development rights but the number and type of buildings that he is allowed to place on his land may be limited by local or state land use ordinances. There are, in fact, a great many things that he may not do with his own property.

In cities, the public control of private property is likely to be even more elaborate. Zoning laws, building codes, health and safety regulations, and regulations defining the obligations of landlords to their tenants are among the many ways in which private control of property is likely to be limited in today's cities.

Private Control of Public Property

Forty-two percent of the land in the United States is owned by one or another level of government—most of it by the federal government. All of this land is considered to be public property, but there are real questions concerning who controls its use and whose interests are served by this use. It is not our purpose to argue that there are no public benefits from this land, and it is certainly not our purpose to argue that there should be no public land, but we do want to emphasize that, as in the case of private property, public property is not altogether what the name suggests.

First, it should be said that most public land is not community land in the sense of a village common. Most public land is controlled by government agencies that are relatively remote from the communities in which the land is located. Even if these agencies are models of uncompromising public service, the public they serve is usually much larger than the communities in which they hold land. As a result, in communities where a great deal of land is owned by federal or state governments, or even by big city governments, there is often frustration and resentment at the community's inability to control the use of, and draw value from, its "own" land. In reality, of course, most public land-management agencies are heavily influenced by private interests that want to use the land for their own profit.

In the western United States, vast areas of land are controlled by the Bureau of Land Management (BLM), an agency within the Department of the Interior. Former Secretary of the Interior Cecil Andrus has observed that in practice BLM seems to stand for "Bureau of Livestock and Mining," for it is primarily livestock and mining interests that benefit from this land. BLM land is not *owned* by these interests. They do not need to own the land. In fact, they are often better off not owning it but letting it be maintained for them at public expense and paying in return only a small part of the value they derive from it. The same kind of situation is common with land owned by the other major federal land-management agency, the U.S. Forest Service, and with publicly owned land generally. This private use of public land may or may not be, ultimately, "in the broad public interest." The point is that, although public ownership does preserve the long-range possibility of public control and benefit, the immediate benefits and often a large portion of control are enjoyed by private entities—many of them the same large corporations that are coming to control more and more of our private land as well.

Housing, Public and Private

Until quite recently, housing was assumed to be an entirely private matter. In the last several decades, however, there have been a number of public efforts to help people in communities where private initiative and capital have not provided adequate, affordable housing. Most of these efforts fall into three general categories: public housing developed and owned outright by government agencies, rent subsidies for tenants in privately owned buildings, and subsidized financing for the purchase of private housing. All of these have been important attempts to balance public and private interests; they have helped many people. But as long-term arrangements, all of them have serious limitations.

Government-owned housing is the most direct means of providing for people who cannot otherwise afford decent housing. But like other rental housing, it gives these people only limited security and does not allow them to build equity in their own homes. As in other situations where government agencies own property within communities, the problem remains that the occupants and their immediate communities do not usually control the use of the property.

Rent subsidies, like government-owned housing, offer no opportunity for equity and only limited security. They can provide crucial assistance to individuals for as long as the payments are continued, but they do not help either these individuals or their communities to improve their basic situations.

Publicly subsidized financing has been made available both for individuals seeking to buy their own homes and for developers of rental housing. Prospective homeowners who qualify for subsidized low-interest loans do receive security and equity, but most low-income people cannot qualify for these loans. Furthermore, when these homes are sold in the open market they may not be affordable for the next generation of prospective homeowners. To keep housing affordable for potential homeowners in a low-to-moderate income community, it may be necessary to provide subsidized financing each time a piece of residential property changes hands.

Perhaps the most basic problem with both rent subsidies and subsidized financing is that the public money put into them flows quickly into the hands of private interests—not only as remuneration for services rendered, but often as very large profits for landlords, developers, speculators, and other investors. Thus the value of public efforts to improve the community is not retained by the community. It passes to people who are for the most part outside of the community.

We do not want to suggest that these public efforts are wrong from the start. There is a tremendous need for assistance to communities that lack the resources to deal with their own increasing problems; private efforts are not likely to solve these problems, which are, in fact, often the result of private interests having diverted capital away from the community. The question is how to apply these subsidies so as to serve both the shorter-term interests of needy individuals and the longer-term interests of their communities. Today, as public subsidies are being reduced and those that remain are being closely scrutinized, there is a rapidly increasing awareness of the importance of this question. City administrators, in particular, are looking desperately for answers.

In Search of New Property Forms

It is no longer meaningful to describe property as either public or private. As simple labels, the terms do not fit the complicated property arrangements we have been discussing, and they divert attention from the dynamic nature of these modern arrangements. If the problems facing American individuals and communities are to be solved, a new understanding of property is needed—an understanding based on a clear view of the ways in which individual and community interests are related. Only through such an understanding can property arrangements be designed to balance and protect these interests.

The need for new and balanced arrangements is urgent. Unstable economic conditions and the rapidly increasing costs of land, housing, and financing are putting conventional homeownership out of the reach of more and more people. In an effort to stimulate a flagging market, private real estate interests and lending institutions are attempting to reduce the purchase costs of homes through new kinds of property arrangements. With shared-appreciation mortgages, for instance, homeowners no longer receive the full amount of any increase in the value of their property; the holder of the mortgage receives part of it. Perhaps even more significant is the fact that some private developers have begun setting up landholding companies in order to separate the ownership of homes from ownership of the land and thus reduce the purchase price of the homes themselves.

These are piecemeal efforts designed to serve the interests of lending institutions and developers. They may be helpful to those people whose incomes and credit ratings qualify them as potential homeowners in today's market, but they do not address the basic problems of communities or the needs of people who do not qualify.

Some of these new arrangements have similarities to some of the distinctive features of the community land trust. But they do not represent the balanced approach that the CLT provides. Given current market trends, conventional access to land and homeownership will continue to tighten, and the nature of ownership will continue to change. The question is no longer whether there will be new approaches to property. The question is whose interests they will serve.

The Community Land Trust Model

What Is a CLT?

A community land trust is an organization created to hold land for the benefit of a community and of individuals within the community. It is a democratically structured nonprofit corporation, with an open membership and a board of trustees elected by the membership. The board typically includes residents of trust-owned lands, other community residents, and public-interest representatives. Board members are elected for limited terms, so that the community retains ultimate control of the organization and of the land it owns.

The CLT acquires land through purchase or donation with an intention to retain title in perpetuity, thus removing the land from the speculative market. Appropriate uses for the land are determined, in a process comparable to public planning or zoning processes, and the land is then leased to individuals, families, cooperatives, community organizations, businesses, or for public purposes.

Normally, the CLT offers lifetime or long-term leases, which may be transferred to the leaseholders' heirs if they wish to continue the use of the land. Leaseholders must use the land in an environmentally and socially responsible manner, but the CLT may not interfere with their personal beliefs, associations, or activities. Leases are given only to those who will use the land. Priority in leasing is usually given to those whose needs are greatest, though individual needs must, of course, be matched with the capacity of a particular piece of land. Leaseholders pay a regular lease fee—based on "use value" rather than "full market value" of the land—but they do not need to make down payments and do not need conventional credit or financing to gain access to the land.

While leaseholders do not own the land they use, they may own buildings and other improvements on the land. In many cases the CLT can help leaseholders to acquire ownership of buildings and improvements by arranging affordable financing, and in some cases by organizing volunteer labor to assist in construction. Where the CLT has purchased property that includes existing housing, the housing may be sold to leaseholders over an extended period of time, either with the CLT holding the mortgage or through a land contract arrangement.

If leaseholders leave the land and terminate the lease, they may sell or remove the improvements which they own. Typically, the CLT retains a first option to buy the improvements at the owner's original invested cost, often adjusted for inflation, depreciation, and damage during the ownership period. This property can then be sold to the next leaseholder. Thus, the first leaseholder is guaranteed equity in the improvements, and the succeeding leaseholder is able to buy the improvements at a fair price. No seller will profit from unearned increases in market value, and no buyer will be priced out of the market by such increases. Any increase in value that is not due to a leaseholder's efforts will remain with the CLT.

Thus, neither the CLT nor the leaseholder holds the land itself as a commodity. The CLT holds it as a basic resource in which the community and individuals within the community are acknowledged to have certain legitimate interests. In this situation the lease agreement becomes the specific, flexible, legal means by which the legitimate interests of both the community and the individual leaseholder are explicitly described and protected in accordance with the policies of the CLT.

Individual Interests

Security

CLT leaseholders have the same basic security of land use that in our society has been traditionally enjoyed only by landowners. The CLT provides and guarantees this security through the long term of the lease and a variety of specific provisions detailing the respective rights and responsibilities of the CLT and the leaseholder. As a nonprofit organization, the CLT does away with the common conflict between the profit motives of some individuals and the security rights of others, and it does so without bringing into being a remote "public landlord." As members of a democratically structured organization, leaseholders are directly represented on the CLT's board; they are assured that the lease agreement will be administered by a group which includes their peers. Should any disputes arise between a leaseholder and the CLT concerning the terms or performance of the lease, a process for arbitration is provided in which each will have equal standing with the other and a fair opportunity to present their cases to a jointly established arbitration panel.

The CLT makes both long-term land use and homeownership possible for people who could not otherwise afford them. These people enjoy security in both their long-term lease and their title to their homes. They have the assurance that they will never be forced from their homes, or from the land they use, by a landlord who finds he or she can make more money by using the property in some other way or by renting to other parties. Such security stands in stark contrast to the vulnerability of most renters, especially in a "landlord's market" of limited housing and high inflation, where leases become less available and their terms shorter, and displacement is a common threat.

As these same economic pressures weigh more heavily on many present and prospective owners of land and homes, they too may find greater security in a CLT. By joining together, CLT members assure themselves of more support from others and greater access to financing than they could command as individuals. As a group they can give support and assistance to one another, both in daily land use and property maintenance as well as in times of hardship and special need. With its broader financial base, the CLT may be able to reduce its lease fees or provide direct financial assistance at such times.

Earned Equity

CLT leaseholders normally have equity for their own investments in buildings and other improvements on their leaseholds. Once again, this is a far better situation than that of ordinary tenants, who rent their housing and other improvements as well as the land beneath them, and have neither equity nor any way of developing equity. By law, any improvements made to land or housing by conventional tenants belong to the owner and remain with the property. The tenant has no permanent claim to them—no security in their use and no return for this investment—regardless of what they have cost her or him in effort or money. Yet most low- and moderate-income people have no choice but to accept the role of tenant. They cannot get the financing necessary to purchase property of their own. They are told by banks and other lending institutions that they cannot afford to own their own land or their own homes. They cannot afford an arrangement that would allow them to keep some of the fruits of their own labor and thus improve their own lot. Ironically, they can only afford to pay rent that will continue to rise as the market permits, and that, in a lifetime, may amount to many times what it would now cost them to purchase the property that they are renting. They are stuck with an arrangement that will not yield them one cent of equity. The CLT offers an alternative to this renter's dilemma.

Some renters of moderate income cling to the hope of owning land and a home. If their luck holds, if they can save enough for a down payment, if interest rates fall, if inflation is checked, this may one day be possible. The CLT can offer them an earlier and more certain opportunity to realize the benefits associated with ownership.

For those with sufficient financial resources to purchase land and housing, becoming a CLT leaseholder may represent an economic sacrifice. As leaseholders, they will build equity only through their own investment in improvements, not through increases in market value due to other factors. Such people may choose to become CLT leaseholders because of lower financing costs required through the CLT, or for the sake of the community of support and friendship which it offers, or out of concern for providing affordable properties within the community for future use by their children, friends, and others.

A Reasonable Legacy

The CLT provides the assurance that not only the leaseholders' property (the buildings and improvements which they own) but the leasehold itself (the right to continue the use of the land) may be passed on to their heirs. Obviously the right to bequeath property means nothing to someone who has no property to bequeath. The CLT first makes it possible for many people who could not otherwise do so to acquire property that they can leave to their heirs. Children who have grown up in homes on CLT land can continue to live in the homes that they know and have helped to maintain, or they may realize the value of the improvements through liquidation of the estate. Children who have grown up in families that farm CLT land can continue to work the land in which they already have a real stake. The parents of these children can live their lives with the knowledge that the fruits of their labor will not wither when they die.

Community Interests

Because a community is a collection of individuals, it is true that the advantages for individuals outlined above tend, at least indirectly, to be advantages for their communities. Certainly a community is healthier when its people enjoy security and can earn equity and leave it to their children. These opportunities are not only important in themselves but foster the development of supportive social relationships and services, providing personal benefits to community residents and reducing the burden on public agencies and appropriations. However, a community does have certain legitimate interests . . . that must be protected and balanced with the interests of individuals.

Community Access

Increasing numbers of communities are suffering from a lack of access to their own lands and therefore a lack of security for present and future generations of residents. For many communities, access is severely limited by high rates of absentee ownership. This has long been true for communities with a substantial base of valuable resources. It is increasingly true for agricultural communities. It is true for urban neighborhoods where a large percentage of the housing stock is owned by absentee landlords, or sometimes city governments and redevelopment agencies, and is made unavailable or unaffordable for neighborhood residents. Always, it is low-income communities whose needs are most consistently neglected and denied.

When land, housing, and commercial developments are offered for sale, they are subject to a market which recognizes only the potential for profit, not the needs of the people whose security depends on this land and property. Confronted on the one hand by monopolization and absentee ownership, and on the other by tight credit and the financial barriers of a speculative market, communities are becoming more and more aware that their security depends on community acquisition or control of land.

The CLT can be an important tool for communities seeking to regain control of their own lands. As a flexible nonprofit organization it can utilize a variety of acquisition techniques. It can receive donations of land from people and institutions motivated by sympathy with the CLT's goals and by an interest in the tax savings resulting from the donation. It can arrange to acquire land from elderly people who want to live out their lives in their own homes but can no longer maintain these homes. (CLT acquisition can both help these people to stay in their homes and secure long-term community control.) In purchasing land, a CLT can draw on a wide range of both conventional and nonconventional sources of financing. It can utilize private grants and a variety of public grants and subsidies. It can borrow from conventional private and public sources of capital and from the growing number of individuals and institutions that are seeking socially responsible ways of investing their savings and endowments.

The lease fees that a CLT receives for the use of its land can be utilized to acquire more land and, as the value of its accumulated resources increases, the CLT's ability to borrow in order to finance further acquisitions will also increase. Thus for the long term a CLT can become a powerful means of acquiring land for the community.

But the importance of the CLT is not simply as a community land-acquisition tool. It is designed to hold in perpetuity the land that it acquires, and to provide secure access to that land for individuals within the community—particularly for individuals who have previously been denied the access to and the benefits of land. For the land that it holds, the possibility of absentee ownership and monopoly is eliminated. In its leasing policies, the CLT typically offers use rights only to those who will use the land themselves, or to organizations that will manage the land for the direct benefit of community residents. Land is allocated only in the amounts required for use.

The CLT also provides a means of assuring that the benefits of access are fully realized by those to whom the land is leased. Its resources can be utilized in developing housing on its land, and in helping leaseholders to maintain their homes and use their leased land effectively.

It goes without saying that a community land trust cannot be the sole means of assuring access to land and resources for all members of a community. In this effort it must be a partner with government as well as with other community organizations. Public legislation is still extremely important. Civil rights legislation has prohibited discrimination in housing and in the workplace. State and local laws give tenants a greater degree of security—and in some cases help them to purchase their own buildings. Such laws represent real progress, though a great deal remains to be done in enforcing them. As an active community organization concerned with questions of access, a CLT can work effectively to see that such laws are enforced, and that further necessary legislation is passed. It can be particularly effective in these efforts if it works in cooperation with other community organizations.

Community Equity

No element of a local economy is more basic than the community's land and natural resource base. On this land, and from this land, the wealth of the community and most of its individual members is produced. The community's land is the original "commonwealth." Yet present patterns of landownership and transfer often render land and resources and their economic value unavailable to the communities that occupy them. In these situations the economic benefits of community development are continually captured by a privileged few or drained away by outside interests. In other words, the community is deprived of its equity.

The community's claim to this equity rests on two principles: that the inherent value of the land is not of human creation and thus cannot rightfully be regarded as personal income for any individual, and that the appreciated value of the land (as opposed to the value of improvements made to the land) is the result of the activity and efforts of individuals, organizations, and public agencies throughout the community, and economic forces outside the community. By holding land permanently in trust, a CLT preserves for the community both the original, inherent value of the land and any value that is added to it by the efforts of the community or larger economic forces. Individuals who use the land may retain the value of what they invest as individuals, but they may not claim or remove for themselves what belongs to the community as a whole.

As outlined here these distinctions are necessarily abstract, but the importance of the CLT as a means of preserving community equity is not merely a matter of abstract justice. What is at stake in this matter is the survival of whole communities and the basic well-being of their residents. Contemporary problems . . . are directly related to the loss of community equity.

The process of gentrification, for instance, stems from recent drastic increases in the costs of transportation and home heating and from changes in family values and lifestyles that make urban living newly attractive. Both of these changes have encouraged speculation by investors who themselves had no role in making these neighborhoods more attractive, but whose financial resources and access to credit allow them to profit greatly from them. In such situations the existing community retains little of the increased value of its land base, and may be powerless to prevent the large-scale displacement of its members.

Even more ironic is the grim paradox faced by many low-income neighborhoods—and by an increasing number of middle-income communities as well—when residents try to improve their community and the quality of their lives in it, for if they succeed in this effort they will make the community's land more attractive for speculation. By making their streets cleaner and safer, creating community gardens and playgrounds, renovating their homes, and building a stronger local economy, they may initiate or accelerate the market forces which will increase property values, raise property taxes and rents, and ultimately drive them from the community.

The loss of community equity is also a problem in rural areas, where the concern is often less with housing than with preserving the community's economic base. Many rural communities whose land has been cultivated by generations of family farmers are losing control of the land necessary to local enterprises. At the same time that new technology and marketing systems are driving small farmers out of business and depressing the economies of farming communities, the market value of land in these communities has tended to rise sharply as it is sought sometimes by agribusiness but in many cases by people seeking vacation homes, and by developers, speculators, and other outside investors. With the increase in market value, taxes often increase and resident landowners find that not only is it difficult to make a living from their land, but they can no longer afford to own it. As properties change hands, the community also changes. Social networks are broken. As land is withdrawn from cultivation, agricultural support services may be lost, further increasing the difficulty for those still trying to farm their land. The result may be increased control of the community's land by absentee owners. Community equity is again eroded.

In all of these situations, urban and rural, the CLT offers a means of preserving community equity. Any increase in the value of the CLT's land is retained and residents need not be displaced by real estate market forces. On the contrary, the increased value of the community equity held by the CLT can be used, judiciously, as collateral to leverage financing for further land acquisitions, to meet the needs of some of those who may be displaced from other community land. From this equity base the CLT will also receive direct income in the form of lease fees.

Lease fees represent the fair return to the community from those who have been given use of the community's land and resources. They reflect the value of the land as it appreciates through community investment and development. They are similar in principle to local property taxes which landowners now pay, but with a significant difference: The lease fee is based on the value of the land alone, with no consideration for the value of the improvements which the leaseholder may construct upon the land. In contrast, many local property tax structures not only tax improvements, but tax them at a higher rate, while undeveloped land and extracted natural resources are often taxed at considerably less than their full value. Such a tax structure tends to discourage constructive development and to encourage the monopolization of potentially productive land and resources.

Typically, the CLT makes an effort to base lease fees on the use value of the land, so that leaseholders are not penalized for land uses which are consistent with the interests of the community but are less profitable than the "highest and best use" of the market. This practice is similar to the "current use" taxation policies of many local governments, which allow farmers and owners of forest land to pay lower taxes on productive land that has a higher market value based on its development potential.

The CLT may also choose to lease land for less than a full-value fee, to facilitate access to the land by low-income families or to respond to a situation of personal hardship for the leaseholder. When the real value of its land has in fact increased, the CLT can afford to hold lease fees at a level below real value, thus providing a form of subsidy for needy members of the community and reducing their dependence on public assistance and subsidies. This use of increases in community equity to assist needy residents reduces the public expenditures necessary to meet the basic needs of these people; and, since many of those assistance funds have come from federal or state governments, it reduces the uncertain dependence of local communities on policies and appropriations beyond their direct control.

However, when government subsidies *are* provided to a community, the CLT can be the most effective recipient and administrator of these subsidies. Many current government efforts to subsidize housing and other facilities within a community can be likened to an attempt to help a hemorrhaging patient by administering repeated transfusions without any action to stop the bleeding. Transfusions of public money—in such forms as acquisition and development funds, or rent and interest subsidies—offer short-term benefits to individuals and communities, but the value of the subsidy normally passes *through* the community, often quite rapidly. It is not retained, so the transfusions must be repeated over and over again at increasing expense or, as is the current trend, the community must be abandoned to its own limited resources. Through the CLT, public funds can be retained within the community for repeated use with multiple effect. They achieve their original purpose and still remain in the community as a type of revolving fund. The benefits pass on to a succession of individual recipients, and the need for further transfusions is reduced.

Community Legacy

Every community has a legitimate interest in its development over time and in the preservation of its natural environment for both present and future generations. At present, many critical land use decisions are made by individuals and interests outside the local community, by people who are leaving the community, and by the operations of the commercial market. Through a CLT, while leaseholders have secure tenure and considerable freedom in their use of the land, decisions about redistribution and long-term community planning and development are made by the community.

Using its ownership of the land and its power to grant or withhold leases, the CLT exercises effective community control over development. Specific land use plans can be formulated through democratic procedures and with expert advice where needed. The stability and character of established neighborhoods can be protected. Undeveloped land can be divided, appropriate building sites identified, roadways, sewage systems, and other facilities mapped out, all with a concern for the long-range effects on the land and on the community. Sites that are appropriate for commercial or industrial use can be identified, and the use of these sites allocated to enterprises that will offer long-term benefits to the community. Productive agricultural land may be reserved for agricultural purposes. Forest land may be preserved and the forest itself managed so as to provide a continuing supply of firewood, timber, and jobs for community residents. Limited fragile areas such as wetlands may be protected in an undisturbed state; other areas may be kept in a relatively natural state for recreational use or for aesthetic reasons.

Of course, one may ask why control of present and future land use should not be left to established local governments, which are already involved in such matters as zoning and community development. Zoning boards and planning commissions have made efforts to evaluate and regulate development in their own communities. But in many instances, the initiative is in the hands of the owner/developer; land use hearings take on the character of adversarial proceedings, and the community lacks a firm economic base from which to offer or implement alternatives.

Certainly the CLT does not replace local government in these matters. It is itself, as a landowner, subject to prevailing regulations. Ideally, the CLT should work in partnership with local government for the good of the community. In the complicated process of land use planning and environmental protection, such a partnership can provide a valuable additional layer of protection.

However, there are some ways in which the CLT offers distinct advantages. Land owned by the CLT is removed from the market. Community control over its future development is direct and long-term; the potential for speculative gains is removed as an incentive for land acquisition and development. CLTs are also more likely to avoid the sort of "public versus private" or "owner versus regulator" controversies that often paralyze attempts to establish or implement public ordinances affecting private land. In planning the use of CLT land, community members are more likely to come together as equals, rather than adversaries, to do what is best for all concerned. The land is theirs; it will remain theirs; and ultimately, they all have an equal interest in it.

As an association of community members, the CLT may also be able to promote sound policies beyond the boundaries of the land it actually owns. The CLT's outreach and educational programs can contribute importantly to public understanding of land and development issues, and the organization can exert a degree of influence that its members as individual citizens may not be able to muster. The CLT can mobilize community members to respond to these issues, and can serve as a critical vehicle for community-based voluntary initiatives when there is not yet an effective public policy or a political consensus to support governmental action. This may be particularly important in low-income communities whose members typically lack the economic and political power necessary to protect the community from exploitation by outside interests. Even indirectly, a CLT can have a healthy effect on local politics as people realize that through the CLT they really can influence the future of their community.

Roots of the CLT

The CLT is both a practical, multipurpose tool for dealing with immediate problems and an institution based solidly on deeply rooted and durable assumptions about the land and our relationship to it. As a specific model, the CLT is still new in America; the earliest developments in the CLT movement occurred only some 15 years ago, and only in the past few years has the model begun to achieve rather wide recognition. As a basic approach to landownership and control, however, the CLT model is very old— far older than the property institutions that surround us today.

In its basic approach, the CLT model stems from the ancient view of the earth as something naturally given, or God-given, to all people in common—something which, like the air above it, can never be owned in any absolute sense by individuals. The principle that people can never own land absolutely and the recognition of the duality of individual and community interests in land are deeply embedded in the Judeo-Christian tradition, as they are in other major religious and ethical traditions. In this sense the CLT is a deeply traditional approach to land.

In its approach to the economic significance of land, the CLT model draws on Henry George, the author of the influential book *Progress and Poverty* (published in 1879). George reaffirmed the principle that land is a common trust, and traced the origin of much of the poverty and social distress of his times to the maldistribution of land and the failure of society to claim its economic value. To remedy the situation—to make land available to all, and to retain for the community the value which it created through municipal development and services—George proposed having a single tax on the full value of land (known as site value, or land value, taxation), and no tax on private improvements. This "single tax," as it was commonly known, is comparable to the lease fees charged by CLTs, although most CLTs take other factors into account along with the value of the land in determining their fees.

Based on George's analysis and proposals, a number of "single tax enclaves" or communities of "economic rent" were established in Alabama, New Jersey, Delaware, Massachusetts, and other states. In the wake of the Depression, the social philosopher Ralph Borsodi (who is sometimes called the grandfather of the CLT) assisted in the development of several new communities based in part on Georgist principles. Some of these single tax communities are still flourishing, although in several instances an element of speculative gain has been allowed to creep into their methods of operation.

As a practical tool, the CLT has been influenced or inspired by more recent land reform policies in several other countries. Vinoba Bhave, a close coworker and successor to Mahatma Gandhi, initiated a voluntary land-gift program in India known as Bhoodan. In a series of long walks across the Indian countryside, Bhave and his companions collected gifts of land from landowners, and distributed the land to landless peasants. When it became clear that many of the new landowners soon lost their land—to creditors or the temptations of cash offers—the program was changed to Gramdan, or village gift. A Gramdan village acts as trustee of the lands, which are made available for individual use but not individual ownership.

The Jewish National Fund of Israel is a land trust on a national scale. Founded in 1901, the JNF is a nongovernmental public institution which predated the founding of the state of Israel. It currently owns most of the productive land of Israel and considerable additional land in both rural and urban areas. The land is held in trust and leased out for use. Improvements on the land may be owned by the leaseholders.

In Mexico and Tanzania, government land reform policies have given trusteeship of local land to village communities, which grant use rights to individuals but retain a degree of control, so that these individuals cannot sell the land and wealthy people cannot reacquire large landholdings.

In a number of western countries, local and regional governments have created land banks. A land bank is a public agency which acquires land, holds the land for varying lengths of time, and sells or leases the land to private or public parties for a variety of purposes. The technique had developed largely as a response to the perceived failure of planning strategies and land use controls in regulating metropolitan growth, and in anticipation of the problems often associated with the rapid increases in land prices which result from development. Metropolitan land banking has been successfully used in Sweden since 1904, and in a number of other countries as well. In recent years rural land banks have been established in the Canadian provinces of Saskatchewan and Prince Edward Island to purchase and lease farmland in an effort to preserve family farming and reverse the trend toward greater absentee ownership of rural land. In the United States, public land banking has remained a relatively undeveloped technique, despite early programs of public acquisition and planning which played important roles in the development of such cities as Washington, Austin, Savannah, Detroit, and Chicago. Currently, public land banks in Puerto Rico, New York State, and Massachusetts are operating with an emphasis on job creation and economic development.

Comparisons and Confusions

The CLT bears some resemblance not only to the forerunners mentioned above but to a variety of other contemporary landholding entities. In some instances the apparent similarities are deceiving. In other instances they are real and significant. In any event, it is important to understand the similarities and differences, and to avoid the likely confusion.

Real Estate Trusts

A CLT is a trust in the basic sense that it holds land in trust for the entire community, but it is not a trust in the traditional legal sense. A CLT is a nonprofit corporation. A legal land trust or real estate trust, on the other hand, is a private entity with private purposes. It is a means of holding property for the good of certain specified "beneficiaries," and it is controlled by specified trustees. The legal land trust is a closed arrangement, while the CLT is open and democratic.

Real estate trusts may be relatively small, established to manage a fixed amount of property for the benefit of a very limited number of individuals; or, they may be quite large and commercially active. In the past few years, an increasing number of private land trusts (legal trusts and other legal entities) have been created by major financial institutions turning to land as a sound investment, and by private developers seeking to reduce the sales price of their properties, increase sales, and realize long-term speculative gains.

Enclaves and Communes

There is a long history in America of intentional communities and cooperative settlements in which land is held in common. Some of these communities may be regarded as forerunners of the CLT, particularly those which have focused on land as a basic economic issue and have distinguished between land and human improvements on the land. For the most part, however, these communities have been enclaves, or private trusts created by and for groups of people who share a specific philosophical commitment or personal affinity. Their memberships are not open to all members of the larger communities in which they are established, and they are not designed to relate to the various needs and interests of these communities.

A CLT is not a commune. Communes, or intentional communities, may lease land from a CLT, or choose to put the land they already own into a CLT; but the two are not synonymous.

Conservancy Trusts

Conservancy or land conservation trusts seek to prevent the development of certain undeveloped lands so that their natural characters can be preserved. They provide maximum protection for particularly distinctive or fragile natural areas and ecosystems. With a history in the United States that reaches back over a century, the local land conservation movement has grown tremendously in recent years—as environmental problems have grown and as the economic trends which now oppress individual families and communities also pose new threats to environmental protection efforts. Currently, there are more than 700 local conservation trusts across the country.

The organizational structures and land acquisition techniques of conservancy trusts and CLTs are often quite similar. Most, though not all, conservancies are local organizations, and many, though not all, have open memberships. Their obvious and principal difference lies in the goals of their land acquisition programs. Conservancy trusts normally withhold their lands from all human use except for limited scientific or educational field study and some carefully regulated recreational use. CLTs, on the other hand, are usually concerned with housing, agriculture, economic development, and other basic human land uses.

The purposes of these two types of trusts are surely not mutually exclusive, and should be complementary. Conservancy lands can offer recreational, educational, and psychological benefits to local residents and can often protect water supplies and other vital resources. CLTs frequently do set aside or protect natural land areas and they work to develop land-use plans to protect both social and natural characteristics of local communities.

Some communities now include both types of trusts. It is natural to assume that the two would be allies, and in some communities this is the case. In others, however, differences of orientation and strategy, or differences in the backgrounds of the respective memberships, have prevented them from becoming effective partners. As with many other environmental groups, conservancies are often associated (whether in fact or in the public mind) with more affluent communities, while many (though by no means all) CLTs are based in low-income communities whose members face a daily struggle to meet their basic needs. When communication between the two groups is weak, some community residents may see a conservation organization's concern with "wilderness" as disregard for human needs; others may worry about the effect of conservation acquisitions on property values, access barriers, and tax rates throughout the community.

But the real differences between conservancies and CLTs need not prevent cooperation or cause tension between the two. There is a strong basis for common effort, and each has resources which can be critically useful to the other. With current economic problems so often used to justify environmental compromises, environmentalists need a broader grass-roots base of public and political support, in local communities as well as on the state and national levels. CLTs can help to provide this kind of community support for conservancy trusts. At the same time, as economic problems raise traditional access barriers even higher for low- and moderate-income people, they and their local CLTs may need the help of the frequently greater technical skills and financial resources of the conservancy trusts.

Limited Equity Cooperatives

As legal entities, cooperatives differ from nonprofit corporations in that co-op members each own an equity share of the co-op's assets, while the assets of a nonprofit corporation cannot be held by or distributed to its members. In a housing cooperative, each member owns a share of the value of the co-op's building and land; in a CLT, members and leaseholders never have personal ownership of the corporation's land. Both organizations are democratically structured, with boards elected by their members.

The value of a traditional housing co-op's assets increases with the market value of its property holdings, and the value of each share appreciates accordingly. As with other real estate on the commercial market, this inflation in the price of co-op shares may threaten the future availability of its housing units to lower-income people. As a result, a number of co-ops—particularly those composed of low- or moderate-income people—have chosen to limit the value, or the potential for inflation in the value, of each member's share. These co-ops retain an option to purchase and resell the share of any departing member at the established value. These are "limited equity" or "low yield" co-ops.

Obviously, limited equity co-ops and CLTs share the same basic social commitments and function in a very similar manner, though they normally differ in the scale and diversity of their landholdings. Most limited equity co-ops include only one or a limited number of buildings, in a single location, and these buildings are limited to housing. The CLT, on the other hand, may own land throughout a much larger area and its land may be put to a variety of uses.

Limited equity co-ops do not necessarily separate the ownership of their housing from ownership of the land on which it is situated. Normally, cooperatives own both in the traditional way, but the separation of landownership may serve the purposes of a limited equity co-op very well when there is a CLT that can take title to the land. In fact, there are important opportunities for collaboration between the two organizations.

When a limited equity co-op turns its land over to a CLT, or when it is established on CLT land, the CLT retains ownership of the land and its value, while the co-op holds a renewable lease to the land and its members each own an equity share in their building. The co-op will control the resale of shares and the admission of new members. Only in the event that the co-op proposes to sell the entire building will the CLT exercise its option to purchase the improvements on the land. Such an arrangement gives greater stability and security to the co-op. In a number of legal jurisdictions, a co-op's provisions for equity limitation cannot be made perpetual—thus the CLT's option provides an additional layer of protection, an assurance that these housing units will continue to be available to those who need them most. At the same time, co-ops offer a strong organizational base for CLT members, particularly those who live in multiunit buildings. Such co-ops can effectively provide both maintenance and personal services for buildings and people, and reduce the administrative burdens of the CLT. While each co-op normally includes a limited membership who share common circumstances, the CLT can link a number of co-ops together across the community, forming a larger "cooperative" of shared purpose and resources.

One Model—A Variety of Actual Forms

If a representative group of people involved in starting CLTs were brought together in one place, it might be hard to say what they had in common. They would be urban and rural people; low-, middle-, and upper-income people; farmers, factory workers, public officials, professionals, and unemployed people. They would be people concerned with preserving traditional communities, and people concerned with bringing about changes in afflicted communities. They would be philosophically oriented people with a theoretical interest in the question of property, and pragmatically oriented people looking for practical ways of meeting immediate needs. The group would consist of all sorts of people, from all sorts of communities. Members would have a common interest in community land trusts, but the CLTs with which they were associated would vary widely.

Because communities vary, CLTs vary both in the emphasis that they place on specific issues and interests and in the strategies and techniques that they use to realize their goals. CLTs in rural areas are working to provide access to land and decent housing for low-income people, to preserve family farms and farmland, and to facilitate sound, long-term land and forest management. Urban CLTs have formed to combat speculation and gentrification, to preserve and develop low- and moderate-income housing, and to maintain useful urban open spaces.

Some CLTs have been created in response to specific and pressing needs, others in response to long-range concerns with land use planning and future management of community resources. Some are concerned with a strictly defined locality, others with a larger and less clearly defined area. Some have moved rapidly to acquire substantial amounts of land; some own only a little land and are moving slowly toward long-range goals; some have focused on the acquisition of partial interests in land.

CLTs also vary in the kinds of roles they adopt in relation to their communities and to other community organizations. In some cases, a CLT may be *the* organization in a community that is concerned with giving people access to land and with helping them preserve and take advantage of this access. In such cases the CLT may initially play an active and varied role as the primary organizing force in the community and as the planner and developer for the land it acquires. It may even serve to enfranchise people in a community that lacks its own representative government, as in unincorporated rural areas and some urban neighborhoods.

In other situations, however, some or all of these functions will be performed by other specialized community organizations, and the CLT's role may be limited essentially to land stewardship—simply acquiring, holding, and managing the transfer of land, making sure that it is used appropriately and in the best interest of the community. In fact, the CLT is often initiated by other organizations that have been active in the community and have come to appreciate the underlying importance of land-ownership as a community concern. It may also be the initiator of other organizations as it comes to feel the need for them. . . .

Prospects and Possibilities

Community land trusts have many important capabilities; they can undoubtedly make critical contributions to the stability and responsible development of many very different communities, on their own and in partnership with other organizations. They are not, of course, a panacea. As with any other institution or program, CLTs hold a potential for failure or abuse. They are subject to the same organizational problems—problems of both initial organization and efficient operation—that other community groups face. While they are democratically structured to provide an opportunity for broad participation and a fair representation of the different interests in the community, their members can (like the members of other groups) become less active or vigilant, and the CLT can become less truly representative and democratic.

CLTs also must struggle within the limits of their resources: human resources, technical skills, and financial resources. The most obvious problem to date has been limited access to affordable financing for land acquisition and development. In the past several years, as interest in CLTs has grown, considerable progress has been made and new sources have been opened. But social problems are growing also, and in many communities CLTs may not be able to acquire sufficient resources soon enough to meet pressing human needs and to prevent displacement of the existing community. Also, while they are founded on traditional values and utilize conventional legal forms, CLTs may some day face legal or political challenges.

Nevertheless, the CLT is one of the best tools available to local communities in their efforts to meet land and housing needs with respect for both individual and community interests. CLTs do meet the strategic criteria required of a land and housing program for success in our current economic circumstances, and they offer greater security and long-term benefits than many other models. With the collective resources they assemble, the advantages of a nonprofit corporation, and their own base of collateral and income potential, CLTs can offer access and equity to people in need today. By limiting individual equity to the value of the leaseholder's own investment and retaining an option to purchase and resell these improvements, the CLT can insure that this land and property will remain available to those who need it, regardless of the forces of a speculative market. And ultimately, through its landownership and lease fees, a CLT will enable the community to re-create, and to retain, its own economic base.

As neither "public" nor "private" institutions, CLTs incorporate some of the best features of each with considerable flexibility. In some communities they may be able to build new bridges between individual and community interests, and may help to overcome traditional political dichotomies. As voluntary local initiatives, they may be able to effect community control and land reform without the controversies and uncertainties that surround new public land use policies. In any case, CLTs offer incentives and opportunities for responsible community development, and discourage or prevent inappropriate development.

Implementation of the CLT idea in America is still experimental, still evolving. Most of the CLTs examined in the second section of this book are only a few years old. None of them can yet stand as proof of the long-term effectiveness of the model. One thing that they all do demonstrate, however, is the stimulating effect that the idea has had in communities where it is being tried.

Ours is a time in which most people feel helpless before the powerful and often paralyzing economic forces that affect their lives. They may sometimes benefit from these forces and sometimes suffer from them, but in either case they feel little or no hope of altering the forces themselves. As a result, they are often encouraged to look out for themselves, as individuals, as best they can—to take what profit they can get when and where they can get it, regardless of the effect on a community which they may expect to leave before long anyway. In this way community relationships are weakened. People are alienated from their neighbors and from their localities.

The community land trust offers opportunities for reversing this tendency. By joining together to form a CLT, people find that they can affect the economic structures that surround them. By seeking control of land *as a community* they can hope to benefit as individuals *without* sacrificing community interests. In fact, they can hope to benefit through promoting community interests. It is an exciting discovery—one that nourishes the roots of community life, that stimulates the side of human nature that needs community and wants to work for it.

It is true that in the long run CLTs must acquire significant amounts of land if they are to be seen as important institutions. For the present, however, we can best measure the success of newly formed CLTs not in terms of total acreage or total housing units but in terms of the constructive community activity being generated. Without this sort of activity—and the sense of community that goes with it—no amount of institutional change can solve our problems. The open and democratic structure of the CLT is thus a centrally important feature of the model. A community land trust cannot succeed as something created merely *for* a community. It must represent an effort *of* and *by* the community. . . .

Federal Definition of "Community Land Trust"

United States Federal Register
(1992)

SEC. 212. HOUSING EDUCATION AND ORGANIZATIONAL SUPPORT FOR COMMUNITY LAND TRUSTS

(a)   COMMUNITY LAND TRUSTS.—*Section 233 of the Cranston-Gonzales National Affordable Housing Act (42 U.S.C. 12773) is amended–*

(1)   *in subsection (a)(2) by inserting "including community land trusts," after "organizations";*

(2)   *in subsection (b), by adding at the end the following:*

(6) COMMUNITY LAND TRUSTS.—Organizational support, technical assistance, education, training, and community support under this subsection may be available to community land trusts (as such term is defined in subsection (f) and to community groups for the establishment of community land trusts); and

(3)   *by adding at the end of the following:*

(f) DEFINITION OF COMMUNITY LAND TRUST.—For purposes of this section, the term "community land trust" means a community housing development organization (except that the requirements under subparagraphs (C) and (D) of section 104(6) shall not apply for purposes of this subsection)–

"(1) that is not sponsored by a for-profit organization;

"(2) that is established to carry out the activities under paragraph (3);

"(3) that–

"(A) acquires parcels of land, held in perpetuity, primarily for conveyance under longterm ground leases;

"(B) transfers ownership of any structural improvements located on such leased parcels to the lessees; and

"(C) retains a preemptive option to purchase any such structural improvement at a price determined by a formula that is designed to ensure that the improvement remains affordable to low- and moderate-income families in perpetuity;

"(4) whose corporate membership is open to any adult resident of a particular geographic area specified in the bylaws of the organization; and

"(5) whose board of directors—

"(A) includes a majority of members who are elected by the corporate membership; and

"(B) is composed of equal numbers of (i) lessees pursuant to paragraph (3) (B), (ii) corporate members who are not lessees, and (iii) any other category of persons described in the bylaws of the organization."

FROM *Development without Displacement*

Organizational and Operational Choices in Starting a Community Land Trust

John Emmeus Davis
(2006)

The community land trust (CLT) is a model of great versatility, leading to wide variation in the ways in which the CLT is structured and applied. The key features of the "classic" CLT are described in the present chapter, along with the model's most common variations.

Variations on a Theme of "CLT Classic"

The community land trust combines a new approach to the *ownership* of land, housing, and other real estate with a new approach to the *organization* of the nonprofit steward of this property. The basic features of the CLT model were outlined in *The Community Land Trust: A Guide to a New Model for Land Tenure in America,* published by the International Independence Institute in 1972. Ten years later, the Institute for Community Economics (ICE), successor to the International Independence Institute, refined and extended the CLT model in another publication, the *Community Land Trust Handbook,* in which a new emphasis was placed on the CLT's potential for producing and preserving affordable housing and for developing lower-income communities without displacing lower-income people. In 1992, ICE's refinement of the CLT model was enshrined in federal law in a definition approved by Congress. Although there is much variation among the CLTs already in existence or under development in the United States, there are ten key features that are found in most of them. These features, defining and distinguishing what may be called the "classic" CLT, are described below. Described as well are the most common variations occurring in each of these features.

This selection is chapter 1 of a manual written by John Emmeus Davis in 2001 and revised in 2006. The revised manual, *Development without Displacement: Organizational and Operational Choices in Starting a Community Land Trust,* is available online at the CLT Resource Center. It may be downloaded in its entirety free of charge (www.burlingtonassociates.com). It is reprinted by permission of the author.

Nonprofit, Tax-Exempt Corporation

CLT Classic. A community land trust is an independent, not-for-profit corporation that is legally chartered in the state in which it is located. Most CLTs target their activities and resources toward charitable activities like providing housing for low-income people, combating community deterioration, and lessening the burdens of government. Most CLTs, accordingly, seek and obtain a 501(c)(3) designation from the IRS.

CLT Variations. Although CLTs are usually created "from scratch," as newly formed, autonomous corporations, some have been established as successors, affiliates, or programs of an older nonprofit. Either a preexisting nonprofit transforms itself into a community land trust or grafts selected elements of the CLT model onto its own structure and programs. Sometimes, when a new CLT is established within the corporate shell of a preexisting nonprofit, the CLT becomes a permanent part of the nonprofit's on-going operations. Alternatively, this may be a temporary, transitional arrangement, where the CLT is spun off as a separate corporation when it has the capacity and constituency to thrive by itself.

Nearly all CLTs are chartered as a nonprofit corporation or housed within a nonprofit corporation. Most have a 501(c)(3) tax exemption from the IRS. In a few cases, however, a local government or municipal corporation (like a public housing authority) has developed and managed resale-restricted, owner-occupied housing on leased land, administering a program that resembles a CLT. Not every CLT has secured a 501(c)(3) designation, moreover, either because they have chosen not to serve a population that is "poor, distressed, or underprivileged" or because the IRS has determined that the applicant fails to meet the organizational and operational tests for receiving 501(c)(3) status.[1]

Dual Ownership

CLT Classic. A nonprofit corporation (the CLT) acquires multiple parcels of land throughout a targeted geographic area with the intention of retaining ownership of these parcels forever. Any building that is already located on the land or that is later constructed on the land is sold to another party. The building's buyer may be an individual homeowner, a cooperative housing corporation, a nonprofit organization or limited partnership developing rental housing, or any other nonprofit, governmental, or for-profit entity.

CLT Variations. Although dual ownership is a characteristic of every organization that calls itself a community land trust, buildings that are renter-occupied are sometimes treated differently than buildings that are owner-occupied. Some CLTs, when dealing with multiunit rentals, whether residential or commercial, retain ownership not only of the underlying land but of the buildings as well. Some CLTs, when accepting limited-equity condominiums into their portfolios, have not owned the underlying land. They have retained ownership only of a durable right to repurchase these condominiums for an affordable, formula-determined price when their current owners someday decide to sell.

Leased Land

CLT Classic. Although CLTs intend never to resell their land, they provide for the exclusive use of their land by the owners of any buildings located thereon. Parcels of land are conveyed to individual homeowners (or to the owners of other types of residential or commercial structures) through inheritable ground leases that typically run for 99 years. This two-party contract between the landowner (the CLT) and a building's owner protects the latter's interests in security, privacy, legacy, and equity, while enforcing the CLT's interests in preserving the appropriate use, structural integrity, and continuing affordability of any buildings located upon its land.

CLT Variations. Every CLT uses a long-term ground lease for the conveyance of land. Most of these leases are based on the "model CLT ground lease" developed and refined by ICE over the past 30 years. The exact terms and conditions contained in these two-party contracts, however, can vary greatly from one CLT to another, especially with regard to restrictions on using, subletting, improving, and reselling the buildings that are located on the CLT's land.[2] Condominiums present a special case, however, where ground leasing is not always possible. Although some condominiums are located on land that is leased from a CLT, there are many cases where a CLT has acquired title to a portion of the condominiums in a large, multiunit project for which the CLT does not own the underlying land. This has happened most frequently when a CLT has been the beneficiary of a municipality's inclusionary housing program and been assigned long-term responsibility for monitoring and enforcing durable controls over the occupancy, eligibility, and affordability of these inclusionary units required by the municipality.

Perpetual Affordability

CLT Classic. The CLT retains an option to repurchase any residential (or commercial) structures located upon its land, whenever the owners of these buildings decide to sell. The resale price is set by a formula contained in the ground lease that is designed to give present homeowners a fair return on their investment, while giving future homebuyers fair access to housing at an affordable price. By design and by intent, the CLT is committed to preserving the affordability of housing (and other structures)—one owner after another, one generation after another, in perpetuity.

CLT Variations. While perpetual affordability is a commitment of every CLT, the formula that defines and enforces affordability varies greatly from one CLT to another. This is due, in part, to the different methods that CLTs can adopt in calculating the resale price of housing that is located upon the CLT's land. Different formulas may also result from the different goals that particular CLTs are trying to achieve or the different populations they are trying to serve. Furthermore, while the vast majority of CLTs adopt a single resale formula, covering all types and tenures of housing within their portfolio—and covering every neighborhood in which they work—a few CLTs have begun to fine-tune their resale formulas to allow some variation among different portions of their housing stock (distinguishing, for example, among detached, single-family houses, condominiums, and cooperatives). A few others have tailored their resale formulas to account for varying conditions within hot and cold sub-markets of their regional service area.

Perpetual Responsibility

CLT Classic. The CLT does not disappear once a building is sold to a homeowner, a co-op, or another entity. As the owner of lands underlying any number of buildings and as the owner of an option to re-purchase those buildings for a formula-determined price, the CLT has a continuing interest in what happens to these structures—and to the people who occupy them. The ground lease requires owner-occupancy and responsible use of the premises. Should buildings become a hazard, the ground lease gives the CLT the right to step in and to force repairs. Should property owners default on their mortgages, the ground lease gives the CLT the right to step in and cure the default, forestalling foreclosure. The CLT remains a party to the deal, safeguarding the structural integrity of the building and the residential security of the occupants.

CLT Variations. Some CLTs provide a full menu of prepurchase and postpurchase services. They go to great lengths to prepare people for the responsibilities of homeownership and to support their homeowners, in good times and bad. Other CLTs do little more than monitor and enforce the occupancy, eligibility, and affordability controls embedded in the ground lease and intervene only to prevent the loss of a building faced with foreclosure. The intensity of a CLT's postpurchase involvement in the housing situations of its leaseholders depends largely upon a CLT's capacity. It is also affected, however, by the CLT's own preferences and concerns, as each CLT struggles to find an acceptable, sustainable balance between "backstopping" the success of its newly minted homeowners and leaving them alone to enjoy the privacy and independence that homeownership is supposed to bring.

Place-Based Membership

CLT Classic. The CLT operates within the physical, geographic boundaries of a targeted locale. It is guided by—and accountable to—the people who call this locality their home. Any adult who resides on the CLT's land and any adult who resides within the geographic area that is deemed by the CLT to be its "community" may become a voting member of the CLT.

CLT Variations. Nearly every CLT is a membership organization, drawing its members from a community that is geographically defined. Within the diverse world of CLTs, however, there is considerable variation in the size of that "community" and in the make-up of that membership. A decade ago, the community served by most CLTs was a single urban neighborhood or a small rural town. That has changed. Many CLTs created in recent years have staked out a much wider service area, encompassing multiple neighborhoods, an entire city, an entire county, or, in a few cases, a multicounty region. There are many variations, as well, in the composition and role of the CLT's membership. Some CLTs have opened their membership to individuals who reside outside of the CLT's target area. Other CLTs have expanded their membership beyond individuals, allowing nonprofit corporations, local governments, or private institutions like hospitals, churches, businesses, or a community foundation within their service area to become voting members of the CLT. There are a few CLTs with no membership, although these tend to be situations where the CLT has been established as a subsidiary or an internal program of an existing community development corporation that has a membership of its own, or no members at all.

Resident Control

CLT Classic. Two-thirds of a CLT's board of directors are nominated by, elected by, and composed of people who either live on the CLT's land or people who reside within the CLT's targeted "community" but do not live on the CLT's land.

CLT Variations. Nearly every CLT has a board of directors that is elected, in part, by the residents who make up its membership. There are many variations, however, in the process of nominating new directors, in the process of selecting those directors, and in the percentage of the board that is directly elected by the CLT's membership. There are a few CLTs where the board is appointed in its entirety by a municipal government, by a community foundation, or by some other corporate sponsor.

Tripartite Governance

CLT Classic. The board of directors of the "classic" CLT is composed of three parts, each containing an equal number of seats. One third of the board represents the interests of people who lease land from the CLT ("leaseholder representatives"). One third represents the interests of residents from the surrounding "community" who do not lease CLT land or live in CLT housing ("general representatives"). One third is made up of public officials, local funders, nonprofit providers of housing or social services, and other individuals presumed to speak for the public interest ("public representatives"). Control of the CLT's board is diffused and balanced to ensure that all interests are heard but that no interest is predominant.

CLT Variations. Although every CLT board is distinguished by both a diversity of interests and a balance of interests, the exact make-up of this governing board can vary widely from one CLT to another. Every CLT board has leaseholder representatives, for example, but some CLTs subdivide this leaseholder category among directors who represent the interests of leaseholders occupying single-family homes and those occupying co-op units or commercial buildings. CLTs that are managing rental housing may reserve a leaseholder seat for a tenant. Every CLT has public representatives, but some CLTs fill these seats exclusively with representatives of local or state government, while others include representatives of local churches, foundations, banks, social service agencies, tenant rights organizations, or community development corporations within this "public" category. Many start-up CLTs, moreover, have interim boards that may be composed (and appointed) quite differently than the broadly representative, membership-elected, tripartite board that will ultimately govern the CLT.

Expansionist Acquisition

CLT Classic. CLTs are not focused on a single project that is located on a single parcel of land. They are committed, instead, to an active acquisition and development program, aimed at expanding the CLT's holdings of land and increasing the supply of affordable housing (and other types of buildings) under the CLT's stewardship. A CLT's holdings are seldom concentrated in one corner of its service area, moreover, but tend to be scattered throughout the CLT's territory so they are indistinguishable from other housing within the same community.

CLT Variations. Every CLT has an eye toward expanding the number of acres and buildings that are brought into its domain of nonspeculative ownership, but the scale and pace of acquisition can vary widely from one CLT to another. This is due, in large measure, to factors outside of a CLT's control, like the cost of buildable sites and the availability of grants and loans. An acquisition strategy is also a function, however, of a CLT's own priorities in choosing whom to serve, what to build, and where to work. Some CLTs have grown quite slowly, each year purchasing a few parcels of land on which are constructed (or rehabilitated) a handful of single-family houses. Other CLTs have grown rather rapidly, benefiting from private donations or public largess that have allowed for the acquisition of larger parcels of land and the steady development of many units of housing. Regardless of the magnitude of their development activity, which may ebb and flow over the years, most CLTs stay committed to adding more land to their holdings and to bringing more resale-restricted, owner-occupied housing under their stewardship.

Flexible Development

CLT Classic. The CLT is a community development tool of uncommon flexibility, accommodating a variety of land uses, property tenures, and building types. CLTs around the country construct (or acquire, rehabilitate, and resell) housing of many kinds: single-family homes, duplexes, condos, co-ops, SROs, multiunit apartment buildings, and mobile home parks. CLTs create facilities for neighborhood businesses, nonprofit organizations, and social service agencies. CLTs provide sites for community gardens and vest-pocket parks. Land is the common ingredient, linking them all.

CLT Variations. There is enormous variability in the projects CLTs pursue and the roles they play in developing them. Some CLTs focus on a single type of housing, like attached townhouses. Some focus on a single tenure, like owner-occupied housing. Others, embracing a more comprehensive mission like revitalizing an entire neighborhood, rebuilding a locality's housing tenure ladder, or redistributing the benefits and burdens of regional growth, take full advantage of the model's flexibility in undertaking an array of residential and commercial projects. Most CLTs do their own development, initiated and supervised by their own staff. Others leave development to nonprofit or governmental partners, confining their efforts to assembling land, leasing land, and preserving the affordability of any housing located upon it. Between these two extremes of the CLT-as-developer and the CLT-as-steward lie a variety of roles that different CLTs have embraced in expanding their domain.

Causes of Continuing Variation

The majority of the nation's CLTs incorporate into their organizational structure and their on-going operations most—if not all—of the ten features characteristic of the "classic" CLT. Most of the variations occurring in the model are the result of tailoring the model's most flexible features, especially the resale formula and the development agenda, to meet local circumstances and needs. These variations occur within the framework of the model's basic structure. They do little to alter the structure itself.

Other variations, like establishing a CLT within the corporate shell of another nonprofit, extending the CLT's service area beyond a single neighborhood or town, or modifying the make-up of the CLT's membership or board, go much further in altering the CLT's "classic" structure. Despite these variations, the model's core commitments to land stewardship, perpetual affordability, perpetual responsibility, a balanced structure of governance, and organizational accountability to the people housed by the CLT and to the people residing in the surrounding locale are retained by most organizations that call themselves a CLT.[3]

Experimentation and variation in the model's make-up continues, as the CLT is adapted to new conditions and is applied in different ways. The most common and influential of the factors giving rise to such innovation are the following:

- *Density of the Organizational Landscape.* In communities where many non-profit housing development organizations already exist, it has sometimes made more sense to establish a CLT under the sponsorship—or inside the corporate shell—of another nonprofit, instead of starting a new corporation from scratch. At other times, in other places, an independently incorporated CLT has sought a special niche within a densely populated organizational landscape by focusing on functions or roles that are not only different than those of existing nonprofits but also different than those that "classic" CLTs have traditionally embraced.

- *Density of Residential Development.* In communities where buildable land is very expensive, housing development is usually more practical and economical when it takes the form of multiunit condominiums, cooperatives, rentals, or densely sited manufactured housing. Multiunit housing works well with a CLT, but it requires modifications in the CLT's ground lease. It may also engender modifications in the structure of a CLT's membership and its governing board. That is not to suggest that the "classic" CLT is to be found only in communities where detached, single-family houses on separate parcels of land are the primary form of housing production. It *is* to say that the experience of developing multiunit housing has often been a spur to innovation, causing several variations in the "classic" model.

- *Priorities & Requirements of Funders.* Changes in the model are sometimes provoked by the demands—some reasonable, some not—of public agencies and private lenders on which a CLT must depend for the funding that makes its projects possible. Innovation may also occur when a municipality looks to a CLT to serve as the long-term steward for occupancy, eligibility, and affordability controls mandated by the municipality—not only for publicly-subsidized housing on a CLT's land but for inclusionary housing scattered throughout larger residential projects under which the CLT does not own the underlying land.

- *Marketing an Unfamiliar Model.* The CLT is sometimes modified to make an unfamiliar model of homeownership look and feel more like the deal that is typically offered to more affluent households when buying a home on the open market. By tinkering with the bundle of rights and responsibilities that are provided to a CLT leaseholder/homeowner, especially those affecting the use, improvement, and resale of the CLT home, CLTs seek a workable balance between a form of property that is different enough from traditional homeownership to protect the long-term interests of the community, but close enough to traditional homeownership to attract the investment and support of the individual homebuyer.

- *Development vs. Organizing.* It is difficult for any community-based housing development organization to wear two hats. As a developer, a CLT is accountable to a constellation of funders, contractors, deadlines, and demands that drive the business of getting affordable housing constructed and occupied. As an organizer, the CLT is accountable to a constellation of interested parties who lease its land, reside in its community, make up its membership, and serve on its board. While the "classic" CLT serves both sets of interests, this balancing act is not always to everyone's liking. For CLTs that favor development over organizing, especially where a CLT program has been grafted onto the structures and programs of an existing community development corporation or where a CLT has been initiated by a municipal government, there has been a tendency to modify, dilute, or even abandon membership features or board features that make a CLT directly accountable to a local constituency of lower-income residents. For CLTs that favor organizing over development, there has been a tendency to spend more time building and sustaining the organization than building and managing an expanding stock of affordable housing. The most successful CLTs have found a balance between these two extremes, even when modifying basic features of the "classic" CLT.

- *Regional Opportunities & Resources.* Many CLTs are tempted to expand the territory and to modify the structure of the "classic" model because of opportunities and resources available to them only if they operate on a regional basis. Pulled by the prospects of doing more (or getting more), they may also be pushed by the demands of local constituents who want a wider choice of place in seeking a CLT home.

Because of factors such as these, the world of CLTs has become increasingly diverse. The model has continued to change. Indeed, much of the growth in the CLT movement in recent years can be attributed to the model's unique plasticity. Something is lost whenever fundamental features of the "classic" CLT are altered, for there are sound philosophical and practical reasons for every one of them, but something of value may also be gained. Over time, some of these variations will be discarded, while others may prove so beneficial, so successful that they eventually become a permanent part of what the "classic" CLT is defined to be. The community land trust remains a dynamic model, which is a large part of its strength and appeal.

NOTES

1. See "Tax-Exempt Status for Community Land Trusts," Chapter Six in the *Community Land Trust Legal Manual* (Springfield, MA: Institute for Community Economics, 2002).

2. See "Design: Contractual Controls over Use and Resale," Chapter Three in John Emmeus Davis, *Shared Equity Homeownership: The Changing Landscape of Resale-Restricted, Owner-Occupied Housing* (Montclair, NJ: National Housing Institute, 2006).

3. The National CLT Network, incorporated in 2006, has recognized—and embraced—the model's variability in its own criteria for membership. An organization may become a member of the Network either by exhibiting characteristics of a "classic" CLT, based upon the federal definition of a CLT, or by meeting organizational and operational criteria for a "CLT Variation." The latter criteria include the "core commitments" listed above.

Bob Swann

An Interview

Conducted by Kirby White
(1992)

A founder of ICE [Institute for Community Economics] and its Executive Director until 1980, Bob Swann is the source of many of the ideas that have kept the Institute busy for the past 25 years. Since 1980, he has lived in Great Barrington, Massachusetts. He is a founder and board member of the Community Land Trust in the Southern Berkshires, and is President of the E. F. Schumacher Society—in which capacity he continues to promote community-based approaches to basic economic issues. In the interview published here we asked him to talk about the experience and thinking that shaped the community land trust model and to comment on the state of the CLT movement today.

COMMUNITY ECONOMICS: Would you talk about how the community land trust model was developed, and how your own experience led to the development of the model.

BOB: As a conscientious objector during world War II, I spent two years in prison. It was a great chance to get your head together and learn about a lot of things that you never get a chance to on the outside. I was lucky because there was a group of us—40 COs, down in Ashland, Kentucky—and we put together a sort of post graduate course for ourselves on economics, with a heavy emphasis on the kinds of things that Gandhi was doing in India, things related to nonviolence and the peace movement. Also we had a correspondence course with Arthur Morgan, who at that time had left TVA and returned to Yellow Springs where he had been President of Antioch College. He had set up a course at the college in what he called "the small community."

Partly as a result of that course, I learned about things like Celo Community in North Carolina, which Arthur Morgan had helped to found. There were several Henry George communities, too, in Fairhope, Alabama, and Arden, Delaware. Also I learned about Ralph Borsodi's work in setting up several communities of this kind. Suffern, New York, was the first one. I think the second was Bryn Gweled, outside of Philadelphia.

This interview was originally published in *Community Economics* (Summer 1992): 3–5. It is reprinted by permission of Equity Trust, Inc.

All of these communities had a similar approach to land ownership—using a leasehold approach rather than individual ownership of land. Later, after the war, the leasehold concept kept intriguing me. But the thing that stuck with me was, well, these were nice communities; they were good for the people there, and they were interesting experiments for the time; but they were what I call *enclaves*. There was no effort at reaching into the larger community with the concepts—and that kept bugging me.

After Gandhi's death, one of his followers, Vinoba Bhave, began a movement in India which came eventually to be called the Gramdan, or Village Gift, Movement. What was interesting about this movement was that it was reaching out constantly and growing larger and larger, and had the element of true land reform in it. Vinoba wasn't just setting up enclaves; he was getting whole villages to adopt his concept—that the land should be held by the village and leased to the members of the village—and that seemed to me to be what was needed.

I moved to Yellow Springs shortly after getting out of prison. Arthur Morgan had asked me to work with him, but I was more interested in building and architecture. I got interested in Frank Lloyd Wright's work, so I left what Morgan was doing and got into the building field for a while. I moved to Michigan and built some houses for Frank Lloyd Wright, and then to Chicago where I designed my own houses. That experience gave me a lot of direct experience with the high cost of land and the high cost of financing. All of that was sort of grist for the mill. I kept thinking that something ought to be done about those costs.

Then in 1956 I moved back to Philadelphia to work with Morris Milgram on the first inter-racial housing project in the country—at least the first one built by a builder. What Milgram was doing was only a stone's throw from Bryn Gweled, so I learned more about that community at that time also.

Then came the whole peace movement. My wife and I moved to Connecticut and through most of the '60s we were mostly occupied with the peace movement. We were given a tract of land and building outside of Norwich, Connecticut, in the town of Voluntown. We set up a kind of land trust to own the property, and it became the base for the Community for Non-Violent Action—CNVA.

One of the focuses of CNVA was the effort to bring together the peace movement and the civil rights movement, the nonviolent aspects of them. In 1963 CNVA organized a walk from Quebec to Guantanamo—that was the plan anyway. We had sponsored many walks, including the San Francisco to Moscow walk, but part of the purpose of the Quebec to Guantanamo walk was to break down segregation along the way. And one of the points where that effort came to be focused was Albany, Georgia, where one of Martin Luther King's coworkers, Slater King—in fact he was also a relative—had been leading an effort to break down segregation. Members of the march—and I wasn't on the march at the time—spent a month or more in jail in Albany and went on a fast, which helped to cement the relationship between the members of the walk in CNVA and the members of the black civil rights movement in Albany.

I became acquainted with Slater King through all of this, and I proposed to Slater that we start a movement out of the civil rights movement that would break the pattern of land-holding in the South. There was a growing awareness of the whole problem of blacks being pushed off the land. Slater was very interested and agreed to help in any way he could.

I had become familiar not only with the Gramdan movement but also with the Jewish National Fund, which had acquired large areas of the land in Israel and leased it to individuals and groups like the kibbutzim. I was interested in that situation because it not only had the communities like the kibbutzim, but a larger entity holding the land. There was a much larger process going on. I talked to Slater about that and he agreed that it was the kind of thing that was needed in the South. So we organized a trip to Israel and got some small foundation backing for it.

Six of us, including four black civil rights leaders, spent two weeks in Israel in 1967. There was an awareness of the accusations of discrimination by Jews against Arabs, and the black members of the group were all skeptical about that aspect of the Jewish National Fund, but they agreed that the land tenure system was one they could use. So when we went back we organized a number of meetings around this idea and got more and more people interested and involved, and set up the organization called New Communities.

Eventually a 5000 acre tract of land was found on the market—an old plantation owned by two men who were retiring. The price was a million dollars. In the end most of that had to be borrowed, and that was a tragedy, because the land then had to generate a lot of cash to service the mortgage—about $100,000 a year—a terrible burden.

We were able to get a $100,000 grant from the federal government to do a full-scale proposal on how to develop the land. The planning grant was supposed to guarantee $1 million for the land from a special fund in OEO [Office of Economic Opportunity] that Bobby Kennedy had set up for high impact projects, which didn't have to get approval from the State. It looked like we were going to get that money, but then Nixon took office before the whole thing came through, and it was killed.

With the $100,000 that we did get, we had worked out a proposal that included a large housing development. We had set aside about 500 acres for housing—only ten percent of the tract, but still a lot of land, and the plan called for about 500 houses. But that never happened, partly because they were scrambling all the time to raise the money to pay off the mortgage.

Five thousand acres is a tremendous amount of land—a big piece to try to chew off. It was probably a mistake to try to chew off such a big one in the beginning, but the thought behind it, at least on my part, was that to get the kind of publicity and the kind of impact that we wanted we had to have something pretty big. You

couldn't do it on ten acres. Even a hundred acres wouldn't make much of a difference. But 5000 acres could make an impact. At any rate New Communities was
the first project that could be called a community land trust project. It had the elements not only of the Jewish National Fund but of the Gramdan Movement.

C.E.: The Institute for Community Economics was founded about the same time as
New Communities. Would you talk about how that developed?

BOB: The original name of the Institute was the International Independence Institute. It was named by Ralph Borsodi, who returned in 1966 from India, where he
had been teaching and had met leaders of the Gramdan movement. With them he
had planned to develop an international organization that would train local agents
to make small loans for simple tools and other needs to Third World farmers, such
as the farmers who leased land through the Gramdan movement. This scheme was
in fact similar to the Grameen Bank which developed later in Bangladesh.

However, before the scheme could be carried out, Borsodi's health failed—he
was then 86 years old—and the Indian leaders he had been in touch with were
caught up by political changes in that country. So a few of us who had been working with Borsodi decided to limit our efforts to starting a Gramdan movement in
the U.S. It was at that time in 1968 that the opportunity in the U.S. South opened
up, and we changed the name of the Institute to ICE.

C.E.: One of the things that has been distinctive about the community land trust
model has been the idea that CLTs, unlike the enclaves, should be organized
with open memberships, and that both those who lease land from the organization and other members of the surrounding community who do not lease land
should be represented on the board of directors. How did that idea get built into
the model?

BOB: That was my contribution. Other than that, we were taking things from the
Gramdan movement, the Jewish National Fund, the earlier enclaves and so on,
but my contribution was the idea that, if this was going to be a broader movement,
a land trust should have an open membership. Then quite a bit later—in the early
'70s—we came up with the notion of a three-part board, so that you have one third
elected by the lessees, and one third elected by the larger membership, and then
another third that would be selected by the first two thirds.

C.E.: So New Communities was founded before the idea of the three-part board was
developed?

BOB: That's right, it didn't have the three-part board. It *did* have an open membership. I was interested in the open membership because I thought that if people could
join from all around, then you would build into it a real educational element, not
just an enclave of people getting together for their own benefit to hold land.

You know, in my grandest dreams I see it as the ultimate land reform movement—
that gradually communities will more and more take over and own the land and
lease it out to their members as needed at relatively low cost, so that access to land
is available to everybody. That's the long-range dream.

It's also a fact that all other attempts at land reform that I can think of have failed because they took merely the approach of taking over land and then subdividing it into smaller ownership units for the larger population. It hasn't worked because inevitably the older structures that were there before began to regain control. The reason was that where large holdings were divided into smaller holdings the farmers or peasants who were able to get access to land nevertheless had to borrow money to buy the things they needed to farm the land. Because these farmers were mortgaged to the hilt, the land was gradually taken back by the same people that owned it before. In any case I think the long-range approach has to be something different than simply dividing up ownership of the land among more people.

C.E.: As an approach to land reform, how successful do you think the community land trust movement has actually been over the past 20 years? Are you pleased by what you're seeing now? Frustrated by what you're seeing?

BOB: In the first place it seems to me that there are two somewhat different problems between urban and rural land trusts. My interest has tended to be more in the rural side of it, and ICE has moved more to the urban side. I think that what is happening in the urban area is very encouraging. The idea of creating perpetually affordable housing is a good idea. The only thing is that there is a danger of losing track of the land itself. That's the only thing that worries me about the focus on housing, though I understand the forces that are moving in that direction. Housing is something that everybody needs; therefore it has more power to interest people.

But I think when you look at the rural areas, then the land tends to become more of a focus—because what's happening to the land is not just a question of occupancy; it's a question of how you're using the land, and of the sustainability of the quality and richness and ability of the land to produce. It gets into the environmental concerns more than the urban does.

C.E.: How do you see the relationship between community land trusts and conservation land trusts? Can they work together?

BOB: I think there is an important opportunity for community land trusts, particularly the rural ones, to work with the conservation land trusts. The conservation land trust movement is developing very rapidly. Unfortunately, at any rate in my opinion, conservation land trusts tend to have a kind of self-centered interest. Usually they are not set up by people who are interested in having other people have access to the land. They tend to be more interested in keeping other people off the land, at least off the land near them. But the good side is that they are concerned with the environmental aspect of land use, and I think that they can be appealed to. I think that there is potential for bringing the two kinds of land trusts together in mutually advantageous roles.

That's what we're trying to do here in Great Barrington. We have organized a local conservation land trust. In a small community like this one, the people who carry a lot of the political weight are likely to be interested in helping to form a conservation land trust. There is a genuine concern about seeing that everything isn't just over-built, and it has strong political expression in a town like this. In fact the local planning board and its zoning rules are often deliberately structured to make it difficult for a developer to go ahead. That's a battle that's going on all over the country.

But a community land trust is not interested in trying to maximize profit by putting as many houses as possible on a given piece of land regardless of what they do for the environment. The community land trust has some of the same kinds of interests in preserving the environment as a conservation land trust, so there is a common ground between them. And our thinking is that it's better for the community land trust to work with and be supportive of the conservation land trust movement, because that movement does provide a lot of political strength.

Furthermore, when it gets down to immediate practicalities, conservation land trusts that want to acquire land usually have to come up with the money to buy it. There's a good chance that any tract they want to acquire may have some land that is suitable for housing. So what often happens is that they say, okay, we'll sell that off to a developer and we'll get enough money to pretty much cover the cost of the rest of the land, which can then be protected from any further development.

The problem is that the owners of those new homes have an unfair advantage, because they're surrounded by permanent open space, so the value of their land goes up. You've created a land appreciation situation that is not fair to the community as a whole. But if the conservation land trust works with a community land trust rather than a for-profit developer, it won't sell the community short. The community land trust can capture that appreciated value for the community.

Speech to the Opening Plenary Session of the National CLT Conference, Albuquerque, New Mexico

Chuck Matthei
(2000)

As we start this 12th conference of community land trusts, I find myself thinking back to the first national conference of CLTs, which also overlapped an election season. We gathered that first time together in 1988 in Atlanta, Georgia. Our local host on that occasion was the South Atlanta Land Trust, generally known as SALT. At the same time, Atlanta was hosting the Democratic National Convention. The two events were simultaneous.

Georgia was a very appropriate choice for the first national CLT conference because, in fact, Georgia was the birthplace of the CLT model in the United States. It was 1967 when my predecessors at the Institute for Community Economics [ICE] joined with civil rights activists in southwest Georgia to launch a project called New Communities. Even as the New Communities project struggled to sink roots into the Georgia soil, its seeds were beginning to float upon the air and soon landed on fertile ground in Tennessee, Maine, Massachusetts, New Hampshire, West Virginia, California, and the District of Columbia. By 1980, about a decade later, we had maybe a dozen fledgling CLTs across the country. We had a foothold—or at least a toehold.

Very few people in the U.S. had heard the term CLT and even fewer took us seriously. But that was about to change because the second decade of this movement, the 1980s, saw a dramatic expansion. The 1980s brought a combination of recession and recovery and the advent of gentrification. Cutbacks in federal housing funds, which had begun under the Carter administration, accelerated rapidly under President Reagan. The legacy of the New Frontier and the Great Society antipoverty programs was substantially dismantled. Homelessness became the dominant social issue of the decade. There wasn't a newspaper or a magazine in the country that didn't run hundreds of photos of homeless people on the streets of cities and villages across our nation. But because of the federal cutbacks and dismantling of antipoverty programs, it was clear if there was to be any response, let alone a solution to problems like homelessness, new ideas, new initiatives would be needed. New actors, new sources of funds and new models would not only help us gain ground, but *hold* it once we had it. In this context the number of CLTs grew tenfold in ten years. We went from a dozen fledgling groups in 1980 to about 120 ten years later.

Reprinted by permission of Equity Trust, Inc.

In thinking back to that first national gathering and the democratic convention which paralleled it, I should tell you that the very first thing that Michael Dukakis did on the morning of his nomination for the presidency was to visit SALT, accompanied by leaders of the Bricklayers Union. At the time, SALT was one of the largest, most dynamic, and most publicized CLTs in the country.

Now as I look out at this gathering today, I see a lot of old friends and I see a great many new faces. With all due to respect to my old friends, it is more exciting to see the new faces. You're especially encouraging. The CLT movement is still expanding, especially in the west where the ideas were slower to take hold, and it's maturing. Groups like the Burlington CLT in Vermont and the Dudley Street Neighborhood Initiative in Boston have achieved a significance and a scale that is truly impressive. Newer groups like the Sawmill CLT are beginning in a manner that would have been unimaginable just a few years ago. This is really quite exciting to witness. Students in planning programs in universities across the country now read about CLTs. It's a concept and a phrase that's no longer unknown. Public and private institutions have adapted their lending programs and their insurance programs to accommodate land lease development, bringing down some of the technical barriers that slowed our early efforts. Everywhere we turn we find enhanced recognition and respect. That's exciting and promising. It suggests that you and I today have opportunities that are truly unprecedented.

But that's only part of the story. If there are hundreds of old and new faces in this room today, there are also, sad to say, many faces and treasured friends who are missing. There are new CLTs with very bright prospects, but the overall number of CLTs in the U.S. today has not increased significantly in the last ten years. We saw a tremendous growth spurt in the 1980s and we have seen a very important maturation in the last ten years and an expansion into some new areas, but the overall number has not significantly increased. Some groups have grown dramatically, strengthened and matured, but others are struggling to hold on day by day. A few have fallen by the wayside. SALT, which Michael Dukakis and the president of the Bricklayers Union visited that morning after the convention, is no more.

I've had the privilege of watching the CLT movement evolve over the past 30 years and I come to you today with excitement and a great deal of admiration for what you have done and what you will do. But in a positive spirit of constructive self-criticism, I also come with an admonition . . . admiration, yes, but an admonition as well. If we're broader and stronger today, we're also still quite fragile. We are highly dependent on relatively few sources of funding and, if I can be very blunt, we are at risk of squandering some of our most important opportunities. What is it that will determine our success, the degree of our success? What will determine success or failure?

All the technical, financial, and administrative competence is surely a factor and I'm glad in this conference, as in all such gatherings, we will take the time to learn how to practice our craft more skillfully, but that is not all that will determine our fate. Ultimately, I'm not sure it's our technical competence that is the most important factor. I'd like to suggest that there are at least two other considerations that are equally important—perhaps much more important.

First, how do we present ourselves—to our friends and neighbors, to our members, and to the community, the public at large? How do we describe the rationale for our actions and the principles which guide us? That's one issue I think bears further consideration.

The second is what alliances will we form? Truth be told, we've made a lot of friends along the way—in religious institutions, in financial institutions, in the halls of government—but we've gone to them more often looking for help, for handouts and for money, than we have gone to them to explore with them their own land tenure challenges. We've approached them as potential sources of assistance rather than on the basis of shared purposes and principles. It's time to change that relationship. It's time to form alliances that are substantive and genuine and can build the kind of diverse, powerful constituency that will allow us not only to survive, but to grow and have an impact that's far greater than the number of units we will ever build in Albuquerque or Atlanta or Seattle or Vermont.

These are the concerns that I'd like to spend a few minutes talking with you about. When I was invited to join you this morning, ICE suggested that we call my talk "Property and Values," which is also the title of a book that Island Press just published for the Equity Trust, edited by Gail Daneker and Chuck Geisler. The title *Property and Values* is something of a play on words. It's meant to suggest that property is not merely a tangible or even an intangible commodity. Values are not only monetary calculations. Property is a relationship. Forget the market and the state. Forget the constructs of law and the calculations of the marketplace for a moment. Think of property as a relationship—or, more accurately, as a web of relationships—in which there are many interlocking interests. Property is the manifestation of our relationships: to one another individually; to our communities; and to the earth on which we all depend. Our values are reflected in the character and quality of those relationships. Property involves a recognition of all the interested parties and a delineation of their respective rights and responsibilities. It's an arena of power and powerlessness, of hubris and humility.

The director of SALT at the time of that first national CLT conference was a wonderful man, Craig Taylor, who began his adult life as an air force officer stationed in a nuclear missile silo in North Dakota—until one night he had an epiphany, went to seminary, and studied for the pastorate. But by the time he graduated, he had another epiphany and, instead of going into the pulpit, he went into the streets and became a community organizer and a community developer. I remember Craig reflecting on the dynamics of power and powerlessness, humility and hubris contained in this institution of property. I remember Craig saying to us at that first CLT conference, "you know, when I listen to people arguing about who owns the land, they sound an awful lot like two fleas arguing about who owns the dog."

The duality of property and values is manifest in many ways. The word "property" is etymologically related to "propriety" which suggests responsible behavior. The word "equity" has several meanings as well. Equity is a financial interest in property and equity is a moral principle of fairness—and, for you old scofflaws of the Sixties like myself, equity in the law is the principle that allows you to override the restrictions of statutory law—to do what's right. So the duality of property and values is all around us. It's even in our language.

It was his own understanding of property as a web of relationships that led Mahatma Gandhi, India's Great Soul, to articulate the doctrine of trusteeship from which the word "trust" in CLT is derived. Gandhi understood that the economic relationships of individuals to their communities are inextricable and profound.

But for most of the last century, in both political debate and popular discourse, public and private, individual and community interests have been highly polarized, stereotyped, caricatured, set at odds against one another, right and left, public and private, the market and the state. For a very long time, half a century at least, it seemed that there were two ideological knights jousting on the battlefield of history. Then, not long ago, one of them vanquished the other. Now we're left with a universal secular religion that the author of a newly published book characterizes in his title as "One Market under God."

But despite this turn of events, the old rhetoric still persists. Perhaps you listened to some of the presidential debates over the past several weeks and you heard some people say, "*I* trust in the people; *he* trusts in the government." Public and private have become sectors and the human face has been lost. Wasn't it William Blake who told us that "mercy has a human face and pity a human heart"? I think we've lost sight of the faces and, perhaps, we've lost the capacity for mercy and pity.

Now in this context and faced with these cultural trends, we in the land trust movement began to speak not so often of "public" and "private," these depersonalized phrases. We tried to put the faces back in the picture. We acknowledged the legitimate property interests of individuals: security, equity and legacy. But we also acknowledged the parallel interest of communities. It is our emphasis in the CLT movement on the integration and balance of public and private interests that is our distinction. It's what makes us unique in the policy arena. It's what makes us unique on the street. Community for us is not only a word and a title.

Community is a value and a reflection of our values, but what does it mean to us? What is community when we say "community land trust" or "community economic development"? What is community to us? Early on, when ICE began to publish its own newsletter, *Community Economics,* Kirby White, who was the editor of the publication, tried succinctly (unlike some of us, Kirby has a capacity for clarity and succinctness)— Kirby tried to address that question of what is "community" in a CLT or in economic development. He defined three characteristics that were essential to us. *Community means place.* It is the place where we live, the place where we make our living, the place we care about which nurtures us. But community is more than a commitment to place; *community is a commitment to the people in that place*—to all of the people in that place, but first and foremost to those in greatest need. And, finally and critically, *community is a commitment to development models that protect and preserve*—that retain and recycle the income and the assets of the people derived from that place. Community economic development is not simply any and all economic activity, but that economic activity which both empowers individuals and sustains their communities over the generations.

The models which embody those principles reflect our distinctive and relatively unique analysis of poverty and wealth. Underlying the CLT model is the realization that the roots of poverty lie not in the lack of character or capacity on the part of poor people, nor even in the lack of income, which is how most people understand poverty. So what does it mean to be poor? You don't have enough money to meet your basic human needs, but that's not the story. Is it a factor? Yes, but it is more a consequence than a cause. What is the cause of poverty? The cause of poverty lies in structures and patterns of ownership that systematically deny to low-income people, individually and collectively, what is rightfully theirs.

That is the root of poverty and that is what the CLT model, unlike any conventional development strategies, seeks to address. We bring to our work a different analysis of poverty. Concurrently, we bring a different analysis of wealth, because we recognize that value comes not only from the individual, but from the community as a whole—property and values. Values are monetary calculations; values are moral principles. These are not antithetical concepts. They need to come together.

It's out of that kind of analysis of the origins of property value that the CLT model has come. It is not a confiscatory model. We manage the transfer of property and we control the transfer price in such a way that we can assure our communities a stable supply of decent permanently affordable housing. But permanent affordability is a functional description. It's a valuable function, but an inadequate description. What is really at work here is not simply an effort to control market forces so as to meet human needs, though that we must do. What is at work here is an effort to shape and sustain equitable human relationships. We are not offering to the poor a form of second-class ownership. We are challenging the community as a whole to squarely and honestly look at the question of where value comes from, to acknowledge that value comes from *both* the individual who makes an investment of his or her time, skill, and resources *and* the community and society of which that individual is a part.

Now over the last 20 years, you and I working together have made, I think, a very significant contribution to the poverty policy debate in this country. We've made more of a contribution than you may recognize. We've helped to change that debate in many quarters, at least from the traditionally paternalistic rhetoric of charity to what is now called impressively "asset-based development." This is a very significant step. It's an improvement, because when we've gone from charity to asset-based development, we've implicitly recognized that the poor have assets—human assets as well as financial assets.

So we're inching along in the right direction intellectually, but we haven't gotten to the goal. This is still only a partial understanding of the problem and it still lacks the essential ingredient of a genuine solution. Why? Because when you hear people talk in the legislative halls or in community development conferences, when you hear them talk about asset-based development, they are almost always speaking solely of *individual* assets. Asset-based development is the process by which we are going to turn the poor of the world into first-time homebuyers and micro-entrepreneurs.

Well, there's room for those programs, to be sure, but to suggest that you're going to solve the problems of poverty by the accumulation in the hands of some poor people of individual assets alone is ridiculous. We know full well that kind of entre-preneurship is realistic for some people, but certainly not for all. And even those who get that leg up, whose bootstrap seems to hold, are still going to be the most vulner-able people in the market economy. When the economy goes down, they will be the first to fail. When it goes up too fast, they will be the first to be gentrified out of line.

The poor of necessity have always relied on one another, and so it should be. Now in our work in the CLT movement, we have tried to acknowledge and strengthen the bonds of community. We do it by putting an emphasis on community organizing as a necessary precursor to good community development. We do it by our emphasis on community participation and planning and we do it by using the model which builds an economic base in and for our communities for present and future generations.

So we're trying to pay attention to this value of community and its essential role in our efforts, but having said this, we at times inadvertently shortchange the commu-nity's interests. Sometimes we do it in practical ways. I'll bet there've been days when you realized at the end of the day that your commitment, however genuine to com-munity organizing and education, had somehow fallen prey to that day's demands of development activity. It's hard to be both a developer and an organizer at the same time. So sometimes we miss the boat there.

We've also missed the boat, I think, in our relationship to one of the critical ele-ments of the CLT model, the lease fee. We spend all our time trying to bring those fees down in order to put poorer people into housing and that's the right thing to do today from a functional perspective. But we haven't looked conceptually at the role of the lease fee over time to realize the social appreciation in property value and to create a vital revenue stream for our communities in the future. It may not be a cash flow today, but if we don't understand the concept and the role of that element in this model, there won't be cash flow tomorrow either.

In our haste to do what's in front of us, we sometimes don't look far enough ahead. But more important than these practical oversights, I would like to suggest that we have defined community too narrowly in our work. This will be a fatal flaw if we don't correct it. Our commitment has been to communities that are marginalized and under siege—and so it should be. But in our commitment to those who are most on the margin, we sometimes fall prey to a siege mentality, a tendency to look inward too often. It's time for us to raise our heads, open our eyes, and see what's happening around us. Go to the printed materials and the audio-visual materials with which we currently present ourselves to the world. More often than not, we tell these stories as though they have no context. Here is a case study, a CLT sprouting like a mushroom from the fields of Iowa, but where do we come from, where are we going, and who else has values and objectives that overlap with ours?

When we define our community too narrowly, we limit our own access to the resources, both material and human, which will be absolutely essential if we are to survive. We are now, most of us, very heavily dependent on a relatively few sources of funding and particularly on public support. Look at a state like Vermont, which has perhaps the strongest infrastructure for community development and consequently the strongest network of CLTs that you'll find in any state in this country today. Is it a story to give new hope to warm your heart? You bet it is. But if the political winds were to shift significantly enough in Vermont and the public support was to diminish below a certain point, you would see how fragile even those strongest of our sister institutions still are.

So we need to increase our access to those human and material resources which success will require, but more than that, when we look too often inward, when we define our community too narrowly, we also limit our capacity to influence the larger environment, the larger community of which we, our members, and our neighbors are also so much a part. The CLT movement in recent years has largely presented itself as a low-income housing initiative and that's how most people see us. It's not because they lack the capacity to understand the bigger picture; it's because we haven't painted it.

Low-income communities are an appropriate priority. They're our first and most important allegiance, but a priority need not be a limitation. They're not our only community—and they are part of a larger community. Thanksgiving is coming. If your family is big enough, you may not be able to fit all at the primary table, so a separate table may be set for the children. It's not inappropriate for the kids, who'll have more fun with one another than they would with you and me. But our goal is not to set a separate table for the poor of the world. They belong at the table. It's their table. They're a part of the larger community. They are not a community unto themselves. We need to remember that. Is our allegiance to the poor? Yes it is. But not off to the side, not after the fact, but front and center at the main table, at the head of the table. Similarly housing is a basic human need, but it's not the only human need. Housing by itself does not constitute the creation of a whole and healthy community.

On a practical note, we all know that low-income communities alone, in this country at least, do not have the numbers, the political strength, or the financial resources for security and success. We have to remember where we came from. It was the civil rights movement of the 1960s that very directly gave birth to the first CLT in the U.S. It was quite appropriate that one of our principle speakers at that first conference was Congressman John Lewis, then a newly minted government official, but one of the true heroes of that era. The civil rights movement went through, as all movements do, a number of different stages in its evolution. In its most effective and dynamic period, although deeply and primarily rooted in the African American community, that movement reached far and wide to the churches, to the labor unions, to people of good will in every class and color. It appealed to them, to their consciences and to their compassion, but it changed them as well. It didn't say simply "help us." It said, in the words of Dr. King, "remember that philanthropy is no doubt commendable, but it must not cause the philanthropist to overlook the circumstances of economic injustice that make philanthropy necessary." It challenged the community as a whole to change. We weren't simply asking them to help African Americans change their circumstances; we were saying, we all must change. And so must we.

That is the message of CLTs. It is not simply an affordable housing program, a service to the poor. It's an effort to rewrite and restructure the institution of property itself. That sounds like a dangerous mission, so we phrase it differently. We tell stories because anecdotes constitute the only language that people of different backgrounds and ideologies can speak together. No matter where we come from, how different we think we are, we can talk to one another about people and places and events. If we're honest we can build trust even across ideological divides. So we tell stories and we find a language that isn't off-putting or alienating or frightening. The message remains the same, but we all have to learn how to tell our tale so that our listener can hear it best.

Make no mistake, like the civil rights movement which gave birth to my CLT and yours, we're a movement too. Sarah Page just referred to the Association of Community Development Financial Institutions. I'm sorry to tell you there was a day not many years ago in their annual conference when a pathetic debate took place, about whether it was appropriate any longer to speak of this community development finance initiative as a "movement" or whether we had grown and matured to the point that we should refer to ourselves now as an "industry." Why you would waste time talking about that when you have three days together, I can't fathom. How you could betray your history to even entertain that proposal is even more incomprehensible.

We ought not to forget our roots. Whether it's Gandhi and Vinoba Bhave in India or J. P. Narayan or Ralph Borsodi who brought their ideas here or C. B. and Slater King, civil rights activists in Albany, Georgia, and Bob Swann, their partner from the early ICE, who took their dreams and their difficulties and crafted the CLT model. Whether it's any or all of them, we should not forget where we come from. There was a great old labor activist, Jim Dombrowski, who was also an artist on the side who produced a poster that I particularly like. It's a painting of the Republic Steel strike in the 1930s, where many unarmed steel workers were gunned down by hired Pinkerton guards. The picture is moving, but so is the inscription. In hand-written letters around the perimeter of this painting Dombrowski writes, "Remember well the dead. Acquaint yourselves with their names."

We need to remember our history and we need to find our allies in the present moment. Who should we reach out to? I'm going to give you a short list and it is by no means complete and there isn't time today to plot the strategy or define the basis for these new alliances, but rest assured there are partners there waiting and alliances to be made. Where should we turn?

Let's turn to our brothers and sisters among the conservation land trusts. We have two land trust families in this country and they've developed along parallel but almost entirely separate tracks with very little communication and even less collaboration between them. In the last few years at the Equity Trust, we've been making a deliberate effort to bring down that barrier and bridge that divide. I'm happy to say I see significant movement, the differences are blurring quickly. But there are still differences of class and color. These are much harder to overcome because people don't even want to acknowledge them, but we need to face the challenge. The conservation groups have grown much faster. They're older than we are. The first conservation land trust was established in the mid to late 1800s. By the 1960s, 80 years later, there were still only a few dozen. Now there are almost 2000. They've grown much faster than we have. They're more numerous than we are, in part because of differences of class. The conservation movement is rooted in middle and upper class constituencies. That's a challenge to us, but it's an opportunity. We need the resources that alliances will bring and they need us as well.

Sprawl, smart growth—these are other arenas where we have to work together because if you impose good growth management and conservation policies and protect the environment and the environmental health of human communities, you will make them more desirable and prices will rise and the poor will be pushed aside. Good environmental initiatives will have bad social consequences if the conservationists don't learn to adopt some of the tools and techniques that are characteristic of our work in the CLT movement. But we have as much to learn as we have to teach.

Agricultural land preservation is another arena where we can work together. At the Equity Trust, we have a national program of land tenure counseling and financing and interim stewardship for community-supported agricultural projects and other small farms. In the agricultural conservation arena, more and more conservationists are recognizing that simply removing the development rights does not protect working land. It keeps it from development, but it doesn't guarantee that it will remain available and affordable to farmers. A farm or a ranch in New Mexico goes up for sale today and it's bought by an actor from Hollywood tomorrow at prices no native New Mexican can afford. That's what's happening here and it's not just here. It's on both coasts. It's in the Great Lakes region. It's all over the Rocky Mountains states. We are going to have to redefine conservation.

Last night, as I drove from the airport, I turned on the radio here in Albuquerque and there was a Native American show on talking about a new lawsuit that's just been filed, a class action suit by Native American farmers against the USDA for systematic discrimination in lending. It follows a successful class action suit by black farmers, which yielded a cash settlement larger than the total of all civil rights judgments to date. But where were you and I? Where were we when the black farmers filed suit against the USDA? So now that they've lost their farms, they get a one-time tax-free

$50,000 settlement. Will that restore their land? No, and when you have people who are the most vulnerable people in economic society trying to hold on one by one by one to little bits of land, it's only a matter of time.

I spent time a few months ago on Sapelo Island in Georgia with one of the last marginally intact Gullah communities, descendants of freed slaves in the sea islands, who know that with only 65 people in residence full time on the island and the property going further and further along the line of heirs, it's only a matter of time until more of those white doctors come in and offer $100,000 an acre and there are no more Gullah communities and there is no memory of Gullah culture in this country. So they're trying to create, at this late date, a CLT to hold what is rightfully theirs.

Where were we when the black farmers filed their suit and drove their tractors and marched step by step around the USDA? That's the challenge for the CLT movement, not simply to learn to be good lenders and good developers, but to remember our history and make it a part of our future.

The churches. We've gone to them for meeting space; we've gone to them for money from day one; but now the nuns are facing a crisis of their own. They've been our best friends, but the median age of nuns in this country is 72 and it rises by one year every year. They are going to have to dispose of all the property they own in the next 15 years. It's conference centers and convents, hospitals, schools, houses in low-income neighborhoods. It's hotels and shopping centers that have been given to them. It's oil rights in Oklahoma and mineral rights in Montana. These are actual examples. They need your help. They are trying to figure out how to balance their commitment to the land and to the communities of which that land and these sisters are a part with their own retirement needs. They're looking for partners and models that will carry on when they are no longer here. We all face mortality sooner or later. They are facing theirs now. They need your help. They'll give you help.

When the hotel workers union in Boston launched the campaign that required the first amendment of the Taft-Hartley law in a generation to establish a housing trust fund for low-wage hotel workers, where were we? We should have been helping them to shape the plans and policies for that trust fund that would make the most effective and lasting contribution to the well-being of their members.

When the environmental and labor movement came together in the streets of Seattle, where were we? Whether it's in front of the World Trade Organization meetings, or the World Bank, or in a classroom, or in a Senate conference room, the issues of globalization will continue to be debated. The globalization debate is many faceted, but it's a critical one—and it's a land tenure debate. In the early 1990s, Mexico changed its constitution. Peru changed its constitution under pressure from international lending agencies. How did they change those constitutions to undermine traditional communal landholding and open the market to foreign ownership? Where were we? No, that's not the question. Where *will* we be? *That's* the question.

As we redefine ourselves and our definition of community, we need to do a few simple things, and some that are not so simple. We need to lift our heads and look around us and recognize the property issues that are at play. We need to listen to the people involved and affected, learn their language, hear their values, their hopes and fears in their own words and learn how to talk with them. Study your history. Remember the dead and acquaint yourself with their names. Develop a vocabulary, an anecdotal vocabulary. Find the words that will help people re-conceive property, not as a construct of law or a calculation of the market, but as a web of relationships. Prepare the kind of curricula that can teach ourselves, our children, our neighbors to think in these terms and to negotiate equitable property relationships. Reach out, speak out, proselytize. Develop educational programs, not only in the community, but among your members. It's not enough to give them a home. Give them a vision. Give them values. Give them respect. Give them a reason to fight.

And finally, let's address the policy arena. Let's remember that this is not any longer to be a platform simply of adapting mortgage interest mechanisms to accommodate CLTs or opening this state or federal program so that we have funding. Those are useful concerns, but they're not sufficient; they're not primary. We need to figure out how to change the nature of property and the function of the market. That will involve many different kinds of policies, some of which won't specifically speak to CLTs. We have to sit down with these new allies and enroll them as allies in a political process on our own behalf—but be just as prepared to join them in *their* struggles.

Is this going to be easy? No. It'll take time and effort. It'll require us to challenge those divisions of color and class. Will it be easy? No. Are there risks? Yes there are. There are not only the risks that face anyone who's courageous enough to challenge a prevailing point of view; there are risks that we could lose perspective, lose focus, dilute our efforts.

Are the odds in our favor? Let's not ask a question like that. What difference does it make? The important question is, is it worth the effort? You bet it is.

I'm going to close with a story. It's a personal story that has nothing to do with CLTs in a direct sense, but says a lot about who I am, where I come from, and why I joined with you in building this movement. Two years ago on Christmas Day I received a call from my Aunt Marteen, my mother's sister who was like a second parent to me in all my childhood years. Aunt M. is growing older. She's still pretty feisty, but she's growing older and, although it's inappropriate, unseemly and a bit morbid to think this way, I have had my eye on one of her possessions. I'm embarrassed to acknowledge that because I like to think of myself as someone who isn't materialistic, or at least not very much so, but I had my eye on something that had long hung on her wall. It's the only material possession that, for many years, I've actively coveted. So I was quietly preparing myself for the day when I would have to call my cousins and say it means more to me than it does to you. And I didn't know how those negotiations would go.

Well, two years ago on Christmas Day, Aunt M. calls me out of the blue. I have no idea how she knew or why she did this. She said "I'm sending you a special gift today. I'm sending you Mandy's quilt." That was the quilt on which my eye had so often rested. This is a large quilt, double bed size at least. It has blue borders and blue stripes in both directions, creating white squares. And in each one of those squares is embroidered by hand a scene from the life of Jesus and a little inscription as best the quilt maker could write. On the side, you'll find in the corner embroidered the words, "Made by Amanda Collins, born 1862, May 1945."

Mandy Collins was born a slave of my family. She was freed by the Emancipation Proclamation when she was a year or two old, but she spent almost her entire life living and working for my family. It was the custom of the South that black and white children played together quite closely until they reached a certain age and suddenly, without saying a word, one becomes a mistress and the other is the servant. Mandy Collins was my great grandmother's servant. She wet-nursed my grandmother and her brothers and sisters.

When I was a little boy of eight, my mother and grandmother took us to Shreveport, Louisiana, to meet the extended southern family and, if you understand the protocols of the South, that meant for two weeks. Day after day we went from house to house to meet Great Aunt Josephine three times removed. But one day we went into the black community in Shreveport to a small wooden house to meet Mandy Collins. I didn't know this story at the time. I was eight and she was 95. It was perhaps the last moment in American history when a child could meet a woman who'd been born a family slave.

I remembered Mandy Collins when, just 8 years later, I stood at Soldier's Field in Chicago with tens of thousands of others as Martin Luther King delivered a sermon and then began the march to mail the demands of the Chicago movement. The southern movement had come north to the doors of a city hall whose mayor wouldn't open them. When Martin Luther King said that there would come a day when the sons of former slaves and sons of former slave owners would join hands together to make a better world, I knew he was speaking to me.

So if you are inclined to despair that we can ever change public attitudes or restructure an institution as fundamental for the character of American society as the institution of property, I say to you take heart because our understanding of property is changing. There was a time, almost within memory, when many of our parents and grandparents thought that others of our parents and grandparents belonged to them. Thank God we don't think that way anymore. We have to continue to re-vision our relationships to one another and to the earth on which we live.

As we do so, we should remember the story that Dr. King told us. It was a story from one of the struggles in the streets of a southern city in the early 1960s, when an old and tired black woman came up to Dr. King and said with all the faith and determination and courage that those times required of her and that these times require of us, she said, "you know Dr. King, we ain't what we oughta be, and we ain't what we wanna be, and we ain't what we gonna be, but thank God we ain't what we was."

PART FOUR

AFFORDABLE HOUSING

CLTs

A Growing Trend in Affordable Home Ownership

Julie Farrell Curtin and Lance Bocarsly
(2008)

Community Land Trusts in Context

Home ownership is one of the great opportunities for wealth building in the United States of America. Not only does owning one's own home provide a family with an asset that will appreciate in value over the long term, but home ownership also provides a family with a stable base from which to participate and engage in its broader community. For these reasons, and many others, the promotion of home ownership has long been a goal of various community groups, local and state governments, and even the federal government.

Over time, and especially during the real estate boom from 2001 to 2005, real estate appreciation far outpaced income growth in the United States, making home ownership increasingly out of reach for many low- and moderate-income families.[1] As a result, a wide variety of tools have evolved to make home ownership affordable for families of modest economic means. Soft-second mortgages, limited-equity cooperatives, condominiums, townhomes, and other common-interest communities are just a few examples of affordable home ownership strategies. Community land trusts (CLTs) are another such model that over the past three and a half decades has become an increasingly accepted tool for creating permanently affordable home ownership.

This article will focus on the CLT as an affordable home ownership strategy. First, we provide an overview of the history and economics of the CLT movement, as well as some common issues and challenges faced by CLTs. Second, we detail several examples of CLTs to illustrate the variations in the use of the CLT model. Third, we provide some analysis of new opportunities, and challenges, for CLTs playing a role in creating permanently affordable home ownership.

Community Land Trust: The Basic Model

There are many strategies that community groups and government organizations have employed to make home ownership affordable for low- to moderate-income households. These strategies generally fall into two broad categories: property-based programs and individual-based programs.

Overview of Models for Affordable Home Ownership

Property-based affordable home ownership programs include deed restrictions, limited-equity housing cooperatives (LEHCs), and CLTs. A property-based approach is one in which a particular unit of housing is made affordable to a defined class of home buyers by reducing the price of the unit. Deed restrictions involve attaching resale and other restrictions to title of the home at the time of sale to the low-income family. Because the restrictions are a part of the title to the property, all subsequent transfers of the property are subject to them.[2]

Limited-equity housing cooperatives are corporations that own housing for the benefit of its members. Individual households buy membership shares in the LEHC, giving them voting rights in the corporation and the exclusive use of a particular dwelling unit in the LEHC property. The LEHC is a property-based approach because the LEHC's housing units are made affordable by regulating the price of owning a share therein.[3]

Many nonprofits, municipalities, state governmental agencies, and federal agencies employ individual-based programs to assist low-income families in buying their first homes. Individual-based programs make housing affordable by granting or loaning to the low-income purchaser the funds needed to make a market rate home affordable. This often involves providing the household with a subordinate mortgage that bridges the gap between the purchase price for the home and the sum of the down payment the family can afford and a conventional first mortgage. These "soft seconds" usually have low or no interest, require no payments during the term of the mortgage, and are forgiven after the borrower has lived in the home for a specified period of time.[4] In the event the home is sold or otherwise transferred prior to the end of the mortgage term, the loan must be repaid in full. There are many variations on this soft second mortgage approach to making home ownership affordable.

The Community Land Trust Model

A CLT uses a property-based approach for maintaining affordability that differs in several respects from the property-based and individual-based models discussed above. Typically a CLT is a nonprofit, tax-exempt 501(c)(3) corporation dedicated to the preservation of land for the benefit of the community and for its use as low-income housing. Some CLTs are programs within other nonprofit organizations. Other CLTs are sponsored by local governments.[5]

A CLT's mechanism for meeting its mission is to acquire fee title to land and lease it through a long-term ground lease to the owners of the homes located on that land. Essentially, the ground lease is a contract between the CLT and the home owner giving the home owner exclusive access and rights to use the land, but limiting those rights in certain ways to maintain the home's affordability for subsequent owners.[6]

Typically a CLT's main emphasis is on permanently affordable home ownership. Many CLTs have single-family homes, condominiums, town-homes, multifamily rental, LEHCs, and other forms of housing located on their land. Of the 119 CLTs responding to a 2006 census of CLTs by the Lincoln Institute of Land Policy, 95 percent have home ownership units, while only 45 percent also have rental units, on their land. With the exception of several large CLTs, most CLTs across the country are small, having fewer than 100 housing units in their portfolios.[7]

History of the CLT Movement

Community land trusts are a relatively new arrival on the affordable housing scene. The first CLT was established forty years ago. The two decades following its incorporation saw modest growth in the number of CLTs across the country. Most CLTs that exist today were formed over the past two decades, with a large spike in the number of new CLTs after 2000.

1960s: The Birth of the CLT from the Civil Rights Movement

Several leaders from the civil rights movement in the 1960s, including a cousin of Dr. Martin Luther King Jr., organized the first CLT in 1968 in rural Georgia, called New Communities, Inc., (New Communities).[8] The CLT model was seen by the organizers as a means to provide land tenure to landless sharecroppers and tenant farmers. They believed that economic justice for African Americans in the South required that blacks secure land.

The goal was to lease the land to dozens of families who would own homes on the land, farm individual plots, and participate in cooperative farming. The land would provide housing and income. The combination of land, decent homes, and a means of making a living would help those who had long suffered the injustices of a segregated South gain freedom.[9]

The ground lease was integral to the New Communities model. New Communities' founders countered the argument that land ownership was essential to their equal justice goals by citing the fact that even when poor rural families owned land, their ownership of the land was usually at risk of foreclosure by their creditors (something that sounds familiar in today's subprime crisis). Therefore, they felt that having land owned by the CLT was important to maintain its use by those living on and farming the land. Additionally, the founders felt that the lease structure was needed to prevent land speculation, absentee ownership, and exploitation[10] many of the same reasons that attract people to the CLT model today.

New Communities acquired an approximately 5,000-acre farm near Albany, Georgia. Just as land acquisition is one of the major challenges facing modern-day CLTs, land acquisition was difficult for New Communities. The group had to be very covert about its purchasing efforts since it would have been extremely difficult to find someone willing to sell land to a group whose purpose was to help the African-American community.[11] Although New Communities ultimately failed and the land had to be sold,[12] the founders of the group took the lessons learned from the experience and incorporated them into a book about CLTs that went on to inspire other groups to follow their lead.[13]

1970s and 1980s: CLTs Powered by the Grassroots

The story of the Northern California Land Trust (NCLT) is representative of the generation of CLTs that formed during the 1970s. After the group formed in the 1970s, its first acquisition was a chicken farm in California's Central Valley. The group intended that the farm be a place where families would live and work on the land together. Like New Communities, the farm effort eventually failed.[14] However, NCLT still exists today as a successful CLT that owns and leases land for use as low-income housing in Berkeley, Oakland, and other San Francisco North Bay communities.

The Lincoln Institute's census of CLTs found that only four CLTs existing today were established in the 1970s.[15] Like NCLT and New Communities, small groups of activists or an energetic individual created these CLTs. Only one such group cited rising housing prices as a reason for its formation.[16]

Twenty-four of the CLTs existing today formed during the 1980s.[17] Again, many groups were community-based and fueled by the energy of a single leader. The first inner-city CLT, the Community Land Cooperative of Cincinnati (CCLC), formed in 1980.[18] CCLC's organizers created a CLT as a means to combat gentrification in a low-income, African-American neighborhood in Cincinnati. In fact, during the 1980s, a majority of the people who formed CLTs were motivated to do so by the rising cost of housing in their locality. Also in this decade, local governments played a role in the formation of 40 percent of these CLTs, signifying an emerging trend in the CLT movement.

1990s and 2000s: Local Governments Invest in CLTs

The 1990s and the 2000s have seen a boom in the creation of CLTs. Eighty percent of the CLTs that responded to the Lincoln survey were formed since 1990. Fifty-two CLTs formed during the first six years following 2000, compared to thirty-nine during the previous decade. The activists, individuals, community groups, and local governments who formed these CLTs did so in response to the rising cost of housing. The role of local government support in the formation of CLTs increased during this timeframe.[19]

Why has there been a recent rise in the interest in CLTs? The explanation most likely comes from a combination of the following factors: (i) greater acceptance of the CLT as a mechanism for providing affordable housing; (ii) more resources available to help start-up CLTs, such as consultants, funding, and educational literature; and (iii) the growing appeal of permanent affordability restrictions for home ownership.

Riding the CLT Trend Along the Roller-Coaster of the Real Estate Market

A CLT is a long-term affordable housing strategy that is designed to provide housing benefits to the community during the ups and downs of the real estate market.

Why CLTs Appeal to Policymakers During the Boom Times

From 2001 through 2005, real estate values increased at record rates in many parts of the country. The rising cost of housing may be the primary reason that a relatively large number of new CLTs were established during this time.[20] Why have so many government entities and community groups turned to the CLT model?

LEVERAGING LIMITED SUBSIDY FOR MAXIMUM BENEFIT

One reason CLTs have been more popular is because a CLT leverages limited housing dollars to benefit the maximum number of low-income families. Jurisdictions that used soft second mortgages, for example, did not have sufficient funds to cover the rapidly expanding gap between affordability and housing cost. Additionally, local government policies generally did not allow for large loans. Consequently, fewer and fewer people could take advantage of soft second programs.

By contrast, a CLT can lock a limited housing subsidy into permanently affordable housing. The CLT uses the funds to lower the sales price of the home for the initial buyer *and each subsequent buyer* without the infusion of additional public dollars. This guarantees that the units created with public dollars will stay affordable as the CLT maintains the low-income use of the properties for many generations.

The potential for "windfalls" may be another reason more jurisdictions turned to the CLT model of affordable home ownership. Real estate values rose so quickly in some areas, allowing a low-income home owner to sell the home, pay off the soft second, and receive a large "profit." Even though the jurisdiction recovered its subsidy, the dollars recovered no longer were sufficient to help another low-income family buy a home. A CLT's ground lease prevents this problem by regulating the resale price of the home to provide a fair return to the seller while keeping the home affordable to the buyer.

TAKING THE COST OF LAND OUT OF THE EQUATION

CLTs serve as "land banks." By retaining the ownership of the land, the CLT preserves the land for low-income use long into the future. Subtracting the land cost from the cost of housing makes the housing more affordable. This is especially true in a rapidly appreciating real estate market where the demand for land far exceeds both the supply of this limited resource and appreciation in income levels for low- and moderate-income families. Viewed over the long term, this aspect of the CLT model seems essential to meeting the need for affordable home ownership since land values will continue to rise despite any temporary downturns in the housing market.

Why CLTs Appeal to Policymakers During the Bad Times

If the rising cost of housing was a major factor inspiring the creation of the majority of CLTs formed since 2000, are CLTs still an attractive model after the "crash" in the real estate market? Arguably the rationale for using a CLT to create affordable home ownership opportunities is even more compelling in a market such as today's when we see record foreclosure rates and dropping home values.

TOOL FOR PREVENTING PREDATORY LENDING

Many parts of the country have reported record foreclosure rates in recent months.[21] The diverse array of mortgage products that helped fuel the boom of the earlier part of the century has contributed to the housing market's downturn. People who previously did not qualify for a mortgage were able to get one; however, these mortgages came at a price: higher interest rates, variable rates, and/or little to no underwriting to verify that the borrower's income could support the loan. Borrowers may not have understood the terms of their loans and the lenders or mortgage brokers selling the loans did not adequately explain the risks involved in the transaction.

CLTs work very closely with their home buyers to ensure a comprehensive understanding of the home purchase process. Many CLTs provide home buyers with home ownership training and financial counseling. This alerts the home buyers to the risks and responsibilities associated with home ownership before they purchase a home.

Also, the CLT builds protections against predatory lending into its ground lease. A CLT ground lease typically includes a prohibition on mortgaging the leasehold estate unless the mortgage is a purchase money mortgage from an institutional lender. All other mortgages require CLT approval. This gives the CLT an opportunity to spot a problem loan before the home owner signs the loan documents and runs the risk of becoming financially overextended and losing the house.

ASSISTANCE FOR HOME OWNERS IN DEFAULT

The CLT serves as a safety net in the event that a home owner gets into financial trouble. A CLT conditions its approval of a leasehold mortgage on the home owner's lender agreeing to provide the CLT with notices of default under the mortgage and to give the CLT the right to cure such defaults before the lender accelerates the note. This allows the CLT to work with the home owner to find a way to solve the financial problem and prevent foreclosure. This kind of close relationship between the CLT and home owner is not available to a non-CLT home owner, who often faces the loss of his or her home alone.[22]

Common CLT Issues

Each CLT varies considerably depending on the individuals involved, its geographic location and scope, its sources of funding, and many other factors. However, almost all CLTs face several common issues. The issues vary depending on whether the CLT is in the formation process and whether the CLT owns land, develops and sells housing on that land, and/or manages the resale of homes on its land. In this part we will highlight some of these key issues, starting with those that arise in the formation process and concluding with those that impact more established CLTs.

CLT Organizational Structure

A CLT's organizers must decide what corporate structure is appropriate for the CLT's goals. This decision determines who has the power to make important decisions regarding the CLT's activities. Various CLT structures have evolved over time and across localities.

Classic CLT Structure

The Institute for Community Economics (ICE) has been a leader in promotion of the CLT concept. Through its *Community Land Trust Legal Manual* it has supplied scores of new CLTs with model articles of incorporation, by-laws, and ground leases. These model documents reflect ICE's philosophy regarding the purpose of CLTs, and their use has influenced the structural and other decisions made by many CLTs.

ICE incorporated the "classic CLT structure" in its model articles and bylaws. The model documents reflect ICE's belief that the purpose of a CLT is to allow the community, rather than the private market, to make decisions regarding the use of land. Therefore, the classic CLT is a democratically governed, nonprofit membership corporation. Membership is typically divided into classes: (i) persons who own homes on land leased from the CLT (the Lessee Members), (ii) persons residing within the CLT's community (the Non-Lessee Members), and (iii) members of the general public who support the CLT.

Lessee and Non-Lessee Members elect the board of directors (the Board) and vote on important CLT matters such as changes to the CLT's purpose and resale formula. In the classic structure, the CLT's Board typically has nine, twelve, or fifteen members. The Board consists of one-third Lessee Members, one-third Non-Lessee Members, and one-third representatives of the general public who have important knowledge, relationships, and/or resources to contribute to the CLT's efforts. This is called the "tri partite" structure.[23]

Not all CLTs have adopted the tripartite structure. Nor are all CLTs independent corporations. Some CLTs are programs of larger nonprofits. Typically, the parent nonprofit has a mission to provide affordable housing and the CLT is another tool for the parent to meet this mission. One of the advantages to this approach is that the CLT benefits from the experience and reputation of the parent, especially in technical areas such as housing development. Also, the CLT may have lower operating expenses since they are shared with the parent.

Not all CLTs have members. The Lincoln Institute survey found that 70 percent of CLTs established as independent corporations have members, while only 20 percent of the CLT programs have members.[24] The advantage to having members is that they make the CLT more responsive to the community's needs. The disadvantage of maintaining a membership is the large amount of time and resources required to develop the capacity of the members. Another challenge is that the CLT cannot make certain decisions quickly because they entail calling a membership meeting, assembling a quorum, and garnering sufficient membership support for the decision.

Conflicts of Interest and the Classic Structure

The tripartite structure presents an increased potential for conflicts of interest because Lessee Members, who have ground leases with the CLT, serve on the Board. This raises an issue for CLTs (i) seeking a determination by the Internal Revenue Service (IRS) that it is a tax-exempt organization under § 501(c)(3) of the Internal Revenue Code (the Code) and (ii) receiving federal funding under the HOME Investment Partnership Program (HOME).

The IRS strongly encourages each tax-exempt organization to adopt a conflict-of-interest policy.[25] The IRS defines conflict of interest as "when a person in a position of authority may benefit personally from a decision he or she could make."[26] Lessee Members serving on a CLT Board may benefit from decisions affecting their ground leases; therefore, a conflict of interest may exist. CLTs applying for tax exemption should adopt a conflict-of-interest policy and clearly tell the IRS how the CLT will handle such conflicts in a manner that is in the best interests of the organization.

The rules for HOME funding prohibit persons with the authority to make decisions regarding the use of HOME funds (i.e., Board members) to personally benefit from the use of the HOME funds.[27] This rule would likely apply to a Lessee Member sitting on a CLT Board whose home was built with HOME funds, possibly warranting recusal from any HOME-related decisions. However, HOME rules allow the governmental entity that allocates the HOME funds to request an exception to the conflicts rule. One factor weighing in favor of granting the exception is "whether the person receiving the benefit is a member of a group or class of low-income persons intended to be the beneficiaries of the assisted housing, and the exception will permit such person to receive generally the same interest or benefits as are being made available or provided to the group or class."[28] This scenario seems to apply to a Lessee Member of a CLT Board. Nevertheless, a CLT should carefully evaluate these conflicts rules when making decisions regarding the use of HOME funds.

Obtaining Tax Exemption for Affordable Home Ownership Activities

Obtaining tax exemption under § 501(c)(3) of the Code for a new CLT can be a challenging process. Typically CLTs qualify for tax exemption as organizations organized for a "charitable" purpose. Some of the charitable purposes recognized by the IRS include relief of the poor, the distressed, or the underprivileged; lessening the burdens of government; lessening of neighborhood tensions; and combating community deterioration and juvenile delinquency.[29] In Revenue Procedure 96-32, the IRS has provided a safe harbor for housing organizations to demonstrate that they provide relief of the poor and distressed. This safe harbor sets maximum income limits for persons occupying the housing produced by the charitable organization.[30] Depending on the

CLT's particular real estate market and its target population, it may not be able to produce for-sale housing at low enough prices to be affordable to persons whose income levels fall within the safe harbor.[31] If this is the case, the CLT must find alternative grounds for qualifying for exemption.

Land Acquisition and Development Financing

Due to the high cost of real estate in many parts of the country, CLTs have increasingly struggled to acquire land. CLT land acquisition strategies are as diverse as are CLTs. Some strategies include seller financing, land donations from private parties and public entities, the use of eminent domain, inclusionary zoning, and traditional real estate financing.

Sources of financing for the development of housing on CLT land are similarly diverse. These sources include federal funds, such as HOME[32] and Community Development Block Grant (CDBG) funds, and, in the case of rental housing, Low Income Housing Tax Credits (Tax Credits) pursuant to § 42 of the Code. CLTs commonly fund housing development with state and local dollars. Public funds almost always come with specific affordability restrictions applicable to the housing. Therefore, the terms of these restrictions and the CLT's ground lease must be compatible.[33]

CLTs and Resale Restrictions

A CLT maintains the affordability of the housing on its land through its ground lease. The ground lease gives the CLT an option to buy the home at a "formula price" in the event the home owner decides to sell. The CLT then either exercises its option and sells the home to an "income-eligible buyer" at the formula price or assigns the option to an income-eligible buyer who buys the home at the formula price. Either the CLT or the seller may find the income-eligible buyer who purchases the home for the formula price.

A CLT balances the competing goals of affordability and wealth building in its resale formula. The ground lease usually sets the maximum price of a CLT home at the lesser of (i) fair market value or (ii) the formula price. The type of resale formula that a CLT adopts depends on the CLT's philosophy regarding home ownership.[34]

The Great Debate: Wealth Building versus Affordability

CLTs focused on preserving affordability will likely adopt a resale formula that links the resale price to a fixed index that measures the increase in a low-income household's buying power. A commonly used index is area median income (AMI). By linking the resale price to AMI, a CLT ties housing appreciation to income appreciation. Housing prices will remain affordable if they grow with people's earning power. Allowing some growth in the resale value of the home gives the seller an opportunity to build a modest amount of equity in the home.

Another formula that favors affordability is a mortgage-based formula. This formula provides that the resale price must be affordable to a family at a predetermined income level. The amount of down payment and monthly mortgage payment the income-eligible buyer can afford given the interest rates and underwriting standards at the time of the sale determines the resale price.

Many CLTs use an appraisal-based formula that often favors the wealth-building side of the equation. This formula requires two appraisals, one at the time of the original purchase and the other at the time of the subsequent sale. The seller recovers the original purchase price plus a specified percentage (e.g., 20 percent) of the difference between the original appraisal and the subsequent appraisal. Alternatively, the percentage of appreciation recovered by the seller may grow based on the number of years the seller has owned and occupied the home (e.g., 1 percent per year). Depending on the amount of appreciation, the home may or may not be affordable to a low-income buyer at the time of resale.[35]

The CLT Home: An Asset to Pass On to One's Heirs

Because CLTs often want to provide a product that is as close to fee simple home ownership as possible, they permit transfers of the home to certain family members upon death. Commonly a CLT home and ground lease may be passed to a spouse or child without violating the prohibition on transfers in the ground lease. This raises questions about who qualifies as a "family member" for purposes of inheritance; if spouses qualify, do domestic partners also qualify, and, if so, how should "domestic partner" be defined? Should grandchildren be allowed to inherit the home? Regardless of how the CLT decides to define permitted transferees, the inheritability of the home is an important selling point of CLT home ownership. By allowing the home, often a family's most valuable asset, to be inheritable, CLTs provide an important benefit to its home owners.

Home Buyer Financing

The price of a CLT home is less than that of a comparable home sold on the conventional market because it does not include the value of the land.[36] Nevertheless, a CLT home buyer needs a mortgage and other forms of financial assistance to purchase a CLT home. This requires the CLT home buyer to find a lender willing to have its mortgage secured against the ground lease. Adequate home buyer financing is an additional challenge for CLTs as they pursue a successful home ownership program.

Protecting Mortgagee Interests in the CLT Ground Lease

CLTs must design their ground leases to enable CLT home buyers to obtain financing. A CLT home buyer's lender wants assurance that the ground lease will remain in place for at least five years following the end of the loan term. Therefore, the lender cares about the CLT's termination rights. Lenders require that the ground rent be reasonable, thereby mitigating the risk of monetary default under the lease. At a minimum, a lender will require that the CLT give it notice and cure rights under the ground lease.

CLT lenders also are concerned with the marketability of the collateral. Therefore, most lenders require that the affordability restrictions in the ground lease expire in the event of foreclosure. For example, Fannie Mae will not purchase a leasehold mortgage on a CLT ground lease unless it conforms to their standards. In recent guidance, Fannie Mae stated that: "[t]he resale restrictions in the ground lease must terminate automatically on foreclosure (or the expiration of any applicable redemption period) of, or acceptance of a deed-in-lieu of foreclosure for, the leasehold mortgage."[37] The guidance provides that Fannie Mae will only purchase mortgages secured by a CLT ground lease if that lease uses its preapproved lease language.[38] This language builds in some protection for the CLT's resale restrictions by granting to the CLT an option to purchase the home in the event that the lender acquires it pursuant to foreclosure.[39] However, if the CLT does not exercise the option, or it is not able to because the purchaser at the foreclosure sale is not the lender, the affordability of the unit will be lost. The terms of the ground lease must balance the CLT's interest in preserving affordability with the lender's interest in being repaid.

Down-Payment Assistance

Some CLTs help their home buyers through down-payment assistance programs. Down-payment assistance may come in the form of a soft second, as described [previously]. It also can take the form of a matched savings program wherein the home buyer saves toward the purchase of a home. The CLT, or another third party, then matches, sometimes at generous ratios such as 1:5, the savings to increase the amount the buyer can put toward a down payment on the house. CLTs often educate potential home buyers about available programs and guide buyers through the application and qualification process.

FHA-Insured Mortgages

Another way low-income home buyers can afford to buy a CLT home is by obtaining a mortgage insured by the Federal Housing Administration (FHA). With FHA mortgage insurance, a low-income home buyer who would not otherwise qualify for a conventional mortgage can get a mortgage, often with more favorable terms. However, like Fannie Mae, FHA has imposed some restrictions on the CLT model.

Although FHA permits the use of resale restrictions, FHA regulations prescribe limitations on the precise formula used. FHA regulations provide that the resale formula should not prohibit the borrower from recovering the original purchase price, reasonable costs of the sale and improvements made by the borrower, any negative amortization on a graduated-payment mortgage insured under 24 C.F.R. § 203.45 and a "reasonable share, as determined by the Secretary, of the appreciation in value."[40] A home buyer may not be able to obtain FHA-insured financing if FHA determines that the CLT's resale formula fails to meet these requirements.

Like Fannie Mae, FHA requires that resale restrictions terminate upon foreclosure or transfer of a deed-in-lieu of foreclosure.[41] Additionally, FHA regulations limit the

CLT's ability to enforce violations of the resale restrictions. A CLT cannot terminate the ground lease, void a transfer of the home, or impose other contractual liability on the home owner if the home owner violates the resale restrictions.[42] This leaves the CLT with few options for enforcing the ground lease to maintain the affordability of the unit.

CLT Home Owner Protections

As the current foreclosure crisis illustrates, while purchasing a home may be difficult, holding on to that home can be equally challenging for low-income home owners. The CLT serves as a safety net for its home owners to help them stay in their homes. CLTs build terms into their ground leases to prevent home owners from falling prey to predatory lenders. CLTs also provide training and financial counseling services that help home owners obtain and maintain the dream of home ownership.

Predatory Lending Protections

As discussed above, the CLT ground lease prohibits a home owner from mortgaging its leasehold interest without the CLT's approval unless the loan is a purchase money mortgage from an institutional lender. The home owner must submit all mortgage documentation to the CLT for approval. This allows the CLT to identify potentially predatory practices and prevent its home owners from falling victim to any schemes that might result in future disaster.

CLT Home Ownership Training Services

Many CLTs provide home ownership training.[43] Education is a powerful tool against predatory lending practices. When home buyers understand the terms of their loan and how those terms relate to their personal financial situation, they are able to assess their ability to make mortgage payments. Educated home owners also understand the consequences of defaulting on a mortgage, including the risk of foreclosure and loss of one's home. Often, CLTs require potential home buyers to participate in home ownership training and/or financial counseling to become eligible to purchase a home on CLT land. Some CLTs partner with other nonprofits that provide training to their home buyers. Whether a CLT conducts the training or outsources it to partners, the CLT plays an important role in giving low-income home buyers the tools to become, and remain, successful home owners.

Issues in Context: CLT Case Studies

Each of more than 180 CLTs across the country is a unique organization with a slightly, or sometimes significantly, different take on the CLT model. However, all CLTs face similar issues of how to finance land acquisition and how to make home ownership affordable yet meaningful. By highlighting CLTs in two different regions in the country—the Northeast and southern California—we hope to illustrate some of the diversity and creativity across the CLT community.

CLTs and Local Governments

Many local governments are eager to increase home ownership rates in their jurisdictions. As we have discussed, local governments have a long history of supporting home ownership initiatives with public dollars and other programs. Here we contrast two CLTs and their relationships with their local governments.

Dudley Street Neighborhood Initiative: Boston, Massachusetts

Formed in 1988, Dudley Neighbors Inc. (DNI), the CLT affiliate of the Dudley Street Neighborhood Initiative in Boston, Massachusetts, is one of the country's oldest CLTs. At the time of formation, the Roxbury neighborhood, home of DNI, faced disinvestment and abuse. For example, many vacant lots throughout the neighborhood had become illegal dumping grounds for discarded personal refuse.

In 1987, the community developed a resident-driven plan for the future of land use and development in the neighborhood. The formation of DNI followed as a method of implementing the housing development portion of the plan. DNI has played an important role in transforming the vacant land in the neighborhood from a liability into an asset.

In the fall of 1988, the Boston Redevelopment Authority granted the power of eminent domain to DNI, giving DNI a powerful tool for transforming the vacant land in the neighborhood into permanently affordable housing.[44] Additionally, DNI established a partnership with the City of Boston so that any city-owned land could be transferred to DNI at minimal cost.[45] This combination of eminent domain power and a strong partnership with the city forms the basis of DNI's land acquisition strategy.

DNI currently has 155 units of housing on its land. This housing consists of a mix of home ownership, cooperative housing, rental housing, and commercial space.[46] Arguably, 155 units are not enough to meet the need for affordable housing in the greater Boston area.[47] Nevertheless, the low-income people in Boston's Roxbury neighborhood drive DNI's efforts, making DNI's 155 homes a true community asset.

Irvine Community Land Trust: Irvine, California

Fast forward almost twenty years and we arrive at another example of a CLT-city symbiosis, this time in Irvine, California. Unlike DNI, the Irvine CLT arose from the efforts of city officials in search of a citywide affordable housing strategy. Two key factors compelled the City of Irvine (the City) to develop a comprehensive affordable housing plan: one, the relatively high cost of housing, and two, the annexation and pending redevelopment of the recently closed El Toro Marine Corps Air Station (El Toro).[48] The plan resulted in the City adopting a housing goal of having 10 percent of the City's housing stock maintained as permanently affordable through the newly formed Irvine CLT by 2025.

Although the Lennar Corporation, a private entity, owns and plans to develop El Toro, by annexing the former base the City subjected it to the City's inclusionary zoning ordinance.[49] Additionally, the City designated El Toro as a Redevelopment Project Area, which, under California law, allows the City to capture future increases in property tax revenues for affordable housing and other related uses. Specifically, California law requires that the City use 20 percent of these funds for affordable housing[50] which in this case is estimated to be approximately $143 million.[51]

Since its incorporation in 1971, the City has implemented various affordable home ownership strategies, including the use of deed restrictions, which are difficult and costly to enforce. Additionally, the City's down-payment assistance program no longer meets the needs of low-and moderate-income residents. The City made only one loan through its down-payment assistance program in 2005. This history, plus the housing prices that grew increasingly faster than incomes in Irvine, undoubtedly influenced the Irvine City Council's decision to form Irvine CLT.

The City's affordable housing plan calls for an alignment of all of its housing policies in support of Irvine CLT. For example, the City's inclusionary zoning ordinance requires all new development in the City to have an affordable component, through either the production of units or the payment of an "in-lieu fee." One way a developer can comply with the ordinance is to donate land of equivalent value as the calculated in-lieu fee.[52] Irvine CLT's land acquisition strategy is to encourage developers to select this land donation option. The strategy is particularly viable in the City of Irvine, where a large tract of land, El Toro, will be developed in the near future, and will be subject to the inclusionary zoning ordinance.

To achieve this integrative approach, the City Council has retained a high degree of control over the Irvine CLT. All seven initial members of Irvine CLT's board of directors are City appointees. Also, Irvine CLT is initially staffed with City personnel. Eventually, Irvine CLT's board will consist of the following: two City appointees, three lessees of Irvine CLT land (elected by other lessees), and two at-large seats appointed by the other board members.[53] By maintaining two seats on the board, the City will have a permanent decision-making role in the organization.[54]

The City will also have control over Irvine CLT through contractual agreements. When the City transfers, or causes to be transferred, land to the Irvine CLT, the transfer will be made subject to a "performance agreement." The performance agreement will include performance standards and reporting requirements applicable to the Irvine CLT. If the City determines that the Irvine CLT has failed to meet the standards, it will enforce its rights under the agreement to "take over the lessor function of the TRUST and restructure the organization, with the intent of correcting the problems."[55]

Irvine CLT is perhaps the most extreme example of the latest generation of city-sponsored CLTs. The City's high degree of control over the Irvine CLT distances it from the earlier generation of grassroots CLTs. However, by investing in the Irvine CLT from its inception, the City is, and will most likely continue to be, a strong supporter of the Irvine CLT. This not only will lead to funding and land donations for Irvine CLT projects, but also will ensure that the City will design its other affordable housing policies, such as its inclusionary ordinance and down-payment assistance program, to support Irvine CLT's efforts.[56]

CLTs in Partnership

A CLT can further its mission by partnering with like-minded nonprofit organizations to augment its skills and resources. This is especially true for newly formed CLTs. As the broader affordable housing industry has matured, nonprofits have become more specialized. Some are expert housing developers, while others are effective housing educators. Similarly, funding for housing-related nonprofits, including financing for affordable housing development, is highly competitive. As meeting the growing need for affordable housing becomes more complicated, new and old CLTs alike must build relationships with other housing nonprofits in order to accomplish their goals. This section highlights the partnership approach taken by two southern California CLTs.

Figueroa Corridor Community Land Trust

In 2004, the low-income residents of the Figueroa Corridor, an approximately forty-block area south of downtown Los Angeles, faced rising rents, illegal evictions, gentrification, and displacement. The community had recently won an extensive community benefits agreement (CBA) with the developer of the Staples Center, a mega-sports and entertainment complex, whereby the developer promised to make jobs, parks, and housing available to the low-income residents. Despite this victory, the development associated with the Staples Center and the overall real estate boom brought intense gentrification pressures to the neighborhood. Faced with losing the hard-fought benefits of the CBA, community leaders sought a way to prevent displacement and ensure that the people who lived and worked in the community would always have a place there. Hence, the idea for the Figueroa Corridor Community Land Trust (Land Trust) was born.[57]

The Land Trust is a membership corporation with a classic tripartite board structure. Representing the low-income community of the Figueroa Corridor is central to the Land Trust's mission. The majority of the people who live in the Figueroa Corridor are very-low-income families of Latino descent. Many do not speak English as a first language. All Land Trust board meetings are conducted in both English and Spanish. The Land Trust spent most of its first year focused on board development, thereby ensuring that community members are actively engaged decision makers in the organization.

As a start-up CLT with a strong grassroots base but little affordable housing development or real estate experience, Land Trust organizers knew that, to reach its goal of owning land for the benefit of the low-income community, the Land Trust had to form significant relationships with other groups. From the beginning, Land Trust leadership included experienced and well-respected nonprofit affordable housing developers.

Land acquisition is one of the Land Trust's biggest challenges. To overcome this barrier, the Land Trust's affordable housing developer partner formed an affiliate called the Figueroa Corridor Land Company (the Land Company). The Land Company and the Land Trust entered into a joint venture agreement whereby the two organizations agreed to collaborate to establish a dedicated acquisition financing pool. The Land Company will use this funding to acquire and entitle properties in the neighborhood and thereafter transfer them to the Land Trust. The Land Trust will partner with developers, including the Los Angeles Community Design Center, to build low-income housing on this land.

Housing on Land Trust land will be rental housing. Because land and development costs are so high, and Land Trust members' incomes are so low, affordable home ownership is not economically feasible. The Land Trust will be the long-term steward of this housing through monitoring and enforcement of its ground lease, which will include affordability restrictions. The Land Trust plans to engage its members in the process of identifying properties for acquisition, obtaining land use approvals, and designing the projects that will ultimately be home to the low-income people of the neighborhood.

Community Foundation Land Trust

The Community Foundation Land Trust (CFLT) builds critical partnerships to bring permanently affordable rental and home ownership housing to Los Angeles County.[58] As a supporting organization of the California Community Foundation (CCF), a large philanthropic nonprofit organization in Los Angeles, CFLT is an example of a CLT program of an existing nonprofit. CFLT is a stand alone 501(c)(3) nonprofit corporation. However, seven of CCF's board members, including CCF's CEO, sit on the CFLT board, giving CCF a significant presence among the other real estate, nonprofit, financial, and community leaders that serve on the CFLT board.

Since its formation in 2002, CFLT, through its relationship with CCF and others, has secured over $20 million in loans for site acquisition, which it has leveraged into the development of over 280 homes in six innovative development projects. Like the Figueroa Corridor Community Land Trust, CFLT partners with experienced affordable housing developers to build affordable housing on CFLT land. Unlike the Figueroa Corridor Community Land Trust, however, CFLT uses its land for both affordable rental and home ownership opportunities.

CFLT partners with developers, local governments, and other funders. Through these partnerships, CFLT implements its two main strategies for meeting the affordable housing needs in Los Angeles County: First, CFLT brings permanent affordability to all of its projects through its ground lease. CFLT's resale restrictions serve to ensure that the limited housing subsidy in Los Angeles County benefits the maximum number of people. Many jurisdictions in the county lack the capacity to monitor and enforce their affordability restrictions. CFLT solves this problem by overseeing the resale restrictions applicable to its projects.

Second, CFLT has the capital and internal capacity to be an innovator in a challenging affordable housing marketplace. For example, two of the most significant barriers to affordable housing development in Los Angeles are the high cost of land and the lengthy entitlement process. Through its acquisition fund, CFLT can acquire properties that are suitable for affordable housing development. After acquiring the land, CFLT enters into a disposition and development agreement with its development partner. This frees CFLT's development partners from the need to obtain multiple sources of acquisition financing, minimizes their risk, and allows them to focus their resources on the development of the housing. CFLT and the developer enter into a ground lease at the end of the entitlement process and the beginning of construction. In the implementation of these strategies, CFLT plays a strategic role in expanding the opportunities for affordable housing production, and preservation, in Los Angeles County.

CLTs of the Future: Challenges and Opportunities

As the evolution of the CLT model over the past forty years illustrates, the challenge of creating equitable housing options is one that people in the United States have struggled with for a long time. The need for affordable housing seems to be the only constant in a real estate market that ebbs and flows, and neighborhoods that pass through cycles of prosperity and peril. Although this article describes the CLT model as a viable means for making housing, and in particular home ownership, affordable, the use of the CLT model raises many difficult questions for those who wish to engage this model in solving the affordable housing problems of the future.

CLT Challenges: A "Perpetual" Model in Changing Times
Mission and Marketplace
Community land trusts promise permanent affordability. Through the use of a ninety-nine-year ground lease, a CLT commits to keeping the cost of housing on its land affordable for multiple generations of home buyers. Delivering on this promise may seem easy in the first few years of the ground lease term; however, ninety-nine years exceeds the average human life span. Therefore, the promise of perpetual affordability must remain intact over several generations before a CLT can say that it has fulfilled such promise.

Anyone involved in the real estate market knows that perhaps the only prediction about the market that will come true is that the market will change. The forces of gentrification can suddenly overtake a neighborhood that has suffered from blight for decades. Likewise, a stable neighborhood can slip into decline and disrepair from neglect and disinvestment. A CLT's board cannot forecast what will happen over ninety-nine years to the neighborhoods where the CLT owns land.

The tension between a long-term commitment to affordable housing and short-term changes in the marketplace raises some difficult questions for CLTs. How will a CLT's board respond when its properties are worth five times, or more, what the organization originally paid for them? Will a CLT meet its mission to provide affordable housing when it must spend more resources to build fewer units? Should the CLT shift its focus away from housing low-income households to selling homes to moderate-income households? Will the opportunity to sell its land for a high price tempt the CLT to leave a community and pursue its affordable housing goals elsewhere?

Similarly, a CLT that owns property in a declining neighborhood may find itself in a situation where all of the homes on its land are uninhabitable. Is a CLT's mission compatible with being a slumlord? What options does a CLT have when it has decades remaining on land leases where the use of the property is contrary to its core values? Is it possible for CLTs to have adequate safeguards in their lease documents to prevent CLT homes from becoming hosts to drugs, gangs, prostitution, or other unsavory activities?

The answers to the above questions reside largely with an unknown group of people—the CLT leaders of tomorrow. Just as the real estate market is guaranteed to change, organizational leadership, and the strength and capacity thereof, also will change. Over time, the composition of boards will shift and executive directors will come and go. The local officials and funders that influence a CLT's activities also will change. As new people take control of the CLT, how they answer the questions posed above will be the true test of the CLT's ability to keep its promise of perpetual affordability. Will new leaders bring new priorities? Undoubtedly they will, but will those priorities also change the CLT's fundamental mission? Does this make CLT home owners vulnerable to the whims of evolving CLT management?

We raise these questions primarily to illustrate that although perpetual home ownership is an attractive component of the CLT model, it is not without its limitations, many of which will only become apparent with the passage of time. To the extent that a CLT's board can consider these questions today and draft the CLT's form of ground lease accordingly, the CLT will be better prepared for the uncertainties of tomorrow.

Affordable Home Ownership, Responsible Home Ownership?

The current record foreclosure rates across the country are the painful consequence of a failed affordable housing model. Subprime loans allowed people who otherwise could never have qualified for a mortgage to buy a home through the use of exotic lending products. In a lending binge with loose underwriting practices, banks and other financial institutions made housing temporarily affordable to low-income people, until interest rates increased on their adjustable-rate mortgages. Sadly, and not surprisingly, interest rates rose faster than borrowers' incomes, and higher mortgage payments, in many cases, led to defaults.

The subprime example raises some similarly difficult questions for CLTs. CLTs and their supporters often advocate for home ownership for the same low-income, and in some cases very-low-income, demographic. At what point is someone's income simply too low to bear the responsibility of monthly mortgage payments on a thirty-year, or even longer, mortgage? Do CLT low-income home buyers have an adequate safety net if their home needs a major repair, such as a new roof or furnace, and the home owner cannot afford to pay for it? How does the CLT strike the proper balance between serving as a hands-off ground lessor and hands-on landlord? Would low-income households be better served by the increased availability of decent, affordable rental housing? Do CLTs run the risk of behaving like subprime lenders by focusing on getting people into houses, not on keeping them there? CLTs must assess their affordable housing mission honestly and seek responsible ways in which to provide affordable home ownership without setting people up to fail.

Opportunities: Tools to Take CLTs into the Next Decade

Condominium Development

As many urban areas in the United States have reached their limits of suburban growth, and little buildable land remains within their boundaries, they have turned to higher-density development to create livable and affordable communities. Condominium development in these areas provides for a more efficient use of space than single-family homes, thereby reducing the price of the units. Therefore, the future for CLTs operating in urban areas may mean seeking ways to implement the CLT model with condominiums.

A condo owner owns title to his or her individual unit and an interest in the common areas, which are governed by the condominium association. Combining this structure with a CLT ground lease is complicated. The CLT condo owner would enter into a CLT ground lease for his or her unit, and also would own a membership interest in a homeowners association (HOA) that holds the ground lease on the common areas. What if the HOA defaults on its lease with the CLT? A termination of the HOA ground lease unfairly impacts the condo owners since it would cause them to lose their rights to the common areas. HOAs raise an additional challenge for affordable home ownership. An HOA is responsible for the maintenance of the common areas. The HOA pays for these costs by charging all condo owners HOA fees. Higher HOA fees have a negative impact on affordability. For a CLT condo project to be successful, HOA fees must be addressed at the project's inception in order to prevent rising fees from eroding affordability.

Lease-Purchase: CLTs and the Low-Income Housing Tax Credit Program

Tax Credits are one of the largest sources of funding for affordable housing development. In order to qualify for Tax Credits, a project must be operated as affordable *rental* housing for an initial compliance period of fifteen years (the Compliance

Period). Historically, the rental housing requirement has been a barrier to CLTs' use of Tax Credits for home ownership development. However, the Code provides a way in which a CLT can participate in a Tax Credit project to ultimately create affordable home ownership opportunities.

LEGAL BACKGROUND

The owner of a housing development financed with Tax Credits (a Project) may grant a right of first refusal (ROFR) to the tenants of the Project, or to a "qualified non-profit" as defined in the Code,[59] which they may exercise at the end of the Compliance Period for at least the minimum purchase price prescribed by the Code.[60] However, the owner of a Project must record an extended-use agreement against the Project, which requires, among other things, that the affordability period last for at least thirty years.[61] This conflicts with the tenants' right to purchase the Project at the end of year fifteen. Revenue Ruling 95–49 resolved this conflict by providing that the exercise of a ROFR by a tenant that terminates or suspends the thirty-year extended-use period does not violate the relevant provision of the Code.

Each state has a Tax Credit allocating agency (Agency) that may require a longer extended-use period. Parties considering lease-purchase Tax Credit transactions should be aware of the potential conflict between a tenant purchase at year fifteen and a restricted-use period that extends beyond fifteen years. For example, the extended-use period in California is fifty-five years. Recognizing the conflict between the tenant purchase option and the extended-use period, the California Tax Credit Allocation Committee addressed this issue in its regulations implementing the Tax Credit program.[62]

As long as the applicable Code and Agency requirements are met, a lease purchase Project that involves the sale of the Project's units to tenants at the end of the Compliance Period is legally possible. One way to structure a lease-purchase transaction is to sell the Project to a CLT in year fifteen. Assuming the CLT meets the Code's definition of a "qualified nonprofit organization," the CLT would acquire the Project through the exercise of a ROFR to purchase the Project at a price that is greater than or equal to the minimum price prescribed by the Code. Once the CLT exercises its ROFR with the Project owner, the CLT would own the Project in its entirety. Assuming compliance with state condominium requirements, the CLT could then sell the individual units to the Project's tenants. Each tenant would then enter into a long-term ground lease with the CLT containing various provisions designed to preserve the affordability of the unit.

PROS: CLT LEASE-PURCHASE TRANSACTIONS

A CLT lease-purchase transaction ensures the long-term affordability of the Project, even after the acquisition of the units by the initial tenants and the extended use agreement has been released. Also, in jurisdictions where there is a conflict between the tenants' right to purchase and the extended-use requirement, the CLT's ground lease may serve to satisfy the long-term affordability restrictions applicable to the Project pursuant to the Agency's extended-use requirement. Moreover, many CLTs have experience working with low-income home buyers and providing them with the training and resources that they need to successfully buy and own a home. Finally, selling the Project to a CLT is a simpler transaction for the Project owner than multiple sales to individual tenants. This may be attractive to the Project owner, and its investors, because the CLT assumes any risks associated with the tenant sales transactions.

CONS: CLT LEASE-PURCHASE TRANSACTIONS

For a CLT to meet the definition of a "qualified nonprofit" under the Code and thereby be eligible to have a ROFR to purchase the Project, it must have an ownership interest in the Project throughout the Compliance Period. Therefore, a lease-purchase Project must engage the CLT from the beginning. Presumably, this could be satisfied by allowing the CLT to act as a partner in the Tax Credit partnership owning the Project during the Compliance Period.

Other Opportunities

Despite the current dip in the housing market, home prices will rise again, especially in places close to work and transportation centers. As people seek a higher quality of life, their willingness to commute long distances to work will diminish. Even in the current market downturn, homes close to centers of work and transportation have held their value, while homes in the more distant suburbs have suffered the greatest losses in value.[63]

The environmental benefits, such as reduced carbon emissions from less automobile use, of "live-work" communities and "transit-oriented development" are significant and have caught the attention of planners and policymakers. Basic economics tells us that as the demand for these kinds of communities, which by their nature are limited in supply due to restricted amounts of buildable land, increases, so will their cost.

There is an important opportunity for CLTs to play a role in the development of live-work communities from their inception. By maintaining a percentage of the housing units in these areas for low- and moderate-income families, CLTs can support mixed-income communities. Perhaps more importantly, CLTs can ensure that the social, environmental, and other benefits associated with living in such "walkable communities" will not be reserved exclusively for high-income people.

The CLTs of the future should consider focusing their efforts on major centers of employment for low-income workers. Such centers include universities and hospitals, institutions that require a large labor force of both professionals and low-wage workers. These institutions would benefit from partnerships with CLTs that ensure permanently affordable housing for their employees located close to work. Schools, police, and fire departments are examples of other large employers that directly benefit from having employees live in the communities where they work. However, teachers, police officers, and fire fighters often cannot afford to buy homes near work. Again,

CLTs have a role to play in the future design of our communities to make them more enjoyable places to live for people of all income levels.

What are other potential applications of the CLT model? We raise the question because we do not presume to know all of the diverse and viable possible answers. Rather, as the market changes and people's demand for housing grows, there is certain to be a role for CLTs, but the nature of that role will continue to evolve, as it has for the past forty years.

CLTs Distinguished from Other Affordable Housing Models

In most respects, CLTs are no different than other affordable housing development organizations; they share the same sources of funding and process for successfully constructing and operating affordable housing. What distinguishes the CLT model from other housing models is that it preserves affordability for ninety-nine years. No other model—from Tax Credits to HUD programs—offers such long-term affordability. This ensures that dollars spent making CLT housing affordable today will provide a long-term benefit; it eliminates the need to find additional subsidies to preserve expiring use units and ultimately contributes to the stability of the communities in which CLTs operate. Understanding this distinction is imperative for those wishing to implement the CLT model as an affordable housing solution for the future.

Conclusion

CLTs will play a role in the affordable housing arena for some time to come. As the CLT model has evolved over time and been adopted by various communities, it has been applied in different ways. When considered in the broader context of affordable housing development, what distinguishes the CLT model from other strategies is its commitment to the preservation of affordability over the long term. A CLT's promise, and its challenge, is to provide housing, whether rental or ownership, that will be affordable to many generations of low-income households.

NOTES

1. Home ownership rates are especially low in certain regions in the country. For example, in 2005 the home ownership rate in Los Angeles was 47.4 percent, compared to 70 percent nationally. In fact, 2005 home ownership rates in Los Angeles represented a 1.5 percent drop since their 48.9 percent level in 1994. Alan Nevin, *Home Ownership in California: A CBIA Economic Treatise,* California Building Industry Association, Mar. 22, 2006, at 3, 7. Home ownership rates in New York are also far lower than national levels. New York State's home ownership rate in 2006 was 55.7 percent, and New York City's, at 30.2 percent in 2000, is even lower. U.S. Census, available at http://www.census.gov/hhes/www/housing/hvs/.

annual06/ann06t13.html and http://quickfacts.census.gov/qfd/states/36/3651000.html (last visited Feb. 28, 2008).

2. One drawback to this approach is that the lenders and buyers involved in the subsequent sales of the deed-restricted homes often are not made aware of the restrictions during the title review process and the homes therefore inadvertently get sold at the market, rather than restricted, price, in violation of the restrictions. Enforcement of the terms of the deed restrictions after such a sale can be difficult and costly. One group has addressed this problem by securing a $100 note and recording a deed of trust against the property concurrently with the deed restrictions.

3. The LEHC's bylaws provide a formula for determining the initial and subsequent sales price of a membership share designed to maintain the affordability of the share (and thereby the housing) while allocating a limited percentage of the LEHC's equity to the shareholder. LEHC members often have a separate use agreement with the LEHC that governs the terms of their use of the dwelling unit and requires the payment of a monthly "rent," the amount of which is set by the LEHC board and is designed to cover, at a minimum, the operational costs and debt service of the LEHC. To be successful, an LEHC requires a high level of participation and a reasonable degree of training in group process and real estate management for its members.

4. We note that the IRS may characterize this "loan" as taxable income to the borrower, either at the time that the loan is made or at the end of the term when it is forgiven. A detailed analysis of the tax consequences of soft second mortgages is beyond the scope of this article.

5. Basic issues relating to the structure of the CLT will be discussed later in this article.

6. Issues related to a CLT ground lease will be discussed in greater depth later in this article.

7. Yseim Sungu-Eryilmaz & Rosalind Greenstein, *A National Study of Community Land Trusts* 16 (Lincoln Institute of Land Policy 2007). Of surveys distributed to 183 CLTs with known addresses, the Lincoln Institute received 119 completed surveys. This is the first comprehensive survey of CLTs in the United States.

8. John Emmeus Davis, *Shared Equity Home Ownership: The Changing Landscape of Resale-Restricted, Owner-Occupied Housing* 20 (Nat'l Hous. Inst. 2006).

9. International Independence Institute, *The Community Land Trust: A Guide to a New Model for Land Tenure in America* 16–17 (1972).

10. *Id.* at 18.

11. *Id.* at 22.

12. Davis, *supra* note 8, at 21.

13. *Id.*

14. Personal communication with Ian Winters, Executive Director, Northern California Land Trust (Mar. 2005).

15. Sungu-Eryilmaz & Greenstein, *supra* note 7, at 10.

16. Davis, *supra* note 8, at 21.

17. Sungu-Eryilmaz & Greenstein, *supra* note 7, at 9.

18. Davis, *supra* note 8, at 21.

19. Sungu-Eryilmaz & Greenstein, *supra* note 7, at 10.

20. The Lincoln Institute's survey found that the majority of CLTs established during the 2000s stated that the rising cost of housing was one of their main motivations for forming a CLT.

21. Chris Isidore, *Home Ownership in Record Plunge,* CNNMoney.com, Jan. 29, 2008, *available at* http://money.cnn.com/2008/01/29/news/economy/home_ownership_vacancies

(last visited Feb. 28, 2008). *See also* Dina ElBogh-dady & Nancy Trejos, *Foreclosure Rate Hits Historic High,* Wash. Post, June 15, 2007, *available at* www.washingtonpost.com.

22. At least one community is considering the use of a housing model similar to a CLT to respond to its own foreclosure crisis. The City of San Diego has recently seen an alarming number of foreclosures. Citizens and decision makers in that community are concerned about the debilitating effect that foreclosures will have on the health of entire neighborhoods. In response to this crisis, the community is considering the formation of a "land bank"—a governmental entity that will purchase foreclosed properties and use a combination of public and private resources to sell the homes to people from the community at affordable prices. *A Land Bank for Foreclosed Properties?* San Diego Union-Trib., Feb. 17, 2008.

23. Sungu-Eryilmaz & Greenstein, *supra* note 7, at 22. Thirty percent of all CLTs reported using the tripartite structure.

24. *Id.* at 23.

25. Internal Revenue Service, Instructions for Form 1023 (Application for Recognition of Exemption) (rev'd June 2006) at 9. *See also* Governance and Related Topics—501(c)(3) Organizations, *at* www.irs.gov/pub/irs-tege/governance_practices.pdf (last visited Feb. 27, 2008).

26. IRS Instructions to Form 1023, *supra* note 25.

27. 24 C.F.R. § 92.356.

28. *Id.*

29. Internal Revenue Service, Publication 557, Tax-Exempt Status for Your Organization (rev'd June 2008), at 24.

30. An organization will be considered charitable if it establishes for each project that (a) at least 75 percent of the units are occupied by residents that qualify as low-income and (b) at least 20 percent of the units are occupied by residents that also meet the very-low-income limit for the area or at least 40 percent of the units are occupied by residents that also do not exceed 120 percent of the area's very-low-income limit. Rev. Proc. 96-32, 1996-1 C.B. 717.

31. CLTs have successfully obtained tax exemption under the IRS safe harbor for their home ownership activities, including the production and sale of homes on CLT land, because the income levels of the CLT's eligible buyers fell within the safe harbor guidelines.

32. "Community Land Trust" is statutorily defined under the HOME Program within the broader context of Community Development Housing Organizations and their special status under this law. 42 U.S.C. § 12773.

33. For example, HOME regulations provide requirements pertaining to the affordability period and resale price for HOME-assisted home ownership units. HOME-assisted home ownership units must remain affordable for five to fifteen years, depending on the amount of HOME funds invested in the units. 24 C.F.R. § 92.254(a)(4). Also, the resale price of HOME-assisted home ownership units "must ensure that the price at resale provides the original HOME-assisted owner a fair return on investment (including the home owner's investment in any capital improvements) and ensure that the housing will remain affordable to a reasonable range of low-income buyers." *Id.* § 92.254(a)(5)(i). Also, the HOME regulations require that the price of HOME-assisted home ownership units be capped at 95 percent of the median purchase price for the area. *Id.* § 92.254(a)(2). This may pose a problem for CLTs in high-cost areas.

34. Most CLT ground leases define an "eligible buyer" as someone at or below a certain income level (e.g., 120 percent of area median income). Arguably, requiring the seller to sell to an "eligible buyer" serves to limit the resale price. Since most eligible buyers can only pay what their income will support, limiting the pool of buyers effectively limits the sales price.

Nevertheless, CLTs do not rely on buyer eligibility requirements alone to regulate the resale price of their homes.

35. Over half of CLTs use appraisal-based formulas, with index-based formulas falling in a distant second place. Only four CLTs reported using a mortgage-based approach. Sungu-Eryilmaz & Greenstein, *supra* note 7, at 31–32.

36. CLT home owners do have to pay ground rent to the CLT. In keeping with their affordable housing mission, CLTs do not charge market rent. Instead CLTs typically design rent payments to be low enough to be affordable to the home owner, yet high enough to cover the CLT's costs of monitoring the lease.

37. Fannie Mae, Announcement 06-03, Amends These Guides: Selling and Servicing, Properties Subject to Resale Restrictions or Located on Land Owned by Community Land Trusts 9–10 (Mar. 22, 2006).

38. *Id.* at 10.

39. Community Land Trust Ground Lease Rider, Fannie Mae Form 2100 at 3 (Mar. 2006) *available at* www.efanniemae.com/sf/formsdocs/forms/2100. jsp (last visited May 19, 2008).

40. 24 C.F.R. § 203.41(d).

41. *Id.* § 203.41(c).

42. *Id.* § 203.41(d).

43. After housing development, home ownership counseling ranks as the second most common activity conducted by CLTs. Sungu-Eryilmaz & Greenstein, *supra* note 7, at 24.

44. Dudley Neighbors, Inc., www.dsni.org/dni/.

45. Personal communication with Jason Webb (spring 2006).

46. Dudley Neighbors, Inc., www.dsni.org/DNI_Web_Pages/products.htm.

47. One of the critiques of the CLT model is that it fosters only a low rate of production of housing. In fact, DNI represents one of the largest producers of housing among CLTs, with most CLTs reporting a housing stock of less than 100 units. Also, few, if any, CLTs other than DNI have the power of eminent domain, indicating that other jurisdictions have been either unable or unwilling to adopt this strategy. Perhaps this will change with the increasing popularity of the CLT model.

48. Adam Elason & John Trauth, City of Irvine Housing Strategy & Implementation Plan at i (Mar. 14, 2006), available at www.cityofirvine.org/civica/filebank/blobdload.asp ?BlobID=8842 (last visited Mar. 3, 2008).

49. *Id.* at 3.

50. Cal. Health & Safety Code § 33334.2 (Deering 2008).

51. Eliason & Trauth, *supra* note 48, at 7.

52. Irvine Mun. Code ch. 2-3 § 2-3-5(B).

53. Eliason & Trauth, *supra* note 48, at 20.

54. Arguably the influence of the City appointees will be significant since such a large amount of the Irvine CLT's funding will come from City sources such as the housing set-aside funds, in-lieu fees generated through the inclusionary zoning program, and other traditional sources of affordable housing funds such as Community Development Block Grants and the HOME Investment Partnership Program.

55. Eliason & Trauth, *supra* note 48, at 24.

56. Irvine CLT's progress toward its affordable housing development goals has not been as fast as originally projected due to the recent downturn in the housing market, which has slowed the pace of the private development upon which Irvine CLT's core strategies (inclusionary zoning and redevelopment) depend. As a result, the City recently voted to provide Irvine CLT with funding to jumpstart its development program and acquire several housing units. Personal communication with Rick Jacobus, Partner, Burlington Associates in Community Development (May 17, 2008).

57. One of the authors served as counsel to Figueroa Corridor Community Land Trust from 2005 through May 2007. One of the authors continues to serve as counsel to the Figueroa Corridor Land Company, a partner organization.

58. One of the authors currently represents CFLT.

59. The Code defines a "qualified nonprofit organization" as an organization that (i) owns, directly or indirectly through a partnership, an interest in the project throughout the Compliance Period; (ii) is determined by the state housing credit agency to not be affiliated with or controlled by a for-profit corporation; (iii) has as one of the exempt purposes of such organization the fostering of low-income housing; and (iv) is described in paragraph (3) or (4) of § 501(c) and is exempt from tax under § 501(a). IRC § 42(h)(5).

60. 26 U.S.C. § 42(i)(7)(B) provides that the minimum purchase price is "an amount equal to the sum of (i) the principal amount of outstanding indebtedness secured by the building (other than indebtedness incurred within the 5-year period ending on the date of the sale to the tenants), and (ii) all Federal, State, and local taxes attributable to such sale."

61. *Id.* § 42(h)(6).

62. California's regulations provide that "[a]ll projects, except those applying under section 10326 of these regulations [pertaining to projects financed at least 50 percent by tax-exempt bonds], will be subject to the minimum low income percentages chosen for a period of 55 years, unless they receive Federal Tax Credits only and are intended for eventual tenant home ownership, in which case they must submit, at application, evidence of a financially feasible program, incorporating, among other items, an exit strategy, home ownership counseling, funds to be set aside to assist tenants in the purchase of units, and a plan for conversion of the facility to home ownership at the end of the initial fifteen-year compliance period. In such a case, the regulatory agreement will contain provisions for the enforcement of such covenants." Cal. Code Regs. tit. 4, § 10325(c)(9)(b).

63. Kathleen Schalch, *Home Prices Drop Most in Areas with Long Commutes,* NPR: Morning Edition (Apr. 21, 2008), available at www.npr.org/templates/story/story.php? Story 1 & 2 89803663.

Diminishing Returns

A Critical Look at Subsidy Recapture

Helen S. Cohen
(1994)

Long-term protection of the public's investment in affordable housing is gradually becoming a credo among municipalities—even a litmus test for public policy. Whether the result of obvious economic constraints or lessons gleaned from poorly planned programs of the past or conclusions derived from a far-reaching analysis of private property and publicly assisted housing, it is slowly dawning on many municipal officials that public dollars should be safeguarded against the whims of the market and the speculative desires of individual investors. There is a growing agreement that cities have a responsibility to somehow *recycle* their scarce subsidies for affordable housing.

But there are questions: How should cities accomplish this? Which programs most effectively protect the public's investment while providing low- and moderate-income people decent, affordable, secure places to live? How long should the public's investment be protected? Which mechanism is most fair? Most efficient? Most marketable? And, more fundamentally, should permanent affordability be a municipality's bottom-line requirement, or is the recapture of public subsidies enough?

In spite of widespread agreement on the need to preserve public dollars, municipal officials in different regions of the country have answered these questions in different ways and have arrived at different conclusions about how to proceed. The basic policy debate has been framed around two options:

1. *Subsidy recapture.* A municipality's investment in affordable housing is recycled through a "shared equity" type of program, whereby the city subsidizes the initial purchase of a home for a low- to moderate-income buyer and gets back its subsidy plus a percentage of the appreciation when the unit is resold. With this technique, homes are resold at the highest value the market will bear, with no restrictions on price. The city then uses its "recaptured" capital to finance the next eligible buyer in the same or in another home.

2. *Subsidy retention.* The affordability of publicly assisted, privately owned housing is preserved through price restrictions on future sales (or rents), which

ensure that the units do not escalate in price beyond what might be affordable for a low- or moderate-income buyer. With this approach, municipal subsidies are locked in place, creating and retaining a permanent stock of affordable housing.

The relative effectiveness of subsidy recapture versus subsidy retention is the subject of the present chapter. I provide both a descriptive overview of these programs and a critique of their financial, social, and political consequences, drawing on examples from several municipalities with very different market conditions. My focus is on homeownership programs, though my conclusions extend to rental housing as well.

Although subsidy recapture and subsidy retention are both enormous improvements over housing programs requiring *no* recycling of the public dollar, subsidy retention is the more effective policy. It simply makes more sense, economically and socially, to use scarce public resources to produce and preserve a permanent stock of affordable housing. This is particularly true in urban or suburban areas with rapidly inflating real estate markets, limited access to land, and median incomes that lag behind a rapid rise in housing costs. In these settings, affordability is difficult to achieve at the outset, but once that feat has been accomplished, it can be—and should be—perpetuated for as long as possible. What is needed is not simply a program that recycles a municipality's housing dollars but one that invests those dollars in the kind of housing that is itself recycled from one owner-occupant to another without losing any of its publicly subsidized affordability.[1]

Subsidy Recapture

Subsidy recapture or equity-sharing programs vary in structure, mechanics, and scale, depending on the demographics of the city, the goals of the particular program, available sources of financing, and various political and legal realities. These programs also go by a variety of names: homeownership coinvestment (HCI), equity participation, shared appreciation, and equity partnership, among others. They may be administered by various entities: public, private, or nonprofit. I will concentrate here solely on programs administered by a municipal agency that subsidize homeownership for low- or moderate-income residents.

Despite the variation among subsidy recapture programs, most of them adhere to a few key features:

- Public or private subsidies are coinvested with the funds of a prospective homebuyer to reduce the principal of the homebuyer's mortgage.
- Repayment of all or part of this subsidy—both principal and interest—is deferred until the property is resold. Because repayment is deferred, the homeowner's

monthly mortgage payments are reduced, enhancing the affordability of the housing unit.

- The homes are sold and resold at their highest market value.
- Coinvestors share in the home's appreciation, usually in proportion to the amount of their initial investment. The financial commitment of the municipal agency is treated as an investment made with the goal of getting back a proportionate "fair return" on the municipal dollars put into the property.
- Subsidies that are recaptured are used again by the municipal agency to refinance the same home with a new buyer or to finance another home.

A simple example helps to illustrate the financial obligations of each party. Say municipal agency X lends $20,000 at a simple annual interest rate of 5 percent to help finance a $100,000 home. Repayment of principal and interest is deferred until the home is resold. At the time of resale, the homeowner/borrower owes the agency $20,000 plus interest—plus 20 percent of the home's appreciation. If the home resells for $150,000 after five years, the homeowner/borrower pays back the $20,000 subsidy, plus $5,000 in interest, plus $10,000 (20 percent of $50,000 appreciation). The municipal agency then uses its $35,000 to subsidize the next purchaser of that same home, which now costs $150,000, or to locate another unit to finance with the recaptured and augmented subsidy.

The goal of most subsidy recapture programs is twofold: to assist lower-income households in purchasing homes they could not otherwise afford, and to preserve and recycle the public's investment in housing. Continuing affordability of the housing itself has historically not been a goal. Equity-sharing programs directly assist homebuyers in purchasing homes at prevailing market rates, enabling them to get into the market and to profit from the deal, if and when they resell. These programs also serve as a mechanism for the city to recoup at least some of its investment. According to advocates of this approach: "With an equity sharing program, units can be sold and resold at market value without artificial controls or restrictions. Agencies can place the return on their investments in a revolving fund and then use those resources to help other potential buyers. Recycling public resources in this way is consistent with the current realization that both resources and the tax base are finite."[2]

Recycling funds in this way is also consistent with the common belief that cities should not unreasonably intervene in the market or unduly restrict an individual's rights as a homeowner. There is a premise that all parties involved should get their "fair return," based on whatever the market can generate, allocated according to whatever each party has invested in the deal.

Unfortunately, these same premises and practices compromise efforts to preserve the affordability of housing over time, particularly in inflating markets. The subsidy recapture model assumes that the market will stay flat enough for the pool of recycled funds to keep pace with rising housing costs. As the constant dollars available for housing shrink, however, and as housing costs escalate relative to household income, many cities are faced with the troubling reality that they cannot maximize the return on their investment without minimizing the affordability of the housing they subsidize. Conversely, they cannot ensure the affordability of the subsidized housing, as it changes hands at an unrestricted price, without assisting fewer and fewer buyers or adding more and more dollars to their original investment. This is the paradox at the heart of subsidy recapture: the preservation of the public subsidy is incompatible with the preservation of affordability, and vice versa.

Subsidy Recapture in Action: San Francisco's First-Time Homebuyer Program

San Francisco is a prime example of a city whose housing costs have escalated at an astronomical rate in the last decade while average incomes have lagged far behind. In the Bay Area between 1980 and 1990, median household income increased by 76 percent (not adjusted for inflation), while the median value of owner-occupied units increased by 162.8 percent and median rents increased by 131.8 percent. In the city of San Francisco between 1980 and 1990, the median home value increased from $104,600 to $298,900. This profile is typical of many West Coast cities where real estate values are still soaring—cities like Seattle, which is currently experiencing some of the same inflationary trends that swept California in the middle to late 1980s.

San Francisco was one of the first cities in California to institute a homeownership program using a subsidy recapture model based on shared equity. The San Francisco First-Time Homebuyer Program, begun in 1984, is administered by the mayor's Office of Housing and Community Development. The program is targeted to first-time homebuyers earning up to 120 percent of the median income for San Francisco; it is not exactly a "low-income" housing program, but it makes a highly inflated homeownership market more accessible to moderate-income residents.[3]

Through the First-Time Homebuyer Program, the city provides deferred payment, shared appreciation, and second mortgages ranging from $35,000 to $65,000. The city will make a loan to an eligible buyer if his or her downpayment, combined with a conventional loan from a local bank, does not cover the cost of the home. The city's loan is subordinated to the conventional financing, and payment of the principal is deferred until the unit is sold or rented.

The deferred loan from the city serves to write down the initial cost of the property and thus to reduce the amount of debt the homeowner(s) must cover. When the unit is resold to another homebuyer, the subsidy must be repaid, along with a percentage of the appreciation proportionate to the city's initial investment in the property, plus an additional 10 percent of the appreciation.

The directors of the First-Time Homebuyer Program have tried to adapt the terms and policies of the program to accommodate changing market conditions. When the program first began in 1984, the city either collected a simple 6 percent annual interest rate on its loans or recaptured 20 percent of the appreciation, whichever was less. The high rate of inflation of land and housing costs in San Francisco quickly convinced the city that it needed to increase the percentage of recaptured appreciation. Otherwise, the program would never keep pace with the market, and the amount of subsidy needed to make the housing affordable to subsequent buyers would have to be increased substantially with each transfer. Since 1988, the city has taken back a portion of the appreciation that is equivalent to its proportionate share of the initial investment plus an additional 10 percent. Interest on the city's investment is no longer charged to the homeowner.

To preserve the affordability of these publicly subsidized homes, the city has tried to enforce contractual obligations of owners to sell to other eligible buyers. When buying into the shared equity arrangement, property owners must agree to restrictions that either limit the sale of the property for thirty years to another low- or moderate-income household or grant the city a right of first refusal to repurchase the property at the market rate if the homeowner decides to sell. The city may then assign its purchase right to another entity or individual, or it may repurchase the property and refinance it for another eligible buyer.

Despite these restrictions, assisted homeowners have been able to sell their homes at the highest possible price. An inflationary market and the lack of municipally imposed restrictions on profits or prices have meant that they could repay the city both the deferred loan and a share of their homes' appreciated value and still walk away with a substantial windfall. Many of the program's homeowners have done just that. Consequently, the subsidized homes themselves have become less and less affordable to subsequent moderate-income buyers, who require greater amounts of subsidy from the city.

The First-Time Homebuyer Program was established on the assumption that the city's initial investment of $35,000 to $65,000 would be "recycled" with little erosion and little need of replenishment as long as the rate of appreciation in housing costs was not 4 percent higher than the rate of increase in median income. This assumption proved way off the mark. As noted earlier, there has been a much larger gap between housing costs and household incomes in the Bay Area over the last decade.

The City of San Francisco responded by revamping the program's terms and conditions to capture a greater portion of an assisted property's equity upon resale, but this has not prevented the gradual depletion of the original subsidy pool. According to Joe LaTorre, director of the mayor's Office of Housing and Community Development, it now takes the recycled subsidy from *two* homes, on average, to finance each new homebuyer in the current market. In a market like San Francisco's, simply recycling a portion of the market appreciation does not ensure the preservation of affordability or the preservation of the original subsidy pool.

The most glaring weakness of San Francisco's First-Time Homebuyer Program is its inability to fulfill its own objective of preserving a pool of public subsidies for affordable housing. The recapture mechanism, while allowing initial homeowners to reap the benefits of traditional homeownership, simply does not keep pace with the cost of housing. Without any limits on resale prices or profits, individual homeowners walk off with huge equity windfalls while the pool of public dollars for future deals steadily shrinks.

Even when the original homeowner sells to another eligible buyer (of which there are many on a long waiting list), the sale price is still at the highest possible market rate. The city must compensate for an ever-widening affordability gap with an ever-higher subsidy, reducing the total subsidy pool over time; this is precisely what subsidy recapture programs profess, or at least aim, to avoid. The city gets something back on its original investment, but it must reach into its pockets again and again to refinance other homes (or the same homes) at inflated prices. These outcomes have led policy analysts and the managers of these publicly financed loan programs to question the benefits resulting from the subsidy recapture approach.

Does Subsidy Recapture Work?

Are there circumstances under which a subsidy recapture program might work? Is the paradox—and failure—I have noted in San Francisco unique to that city's particular homeownership program, or is it intrinsic to subsidy recapture itself? While many market conditions and political constraints affect the success of any municipal housing program, my own conclusion is that there is a fundamental problem with the recapture approach to preserving public dollars. Under inflating market conditions, in particular, it is ineffective, judged solely by the standards that most subsidy recapture programs set for themselves.

The San Francisco scenario of spiraling housing costs and shrinking recaptured subsidies has, in fact, been played out in a number of other communities in California, as well as in other parts of the country. Two studies from other cities, one on the West Coast and the other on the East, further illuminate the concerns I have raised and support my conclusion that, in most cases, subsidy retention, rather than subsidy recapture, is a more effective means of recycling public dollars invested in affordable housing.

San Mateo, California

The Community Development Department of the City of San Mateo, California, commissioned an analysis of different shared appreciation models in 1990 to determine whether the recapture approach would be an effective use of municipal resources for a first-time homebuyer program. A careful analysis led to the conclusion that only by intervening in the market and restricting the resale prices of subsidized housing would the city be able to maintain the initial level of affordability and to recycle its subsidy efficiently.[4] The study showed that if no resale restrictions were imposed, the city would have to recapture almost all of the appreciation in order to maintain affordability with the same level of subsidy (see chart in Appendix showing diminishing returns of subsidy relative to housing costs).

Given the high inflation rate of housing in the area, even a fifty-fifty split in the appreciation between the city and the homeowner would not allow the city to recapture enough funds to sustain the unit's affordability (that is, its affordability to another buyer at the same relative income level). The city would be obliged either to pump additional dollars into the unit for a new eligible owner or to lose the unit to the market when it resold. According to the city's assumptions, only if the rate of inflation in housing prices dropped significantly below the twenty-year historical trend of 12.31 percent would the fifty-fifty split be sufficient to maintain the unit's affordability.

Based on the above analysis, the Community Development Department of San Mateo concluded that the only model that would maintain the affordability of assisted units and not require the city to continue to refinance units with ever-greater amounts of public money would be one in which resale prices were restricted to the rate of increase of San Mateo's median income. Applying such a resale restriction, homeowners would be allowed to resell their homes only for an amount equal to what would be affordable for a moderate-income buyer.[5] The units themselves would remain affordable to the low- to moderate-income group for whom the program was originally designed.

Boston

In Boston, Massachusetts, a similar conclusion was reached in 1988 by the Public Facilities Department (PFD) in its analysis of different options for the use of municipal housing subsidies. PFD concluded that programs that attempt to recapture city subsidies and then rebuild or refinance new units are not self-sustaining and are not efficient from an economic standpoint. Without restricting resale prices, such programs would require significant additional public investment to maintain the initial affordability level over time. According to PFD's assistant director at the time, "Restricting resale prices to a fixed 5–6 percent increase is at least twice as efficient at maintaining the availability of an affordable housing stock as options that rely on the recapture and recycling of funds."[6]

Tables 1 and 2, developed by PFD, give an indication of the level of additional subsidy required over a ten-year period using a simple recapture mechanism.

Given projected inflation in the Boston housing market, PFD's conclusion was that it would cost the city $79,422 per unit in subsidy to make homeownership affordable to a low-income buyer in 1998, compared to $25,000 per unit in 1988. Even if the full $33,597 of city funds were recaptured, there would still be a funding gap of $45,825 in 1998. In other words, unless the city were to continue to pump additional subsidy into the program, there would be a dramatic reduction in the affordable housing stock. Under this "recycle and rebuild" scenario, for every one hundred units lost through resale, only forty-two new homes could be rebuilt with the remaining funds.

TABLE 1: Subsidy Recapture: "Recycle and Rebuild"	1988	1998
Construction cost	$100,000	$208,997
Affordable price	75,000	129,575
Subsidy required	25,000	79,422
Recapture, 1998 (lend at 3%)	N/A	33,597
Resubsidy required in 1998	N/A	*45,825*

Source: Public Facilities Department, City of Boston, unpublished paper, 1988.

TABLE 2: Subsidy Retention: "Restrict and Retain"	1988	1998
Construction cost	$100,000	$208,997
Affordable price	75,000	129,575
Restricted price	75,000	129,575
Recapture, 1998	N/A	10,914
Resale price for homeowner, 1998	N/A	118,661
Subsidy required	*25,000*	0

Source: Public Facilities Department, City of Boston, unpublished paper, 1988.

More than half (58 percent) of the units financed with municipal funds would be permanently lost when the first owners decided to sell.

Cost efficiency is even poorer in programs that recapture funds from assisted units resold at market rates and then use these funds to refinance the *same* home for the next buyer. Using a finite allocation of public funds, only thirty-eight units out of every one hundred that were initially subsidized would remain affordable.

Compared to the above, the option of restricting resale prices, as shown in Table 2, was found to be a much more efficient mechanism for maintaining affordability and preserving public funds.

Using this "restrict and retain" approach, limiting appreciation to an income growth rate of 5.62 percent (the average neighborhood growth rate over fifteen years), *no additional subsidy would be required* over time. One hundred units subsidized by the city would result in one hundred units of affordable housing even after resale. Not only would the city not need to replenish its original subsidy pool, but additional revenue would be generated for the city to finance more homes. Though the homeowner would not get the maximum appreciation that the home could produce, linking the return to average income growth would still yield significant annual increases in equity for the homeowner, well above what might be earned, for example, had that money been placed in a conventional investment such as a CD or government bond.

Conclusion: Pitfalls and Popularity of Subsidy Recapture

The success of a subsidy recapture program, in terms of financial efficiency, depends to a great extent on the local real estate market, the availability of developable land, and the amount of subsidy a municipality is able to recapture when homes are resold (that is, the percentage of appreciation that accrues to the municipality with each resale). In rural areas or more depressed urban areas, where inflation in real estate is relatively low, subsidy recapture may be a financially viable model for assisting first-time homeowners and recycling scarce public dollars.

The economics of this program simply do not work, however, in urban and suburban areas where steady appreciation in land and housing prices is the norm. Public subsidies will eventually be depleted and private affordability will eventually be compromised. Municipalities will be in the position of continually pumping additional funds into the same (or similar) units in order to keep them within the financial reach of potential low- to moderate-income buyers. Without price restrictions, initial homeowners will walk off with substantial equity due to market appreciation. Prospective homebuyers of modest means will walk into closed doors—priced out of the appreciating market altogether.

Subsidy recapture does nothing to limit the endlessly spiraling cost of real estate that makes affordable housing a more and more remote dream for most lower-income people in this country. Instead of controlling the cost of housing, the municipality with a subsidy recapture program is actually given a stake in the kind of petty speculation that helped create its housing problem in the first place. It also, inadvertently, is given a stake in all the antisocial consequences of our national obsession with appreciating property values: the temptation to weigh in on the side of anyone who resists the "invasion" of minorities, the siting of public facilities, the development of homeless shelters, or any event perceived as a "threat to property values."

Subsidy recapture also does nothing to expand the *supply* of affordable housing— and may do just the opposite. Housing that may have been relatively affordable when first purchased with a public subsidy tends to become less and less affordable over time. Indeed, many subsidy recapture programs should not really be called affordable housing programs at all because they eventually lose affordable units to the market rather than preserve them.

In addition to these problems associated with the cost and supply of housing, subsidy recapture is flawed in its underlying assumption of limitless growth. The proponents of recapture programs seem to assume that there is an infinite amount of land on which to build new housing as homes are sold off and subsidies are recycled. But the economic, social, and environmental conditions most communities face do not allow for the ongoing development and loss of affordable housing, compromising the integrity and accessibility of existing neighborhoods. The limitless growth mentality becomes particularly problematic as more and more cities and rural communities institute strict antigrowth and infrastructure regulations.

With all the problems accompanying the subsidy recapture approach, why is it embraced by so many cities? Why does subsidy recapture seem an attractive and justifiable alternative to subsidy retention?

The first answer is that subsidy recapture programs are easier to sell politically—to city councils, to financial institutions, to current homeowners, and to potential homeowners alike. These programs tend to be perceived as "fair," with each party getting a fair return on its investment, and as a way to help moderate-income families get a "foot in the door." Tampering with the market—or the right to profit from it—is a more difficult policy for most municipalities to contemplate or defend.

Public officials are more likely to view appreciation through the eyes of bankers than through the eyes of low-income communities. The idea of using public money to push up property values is often perceived as positive—a way to "improve" local properties and neighborhoods. Appreciating property values are seen by bankers and public officials alike as a welcome opportunity to share in the action rather than as a dreaded threat to neighborhood stability and the long-term affordability of housing.

These prejudices and preconceptions aside, subsidy recapture does not measure up, not even to the minimal standard that it sets for itself of "recycling" and protecting a pool of public subsidies. Public dollars are better protected through subsidy retention, leveraged over time into greater and greater *community* wealth. A permanent pool of affordable housing can, in the end, assist many more first-time homebuyers than a typical recapture program without additional infusions of capital. Subsidy retention yields a perpetual return on the public dollar in the form of a permanent—and expanding—stock of affordable housing. This is a lasting benefit that is enhanced, not diminished, with the passage of time.

APPENDIX

San Mateo Analysis

Model 1: Shared Appreciation (No Resale Price Control)*

	At 12.31%	At 9.5%
Resale price 2000	$574,721	$446,081
First mortgage 1990 (repaid)	$157,184	$157,184
City subsidy 1990 (repaid)	22,816	22,816
Deferred city interest	36,363	36,363
Subtotal A	($216,363)	($216,363)
Total appreciation (resale minus subtotal A)	$358,357	$229,718
50% Owner share	$179,179	$114,859
50% City share	179,179	114,859
	$358,357	$229,718
Funding available for unit		
50% City share	$179,179	$114,859
Mortgage differential	146,858	146,858
Subtotal A	$216,363	$216,363
Total funding for unit	$542,400	$478,080
FUNDING GAP (city surplus in parentheses)	$32,321	($31,999)

Model 2: Subsidy Retention (Resale Price Control)*

	At 12.31%	At 9.5%
First mortgage 2000 (paid to owner)	$304,042	$304,042
First mortgage 1990	(157,184)	(157,184)
Owner's share of appreciation (mortgage differential)	$146,858	$146,858
City's share:		
Resale price 2000	$574,721	$446,081
First mortgage 2000	(304,042)	(304,042)
City's share	$270,679	$142,039
% Owner's share	35	51
% City's share	65	49
FUNDING GAP	0	0

(continued)

Assumptions for Both Models *(continued)*
Sales Price 1990: $180,000
Resale Price 2000: @12.5% appreciation = $574,721
@ 9.5% appreciation = $446,081
110% Median income 1990: $50,160
110% Median income 2000: $97,020
Income increase: 6.28%
First mortgage 1990: $157,184
First mortgage 2000: $304,042
City subsidy: $22,816

Source: Analysis prepared for the Community Development Department of the City of San Mateo by the law firm of Goldfarb and Lipman, San Francisco, 1990.

*In model 1, the city receives 50% of the appreciation plus 10% compounded interest. In model 2, the city guarantees affordability; the owner's share of the appreciation is equal to the amount that is affordable to a new buyer at the same relative income level.

NOTES

1. The choice between subsidy retention and subsidy recapture has become very real for every municipality that is a "participating jurisdiction" under the National Affordable Housing Act of 1990 (NAHA). Title II of NAHA, the so-called HOME program, originally required resale restrictions on assisted owner-occupied units. Section 209 of the Housing and Community Development Act of 1992, however, amended NAHA to allow participating jurisdictions the option of either restricting the resale prices of HOME-assisted, owner-occupied units or recapturing the HOME subsidy upon resale of the assisted units. No restrictions on price are required under the latter option.

2. See *Equity Sharing Handbook*, State of California Department of Housing and Community Development, Division of Community Affairs, Sacramento, Calif., June 1982.

3. The city also administers a first-time homebuyer program for condominium purchases for moderate-income residents. Price restrictions are set on these properties, and no city financing is provided. This price-restricted variation is not a part of the First-Time Homebuyer Program discussed here.

4. This analysis assumed twenty-year historical trends in housing costs and median incomes. It also assumed individual expenditures of 33 percent of gross income on housing costs.

5. The city would have to add an additional subsidy to these units only if the first homebuyer resold the house to someone earning less—for example, if a homeowner earning 120 percent of median income sold to someone earning 110 percent. The city would make up the difference.

6. Memo from Kevin McColl, Public Facilities Department, City of Boston, February 26, 1988.

Deed Restrictions and Community Land Trust Ground Leases

Two Methods of Establishing Affordable Homeownership Restrictions

David Abromowitz and Kirby White
(2006)

Before discussing deed restrictions and community land trust ground leases as methods of establishing "affordable homeownership restrictions," let us first note the types of restrictions that are common to affordable homeownership programs. In general these programs—which employ public and charitable subsidies to reduce the cost of home-ownership to an affordable level for lower income households—commonly impose four types of restrictions: price restrictions, buyer eligibility restrictions, occupancy and use restrictions, and restrictions on mortgage financing. Any of these restrictions may be established for a shorter or longer period of time. In practice the periods range from as little as five years to as much as 99 years, and can, in effect, be perpetual in some cases.

Price restrictions

Resale price restrictions limit the price for which a home can be sold, with the intention of keeping the price affordable for households of a designated income level (generally identified as "income-eligible" or "income-qualified" households). These limitations on resale prices are usually established through formulas that allow the seller to recoup her investment (i.e., the downpayment and the amortized portion of her mortgage) plus a limited amount of appreciation. The four basic types of formulas are identified below—the first two being the most common, the last two being used only occasionally.

1. "Appraisal-based formulas" limit the resale price to the original purchase price plus a specified percentage (e.g., 25 percent) of total market appreciation as determined by the difference between appraised value at the time of purchase and at the time of resale.
2. "Indexed formulas" allow resale prices to exceed the original purchase price only in proportion to increases in indexes such as the consumer price index or area median income.

This selection is a slightly revised version of an article written for Florida Housing Coalition and originally published in *Housing News Network Journal* 22 (May 2006): 7–10, 24. It is reprinted by permission of the Florida Housing Coalition.

3. "Itemized formulas" add to the original purchase price a set of specifically itemized factors such as the value of improvements made by the owner and adjustments for monetary inflation.

4. "Mortgage-based formulas" establish the resale price as the maximum price for which mortgage payments including principal and interest (at the then prevailing rate) plus taxes, insurance, and lease fee—would be affordable for a household at the targeted income level.

Buyer Eligibility Restrictions

These restrictions determine what categories of people will be permitted to buy a home when the owners want to sell it. Programs designed to provide homeownership opportunities for lower income households typically limit subsequent, as well as initial, buyers to households that have incomes in the range targeted by the program (or to public or nonprofit sponsors that will see that the homes will be resold to income-qualified households). Maximum incomes for eligible buyers are usually established as a percentage of median household income (adjusted for household size) for the geographical area in question, as defined by the U.S. Department of Housing and Urban Development (HUD).

Occupancy and use restrictions. Homeownership resale restrictions are normally accompanied by occupancy requirements, and often by other types of use restrictions. Programs designed to provide homeownership opportunities for lower income households have reason to require that owners occupy the homes they own as their primary residences. Occupancy restrictions thus prohibit absentee ownership and require that an owner who moves out of a home must sell it. Other types of use restrictions are designed to regulate subletting, promote proper maintenance, and prohibit uses that would diminish the quality the homes for future residents or that would be detrimental to the surrounding community. In the case of homes that include one or more rental units in addition to the units occupied by the owners, restrictions may require that tenants be income-qualified and that the rents not exceed an affordable amount.

Mortgage Financing Restrictions

Homeownership restrictions are usually subordinated to the homebuyer's first mortgage. The restrictions can therefore be eliminated by a mortgage foreclosure—with the result that the public's investment in the affordability of the home will be wiped out. The funders and sponsors of affordable homeownership programs have an obvious interest in preventing foreclosure, and therefore have an incentive to seeing that homeowners do not take on more mortgage debt than they will be able to manage. They also have an interest in seeing that mortgage lenders understand the price restrictions and do not allow mortgage debt to exceed the restricted resale price. For these reasons, mortgage financing restrictions usually require approval of a mortgage by the sponsoring agency, and often require the mortgagee to agree to notify the sponsoring agency if a resale-restricted home is in default and to give the agency certain rights to intervene to prevent foreclosure.

Vehicles for Restrictions: Deed Covenants and CLT Ground Leases

Deed Restrictions

Deed restrictions (or deed covenants) are restrictions that are attached to the deed of a property and that are binding on subsequent as well as initial owners. The restrictions themselves can vary from very simple requirements to very elaborate and complex requirements. They can be established for various types of property and can be used to serve a wide variety of purposes. They are common, for instance, in subdivisions where developers have established restrictions to prevent owners from modifying their homes in ways that might be inconsistent with the conventional expectations of their neighbors, and they have become an essential feature of "common interest developments" such as condominiums, where they are a means of defining and protecting the elements of housing that are shared by a number of owners of separately deeded units.

In recent years deed restrictions have also become increasingly common as a way to preserve affordability and other intended effects of affordable homeownership programs. Covenants attached to the deeds of homes developed or sponsored by such programs can also give a preemptive option to the developer or sponsoring agency, allowing that entity either to purchase the home for a limited price when the owner wants to sell or to see that the home is sold to another income-qualified household for a price not exceeding the purchase option price. Such covenants also commonly include restrictions on occupancy, use, and mortgage financing.

Ground Lease Restrictions

Community land trust homeownership programs allow people to buy houses on land that is leased to them by the CLT through very long-term ground leases (typically, renewable and inheritable 99-year leases). The lessee/homeowners pay a modest (usually subsidized) monthly ground rent to the CLT for the use of the land. The terms of the ground leases give the homeowners most of the rights of conventional homeownership, but also impose the four types of restrictions noted above.

The CLT itself as ground lessor retains a preemptive option that allows it either to buy the house when the lessee/homeowner wants to sell or to assign the option to another income-qualified household, or simply to oversee the sale of the home directly to another income-qualified household for a price not exceeding the purchase option price. The lease normally includes restrictions on occupancy, use, and mortgage financing as well.

In its role of overseeing the resale of affordable homes, the CLT makes sure that the buyer is income-eligible and that the price does not exceed the limit established by the "resale formula." Most CLTs also play an active role in helping lower income buyers to qualify for mortgage financing, and often play a role in negotiating with lenders to see that appropriate mortgage financing is available to these CLT homebuyers. CLTs may also provide a variety of training and support services to these households once they have become homeowners, including assistance in cases of mortgage default. The costs incurred by the CLT in carrying out this work can be defrayed in part by the lease fee that is collected, and can also be defrayed by a mark-up of the resale price or transfer fee added to the price paid by the new homebuyer.

Strengths and Weaknesses of Deed Restrictions

When compared to CLT ground leases, deed restrictions can be seen as the "simpler and easier" means of establishing restrictions. This does not mean that the restrictions themselves will be simpler and easier to read than when written into CLT ground leases—the language will be essentially the same in either case. Nor is it true that deed covenants are "self-enforcing" in the simple sense claimed by those who assume that the sale of a home in violation of resale restrictions would compromise a buyer's title to the property (and a mortgagee's claim to the property as collateral) and would therefore not happen. As noted below, "self-enforcement" is uncertain in the case of resale restrictions and virtually impossible in the case of occupancy and use restrictions. Nonetheless, deed covenants can be easier to use in some respects, and they do have certain advantages over CLT leases as means of establishing and enforcing restrictions, including the following:

- They do not require the creation of separate ownership interests in land and buildings, and they avoid the possible complications of separate tax assessments on the separate ownership interests.
- They are likely to be more acceptable to homebuyers who want to "own the land as well as the house."
- They can be used with condominiums on a unit-by-unit basis.[1]
- Deed-restricted properties do not require "leasehold mortgages," so many mortgage lenders are more comfortable with them.

Most deed restrictions are designed to last for relatively short periods of time—typically for periods ranging from 5 to 20 years, rarely for more than 30 years. If a program strives to preserve affordability only for a relatively short time, it can be argued that a deed restriction is a relatively easy way of doing so.

The enforceability of deed restrictions lasting longer than 20 or 30 years, however, is more problematic, depending on a number of factors, both legal and practical. Some states have statutes specifically limiting deed restrictions to a certain period, such as 30 years, and in almost every state, "perpetual" deed restrictions are considered invalid as an unacceptable "restraint on alienation" or violation of the "rule against perpetuities." Generally, the longer the duration of the restriction and the farther the party imposing the restriction is removed from the property, the less defensible is the restriction. (Enforceability rests on meeting legal tests of "privity," "touch and concern," and benefit to a nearby parcel owned by the same party who is imposing the restriction.) In recent years, a few states, including Massachusetts, Vermont, Maine, Rhode Island, and Oregon, have enacted laws explicitly authorizing "perpetual" deed restrictions for the purpose of preserving the affordability of publicly subsidized owner-occupied housing. As shared equity housing becomes more common it can be hoped that other states will follow, but for the present most states do not have such legislation.

Even if all the legal obstacles to enforcement of the deed restriction are satisfied, they are seldom effectively enforced. In the case of resale price restrictions, if the difference between the allowable "purchase option price" and the then market price is great, the owner of the property has a financial incentive to seek ways to avoid compliance with the restriction. There may well be a speculative purchaser who would be willing to pay more than the purchase option price but less than the property's market value, with the difference serving as either the reward for the risk that the restriction will ultimately be enforced or the incentive to spend substantial sums on a legal challenge to enforceability. Or it may simply be that the necessary title work is not done carefully enough at the time of resale and the existence of a price restriction that was attached to a deed decades before may be missed.

In the case of buyer-eligibility restrictions, a purchase by a nonincome eligible person could also compromise the buyer's title to the property, but, in the absence of diligent oversight by an experienced monitoring agency, it can be difficult to establish who is and is not income-eligible. And in the case of occupancy and use restrictions, enforcement depends absolutely on diligent monitoring on an ongoing, month-to-month basis.

Until relatively recently, deed restrictions generally were *not* monitored, and programs were generally not funded or put in place to support monitoring. As the failure of "self-enforcement" has become more apparent, however, a growing number of programs *are* now being established to monitor and enforce deed restrictions established through state and municipal efforts to create affordable homeownership opportunities.

Strengths and Weaknesses of Ground Lease Restrictions

Compared to deed-restricted homeownership, ground-lease-restricted homeownership may require more effort by the CLT as sponsoring agency and is generally less familiar (and in some cases less acceptable) to homebuyers. However, it can also provide a stronger basis for the enforcement of restrictions, a better basis for the support of economically vulnerable homeowners, and a more complete set of tools for preserving the public's investment in the home even in situations where a mortgage is foreclosed.

Restrictions established through a CLT ground lease are likely to be more enforceable for both legal and practical reasons. The fact that the lease represents an agreement between two parties, each of which has a continuing ownership interest in the property, provides a strong legal basis for the CLT's enforcement of restrictions. The CLT's preemptive right to purchase the house for a restricted price (and thereby to ensure that it will be passed on to another income-eligible household) is part of this ongoing agreement and is strengthened by the fact that the house is located on land that the CLT owns and by the fact that the lessee's ownership of the house is explicitly subject to the terms of the lease.

Although theoretical questions have been raised as to whether the 99-year term of the CLT's preemptive option might be held to violate the rule against perpetuities (potentially exceeding the traditional common law measure of a "life in being plus 21 years"), the CLT option has never been challenged in court and there are reasons to believe that such a challenge would not succeed.[2] Notwithstanding this presumed long-term enforceability of the option, most CLT ground leases contain a backup provision. As expressed in the Model CLT Ground Lease, this provision states, "It is the intention of the parties that their respective options to purchase and all other rights under this Lease shall continue in effect for the full term of this Lease and any renewal thereof, and such options and other rights shall be considered to be coupled with an interest. In the event any such option or right shall be construed to be subject to any rule of law limiting the duration of such option or right, the time period for the exercising of such option or right shall be construed to expire twenty (20) years after the death of the last survivor of the following persons . . ." [e.g., all children born in a specified local hospital in the year the lease is executed].[3] Similar language can of course be written into deed covenants that are intended to be perpetual or very long term.

When the homeowner eventually wants to sell, the possibility that the sale could be carried out in violation of the lease's resale restrictions is extremely limited. Any but the most woefully ill-informed and ill-advised buyers would understand that they could not buy the land from the existing homeowner and would *have* to deal with the CLT landowner. Similarly, only the most woefully negligent lender would offer financing to the buyer of a CLT home being resold by the first homeowner without noticing that the underlying land is owned by the CLT.

The CLT ground lease provides a strong basis for enforcing the CLT's occupancy and use restrictions as well as its purchase option. The legal mechanism for enforcement of these restrictions is the relatively familiar process of declaring a default under the terms of the ground lease and, if the default remains uncured, obtaining judicial relief through the typical landlord-tenant summary process. The exact procedural details and substantive requirements will differ from jurisdiction to jurisdiction, but will have significant elements in common from one jurisdiction to another. The ground lessee's rights of possession of the land depend upon compliance with the lease terms. Failure to comply gives rise to the right of the landlord to evict the ground lessee or seek other remedies, such as damages or injunctive relief, where appropriate.[4]

On the practical level, the likelihood that the CLT's restrictions will be enforced in practice is supported by the necessary ongoing interaction between the parties. The homeowner is responsible for making monthly lease fee payments to the CLT. If payments are not received, the CLT will contact the homeowner and, in so doing, may learn of other violations or problems. For instance, it may become clear that the homeowner no longer occupies the home and has rented it to others. (It should be noted that some organizations that now monitor affordable homeownership deed covenants maintain a similar month-to-month relationship with the homeowners by charging a monthly "stewardship fee.")

In the event of a mortgage default by the lessee-homeowner, the ground lease provides important protections for the CLT as steward of the public's investment in the property. Although different terms may be negotiated with different lenders, CLT ground leases typically provide for notification of the CLT in the event of a mortgage default and, thereupon, give the CLT an opportunity to cure the default (as well as to help the homeowner herself to work out the problem). In the rare event that the problem does result in foreclosure, the CLT often has an option to buy the house back from the mortgagee. In the worst case scenario, if the house is not repurchased by the CLT subsequent to foreclosure and the resale restrictions are removed from the lease (as CLT leases normally permit in such situations), then the CLT normally has the right to charge a higher ground rent to the new owner of the now less restricted home. Thus the property will continue to provide significant support for the CLT's affordable homeownership program. (The *public's* interest in a deed-restricted home, on the other hand, can be completely wiped out by a foreclosure, with a loss of any subsidies originally invested in the foreclosed home.)

It should also be noted that the CLT ground lease provides an opportunity for flexibility and adaptability that is usually lacking with long-term deed restrictions. If, at some point in the future, certain ground lease restrictions no longer serve the community's interest, the parties to the lease can negotiate reasonable modifications. And if, at some point, the community's interest is better served by an altogether different use of the property, then when the then-current owner wants to sell, the CLT can exercise its option and dedicate the property to that different use.

Finally it should be said that the CLT's approach to ownership brings a kind of perspective and understanding to CLT homeownership programs that is less clearly and emphatically present with homeownership programs that utilize deed restrictions. The community land trust model embodies a commitment to the principle that a community has an interest in the way that its land base is used and in the way that its land is allocated to individual members of the community. The CLT directly expresses and acts upon this principle when it enters into a ground lease as steward of the community's land and guardian of the community's interests. Through the ground lease the community's interests are affirmatively stated and are balanced with the stated interests of the individual.

NOTES

1. Ground leases can also be used with condominiums on a unit by unit basis, but only in states where the condominium law allows each unit owner to hold a direct undivided interest in the land, as opposed to requiring that the association own the land.

2. For a survey of the applicable law, see the discussion by Professor Deborah H. Bell set out in *The Community Land Trust Legal Manual.* But also see C. A. Seeger, "The Fixed Price Preemptive Right in the Community Land Trust Lease: A Valid Response to the Housing Crisis or an Invalid Restraint on Alienations?" 11 *Cardozo L. Rev.* 471 (1989). A detailed analysis under Florida law is found in S. J. Pastel, "Community Land Trusts: A Promising Alternative for Affordable Housing," 6 *Fla. J. of Land Use & Envtl. L.* 293, 301–12 (1991).

3. The Model Community Land Trust Ground Lease, developed by the Institute for Community Economics (ICE) appears in *The Community Land Trust Legal Manual* (Institution for Community Economics, 1991; 2002), which can be obtained from Equity Trust, Turners Falls, Massachusetts.

4. For a discussion of this process under Mississippi law, see: Deborah H. Bell, "The Mississippi Landlord-Tenant Act of 1991," 61 *Miss. L. J.* 527 (1991).

City Hall Steps In

Local Governments Embrace Community Land Trusts

Rick Jacobus and Michael Brown
(2007)

Once exclusively a tool for grassroots activists seeking to change local policies, the community land trust (CLT) is increasingly being adopted by local governments facing urgent housing-affordability needs. Frustrated by housing costs that are rising rapidly beyond the reach of low- and moderate-income families and concerned about the steady loss of affordable homes created through the dollars or powers of local government, municipalities as different as Irvine CA, Chicago IL, Austin TX, Burlington VT, Delray Beach FL, Highland Park IL, St. Tammany Parish LA, Tucson AZ, Whitefish MT and Carver County MN, have taken the lead in creating their own CLTs. This trend represents an important evolution of the CLT model and a significant rethinking of the goals and roles of municipal government in promoting and preserving affordable housing.

A community land trust is a nonprofit organization formed to hold title to land to preserve its long-term availability for affordable housing and other community uses. Typically structured as a community-based, open-membership organization with a broadly representative board of directors, a CLT receives public or private donations of land or uses government subsidies to purchase land on which housing can be built. The homes are sold to lower-income families, but the CLT retains ownership of the land, entering into a long-term lease with the homebuyer. The CLT also retains a long-term option to repurchase the home at a below-market price, should the homeowner decide to move. Ownership of the land, along with the imposition of durable affordability controls over the resale of any housing located on its land, allows the CLT to ensure that homes will remain available for lower-income homebuyers for generations to come. CLTs can play a similar role in preserving the affordability of rental housing, limited equity co-ops and condominiums, and even commercial property.

This chapter is a slightly revised version of an article published in *Shelterforce* (Spring 2007): 12–15. It is reprinted by permission of *Shelterforce: The Journal of Affordable Housing and Community Building.*
Copyright © 2007 National Housing Institute.

In the 1970s and 1980s, municipal support for neighborhood-based CLTs was very limited. From the mid-1980s into the 1990s, the number of CLTs increased and so did the level of municipal support. Since 2000, a growing number of cities and counties have chosen to play a larger role not only in creating CLTs but also in guiding their development and sponsoring their affordable-housing initiatives.

Two primary reasons are driving this new municipal interest in—and support for—community land trusts:

- *Long-term subsidy preservation.* As housing costs rise, the level of subsidies required to create housing affordability also increases. With much of the burden for creating affordable housing now shifted to city and county governments, local policymakers are looking for ways to ensure that their investment has a long-term impact. The proven ability of the community land trust model to create a permanent supply of affordable housing, where public dollars are not pocketed by individuals when they resell their homes, is very attractive to municipalities searching for ways to make their scarce resources go further and last longer than before.
- *Long-term stewardship.* Preserving long-term affordability requires long-term monitoring and administration, a workload that local governments are neither well-equipped to tackle nor much interested in taking on. In addition to developing projects and finding, educating and screening buyers, CLTs can play a long-term stewardship role, relieving local government of this ongoing responsibility: monitoring and enforcing affordability and occupancy restrictions and providing long-term backstopping support to their low-income homeowners. In hot markets, the CLT's proven effectiveness in preserving the affordability of publicly assisted owner-occupied homes (especially those created through municipal mandates like inclusionary zoning) has been the principal reason for growing governmental support of this unusual model of tenure. In cold markets, the CLT's proven effectiveness in reducing defaults and preventing foreclosures has commanded the attention of municipal officials.

The impact of municipal involvement in initiating and supporting community land trusts can be illustrated by two new city-sponsored community land trusts. The governments of Irvine, California, and Chicago, Illinois, have spurred the creation of citywide CLTs as a means to preserve affordable housing developed through regulatory mandates (or incentives) and financial resources provided by the municipality.

Irvine, California

The City of Irvine came slowly to the community land trust model. By learning from earlier policy mistakes and by seizing an opportunity to create thousands of moderately priced homes, however, Irvine found its way to this innovative model of permanently affordable housing.

In 1975, housing advocates in southern California sued the still brand-new City of Irvine. The Irvine Company, the private development company responsible for the city's planning and construction, was preparing to build office and industrial parks that would make Irvine a major regional employment center. But Orange County's tracts of ranch houses didn't offer reasonable housing options for the people who would work in the newly created jobs. To settle the suit, Irvine launched one of the nation's first inclusionary housing programs. The program's initial success led the city to expand its scope, requiring that 15 percent of all newly built housing must be affordable to low- or moderate-income households. Since the mid-1970s, Irvine has produced more than 4,400 units of affordable housing—a significant achievement for a town of 62,000 housing units.

Unfortunately, Irvine's inclusionary housing program required the units to remain affordable for only 13 to 30 years. When the control period ends, the housing can be converted to market-rate. As a result, more than 1,000 affordable units already have been lost. Many of the remaining affordability controls will expire during the next 10 years, leaving Irvine with little to show for its pioneering effort to make room for working families.

Faced with the impending loss, the Irvine City Council convened a housing task force in 2005. Led by Mayor Beth Krom, the task force was charged with searching for strategies to preserve affordable housing and developing a plan for capitalizing on a unique opportunity to increase the affordable housing supply. In 1999, the Marine Corps had closed the El Toro Air Station, a 4,700-acre military base adjacent to the city. After years of public debate about how to reuse the El Toro site, including a proposal to develop an international airport that was rejected by voter referendum, the city decided to create one of the nation's largest urban parks and a new mixed-income, mixed-use community surrounding it.

The Housing Task Force drafted a strategy in 2006 that called upon Irvine to develop 9,700 new affordable-housing units—10 percent of the city's housing stock—at the El Toro site and to place these units under the stewardship of a municipally sponsored CLT. The community land trust is still a relatively new idea in California, but the model was familiar to many in Irvine because the University of California has long used land leases to preserve faculty housing around its Irvine campus. The task force's recommendations were unanimously supported by the city council.

The Irvine Community Land Trust (ICLT) was incorporated in mid-2006. The City Council budgeted $250,000 in start-up funding for the land trust. In addition, the city's redevelopment agency is providing staffing to the organization while the land trust's first projects are developed. Irvine is well served by existing nonprofit and for-profit developers of affordable housing, so it is not intended that the ICLT will serve as a developer. Instead the land trust will focus on long-term stewardship, finding and screening buyers for homeownership units and monitoring those units over time.

Mayor Krom regards the land trust as an integral part of Irvine's sustainability plan. Given the city's history of creating high-quality, affordable housing that is integrated into the community, Krom is excited about the opportunities the Irvine Community Land Trust presents. "Irvine has a once-in-a-lifetime opportunity to significantly expand affordable housing to meet the needs of a broader spectrum of people—particularly those who work in our city but cannot afford housing here," she says. "The city and the land trust board will work with our private and nonprofit developers to effectively leverage our resources, tripling our inventory of affordable housing over the next 15–20 years and establishing permanent affordability."

Chicago, Illinois

The City of Chicago has a longstanding commitment to creating affordable housing for its residents. In 2005, for example, the city provided or leveraged $67,370,461 in land and public and private resources to create 1,042 for-sale homes, the majority of which were affordable to households earning 100 percent or less of Chicago median household income. As in many municipalities, the city offered "soft second" mortgages to help qualified homebuyer households purchase a home. In exchange, homebuyers agreed to repay these loans whenever they sold their home. While the principal balance was returned to the city for re-use, the affordable unit was lost and, because of rapid appreciation and increasing development costs, recaptured funds were insufficient to cover the cost of a new affordable unit.

Alarmed by the loss of housing made affordable through city investment—at a time when the amount of subsidy needed to make housing affordable was increasing and public affordable-housing funding was diminishing at all levels of government—the city began to focus on permanent housing affordability. The city began to work with Burlington Associates in Community Development and community constituents to determine how the city might best support community land trust development in Chicago's neighborhoods as a way to maintain long-term affordability.

Through this process, the Chicago Community Land Trust (CCLT) was created in 2006 to preserve the long-term affordability of housing units developed by nonprofit and for-profit developers with the financial support of various city programs. The CCLT will preserve the affordability of single-family homes and condominium units, using 99-year deed covenants nearly identical in content and format to the ground lease used by other CLTs across the country.

The city determined that the Chicago CLT would be citywide, in order to more easily standardize many of the processes associated with resale-restricted housing. "We were able to work with the county on a standard means for assessing property taxes based on the home's affordable price. Being citywide also ensures that the homes are spread out among the city's neighborhoods," stated Commissioner John G. Markowski of the Chicago Department of Housing (DOH).

The CCLT is incorporated as a private, nonprofit Illinois corporation and is currently seeking 501(c)(3) tax-exempt designation. Funding for start-up costs and operating revenue for CCLT's first several years was provided through a $396,000 grant from the John D. and Catherine T. MacArthur Foundation. The board of directors is comprised of community leaders and public members representing a broad spectrum of interests and perspectives with one-third of the seats reserved for lessee/homeowners once CCLT's portfolio reaches 200 units.

Homes made affordable with DOH funding and targeted for the CLT are currently under construction and will be brought into the Chicago CLT's portfolio upon sale. While the anticipated growth of its portfolio has been slowed by the recent economic recession, the Chicago CLT could still become one of the fastest growing and largest CLTs in the country.

Opportunities and Challenges

Municipally sponsored CLTs represent only a minority of the 200 or so existing CLTs, but the expanding role of municipalities in initiating, staffing, and governing community land trusts is a significant development. This recent phenomenon brings both opportunities and challenges. For example, the infusion of additional financial resources is likely to increase the number of CLT units nationwide and to raise the profile of CLTs. That very visibility, however, will stretch the nascent CLT movement in new and untried directions.

Most CLTs have an open membership made up of community members and people who live on the CLT's lands. At the annual membership meeting, the CLT's membership is responsible for electing the CLT's board of directors. The CLT's open membership is intended to make it directly accountable to a broader community of neighborhood residents in which it operates. One-third of the seats on the CLT's governing board are usually reserved for persons living in land trust housing. The framers of the CLT model developed this unique form of governance to ensure that these organizations would remain responsive to the needs of the communities they were serving. The governance structure offers balanced accountability: Giving residents one-third of the board seats provides them with a real voice in the governance and operation of the organization, while balancing their concerns with other community interests ensures the long-term protection of the organization's core values.

Municipalities tend to be more interested in the community land trust's ability to preserve housing affordability and to retain public subsidies than they are in the more community-based characteristics of the CLT model, such as recruiting and nurturing a broadly based membership. Consequently, the new wave of municipally sponsored CLTs are experimenting with ways to maintain accountability to the CLT residents and broader community, while allowing local government to play a greater role in directing the organization.

In Chicago, the CLT board of directors is comprised of community leaders and public representatives, with one-third of the seats reserved for CLT households. Unlike most CLTs, however, the Chicago CLT's board of directors is appointed by the mayor and City Council (rather than elected by the CLT's membership). Chicago CLT's executive director is accountable to the CCLT board. She is also a city employee, however, so she has many other bosses as well.

In Irvine, the city appointed the initial board and will retain a permanent right to appoint one-third of the land trust board. Initially, the mayor and a city council member are serving on the land trust board to insure close coordination between the new organization and the city's housing programs. While at some point in the future, the city's board seats may be filled with appointed representatives rather than elected officials, Irvine's leaders felt that the CLT should be directly accountable, at least in part, to the city. Like Chicago, Irvine has also reserved one-third of the board seats for land trust residents.

While sponsoring municipalities require some degree of control over the CLT's governance and operation, these new partnerships between local governments and CLTs are creating exciting new opportunities for spurring the growth and development of this innovative model of housing, including:

Removing competing municipal programs. A distinguishing factor of the new municipally sponsored land trusts is the local government's commitment to use the CLT as its primary tool for preserving the affordability of housing created with municipal assistance. Local government uses its financial resources or regulatory powers to create affordably-priced homes and then asks the CLT to play a long-term stewardship role for virtually all of these new homes.

The participation of a community land trust saves local governments from having to create an administrative structure of their own to monitor and enforce long-term affordability provisions. Programs like the new Chicago and Irvine land trusts formalize such close coordination by allowing their municipalities to influence the organization's direction. And in exchange for this accountability, the land trusts expect their local governments to provide long-term operating support and ongoing access to housing subsidies.

Raising the profile and productivity of CLTs. Until recently, the growth of the community land trust movement has been steady but slow. Local governments often are unfamiliar with the model, and some public officials are personally or politically unwilling to support the creation of permanently affordable housing. As a result, there is a relatively small number of CLT homes nationwide—a major criticism of the productivity of CLTs.

The growth of high-profile, municipally sponsored CLTs, however, that have the potential of quickly adding hundreds of units of permanently affordable housing to their portfolios will serve to enhance the model's credibility and to expand the municipal commitment to permanent housing affordability. The new phenomenon of larger, well-capitalized community land trusts may, in rather short order, double or triple the number of permanently affordable CLT homes nationwide, helping to bring the community land trust approach into the mainstream. Furthermore, CLTs with a sufficient number of homes should be able to generate enough revenue internally to support their organizational operating budgets—leading to the financial sustainability of these individual CLTs and a strengthening of the CLT movement.

Municipal engagement in the creation and sponsorship of community land trusts represents a significant rethinking of the role of local government in meeting the need for affordable homeownership. At a time when the gap between what housing costs and what many working families can afford to pay is increasing, alongside a soaring demand for limited public resources, local governments are increasingly recognizing the critical importance of preserving housing affordability created through the investment of public funds.

While many jurisdictions work closely with nonprofit housing developers to build and manage rental housing, most local governments still manage their homeownership programs in-house. Requiring lasting affordability in homeownership programs, however, creates a new set of long-term management and administrative responsibilities, which many jurisdictions are not prepared or not willing to take on. As a result, we are likely to see more municipalities form creative partnerships with community land trusts to preserve the affordability of publicly assisted owner-occupied homes for many years, ensuring a lasting return on the public's investment.

Community Land Trust Keeps Prices Affordable—For Now *and* Forever

Daniel Fireside
(2008)

Since the recent housing boom went bust, the news has been filled with stories of panic-stricken homeowners, skyrocketing foreclosure rates, and multibillion-dollar taxpayer bailouts.

It's especially striking, then, that not a single owner of a house, condo, or co-op purchased through the Vermont-based Champlain Housing Trust (CHT) has experienced a foreclosure in the past year. Nor do any of the renters in the more than 1,600 CHT apartments have to fear eviction because of the mortgage meltdown. It's the kind of track record that has brought the CHT international accolades and sparked an affordable housing revolution.

Over the past 25 years, the CHT has become one of the largest providers of affordable housing in the tri-county area surrounding Burlington, the state's largest city, and home to its priciest homes and tightest rental market.

The genesis of the idea took form in the late 1970s, when environmentalist Rick Carbin formed the Vermont Land Trust to preserve open space as developers bought up farms. Instead of buying and holding land, as some land trusts do, the trust bought undeveloped properties at the edge of urban areas and resold them, often at a profit, but with strict limits on future development.

Then, in the early 1980s, wealthy out-of-town speculators began driving up the cost of housing in Burlington. Longtime working-class residents were being priced out of their homes and neighborhoods. Frustration reached a boiling point when the political establishment cut a deal with big-time developers to put upscale apartments on the city's scenic waterfront. Voter disgust with this plan to privatize public space led to an upset mayoral victory in 1981 by socialist gadfly Bernie Sanders and his ragtag Progressive Coalition.

Sanders and the coalition quickly sought to develop institutions that would have a lasting impact. They established the Burlington Community Land Trust as an independent nonprofit corporation in 1984 with backing from the Burlington City Council and $200,000 in seed money. While the land trust was designed primarily to promote sustainable home ownership in the city, the Lake Champlain Housing Development Corporation, set up at the same time, focused on rental properties in

This selection is reprinted from "Purple America," the Fall 2008 issue of *YES! Magazine*. It is reprinted by permission of Positive Futures Network/*YES! Magazine*.

the areas surrounding Burlington. The two organizations merged in 2006 to form the nonprofit CHT.

The trust became a central part of the area's affordable housing effort—one that bridges the ideological divide between a flawed free-market approach and heavy-handed government intervention. Both Democratic and Republican politicians found it difficult to oppose a program that promotes home ownership and offers life-long renters a "piece of the American Dream."

Housing Trust 101

Buying land through a housing trust starts when the trust acquires a parcel through purchase, foreclosure, tax abatements, or donation. The trust arranges for a housing unit to be built on the parcel if one does not yet exist, then sells the building but retains ownership of the land beneath. The new homeowner leases the land for a nominal sum (for example, $25 per month), generally for 99 years or until the house is resold.

This model supports affordable housing in several ways. First, homebuyers have to meet low-income requirements. Second, the buying price of the home is reduced because it does not include the price of the land. Third, the trust works with lenders to reduce mortgage costs by using the equity of the land as part of the mortgage calculation. This reduces the size of the down payment and other closing costs, and eliminates the need for private mortgage insurance. In all, the trust can cut the cost of home ownership by 25 percent or more.

For longtime CHT member Bob Robbins, purchasing a home through the trust was the only affordable option. "We did not have access to money for a down payment on a regular home, and at our income level, we wouldn't have qualified for a mortgage," Robbins says. "Through the CHT, we were able to purchase a $99,000 home with just $2,500 down."

Unlike federal programs that only help the initial buyer, the CHT keeps the property affordable in perpetuity by restricting the profit buyers are able to take when they sell the house. According to the terms of the CHT leases, homeowners get back all of their equity plus the market value of any capital improvements they made. However, they only get 25 percent of any increase in the value of the house, and none of the increase in the value of the land.

This model gives the buyer access to the benefits of homeownership otherwise beyond her means, including tax deductions, wealth accumulation through equity, and stable housing costs. In return, she gives up her chance at windfall profits. A study of trust homes sold to a second generation of buyers showed that members were realizing a net gain of 29 percent on the money they had invested. "These aren't sky-high returns," says CHT executive director Brenda Torpy. But most CHT homeowners would never have been able to buy homes otherwise.

"We're trying to stop the concentration of land in the hands of a wealthy minority," says Torpy.

The CHT has become an increasingly important force in Burlington's housing market as well as in the surrounding counties, even as city administrations have come and gone. After 25 years, the trust has over 2,100 households living in its homes, condos, and apartments, not concentrated in pockets of poverty, but spread throughout the area. Since the 2006 merger of the Burlington Community Land Trust and the Lake Champlain Community Development Corporation into the CHT, the trust has become one of the region's largest managers of rental property.

The CHT is remarkable not only for its size, but for its promotion of community empowerment. CHT tenants and owners vote for and serve on its governing board, along with government officials and other city residents with technical expertise, such as architects and urban planners. The system is designed so that all interested parties have a voice and a vote, making it an experiment in democratic self-governance as well as an affordable housing program.

Booms Without the Bust

CHT employs several strategies to make sure their model succeeds, even during tough times. They offer homes below the market rate—typically half the price of a comparable open-market unit. Unlike shady mortgage brokers, "we're not going to let people take risky mortgage products," says Chris Donnelly, CHT's director of community relations. And if residents run into trouble, the land trust works with them. "It's not hand-holding," Donnelly says. "It's standing next to the homeowner."

A study conducted in December showed that foreclosure rates among members of 80 housing trusts across the United States were 30 times lower than the national average.

Tenants in the trust's rental properties are also benefiting from CHT's commitment to affordability and community building. By leveraging grants and subsidies, and because they aren't seeking a profit, CHT is able to keep rents up to 30 percent below market rate, even though they use the most environmentally rigorous building standards and set aside funds to cover future maintenance and repairs. The trust fixes up the buildings that for-profit companies won't touch. "When a fire destroys a block, we're the ones who come running in to restore the neighborhood," says Donnelly.

"We're going to steward these places forever," says Donnelly.

Housing advocates in Burlington have created a sustainable model for affordable housing through shrewd politics and a belief that housing is a fundamental human right rather than a commodity. Their model is being emulated across the country. There are 200 community land trusts in the United States today, including in large cities like Atlanta and Cincinnati. Washington, DC, is in the midst of creating a

1,000-home land trust with advice and support from the CHT. Half of these trusts started up in just the past seven years.

Back in Burlington, the main obstacle to CHT's expansion is money. The trust relies on government programs, grants, and donations to bring new properties into its model. "We're doing about 25 new homes each year, and about 25 to 30 resales. We could easily do 100 sales a year if we just had enough cheap capital. The model has been proven to work. It's gone to scale. It would be a great way to fill the need without the problems we're seeing nationally," says Donnelly. But public funding has been flat or falling in recent years, and the economic downturn will make other funding harder to find.

Donnelly hopes that the recent troubles in the conventional housing market and some international accolades will help spur more interest in the land trust model.

In October, CHT will be honored with a World Habitat Award at the annual gathering of UN-HABITAT, the global agency dedicated to sustainable living. The award is one of only two given out each year. Donnelly is proud of the achievement. "It's like the Nobel Prize for sustainable development and housing."

No Foreclosures Here

Holly Sklar
(2009)

When I first visited the Dudley Street neighborhood in 1988, less than two miles from downtown Boston, it looked like tornadoes had struck, leveling whole sections of homes and shops that were never rebuilt.

Beginning in the 1950s, an escalating unnatural disaster of government negligence, banking discrimination, racism, and arson for profit had stripped the Dudley neighborhood of services and destroyed many homes and businesses. Nighttime often carried the smell of smoke and fear as fires struck abandoned and occupied buildings, orchestrated by absentee landlords who wanted to collect on insurance and speculators clearing out properties for later redevelopment.

By the early 1980s, nearly one-third of Dudley land lay vacant. The empty lots became illegal dumping grounds for garbage, construction debris, and toxic waste from around the state. The community worried it would be driven out altogether by "urban renewal," favoring costly housing, office towers, upscale retail, and high profits for developers over affordable homes and local businesses.

But instead of leaving their fate in the hands of city planners and private developers, residents did something extraordinary. They founded a community organization called the Dudley Street Neighborhood Initiative (DSNI). They organized a "Don't Dump On Us" campaign to fight illegal dumping, clean up the vacant lots, and build community hope and power. They "flipped planning on its head": Instead of trying to influence a top-down urban renewal process led by city government and developers, they created their own "bottom up" comprehensive revitalization plan and, in 1987, convinced the City of Boston to formally adopt it. Then, DSNI made history in 1988 as the only community group in the nation to win the power of eminent domain to acquire vacant land for resident-led development.

Over the past two decades, the community has rebuilt much of the vacant land with housing affordable to low-income families and revitalized the neighborhood. Today, Dudley is much more prepared to weather the storm of predatory lending, fraud, and foreclosures sweeping the country.

Residents Claim Control

Dudley was hit hard by the widespread discriminatory practice known as "redlining" that denied home and business loans, insurance, and other services to people in low-income neighborhoods—or offered them only at exorbitant rates. In the late 1960s, Dudley temporarily experienced a reverse form of redlining in a devastating preview of today's nationwide foreclosure crisis. Mortgages insured by the Federal Housing Administration (FHA) were finally made available to black buyers in Boston, but only within specific areas like Dudley that were designated by the Boston Bankers Urban Renewal Group (B-BURG). Realtors used racist fear-mongering and arranged break-ins and other "scare the hell out of them" tactics to orchestrate blockbusting and flight by longtime white homeowners with paid-off mortgages. FHA inspections deliberately played into the hands of speculators. They undervalued good properties so speculators could buy them cheap, while overvaluing properties that homebuyers would find out later needed major repair. Buyers who had no reserves to pay for repairs and had mortgages that were greater than the actual value of their homes often faced foreclosure. More than half of all B-BURG purchasers lost their homes by 1974. The bankers, meanwhile, made money on mortgage processing fees while passing on the costs of foreclosure to the federal government—and the Dudley community.

DSNI confronted the devastation by shifting control over development from city planners, speculators, and private developers to neighborhood residents. Residents' vision of a diverse, dynamic, sustainable "urban village" has guided Dudley redevelopment since the late 1980s.

DSNI's eminent domain proposal targeted the center of the Dudley neighborhood—a 64-acre triangular section with 30 acres of vacant land, nicknamed the "Bermuda Triangle." About half of this land was city-owned, but scattered throughout were 181 private vacant lots, many held by tax-delinquent absentee owners. Acquiring private lots one by one would have been a complex and piecemeal ordeal. Eminent domain gave DSNI the chance to pursue a coherent plan for the area that would meet community needs.

Dudley's approach turned the long-abused power of eminent domain into a tool for development without displacement. Eminent domain applied only to vacant land: No one lost their home or business in the process. DSNI worked with residents who owned vacant land in the Triangle and wanted to develop their lots as homes or gardens, for example.

And the strategy placed control over vacant Triangle land in the hands of a community land trust, Dudley Neighbors, Inc., to institutionalize resident control over the land and its development, and ensure that housing created is not only affordable to the first buyers but future homeowners.

How It Works

In a community land trust, families purchase homes but a nonprofit organization owns the land. This approach "protects affordability in perpetuity," says May Louie, DSNI director of capacity building.

In the Dudley Neighbors land trust, homebuyers receive a 99-year renewable and inheritable lease for use of the land. They agree that all future sales will be made to a low- or moderate-income buyer and follow a resale formula at a price that allows them to recoup the cost of home improvements and benefit from modest price appreciation.

Dudley Neighbors prohibits the shoddy construction that so often undermines affordable housing. Homebuyers often qualify for downpayment and closing cost assistance through the Boston Home Certificate Initiative.

Homeowners benefit from city and state affordable-housing subsidies, and get a quality home they couldn't otherwise afford. And land trust homeowners pay significantly lower property taxes because the city recognizes the resale restrictions.

Land trust subsidies aren't lost if the homeowner leaves. "The subsidies stay with the home generation after generation," Louie says. "They can't be cashed out. In the land trust model, the investment is shared, and the equity is shared. It builds family wealth and community wealth." And the housing remains affordable for future buyers.

Homeowners also get protection from predatory lenders. Dudley Neighbors restricts loans to reasonable terms from approved lenders and steps in to help if homeowners miss payments due to job loss or medical crises.

"Homeowners get more than a financial subsidy," explains John Barros, executive director of DSNI. "They get an ongoing partner in dealing with lenders."

The land trust provides stability and opportunity that low-income neighborhoods generally don't have. "Turnover in the land trust is very low," says Jason Webb. "People really plant roots in the community."

He should know. Jason grew up in the neighborhood and started volunteering with DSNI when he was seven years old. By 13, he knew he wanted to work for the group as an adult, and he's never wavered, going from volunteer to DSNI board member to full-time community organizer to director of the Dudley community land trust.

John Barros is another of the many residents who prove that moving up in a low-income community doesn't mean moving out. John's parents emigrated from Cape Verde to Boston before he was born, and as a teenager, he was the founding cochair of DSNI's youth committee and the first youth to serve on the DSNI board. A graduate of Dartmouth College, John became DSNI director in 2000. "It's a real sign of progress that so many kids move up and stay [in Dudley]," John says.

Weathering the Next Disaster

The strategies that enabled Dudley to overcome the housing disasters of earlier decades are now helping protect it from today's foreclosure crisis. There were 713 foreclosures in the city of Boston in the first seven months of 2008, but none in the Dudley land trust.

"The community land trust secures the wealth and assets [people] worked for," says Barros. "Without the land trust, the risk is not just to homeowners, but the community. Foreclosure destroys communities. With the [land trust], public funds are used more efficiently and responsibly. Society gains from the more stable market the community land trust provides." DSNI cannot stop all foreclosures on neighborhood homes outside the land trust, but it is helping homeowners negotiate with lenders to avoid foreclosure, and supporting tenant rights in foreclosed apartment buildings. It is also working with the City of Boston to purchase and repair vacant foreclosed neighborhood properties and add them to the community land trust where possible. Without the land trust and these other actions, says Barros, the situation "could have been catastrophic."

"We've learned from the past," says Jason Webb. "We want to intervene before the [foreclosed] homes are stripped and burned. We want to rebuild while the homes are still standing."

DSNI is working with Boston City Council president Maureen Feeney, who is exploring whether the community land trust model can help fight foreclosures citywide and strengthen Boston's affordable housing strategy.

Meanwhile, housing experts across the country have their eye on community land trusts as proven means of preventing foreclosures. In a survey released March 2008, the National Community Land Trust Network found only two foreclosures among a national sample of 3,115 land trust homeowners. A report on land trusts (including the Dudley example) by the Lincoln Institute of Land Policy concluded, "The traditional subsidy temporarily creates affordable payments, while the [community land trust] model permanently creates affordable housing."

A Vision Realized

Dudley's plans for an urban village are coming to fruition. The Dudley Triangle looks nothing like it did in 1988. The Dudley Town Common, created from fragmented vacant lots, welcomes residents and visitors with colorful permanent artwork, farmer's markets, performances, and inviting green space. The land trust has 205 affordable homes, including co-ops, rentals, and homeownership units—with plans for more in 2009. There's a 350-person waiting list to rent apartments in Dudley Village, a new mixed-use development that will have a laundromat, beauty supply store, and Caribbean restaurant. A once-contaminated "brownfield" site is now a greenhouse.

Across the Dudley neighborhood, vacant land once used as a dumping ground now hosts playgrounds, parks, community gardens, and multicultural festivals. More than 450 affordable homes (including those in the land trust) have risen from the ashes of burned-out buildings, along with businesses, nonprofits and community centers. More than 700 homes have been rehabilitated. And the neighborhood is planning a major new community center for indoor and outdoor recreation, the arts, education, and events. Kids who grew up with DSNI have become community leaders, businesspeople, politicians, and teachers.

"Long-term vision has been the most valuable skill I've cultivated over the years," says Jason Webb. Long-term vision has guided Dudley's revitalization for 24 years, and kept Dudley moving forward through economic ups and downs and changing government policies. Today, that vision is helping Dudley confront a widening recession and harsh government cutbacks.

Dudley's spirit is evident in the preamble to the Declaration of Community Rights written by Dudley residents in 1993. It reads, "We—the youth, adults, seniors of African, Latin American, Caribbean, Native American, Asian, and European ancestry—are the Dudley community. . . . We were Boston's dumping ground and forgotten neighborhood. Today, we are on the rise! We are reclaiming our dignity, rebuilding housing, and reknitting the fabric of our communities. Tomorrow, we realize our vision of a vibrant, culturally diverse neighborhood, where everyone is valued for their talents and contribution to the larger community."

PART FIVE

BEYOND HOUSING

Land Trusts as Part of
a Threefold Economic Strategy
for Regional Integration

Robert Swann
(1978)

Today in the large agribusiness complex we see the movement towards "vertical integration" (that is, control of production from the farm through the processor to the ownership of the wholesale or retail store, and often including ownership of production of equipment and machinery) carried out to an extreme degree. Vertical integration spells a higher degree of monopoly control, maximum profit to the few owners of the corporations, and high prices to consumers, along with reduction in quality of food and ecological danger to the land through monoculture practice. While this process is a widely discussed symptom of the growing concentration of corporate power, the forces behind the concentration are not always recognized as the enemy in that they exemplify control over resources, production, and people, which the giant corporations exert for the benefit of a few people.

However, more than recognition is needed. We must analyze the sources of power upon which it depends and create a commensurate alternative strategy. Without denying the need for a legislative program (and the California Land Conservation Fund is the best proposal I have seen), I submit that by itself this is not an adequate strategy. A parallel economic strategy is also needed. It is in this context that the community or regional land trust belongs. First, let's look at some of the economic forces which have helped shape vertical integration (and monopoly control), because it is necessary to have a clear understanding of these forces before a comprehensive opposing strategy can be mapped out.

Basically, those forces, in my opinion, have consisted of three major factors, long in existence and deeply entrenched in the American and Western economic systems. As I list these factors I will also note hopeful signs of countervailing forces.

1. Built into the very core of the U.S. constitution, written as it was by land owners, is the proposition (although not explicit) that property rights take precedence over human rights or ecological realities. The notion of ownership of land and national resources in private hands and for private profit was incorporated into the Constitution, thus perpetuating the myth of divine rights in ownership first promulgated by

This piece is from an online article and is reprinted by permission of E. F. Schumacher Society, 140 Jug End Road, Great Barrington, MA, 01230. www.smallisbeautiful.org.

Roman Law. Only the American Indians, the original inhabitants of this soil, dared to question the supposedly divine right of kings to bestow legal title to land. The Indians did not claim ownership, but rather they questioned the *notion* of ownership of land and resources which, in fact, had no place in Indian culture. In accepting the white man's trinkets (for which they had no use) the Indians did not think they were "selling" the land, but rather acknowledging in a symbolic way the white man's request to share the *use* of the land which was, to the Indians' way of thinking, the gift of the Great Spirit for *all* men to use without exception.

While private ownership in land and resources remains strong and relatively entrenched, the ecology or environment crisis is bringing about a change in thinking about the right to exploit and pollute and, therefore, the public is today more open to the concept of trusteeship in land use rights rather than ownership rights. It may also be becoming more sensitized to the legal robbery which takes place under the form of what is euphemistically called "speculation in land."

2. The second factor is special privileges which have been granted by law to private for-profit corporations, and which have provided them with advantages over individuals or "natural persons." Such privileges as personal immunity from suit had only been accorded to board members of *public nonprofit* corporations such as schools, government institutions, etc., previous to 1811. In 1811 the state of New York passed the first law, in the face of considerable opposition and public indignation, granting the same privileges to for-profit corporations. The Civil War gave a great impetus to these for-profit corporations which, as they moved West, began to acquire huge holdings in land and other resources through government grants (to the railroads, for instance). By the end of the Civil War, Abraham Lincoln remarked, "The corporations are in the saddle and control the country."

Today a resurgence of opposition to the private profit corporation is sweeping the country (Ralph Nader says, "Finally the public is beginning to understand that corporate crime, corporate pollution and corporate distortion of our laws takes more lives, destroys more property and depletes more consumer incomes than all the street crimes put together.") But not until the special privileges granted these monstrous corporations are revoked, can imbalance of power be rectified. Meanwhile, a strategy of developing nonprofit corporations to replace profit corporations must grow.

3. The third force, and perhaps the least understood or recognized, behind monopoly is the power of the centralized issuance of money. By the time Alexander Hamilton had overcome the opposition of the Jeffersonians and established the first bank of America modeled after the central bank of England, this force had already been established. The centralized monopoly control over issuance of money has grown ever stronger (not without periods of populist opposition) until today it remains almost unquestioned even by the foremost critics of the "system." This system has worked badly for the majority of the people, especially those in the rural and underdeveloped parts of the U.S. In the 1930s the Keynesian band-aid was applied to patch up the system and it has been staggering along ever since, but even more inexo-

rably at the expense of those outside the main centers of commerce. In short, the rich have been getting richer and the poor, poorer, without change, as a result of the Keynesian reforms of the monetary system. In fact, the very centralization of the system and privileged monopoly control which is built into the profit banking system makes such a maldistribution of goods and services a virtual certainty. Any strategy to oppose monopoly control must take this factor into account.

The often drawn conclusion from the above analysis by those in opposition to special privilege and injustice of the system is that more government control is needed—usually implying the Federal government. We are, of course, somewhat more sophisticated today, and most of us recognize that Federal bureaucracies tend to become the captives of the vested corporate interests. (Nader might put it, "The supposedly regulated end up controlling the regulators.")

Nor has socialism as practiced in other countries given a great deal of insight or hope regarding our problems in the U.S. This is because the limited success of socialism (at the very least, people are usually better fed and better housed than they were prior to the socialist regimes) has generally taken place in the so-called undeveloped countries. As their socialist systems developed, these countries have been isolated from the exploitative system which controlled them previously—usually called imperialism. Basically this had meant a "closed economy" whereby the depredations of the international monetary and corporate system could not invade the country and exploit the local population. Certainly, this has been effective in China and Cuba when accompanied by land reform programs, and perhaps to a lesser degree in other socialist countries, or even nonsocialist countries where nationalism has to some degree produced the same "closed economy."

But because the U.S. is an overdeveloped nation, it is not likely that identical solutions will be applicable here, certainly not on the national level at any rate. As we see in the case of Russia, centralization of power under the name of socialism merely leads to bureaucratic control from the center and not very much difference in the inequality of distribution results. As has been observed by many people, Russia and the United States are growing closer together, as ever larger bureaucracies control both countries from centralized points.

On the other hand, one might take the view that essentially the entire United States is divided between affluent centers of power (the large industrial and financial complexes of the East, Midwest, and far West), and the rest of the country is, in effect, "colonial" hinterland. Then an analogy can be drawn between the situation of the third world and these "colonial" areas of the U.S.—generally the rural areas and the inner cities. Here is where the concept of regional decentralization enters in as the alternative strategy to a purely political strategy. Within the regions defined as "undeveloped" (Appalachia, South, Southwest, North Central, inner cities), sub-regions can begin to create a comprehensive strategy which includes land trusts, relatively closed economies, and community development corporations. I will try to describe each component and its role in an overall economic strategy.

The Community Land Trust

The community land trust is a legal entity, a quasipublic body, chartered to hold land in stewardship for all mankind present and future while protecting the legitimate use-rights of its residents.

The community land trust is not primarily concerned with common ownership. Rather, its concern is for ownership for the common good, which may or may not be combined with common ownership. The word "trust" is used more to connote the idea of trusteeship or stewardship than to define the legal form. Most often the land trust will be a nonprofit corporation rather than a legal trust.

The following key features differentiate the community land trust from the ordinary real estate trust or conservation trust, and enable it to achieve its goal of "ownership for the common good":

1. The trust holds land only.
2. The land user is protected by his long-term lease—99 years, renewable and inheritable.
3. The land itself is protected by the charter of the trust.
4. The trustees do not "control" the users of the land; they implement the trust charter and ensure that the provisions of the charter and of the lease contract are fulfilled.

Some reasons why land trusts are advantageous in a strategy of regional decentralization:

Immediate Implementation

Trusts can be established immediately. They do not require any legislation for implementation. Land trusteeship utilizes the legal principle of the leasehold, but in perpetuity (99 years, renewable and inheritable). Such long term leasehold systems as a substitute for ownership are being utilized increasingly in urban areas (in New York City most skyscrapers are on leased ground) and even new towns (Irvine, California, for instance), but generally for maximizing profit (Leavitt retains the commercial areas of his town and leases them out—thereby reducing taxes and spreading profit over years). In the concept of trusteeship, these profits return to the trust which, in turn, can donate them to the community via special agreements.

Built on Tradition

Trusteeship and stewardship can be built on a long tradition in many societies. For example: Indians of North and South America, the Ejidos of Mexico, the tribes of Africa, the "commons" in England and New England, the Crofter system in Scotland, the Eskimos of Alaska. And in recent history, the Gramdan movement in India and the Jewish National Fund in Israel.

Broad Base for Political Coalition

One of the problems with traditional land reform is that it often implies or has, historically, involved forcible expropriation. This fact has led to a great deal of fear regarding the term on the part of the land owners, including homeowners, who fear (irrationally) loss of their homes. Such fear is not associated with the words "trust" or "trusteeship" (nor is expropriation advocated under the land trust concept). In fact, since trusteeship implies and includes a concern for the land itself in a conservation or ecological sense, new allies are found in the environmental movement who want to ensure that the land is not violated (in Maine these people are called "land advocates," and their number is growing rapidly). This creates a basis for a broader political coalition than land redistribution, per se.

At the same time, it should be pointed out that under traditional land redistribution, land typically reverts to its former absentee landlords (or new ones) in about twenty years, partly because other factors or forces in the economy (control of money, etc.) are not changed. Under land trusteeship, on the other hand, land is taken out of private ownership (voluntarily) and placed in trusteeship "in perpetuity."

Tax Reform

As land trusts grow and the amount of nontrust land in a given region decreases, the value of the remaining land may decrease, resulting in lower prices and increasing opportunity for more people who need land to purchase it. On the other hand, due to the community development which takes place on trust land, it is possible that land values may increase. In this case, the trust with its broad-based membership is in a good position to form a coalition with small farmers, homeowners and environmentalists to drive speculation out through changes in the application of local tax assessment. That is, either through election of a candidate for local tax assessor or through statewide tax reform, to place the burden of the property tax on unimproved land and big private landowners.

Planning Advantages

A trust can be used as a holding mechanism for all sizes and tracts of land. Some of these tracts may be large enough to build entire new towns (large or small) or simply used as farms or as conservation tracts. Because large segments of land are held as a unit, the trust can utilize the greatest flexibility in planning, taking account of the entire region. This is, from a planning viewpoint, the most logical unit for resource planning. Most regions have regional planning commissions already—usually frustrated planners who are unable to utilize their best knowledge of the region. (In planning New Communities, Inc., in Southwest Georgia, we received enthusiastic support from the regional planning commission.) This flexibility permits both short and long range strategies which can include small farms, large farms, or combinations of both. In this way, the modern technology of the large scale farm can be utilized while, at the same time the trust can encourage and promote the new ecological fertilizers and farming systems to avoid dangers of monocultures and pesticides. In the short range, at least, large scale use of machine technology is necessary to compete with the agri-business farm system. Land redistribution or resettlement creates more small farmers, but does nothing to ensure their survival.

Mechanization and Farm Workers

Another aspect of this same issue which must be considered is the assumption that farm workers and agriculturalists want small farms—I doubt this is true in most cases if it means giving up labor-saving machine technology. Farm laborers want a share, real participation in ownership of their production, but not at the expense of more "stoop labor." In our planning sessions for New Communities, Inc., we ran into this issue any number of times. Farmers did not want to divide the farm (about 6,000 acres) into small individual tracts because it would make the use of machinery more difficult. Cucumbers, which meant a great deal of stoop labor, were voted out as a cash crop even though they bring good prices.

Removes Burden of Payment from the Land

To those who are concerned about chemical fertilizers and pesticides distributed with large scale machinery, as well as those who believe in the small farm system, this attitude presents a problem and a challenge. I suggest that a land trust mechanism, which helps to remove the burden of land payments from the back of the farm worker, is a form which offers the best approach to solve this problem. Since so-called "organic" farming generally costs more in terms of labor, and since present markets do not offer any price incentives to the farmer, he is often forced to use pesticides and chemicals on his fields against his better judgment, in order to meet his obligations (mortgage) on the land. In our planning at New Communities we have, at least in theory, developed a plan for combining large scale farming with small plots mainly for home gardens and animals. However, larger plots could be provided for individual families to live reasonably close together in villages where other needs such as schooling, recreation, buying clubs, marketing co-ops and other stores can easily be provided.

In Israel, the advantages of flexibility in planning can be seen very clearly, since over two-thirds of the best land is held in trust by the Jewish National Fund. There, everything from small farms, Kibbutzim, Moshavim and whole new towns are planned and established on trust land.

In short, the trusteeship concept is an activist approach to the problem of redistribution of resources, and while it is initially aimed at the land, as it grows and develops strength as a movement it can begin to reach out into other areas of resource management.

The Community Development Corporation

The second element in the threefold strategy of regional integration is the concept of the nonprofit Community Development Corporation (CDC). The concept of the CDC provides the mechanism which can substitute for the present vertically integrated corporation on a local or regional level. As an umbrella nonprofit organization it can even spin off and control for-profit corporations which return profits to the CDC, which, in turn, uses those profits for the benefit of the community. As the land trust is the land use planning organization, the CDC is the development organization. It can develop businesses (ecologically sound industries), and it can provide for recreation, health, schools, etc., which the community may need and which are not provided for in the present institutions. Its job is overall development planning, using the savings of the local members as initial capital to start the process.

Community Money

The third necessity in such a strategy is the one least likely to be understood or considered. It is comparable to the process of a newly established country creating its own money-of-account, or currency, and operating as a semiclosed economy that produces primarily for local consumption and exports the surplus for "foreign exchange." This is not to imply that all newly formed countries do this. Unfortunately, they often fail to do so because they have accepted the colonial banking system which they have inherited from their former Colonial masters. In these cases, and it is the majority of them, the former "mother" country continues to exert economic control through the power of the dollar, the pound, the franc, etc. While these countries are politically independent, they continue to be economically controlled from the outside.

In the same way, a regional integration strategy will not be complete or successful until some form of isolation from the larger economy and independence from the dollar is achieved. An illustration of such isolation within a country is Israel, in the case of the Kibbutz, where national currency is not required within the internal mechanism of the Kibbutz—but only a bookkeeping system is used to determine each family's allocation. Exports and imports of the Kibbutz are paid in terms of the Israeli dollar; any surplus of export income over import cost being allotted on an equitable basis to each workerfamily. The amount of national cash or currency needed is thus reduced to a minimum. Coupons, or credit vouchers, are used as internal currency within the Kibbutz, but they are good only for purchases at the Kibbutz clothing or Kibbutz "supermarket." Such a system can be applied on a wider level and there are many examples of "scrip" money, as it has been called in U.S. history, especially during the Great Depression of the 1930s.

It is my opinion that such a system, on a more sophisticated level, must be utilized in order to insure successful regional integration. We are now involved with an experiment in New Hampshire which is demonstrating that such a system can utilize the existing banking system. We intend, of course, to use it as a means for financing land trusts in New Hampshire and Maine, and for creating the currency needed to develop the related CDCs.

The international monetary crisis and the continuing devaluation of the dollar is helping to bring about a favorable climate for accomplishing this objective. The New Hampshire experiment uses a scrip called "Constant" which does not devalue with inflation but is linked to a noninflationary index (Bureau of Labor commodity price index at present, but eventually a world commodity index). A checking account system is already in operation, which moves through the bank clearing house. However, it is a separate corporation, a nonprofit corporation, which provides financing and local currency within a developing regional system. At present, U.S. dollars are being exchanged for the Constants, but eventually it will rediscount loans and, in the process, issue new credit.

Most of us have been intimidated by our lack of knowledge of the banking mechanisms or by our naive assumptions or fears that only the government can issue credit or currency. The result is that we have retained our dependence upon the centralized system and its ability to exploit us through the mystery of its operation. Without intending to oversimplify what is not necessarily an easy subject, I submit that the time is long past for demystifying this process which has kept us at the mercy of Wall Street and its manipulations.

Long Range Political and Social Implications

Finally, a word regarding the long range political and social implications of such a threefold strategy. It should be clear that the implications of the CDC would be to gradually replace the multinational corporation. With its emphasis on the local community, and transformation of the purely private profit system in order to make it serve the needs of the community and region, the CDC represents a unique form for releasing new energy, imagination and power around the concept of local control and local participation in economic decision making.

It should also be clear that control and issue of money, or currency, on the local or regional level will lead away from control and domination at the national level over monetary decision making. I may not be as clear that, at the same time, issue of currency whose value is regulated by the use of an index based on world production of commodities could eventually remove the necessity for international monetary regulation as embodied in the concept of the International Monetary Fund. (*Newsweek* says we are "groping for a new international monetary system." Rather, I would say we are searching for a noninternational monetary unit of exchange, a money for world-wide use to replace gold. This is what is proposed in the use of the constant.) In effect, this means one raison d'être of the nation-state will have been removed.

From another dimension, the very concept of trusteeship when applied in the broadest fashion to all natural resources, challenges the political sovereignty of the nation-state.

The concept is being applied to the oceans in the Seabed Committee of the UN General Assembly. A general conference is being planned on the law of the seas to draw up a treaty establishing an "international ocean regime" for the peaceful uses of oceanspace and resources for *the benefit of mankind as a whole.*

As Elizabeth Borgese writes in *The Center Magazine,* "In trying to establish an organization for the management of ocean resources, we must tackle all the problems of world government. This includes questions of constitutional structure, distribution of voting power, relations between large and small and developed and developing nations, planning and resource management, conservation, regional and global development, taxation, diversity, and unity, sovereignty and poverty, rights and responsibilities, a new science policy, and the control of technology for the benefit of mankind."

With the exception that its scale is regional instead of global, most of the above applies to the problem of organizing a regional land trust. What is learned in the process at the global level may be applied at the regional level and vice versa. In fact, it will be the interaction between the nucleus of the "new politics" of the transnational period we are entering—a period in which the new technologies of war are rapidly making the political institution of the nation-state untenable. As it becomes increasingly clear that "we will abolish war or war will abolish us," war as an instrument of political policy becomes increasingly unfeasible.

Without war as an instrument of national political policy the nation-state cannot endure. Even the very cost of maintaining an outmoded and obsolete "defense" establishment will help break down the nation-state itself. Resentment and resistance to the taxes required to maintain this establishment will bring about decentralizing forces and new alternative institutions. New institutions of many kinds are needed to replace present outmoded nation-state institutions, but central to all such institutions must be the institutions of land and resource management on a global and regional level. Trusteeship is simply the underlying concept which can give coherence and unity to all such planning, whether "conservative" or "radical."

Reallocating Equity

A Land Trust Model of Land Reform

John Emmeus Davis
(1984)

Land reform is commonly equated with land redistribution. Some people own more land than they need (or deserve). Others need more land than they own. So the deck is reshuffled at the command of the state and dealt out differently than before. Large estates are broken up and placed in the hands of landless peasants, agricultural laborers, or small farmers. However, redistributing the ownership of land is only one "tradition" of land reform,[1] and transferring title to small producers but one "model" by which this tradition has been made a reality. There are other traditions and other models. Particularly within the United States, a more politically acceptable approach has been to leave untouched the distribution of land and to focus instead on restricting the use to which the land is put. This is the only tradition of land reform to which most Americans have been willing to submit. Nonetheless, a third tradition of land reform is alive and well in this country—though it is often obscured by the rhetoric and reality of the more familiar approaches of redistributing ownership and restricting use. This third tradition may be conveniently called "reallocating equity."

Equity refers to the value inherent in land and buildings: that portion of a property's market value that is unencumbered by a mortgage or lien; the value that exists free and clear once any liability on a parcel of property has been paid off or subtracted.[2] Part of this value is created by the dollars and labor of the property's owner, poured into the property over a period of time to purchase, build, maintain, and improve it. Another part of the property's value, however, is less a product of the owner's investment than a gratuitous windfall, bestowed by changes in the larger society. Changes in the level of private investment in surrounding parcels, changes in the level of public investment in the surrounding neighborhood, changes in the population of the region or in the price of oil throughout the world—any of these may add considerable value to an individual parcel of real property. To the value created by the capital and labor of the property's owner, there is thus added a "social increment" created by the investment and development of society. Equity is a mix of both kinds of value, one earned and the other unearned by the investment of the property owner, yet *both* are claimed by the individual owner as a proprietary right, guaranteed by

This selection was originally published as a chapter in *Land Reform, American Style* edited by Charles C. Geisler and Frank J. Popper (Totowa, NJ: Rowman & Littlefield, 1984), 209–232. Copyright © Rowman & Littlefield. It is reprinted by permission via Copyright Clearance Center.

custom and law. In the United States, equity is usually synonymous with the "owner's interest."

The third tradition of land reform confronts this custom head-on by reallocating the equity embedded in real property between the individual owner and the larger community. To the individual goes the fruits of individual labor; to the community goes the social increment. There are several ways to accomplish such a result. This paper will focus on a model of reallocation that is being used increasingly in urban and rural communities across the United States, particularly by grass-roots groups which are struggling against land speculation, absentee ownership, and residential displacement. This model is the community land trust.

The community land trust (CLT) is a mixed-ownership arrangement. Title to land is held by a nonprofit corporation—the CLT—based in and accountable to the local community. Title to buildings and other improvements on the land is held by an individual owner—a person, a family, a business, or another nonprofit organization. Though never sold by the CLT, lands are leased to individuals under long-term, renewable, inheritable leases. By holding the land beneath the buildings and controlling the price at which these buildings may be resold, the CLT is able to achieve a just and lasting reallocation of equity between individual leaseholders and the local community. It is able to reverse the worst effects of land speculation. It has the potential of altering, quite fundamentally, the ways in which local lands are held, used, and developed. In short, the CLT is a community-based model of land reform, effective both in its own right and as a complement to other land reform measures.

Three Traditions of Land Reform

Land reform is a term with innumerable meanings and connotations. It is like a suitcase that is seldom packed the same way twice. Any discussion of land reform should therefore begin with a mutual understanding of how the term is to be used. Our "suitcase" will be filled with three elements. First, land reform is a purposeful response to a land-related problem that is deemed socially harmful; it is undertaken to correct a tenure system that is considered defective from the point of view of the broader public interest. Second, land reform restructures the institutional framework of land-ownership and use. It is, to paraphrase Peter Dorner (1972:17–18), a significant change in the rules and procedures governing the rights, duties, and liberties of individuals and groups as to the control and use of real property. Finally, land reform transfers power, property, and status from one group to another (Galbraith, 1951:695). To the extent that this transfer occurs across class lines, land reform represents a revolutionary step. Although other elements are commonly included in definitions of land reform,[3] these three should suffice to provide both a shared sense of the term and a general standard with which to compare the various traditions of land reform reviewed below.[4]

Redistributing Ownership

Outside the United States, land reform has usually meant redistributing the ownership of landed resources from one social class to another in order to achieve a more equitable allocation of wealth, income, and political power. The state condemns or confiscates land from the largest owners and either parcels it out among numerous small holders (distributionist reform) or transfers undivided estates to cooperatives, collectives, or state-run farms (collectivist reform).[5] The land-to-the-tiller programs of Taiwan and Japan are effective examples of distributionist reform. The most striking examples of collectivist reform are the state farms of Eastern Europe and the Soviet Union.

A less drastic means of redistribution is found in the attempt of some countries to *buy* lands from large landowners, without the imminent threat of seizure, for the purpose of making these lands available (and affordable) for small farmers, small businesses, and low-income housing. The land reform programs of Venezuela and Iran (Dorner, 1972:47), the land bank programs of Canada and Western Europe (McClaughry, 1975; Strong, 1979), and the New Deal community programs of the Resettlement Administration and the Farm Security Administration in the United States (Conkin, 1959) have all had ingredients of distributionist reform.[6]

Redistributing ownership is often accompanied by a fundamental change in the institutional framework within which land is held and used. There is, however, no necessary link between the two. It is possible to alter the pattern of ownership through the intervention of the state without changing the rules, procedures, or prerogatives of the tenure system itself. Distributionist reform is especially problematic in this regard. Parceling out large estates, while leaving intact a private, market-based system of land tenure, leaves open the possibility that what is owned today by a multitude of small, low-income producers may be owned tomorrow—because of sale, foreclosure, or unpaid taxes—by an exclusive coterie of wealthy individuals and corporations. Collectivist reform, on the other hand, may significantly alter the tenure system but do nothing to alter the concentrated pattern of ownership that was regarded as undesirable in the first place. Furthermore, as the history of eminent domain in the United States shows, lands that are taken by the state for a public purpose often benefit only a narrow range of private interests—and often end up in the hands of private corporations (see Scheiber, 1975).

At any rate, the United States has shied away from dissolving *or* collectivizing the holdings of its largest landowners.[7] American policy has periodically disbursed public lands and provided public funds to make land and housing more affordable for persons of modest means, but this has been more a matter of passing out subsidies to would-be buyers than of redistributing lands held and hoarded by a privileged few. The simple fact is that redistributing the ownership of land has had scant acceptance in the past and is likely to prove politically unacceptable for the foreseeable future. Land reform in the United States, such as it is, has customarily followed a different course.

Restricting Use

Americans have embraced, however reluctantly, a tradition of land reform that places public restrictions on the use of private property. The ends here have less to do with how the ownership of property might be made more widely available than with how the use of property might be made more safe, healthy, efficient, secure, or environmentally sound for the public at large. The means of this tradition are different, too. While the redistribution of ownership relies primarily upon the power of the state to seize private property, restrictions on use rely primarily upon the power of the state to police the behavior of property owners—regulating the ways in which they manage, develop, or dispose of their property.[8] Zoning laws and health and building codes are long-established representatives of this tradition. More recent additions include environmental regulations, prohibitions designed to preserve historic structures, and various ordinances intended to retard or prevent tenant displacement due to condominium or cooperative conversions.

Restricting use alters the tenure system by diminishing the rights that owners have traditionally held when holding title to real property. Private rights of ownership are subordinated to the public purpose of relieving society of a prospective or actual harm believed to be associated with the unrestricted use and development of land. This "harm"—whether defined as "urban sprawl," "congestion," "pollution," "displacement," or something else—is eliminated in the public interest, either by preventing certain kinds of use and channeling development in more socially desirable directions, or by forcing private developers to bear the cost of certain "externalities" previously inflicted on society as a whole.

Although this tradition does not produce a redistribution of property *titles* among social classes, it does engender a redistribution of property *rights* (Geisler, 1980a:497). The results have been rather mixed. Restricting use has, on the one hand, preserved the status quo in the distribution of land, transferred power to large developers, and in many cases enhanced the value of private property held by the few (Walker and Heiman, 1981). Yet restricting use has also tended to transfer substantial power from landowners to local units of government and, increasingly, from local government to higher units of government (Popper, 1981). The exercise of this power, to the extent that private owners are forced to internalize costs previously borne by the public, tends to shift wealth away from individual property owners toward the larger society (Hite, 1979:37).

Restricting use allows the community to avoid costs that it did *not* create. The third tradition of land reform—reallocating equity—takes a different tack. It enables the community to reclaim value that it *did* create.

Reallocating Equity

Each tradition of land reform tends to stress a different land-related problem. Redistributing ownership confronts the problem of concentration—the accumulation of property and power by a landed elite. Restricting use is a response to the private abuse of landed resources and the private landowner's imposition of costly externalities on the general public. The problem that motivates the third tradition of land reform is speculation and the land monopolization and absenteeism which accompany it.

Under the fee-simple concept of private property, Americans have considered the "right to speculate" a basic prerogative of landownership.[9] Landowners claim most, if not all, of the increases in value which accrue to their property. Since appreciation will often occur even if the landowner does nothing to improve or develop the property, land has long been seen as a low-risk investment.[10] It has, from America's earliest days, attracted persons with less interest in *using* the land to meet their own productive, residential, or aesthetic needs than in holding it and later selling it for profits they did little to earn.

This is the heart of the problem: speculation so inflates the commodity value of land that socially desirable uses of land are often thwarted. For the local community, there are a number of negative consequences. Speculation makes access to land and housing more and more difficult for those of modest means: small farmers, small businesses, and low- and moderate-income residents. As the price of land is bid ever higher, only a few investors—many of them from outside the local community—can afford to acquire and hold the land. Concentration increases, as does absentee ownership and control. Agricultural producers are unable to compete with nonfarm investors for farmland that is soaring in price (USDA, 1981:77). Urban land for commercial and residential development is priced so high that one-fourth of all privately held land is left vacant in America's largest cities (U.S. House Subcommittee on the City, 1980). Speculation in land is also one of the factors that has helped to push the cost of new homes beyond the reach of three-quarters of the nation's families.[11] In urban neighborhoods, speculation in land and housing by brokers, developers, and affluent professionals has spurred gentrification and helped to displace the poor, the elderly, and the working class (see LeGates and Hartman, 1981); and in residential communities throughout the country, petty speculation by those selling a home and claiming the unearned increment as their rightful due has helped to nudge the price of housing beyond the means of a growing number of households.

Speculation also prevents a community from using its land as an equity base for its own development. A community's land is the original "commonwealth"; on that land and from that land is produced much of the community's wealth. If most of the land is held by investors who reside outside the community, much of this wealth will be drained away. Furthermore, if most of the value that accrues to land is captured by a privileged few, wherever they reside, much of the "commonwealth" will be unavailable to promote the development and prosperity of the community as a whole.

Finally, speculation makes it more and more difficult for the community to guide the pace and direction of its own development. Restless buying and selling of real estate tends to undermine whatever legacy of careful planning and thoughtful preservation the community would leave to future generations. Speculation is a threat to nearly every use of land that cannot be measured in the highest monetary terms. Aesthetic uses are the most vulnerable of all, for the single-minded pursuit of unearned profits in land has little regard for ornate structures of yesteryear, urban belts of green, or amber waves of grain.

The third tradition of land reform seeks to reverse the ravages of speculation by removing the *incentive* to speculate. Individual landowners are no longer permitted to exercise an undivided claim over the equity that accrues to real property. Local communities are empowered to recover the value which society had a hand in creating. There are two principal means by which this may be done: one model employs the public power to tax; the other mixes public and private elements of ownership. Both models attempt to reallocate equity between individual property owners and the larger community.

The proposition that the state can and should discourage speculation by taxing away increases in land value that are not the result of the owner's investment was popularized in the United States by Henry George (1839–1897).[12] He believed that individual landowners have no right to the equity created by others, private or public. Owners do, however, have an absolute right to the fruits of their own labor. To allow individual landowners to profit from appreciation caused by others is to handsomely reward those who monopolize and idle land instead of those who put the land to productive use.[13] George therefore proposed a "single tax" which would confiscate the socially created value of land and generate enough public revenue, so he claimed, to eliminate the need for all other levies on owner-made improvements.

Whatever the merit of George's single-tax proposal, his provocative idea that equity buildup contains a "social increment" has surfaced again and again since the turn of the century, inspiring many taxation schemes. There are Georgist elements, for instance, in the "betterment recapture" provisions of the 1967 British Land Commission Act and in the "unearned increment" taxes of Australia, New Zealand, and Alberta, Canada (Glickfeld and Hagman, 1978). There are echoes of Georgist ideas in the American planning system proposed by Donald Hagman which would tax away "windfalls" bestowed on lucky landowners by governmental activity, in order to compensate unlucky landowners for "wipeouts" in property value caused by other governmental activity (Hagman, 1974; Hagman and Misczynski, 1978). There is also a certain Georgist logic in Vermont's special capital gains tax on land sales, enacted in 1973 to discourage the rapid turnover of land by out-of-state speculators. Land that is purchased and quickly resold, presumably to reap speculative gains, is taxed at a higher rate than land that is held for many years (Glickfeld and Hagman, 1978). Implicitly acknowledged is the community's need to stop speculation and its right to share in the short-term surges in property value that the community, not the individual owner, happens to create.

Mixed-ownership models of equity reallocation attempt to accomplish similar ends by other than Georgist means. These models give the community a direct ownership interest in lands that are used and developed by private individuals. Outside the

United States, mixed ownership has usually entailed *public* ownership of land, either by the state or by a quasipublic association. This has been accompanied by *private* ownership of the structural improvements upon these lands, with private owners leasing the land beneath their buildings. The Ujamma program of Tanzania, the *ejidos* of Mexico, and the settlements founded upon the lands of the Jewish National Fund in Israel are representative examples (Dorner, 1972; Tai, 1974; Orni, 1972). Public acquisition and permanent municipal ownership of lands, dispersed into private hands by means of long-term leases, is also a mainstay of England's Garden Cities.[14] All of these programs permanently remove land from the speculative market, while making it available for private use. Equity buildup is allocated between the leaseholder, who receives a just return on any investment of capital or labor, and the larger community, which retains the unearned increment.

The mixed-ownership model need not depend, however, upon public subsidies and public ownership. In India, the Bhoodan and Gramdan movements—part of Gandhi's political legacy—have placed nearly 4½ million acres of privately donated land into "village republics," private associations that combine local self-government with the common ownership and private use of local lands. Gandhi hoped that such independent village republics would form the basis for a decentralized structure of economic and political development for all of India (Linton, 1970).

Private associations figure prominently, as well, in the mixed-ownership model that is quietly taking root among urban and rural communities of the United States. This American model is the community land trust, a distinctive approach to land reform which interweaves many strands of thought and practice found within the larger tradition of reallocating equity. From Henry George, the CLT draws its focused opposition to speculation. George's influence is also apparent in the CLT's preoccupation with the origins and allocation of property value. From Gandhi, the CLT draws its emphasis on decentralization—political and economic development that proceeds from the bottom up, controlled by community-based associations. From the mixed-ownership models of Israel and England, the CLT draws the practical details of leasing land and guiding local development. In addition, the CLT implements a conception of land that is, at once, both Gandhian and Native American in regarding land as a common trust rather than a commodity, a common heritage that may be individually used but not individually owned. The community land trust combines these disparate strands within itself to form a community-based model of land reform—a grass-roots approach to the reallocation of equity.[15]

The Community Land Trust

Land trusts are neither new nor uncommon. For years, environmentalist and preservationist groups have been using local nonprofit corporations to protect endangered lands and buildings. The Nature Conservancy has established hundreds of local organizations to preserve unusual natural areas for posterity. The National Trust for Historic Preservation has helped local chapters to protect hundreds of historic landmarks from destruction and decay. The Trust for Public Land has helped to establish many local land trusts to defend open space against needless development. Organizations of this sort are painfully aware of the threat that is posed by speculation. All act decisively to remove property from the speculative market by acquiring selected parcels and holding them in perpetual trust.

Land trusts, then, are nothing new. Reallocating equity via a community land trust, however, is very new indeed. It is the question of equity that sets the CLT apart: how is property value created; how does the present allocation of value generate or aggravate the land-related problems that bedevil a local community; how might the reallocation of value begin to alleviate these troublesome problems? Like the more familiar trusts of the environmentalists and preservationists, the CLT removes property from the speculative market. Unlike these trusts, the CLT returns property to individual use, attempting to balance the legitimate interests of the individual user and those of the surrounding community through a just allocation of equity.

The CLT Model
The CLT is legally established as a nonprofit organization, with a membership that is open to any resident of the surrounding community. Out of this membership is elected a board of trustees that is empowered to acquire land, housing, and other real property by purchase or gift. Land is held by the CLT with the intent of retaining title forever. It is never resold, though it *is* made available for individual use. Appropriate uses are determined for the land by a committee of the CLT. Then the land is leased to individuals, families, businesses, or another nonprofit organization. The lease is a long-term use agreement, typically guaranteeing lifetime occupancy and specifying the uses to which the land may be put. This agreement may be transferred to a leaseholder's heirs, should they wish to continue using the land. Leaseholders pay a nonrefundable annual lease fee to the CLT, based on the current "use value" of the land, not its "exchange value."

Improvements on the land are treated differently. Any buildings acquired by the CLT are sold off to whoever leases the land beneath them. Any buildings constructed on lands that are leased from the CLT are owned by whoever had them built. The CLT retains title to the land; the leaseholder obtains title to buildings and other improvements.

If leaseholders later wish to leave the land, they may sell their improvements. They cannot sell them, however, for whatever the market will bear. Were the land to be removed from the speculative market, but not the house that is on the land, any social increment that would have accrued to the land would merely be transferred to the house. To prevent this, the CLT removes one "stick" from the bundle of rights held by the home owner—the right to an undivided claim on the appreciating equity in the house which the leaseholder owns. Utilizing a resale formula that is incorporated both into the home owner's lease and into a first-option agreement which the CLT retains on all improvements, the CLT limits the owner's equity in any improvements on CLT land.[16] The leaseholder/home owner is guaranteed a fair return on any personal investment in structural improvements, but is not allowed to profit from increases in the improvements' market value.

Applications of the CLT Model

CLTs have recently appeared in Cincinnati, Trenton, and Dallas to oppose gentrification and secure a base of decent, affordable housing for the neighborhood's present population.[17] A CLT was founded in an Appalachian community of east Tennessee to promote access to lands long monopolized by absentee land and mineral companies. In a middle-class neighborhood of Minneapolis and in one of the poorest counties of rural Maine, CLTs have been established to complement ongoing programs of community-based economic development. Variations on the basic CLT model have sprung up in Marin County, California, to deal with the loss of farmland; in Vermont to preserve open space and promote low-density development; and in New Hampshire to improve the management of forest lands. Their numbers are few—less than fifty in the United States—and their holdings not yet large, but CLTs are attracting serious attention and winning steady acceptance among a remarkably diverse population. By mixing various features of private and "public" ownership, the CLT is able to secure—and to balance—the legitimate interests in real property of both private individuals *and* the larger community.[18] These interests, which the CLT is designed to meet, are mirrored in the scattered struggles of numerous local groups to defend or develop their own communities. Among such groups, the CLT is finding a natural constituency.

The political acceptability of this model has much to do with its "conservative" promise of fulfilling the most fundamental expectations that Americans have traditionally held regarding the ownership of real property. Three of these are paramount: *security* against unfair eviction, unexpected increases in shelter costs, and unwarranted invasions of privacy; *equity* for one's personal investment; and a *legacy* for one's children. Because the CLT is able to meet the security, equity, and legacy needs of individual leaseholders, it is possible to persuade a diverse cross-section of the community that this alternative institution—this new approach to land reform—is worth supporting. Security of tenure is assured by means of a long-term lease for the land and a clear title to the land's structural improvements, both of which are placed in the leaseholder's possession. The CLT guarantees the leaseholder a fair equity in the resale of these improvements. Furthermore, the leaseholder may bequeath these improvements to designated heirs, along with the use rights in any lands that are currently leased from the CLT.

At the same time, the community has its own set of legitimate interests. A unique advantage of the CLT is that individual needs for security, equity, and a legacy may be met even as the CLT is serving the more general interests of the community at large. The first of these community interests is *access,* extending the privileges and prerogatives of property to those who would be denied them otherwise. CLTs have used their tax-exempt status[19] as a vehicle for low-cost acquisition by coaxing donations and bargain sales from local governments, charitable institutions, and wealthy individuals. As for raising funds, CLTs have been able to attract low-interest loans from a growing number of institutions and individuals seeking socially responsible ways to invest their money. Then, too, since they are mixed-ownership organizations, CLTs provide greater access to land and housing: leaseholders do not need a large downpayment to gain long-term use of land, and prospective CLT homeowners do not need to purchase the land that is under a house—a cost which now makes up 25 percent of the purchase price of most new homes (Cigler and Vasu, 1982:91).

As useful as the CLT may be in making property available now, its greater effectiveness lies in assuring that whatever is made affordable today will remain so tomorrow. By removing land from the speculative market and limiting the equity which leaseholders may claim as their own, the CLT should make it possible for future leaseholders to purchase homes at a price below the inflated market rate. In effect, this feature reallocates equity not only between the present leaseholder and the broader community, but between the present generation of home owners and those of the future.

The second interest of the broader community is *development,* exercising enough control over local land and housing to promote local economic development. The CLT attempts to place an increasing proportion of local lands under its stewardship. As absentee ownership is gradually reduced, the drain on the community's financial resources diminishes; rents and mortgage payments are no longer siphoned off to other neighborhoods or regions. These local resources may be augmented by using the CLT's lands as collateral in leveraging new funds into the community.[20] Equally important, over the long run, is the prospect that lease fees will eventually reach a volume sufficient to fund community services and other community development efforts.

There is the additional prospect that CLTs will either generate jobs themselves or support the development efforts of other community-based organizations. New Communities, a CLT in Georgia, has created new jobs in agriculture. The Community Land Association in Tennessee is engaged in housing construction; the Community Land Cooperative of Cincinnati and the Mill Hill II CLT in Trenton, New Jersey, are engaged in housing rehabilitation. These are labor-intensive activities, employing skilled and semiskilled people from the surrounding area. In other communities— where cooperatives, community development corporations, and the like have already begun tackling problems of unemployment and underdevelopment—CLTs may serve a more passive role, holding lands that other organizations utilize and develop. This is the nature of the relationship that currently exists, for instance, between the H.O.M.E. Co-op and the Covenant CLT in Hancock County, Maine.

The community also receives a developmental bonus in that increases in property value (unrelated to the leaseholder's personal investment) are retained by the CLT.

They are neither removed by absentee landowners nor captured by individual home owners. Consequently, any general improvement in community well-being—whether due to public investment from outside or indigenous self-help—will benefit the community's present population. Many low-income communities, and an increasing number of middle-class ones, face the dilemma that creating parks, rehabilitating houses, or strengthening the local economy tends to fuel market forces that accelerate speculation, increase property values, raise taxes and rents, and ultimately—perversely—drive many residents out of the area. By capturing the social increment in land and housing, the CLT can control these market forces, while securing the community's present residential base and locking in the benefits of outside subsidies and internal improvement for long-time community residents.

Finally, every community has an interest in leaving a long-term *legacy* of thoughtful planning and preservation for its future members. This legacy is secured by the CLT's perpetual ownership of local lands. In the end, no method of land use control can be as effective as outright ownership—the method employed by the CLT. The use and development of CLT lands are guided by plans drafted by a committee of the CLT and enforced by means of the lease agreement negotiated between the CLT and individual leaseholders. Some lands are leased for residential use. Some are reserved for present and future productive, commercial, or industrial activity. Some, requiring a more conservationist approach, may be managed directly by the CLT as forests, farmland, urban parks, or protected wilderness. Urban CLTs in Trenton and Boston have proceeded in conjunction with ongoing community garden programs. New Communities, Inc., directly manages all of its arable land as a cooperative farm. The Monadnock CLT has joined with other landowners in southern New Hampshire in developing a cooperative forest-management program for the owners and leaseholders of small woodlots.

Of equal importance to local planning is the social legacy. Here, the diverse interests of individuals and communities coincide. Since the time of Jefferson, Americans have professed a policy goal of giving as many citizens as possible an ownership interest in real property. Not only has this been seen as a matter of simple justice, but also as a way of promoting good citizenship and stable communities. As fewer households come to have the security, equity, and legacy that ownership affords—and as those that have them are threatened with their loss—the character and stability of many communities are jeopardized, along with whatever private investment and political participation that these ownership interests encourage. One of the finest legacies which a community may bequeath to the next generation, therefore, is the opportunity for most of its members to acquire these interests for themselves, their families, and their heirs. The CLT—by promoting access, limiting owner equity, and guiding community development—becomes the locally accountable steward of this social legacy.

These are the kinds of community interests that speculation does the most to thwart. Moreover, these are the kinds of individual interests that the private market in real estate is less and less able to secure—*even for families of the middle class.* This impasse occurs at a time when the other traditions of land reform appear to have reached, perhaps temporarily, the limits of their own political acceptability. Out of this situation, among grass-roots groups struggling to realize these *same* community and individual interests, there has arisen a growing willingness to experiment with the CLT model, adapting it to meet particular circumstances and needs.

The Land Trust as Land Reform

The strengths and weaknesses of the CLT as an actual method of land reform can now be explored in some detail. The three definitional elements of land reform, discussed earlier, serve as something of a general yardstick against which to measure the model's effectiveness. What, then, is the CLT's potential—and its limitations— in (1) solving the land-related problems caused by speculation; (2) changing the tenure system; and (3) transferring property, power, and status from one social class to another?

Land Reform Potential of the CLT

The effectiveness of the CLT in treating the *symptoms* of speculation has already been examined. The CLT is capable of ameliorating the most harmful social, economic, and environmental consequences of valuing land primarily as a profitable commodity. It is able to secure precisely those community interests that are made so precarious by speculation and its twin offspring, absenteeism and land monopolization. But the CLT goes further than this, for it treats the *causes* of speculation as well. The underlying system of land tenure that permits and promotes speculation is fundamentally changed within the CLT's domain.

Reallocating equity, by whatever means, removes the speculative incentive from land. The imbalance produced by the private market in real estate, where a property's use value becomes subordinate to its exchange value, is reversed. The exchange value is taxed or taken away. Land, for the most part, ceases to be a commodity. The CLT, in particular, accomplishes this feat by permanently removing land from the marketplace. Once land is acquired, it is never again resold. Future transactions occur by lease, not by sale.

The lease itself represents a significant tenure reform, a marked departure from the way that land is usually rented in the United States. The lease is long term, typically extending for many years. It is automatically renewable, upon the leaseholder's request. It is inheritable, with the leaseholder able to bequeath use rights to specified heirs. Furthermore, it contains provisions which protect both the quality of life for the leaseholder (privacy, quiet enjoyment of property, freedom of association and belief, flexibility of land use and development within negotiated parameters, etc.) and the environmental quality of the leasehold itself.[21]

The tenure system is further transformed by limiting the equity that homeowners receive from the property they own. The CLT goes one step beyond the reallocation prescribed by Henry George. It claims not only the socially created value embedded in land, but the socially created value that becomes attached to structural improvements as well. Achieved by means of the lease agreement and a first option (held by the CLT) on any improvements, a ceiling is placed on the owner's equity. Housing and other improvements are made less a commodity than ever before.

The third element of land reform is, in many respects, the most important. Unless a model can redistribute property, power, and status among social classes, transferring control over land-based resources from those who have to those who have not, the land reform potential of that model must be considered rather small. This will usually be true even if the model is quite effective otherwise in solving various land-related problems or in actually changing the established system of land tenure.

The CLT distributes the privileges of property more widely than before. Access to land and housing is increased for the community's current residents and preserved for the low- and moderate-income residents of future generations. There is, moreover, an implicit transfer of landed wealth in the CLT's enforcement of equity limitation. Value embedded in real property, customarily reserved for the home owner alone, is now shared with members of the larger community—present and future.

As a complement to equity transfers of this type, the CLT may also be effective in *preventing* the transfer of land and housing *away* from low- and moderate-income families. This is, in fact, precisely the hope of those who have organized CLTs in the rapidly changing inner-city neighborhoods of Cincinnati and Trenton. Their expectation is that the CLT may be able to acquire enough of the neighborhood's real property, in advance of the invasion of affluent investors, to reserve a portion of the locality's land and housing for less affluent families who already live there.

The transfer of power and status may be less apparent than the transfer of property, but still may be very real. Propertylessness and powerlessness tend to go together. As more property is brought under the control of the CLT and gradually removed from the grasp of absentee owners or indigenous landlords, the power to plan and develop the local community is returned to local hands and distributed among the many, not just the privileged few. The CLT provides the institutional vehicle by which such power may be both wielded and shared.

The contribution of the CLT to local empowerment, however, may go beyond granting local people greater control over the use and development of lands within its domain. Inherent in the base of community support on which the CLT is founded is a potential *political* base from which may be mounted local demands for further transfers of property, power, and status. The CLT is a membership organization, with a community-wide constituency. This constituency includes not only the CLT's lease-holders, but anyone who wishes to support the CLT's attempt to solve the many land-related problems that plague most local communities. In striking a unique balance between individual and community interests in land, the CLT has a special ability to pull together diverse groups of people—even across ideological and class lines. The CLT either puts together its own grass-roots organization or works to strengthen community-based organizations which already exist. Organizations of this sort will often perform an advocacy role on behalf of powerless groups within the community or in defense of the community itself, often exacting significant transfers of wealth and power from economic and political elites.

Finally, it should be noted that empowerment also has a personal dimension. The CLT provides a modicum of residential and (perhaps) economic security for persons who are normally reluctant to participate in political action because of the precariousness of their own circumstances. Political activism and personal security may be closely linked. Persons without security of tenure, in residence or job, are often slow to press for improved conditions or to confront powers-that-be for redress of grievance; conversely, the same persons, when granted more security, will frequently display a greater willingness to act politically in the interests of themselves and their neighbors (see Salamon, 1974; Cox, 1982). The community land trust may underwrite the expanded political involvement—and empowerment—of persons of modest means.

Land Reform Limitations of the CLT

There are, however, several limitations in the land trust model of land reform. The model makes no frontal assault on the large concentrations of property and power which already abound in the United States. Only within its own domain does the CLT effect an actual transfer of property; only within the confines of its own beachhead does the CLT change the inequitable tenure system. The pattern of landownership and the institutional framework of land tenure in the rest of the country remain intact. Although there may eventually be enough CLTs with enough property to constitute an alternative to the status quo, the current reality is that CLTs are still few in number and most are fairly small. Established one community at a time, CLTs would seem a painfully slow, expensive, and piecemeal approach to land reform.

As a community-by-community affair, CLTs may also contribute to the "balkanization" of a city or region. The public interest of the individual community, organized around a CLT, may not be consistent with the public interest of society as a whole—or the interests of other communities in the same city or region. A region dotted with CLTs, each with a political base in its local community, may degenerate into a struggle of each against all, each community competing with every other for land, subsidies, loans, and political support.[22]

There may even exist serious legal limitations that will render the CLT model ineffective. Land and housing in the United States are legally treated as commodities, freely traded at the highest price agreeable to both buyers and sellers. The value inherent in a parcel of property (minus outstanding liens and liabilities) belongs to the person who holds the deed. But the CLT operates on the assumption that land and housing should *not* be commodities and that equity buildup does *not* necessarily or entirely belong to the individual property owner. Because the CLT acts to limit the equity of its leaseholders, it risks someday running afoul of the legal prohibition against "unreasonable restraint" on the buying and selling of property. This is not idle conjecture. As CLTs begin to amass larger holdings, the likelihood grows of legal challenges from local real estate interests, threatened by the CLT's expanding store of property and power, or from a disgruntled leaseholder, rebelling against the CLT's attempt to impose a ceiling on the profitability of his home.

There are reasons, however, for believing that these limitations will prove less of a problem than they might at first appear. It is true that CLTs will not soon have a major impact on national, regional, or city-wide patterns of landownership and land use. Even so, at the community level, CLTs can—and do—make a difference now. CLTs can reduce the absentee ownership of land and housing and spread the benefits of ownership more widely. They can retard speculation and give communities a new way of resisting displacement and guiding their own development. They also perform an important pedagogical function: teaching people to understand and accept new tenure arrangements, while encouraging them to develop innovative arrangements of their own. The community land trust is perhaps at a stage of development and acceptance today comparable to the stage that zoning had reached in the early 1920s. The CLT stands on the brink of wider adoption, legal sanction, and years of experimentation and fine-tuning. There is ample reason to proceed.

This does not, of course, completely address the problem of expense. Land and housing are costly acquisitions. Unless public powers and public funds are eventually offered in support of land trust expansion, it is difficult to see how CLTs can ever control enough property to have an appreciable effect on speculation, absenteeism, and long-term community development. But even without state support, CLTs have made significant progress. The Community Land Cooperative of Cincinnati (CLCC), to take a single example, started out in 1980 with no assets whatsoever. In the next two years, by combining gifts and bargain sales of property with grants and low-interest loans from individuals, churches, and religious orders, CLCC managed to acquire ten buildings—over twenty units of housing—valued at more than $250,000. More acquisitions are underway. Admittedly, this barely begins to meet the land and housing needs of this inner-city community. Yet twenty families that would have faced displacement from the next wave of gentrification have found secure housing through the CLT. Land is being gradually acquired; housing is being provided; people are being helped. However difficult, a start has been made.

Meanwhile, community land trusts have already begun confronting the problem of balkanization. Most CLTs reserve at least a third of the seats on their boards for public-interest representatives—persons who are not necessarily members of the CLT or even members of the immediate community. CLTs are also urged to include at least one representative from *outside* the community—preferably someone from another CLT.[23] This strategy offers a possible long-term solution to the problem of intercommunity rivalry: municipal or regional federations of CLTs, linking one community with another.

The prospect of legal challenge will probably loom over CLTs for many years to come. Yet the notion that equity buildup contains a social increment that society may claim as its own—an idea at the heart of the CLT—has recently won unexpected endorsement from an influential corner of the legal community, the New York Court of Appeals. In the case of *Penn Central Transportation Company* v. *New York City*,[24] the court had to decide whether the plaintiff was unconstitutionally deprived of a "reasonable return" from its investment in Grand Central Terminal when the city's Landmarks Preservation Commission refused to allow construction of an office tower above the terminal. Deciding against the plaintiff, the court noted that "society as an organized entity . . . has created much of the value of the terminal property."[25] A private owner has the right to a reasonable return only on that portion of a property's value created by his own investment:

> It is that privately created and privately managed ingredient which is the property on which the reasonable return is to be based. All else is society's contribution by the sweat of its brow and the expenditure of its funds. To that extent society is also entitled to its due.[26]

Appealed to the U.S. Supreme Court in 1978, the ruling of the New York court was upheld, but on different grounds.[27] Nationally, the question of socially created value was put aside for another day, even though "the social increment theory should still be considered good law in New York" (Scott, 1978:317). The case suggests that a new idea of property value is clearly in the air—one that seems remarkably consistent with the reallocation of equity pursued by the CLT.[28]

> What seems to be emerging is a concept of property value more relevant to the reality of the contemporary, highly interdependent system of urban land use. The concept would not seek to deny an individual the fruits of his labors but would examine increments in property value to ascertain what proportion might have been directly the result of collective action. . . . (Conrad and Merriam, 1978:24–25)

Whatever the present limitations in the land trust model of land reform, there is reason to believe that they will neither undermine nor unduly restrict the model's effectiveness. Considered by itself, the CLT holds great potential. Yet the CLT will seldom function *by itself*; in the short run and in the long, CLTs will coexist with other land reform measures. There is much advantage in this, for there are many ways in which the CLT may complement these other models and programs, representing other traditions of land reform. Such complementarities enhance the effectiveness of the CLT while reducing the most common flaws in these other approaches to land reform.

Complements and Conclusions

Redistributing ownership is not completely alien to the United States. There seems little chance of the state soon moving to dissolve the huge holdings of our latter-day land barons, but sporadic redistribution does occur and is likely to increase. In the 1970s, for instance, West Virginia's governor used the power of eminent domain to seize lands of an absentee-owned land company in order to provide housing for victims of a devastating flood. In the nation's largest cities, where housing shortages are beginning to reach crisis proportions, pressure is mounting on municipal officials to move more quickly against the owners of tax-delinquent, substandard, and abandoned properties and to turn them over to tenants' unions and other community-based organizations. Such a strategy avoids a common problem of public ownership— the tendency for condemned property either to deteriorate while awaiting a public use or to slip back into a private use that benefits only a privileged few. CLTs provide an excellent vehicle for receiving such property, developing or rehabilitating it for residential (or other) use, and keeping it available and affordable for community residents, one generation after another. A Boston CLT has already been offered a multi-unit apartment building taken in receivership by the local housing court. The Cedar-Riverside CLT in Minneapolis may eventually acquire nearly 300 housing units that the city's community development agency was left holding upon the collapse of a large federal project.

Should the federal government eventually return to a distributionist policy of subsidizing home ownership for families of limited means, CLTs would also be effective guardians of these public funds. When a public subsidy goes into a property to improve its condition or increase its affordability for low- and moderate-income families, the subsidy should remain with the property. Otherwise, the subsidy must be repeated again and again—at increasing amounts—each time the property is sold. This has been the flaw in many housing and community development programs of the past. The CLT, on the other hand, is able to lock in public subsidies, assuring that public monies continue to provide public benefits—not unearned profits for a small handful of lucky homeowners.

Within the tradition of *restricting use,* land use planning and environmental protection can both be strengthened by a CLT. The Ottauquechee Regional Land Trust in Vermont, for example, was founded in 1977 to retain open space and preserve agricultural land in ways that public restrictions could not. The situation demanded a private nonprofit entity that could acquire threatened lands and channel them into the hands of individuals willing to put them to environmentally benign uses. The Ottauquechee Trust deviates somewhat from the basic CLT model, but its success in working with local planners to guide development in socially desirable directions has been repeated by CLTs of every kind. The willingness of CLTs to participate actively in land use planning and environmental stewardship was clearly revealed in a 1980 survey of American CLTs. Over half of the thirty-one respondents included "environmental preservation" among their founding ratio-nales (Geisler, 1980b).[29]

Community land trusts may even complement models of land reform that *reallo-cate equity* through taxation. As John Costonis (1977:417) has remarked, the innova-tive reasoning in the Grand Central Terminal case lends "implicit support for public measures that seek partial recapture of private property's social increment of value to finance community amenities." Such measures may take the form of a tax on prop-erty sales (as is done in Vermont's land gains tax) or an annual assessment on the ap-preciating value of property, but the problem will remain of ensuring that recaptured value is productively and equitably reinvested in the local community—a problem which the CLT may help to solve.

Tax increment financing is a case in point. Tax increment financing implicitly ac-cepts the Georgist notion, mirrored in the Grand Central Terminal opinion, that the community has a right to share in increases in property value brought about by com-munity development. (Contrary to Georgist theory, however, the community shares in the appreciating value of buildings, as well as land.) In a typical project making use of this financing tool, a municipality designates certain neighborhoods as "tax increment districts" and records the current volume of property taxes being collected from these districts. Then, in ensuing years, any increments collected over this base volume are returned directly to each district and used to capitalize local redevelop-ment projects. Variations of this scheme are used in fourteen states, most extensively in California and Minnesota (Davidson, 1979).

Minneapolis provides an instructive example of both the use and abuse of such social increment financing. Specified districts in Minneapolis receive millions of dol-lars in tax increment funds to promote community development. However, local resi-dents contend that only in the Cedar-Riverside neighborhood have these funds been used to benefit the entire community. The difference in Cedar-Riverside has been the presence of a strong tenants' union, a community-controlled development corpora-tion, and a community-wide technical assistance and advocacy group. A community land trust was added to this ensemble in 1981. A local activist had this to say:

> If [tax increment financing] is not abused, it's a really good tool for the city to
> use to get neighborhoods developed. Unfortunately, in Minneapolis this is
> the only project that is not a prime example of abuse of tax increment funds.
> What it has turned out to be is just a free pot for big developers. And I think
> without the strong neighborhood involvement in this project, that's exactly
> what it would be here, too.[30]

Recapturing the social increment in property is not enough. Just as public subsidies for housing and community development often wind up in private pockets, socially created value may be returned to private developers and do little to promote wider access to land and housing, encourage local development, or preserve the community's legacy for its future members. Community land trusts, like the one in Cedar-Riverside, can serve as community-based complements to state and municipal programs that reallocate equity through taxation, ensuring that these public funds are put to more equitable, productive, and permanent use.

The CLT, therefore, may enhance the effectiveness of a wide assortment of public measures designed to correct various defects in the present system of land tenure. Complementing these public programs, drawn from all three traditions of land reform, the CLT may itself be made more effective. There is another complementarity, however, that is *not* dependent upon public policies or programs. The CLT may support—and be, in turn, supported by—"private" indigenous efforts to defend or develop the local community. As in Cedar-Riverside, the CLT can complement existing organizations and ongoing movements of insurgency, improvement, or reform. Land is a thread running through many community-based endeavors. Issues intersect. Constituencies overlap. The CLT may become advantageously entwined in an ever-widening web of local affiliation and mutual aid.

Within such a web, land reform and community reform are drawn together, meeting and mixing in the CLT. The CLT expands the focus of traditional community development practice, interjecting issues of landownership and land use into the midst of other efforts to empower and rehabilitate the local community. At the same time, the CLT's involvement in such grass-roots endeavors expands the focus of its own tradition of land reform. Reallocating equity becomes a means not only of stopping the reign of speculation, but of starting community redevelopment; a means not only of removing socially created value from private hands, but of returning the power to plan and develop to local hands. Land reform and community reform tend to become two sides of the same movement—the warp and woof of a changing pattern of property and power, given form by the CLT.

By itself, therefore, the CLT may begin to address many of the land-related problems that plague urban and rural communities throughout the United States. The CLT is an effective instrument of land reform. Its effectiveness, however, does not depend upon itself alone. The community land trust is a remarkably gregarious model, teaming well with other measures of tenurial, political, and economic reform. It is in conjunction with these other measures that the CLT will have its greatest effect and fulfill its highest potential, now and in the foreseeable future.

NOTES

The critical comments of Charles Geisler and Chuck Matthei at various stages of this manuscript's preparation are gratefully acknowledged.

1. "Tradition" is used in preference to terms like "strategy" or "technique" because I wish to suggest a more general and long-standing pattern of perception and practice—a distinctive way of seeing and doing land reform that has been handed down by example, writing, and word of mouth. There is, as well, an older meaning that makes the term especially

appropriate here. In Roman, civil, and Scottish law, tradition has meant "the transfer or acquisition of property by mere delivery with intent of both parties to transfer the title . . ." (*Webster's Third International Dictionary*). A "tradition" of land reform therefore has the connotation of one party surrendering property to another.

2. Excepting the question of ownership—i.e., to whom the equity belongs—this definition is consistent with the conception of equity generally held by those who deal in real estate. See, for instance, the definition of "equity" proposed by Wiedemer (1980:346).

3. Two definitional criteria of land reform that are frequently mentioned—but rejected here—are land reform as a rapid, drastic process (see Tai, 1974) and land reform as a product of compulsory state power.

4. There are three clarifications that should be noted at the outset. First, while the focus here will be on land, the discussion will frequently extend to housing and to other forms of real property. Second, despite the habit of many writers of using "land reform" and "agrarian reform" interchangeably, the present discussion will consider land reform as both a rural and urban phenomenon. Finally, examples of land reform in other countries will be presented only in passing; the focus will be on land reform in the United States.

5. This distinction between "distributionist reform" and "collectivist reform" is suggested by Lipton (1974).

6. The Resettlement and the Farm Security Administrations contained certain collectivist ingredients as well. Even though the establishment of viable family farms and subsistence homesteads remained the primary objective of these New Deal agencies, both supported the development of model communities and large-scale agricultural cooperatives. Such "collectivist" elements later made the FSA quite vulnerable to red-baiting attacks from the Right.

7. During the final years of the Civil War, Northern military authorities distributed a number of confiscated and abandoned plantations to over 40,000 former slaves, who successfully worked the land as small farmers until President Johnson returned these estates to their original white owners (Moore, 1966:145). Such cases of redistribution are rare in U.S. history. Redistributing the ownership of land has not been a topic of serious discussion among policymakers since the Great Depression, when the need for agrarian land reform was a subject of intense national debate, with those who favored distributionist reform pitted against those who favored a more collectivist approach. For an excellent review of this debate, see Gilbert and Brown (1981).

8. Though the police power is the principal means of carrying out this tradition, the importance of tax incentives and disincentives in restricting and guiding the use of land should not be ignored, nor should the utilization of private restrictions on land, such as covenants and easements.

9. "The dubious tradition of land speculation is so strongly embedded in the American character that it is probably only realistic to take it as a given. Many Americans who are not land speculators at least aspire to be. As a result, the public at large seems unwilling to constrain the freedom to speculate. Indeed, such constraints, when proposed, are attacked as outright un-American" (Hite, 1979:65).

10. As of 1979, land prices had declined in only nine years of the twentieth century. Eight of these years were during the Great Depression (Hite, 1979:62).

11. "According to a recent study by the Harvard-MIT Joint Center for Urban Studies, less than one-quarter of U.S. households can now afford to buy a home, compared to two-thirds in the 1930s" (Atlas and Dreier, 1980:14).

12. An introduction to the thought of Henry George can be found in George (1975), Andelson (1979), and Ross (1982).

13. In Georgist thought, there is a decided bias in favor of pushing all land to its "highest and best" use. Land which is "idle" is regarded as one of the worst symptoms of land

speculation. This bias has been a source of much antagonism between Georgists and conservationists. Even more antagonistic have been the relations between Georgists and social reformers of the Marxian Left, who have accused George of being so concerned with the monopolization of land that he ignored the monopolization of capital—and the exploitation of labor.

14. Under the New Towns Act of 1946, twenty new towns were founded in Great Britain, essentially conforming to the "garden city" model proposed by Ebenezer Howard in 1898 (see Howard, 1965). Howard proposed the permanent municipal ownership of land as a means whereby equity buildup could be used to promote the public good rather than to enrich a privileged few.

15. The credit for this synthesis belongs, in large measure, to Robert Swann and the late Ralph Borsodi, the intellectual fathers of the CLT model. For the original formulation of this model, see Swann's book, *The Community Land Trust: A Guide to a New Model for Land Tenure in America* (International Independence Institute, 1972).

16. This limited-equity formula varies from one CLT to another. Each CLT must decide for itself the precise balance that it wishes to strike between fairness to the present lease-holder and fairness to future ones. Some CLTs, wishing to make housing as affordable as possible for future generations, will allow present leaseholders only a dollar-for-dollar return on anything invested in acquisition and capital improvement. Other CLTs, wishing to be more generous to present leaseholders, will factor in adjustments for inflation and the time value of money. For an excellent discussion of the kinds of choices and trade-offs that confront a CLT in deciding upon a limited-equity formula, see Kirkpatrick (1981). Even though his subject is equity limitation in housing cooperatives, Kirkpatrick's remarks are relevant to CLTs as well.

17. Specific CLTs will be mentioned only to illustrate specific points in the text, not to hold these few cases up as ideal applications for the CLT model. The fact remains that the CLT is a fairly recent innovation. Few CLTs are old enough or large enough to serve as full-blown examples of what a CLT can do.

18. This discussion of community and individual "interests" draws upon material in chapters 1 and 2, Institute for Community Economics, *The Community Land Trust Handbook* (1982:1–35). An earlier version of some of the same ideas appeared in Matthei (1981).

19. While all CLTs are chartered as nonprofit corporations, not all are exempt from federal and state income taxes. Those that have obtained tax-exempt status under 501(c)(3) of the IRS Code tend to work primarily on low-income housing or environmental protection. None have sought exemption from local property taxes. CLTs do not remove land and housing from local tax rolls.

20. But many CLTs will not use lands held in trust as collateral, fearing that these lands might be lost through foreclosure.

21. See "Model Lease Agreement" for CLTs, available from the Institute for Community Economics, 151 Montague City Road, Greenfield, MA 01301.

22. A more general political critique—one leveled against the entire neighborhood movement and the institutions arising out of it—is that organizing around place instead of class will inevitably diffuse the power of low-income, minority, and working-class populations. According to this view, territorial consciousness and class consciousness are incompatible. Yet the CLT is merely a means to an end, not an end in itself. Incumbent upon the organizers of a CLT is the responsibility for determining the uses and ends to which this instrument will be put.

23. See "Model CLT By-laws," available from the Institute for Community Economics, 151 Montague City Road, Greenfield, MA 01301.

24. 366 N.E. 2d 1271 (1977).

25. Ibid., at 1275.

26. Ibid., at 1273.

27. 438 U.S. at 121 n. 23 (1978).

28. New ideas of property *rights* are in the air as well—and these, too, are conducive to CLT development. John Cribbet (1978:677), for instance, has predicted that in the near future: "The non-freehold estate will come into its own. . . . The diminishing fee will be further eroded as the lease becomes more like 'true' ownership and, at times, it will be difficult to say who has the greater bundle of sticks, the landlord or the tenant. Even today, the long-term leasehold is a major form of land holding with great advantages in terms of financing, land use control, and investment opportunities."

29. Land use planning and environmental protection, placed in the hands of CLTs, would also seem to satisfy those critics of traditional restrictions on use who decry the confiscatory nature of zoning and other police-power regulations, and who fear the centralization of land use planning in higher and higher units of government. See, for example, McClaughry (1976:528–29, in particular).

30. Dorothy Jacobs, quoted on pp. 112–13 of Institute for Community Economics (1982).

REFERENCES

Andelson, Robert V. (ed.). 1979. *Critics of Henry George.* Cranbury, NJ: Associated University Presses.

Atlas, John, and Dreier, Peter. 1980. "The housing crisis and the tenants' revolt." *Social Policy* 10 (January/February).

Cigler, Beverly, and Vasu, Michael. 1982. "Housing and public policy in America." *Public Administration Review* 42 (January/February).

Conkin, Paul K. 1959. *Tomorrow a New World: The New Deal Community Program.* Ithaca, NY: Cornell University Press.

Conrad, Jon M., and Merriam, Dwight H. 1978. "Compensation in TDR programs: Grand Central Station and the search for the Holy Grail." *University of Detroit Journal of Urban Law* 56 (Fall).

Costonis, John J. 1977. "The disparity issue: a context for the Grand Central Terminal decision." *Harvard Law Review* 91 (December).

Cox, Kevin R. 1982. "Housing tenure and neighborhood activism." *Urban Affairs Quarterly* 18 (September).

Cribbet, John E. 1978. "Property in the twenty-first century." *Ohio State Law Journal* 39.

Davidson, Jonathan. 1979. "Tax increment financing as a tool for community redevelopment." *Journal of Urban Law* 56.

Dorner, Peter. 1972. *Land Reform and Economic Development.* Baltimore: Penguin Books.

Galbraith, John Kenneth. 1951. "Conditions for economic change in under-developed countries." *Journal of Farm Economics* 33.

Geisler, Charles C. 1980a. "The quiet revolution in land use control revisited." In *The Rural Sociology of the Advanced Societies.* Edited by F. H. Buttel and H. Newby. Montclair, NJ: Allanheld, Osmun.

———. 1980b. "In land we trust." *Cornell Journal of Social Relations* 15 (Fall).

George, Henry. 1975. *Progress and Poverty.* New York: Robert Schalkenbach Foundation.

Gilbert, Jess, and Brown, Steve. 1981. "Alternative land reform proposals in the 1930s: the Nashville Agrarians and the Southern Tenant Farmers' Union." *Agricultural History* 55 (October): 351–69.

Glickfeld, Madelyn, and Hagman, Donald G. 1978. "Special capital and real estate windfalls taxes." In *Windfalls for Wipeouts: Land Value Capture and Compensation.* Edited by D. G. Hagman and D. F. Misczynski. Chicago: American Society of Planning Officials.

Hagman, Donald G. 1974. "Windfalls for wipeouts." In *The Good Earth of America: Planning Our Land Use.* Edited by C. L. Harriss. Englewood Cliffs, NJ: Prentice-Hall.

———, and Misczynski, Dean F. 1978. *Windfalls for Wipeouts: Land Value Capture and Compensation.* Chicago: American Society of Planning Officials.

Hite, James C. 1979. *Room and Situation: The Political Economy of Land-Use Policy.* Chicago: Nelson-Hall.

Howard, Ebenezer. 1965. *Garden Cities of Tomorrow.* Cambridge, MA: M.I.T. Press.

Institute for Community Economics. 1982. *The Community Land Trust Handbook.* Emmaus, PA: Rodale Press.

Kirkpatrick, David H. 1981. "Limiting the equity in housing cooperatives: choices and tradeoffs." In *Legal Issues in the Development of Housing Cooperatives.* Report XI. Berkeley: Economic Development and Law Center.

LeGates, Richard, and Hartman, Chester. 1981. "Displacement." *Clearinghouse Review* (National Clearinghouse for Legal Services) 15 (July).

Linton, Erica. 1970. *Gramdan—Revolution by Persuasion.* London: Headley Brothers.

Lipton, Michael. 1974. "Towards a theory of land reform." In *Peasants, Landlords, and Governments: Agrarian Reform in the Third World.* Edited by D. Lehman. New York: Holmes & Meier.

Matthei, Charles. 1981. "Community land trusts as a resource for community economic development." In *Financing Community-Based Development.* Edited by Richard Schramm. Ithaca, NY: Cornell University, Department of City and Regional Planning. pp. 99–106.

McClaughry, John. 1975. "Rural land banking: the Canadian experience." *North Carolina Central Law Journal* 7.

———. 1976. "Farmers, freedom, and feudalism." *South Dakota Law Review* 21 (Summer).

Moore, Barrington. 1966. *Social Origins of Dictatorship and Democracy.* Boston: Beacon Press.

Orni, Efraim. 1972. *Agrarian Reform and Social Progress in Israel.* Jerusalem: Ahva Cooperative Press.

Popper, Frank J. 1981. *The Politics of Land-Use Reform.* Madison, WI: University of Wisconsin Press.

Ross, Steven F. 1982. "Political economy for the masses: Henry George." *Democracy* 2 (July).

Salamon, Lester M. 1974. "The time dimension in policy evaluation: the case of the New Deal land reform experiments." Paper presented at the annual meeting of the American Political Science Association, Chicago, Illinois.

Scheiber, Harry N. 1975. "Property, law, expropriation and resource allocation by government: the United States, 1789–1910." *Journal of Economic History* 33.

Scott, Thane De Nimmo. 1978. "Alas in Wonderland: the impact of Penn Central upon historic preservation law and policy." *Boston College Environmental Affairs Law Review* 7.

Strong, Ann L. 1979. *Land Banking: European Reality, American Prospect.* Baltimore: Johns Hopkins University Press.

Swann, Robert (International Independence Institute). 1972. *The Community Land Trust: A Guide to a New Model for Land Tenure.* Boston: Center for Community Economic Development.

Tai, Hung-Chao. 1974. *Land Reform and Politics: A Comparative Analysis.* Berkeley: University of California Press.

U.S. Congress, House Subcommittee on the City. 1980. *Compact Cities: Energy Saving Strategies for the Eighties.* Subcommittee Report, Ninety-sixth Congress, Second Session (July). Washington, DC: U.S. Government Printing Office.

U.S. Department of Agriculture. 1981. *A Time to Choose: Summary Report on the Structure of Agriculture.* Washington, DC: U.S. Department of Agriculture.

Walker, Richard A., and Heiman, Michael K. 1981. "A quiet revolution for whom?" *Annals of the Association of American Geographers* 71 (March).

Wiedemer, John P. 1980. *Real Estate Finance.* Third Edition. Reston, VA: Reston Publishing Co.

U.S. Land Reform Movements

The Theory Behind the Practice

Chuck Matthei
(1992)

In the course of the 1980s, housing became a topic high on anyone's list of social ills in the country. From the *Wall Street Journal* to *The Nation* to *Better Homes and Gardens,* magazines and newspapers featured major articles drawing the public's attention to "the housing crisis." Since then, the crisis has grown, but housing is only the very tip of what are in fact a series of real estate problems ranging from homelessness to an increasingly difficult struggle for middle-class people to own a home, from small businesses unable to pay inflated rents to the collapse of family farms, and culminating in the savings and loan debacle—which is, in significant measure, a real estate fiasco.

In the prevailing economic circumstances, budget constraints are seriously limiting the availability of subsidies at a time when needs are growing. Many traditional housing and social welfare programs are diminishing or disappearing. Resistance to increased taxation is strong, and policymakers are stymied in their efforts to address the problems. Yet ironically, this dilemma may also create an opportunity for innovation and reform, if advocates can reinterpret the economic roots of social problems and offer a renewed vision of the relationship between individuals and communities. With housing on the public agenda amid a continuing atmosphere of crisis, we may be able to broaden the issue and change some of the most fundamental aspects of how we think about real estate and property.

What Can Be Done?

Today, in the midst of a recession and faced with an ever-mounting national debt, the capacities of states and cities are diminished, and the prospects for renewed federal commitment are slim. Real estate markets have softened, but the lot of the poor has not materially improved, and many people have been added to the ranks of the unemployed.

Traditional housing programs are simply inadequate and economically inefficient in this situation. Public housing, while an important component of the low-income housing stock, provides only limited opportunities to residents and meets consider-

---

This article was originally published in *Social Policy* (Spring 1992): 36–45. It is reprinted by permission of *Social Policy.*

able opposition in many communities. Public subsidy of private rental housing, on the other hand, perpetuates patterns of absentee ownership. And even subsidized homeownership ultimately results in a loss of subsidies and a loss of affordability: since when any private housing is resold on the open market, the substantial amounts invested by government are reaped by the current owner. The seller benefits, but the community's need for affordable housing is not met unless the same units are subsidized over and over again—an increasingly difficult prospect.

An effective housing program must achieve three objectives. It must provide decent, affordable housing to those who most need it today, with the essential benefits of homeownership where appropriate. It must preserve the affordability of these units, without requiring an endless succession of subsidies. And it must build an economic base in these communities, to enable them to meet a greater share of their own needs over time. These are simply practical necessities. Meeting them, however, will ultimately produce a different conception of "public/private partnerships," and of property itself.

The Wrong Approach

The housing crisis is primarily a structural problem, rooted in our failure to acknowledge the legitimacy, quantify the contributions, and craft a fair balance of both private and public interests. Unfortunately, most policymakers, the general public, and even a large segment of the nonprofit development sector still treat housing as a social service or commodity supply problem. As such, it is considered to be uniquely a problem of poor people and their deficiencies, to be addressed by providing charitable subsidies to the needy or incentives to the market to enhance production.

Three prevalent myths distort our perspective and prevent us from striking at the true roots of the problem:

The Myth of Poverty
Poverty is not simply or even primarily a lack of income. There are many people who lack sufficient income to adequately meet their basic needs in the marketplace, but an examination of the housing economy of many low-income communities makes it clear that the problem is deeper and more comlex.

Over their rental lifetimes, many low-income people will pay not only a higher percentage of their incomes for (often substandard) housing, but a great number of times the original market value of the units they occupy. In other words, they will pay more than would have been required to purchase their homes, and more than many homeowners pay for far better housing.

The problem is not simply the amount of cash flowing *in* to the community, but the rate at which it flows *out*. Low-income communities are unable to retain and reinvest their earnings and build equity. Their poverty is misinterpreted by many as a lack of economic capacity, or even a deficiency of character. But the problem is rooted in patterns of ownership and the credit barriers that prevent those affected from changing them.

While American society in general offers broader opportunities for property ownership than most others, the rate of absentee ownership in low-income communities is often as high as 75 and even 90 percent. This is true in both small urban neighborhoods and large rural areas. "Land reform" is a concept typically associated with underdeveloped countries, yet the statistical realities and human needs are very similar in many parts of the United States.

The Myth of Wealth

The prevalent view in the United States is that property value is a single sum earned by the owner through hard work, wise investment, or good luck. What this view leaves out is the public contribution to property value.

When individuals purchase properties, they acquire something of value; when they improve their properties—by investing additional capital or labor—they add value. But value is also added by public investment in infrastructure and services, community development activity, and larger economic and social forces. The law describes property as a "bundle of rights," but the corollary principle that "property value is a bundle of values" is not equally recognized.

Recent federal court decisions have required that property owners be compensated when new zoning regulations significantly *reduce* their property's market value (a "partial taking"). On its face, this principle seems reasonable and fair, but, if so, it should be fairly applied to both "partners." When a new subway line is installed in a low-income neighborhood of Washington, DC, not only will there likely be substantial windfall profits to absentee owners of properties near each subway station, but renters may be disadvantaged or displaced as a result—and the same taxpayers who paid for the subway may be asked to pay for emergency shelters and higher rent subsidies. Value can be reduced by public actions and public policies, but it can also be enhanced; the public should share responsibility for reducing property values, but it should also share in the benefits of increasing them.

In a sense, property taxes and capital gains taxes lay some claim to this social appreciation in value, but they do not effect an equitable distribution of value according to its source. Moreover, the common perception is that taxation is a confiscation of privately generated wealth, rather than an acknowledgment of the community's contribution and an assertion of its legitimate interest.

The Myth of Public Assistance

The notion that public assistance is a process by which government takes from those who have earned it and gives to those who haven't (but probably should have) is a simplistic attitude that results in both economic and social discrimination.

In reality, there are two ways in which government typically subsidizes housing. Most assistance to the poor is provided through tax collections and budget appropriations. Recipients benefit, but they are also stigmatized by their dependence (the assumption often being that their lack of economic resources reflects a deficiency of capacity and character). Allocations are usually annually determined, forcing the poor and their advocates to "beg" year after year.

The other major avenue for subsidies is the tax code, which provides a variety of deductions and benefits to property owners (but usually not to renters). In contrast to direct appropriations, these tax benefits are rarely acknowledged to be subsidies, they are not stigmatized, they are not annually reviewed—and, in great disproportion, they accrue to the wealthiest sectors of society, not the poor or even the middle class (who bear a heavy share of the tax burden, but do not qualify for appropriated subsidies). The home mortgage interest deduction alone represents many times as much in foregone revenue as the total amount spent on housing subsidies for the poor each year. The national commitment to facilitating homeownership is understandable, but it can hardly justify deductions on $1 million of investment and on second homes as well as primary residences.

From Subsidy to Equity

It is time now to move from a policy of subsidy to one of equity. "Equity" is commonly defined both as a financial interest in property and as justice. An equitable policy would recognize the economic capacity—and the dignity—of the poor, developing their assets rather than lamenting their deficiencies. It would respect private interests, but treat the community as an economic partner and public contributions as legitimate business investments for the common good. In so doing, it would also make the most efficient use of public and private charitable resources, and reduce the need for future appropriations. Without such policies, and in the face of the economic challenges ahead, it is difficult to imagine that real progress will be made toward solving social problems such as the housing crisis.

A foundation is being laid and precedents set for an equitable housing policy in the efforts of progressive community development organizations. The housing stories of the 1980s were the "crisis" stories, with homelessness the focal point of public attention, and the "thousand points of light" shining from myriad community-based voluntary initiatives. But for the 1990s, as concerned people grapple with the problem across the country, a growing number of them are beginning to ask fundamental questions about the institutions of property and to experiment with new models of ownership.

Neither "public" nor "private" in traditional terms, these new models blend the best features of both in a variety of combinations. *Limited-equity cooperatives* (in which residents own shares in the cooperative corporation that owns the property, but the sales price of shares is restricted to preserve affordability) and *mutual-housing associations* (in which housing is owned by a resident-controlled nonprofit corporation) both provide their members with the security and control normally associated with ownership. Some *land conservation trusts* make creative use of partial interests by holding development rights and conservation easements for public benefit, while the rest of the "bundle of rights" is privately owned.

Perhaps the most distinctive and deliberate balance of interests is represented by the *community land trust* (CLT) model. CLTs are democratically structured, community-based nonprofit corporations that typically separate the ownership of land from that of buildings. Land is held in perpetuity by the CLT, but individuals, cooperatives and other organizations may own their buildings. Long-term or lifetime inheritable leases detail the "partnership" between these individuals (or groups) and their community, as represented by the land trust. The private contribution to property value is fully respected, but the social appreciation in land (location) value is retained for community benefit. The property remains accessible and affordable for succeeding generations. And any subsidies remain with the property and are treated as long-term community investments. In essence, land trusts preserve the opportunity for individual ownership, but protect the public interest by preventing monopolization, absentee control, and speculative gain.

These innovative models are not mutually exclusive, and can often be used in combination with one another in a multifaceted, integrated community development program. A single CLT, for example, might hold tracts of land used variously for individually owned homes, multiunit cooperatives, and rental housing—and other tracts used for commercial or public services facilities, agriculture, open space or conservation. Together, they are beginning to give form and credibility to alternative concepts of property, and to stimulate public and policy discussions.

Expanding the Movement

Efforts like these constitute what Mahatma Gandhi used to call the "constructive program." There are now approximately 100 operating or developing CLTs in 23 states, and many more co-ops, MHAs, and conservation trusts. However, despite the impressive growth of this progressive community development sector, the number of such initiatives in the foreseeable future will still be limited, and most of them will take place in lower-income communities. What is needed now is to build upon this foundation, with complementary initiatives that apply these principles to the other arenas of social change: individual action and public policy.

Additional vehicles are needed to enroll a larger, more geographically dispersed population of socially concerned property owners in this nascent land reform movement. *Community development loan funds,* which pool capital from many socially concerned investors and provide financing for land and housing, business, and social service ventures, are a precedent for this. The 41 member funds of the National Association of Community Development Loan Funds, with several thousand investors, have provided nearly $100 million in loans to date for projects throughout the United States. Unlike other financial institutions, they target all of their assets under management to low-income communities, and give priority to projects designed both to meet immediate needs and to change the structures of ownership perpetuating poverty.

Another vehicle for expanding the land reform movement is the newly instituted *"Equity Pledge"* of the Equity Trust, Inc., which asks property owners to voluntarily tithe a portion of the social appreciation in their property value. When the property is sold, the designated amount is paid to the Equity Trust Fund, to be used to finance acquisition and development by CLTs and similar projects.

The Equity Trust Fund asks participants to go beyond reinvestment to examine the origins of wealth and acknowledge the "social mortgage" on property. Though commitments may be modest in number, the human interest stories of "average Americans" voluntarily making significant changes in their own economic lives may add visibility and credibility to the broader effort for economic reform.

As interest and involvement grow, so does the opportunity to build effective *political coalitions*. It was the determined effort of community developers, social service providers, environmentalists, and farmers to overcome their social divisions and resolve their competing claims for properties and dollars that led to the most significant state support for land trusts. The Vermont Housing and Conservation Trust Fund has been capitalized with more than $30 million in direct appropriations and a dedicated annual revenue stream from property transfer taxes to finance both permanently affordable housing through CLTs and agricultural and open-space preservation through conservation trusts.

Maine has also dedicated funds to CLTs, through a statewide bond issue referendum, and begun to require commitments of very long-term affordability in conventionally subsidized developments. Connecticut has made CLTs a line-item appropriation in its housing budget. And numerous cities have provided grants, loans, and unused properties to CLTs. Following a four-year community organizing and planning process in the Central Roxbury neighborhood, the City of Boston has agreed to transfer all vacant city-owned properties in the area to a proposed CLT—and to delegate its power of eminent domain to allow the CLT to acquire vacant privately owned parcels for redevelopment. This was the first time that a municipal government had gone beyond lot-by-lot transfers, regarding all of its holdings in a particular area as a public investment and public trust, to be managed for long-term public benefit while offering private development opportunities.

Policy Options

These and other examples of public support for innovative community development indicate that the climate for policy reform is steadily improving. Indeed, many legislators—uncomfortable with some traditional social programs, and unable to fund others—are looking for new ideas. Though the comparison is not often made, their interest parallels the search underway in other countries for alternatives to communism or state-ownership and to private markets that cannot (or will not) adequately meet the needs of the poor and working class.

What is needed is an incremental, but comprehensive, approach to policy reform—an "American land reform" program—that reflects understanding of the structural roots of the problems, but respects traditional American values and realistically accepts financial constraints. Such a program would be designed to strengthen the progressive community development sector, equalize opportunity and increase market access for the disenfranchised, reshape public perception of the community as an economic partner, and bring good consumer and business practices into the management of the public investment.

At the outset, significant tax reforms and increased appropriations may be volatile or unproductive issues. But there are other policy options available, many of which would have little or no budgetary impact, but could nonetheless have a meaningful effect on housing needs.

Appropriations

Rather than requesting substantial increases in the overall volume of housing appropriations, attention should be given to the effective use of existing funds. If the regulations governing all current funding programs are amended to rank applicants according to their ability to deliver long-term public benefit, the most progressive developers will have far greater resources available, even if spending remains constant. Because CLTs, MHAs, limited-equity co-ops and the like "recycle" subsidies for future generations, they represent a better value for each public dollar spent, and thus would be given priority over conventional homeownership and private rental housing on which state housing finance agencies and other programs still spend very large amounts.

Publicly Held Properties

Rather than treating tax-default and other surplus properties as disposable items, they should become long-term assets, an "investment trust" for public benefit. They can serve as the public contribution to genuine "public/private partnerships," as in the Boston example. If the Resolution Trust Corporation would place the land under the enormous number of S&L properties it holds into quasipublic trusts, sell only the buildings, and use long-term lease fees and resale controls, it might well be possible to slowly recoup the enormous public investment that cannot be retrieved in the current auctions.

As it stands, because of the federal government's commitments to S&L depositors, taxpayers are investing half-a-trillion dollars in the purchase of a vast inventory of real estate for considerably more than its current value. While it may make sense to protect depositors in this way, to subsequently auction the properties as fast as possible, under very unfavorable market conditions, is inexcusable. Use of CLTs or quasi-public regional land trusts would allow for privatization of the buildings, relieve government of most of the management responsibilities, create incentives for private investment and, at the same time, protect the public interest. It would be both more business-like and more equitable than current policy, which nationalizes the liabilities but privatizes the assets.

Investment

The City of Burlington, Vermont, has invested significant amounts of its public employees' pension fund in the Burlington CLT, in the form of loans and hybrid debt-equity instruments. The performance of community development loan funds, community development credit unions, and community development banks justifies amendment of regulations to increase investment of public funds. In addition, there are a variety of ways government might enhance the flow of private investment dollars, ranging from continued strengthening of the requirements of the Community Reinvestment Act (which regulates banks) to measures supporting the nonprofit community development lenders. A program of "liquidity guarantees," for example, would allow loan funds to utilize some of the funds institutional investors now maintain (at modest rates of return) in money market accounts and short-term certificates of deposit, while at the same time not asking government to bear any risk of loss.

Regulation of Market Activity

Without compromising the legitimate independence or flexibility of the market, it would be possible to broaden access to its opportunities. The "tenants' first-right-to-purchase" laws enacted by the District of Columbia and by the states of New Hampshire, Vermont, and Massachusetts for mobile home parks are important steps in that direction. Because the laws apply equally to all property owners, they do not disadvantage any unfairly. Tenants cannot always afford to purchase their properties, but if they were clearly permitted to assign their option to a qualified CLT or nonprofit developer with greater financing capabilities, they would be able to do so more often. In any event, such measures give tenants notice of impending risks of displacement—they are a real estate equivalent to the popular "plant-closing" legislation.

The Chances of Success

Even initial measures such as these could have the effect of expanding the supply of permanently affordable housing, nurturing the development of a nonspeculative market sector, and democratizing access. Those with some financial means would have opportunities for a valuable form of homeownership; those for whom rental housing is more desirable would be served by nonprofit housing corporations and other appropriate providers. In either case, the long-term cost to government and the burden on taxpayers would be reduced.

Admittedly, any proposal to redefine property rights, limit equity or profitability, or regulate market activity is potentially controversial. The political atmosphere that has developed around traditional social welfare policy is adversarial: government is typically cast in the role of "regulator" or "confiscator," using its police powers to infringe on private initiatives and earnings. The process of reform will have to begin with public education and a reinterpretation of the housing issues, and will have to include voluntary initiatives as well as legislative and regulatory changes.

The central themes of this advocacy must be the compatibility of social concern and fiscal responsibility, and the affirmative partnership of individual and community interests in property. The goal must be clearly identified as "equity" or fairness, with benefits for many. With this reassurance, it should be possible to bridge some of the traditional gaps between "liberal" and "conservative" and gain a broad hearing for reform proposals. The challenge is formidable, but with the increasing pressure of circumstances and the failure of traditional programs, the opportunities are also very great.

The Value of Land in Economics

Chuck Matthei
(1993)

Land

Traditionally, land is the first leg of the economic triangle. Even in a modern economy, it is the source of shelter, nourishment, and raw materials for production—and literally the common ground on which all social and economic activity takes place, all shaped by the character of American society. And, for many individuals, real property remains their greatest personal investment and economic asset.

Nevertheless, the most prominent domestic problem in the United States in the past decade was homelessness and the crisis of affordable housing. In the same period, tens of thousands of family farmers left the land, and an already troubled national economy was further burdened with nearly a trillion dollars in debt, significantly related to the involvement of financial institutions in speculative real estate ventures.

Despite many good efforts, the problems still persist. In housing, as in health care, the evidence is that conventional social welfare programs simply aren't working. The subsidies are inadequate and inefficient. Needs are growing faster than available resources, and political will is limited. But more fundamentally, conventional programs cannot ultimately succeed because they are based on false premises.

The Myth of Poverty

Three widespread myths distort popular perspectives on poverty. First is the "myth of poverty," or the tendency to judge the poor by their apparent deficiencies, ignoring very real economic capacities.

Most low-income people are renters. Before Mrs. M became one of the first homeowners in a new community land trust in Cincinnati, Ohio, she was paying $350 a month for a dilapidated apartment with a market value of less than $15,000. Over her lifetime, with normal rent increases, she would have paid several hundred thousand dollars for a slum dwelling, far more than would have been required to purchase the same (or better) housing on conventional terms. In fact, many low-income families

This article was originally published in *Sojourners* (November 1993). It is reprinted by permission of *Sojourners*. www.sojo.net.

pay not only a higher percentage of income, but a greater total amount than many homeowners pay—with none of the same benefits.

Poverty is not simply a lack of income. Examine the economy of most low-income communities and you will find far more money flowing than one might suspect. The problem is that what flows in flows right back out: and that is a problem of ownership.

From small urban neighborhoods to large areas, one of the most common characteristics of low-income communities is a prevalence of absentee ownership that rivals any third world country. These patterns may not represent our national average, but they are the circumstances of the poor and a root cause of their continuing poverty.

The poor need equity before subsidies.

The Myth of Wealth

Next is the "myth of wealth," which is very respectful of private initiatives and protective of private investment, but often ignores the social contribution to property value. When individuals purchase or improve properties, they create value. But when a city government installs a subway line, giving another neighborhood the amenity of convenient transportation, that also adds value.

And when low-income tenants organize to transform vacant lots into mini-parks or otherwise make their community more desirable, that too enhances property values. They themselves will receive no economic return for their investment and may inadvertently accelerate a process of gentrification that will displace them altogether.

The legal conception of property as a "bundle of rights" (air rights, development rights, timeshares, etc.) has an economic corollary. Property value is a "bundle of values." It comes from many sources both individual and communal. And this realization may hold a key to solving our land and housing problems.

When we fail to measure the social contribution then we also fail to utilize the social increment in value, the "commonwealth," for the common good. This is true when public funds are used to subsidize housing in the private market, and it has been true of the management of public timber, mineral, and grazing lands in the West and elsewhere. If private trustees or investment managers were so heedless they would be dismissed or held legally liable for breach of fiduciary duties. But we have become accustomed to the neglect of public interests.

The Myth of Public Assistance

Last is the "myth of public assistance," which portrays efforts to bridge the economic gap as a process of taking from those who have fairly earned and giving to those who have not (but probably should have). This characterization stigmatizes the poor and fosters resentment among the taxpaying public, creating a political climate in which appropriation levels will never be adequate.

Even more important, it reflects only a partial understanding (perhaps a willful blindness) of subsidies in the housing market. In fact, while the poor receive some services through direct appropriations, a second set of indirect but very substantial subsidies are embodied in the tax code. It is significant that these subsidies are not even acknowledged as such: they are not subjected to annual review and renewal; and, in great disproportion, they benefit the wealthier sectors of society, not the poor.

If you ask a group of middle- or upper-income homeowners, "How many of you live in subsidized housing?" no hands will be raised. But ask, "How many of you take advantage of the federal and state home mortgage interest deductions?" and virtually every hand will rise. Through this deduction alone, the federal treasury gives up several times as much each year as the total amount spent on housing assistance for the poor—and 80 percent of the financial benefit accrues to the wealthiest fifth of the population. The rationale for this policy is the national commitment to helping every family realize the American Dream of home ownership. But this can hardly justify the deductions on million dollar homes, second homes, or equity loans unrelated to housing acquisition.

Property as Partnership

Property can never be wholly private or wholly public, but must be seen as a partnership between the individual and the community. This realization is implicit in the religious doctrine of stewardship or Gandhi's concept of trusteeship. "The Earth is the Lord's." It is not of our making and cannot be, in absolute terms, a private possession.

There is growing public awareness of the environmental dimension of land stewardship, but less attention to the social and economic implications. A half-century ago, the early environmentalist Aldo Leopold observed, "We abuse the land because we regard it as a commodity belonging to us. When we see land as a community to which we belong, we may begin to use it with love and respect." It is not only the land itself, but also the entire community that is affected.

In this partnership, individuals have a legitimate economic interest and the community has a legitimate interest. The original, essential value of the creation may be considered, in the spirit of the gospel, to be held in trust for the good of all and especially for the poor.

Historically, the church has affirmed the legitimacy of private ownership—but always qualified its affirmation by recognizing that this private interest is not singular or absolute and that there is a "social mortgage" on property. Our challenge is to give this principle a practical, personal application in a modern market economy.

Models for Community Development

A number of community development practitioners are doing just that today. Perhaps the most distinctive of these new models, and the most deliberate in its delineation of individual and community interests and the relationship between them, is the community land trust (CLT).

CLTs are democratically structured, nonprofit corporations that own land and make it available to individuals and organizations for residential, commercial, agricultural, public service, or other appropriate purposes. Occupants may own the buildings and other improvements they make on the land, and a lease agreement defines the relationship and the rights and responsibilities of each party.

Through a CLT, individuals gain the essential benefits of ownership: lifetime security and a legacy for their heirs, as long as they will actually use the land; and fair equity for their personal investment of capital and labor. But the community democratizes access, protecting itself from the effects of absentee ownership and monopolization; it has a stronger voice in planning decisions. And it reserves subsidies and the social appreciation in land value for multigenerational benefit.

In different ways, public and private interests are also balanced by limited equity cooperatives (in which every resident owns a share but the transfer value is limited to preserve affordability) and mutual housing associations (MHAs, which are resident controlled, not-for-profit housing corporations), and by deed restrictions, "sleeping" mortgages, and other legal and financial devices.

Many of these techniques can be used in combination with one another. For example, it is common for a CLT to hold land on which a group of families own their building as a limited equity co-op.

These models can be applied in cities, towns, and rural areas. Over the past 15 years, there has been dramatic growth in the number of such organizations, the scale of their development activity, and the breadth of popular and institutional support. In important ways, they bridge traditional political divisions. On the one hand, they are cost-effective and create opportunities for individual homeownership; on the other, they give low-income communities security, economic power, and greater control over their own destinies.

For churches in particular, these efforts have both practical appeal and spiritual affinity. From the outset, churches have provided facilities, board and staff members, volunteers, and substantial amounts of investment capital. For example:

- The West End Alliance of Ministers and Ministries initiated the development of the Community Land Co-op of Cincinnati (a CLT); black and white churches joined together to establish the Time of Jubilee CLT in Syracuse, New York.
- The United Methodist Church sponsored a pastor/organizer to work with developing CLTs in Atlanta, Georgia; the Catholic archdiocese in New York

City assigned personnel to the sweat equity homesteading projects of the RAIN CLT.
- The Dominican Sisters of the Sick Poor donated property in Ohio and have now offered to donate land adjacent to their motherhouse in Ossining, New York.

Companion Initiatives

There are now more than 100 CLTs across the country, and many individual co-ops or MHAs. Yet their numbers are still limited and most of this development takes place in low-income communities where the need is most urgent and where these models have obvious advantages over conventional market or public sector options.

Companion programs are now needed to engage socially concerned property owners in every geographical and economic sector, to make it clear that the social mortgage is not a form of "second class ownership for the poor" but, rather, a guiding principle for an equitable market. The new Equity Trust Fund [administered by Equity Trust, Inc.] is designed to be a vehicle for this commitment. It invites gifts from the social appreciation in property value and gifts of property to be used to meet the needs of those who are disenfranchised or disadvantaged by the same market that gives current owners a windfall profit.

The Equity Trust Fund is unique. There are many conservation organizations that solicit land gifts, but this program addresses human needs as well. It does draw inspiration, however, from the Bhoodan/Gramdan ("land gift/village gift") movement of Gandhi's successors, Vinoba Bhave and Jayaprakash Narayan, in India in the 1950s. While that effort failed to meet its ambitious goal of providing for poor landless peasants, it did redistribute more than a million acres, achieving more than any government program.

The purposes of the Equity Trust Fund are educational and political, as well as financial. It is designed to focus public attention on basic questions of property and equity as participants go beyond traditional charity to reform their own economic relationships.

Of course, CLTs and Equity Pledges alone cannot equal the volume of need, but they can play a role in developing a political constituency for property reform. In Gandhi's conception, social change has three dimensions: personal commitment; the "constructive program"; and political campaigns. CLTs, co-ops, MHAs—this emerging "third path" between the strictly public and private—represent our constructive program.

The Equity Trust Fund offers individuals and institutions an opportunity to express the values that underlie these efforts and to demonstrate the will to make the personal changes that meaningful political reform will require. For religious persons, it effectively combines practical economic action with prophetic witness.

An American Land Reform

Land reform in the United States will not take the same forms as in the third world, but land reform is what we need. It should not be seen as a confiscatory program but rather, one that reflects renewed respect for one another and a new regard for equity in the economic relationship between individuals and communities.

Three principles should guide the development of a platform for reform. First, public contributions should be treated as long-term investments for the common good. Second, the poor should be able to make full use of their assets. And third, the playing field should be leveled so that all have the same opportunities, and preferential subsidies are allocated to those who genuinely need them.

Conventional land and housing programs are constrained by budget limits that may well be a permanent feature of our political economy. But many reform measures need not be costly, and some will actually increase revenues or reduce the demand for future spending.

- Appropriations can be used much more efficiently if they are allocated on a priority basis to projects that ensure long-term affordability.
- Tax-default properties and the inventories from failed banks and S&Ls should be placed in land trusts, with only buildings sold, and long-term lease fees used to recoup the public investment.
- The flow of investment capital could be increased by encouraging public and private pension funds, ensuring liquidity to give community development funds greater access to institutional assets, and applying the Community Reinvestment Act to insurance companies and even charitable institutions.
- Tenants and community trusts should have a first right of refusal for the purchase of rental properties and properties that have received public subsidies, as is true for housing in Washington, DC, mobile home parks in Massachusetts, and farmland in Vermont.

Tax reforms should be pursued, including capping mortgage-interest deductions (or relating them to the percentage of income paid for housing) and legislating more progressive capital gains and property taxes.

Facing the Challenge

These are but a few of the measures that might be included in an American land reform agenda. They reflect the moral imperative to help first those in greatest need. But this would not be a "poor people's policy." Rather, it would be an inclusive effort to establish a socially, as well as environmentally, responsible land ethic and more equitable market.

It is interesting that in the current national debate on health care, an unusual degree of consensus has emerged: the private market alone cannot solve the problems; traditional subsidy programs are financially ruinous; and structural reform of some kind is required.

In the previous years, during which homelessness and the housing crisis were in the spotlight of national concern, no similar call for structural reform was heard. Property is both a very basic issue and, perhaps, the most controversial. Genuine reform will be a very difficult challenge. Nevertheless, as both social and environmental problems related to land continue to mount and resources dwindle, it will become clear to more and more people that we have only four alternatives. We can ignore these problems and suffer the terrible social and economic consequences of that neglect. We can continue subsidizing the private market, generation after generation, at ever-higher levels of spending. We can expand the public housing sector, which, though it provides an important service, offers only a limited range of housing benefits to residents and meets considerable resistance in many communities. Or, finally, we can renew the covenant between the individual, the community, and the land on which both depend—and embark together on the path of economic reform.

For some, this process will bring new opportunities. From others, it will also ask for sacrifices. It is appropriate—and perhaps even necessary—that the initiative be taken by people of faith. As the French philosopher Albert Camus said in response to a question from a group of Dominicans, what the world expects of Christians today is that they "speak out clearly and pay up personally."

Community and Conservation Land Trusts as Unlikely Partners?

The Case of Troy Gardens, Madison, Wisconsin

Marcia Caton Campbell and Danielle A. Salus
(2003)

Introduction

Over the last two decades, private nonprofit land trusts have gained increasing popularity among those who wish to conserve land or preserve access to affordable housing in the United States. Currently, there are approximately 1200 conservation land trusts (Land Trust Alliance website), and nearly 200 community land trusts in the US (Levin, 2000). Among the several theories explaining this rise in popularity is, most notably, that people have cited a "dissatisfaction with regulatory planning's failure" (Jacobs, 2000, p. 425). That is, the limitations of zoning, taxation, and other public land use control measures have spurred private citizens into action. Where the public sector has not been able to respond quickly enough (or at all), private land trusts provide a focused, long-term solution to land conservation and community preservation (Jacobs, 1999).

Land trusts have grown at the same time that decreasing public funds and devolution have caused a rise in private nonprofit corporations throughout the US. Nonprofit corporations are responding to such wide-ranging problems as job training, environmental preservation, and housing. Land trusts use the tools of the private market to protect land, and environmental and community resources (Jacobs, 1999).

The two most common types of land trusts are conservation trusts and community land trusts, both of which use many of the same land-saving tools, but for different purposes. Conservation land trusts typically acquire land or land rights to preserve open space or protect ecological resources. Community land trusts typically acquire land and the improvements upon it to ensure long-term access to affordable housing or community resources. The focus of conservation land trusts is the land itself; the focus of community land trusts is more often the people who will be using the land. Community land trusts divide the rights to the improvements and the rights to the land between individuals and the community through a dual ownership agreement (for further explanation of both types of land trusts, see Davis, 1984; Institute for Community Economics, 1982; Daniels and Bowers, 1997).

This article was originally published in *Land Use Policy* 20,2 (2003): 169–180. It is reprinted by permission of Elsevier. Images have not been reprinted.

Debating the Appropriate Role for Land Trusts

In a recent issue of the *Journal of Planning Education and Research*, a series of comments debate the appropriate role for land trusts in regulating and controlling land (Wright and Czerniak, 2000; Jacobs, 2000; Nelson, 2000). In their opening comment, Wright and Czerniak contend that the standard land use regulatory mechanisms (primarily zoning) have had limited effectiveness, failing to preserve important agricultural, open space, and other ecologically sensitive lands in sufficiently large quantities. They fault the regulatory focus of Euclidean zoning, which has been on *how* land should be developed rather than *whether* it should be (p. 419).

Stepping into the breach, large conservation land trusts such as the Nature Conservancy have engaged in significant amounts of voluntary land preservation, in essence conducting de facto land use and open space planning at the same time. Wright and Czerniak proclaim these voluntary efforts superior to traditional land use regulation because they combine cooperative agreements with economic incentives for not developing private land, thereby affording important lands the permanent protection from development that is neither politically feasible nor legally possible under standard land use controls.

Jacobs (2000) questions, however, whether it is appropriate for land trusts to operate in this way, arguing that they lack the accountability to the public at large of public land use planning agencies. Although most are registered nonprofit organizations with a public interest mission, land trusts report only to their private member clientèle and are not legally required to obtain public input on their planning and decision making. Citing his own earlier research into land trusts (Foti and Jacobs, 1989), Jacobs notes that most conservation land trusts are created in response to a crisis involving a specific property threatened by development, and have limited staff and budgets, small memberships, and few land holdings. This means that comprehensive or coordinated impact over large areas is minimal. Acquiring land can be costly, and it is sometimes only possible to affect small pockets of land within larger tracts. Typically, these small land trusts do not coordinate their efforts within larger public planning processes, nor do they seek the active involvement of a broader, more diverse public beyond their membership.[1]

The advantages of land trusts over public sector alternatives are their focus, flexibility, and ability to provide long-term conservation and affordability. Yet, despite these advantages, those who have supported land trusts *over* public sector land control methods have come under heavy criticism. Precisely because of their fragmented impact, Jacobs (1999, 2000) argues, conservation land trusts are viewed more appropriately as a complement to standard land use regulations within a clear public sector planning framework that incorporates public input. Because of their small number and size, community land trusts are similarly more likely to be effective in conjunction with other types of land reform measures and organizations (Davis, 1984).

Both types of land trusts have collaborated with government agencies on a fairly regular basis; however, they have rarely worked together. In fact, because of differing goals—one type of trust is used for housing and development, the other used for preservation of farmland and natural habitats—there are few examples of collaboration between community and conservation land trusts. The most extensive collaborations have occurred in Vermont and New Jersey (see Libby and Bradley, 2000; Axel-Lute, 1999; the Vermont Housing and Conservation Board website for examples). Although Wright and Czerniak and Jacobs write specifically about conservation land trusts, the issues that they raise are also pertinent to the new type of land trust collaboration. Do collaborations between conservation land trusts and community land trusts result in the preservation of land as common property? Does their work take place in a public sector planning framework with adequate public input? To whom are the land trusts accountable? And finally, given that such collaborative efforts include housing development as well as land preservation, do the results constitute good land use and community development planning?

Amid the Northside neighborhoods of Madison, Wisconsin, there exists an unusual example of this new form of land trust partnership. The Madison Area Community Land Trust (MACLT), a community land trust, and the Urban Open Space Foundation (UOSF), a conservation land trust, have teamed together with other community organizations and departments from a major university in an innovative, community-based development effort to preserve the majority of a large tract of land in the city from development, while providing some much-needed affordable housing on a small portion of the site. This paper explores the lessons learned from this collaborative effort and asks whether it offers a viable model for land conservation and community development elsewhere in the United States. In the pages that follow, we provide background on the Troy Gardens project, highlight the strengths of the collaboration, identify tensions that currently exist and challenges that lie ahead, and offer suggestions for ways to increase collaborations between the two types of land trusts in Wisconsin and across the United States.

Troy Gardens History

In October 1995, the State of Wisconsin announced its decision to place on the State's surplus land list a 6-ha (15 acres), undeveloped site abutting the Mendota Mental Health Center grounds on the city of Madison's Northside. The State intended to sell the site, most likely to a private developer, for a standard residential subdivision. However, Northside area residents and people from other city neighborhoods had been gardening on approximately 2 ha (5 acres) of the site for 15 years, using much of the rest of the land to bird-watch, walk their dogs, and simply wander the land and gaze at the beauty of the landscape. Alarmed at the prospect of losing this valuable common resource, and at the potential development of the site in ways undesirable to the community, concerned community gardeners, citizens living near the site, and the Northside Planning Council (NPC)[2] joined together with several nonprofit groups—the MACLT, the UOSF, the Community Action Coalition of South Central Wisconsin (CAC), and the Design Coalition—to form the Troy Gardens Coalition (see Table 1 for descriptions of the major partner organizations).[3] Representatives from the University of Wisconsin–Madison joined the Coalition in the fall of 1996 when the State added to the surplus land list an additional 6.5 ha (16 acres) of landlocked, undeveloped land directly north of the original site. This increased the total site area to 12.5 ha (31 acres).

After many hours of organizing and community meetings facilitated by NPC, the Troy Gardens Coalition devised a mixed housing/open space plan that was accepted by the community residents, and ultimately by the City of Madison Planning Department and Common Council. The Coalition's intent was to develop the site at a lower density than it would be if the area were sold to a private developer. In February 1997, the State agreed to take the entire 12.5-ha (31 acre) site off the surplus land list. It gave the Troy Gardens Coalition—through the local nonprofit organizations MACLT and UOSF—a 16-year lease to use the land as the Coalition saw fit (Troy Drive Gardens Letter of Cooperation, 1997).

With this breakthrough, the pressure to allow conventional housing development beyond the original Coalition proposal of 24–30 units to fund open space uses was eliminated, opening up possibilities for an exciting and creative array of integrated open space and food production uses on the majority of the site.[4] By the summer of 1998, the Coalition and the State had reached an agreement that the State would extend the lease to 50 years, with a provision stating that MACLT could acquire full title to the land, with a conservation easement to be held by UOSF. The two land trusts then began to seek the funds to acquire title to the land. In early 2001, after the Coalition had explored numerous funding possibilities to no avail, MACLT succeeded in obtaining a long-term, low-interest loan of community development block grant funds from the City of Madison to buy the entire tract of land from the State. On December 28, 2001, the sale of the land was completed, and Troy Gardens was secured in perpetuity for the Northside community.[5]

Strengths of the Land Trust Collaboration

When MACLT and UOSF were asked to join the Troy Gardens Coalition by Tim Carlisle, lead facilitator and community organizer for NPC, they had no existing relationship with NPC (Levin, 2000). Directors of both land trusts felt that Carlisle called them because he had a general sense of the purpose of land trusts and was looking for any alliance that could be formed to help the Northside community

TABLE 1: Organization Profiles

Community Action Coalition of South Central Wisconsin, Inc., (CAC): A 34-year-old, 501(c)3 nonprofit, antipoverty community action agency serving three South Central Wisconsin counties, its mission is to develop and enhance the social and economic capacities of low-income individuals, families, and communities. Its Community Gardens program provides a holistic strategy of community-based, participant-led, sustainable food initiatives. The program currently manages 14 community gardens over the Greater Madison area, serving a total of 850 low-income participant-gardeners. Troy Drive Community Gardens is the largest of these. CAC has been an active coalition partner since 1995, and provides technical and organizational support to FTG.

Friends of Troy Gardens, Inc., (FTG): An incorporated 501(c)3 nonprofit organization formed in 2000. FTG is responsible for the stewardship of the agriculture and conservation land at Troy Gardens. FTG includes citizen representation from the local community and representation from partnering organizations, including the Northside Planning Council (NPC), the Madison Area Community Land Trust (MACLT), the Community Action Coalition of South Central Wisconsin's Gardens Program (CAC Gardens Program), the Urban Open Space Foundation (UOSF), and the University of Wisconsin–Madison. Replaced the Troy Gardens Coalition.

Madison Area Community Land Trust (MACLT): An active player since the early days of the Troy Gardens Coalition (the precursor organization to Friends of Troy Gardens) and a key player in the development of the project. A 501(c)3 nonprofit, MACLT's mission is to acquire land in Dane County and hold it in trust for the benefit of the community, and to provide permanently affordable housing to first-time homebuyers who are at or below 80 percent of Dane County median income. MACLT owns the land at Troy Gardens and is the developer of the affordable housing component. MACLT has granted Friends of Troy Gardens a long-term, interim ground lease for the open space and agricultural uses and has granted the Urban Open Space Foundation a permanent conservation easement on the 10.5 ha (26 acres) of open space.

Northside Planning Council (NPC): A national-award-winning, nonprofit coalition of 17 neighborhood organizations in Madison's diverse Northside community. As the primary voice for neighborhood residents in the community, NPC spearheaded the Troy Gardens Coalition partnership of a dozen neighborhood and community organizations and led in the formation of the Friends of Troy Gardens, the formal successor to the Coalition. NPC served as fiscal agent for FTG before it received its 501(c)3 status, and continues to provide technical assistance to FTG and its staff in organizational development and community involvement work.

Urban Open Space Foundation (UOSF): A 501(c)3, nonprofit, conservation land trust that works creatively with local governments, residents, businesses, private landowners, and community organizations to acquire urban lands, legally conserve the land's natural and open space values, and involve residents and area businesses in restoring natural, cultural, and recreational features. UOSF was involved in the Troy Gardens Coalition from its earliest days, and has advocated for natural lands restoration and open space preservation on the property. UOSF holds a conservation easement on the 10.5 ha (26 acres) of agricultural and open space land that is managed by FTG. The land trust is deeply involved in developing site plans and facilitating natural areas restoration activities on the land, as an FTG partner organization.

preserve the land. After the first meeting of the Coalition, the community viewed the two organizations as sensitive to their needs, and both land trust directors saw the opportunity to participate in a unique collaborative effort that met their organizations' interests. For MACLT, the opportunity was to build a substantial number of affordable housing units (24–30 total)—more in one place than they had ever developed or acquired before (Levin, 2000). UOSF, a statewide conservation land trust and one of the few in the US that focuses on preserving open space in urban areas, saw the opportunity to preserve a large tract of urban open space with the potential for many activities (Mann, 2000). Clearly this was a unique situation where the interests of two different types of land trusts merged.

MACLT and UOSF have now worked together, first as part of the Troy Gardens Coalition and now as members of the nonprofit Friends of Troy Gardens, for over 6 years and cite many advantages to their collaboration. First, because of the different foci of the two land trusts, they have access to very different pools of financial and technical resources. UOSF is able to access conservation and preservation funding and resources, while MACLT is able to access housing funding, conventional mortgage and development loans and technical assistance, and community development block grant funds (see Table 2 for a summary of the major funding sources for Troy Gardens). Further, the directors of both organizations had strong backgrounds and expertise in their areas (Kaufman, 2000). Sol Levin, an urban planner who had once directed Madison's Community Development Authority, had decades of experience in community development and housing finance, as well as an in-depth understanding of related state and city legislation. Heather Mann, who holds a master's degree from the Land Resources Program at the UW–Madison's Gaylord Nelson Institute for Environmental Studies, is highly experienced in open space preservation and has strong connections to the political power structure both at the City of Madison and in the Wisconsin state legislature (Kaufman, 2000). Savvy strategizers who used their varied expertise and skills to work together, the directors of the land trusts created a synergistic coalition, doubling their skills and expanding their resource base (Levin, 2000; Mann, 2000).

A second advantage of the collaboration is that the two land trust organizations complement each other both in achievement of mission and in combining different mechanisms of land purchase and ownership (Levin, 2000). Although both types of land trusts acquire land through donations and purchase, conservation trusts rely primarily on tools such as remainder interest estates, below cost sales, and conservation easements to restrict land uses and protect land (Daniels and Bowers, 1997). Community trusts use dual ownership arrangements, in which the community owns the land and the individual owns the improvements, and resale formulas to restrict profit from increases in market value to keep housing affordable (Ambromovitz, 2000; Davis, 1984, 2000; Institute for Community Economics website). Again, the collaboration between MACLT and UOSF has served to broaden the mechanisms available to them to achieve their goals.

TABLE 2: Major Sources of Funding for Troy Gardens				
Funding Source	**Recipient**	**Type of Grant**	**Amount**	**Period Covered**
Oscar G. and Elsa S. Mayer Family Foundation[a]	FTG	Program grant (farm, gardens, open space)	$35,000	May 2000–May 2001
Oscar G. and Elsa S. Mayer Family Foundation[a]	FTG	Program grant (farm, gardens, interpretive trail system signs)	$43,350	May 2001–May 2002
Madison Community Foundation[a]	FTG	Program grant (operations and staff support)	$75,000	August 2001–July 2003
HUD Economic Development Initiative[b]	MACLT	Housing construction (subsidizing affordability)	$750,000	September 2001–December 2004
The Evjue Charitable Foundation[a]	FTG/UW–Madison	Program grant (educational programs in urban agriculture)	$19,500	May 2001–December 2002
CDBG Acquisitions/Rehab Fund[c]	MACLT	Land acquisition	$318,000	January–December 2001
Community Enhancement Program[c]	FTG	Capital improvements (signage)	$10,000	January–December 2002
USDA Urban Forestry Grant[b]	UOSF	Program grant (natural areas restoration)	$65,000	October 2001–December 2003
CDBG Futures Fund[c]	MACLT	PUD planning process	$14,000	April–December 2002
W. K. Kellogg Foundation[d] (Food and Society Initiative)	FTG/UW–Madison	Community–University partnership (program, organization, and staff support; research)	$493,603[e]	June 2002–May 2006

[a]Private local foundation.
[b]Federal grant.
[c]City of Madison.
[d]National foundation.
[e]FTG's share of grant is $241,901; UW–Madison's share is $251,702.

A final advantage of collaboration is that the end product is "different and better" than either land trust could have achieved alone (Mann, 2000). Both land trust directors agree that open space preservation and affordable housing make good bedfellows. The Troy Gardens project is a unique and creative combination of housing and open space precisely because of the participation of both land trusts in a broader community coalition.

Relationship Between MACLT and UOSF

One of the reasons the collaboration between MACLT and UOSF has worked so well is because the two organizations had developed a strong relationship even before the 1996 Coalition was formed. Heather Mann turned to Sol Levin before she founded UOSF for his expertise in directing MACLT and to build from his base of experience (Mann, 2000). Once UOSF was founded, Levin was asked to be on the trust's Board of Directors. Since then, each director has had a seat on the other's board (Mann, 2000; Levin, 2000). In addition, both organizations were located in the same office space for close to 5 years; although they now have separate office spaces, colocation fostered a spontaneous and informal relationship that in turn strengthened the respect of each director for the other.[6]

Underlying Tensions

Despite the strength of their relationship, and the advantages of their collaboration, underlying tensions between the two organizations occasionally rise to the surface. One obvious tension has to do with land and resource allocations. This is a natural tension that will most likely occur among most land organizations working in collaboration. However, a deeper tension arises from the changing roles the two trusts have played in the Troy Gardens Coalition over time, and from competition between the organizations as to which group's issues generate the most excitement, and which has center stage.

When the Troy Gardens Coalition was first formed, Sol Levin and MACLT were central. Sol's knowledge about the State, and about housing funding and planning was critical in developing the original plan for the site. Once the State took the land off the surplus land list, however, Levin was concerned that the project would be diverted from its housing goals. This turned out not to be the case, but there was some shifting in priorities and roles such that housing, while still an element of the plan, was not the *key* element of the plan, MACLT, while a major player in the Coalition, was not always the *key* player. For a period of several years, Mann and UOSF took on a more central role, primarily because of her strengths as a fundraiser and her connections to the power structure in Madison (Kaufman, 2000), while sources of funding were pursued through state natural resource and open space programs. MACLT ultimately returned to the role of key player, however, when it became clear that the best opportunity for raising the funds to purchase the land lay in a grant request to the City of Madison Community Development Block Grant Office.[7]

Thus, Sol Levin felt at times that MACLT was somewhat overshadowed by UOSF, not only in interactions within the Troy Coalition (particularly around space and resource allocation issues), but also more generally. Levin felt that MACLT was unable to generate as much excitement around the issue of affordable housing as UOSF was able to generate around open space preservation, that UOSF tapped into "sexier" issues than MACLT, and that therefore MACLT's mission was not viewed as favorably as that of UOSF.

Levin's concerns may be a reality for community land trusts working in collaboration with conservation land trusts. In part, this may stem from conservation land trusts being the more familiar and widely known of the two major land trust models; although the number of community land trusts in the US is increasing, they are far outnumbered by conservation land trusts. Certainly in the Troy Gardens case, much of the attention UOSF has received over MACLT has had to do with the differing strengths of the two directors, but there are other reasons. In general, people find preservation of open space a more palatable goal than preserving affordable housing and community assets. Open space preservation affects us all—whether it is creating and preserving parks in our cities, or protecting farmland and open space outside our cities—and thus is a goal that most can support. However, the idea of enabling permanent access to housing for those who do not have it, is an uncomfortable one for many in this era of devolution and welfare reform and emphasis on personal responsibility. Thus, the underlying tensions between MACLT and UOSF are not just particular to the Troy Gardens project, but will be found in other similar land trust collaborations. Depending on the project, community land trusts may often find themselves in the shadow of their conservation counterparts.

Challenges Ahead

Although the underlying tensions between the two land trusts do not always surface, in part because of the strong relationship between them, there are a number of issues for negotiation in the future where the tension may become more palpable and problematic. For much of the Coalition's history, it has planned only in "generalities" around the site, and the devil may be in the details. Now that the land at Troy Gardens has been secured, detailed site plans need to be made and submitted to the City of Madison in order to rezone the land as a planned unit development and complete the development process. In particular, there may be tensions surrounding the physical interface of the residential portion of the site, which occupies the extreme southwest corner, with the larger open space area that borders it on two sides and with the existing neighborhood fabric.

A second concern has to do with access. As the planned unit development planning process moves forward, there will be issues concerning the spatial arrangement and access to the housing site, the community gardens, and the CSA farm. Related issues, such as the placement of farm structures (e.g., greenhouse, barn, storage shed, and farmstand), utility lines, and roads (whether public or private), could also pose potential conflicts among the organizations (Levin, 2000).

A third challenge has to do with the slow pace of the process (Mann, 2000), which has less to do with the tensions between the two land trusts and more to do with the difficulties of coordinating an effort across five nonprofit organizations, 17 neighborhood groups, and university- and state-level bureaucracies. However, this slow pace has the potential to drain energy and exacerbate underlying tensions between organizations, even as it allows the nascent Friends of Troy Gardens organization to become more financially stable. The recent influx of substantial grant monies into the coffers of Friends of Troy Gardens, MACLT, and UOSF has sped up the pace of certain project components, such as the CSA farm and the natural areas restoration (see Table 2 for a listing of funding sources and amounts received). Much of the staff and project funding is in soft dollars, however, which necessitates continued fund-raising. If long-term funding proves hard to find, the pace of the project will slow once again. For the time being, staff and project funding is secure through to mid-2006.

Finally, Troy Gardens is but one of several important projects undertaken by either of the land trusts. Both MACLT and UOSF have other major projects in different stages of development in the Madison area that fulfill their individual land trust missions. These projects quite reasonably command a considerable amount of the land trusts directors' energies and time, which has occasionally caused Troy Gardens to take a back seat, particularly for UOSF. As the planned unit development process moves forward, however, the directors' attention will return to Troy Gardens. The challenges described here are by no means insurmountable, but land trusts seeking to work in collaboration should be prepared to negotiate them.

Facilitating Future Collaboration

Both land trust directors agree that there are several factors that would help facilitate future collaboration between them, and between other community and conservation land trusts in the United States. First, they note the need for greater public awareness and understanding that housing and conservation *can* coexist (Levin, 2000; Mann, 2000). Typically, these two goals have been viewed as contradictory and pitted against one another, although there are examples to the contrary in the northeastern United States.[8] Funding streams and resources, as well as local, state and federal agencies that deal with housing and conservation, are separated into different silos. In Wisconsin, there is some hope that the new Smart Growth legislation will bring housing and conservation groups together for joint planning in communities around the state.

Second, technical assistance from a third party knowledgeable about both types of land trusts would facilitate future collaboration (Levin, 2000; Mann, 2000). Technical assistance is available for conservation land trusts through the Land Trust Alliance, and through state groups such as Gathering Waters in Wisconsin. Technical assistance is also available for community land trusts through the Institute for Community Economics. However, there are few groups in the US that offer technical assistance to the two types of land trusts working in collaboration, and there is no group of this kind in Wisconsin.

One such technical assistance group that has worked successfully is the Vermont Housing and Conservation Board (VHCB). VHCB was formed in 1987 through lobbying efforts by a coalition of land conservationists and housing advocates (Dennis, 1993). Vermont legislators appropriated $3 million in state funds to create this quasigovernmental agency, which provides grants and technical assistance to both community and conservation land trusts. Since its inception, VHCB has helped land trusts in Vermont preserve over 68,825 ha of open space (170,000 acres) and 5000 units of affordable housing (Libby and Bradley, 2000). Both Levin and Mann noted that a similar agency at the state level in Wisconsin would be desirable to provide funding and assistance. In addition, Mann suggested that a national agency could be formed to play a similar role across the United States. In the current US political climate, however, that remains a distant dream.

Lessons Learned from Land Trust Collaboration

The collaboration between MACLT and UOSF offers several important lessons for other community and conservation land trusts interested in working together.

Projects must meet organizations' interests. For community and conservation land trusts to come together, the project they collaborate on must meet both organizations' interests. In the Troy Gardens case, MACLT's interest in affordable housing was met through the cohousing portion of the development (20 of the 24–30 units to be built will be below market rate[9]),[10] and UOSF's interests were met through the prairie restoration, community gardens, edible landscape, horticultural therapy gardens, and urban agriculture portions of the site. Again, the unique nature of UOSF, as one of the few land trusts focused on urban open space issues, positioned it well for the Troy Gardens project.

Projects must include external pressure/support for the collaboration. In the Troy Gardens case, MACLT and UOSF are not the only organizations taking part in the project. There are several other organizations, as well as community groups and members that participate in the Friends of Troy Gardens. Being part of a broader coalition has helped mediate the tensions between MACLT and UOSF, and kept them focused beyond their own organizational interests and on the community's needs and goals.

Projects must build trust and strong relationships. MACLT and UOSF had developed a solid working relationship with one another before the Troy Gardens Coalition even formed. This relationship, which grew throughout the years the Coalition existed and has continued through the nonprofit Friends of Troy Gardens, has helped both organizations trust each other enough to address challenges as they arise, rather than allowing them to derail the project. In addition, both organizations have earned the trust of the Northside community through their participation first in the Coalition and then as members of FTG, and through their willingness to meet community needs. Conservation and community land trusts that wish to work in partnership will need to find common ground, build trust between open space and affordable housing advocates, and work carefully together to craft a formal decision-making structure (Axel-Lute, 1999).

In addition, projects must build relationships of sufficient strength to weather occasional fluctuations in the balance of power and changes in key personnel. As the history of the relationship between MACLT and UOSF demonstrates, tensions can arise when one organization's goals are being achieved and another's are not (or are less fully realized). The directors of both land trusts recognized, however, that the achievement of a broader goal—saving Troy Gardens—depended on their ability to deemphasize individual organizational goals for the overall good of the project. This both directors were able to do, despite repeated shifts in which organization played the key role. The strong relationship between land trusts has also survived the departure or even loss of key individuals in the organizations themselves and in the broader coalition that is FTG.[11]

Land Trust Collaborations and Community-Based Development

In the light of the debate outlined at the outset of this paper about the appropriate role for land trusts, several questions remain with respect to the Troy Gardens project. Will Troy Gardens, under the future ownership and stewardship of two private land trusts, continue to be an example of common property? From a community-based development perspective, what are the advantages and drawbacks to the Troy Gardens collaborative effort?

Troy Gardens as Common Property

Early in the partnership's history, the Troy Gardens property was owned by the State of Wisconsin, but leased by MACLT and UOSF, the two local land trusts. On December 28, 2001, MACLT finalized the purchase of the land from the State of Wisconsin Department of Administration. Thus, the current status of the land is that it is publicly owned but privately managed, albeit with management strongly influenced by Northside residents. Arguably, this land has been common property, but will it continue to be so now that the title to it has been transferred to MACLT?

Under the land ownership and management structures that went into effect with the sale of the land, MACLT holds title to the entire parcel. Upon the sale, however, MACLT immediately granted UOSF a conservation easement over 10.5 ha (26 acres) of the site. MACLT then entered into a ground lease agreement with FTG for the management of the urban agriculture and open space projects on the site.[12] Because of this conservation easement and ground lease structure, Troy Gardens should remain common functionally and in perpetuity even under its new ownership.[13] Although the primary intent of the land acquisition is to maintain this common resource for the benefit of Northside residents, the greater Madison population will continue as before to have free access to the land, thus maintaining its status as a functional commons. The exception to this would be the cohousing units, which will be privately owned. The common house structure on the cohousing site, however, may well be available to community gardeners and FTG members for meetings, and the possibility that some farm structures could be located on the cohousing portion of the site is still under discussion.

Troy Gardens as Sustainable, Community-Based Development

Madison, Wisconsin, has a strong historical tradition of neighborhood-level planning. Troy Gardens differs, however, from typical community-based development projects in Madison and other central cities in that it is not *comprehensive* community development, but rather was stimulated by a crisis—the threatened loss of Troy Gardens (Pothukuchi, 1999, p. 2; compares Boston's Dudley Street Neighborhood Initiative, described in Medoff and Sklar, 1994). Still, the comprehensive approach to planning for the site taken by the land trusts and the other partner FTG organizations responds to what Campbell (1996, p. 299) calls "the most challenging conundrum of sustainable development: how to increase social equity and protect the environment simultaneously."

Campbell locates sustainable development within a triangle of conflicting planning goals (economic growth and efficiency, social justice, and environmental protection) that engender three associated conflicts over the boundaries between: (1) private interest and the public good; (2) the developed city and the undeveloped wilderness; and (3) social equity and environmental protection (the source of the aforementioned conundrum). Site plans for Troy Gardens call for a project comprised of a variety of land uses: restored prairie and open space, entrepreneurial urban agriculture and community gardens (targeted toward increasing the food security of low- and moderate-income households), and a mixed-income cohousing development. This combination of uses places Troy Gardens in the center of Campbell's sustainable development triangle. Although Troy Gardens is just a single case of land conservation and sustainable, community-based development planning, it may well offer useful lessons for other, similar, collaborative land trust efforts around the country.

Finally, although the City of Madison's Planning and Development Department has not been directly involved as a partner in the Friends of Troy Gardens or in the Coalition's planning process, it has had some input. The City has contributed community development block grant funds on three occasions, facilitating the initial development concept planning, financing the eventual purchase of the site, and mostly recently supporting the Planned Unit Development process. A general concept plan for Troy Gardens was approved in November 1998 by Madison's Common Council, after review by the Madison Plan Commission and city planning staff. Using the latest CDBG monies, MACLT has now contracted with a local planning firm to prepare the General Development Plan (GDP) for the overall site—the first stage in the Planned Unit Development approval process—for review by the Planning and Development

Department and eventual submission to the Common Council in mid-2003. Following GDP approval, MACLT and FTG will engage in more detailed site and architectural planning for the Specific Implementation Plan (SIP) that is required before ground can be broken for the cohousing development or any other permanent structures can be put up. The SIP will also undergo review by the Plan Commission and city planning staff before it can be approved by the Common Council. Thus, any land-use plans that FTG (and its two land trust partners) intend to implement at Troy are in fact subject to public sector planning agency review, which should reduce the kinds of concerns about lack of public sector oversight raised by critics such as Jacobs (2000) and noted at the outset of this paper.[14]

Conclusion

Can a land trust collaboration like that between MACLT and UOSF be formed in other communities? If the conditions specified above are met, the answer is quite likely yes. Collaboration offers clear advantages to community and conservation land trusts, but does pose potential conflict because of tensions between often competing goals. As land trusts continue to grow in popularity across the US, it is important to note that collaboration is only one of a number of viable options and not a replacement for public sector land control and reform mechanisms.

Is community and conservation land trust collaboration a viable strategy for preserving common property while engaging in sustainable community-based development? The Troy Gardens case suggests that it can be. Long-time Northside resident and Troy gardener Marge Pitts, now Chair of the Friends of Troy Gardens, writes:

> We each have a sense of proprietorship over this piece of green earth which we each need and love for our own reasons, but no one of us has ownership. This paradox of loving proprietorship absent of exclusionary ownership . . . gives us a "selfish" reason to cooperate and communicate respectfully with one another. I think it might be the secret to saving the world.[15] (City Farmer, Canada's Office of Urban Agriculture, 2000)

The Troy Gardens project combines land conservation, affordable housing, food production and entrepreneurship, and community building objectives to conserve as common property 12.5 ha (31 acres) of prime, developable land within the city limits on Madison's Northside. When conservation land trusts and community land trusts work in partnerships such as this one, however, a diverse group of voices and interests may be heard in the process of preserving land. The result is the creation of common property for the public good which, in the Troy Gardens case, is yielding sustainable community-based development as well.

NOTES

1. Objections to land trusts have come from other directions as well. Conservation easements—a primary land-saving tool used by conservation land trusts—have been criticized by Grover Norquist, president of Americans for Tax Reform, on social equity grounds. Norquist claims that conservation easements "lock up" areas that upwardly mobile minority populations might wish to move to, such as land near the urban fringe that might be considered for suburban development (Seelye, 2001).

2. NPC is the umbrella organization that represents the 17 neighborhood organizations on Madison's economically, ethnically, and racially diverse Northside.

3. The formation and early history of the Troy Gardens Coalition and its value as a mechanism for citizen participation in community development planning is documented by Pothukuchi (1999) and Brooks (1998). Although involved in the early years of the Troy Gardens Coalition, the Design Coalition ceased to be an active participant after 1998.

4. In addition to the community gardens already on the site, the project includes the Troy Community Farm, which is being developed under the community supported agriculture (CSA) model. CSA is a model of sustainable small farming developed in Switzerland and Japan and adapted for use in the United States. It brings small farmers together with a community of "eaters," who buy individual household shares in the farm in exchange for a weekly allotment of fresh produce over the growing season (see Henderson and van En, 1999). This model has the advantage of providing the farmer with much-needed cash up front to invest in seeds and equipment, while offering the consumer ("eater") a steady supply of fresh (often organic), locally grown produce. This model is now being adapted and modified at Troy Gardens and in other locales (Boston's Dudley Street neighborhood, for example) to provide healthy, nutritious food to low- and moderate-income communities in central cities (see Kaufman and Bailkey, 2000).

5. Sale of the land was contingent upon the resolution of several sticking points. First, the State Department of Administration and the Coalition had obtained widely disparate appraisals of the land's value, which had to be reconciled. The disparity was created when the State's appraiser valued the land at its residential development value ($590,000) and the Coalition's appraiser valued the land at its conservation value ($308,000). The problem was resolved at a January 2001 hearing of the State Building Commission, in which Coalition members and Madison Mayor, Sue Bauman, testified about the importance of the land to the Northside community and requested that the State accept the Coalition's appraisal figure. After brief deliberations, the Commission agreed to accept the Coalition's figure and approved the sale of the land to MACLT. The Commission attached a reversion clause to the sale, which stipulates that ownership of Troy Gardens will revert to the State should the land ever cease to be used for the proposed combination of affordable housing, sustainable urban agriculture, and community open space uses.

6. While Mann remains the Executive Director of UOSF, Sol Levin retired in February 2001 and was replaced by Greg Rosenberg as Executive Director in October of that year. Levin continued to lend his expertise to the Troy Gardens project on an ad hoc basis for the next 12 months, while the land acquisition was negotiated. He represented MACLT at the closing on the sale of the land on December 28, 2001, fulfilling his long-term objective to save Troy Gardens. Levin died less than 2 months later, following complications from back surgery. MACLT continues to play the same strong collaborative role with UOSF and FTG under Rosenberg's leadership.

7. In January 2001, MACLT secured a long-term, low-interest loan of $318,000 in community development block grant funds to purchase the site.

8. See Axel-Lute (1999) for examples in New Jersey and Vermont.

9. The HUD Economic Development Initiative grant described in Table 2 is targeted toward buying down the construction costs associated with the below-market-rate housing units. Qualified buyers will have household incomes at or below 80 percent of Dane County median income, which was $49,223 in 1999.

10. Cohousing is a form of cooperative living that combines individual ownership of housing units with common ownership of land and structures that are used by all who live in the development. The cohousing concept was imported to the United States from Denmark and the other Scandinavian countries (see McCamant et al., 1994; Hanson, 1996). The cooperative living arrangements are characterized by a participatory process through which residents design and manage the housing development to encourage a strong sense of community, including the physical design of the housing units and extensive common facilities that supplement each resident's individual unit (e.g., the "common house," which is used for cohousing group meetings and communal meals) (Hanson, 1996, p. 2). The physical design of cohousing projects is typically characterized by compact development of structures and common open space, with minimal vehicular access to the site. The Troy Gardens cohousing will be developed with the aid of $750,000 in grant monies from the Department of Housing and Urban Development, included in the final Clinton Administration budget signed in January 2001 (see Table 2).

11. In addition to the aforementioned loss of Sol Levin, longtime NPC facilitator and organizer Tim Carlisle left that organization and the Friends of Troy Gardens in August 2001. His replacement, Jim Powell, worked side by side with Tim for the better part of a year before his departure, making the transition very smooth. The critical role Carlisle played in bringing the Coalition together and keeping it on track over a 6-year period has been partially documented by Pothukuchi (1999).

12. The ground leases were set up between MACLT and the Friends of Troy Gardens for the management of all of the open space uses on the site. For the foreseeable future, however, the Community Action Coalition will continue to administer the community gardens on site and other aspects of the project pertaining to open space, such as the natural areas restoration, will be managed by UOSF. UOSF's eventual goal is to turn management of all of the open space uses over to community management through the Friends of Troy Gardens. CAC continues to organize and work with the community gardeners, with the ultimate goal of turning the garden management over to them and the Friends of Troy Gardens.

13. The term "in perpetuity" is a relative one. Under the terms of the sale negotiated with the State of Wisconsin, if MACLT ceases to exist or Troy Gardens ceases to be used for this unique combination of affordable housing, urban agriculture, and other open space, the land would revert to the State. Given that these uses of the land are the repeatedly stated desires of the Northside community (in community meetings dating back to the inception of the Coalition and in subsequent FTG board meetings), exercise of the reversion clause seems highly unlikely. Once the PUD approval process is complete, the land will be rezoned for precisely these uses, solidifying community desires in formal land use regulations.

14. Nor will opportunities for broader public comment be lacking. The process of preparing the PUD documents for submittal also involves a planning charrette to be facilitated in the Fall of 2002 by Smith Group/JJR, the local planning consultants, which will offer FTG members the opportunity to finalize details concerning the location of permanent structures and other features of the site plan. (Membership in FTG is open to anyone who can afford the $5 annual membership fee.) In addition, FTG will hold design charrettes specifically for the community gardeners and for the CSA farmer and farm shareholders to complete physical plans for those projects. MACLT and its architect will hold similar design charrettes for the members of the cohousing community in the spring of

2003. Finally, all development plan documents are subject to broader public review and comment at mandatory public hearings.

15. Marge Pitts' column, *Troy Gardens Journal*, can be found on the City Farmer website, http://www.cityfarmer.org/troygarden.html.

ACKNOWLEDGMENTS

The authors thank Jerry Kaufman, the late Sol Levin, and Heather Mann for their participation in interviews; the two anonymous reviewers for their suggestions; Harvey Jacobs for his insightful comments; and Brian Stone and Doug Miskowiak for their help with the graphics. Any errors or omissions are attributable to the authors alone. They dedicate this article to the memory of Sol Levin.

REFERENCES

Ambromovitz, D. M., 2000. An essay on community land trusts: toward permanently affordable housing. In Geisler, C., Daneker, G. (Eds.), *Property and Values: Alternatives to Public and Private Ownership*. Island Press, Washington, DC, pp. 213–232.

Axel-Lute, M., 1999. A meeting of movements. Shelterforce. *The Journal of Affordable Housing and Community Building* 21, 10–14.

Brooks, D., 1998. *Ours to Decide*. Documentary film about Troy Gardens.

Campbell, S., 1996. Green cities, growing cities, just cities? Urban planning and the contradictions of sustainable development. *Journal of the American Planning Association* 62, 296–312.

City Farmer, Canada's Office of Urban Agriculture, 2000. Urban Agriculture Notes.

Daniels, T., Bowers, D., 1997. *Holding Our Ground*. Island Press, Washington, DC.

Davis, J. E., 1984. Reallocating equity: a land trust model of land reform. In Geisler, C. C., Popper, F. J. (Eds.), *Land Reform, American Style*. Rowman and Allanheld, Totowa, NJ, pp. 209–232.

Davis, J. E., 2000. Homemaking: the pragmatic politics of third sector housing. In Geisler, C., Daneker, G. (Eds.), *Property and Values: Alternatives to Public and Private Ownership*. Island Press, Washington, DC, pp. 233–260.

Dennis, P. M., 1993. A state program to preserve land and provide housing: Vermont's housing and conservation trust fund. In Endicott, E. (Ed.), *Land Conservation through Public/Private Partnerships*. Island Press, Washington, DC, pp. 172–194.

Foti, P. E., Jacobs, H. M., 1989. Private public-interest land use planning: land trusts in the upper Mid-west. *Journal of Soil and Water Conservation* 44, 317–319.

Hanson, C., 1996. *The Cohousing Handbook: Building a Place for Community*. Hartley and Marks, Point Roberts, WA.

Henderson, E., van En, R., 1999. *Sharing the Harvest: A Guide to Community Supported Agriculture*. Chelsea Green, White River Junction, VT.

Institute for Community Economics, 1982. *The Community Land Trust Handbook*. Rodale Press, Emmaus, PA.

Institute for Community Economics. http://www.iceclt.org.

Jacobs, H. M., 1999. Market-based regulatory approaches in a system of decentralized governance (Regolanzioni basate su meccanismi di mercato in un sistema di governo decentro). In Curti, F. (Ed.), *Urbanistica e Fiscalita Locale: Orientamenti di Riforma e Buone Pratiche in Italia e all'estero.* Maggioli Editore, Milan, pp. 135–150.

Jacobs, H. M., 2000. The ambiguous role of *private* voluntary methods in *public* land use policy: a comment. *Journal of Planning Education and Research* 19, 424–426.

Kaufman, J., 2000. Professor, Department of Urban and Regional Planning, University of Wisconsin–Madison, personal interview. 16 November 2000, Madison, WI.

Kaufman, J., Bailkey, M., 2000. *Farming Inside Cities: Entrepreneurial Agriculture in the United States.* Lincoln Institute of Land Policy, Cambridge, MA.

Land Trust Alliance. http://www.lta.org.

Levin, S., 2000. (former) Executive Director, Madison Area Community Land Trust, personal interview, 17 November 2000, Madison, WI.

Libby, J. M., Bradley, D., 2000. Vermont Housing and Conservation Board: a conspiracy of good will among land trusts and housing trusts. In Geisler, C., Daneker, G. (Eds.), *Property and Values: Alternatives to Public and Private Ownership.* Island Press, Washington, DC, pp. 261–282.

Madison Area Community Land Trust. http://www.emill.com/maclt/.

Mann, H., 2000. Executive Director, Urban Open Space Foundation, personal interview, 15 November 2000, Madison, WI.

McCamant, K., Durrett, C., Hertzman, E., 1994. *Cohousing: A Contemporary Approach to Housing Ourselves,* revised edition, Ten Speed Press, Berkeley.

Medoff, P., Sklar, H., 1994. *Streets of Hope: The Fall and Rise of an Urban Neighborhood.* South End Press, Boston, MA.

Nelson, A. C., 2000. Comment on voluntary methods of land use control in planning. *Journal of Planning Education and Research* 19, 426.

Pitts, M., Troy Gardens Journal Collection, http://www.cityfarmer.org/troygarden.html. Accessed September 2000.

Pothukuchi, K., 1999. Nonprofit and resident collaboratives: an alternative model for community participation in planning? Working Paper No. 30, North America Series. Land Tenure Center, University of Wisconsin–Madison, Madison, WI.

Seelye, K. Q., 2001. More Families Adopting Lasting Limits to Preserve Land. *New York Times,* September 12, B1, B10.

Troy Drive Gardens Letter of Cooperation, 1997. April 28, 1997.

Urban Open Space Foundation. http://www.uosf.org.

Vermont Housing and Conservation Board. http://www.vhcb.org/coalitions.html.

Wright, J. B., Czerniak, R. J., 2000. The rising importance of voluntary methods of land use control in planning. *Journal of Planning Education and Research* 19, 419–423.

Troy Gardens

The Accidental Ecovillage

Greg Rosenberg
(2010)

Troy Gardens is a 31-acre project on the north side of Madison, Wisconsin. The project encompasses community gardens, a working farm, a restored prairie, an interpretive trail system, and a 30-unit mixed-income cohousing community. Troy Gardens has won numerous awards, including the 2008 Home Depot Foundation Award for Affordable Housing Built Responsibly.

The master developer for Troy Gardens was the Madison Area Community Land Trust (MACLT), a small community land trust founded in 1991 by Sol Levin. The author of this retrospective served as MACLT's executive director from 2001 to 2010.

Beyond Housing

For my first few years as executive director of Madison Area Community Land Trust, I labored under the mistaken impression that we were blazing entirely new trails at Troy Gardens, developing a strategy for sustainable development that pushed the CLT model into new and uncharted territory. I saw the error of my ways in 2005, when I had the pleasure of presenting a workshop at the National Community Land Trust conference in Portland with Kirby White, one of the most influential writers within the CLT movement. Kirby asked me to do some background reading in preparation for the workshop. For the first time, I started learning about the historical roots of the CLT movement. To my great surprise, it quickly became clear that Troy Gardens was actually the type of project that the founders of our movement had envisioned for the community land trust! I arrived at the Portland conference with a newfound dose of humility and a heightened respect for those who had come before me.

Many, if not most, CLTs are still exclusively focused on building or rehabilitating homes for lower-income families, with community ownership of land viewed merely as a vehicle for keeping housing permanently affordable through long-term ground leases. By the end of 2005, I had finished Camino del Sol, the first residential subdivision I oversaw as MACLT's executive director. As a result of that experience, I had come to believe that the CLT movement needs to look beyond housing. The CLT makes little

---

This chapter was written for this volume.

sense if we are going to limit ourselves only to the development and stewardship of affordable housing. To be sure, ground leases are beautifully tailored to perpetuate housing affordability, but they can be enormously complex. If housing is all that you do, why not take a simpler approach to protecting long-term affordability?

Where the CLT model really and truly shines is in its extraordinary potential for a broad and integrated approach to development. By thinking deeply about the value and uses of land over a very long-term time horizon, the CLT leads inevitably to thinking about sustainable development practices. Ninety-nine-year renewable ground leases provoke questions like: "What will Madison look like 100 years from now? Where will people get their food? How will they get to work, how will they afford to heat their homes, and where will they find open skies and fresh air?" Such long-term thinking requires housing to be included as an important part of the equation, but it is only one piece of the puzzle. If our homeowners, 100 years from now, cannot afford to heat their homes, then our work will have been in vain. If our homeowners, 50 years from now, cannot get to work because there is no mass transit within walking distance, who will buy our homes? And what will our homeowners do as they grow into old age, if they can no longer go up and down stairs?

The real power and potential of the CLT model is that it leads us to think in more holistic terms. The CLT is so expansive and so durable that it encompasses any possible use of land, not just housing. When a CLT purchases a new piece of land on behalf of the community, therefore, we must think more broadly about what the highest and best uses of this land might be. Not in the traditional sense of figuring out the most financially profitable returns from the land, but which uses will benefit the *community* the most? This question is always set within a specific place, moreover, within a specific neighborhood, predisposing the CLT to consult and collaborate with individuals, institutions, and businesses that surround our land.

This is a long-winded way of saying that Troy Gardens is really an "old" idea of sustainable, collaborative development that harkens back to the vision of the practical idealists who founded the CLT movement. Our road is much easier today than it was 40 years ago, when that vision was put forward in the first CLT at New Communities, because the larger society has begun to place a heightened value on sustainable development. This is not to say that it was *easy* to develop Troy Gardens—only that an evolving social consciousness about environmental stewardship, energy efficiency, universal design, and sustainable practices made it *possible* to develop Troy Gardens.

Bringing the Story Up to Date

In December of 2001, the Madison Area CLT stepped into the role of lead developer when we purchased a 31-acre site from the State of Wisconsin. I had just applied for the job as MACLT's executive director. I will never forget taking a walk around Troy Gardens the morning of my job interview. The only thing on the grounds was a community garden, but I could imagine all the things that were to come: a delicious mix of urban agriculture, green space conservation and restoration, and mixed-income cohousing. It seemed so cutting-edge, especially since the ideas that formed the basis for this proposed project had all sprung from the people who lived in the surrounding neighborhood. Troy Gardens was to be developed on a foundation of excellent community organizing, accompanied by the involvement of lots of bright, hard-working people from the University of Wisconsin, local nonprofit organizations, and an increasing number of fans within governmental agencies at the city, state, and even federal level.

It has been an extraordinary journey, more rewarding than I could have ever imagined. It has also been far more difficult. I lost my mentor, Sol Levin, just four months after I started. Sol had been the "godfather" of Troy Gardens for the six previous years. Many times, it was only through the sheer force of his personality that the project had kept moving forward. His sudden death broke all of our hearts and cast the whole project into question.

By 2002, Troy Gardens was in real trouble. We had staked our organizational future on pulling off this hugely complex development. But we had lost our visionary leader. MACLT's sole staff person, myself, had no development experience. And we had a board that had become highly ambivalent about the whole project. Fully a third of MACLT's board members were expressing concerns that Troy Gardens would end up killing the organization.

I'm not the brightest person in the world, but I did the smartest thing I could have possibly done—I asked for help from a lot of people. And this is what saved the project. I could not possibly tell the story of Troy Gardens without saying something about their contributions.

Troy Gardens Hall of Fame

Although I'm not particularly religious, I confess that the first person I asked for help was Sol Levin, who had departed to that "Great Community Resource Park in the Sky," the name he sometimes gave to his own notion of heaven. I'd ask myself, "What would Sol do?" Sometimes it worked. Sometimes it didn't—and that's when I looked to other people for help.

So I asked our woefully underpaid architect, Jim Glueck, if he would agree to be my mentor and teach me about the development process—which he did, spending countless hours showing me the ropes, while allowing me an equal voice in the design process. And there was Bill Perkins, now our board president, whom I consider the Red Auerbach of affordable housing. He made a generous commitment to school me in the business of housing development, just to prove to his departed friend Sol that he did indeed believe in community land trusts.

I also took what might seem to be a somewhat counterintuitive step of asking for help from our primary funding source, the City of Madison's Community Development Office. Both Hickory Hurie and Barb Constans were friends of Sol's who had embraced his vision for Troy Gardens. I decided to confess to them that I didn't know how we were going to pull off this ambitious project, even though we were still determined to try our hardest. These fine city officials were both supportive and patient. They stood by the project and pushed me forward when I was too overwhelmed to take the next step.

Sol's favorite author when it came to housing and community development (and yet another of Sol's close friends) was John Davis. So I called and wrote John a lot after Sol died. John always made time to answer questions and teach me about community land trusts—and to laugh about how Sol had created quite a pickle for us to deal with.

There were also two people who helped me to appreciate the history and destiny of Troy Gardens. Marcia Caton Campbell, a professor at the UW–Madison Department of Urban and Regional Planning, dedicated her academic research to Troy Gardens and was a partner and confidant throughout the arduous three-year planned unit development (PUD) process. For part of this period, she also served as the president of MACLT's board. And there was Marge Pitts, the poet laureate of Troy Gardens, who taught me about the beauty of gardening and made me believe that there was a spirit watching over us at Troy Gardens that would make sure we would always find our way.

That watchful spirit, of course, was Sol. It was hardly a surprise that the day when the Madison Common Council finally approved our PUD application for Troy Gardens was also the third anniversary of Sol's death. There has always been some kind of magic at Troy Gardens—the magic created by people dreaming big dreams and having the courage and tenacity to go after them.

Housing as a "Necessary Evil"

There is a certain irony to the fact that the initial community organizing around Troy Gardens focused on preventing any housing from being built. When Sol introduced the possibility of including an affordable housing component in Troy Gardens, he was met with skepticism and outright hostility. Sol was persistent, however, explaining to the site's neighbors that affordable housing could be a fruitful source of funding to purchase the land and to preserve the vast majority of Troy Gardens for green space and urban agriculture.

When other sources of funding for land acquisition proved to be elusive, members of the Troy Gardens Coalition grudgingly accepted the possibility of including a housing element. Their agenda shifted from resisting all development to debating the maximum number of housing units that might be acceptable—and the type of housing it should be. What came out of this conversation with the surrounding neighborhood was agreement on a plan to develop a 20- to 30-unit mixed-income cohousing community clustered in the southeast quadrant of the Troy Gardens site.

The Madison Area CLT was now committed to a very complex model of housing development, one that would require an extraordinary amount of community participation. It would challenge us to develop and sell market-priced units alongside affordably priced, resale-restricted units, which we had never done before. In order to honor the environmental ethic of Troy Gardens, we also substantially expanded our goals around green building practices, incorporating renewable energy systems, green building materials, low-flow water fixtures, and other green features into the project's design. To respect the beauty of Troy Gardens, we made a commitment to go the extra mile in terms of exterior building materials and architectural design. To make sure that everyone could live at Troy Gardens, we deepened our commitment to accessible design as well.

Green Building and Universal Design

Beginning in 2002, the Madison Area CLT began constructing highly energy-efficient homes that incorporated a commitment to universal design principles, offering a high degree of physical accessibility for persons with disabilities. It took the efforts of one of our board members, Dave Borski, to push me toward making green building a central priority. I was not in a position to argue with him, so I began my apprenticeship as a green builder, learning from him, as well as Len Lenzmeier, a retired homebuilder. In the case of universal design, I brought to the project my years of work as a fair housing advocate. I simply introduced universal design principles into our housing program without asking anybody's permission.

By the time we had finalized our construction plans and specifications for Troy Gardens in early 2006, the commitment to green building and universal design had shifted from a few "burning souls" to a full organizational commitment. At Troy Gardens, we felt an obligation to raise the bar for both of these principles because we wanted the sustainability features of the housing site to be up to the same standard as the rest of Troy Gardens. We wanted the whole 31 acres to work as an integrated unit. Some folks on the board questioned whether there would actually be a market for green-built accessible housing. They worried that the added cost of these features would do little to help us to sell the homes we were about to build. But without the green building and universal design features, the housing would have seemed like an intruder at Troy Gardens.

We spent months sorting out what features we could or could not afford. In the end, we came up with a set of specifications that hit about 90 percent of our goals. We also made a decision to reduce our own developer's fee in order to add green features, hoping that doing things right at Troy Gardens would yield long-term benefits for our organization.

I now see green and accessible design as part of the same thing: they are both elements of sustainability. When I think about accessibility, I simultaneously think about access for persons with disabilities, access for persons of modest incomes, access to public transportation, and access to good schools. To do this well, you must have a long time horizon from the first moments of the design process. Sustainability is not a short-term proposition. Nor is community. To have meaning and value, communities must endure for many years. This brings us back to the community land trust, of course, a model that makes forever possible.

Housing Finally Wins Friends at Troy Gardens

During the initial months of construction at Troy Gardens, the Troy Gardens community (in particular the community gardeners and neighbors), had a range of reactions to the changes they were seeing at Troy Gardens. Although the vast majority of them stayed positive in their words and actions, it was obvious that many folks were still apprehensive about what new housing would mean for Troy Gardens and the surrounding neighborhood.

Now, several years later, with the construction completed, the landscaping growing in, and the cohousing community more firmly established, these fears have largely dissipated. Troy Gardens' new homeowners have brought an influx of new blood and energy to the neighborhood and provided new members for the Friends of Troy Gardens.[1] The housing's design has proved to be compatible with the natural areas of Troy Gardens and does not visually dominate the landscape. Gardeners and residents of the surrounding neighborhood have come to see the new housing as an integral part of the fabric of Troy Gardens.

The housing has been valuable in other ways, for it has proven to be the added element that makes Troy Gardens an "ecovillage," a replicable model for sustainable urban development. The design, affordability, and compatibility of the housing with its natural and social surroundings have also driven much of the national recognition that has focused on Troy Gardens since its completion in 2007.

Evolving Partnerships at Troy Gardens

Relationships at Troy Gardens have shifted considerably since the land was purchased in 2001. MACLT's role was paramount in the overall direction of the process of planning and developing the site. A newly formed association, the Friends of Troy Gardens, played a key role in soliciting input into planning for the site's open space and agricultural areas. The Urban Open Space Foundation (UOSF) played a key role in obtaining funding from the Wisconsin Department of Natural Resources for restoration of the woodlands and prairie areas of the site.[2]

The City of Madison's Evolution Regarding Troy Gardens

When the City of Madison began to consider the development possibilities at Troy Gardens, back in 1995, municipal staff in the Department of Planning and Development expressed a clear preference for a traditional subdivision at Troy Gardens, hoping to maximize property tax revenues. Over the next three years, the combined efforts of the Northside Planning Council (and lead organizer Tim Carlisle), neighborhood residents, and MACLT's Executive Director, Sol Levin, slowly persuaded municipal staff and elected officials to think about Troy Gardens in a more outside-the-box way. By 1998, the Madison Common Council approved a "development concept plan" for Troy Gardens that included the mixture of land uses that exist at Troy Gardens today. By 2002, when MACLT began the PUD application process, there had been a profound shift in the attitudes of municipal staff and elected officials, with virtually everyone having become a fan of the mixed-use project being proposed for Troy Gardens.

Because Madison's zoning code is nearly 40 years old, most new development projects take advantage of a "custom" zoning process tailored to each individual site, known as planned unit development (PUD). The sheer diversity of land uses at Troy Gardens made the PUD process extremely complex. No project remotely like it had ever come before the City's staff; there were no templates from which to start. And because we had agreed to give the neighborhood and community gardeners veto power over major decisions at Troy Gardens, we added even more complexity. Any modifications resulting from negotiations with municipal staff had to be brought back to multiple stakeholders for discussion and approval.

While the level of community engagement in the planning process for Troy Gardens was both intensive and extensive, it was not entirely foreign to MACLT. As a community land trust, we are, by our very mission, tied to the larger community, on whose behalf we hold land in the first place. The experience of working with neighborhood residents and community gardeners at Troy Gardens deepened our appreciation for what it means to put the "community" into a community land trust.

Community Engagement

Community engagement went through two distinct cycles at Troy Gardens. From 1995 to 2001, there was continually and consistently a high level of engagement between residents of the neighborhoods surrounding the site and the multiple organizations that had an interest in using the site. Then, from 2002 to 2005, there was an "inward turning" by MACLT as it began working with various development professionals to produce the documents required for the PUD application to the City of Madison. MACLT worked with a landscape architect, civil engineer, architect, and attorney to develop the site plan, floor plans and elevations, and legal documents necessary for the PUD application, striving to stay with the development concept plan of 1998.

There was a mixed response from the community to this "inward turning" by MACLT. People familiar with the PUD application process understood the need for a more "behind the scenes" approach to assembling the technical materials required for the City's approval of the project. Neighbors and gardeners who were less familiar with the PUD process, however, grew concerned that MACLT's control over the planning process was becoming more closely held and less inclusive. MACLT, for its part, could have done a better job of keeping everyone posted on the project's progress.

Because everyone involved with Troy Gardens was passionate about it, people were quick to speak up whenever they were frustrated or left in the dark. This happened a number of times. Fortunately, the one constant at Troy Gardens has always been a commitment to resolve differences of opinion, taking whatever time is necessary to make sure that everyone has been heard and that a good faith effort to reach consensus has been made. This has not always been a smooth process. Passions and opinions often ran high and solutions sometimes remained elusive for weeks or months at a time. What got the Troy Gardens community through these rocky times was a love of the land, respect for the neighborhood, and the commitment of a remarkable group of individuals to hang on for dear life and to persist in moving forward.

The Power of a Beautiful Dream

Troy Gardens has been propelled by a beautiful dream that was passionately articulated by neighborhood residents and carefully honed by multiple partners in a true spirit of collaboration. Once City staffers and other "outsiders" got over their initial skepticism that a project like this could be brought to fruition, they were helpless to resist. Everyone wanted to be thought of as the "good guy" when it came to Troy Gardens. The City of Madison's staff and the staff of multiple organizations with a stake in the project brought a spirit of creative problem-solving to Troy Gardens, finding a way to get it done.

The Promise and Challenge of Community Building

From my experience at Troy Gardens, I am finding that every CLT defines community in a different way. Indeed, it is not always clear what "community" means. Are we referring to the community of CLT homeowners? Are we referring to the community of people who become members of the CLT? Or is the community everyone who lives within the CLT's service area?

There is no one community that is involved with the MACLT. There is the community of our CLT homeowners, who are scattered across three different development projects (as well as scattered-site single-family homes) in a variety of different neighborhoods across Madison. There is the community of people who reside in the neighborhoods surrounding our residential projects. There is also the community of CLTs across the United States of which MACLT is a part, a community joined together by the National Community Land Trust Network.

Then too, there is the community of the Madison Area CLT's board of directors. As our former board president Marcia Caton Campbell has said:

> MACLT's board feels different than any other board I've ever been involved in or had occasion to observe. We share a passion and a commitment to making something happen that is different—we work for *the broader public good,* rather than for *a single public good,* such as a stream or a parcel of land. And if you think of the differences between conservation land trusts and CLTs,

we're really working for the good of all and far into the future. We seek to reach across income levels and bring people into a community of affordable homeownership that provides them stability and affords them the opportunity to participate in society in so many other ways, because they are fundamentally more secure.

To me, putting "community" in CLT means continually asking the question of which community should be involved in every big (and sometimes little) decision that we make. At Troy Gardens, it meant thinking very specifically about who the stakeholders were for any given issue, and figuring out what was the best way to engage with them to make a decision that we all could live with. Sometimes it meant having coffee, sharing a few beers, holding community charrettes or email exchanges—whatever venue or form of communication might work best for the persons and issues involved. This also led us to look for partners who could help facilitate community involvement, so we could involve local neighborhood residents more efficiently and effectively. Above all, it meant being willing to take more time to do our projects so as to honor the voices of our stakeholders.

The Recipe for Troy Gardens

Over the past few years, I have been asked by a number of people for advice on how they can develop a project like Troy Gardens in their own community. What is the replicable recipe for completing a project like Troy Gardens? Obviously, it is NOT "Buy 31 acres in a prosperous city at $10,000 an acre—no brownfields allowed." If that is what it takes, there is little chance of spreading the seeds of Troy Gardens more widely. Furthermore, we need to be very clear about just what "seeds" we are talking about. Troy Gardens has been, and still is, far from a perfect project. But there are many lessons embedded within our experience at Troy Gardens that might be instructive to other communities wanting to do a sustainable development project that incorporates the elements of Troy Gardens.

First, we start with *community organizing,* because that is the only way to pull together a community to figure out what vision it might have for itself. We were fortunate to have great organizing by Tim Carlisle of the Northside Planning Council. If not for his diligence and skill, these 31 acres might have been turned into just another vinyl-clad subdivision.

The second ingredient in our recipe is *tenacity.* Projects like this are very challenging. You must push through more than one brick wall to make them happen.

Third is *patience.* Projects, particularly outside-the-box projects, take a long, long time. Our system of municipal zoning and development approval does not lend itself easily or swiftly to multifaceted projects that combine housing, open space, urban agriculture, and the many sustainability features that are found at Troy Gardens.

Fourth is putting *agriculture* at the heart of your project. The threatened loss of the community gardens, which had existed on the site for many years, sparked the organizing effort that led to everything else. Community gardens saved Troy Gardens, and remain the heart and soul of the place. Community gardens are the best engine of community building that I have ever seen, crossing every conceivable boundary of class, race, and culture.

Fifth is *partnership*. I don't know of any organization that can carry out all of the elements required to do a project like this alone. Partnering expands your horsepower. It also requires you to give away control. But it really isn't giving away control if you couldn't pull it off by yourself in the first place.

Sixth is dense *clustering of housing* to preserve open spaces. By grouping all the housing in a five-acre portion of the site, 26 acres were freed up for a farm, community gardens, and a restored prairie. If every home at Troy Gardens had been designed and developed with its own backyard, preservation and restoration of so much open space would never have been possible

Seventh is the *community land trust model*. I put it seventh because I talk a lot about building homes for seven generations of homeowners, which is what the CLT model is all about. Because the community was so committed to the permanent protection of the green space at Troy Gardens, people understood the value that the stewardship function of the community land trust model could bring to Troy Gardens. When we talked about our 99-year renewable ground lease, people understood the benefit this type of long-term orientation would bring to Troy Gardens. Nowadays, people talk about Troy Gardens being around forever. It is the CLT model that allows people to have confidence that "forever" might be attainable.

Eight is *accessibility*. This has several dimensions: physical accessibility of housing for everyone, regardless of disability/ability; accessibility to home ownership for people of modest incomes; accessibility to green spaces for the whole community; access to fresh healthy food through urban agriculture; and access to public transportation, including the ability to walk or bike to places important to you.

Ninth is *government support*. Federal, state, county, and city support were essential to Troy Gardens. This project would never have happened without it. A key element of such government support was being very thoughtful when it came to the sale or transfer of publicly owned land. In Madison, we were able to make sure that the conveyance of state-owned land supported the public's interest.

Tenth is *belief*. You can't do a project like Troy Gardens unless you believe in the power and beauty of the dream you are trying to achieve. Belief helps you find a way through interpersonal conflicts that can grind you down unless all the players and partners hold on to a shared vision for what they are trying to accomplish. Sol Levin had faith that things would work out for Troy Gardens long before there was any logical reason to think so. His faith was infectious, and helped to carry a whole lot of people over the finish line, through difficult times and countless obstacles.

The Vision Thing—Community, Land, and Trust

When we discuss CLTs, we often spend much more time talking about "land" and "community." Rarely do we devote as much time to thinking deeply and creatively about the word "trust."

Trust is a dynamic term, with multiple layers of meaning. "Community land trust" does not refer to a trust in a legalistic sense, but instead conveys a commitment to hold land for the benefit of the community, however that community is defined. As a result of my experience with Troy Gardens, I now understand "trust" in a deeper way, where the CLT has an ongoing obligation to earn the trust of the community it serves. I have learned that trust is not a static concept. No matter what you have done in the past, you need to continue to act in a manner that validates the community's trust in your ethics and your work. When people's hopes and dreams are tied up in your work, you simply cannot expect people to trust your intentions based on what you have done in the past. You need to demonstrate a willingness to continue to earn that trust going forward.

So when we think about the "community land trust," we need to pull those words apart and find our own localized meaning. Each word is translated into action very differently in each of our communities.

At MACLT, I now have a notion of community that starts with the neighborhood and goes all the way to the whole world. I know that I cannot be as successful with our own little CLT unless we have a strong national CLT movement. I have put in a lot of time, therefore, working on behalf of a fledgling organization known as the National CLT Network. And I think of myself as part of a global community of people and organizations focused on affordable and sustainable development that respects the wishes of local residents, hoping that our work at Troy Gardens can help contribute to the global dialogue around these issues.

Where Are the Dreamers in the CLT Movement?

Much of the writing to date about the CLT movement has been focused on the technical, financial, and political details of implementing this unusual form of tenure. Very little has been focused on dreaming big dreams. We have become practical—which is important and which has led to an explosion in the number of CLTs around the US—but we don't talk so much anymore about "pie in the sky" topics like land reform.

In these challenging times, we absolutely need to be practical. But if we sacrifice all of our big bold dreams in the service of practicality, we will lose the passion that has fueled our movement since its earliest days. Big dreams have predominated at Troy Gardens. The practical has always been in service to those big dreams. Big dreams take you to a better place. Being purely practical can take you places that are good, but never to places that are magical.

NOTES

1. Friends of Troy Gardens changed their name to Community GroundWorks at Troy Gardens in 2008.

2. Urban Open Space Foundation changed their name to the Center for Resilient Cities in 2007. After completing their initial natural areas restoration work at Troy Gardens, the Center's role was largely confined to matters pertaining to site management and monitoring the conservation easement they hold on the 26 acres of open land on the site.

FROM *Preserving Farms for Farmers*

Kirby White
(2009)

If farms are to be preserved for farmers, they must be kept affordable for farmers. The disturbing reality is that, in many real estate markets today, active farming is dying off because farms are being sold to nonfarmers for prices that are not affordable for farmers. This fact is an obvious problem not only for aspiring farmers who are unable to purchase farms but for local communities that have an interest in preserving a viable agricultural economy and access to locally produced food. Any long-term solution to this problem requires a new approach to farm ownership.

Causes of the Problem

What are the reasons that nonfarmers are willing and able to pay more for farms than farmers can afford? There are two basic reasons. In some cases the price of a farm is unaffordable for farmers because the farm's "development value" (based on the profits to be made from developing the land) is greater than its agricultural value (based on the profits to be made from farming). In other cases the price of a farm is unaffordable for farmers because the farm's "estate value" (based on what some buyers will pay for rural estates) is greater than its agricultural value.

Development Value

In rapidly developing areas there is an immediate demand for open land that can be subdivided for the construction of new homes or used for the construction of new malls, parking lots, etc. And even in areas that are not yet experiencing intensive development but lie in the path of encroaching development, investors with an eye on future development are likely to outbid farmers when farms are put on the market. Existing farmers in these areas may continue farming for a time (though facing a growing array of problems as local agricultural activities decline), but when their farms are eventually sold, they will not be sold to farmers. The simple fact is that developers—or investors who expect eventually to sell to developers—will pay more for this land than farmers can afford to pay.

This selection combines two chapters from a manual entitled *Preserving Farms for Farmers* by Kirby White (Turners Falls, MA: Equity Trust, 2009). They are printed by permission of Kirby White and Equity Trust.

Estate Value

But in a growing number of rural areas around the country the problem of farmland affordability is not a result of current or expected development. In these areas, the price of land is being driven up because of demand from affluent people seeking homes in pleasant rural surroundings. Some of these people are buying second homes, some are buying retirement homes, and some are professionals who, as telecommuters, are able to pursue their careers while living in places chosen for their scenery, serenity, and privacy rather than for their proximity to urban centers. They are people who buy farms, but they buy them neither to farm them nor to subdivide and develop them; they buy farms as places to live amid attractive open space.

The Problem Facing Would-Be Farmers

Young people who want to enter farming—whether as ranchers in California or Colorado, or as dairy farmers in Wisconsin or Vermont, or as growers of fruits and vegetables in New York's Hudson Valley or Oregon's Willamette Valley—cannot compete with the buying power that these affluent people bring into rural real estate markets. In these situations, the inescapable economic reality is that the amount of debt that aspiring farmers would need to assume in order to buy farms in such markets cannot be serviced with the income these farms would generate. Unless they have access to substantial capital from another source, such people are unable to purchase farms.

The Problem Facing Local Communities

It is not only would-be farmers who suffer in this situation. As retiring farmers sell their farms to nonfarmers, the number of farms within a community steadily decreases, often to the point where there are no longer enough farms to support the kinds of secondary businesses—agricultural suppliers, shippers, etc.—that are essential to an agricultural economy. As farming thus dwindles, the face of the local community changes. Fields grow up to brush. Fences, barns and other agricultural improvements deteriorate. Ironically, the pastoral landscape that helped to attract nonfarmers to the area in the first place can be lost as nonfarmers replace farmers. At the same time, consumers in the area are likely to be deprived of the opportunity to purchase locally produced food.

Renting: An Inadequate Solution

Traditionally, secure long-term land tenure for farmers has meant outright ownership of farms. But would-be farmers who cannot afford to purchase farms outright are usually forced to choose between not farming at all and farming rented land. Farming rented land, however, has some significant disadvantages.

The Lack of Long-Term Security

It is common today for some farmers to rent land from nonfarmers (including those who have purchased farms as "estates"). These nonfarmer owners often want to prevent their fields from growing up to brush and may particularly like the idea of having their land used productively. They may therefore be willing to rent land to farmers on an affordable basis. But the long-term availability of this land is usually less secure than the farmer would like. The rental arrangement is often established on a year-to-year basis, and it is rare for individual owners to enter into formal lease agreements for terms of more than five years. In some cases, landowners may assure the farmer that they *intend* the arrangement to continue "indefinitely," and the arrangement may in fact continue for a long time, but there will always be the possibility that owners' situations will change in ways that force them to sell, or that they will die and their heirs will be unable or unwilling to continue the lease arrangement. In such cases farmers who do not have a truly long-term lease (written in terms that will be binding on succeeding owners) could be forced to give up land that they may have spent years developing and on which their operation depends.

The Lack of Affordable Housing

A further problem for farmers who must rent the land they work is that the rental situation often does not include housing for them and their families. Even if there is a house on the farm they are working, it is likely to be occupied by the landowner, not the land renter. Farmers in these situations, if they can find affordable housing at all, may be forced to live some distance from the farm and commute to work. If the owner of the farmland does make housing available on the land, the farm family's situation is of course improved, but it will normally be rental housing, without the long-term security of home ownership.

The Lack of Opportunities to Build Equity

Even if a farmer is fortunate enough to be able to continue renting farmland for the long term—and even if the rental situation includes affordable housing—the situation still does not provide one of the important advantages of conventional ownership. It does not provide the opportunity to build equity through investment in agricultural—and residential—improvements. When farmers who have spent years working rented land eventually retire or move on to another farm or another venture, they have no way to sell any of the value they have built up in their farms over the years—no way to capture that value and use it to meet their future needs or to benefit their heirs.

The Need for New Models of Land Tenure

Conventional ownership does give farmers secure long-term tenure with the opportunity to build equity in both agricultural and residential improvements. The problem with conventional ownership is not that it is a bad deal for those farmers who are fortunate enough to enjoy it. The problem, as we have said, is that, when those farmers or their heirs eventually sell these farms in appreciated real estate markets, the prices will not be affordable for entering farmers. The farms will be purchased by nonfarmers, and the local agricultural economy will be eroded.

The question is whether there are other forms of ownership that give farmers long-term tenure and the opportunity to build significant equity while, at the same time, preventing farms from being eventually priced out of reach of future farmers. Are there ownership models that strike a balance between the existing farmer's interest in owning his or her farm and, on the other hand, the interests of aspiring farmers who want to buy farms for affordable prices and the interests of local communities that want to preserve an agricultural economy and continue to enjoy access to fresh local produce? We will focus here on two ownership models that do allow such a balance to be struck. Before introducing these models, however, let us take a fresh look at what is meant by "ownership" in the first place.

Property as a Bundle of Rights

Attorneys and legal scholars describe the ownership of real estate not in terms of a single all-inclusive right of ownership but in terms of a "bundle of rights" that can be, and often are, separated. Water rights, mineral rights, timber rights, grazing rights, air rights, rights of way, and development rights are examples of specific rights that are often conveyed separately from the other rights relating to a particular piece of real estate. It is thus very common for a person to own a *limited* set of rights consisting of less than the full bundle, and thus to *share* the full bundle with others.

Someone who does own a more or less full bundle of rights related to a parcel of real estate is said to own the parcel "in fee simple" (though even a fee-simple owner's rights are limited in certain ways—notably by the public's right to tax, regulate, and even take possession of the property for public use). A person who holds a bundle of rights can transfer one or more of those rights to another party while retaining the rest of the rights. For instance, he or she may transfer development rights through a conservation easement donated or sold to a land trust, while continuing to own, occupy, and use the land for purposes other than development.

Or a person may transfer the right to occupy and use the property—in specified ways for specified periods of time—by giving a lease to another party. As we have noted, the leasing of farmland on a relatively short-term basis is generally not a satisfactory arrangement for a farmer. However, when a land lease (or "ground lease") conveys occupancy and use rights for a very long time, the rights of the "leaseholder," or "ground lessee," begin to look more like the rights of a conventional owner and may include the right to develop, own, and eventually sell buildings and other improvements on the leased land.

These two ownership arrangements—one involving conservation easements and the other involving long-term ground leases—provide legal frameworks for some of today's more innovative efforts to preserve farms for farmers.

Conservation Easements

Typical conservation easements are a means by which a landowner gives up the right to develop the land by transferring development rights to a nonprofit land trust or government agency that will hold those rights permanently—thus *withholding* them permanently from the marketplace. In markets where land is valued more for its development potential than for agricultural use, the removal of development rights may, by itself, bring the market value of the remaining ownership rights down to a level that a farmer can afford. However, in the increasing number of markets where the price of land is being driven up not by its development potential but by affluent people seeking rural estates, the removal of development rights may not result in a significant reduction in the price of the property. In fact, it is increasingly common for such "easement-protected" estates to be sold for prices just as high as would be the case without those easements—simply because the purchasers of those properties are seeking open space and privacy, not development opportunities.

It should be noted, too, that even in areas where the removal of development rights might bring the price of a parcel of agricultural *land* down to a more affordable level, the market value of a *farm* typically includes not just the value of the available agricultural land but also the value of any existing improvements, usually including a farmhouse. As a result, the price of the farm as a whole—with a potentially very desirable residence surrounded by easement-protected open space—is likely to be beyond the reach of farmers.

It is possible, however, for easements to do more than simply remove development rights from open land. The type of easement described in this manual goes well beyond the removal of development rights. It not only prohibits the development of farmland; it requires that the farmland be actively farmed, and, if there is a farmhouse, it may require that the house be occupied by the farmer-owner. These requirements alone may effectively remove the estate value that the farm might otherwise have for nonfarmers. In addition, however, this type of easement grants a purchase option to the holder of the easement, thus giving that institution a way to insure that when the farm is eventually sold, it will be sold to another farmer for a price that a farmer can afford. Because such an easement removes more rights from the bundle of rights relating to a particular property, it removes a larger share of the unrestricted market value of the property than does a more conventional conservation easement. A land trust purchasing such an easement therefore expects to pay a higher price than it would pay for the conventional easement.

Ground Leases with Lessee Ownership of Improvements

Another approach to preserving farmland is to use the sort of mixed-ownership leasehold structure that has been pioneered in the United States by community land trusts. Under this arrangement, the fee interest in the land is acquired and held by a community land trust or other stewardship institution, while specific rights of possession and use are transferred to the farmer, along with the ownership of buildings and other improvements on the land. Farmers normally buy existing improvements (typically including a farmhouse) when they enter into the ground lease agreement and may later develop and own additional improvements subject to the terms of the lease. Ground leases are often written for terms of 99 years, with provisions for inheritance of the leasehold interest, and may be renewable upon the expiration of that term, so they can provide very long-term, multigenerational land tenure for farm families.

As a legal means of separating one set of ownership rights from another, the ground lease is quite different from the conservation easement, but the two models can be used—and are used in the forms presented here—to establish the same kinds of restrictions and requirements regarding the use and transfer of property.

Similarities and Differences between Ground Leases and Conservation Easements

Both ownership arrangements provide ways of managing the long-term use and allocation of agricultural land. Both involve forms of "shared ownership" that separate the rights in a "bundle" of ownership rights so that farmers can purchase for an affordable price the rights that are important to them, while a land trust or other institution plays a long-term stewardship role. Both provide not only a means of prohibiting or restricting nonagricultural uses and ecologically damaging practices but also a means of *requiring* continued agricultural use and owner-occupancy, and both entail the granting of a purchase option that will give the stewardship institution a significant degree of control over transfers of ownership, allowing that institution to see that the property will be passed on to other farmers for prices that farmers can afford. Both types of instrument are highly flexible as to the kinds of activities they regulate and the extent to which they regulate them. Either one may simply require agricultural use of the property, with such use broadly defined; or, at the other extreme, either one may closely regulate agricultural practices—for instance, by requiring organic or biodynamic farming or by requiring the implementation of a detailed land management plan.

The two types of instrument do differ in fundamental ways, however. In the case of the easement, it is the farmer who owns the fee interest in the property, subject to certain restrictions, while certain rights and a certain portion of the unrestricted market value of the property are held permanently by a land trust or other institution. The farmer's interest in the property can be sold only subject to the restrictions imposed by the easement.

Ground leases differ from easements in that they do not "run with the land" as *perpetual* restrictions in the way that easements do. When a ground lease is given up by a farmer-lessee, the landowner-lessor has an opportunity to buy the improvements and revisit the question of what requirements and restrictions should be applied to the property from that time forward. The holder of a conservation easement, for better or for worse, has much less freedom at such times to change the requirements and restrictions imposed by the easement.

Another difference between the two models involves the ways the restrictions and requirements can be enforced. A land trust that leases land to a farmer is in a stronger position with regard to enforcement than a land trust that holds an easement. As the owner of the fee interest in the land, the land trust has the power, ultimately, to evict a ground lessee who violates restrictions or requirements. A ground lease also gives the land trust certain advantages when it comes to the control of transfers from one farmer to another. The landowner may refuse to approve the transfer of the lease (or refuse to issue a new lease) to a purchaser of the improvements if the transaction is not in compliance with the terms of the lease—for example, if the purchaser is not qualified as a farmer, or if the price exceeds the purchase option price. The landowner does not necessarily have to exercise the purchase option to prevent such transfers, whereas the holder of an easement and option can prevent such transfers only by exercising the option (although, after the transfer, the easement holder will have a right to take action against a new owner who violates the terms of the easement).

Relative Advantages for Farmers

Which of these approaches is more acceptable and more workable for farmers in varying situations depends on several factors. The fact that a ground lessee has "outright title" only to the improvements and is in a "weaker" position with regard to enforcement will mean that many farmers would prefer that their farm be subject to an easement rather than a ground lease. At the same time, the up-front cost of acquiring both land and improvements subject to an easement can be greater than the up-front cost of acquiring just the improvements together with a leasehold interest in the land (the leasehold normally being paid for month by month), so for many new farmers the latter approach is likely to be more affordable. Also, as circumstances affecting the farm change over time, it may be easier for the farmer to renegotiate certain kinds of provisions in a ground lease than in an easement (although a "Restrictions and Requirements Exhibit," with provisions for amendment, can be attached to either type of document).

Relative Advantages for Stewardship Institutions

Stewardship institutions, too, may have specific reasons to prefer one approach over the other. Not surprisingly, many land trusts are more comfortable in the familiar role of easement holder than in the unfamiliar role of landowner-lessor. But, if the easement is to include a purchase option and if easement and option are to apply to house and barns and other farmstead improvements as well as to farmland, the situation may feel not at all familiar to land trusts. Some of them, if they want to see that the farmstead as well as the farmland remains affordable to farmers, or if they want greater freedom to adjust the nature of the restrictions from one farmer's tenure to the next, may decide that fee ownership of the land and the use of a ground lease is a more workable—though potentially more expensive—way of accomplishing their purposes.

Caretaker Farm

The case of Caretaker Farm serves to illustrate some of the advantages, complexities, and challenges in applying the ground-leasing mechanism of a land trust to the preservation of a working farm. Since this particular farm is operated as a CSA (community supported agriculture), this case also illustrates the potential for combining two unconventional models, the CLT and the CSA.

A 35-acre farm in the northwest corner of Massachusetts, Caretaker Farm had been operated as an organic vegetable farm for 35 years and as a CSA for 15 years when its owners, Sam and Elizabeth Smith, decided it was time for them to retire. If they had sold the farm, which included two attractive residences, for its estate value, the proceeds would have been more than enough to finance a comfortable retirement. But the Smiths were determined to see the farm continue as a farm and to see the CSA continue as the vibrant community institution that it had become under their stewardship. They were prepared to sell the farm to new farmers for less than its unrestricted market value, but for years they had invested themselves and their resources in the farm, and, in turning it over to new farmers, they did need to recover enough of that hard-earned equity to support their retirement. The problem was that the price they needed to receive, though a bargain compared to market-rate prices, would still be unaffordable for new farmers.

The eventual solution to this problem entailed sharing ownership of the property among four different parties—the Commonwealth of Massachusetts, a local land trust, the retiring farmers, and the new farmers—with Equity Trust Inc., playing a role as intermediary in distributing these ownership interests. The resulting ownership arrangement involved both a conservation easement (with purchase option) and two ground leases with two separate leaseholders.

Background

In 1969 Sam and Elizabeth purchased an old, run-down dairy farm in a secluded valley near the foot of Mount Greylock, seven miles south of the village of Williamstown, Massachusetts. They named their new home Caretaker Farm and, with a clear awareness of their own long-term role as caretakers, set about the decades-long process of restoring the farm's fertility and its infrastructure. But their goal was not only to be responsible stewards; they also wanted to make a living from this piece of land for themselves and their children. And this would not be easy. Of Caretaker Farm's 35 acres only 9 acres are classified as tillable agricultural land—the remainder being pasture and woodland (20 acres), stream bank and wetland (3.9 acres), and the farmstead (2.5 acres).

A modern dairy operation producing a single commodity and shipping it off into a vast marketplace could not begin to provide a family's livelihood from this small parcel of land. If this land was going to support a family, a very different approach would be required—an approach that was more intensive and that at the same time embraced more diversity. The Smiths did indeed cultivate the tillable land intensively, but not to produce just a single crop year in and year out. They planted six of the nine tillable acres each year to vegetables—30 different types of vegetables—while the remaining three acres were seeded to cover crops, so that every part of the garden was rested and enriched with "green manure" one year out of three. They also raised cows, chickens, pigs, and sheep, yielding meat, dairy products, eggs, and wool—and of course animal manure to be composted and returned to the land as an essential component of the organic farming process. The operation also came to include a small orchard, three greenhouses, a bakery, and an apiary.

Caretaker has been an active trainer of new farmers through its internship program. Each year four interns—and over the years more than 100 of them—have worked on the farm during the growing season, living in rustic cabins on the property and sharing meals, and the preparation of meals, with the Smiths. Caretaker has also participated with other organic farms in western Massachusetts and the Hudson Valley in the Collaborative Regional Alliance for Farmer Training (CRAFT), which provides opportunities for interns at each of the member farms to visit other member farms and hear presentations on particular practices of the host farm.

During their first two decades with Caretaker Farm, the Smiths marketed most of the farm's produce through a farm stand and sales to restaurants, but they were attracted to the kind of cooperative producer-consumer relationship embodied in the CSA model. They launched the Caretaker Farm CSA in 1990. Fifteen years later, as they approached retirement, the CSA had more than 200 shareholders and was providing most of the farm's income. Weekly shares provided fruit and vegetables to the members from June to October, with bimonthly shares from the root cellar continuing through the winter. Meat, eggs, honey, and bread were also available to members for an extra charge.

Because all of its members live in the Williamstown area, it has been possible for the Caretaker CSA to develop a particularly strong community spirit. Members must pick up their weekly shares of produce at the farm. Many labor-intensive items are available on a pick-your-own basis, so members must make their way through various parts of the farm to fill out their shares. All members are required to work on the farm at least two hours each year. "Working Shares" are also available, which require at least ten hours of work each year. Given this level of member involvement in the life of the farm, and given the enthusiastic, welcoming spirit of Sam and Elizabeth, it is not surprising that a strong sense of community developed quickly and has been sustained ever since.

Planning for the Transition

As they approached retirement age, the Smiths were determined to find a way to ensure that what they had spent more than three decades developing—the thriving farm and thriving CSA community—would continue beyond their own tenure on a basis that would be both ecologically and economically sustainable. In their thinking about this subject, they were influenced by several old friends. For many years they had known Bob Swann, a founder of the Institute for Community Economics (ICE) and architect of the community land trust model, and his partner Susan Witt, with whom he had founded the Schumacher Society and the Community Land Trust in the Southern Berkshires. Another old friend was Chuck Matthei, who had succeeded Bob Swann as director of ICE and had later founded Equity Trust Inc., where much of his work became focused on alternative approaches to land tenure for CSAs.

A nearby example of an alternative approach to land tenure was Indian Line Farm in South Egremont, Massachusetts, which had once been owned by CSA pioneer Robyn Van En and is often described as the first CSA farm in North America. When, following Robyn Van En's death, her son was forced to sell the farm, it was purchased by the Community Land Trust in the Southern Berkshires. Part of the price was covered by the Nature Conservancy's purchase of a conservation easement for the purpose of protecting adjacent wetlands. Another part of the price was raised through donations to the CLT, and the final part was covered by the sale of the improvements to the farmers who had been operating the farm as short-term renters and who now received from the CLT a long-term ground lease that was similar in concept, if not in detail, to the model agricultural ground lease developed by Equity Trust. Sam and Elizabeth Smith decided that they liked this approach to ownership and wanted to turn over the farm to a local land trust that would make it available through a similar ground lease to future farmers.

The Williamstown Rural Lands Foundation (WRLF) was such a land trust. Founded with the mission of preserving open space and maintaining the attractive rural character of the Williamstown area, the WRLF had become increasingly aware that there was also a need for preservation of active farms as a part of the landscape, and for affordable access to land and housing for local people of modest means—farmers and nonfarmers alike—who were less and less able to compete in the area's escalating real estate market. The WRLF had a special interest in preserving Caretaker Farm, as an attractive part of the landscape, as an important community resource, and as an ally in pursuit of a shared mission. With energetic leadership from Executive Director Leslie Reed-Evans, WRLF joined with the Smiths in an effort to work out the future of the farm.

> The primary reason that even the most idealistic and conservation-minded agrarians have so fervently supported private landownership is that they saw it as the only available option for preserving the land's integrity. The irony of this system is that it makes what I valued and yearned for—secure tenure in the land in order to care for it, enjoy it and belong to it—irredeemably vulnerable. It allows land to be treated as a commodity. . . . (Sam Smith, in *Holding Ground,* New England Small Farm Institute)

Terms of Sale

The first step for the WRLF was to help the Smiths arrange to sell an Agricultural Preservation Restriction (APR) to the Commonwealth of Massachusetts. The APR not only removes development rights from the land and prohibits ecologically damaging activities but also contains the affirmative requirement that the land continue to be used for agricultural purposes. In addition, the APR gives the state an option to purchase the land for its agricultural value if the owners want to sell. Based on appraisals of both unrestricted market value and the restricted agricultural value that would remain under the APR, it was determined that the APR would remove $252,500 in value from the approximately 33 acres of Caretaker Farm that it covers (it does not cover the farmstead). The price of $252,500 was therefore paid to the Smiths. The WRLF then agreed to raise $50,000 to purchase the fee interest in the full 35 acres of land—including the farmstead.

This was a good start toward a deal that would provide the Smiths with the retirement capital they needed while keeping the farm affordable for new farmers. However, a major problem remained. The farm had an unrestricted market value (as an estate) of more than $1 million. The APR had removed some of this value, but much value remained—because the APR did not cover the 2.5-acre farmstead, with its two houses, barn and other improvements, which would still command a high price as very attractive residential property surrounded by open space. If the Smiths were to receive the full amount they needed for their retirement, the farmstead—or at least the improvements on the farmstead—would need to be sold for more than new farmers could afford. Additional money would need to be raised somehow. Exactly how much would be needed would depend on who the new farmers were and how much they were willing and able to pay for one house and all of the agricultural improvements. And of course it would also depend on how much of the property's unrestricted market value the Smiths would be willing and able to forgo (i.e., donate to the cause).

By 2005 prospective new farmers were on the scene. Don Zasada and Bridget Spann and their young daughter, Gabriela, moved to Williamstown in December of 2004 to participate in the operation of the farm and to explore the possibility of becoming its next long-term owner-caretakers. Don had previously been farm manager for the Food Project in Lincoln, Massachusetts, a nonprofit program that involves young people from the Boston area in the production and distribution of food. Don had loved his work for the Food Project, but the family had paid monthly rent of $1,200 for a (subsidized!) one-bedroom apartment three miles from the town-owned farmland. For the long run they wanted a place of their own where they would have, as Sam Smith had once described it, "secure tenure in the land in order to care for it, enjoy it and belong to it."

During the next year, intensive discussions took place among Sam and Elizabeth, Don and Bridget, Leslie Reed-Evans of WRLF, and Ellie Kastanopolous of Equity Trust Inc. A seemingly endless series of interrelated questions had to be addressed.

What price would Don and Bridget need to pay—and be able to pay—for the improvements? Exactly what ground lease restrictions and requirements would they be bound by, possibly for the rest of their lives? What total amount of proceeds would provide adequate compensation to the Smiths for what they were giving up, and what ground lease restrictions and requirements would be essential to their vision of how the farm was to be used and cared for in the future? How much additional money would need to be raised through grants and donations to reach the total compensation for the Smiths? Where and how would it be raised, and what would be the respective roles of WRLF and Equity Trust (as well as the retiring and new farmers) in raising it?

There were times when it seemed that there was no possible set of answers to these questions that would work for everyone. If the participants had not cared so deeply about finding a way to make it work, the process could not have succeeded. But they did care deeply, and a deal was finally agreed upon. The basic terms of the transfer were as follows.

The Smiths continue to own and occupy one house with a 99-year lease to the ground beneath it. Don and Bridget bought the other house and all of the agricultural improvements for their appraised agricultural value of $177,000, with mortgage financing from a local bank, and received a 99-year lease to all of the land except the small lot on which the Smiths' house was located. Finally, the Smiths received a promissory note from Equity Trust for an additional $200,000. At the closing—after the state, as holder of the purchase option contained in the APR, had approved the deal and waived its option—Equity Trust took title to the entire farm; then immediately transferred ownership of one house back to the Smiths and ownership of the rest of the improvements to Don and Bridget, while also executing the ground leases with both parties. Equity Trust then transferred the land to WRLF subject to the ground leases, with WRLF thus assuming the role of ground lessor. A fundraising campaign was launched to solicit donations to Equity Trust to allow payment of the $200,000 note and to cover fundraising costs and Equity Trust's administrative costs as fiscal intermediary. The Smiths agreed that, if the campaign did not succeed in raising the full amount in the allotted time of 2.5 years, they would forgive the balance of the debt (however, the campaign was fully successful). In summary, the Smiths sold Caretaker Farm (which had an appraised unrestricted market value at the time of $1,100,000) for a total of $679,500 ($252,500 + $50,000 + $177,000 + 200,000), and they retained ownership of a home subject to a ground lease.

The Ground Leases

Before this complicated deal could be consummated, however, it was necessary to reach agreement on the even more complicated details of two ground leases. Negotiation of the terms of the agricultural ground lease with the new farmers was especially time consuming. In fact, well before Don and Bridget were on the scene, discussions of the subject had begun between Equity Trust and the Smiths, who had a profound interest in developing a document that would protect the future of the farm in the way they wished it to be protected. Don and Bridget brought their own concerns to bear in crucial discussions with the Smiths and Equity Trust in 2005. Then, in early 2006, after the retiring and new farmers had reached basic agreement on the issues that concerned them, the drafts of both ground leases were reviewed by WRLF's attorney, who brought to bear that organization's long-term concerns with the exact nature of the obligations it would be taking on with regard to the eventual resale of Don and Bridget's interest in the farm. And of course the agricultural ground lease also had to be reviewed and accepted by the attorney for the bank from which Don and Bridget sought a leasehold mortgage loan.

The agricultural ground lease that evolved through this process was based on the Equity Trust model, but did differ in certain ways. One of the most distinctive features was a relatively detailed set of requirements pertaining to the way the land was to be farmed. Separate requirements are established for each of the several portions of the land—the tillable agricultural land, the pasture and woodland, the stream bank and wetland, and the farmstead. The Caretaker lease does not require certification of organic practices. It does, however, establish requirements and restrictions that are essentially those of organic agriculture, and the lessor-landowner has the right to monitor and enforce these provisions, but without the help of a designated third-party certifier.

To ensure continued farming on a commercial basis, rather than merely as a hobby, the Caretaker lease requires that the farmers either show gross agricultural income of at least $40,000 per year *or* show net agricultural income of at least $15,000 per year, as documented by IRS Schedule F or the equivalent. The requirement is applied to a rolling three-year average, so that a single "bad year" cannot, by itself, result in default.

Another distinctive feature of the Caretaker lease is a leave-of-absence provision for the farmers. Don and Bridget have thought that at some point in their lives they may want to spend some time working beyond Caretaker Farm—possibly, for instance, in a third world country. The lease allows them to be absent from the farm for a period of up to two years in any ten-year period, provided they arrange for someone else to operate the farm, in full compliance with the lease, during their absence.

The other Caretaker lease—the Smiths' residential ground lease—deals with circumstances quite different from those the agricultural lease addresses. Much of the basic framework remains the same, but there are no requirements or restrictions relating to agricultural use or to the lessees' income. Also absent from this lease are certain provisions that are key components of virtually all community land trust residential ground leases. There is no requirement that the lessees occupy the home as their primary residence, and there are no restrictions on their right to sublease the home. The price for which they can sell the home is restricted, but not in the way that resales of most CLT homes are restricted. If the Smiths want to sell, they must first execute a purchase-and-sale agreement with a potential buyer. The landowner-lessor will then have an option to purchase the home for a price equal to the lesser of the price stated in the purchase-and-sale agreement or "the appraised local replacement cost of the improvements less deterioration, obsolescence and damage."

It is appropriate that the strict occupancy and affordability requirements contained in most CLT residential leases, as well as in Don and Bridget's lease and the model agricultural ground lease, not be imposed on the Smiths in this unique situation. The Smiths have certainly earned the flexibility that their ground lease gives them in their retirement. It is possible that the time will come, however, when WRLF may want to consider occupancy and affordability provisions in a new lease to a new owner if their goal is to keep the home affordable for local owner-occupants.

Finally, there is one more level of complication that both of these leases needed to address. The home that the Smiths now own is located close to the agricultural improvements now owned by Don and Bridget, and activities on the adjoining leaseholds necessarily affect each other in ways that the two leases acknowledge and provide for. There is a shared driveway crossing both leaseholds, so each set of lessees is given rights to use the portion owned by the other. The septic system serving the Smith's house is located on the other leasehold, and the Smiths are given the right to maintain and, if necessary, replace it. The farm uses water from hydrants located on the Smith's leasehold, and the farmers are given the right to draw water from the hydrants and a right of way to and from the hydrants. The farmers are also given a right to maintain a deer fence located on the Smith's leasehold. In addition, both leases contain a general provision acknowledging the close proximity of the two leaseholds and stating that the lessees agree not to interfere unduly in each other's activities and to agree upon policies regulating their activities where cooperation is called for.

At the event launching the successful fundraising campaign, the guest speaker was Bill McKibben, who had included Caretaker Farm in his book *Hope, Human and Wild: True Stories of Living Lightly on the Land*. McKibben found hope in Caretaker Farm not only as a place where people lived, and farmed, "lightly on the land," but also as a place where people—both CSA members and apprentices—could come and learn and begin to appreciate the ways we can feed ourselves without doing permanent damage to our planet. Such places are valuable and must be preserved, even if it takes a complicated set of legal documents to defend them against a market system that otherwise assumes everything is for sale, sooner or later, to the highest bidder.

PART SIX

BEYOND THE UNITED STATES

Reviving Community Ownership in England

CLTs Are Ready to Take Over the Land

Jennifer Aird
(2009)

Community land trusts are not a new concept in England, but they are enjoying a recent revival. As a means of providing small-scale community-led housing, they build on traditional forms of community empowerment and existing models of common ownership.

Inspired by the success of the community land trust (CLT) movement in the United States, Community Finance Solutions at the University of Salford launched a pilot demonstration program across England in 2006. The aims were to give practical support to CLTs to help them get started, to provide them with the right tools to succeed, and to influence national policy. At that time, there were only one or two recognized community land Trusts in the entire country and they were virtually unknown among government officials. Three years later, they are being championed by all the major political parties, and there are around 30 CLTs which have already built or gotten permission to build over 150 homes.[1]

This success has been largely due to the assistance provided through the pilot CLT demonstration program, as well as the hard work and persistence of the country's CLT pioneers. CLTs have built up such momentum that politicians have been forced to sit up and take notice. A fledgling CLT movement is taking flight, reviving a rich tradition of common ownership in England. This article provides an overview of the CLT movement in England in the context of that tradition.[2]

The Economic and Social Context for CLT Development

The recent emergence of the community land trust in England has had the advantage of being able to draw on a long tradition of community ownership and management. If you go back to medieval English history, all land and other natural assets were held in community ownership, although the "modernization" or "progress" of society has seen most of these assets gradually privatized for individual gain. Village halls are an example of one type of asset that is still owned by the community. Run

This is a revised and expanded version of the article "Ready to Take Over the Land," by Robert Patterson and Jennifer Aird in *New Start* (November 14, 2008): 22–25. It is printed by permission of Jennifer Aird.

by volunteers, they exist throughout rural England and host all manner of community events and activities.

In the eighteenth century, there was a revival of the ideals of community, cooperation, and social responsibility in response to the grinding poverty created by the Industrial Revolution. People wanted to be able to shape a new and better society. This was when the international cooperative movement was born and nurtured in Manchester. It was also when the Garden Cities movement emerged, with the aim of designing more pleasant environments combining the best aspects of town and country living. Garden Cities such as Letchworth were an early form of community land trust, built on the idea of a community trust owning and managing the town. The trust would earn an income from its landed assets that would be reinvested in the community. The guiding principle of the Letchworth Garden City Heritage Foundation was to "create, maintain and promote a vibrant environment while maximizing the financial returns from the assets we hold in trust, and to reinvest those returns."

In addition to these CLT precursors, there are three other well-established and widely used models in England for the management of land and housing assets for the benefit of the community.

The first of these is the almshouse trust, which has a history stretching back over 1,000 years. Most were founded with sums of money bequeathed by the wealthy to assist poor and vulnerable people. The first charity to provide secure accommodation for the infirm was founded in York in the 10th century by King Athelstan. Today almshouses steward over 30,000 properties, providing sheltered accommodation for over 36,000 people, mostly elderly residents who pay just a small maintenance fee.

Then came the housing associations, which appeared in the 1920s as independent providers of social (affordable) housing for people in housing need. They began as local concerns rooted in their community. As they spread during the twentieth century, many grew to be large organizations and were regulated by the state. (If regulated, they are now known as registered social landlords.) Today many of these housing associations are major concerns, some managing up to 50,000 homes.[3] In total they manage around 2 million homes across England, most of them for rent.[4]

Development trusts are another example of the English tradition of common ownership. They are community organizations that use self-help, trading for social purpose, and ownership of buildings and land to bring about long-term social, economic, and environmental benefits in their community. They operate in both urban and rural areas, often in neighborhoods which have experienced the worst economic decline. They are independent, but work with public sector agencies, private businesses, and other community groups. Since the 1990s, development trusts have put around £500 million worth of assets into community ownership. Empty and derelict buildings have been transformed into busy workspaces, training rooms, conference centres, community-run shops, restaurants, and affordable housing. Wastelands have been reclaimed for parks, community woodlands, farms, and allotments.[5]

With so many well-established models for promoting common ownership, providing affordable housing, and managing assets on behalf of a local community, why were community land trusts needed in England?

First of all, villages were looking for ways to solve the housing problems affecting rural England. At the peak of the housing boom in 2007, many people were engaging in property speculation as a means of achieving large profits. This put immense pressure on the housing market, and added a huge premium to the most desirable homes in the most attractive locations. The homes that were in shortest supply were often in remote rural areas. These homes got snapped up by investors who could afford them. Local residents earning low local wages were unable to access housing. What put further pressure on local markets was that many of the houses were being bought up by outside investors as second homes.

This resulted in situations such as that of East Portlemouth, one of the least affordable places in the country. Seventy percent of the properties are second homes. Houses now sell for an average of £1.5 million[6] in an area where average local wages are just £17,000. Affordable rental properties are in short supply too, since the only profitable way to rent a property is as a holiday cottage. Many of those with jobs in the village are obliged to commute in. The village is practically empty for most of the year.

The problem is similar in other parts of the country, amounting to what the Commission for Rural Communities called a rural housing crisis. Communities such as East Portlemouth have looked for different ways of solving the problem, arriving at the CLT as a solution for taking homes out of the market and putting them into community stewardship.

Housing associations, for their part, have not been considered to be an adequate solution to this rural housing crisis, even though they are better known and better established than the CLT. There are three reasons:

- The rural situation revealed a new segment of people in need who do not meet the traditional "housing needs" criteria of the housing associations. They are not earning very low incomes nor are they unemployed. They are often young people in modest employment wanting to stay in the area where they grew up.
- The location and scale of rural housing developments is restricted by the planning system. In many rural areas, newly built homes may not be sold on the open market, but must be sold at "affordable" levels set by the local authority. Meanwhile, housing associations often rely on open market sales to fund affordable homes. As a result, in rural areas, housing associations find it difficult to find the funding to provide affordable homes and/or do not find it viable to build on the small scale required by local planning.

- Housing associations have found it difficult to find new sources of land. In some rural areas, landowners had previously sold land at an affordable price to local authorities or housing associations for the construction of social or low-income housing. When Right to Buy[7] was subsequently introduced in the 1980s, these homes were sold on the open market. This meant affordable housing was lost to the community and not replaced. The landowners who had sold the land for a discount saw their land exchanged for unrestricted profits. This led to a general distrust of housing associations in very many rural areas.

Community land trusts, in contrast, target the intermediate market of households who are not provided for by either social (public) housing or the open market. They are able to keep costs low enough to build on the small scale required. Finally, they are able to acquire sites because they can guarantee the land will remain affordable and in community ownership.

In some areas, CLTs have been created to complement an existing vehicle for common ownership, such as a development trust or almshouse trust. The CLT is able to draw on the same base of support and community empowerment as these older vehicles, while introducing legal mechanisms specifically designed for the management of housing.

CLTs and development trusts have a slightly different focus, but they are complementary approaches founded on similar principles. The latter have long managed a wealth of community assets. But as housing became a more important, if not *the* most important, issue for their communities, some development trusts found it appropriate to form a separate community land trust specifically to hold land in perpetuity for affordable housing. A few other development trusts were already providing affordable housing, so they did not deem it necessary to form a new CLT as a separate organization. They could meet the legal definition of a CLT themselves (see below), as long as they had an open democratic structure and did not provide profit to their members.[8]

CLTs may also be an appropriate model for taking on and expanding the property portfolio currently held by almshouse trusts. This was the approach taken in a village called Chipping in Lancashire, for example. The almshouse trust in this village was founded in 1684 through the will of a wealthy local merchant. The trust manages the local primary school and rents out cottages to people on low incomes. It has land and financial assets, as well as 330 years of housing management experience. The trust is now planning to invest some of its assets in a CLT, which will take the lead in developing several sites around the village. The CLT will produce and sell permanently affordable, owner-occupied homes in the village for the first time.

In short, CLTs are neither a unique nor entirely new concept in England. They build on older traditions and complement the work of other organizations that promote affordable housing and community ownership. Local interest in CLTs has spiked in the past few years, prompted by a desire for small-scale housing development in rural areas that meets local needs and that is shaped and backed by the local population.

Furthering Public Policy: Where Does the CLT Fit In?

CLTs have been championed recently in English legislation supporting sustainable communities and in two government-commissioned reviews of affordable rural housing. In 2008, an official definition of the CLT was included for the first time in the national Housing and Regeneration Act. At annual CLT conferences, convened by Community Finance Solutions, there has been cross-party political support for the model, with speakers from all three of the major parties attending.

If CLTs are to grow in number and reputation in England, however, they will have to show that (a) they can achieve various objectives of government policy and (b) they can assist in the process of civic renewal. The case currently being made by CLT advocates is that the CLT advances both of these policy goals, an argument that makes the following points:

Providing Durably Affordable Housing for All

The national government's strategic objectives for housing are laid out in what is known as Planning Policy Statement 3. Affordable housing is defined in terms of two specific requirements:[9]

- An evidence base where affordability is "determined with regard to local incomes and local house prices," and
- Arrangements for performance where housing must "remain at an affordable price for future eligible households (or) for the subsidy to be recycled for alternative affordable housing."

Many local public authorities have concluded that national affordable housing initiatives, which try to get first-time buyers onto the property ladder, fail to meet this two-fold definition of affordable housing. Community land trusts do. In England, as in the United States, CLTs are committed not only to *making* housing affordable for income-eligible households, but also to *maintaining* the affordability of this housing in perpetuity.

Fighting Asset Price Inflation

Land and house price inflation are the enemies of sustainable and affordable housing for all. Economic boom and bust has damaging consequences for investment, savings, jobs, and housing. This cycle will simply continue, as has happened regularly over the last 200 years, unless government restricts land price inflation and speculation.

Compared to England, countries like Sweden have consistently provided more housing, more quickly, that is more affordable. This housing is also built to higher sustainability standards, has a greater social and income mix, and has greater diversity of tenure and means of production, responding to local priorities. Sweden and other countries have succeeded in all these respects because they have prevented land price inflation and speculation. CLTs do the same by holding land value out of the market for the long-term benefit of all.

Giving Genuine Value for the Money

CLTs are sometimes compared unfavorably to housing associations, which are the traditional form of public and affordable housing provision in England and have long received large amounts of funding through established routes. A perception has arisen that CLTs are "more expensive" than housing associations because they cannot achieve economies of scale. CLTs also usually require a subsidy in the form of land or a grant to purchase land, in order to provide even a small number of homes.

The current housing association model of producing affordable housing is unsustainable, however. Government-registered housing associations rely on mechanisms such as public grants, housing for sale, staircasing receipts, the sale of older rented homes, and debt secured on other tenants' rents. All these mechanisms are currently at risk due to the national financial crisis and the slow-down of new developments. Most housing associations now need the same subsidies as CLTs.

The issue is not that CLTs are "more expensive," therefore, but that *all* housing land is "too expensive." CLTs are not trying to compete with housing associations; they are not operating on a large enough scale for that. CLTs do provide complementary housing provision in areas where there is a gap. In addition, they provide the extra security of being backed by the community, which often results in discounted land, labor, and other professional costs if sourced locally.

Placeshaping—More Than Just Housing

CLTs do more than create permanently affordable housing. They also deal with issues of employment, public space, local amenities, recreation, and renewable energy. All of these are essential to deliver the community well-being outcomes that local public authorities are obliged to deliver by law. CLTs can contribute, in particular, to:

- *The regeneration of rural areas.* Changing patterns of rural land use and agricultural crises such as the foot and mouth epidemic underline the need and the opportunities for interventions that provide more affordable housing, re-engineer farm-based businesses, and give new life to redundant buildings and lands having important landscape, ecological, and practical value.
- *The regeneration of urban social (public) housing.* Communities are demanding a bigger stake in deciding the future of their neighborhoods when they are redeveloped. They see themselves as joint leaders and partners, and sometimes as joint owners, in local regeneration strategies. They expect to benefit from rising local land values. Tenant-led initiatives are now a standard part of the local authority stock options process.

- *Renewal and stewardship.* CLTs can also contribute to the renewal of obsolete mixed-tenure housing, the stewardship of public spaces, voluntary pooling of land to increase housing supply, and the creation of stewardship trusts for urban extensions and new settlements.

Empowering Communities

As the former Minister for Communities and Local Government, Hazel Blears MP, wrote in her foreword to the *Urban CLT Toolkit,* published by Community Finance Solutions in 2009:[10] ". . . there are few problems that British communities cannot solve for themselves—if only you can unlock their talent and ingenuity and provide a framework that supports them."

Finding "talent and ingenuity" is not the problem. The problem is that CLTs are considered either a risky investment or an optional luxury. Yet, as we have seen, they are based on tried and tested models that have lasted hundreds of years. CLTs enable citizens to work and live together, meeting local needs in a socially active setting grounded in traditional systems of long-term land and property ownership and management. We need the state to be courageous, to allow for failure, to celebrate and nurture its social innovators, and to be a true enabler.

Infrastructure for CLT Development

Prospects for expanding the number and size of England's CLTs improved considerably over the past year because of three additions to the legal, financial, and technical infrastructure. Firstly, a CLT definition was written into national legislation. Secondly, a CLT development fund was created to cover some of the early costs of planning and developing CLT projects. Thirdly, government funding was made available to provide technical assistance for CLTs and to create a supportive framework for CLT formation.

The Legal Definition of Community Land Trusts

Community land trusts received statutory recognition for the first time through a definition included in the Housing and Regeneration Act of 2008. Much of the debate surrounding this legislation was focused on whether or not CLTs should be recognised as a category of "housing provider," distinct from bodies such as housing associations or registered social landlords.

The drivers for a statutory definition were threefold. First, to enable and encourage the Housing Corporation (eventually to form part of the new Homes and Communities Agency) and other governmental grantmaking bodies to provide financial assistance to CLTs in delivering affordable housing for both sale and rent. Second, to help the CLT movement bring clarity and certainty to stakeholders and partners

Statutory Definition of Community Land Trusts

A community land trust which qualifies as an English body is defined in the 2008 Act as a corporate body which satisfies the conditions below (in those conditions "local community" means the individuals who live or work, or want to live or work, in a specified area):

Condition 1 is that the body is established for the express purpose of furthering the social, economic and environmental interests of a local community by acquiring and managing land and other assets in order:

- to provide a benefit to the local community; and
- to ensure that the assets are not sold or developed except in a manner which the trust's members think benefits the local community.

Condition 2 is that the body is established under arrangements which are expressly designed to ensure that:

- any profits from its activities will be used to benefit the local community (otherwise than by being paid directly to members);
- individuals who live or work in the specified area have the opportunity to become members of the trust (whether or not others can also become members); and
- the members of the trust control it.

about the nature of the model. Third, to demonstrate the government's commitment to the expansion and development of CLTs.

The statutory definition is relatively broad. It was designed to capture the aims and distinctive characteristics of the CLT. Significantly, the definition is not exclusively linked to the delivery of affordable housing, but to the wider interests of a community—of which affordable housing is only one crucial part.

Key aspects of the definition are:

- CLTs must be an incorporated body. They must be established as a separate legal entity such as a company, an industrial and provident society or community interest company, but may not be an unincorporated trust (a legal form used by many almshouses).
- Every CLT will need to promote the social, economic, and environmental interests of a local community by acquiring and managing land and other assets for the benefit of the community. This will allow CLTs to acquire land to develop

affordable housing, but also to develop other assets such as post offices, shops, or renewable energy.

- Assets owned by a CLT may only be sold or developed in a manner approved by its members or shareholders, *and* which the CLT's members consider will further the interests of the CLT. Importantly, the CLT's members or shareholders are likely to include both the board and other community members. Members do not have to approve each individual sale or development, but they must establish policies to be followed by the board.
- Any profits generated by a CLT cannot be paid by way of dividend or otherwise to its members, but must be used to further the community's interests.
- People who live or work in the local community must have the opportunity to become members of the CLT.

The definition does not immediately qualify a CLT for financial assistance from public bodies. The national body that distributes housing grants, the Homes and Communities Agency, is still developing its criteria for how CLTs can apply for grant funding through its National Affordable Housing Programme 2008–2011. It is also developing registration criteria for a CLT to become a "registered provider of affordable housing." Any CLT that wishes to obtain financial assistance to develop low-cost rental housing under the Housing and Regeneration Act will need to meet these criteria.

A Development Fund for Community Land Trusts

Community land trusts are an emerging movement, led by people who wish to provide affordable housing and other facilities for their communities. But CLTs are constrained in their ability to deliver on that promise by a need for technical and professional advice and by a need for predevelopment risk capital funding.

Three independent charitable funders have now set up England's first major fund to help community land trusts to develop permanently affordable homes. They are the Esmée Fairbairn Foundation, The Tudor Trust, and Venturesome, the social investment arm of the Charities Aid Foundation.

The purpose of this CLT development fund was described by Joe Ludlow, senior investment manager at Venturesome, as follows: "Community land trusts have long been discussed as a way of providing affordable housing to communities, but this is the first time a fund of this size has been created specifically targeting CLTs. We hope that by managing this fund effectively we can help support specific communities in addressing their housing needs and demonstrate the attraction of community land trusts to other funders and policymakers."

Funding is available for the following activities:

- *Feasibility support*: initial consultancy and guidance to help develop ideas and make projects come alive. After a "scoping day" with expert advisers paid for by the fund, projects should have a clear view of their next steps. These could include gathering more information, approaching other local organizations, or seeking support for business planning.

- *Technical assistance*: grants of up to £2,500 to CLTs or emerging CLTs to employ a consultant or consultants for up to five days, in order to develop the CLT's ideas into a comprehensive business plan that is "investment ready."
- *Investment capital*: predevelopment funding to cover costs such as surveyors' and architects' fees in order to gain planning permission, and development finance to work alongside loans from banks in funding the costs of construction.[11]

The initial investment of £2m in this CLT development fund is expected to help 30 new CLTs to get off the ground during the next four years, creating around 150 new affordable homes in areas of need across England. The next step is to expand the CLT Fund and to persuade the government and other major public investors to contribute.

A Framework for Technical Assistance

Starting in 2006, seventeen CLT projects received advice and assistance through the pilot program administered by Community Finance Solutions. Recommendations for further technical support of CLTs were fed back to the government, which responded by announcing in the summer of 2009 £0.5 million in funding for CFS and other technical assistance providers. The priorities for how this money will be spent over the next three years are as follows:

- A CLT trade body will be created to represent CLTs as a sector. This will ensure that all the policy, fundraising, and communications work already begun will continue, while giving CLTs an official "point of contact."
- Training programs will be developed for CLTs and their partners (housing associations, local public authorities, etc.). Some of the training will be delivered at tailor-made events and some will be delivered online. Standard documentation and toolkits will be produced to guide CLTs through the crucial stages of development.
- CFS, with support of the government, will work with lenders to develop suitable mortgage products for CLT homebuyers.
- The final aim of the government's technical assistance funding will be to create a network of CLT umbrella bodies throughout the country. The pilot research found that CLT "umbrellas" or county-wide CLTs can play an important role in supporting smaller CLTs. They can act as the developer for sites where no CLT is already in place and can provide support services for CLT board members. They can also act as an intermediary between CLTs and the national and local government. They can become key points of contact for local CLTs and house the technical support that CLTs need. Once a pilot umbrella body is fully operational, it will mentor the formation of umbrella CLTs in other counties.

In short, this large allocation of governmental funding will put in place a supportive framework for CLT development. Many of the obstacles and barriers that were faced by England's CLT pioneers will be removed, or at least reduced. CLTs will have the technical support they need to flourish.

CLT Portraits

Presented below are three descriptions of established and emerging CLT projects in England that give a flavor of the different ways in which the model is being used to address social and economic issues in both rural and urban areas. The first one is an example of a development trust providing social housing using a CLT model. The second is an ambitious vision for the regeneration of a multiracial community in inner city London. The third is a CLT in a remote and highly desirable holiday destination, where the CLT has recently completed its first self-build scheme.

Case Study: East Ashington

East Ashington Development Trust shows how a community land trust program can offer more than a traditional social landlord. It currently owns only half-a-dozen homes, but because of its experience in managing assets, the Trust is poised to provide a platform for all sorts of other activities.

Located in a former mining town in Northumberland, the Trust gained its six homes—as well as an office, rented out to a local business—when a local youth housing project folded. It lets out these homes to local people at affordable rents.

"We're a drop in the ocean, but on a personal level for the tenants we have made a difference because these are people who have had problems getting private housing and have waited a long time on council (local government) lists," explains development trust manager Janet Cresswell. "We have even been lenient on things like bonds and enabled people to pay over a period of time rather than up front."

One of the homes has been fitted with solar panels and other improvements as part of the "Lo Carb Lane" energy efficiency project.

The Trust's experience has also given it the confidence—and the financial security— to pursue other projects. It has formed a joint venture to run a childcare center, saving a local business for the town and jobs of the staff who were working at the centre when it was put up for sale.

Future plans include converting a former Co-op store as a business base and providing an "activity barn" to help a local school to improve its sports provision.

Case Study: Brixton Green

Until now, community land trusts in England have been thought of mostly as solutions for rural problems, but you can't get more urban than Brixton in south London.

Coldharbour ward, one of the most challenging in the UK, is where local residents Brad Carroll and Phillippe Castaing intend to create the Brixton Green Community Land Trust, combining affordable housing with flexible business space, on-site childcare, and even an urban farm.

Brixton Green aims to demonstrate all the qualities of a sustainable community. The proposed site will feature rented and owner-occupied homes side by side with a communal garden, a playground, and a nursery. A central aspect of the design is an urban farm, with fruit trees, bee hives, and vegetables grown on a commercial scale using polytunnels.

When completed, Brixton Green could accommodate more than 150 homes on the first of two sites and commercial space including live-work units.[12]

"Brixton is a very good place to start with this kind of project because it already has a very active and close community," Mr. Carroll says. "If we can do this in one of the most deprived wards in the UK then we think it can make a big difference."

Case Study: St Minver in Cornwall

The St Minver CLT, located in a small coastal village on the westerly edge of England, has been supported by Cornwall CLT Ltd., a pioneering "umbrella" project promoting local CLTs. Cornwall CLT Ltd. is hosted by a rural housing association which employed England's first county-wide CLT project manager. The aim is to deliver 180 new homes in Cornwall by 2012. The project manager has helped to register a number of new CLTs, including St Minver CLT, St Just in Roseland CLT, and St Ewe Affordable Homes Ltd. Where there was no local CLT in place, the project manager has developed homes under the umbrella of Cornwall CLT Ltd.

St Minver CLT received a great deal of support from the CLT project manager in developing a self-build housing project in one of the most expensive villages in the UK. Twelve bungalows were completed in December 2008 and sold on a part-equity basis to owners who obtained 100 percent mortgages. Costs were kept down by obtaining the land at an affordable price from a local farmer, by receiving a small grant from the local council, and by the future owners contributing their own labor. These homes are owned and occupied by young people and families with connections to the village, including a young man who makes surfboards. They would not have had a chance of living in the village without the CLT.[13]

What's Next?

It is an exciting time for CLTs. Now that land is being bought and homes are being built, there is a general feeling that CLTs have turned a corner. This excitement was palpable at the third National CLT Conference, held in London in June 2009. The conference was attended by almost 200 people, including: volunteers and board members from CLTs; local and national politicians; public sector staff; funders from charitable trusts; consultants; architects; designers; planners; lawyers; journalists; bankers; developers; nonprofit housing sector staff; campaign group members; and representatives from assorted community groups. All of these people, despite coming from such a diverse range of professions and interests, shared a common interest in community led solutions and the stewardship of land as the basis for building sustainable communities.

Politicians from the Conservative Party stated they wanted to remove obstacles to CLTs. There was even talk of giving community groups the power to grant themselves planning permission, provided they can show community support. A spokesperson from the London Mayor's Office announced he would launch a CLT in London by 2011.[14]

This sudden exposure to the political limelight is a double-edged sword, however. Just as easily as they have been embraced, CLTs could be quickly discarded when the next fashionable political bandwagon comes along.

Despite the government's recent announcement of funding for technical support, there is still the question of how CLTs will be funded. The major strengths and unique selling points of the CLT model are independence and an ability to tailor housing to meet specific local needs. There is some potential to do all of this without the use of public grants, where there is enough local support in the form of fundraising, donations of land, and charitable trust funds. Many CLTs, however, will want to access public housing grants, especially if they wish to provide rental properties. We should think carefully, however, about what we are asking when we call for CLTs to be given public housing grants. The unique features of the CLT model could be threatened if government moves to regulate CLTs and to merge them into the conventional social housing sector.

This has been the experience at Holy Island Community Development Trust, for example, where a tiny organization of nine volunteer trustees wishing to develop four homes went through the process of accessing a social housing grant. They were faced with application forms 100 pages long and had to employ a number of consultants to meet all the certifications and standards required. In total, the Trust spent around £30,000 in order to access a grant of £212,000. CLTs have been promised the process will be streamlined in the future, but there is a risk of small organizations being swamped with regulation in order to minimize the risk to the public bodies (while maximizing cost to the CLT).

CLTs are on the verge of moving from a "movement" to a "sector," from "experimentation" to "standardization." CLTs must find a balance between retaining what marks them as unique (like grassroots accountability and support), while continuing to gain political support and pump-prime funding.

What's next on the horizon for CLTs? Up until now, the groundswell of activity has occurred in developing affordable housing in small rural settlements. In the future, this is likely to change, with CLTs playing an expanded role and developing other types of assets, in both urban and rural areas. CLTs could play a much greater role, for instance, in the regeneration of urban communities in England. Already many inner-city groups are getting excited about the model's potential.[15] The CLT could capture the increase in land values for local people when urban areas improve. There are also many neglected or surplus parcels of land that could be put to better use if they were community owned. Coin Street Community Builders, for example, is a community development trust that has created a 230-home housing cooperative with associated facilities on London's South Bank. An active and widespread CLT movement, paired with an invigorated cooperative sector, could help to replicate Coin Street's success elsewhere.

A CLT is a platform on which to build a sustainable community. The model can underpin not only the development of housing but also: the provision of work-space; the preservation of farmland; the preservation of open space and community woodland; the supply of allotments; and the generation of energy from renewable sources.

CLTs are also part of a wider movement for the empowerment of citizens through land use. This wider movement encompasses the Transition Towns movement, the local food sector, and community supported agriculture. By acting together, all of these initiatives could create a strong community of interest for directing the future of places through community asset ownership.

In a very short time, CLTs have moved from a small group of pioneers to the beginnings of a sector. CLTs have punched above their weight in influencing public policy, taking advantage of the current political consensus in favor of community-based development. They have revived and built upon traditional notions of common ownership, cooperation, community spirit, and self-help in order to improve society and to help those in need. Various aspects of the CLT appeal to parties across the political spectrum. Politicians, lawyers, architects, and many others are eager to associate themselves with all this new activity. The story so far shows how much can be achieved. With ambitious targets for growth and with new resources in place, CLTs are now poised to achieve even more.

NOTES

1. See *Lessons from the First 150 Homes,* published by Community Finance Solutions in 2009. Available from www.communitylandtrust.org.uk.

2. The funding for the CLT demonstration program was for England only. There is also a great deal of activity and support for CLTs in Scotland and Wales.

3. Figure from National Housing Federation.

4. Figure from National Housing Federation.

5. Allotments are a traditional type of community garden, where parcels of land are assigned to individuals or families for cultivation.

6. From 2006 to 2009, 11 homes were sold, at an average of £1,499,682. Data accessed from www.zoopla.co.uk 16 July 2009.

7. The Right to Buy is a policy introduced in the United Kingdom in 1980 that gives tenants of council housing the right to purchase the home in which they are living.

8. For instance, Stonesfield Community Trust and Holy Island of Lindisfarne Community Development Trust. See *Why Community Land Trusts should join the Development Trusts Association* published by the DTA, London, www.dta.org.uk.

9. Published 2006, Planning Policy Statement 3 is available at: www.communities.gov.uk.

10. *Placeshaping: A Toolkit for Urban Community Land Trusts.* Available at: www .communitylandtrust.org.uk.

11. More information on this CLT fund is available at www.cafonline.org/ communitylandtrustfund.

12. See: www.brixtongreen.org.

13. See: www.crha.org.uk.

14. There is also evidence of an emerging *cross-party* political support for the cooperative and mutual housing sector, including community land trusts, provoked in part by a recent report on the benefits of expanding this sector. See: *Bringing Democracy Home,* published by the Commission on Co-Operative and Mutual Housing in 2009 (http://www.ccmh.coop/).

15. *Editor's note:* The coming 2012 London Olympics, in particular, has been a recent spur to CLT organizing in residential neighborhoods likely to be affected by the Olympics. The newly formed London Citizens CLT is attempting to acquire two sites for the development of affordable housing at St. Clements Hospital and Olympic Park (www.londoncitizensclt. co.uk).

Fertile Ground for CLT Development in Australia

Louise Crabtree
(2009)

Australia is just beginning to engage with the community land trust (CLT), as that model has been defined and structured in the United States. Australia has long experience with other tenure forms that carry some of the core features of a CLT, however, and the nation is currently facing a number of problems that CLTs may help to address. The potential for CLT development Down Under is great.

Australian Analogues to the CLT

Australia has a history of developing unconventional forms of tenure that, while not themselves CLTs, share some of the structural and operational elements of a CLT. Their existence and acceptance suggest that adopting the CLT model in Australia would not require the creation of entirely unknown structures. The CLT may, in fact, address some of the functional flaws and inefficiencies that exist in these Australian alternatives.

A direct analogue of the CLT model can be seen in the landholding system in the Australian Capital Territory (ACT). Initially conceived as a public mechanism to capture the "unearned increment" in land value generated by the creation and development of the federal capital territory, the leasehold system in the ACT originally involved land rents paid directly to the Commonwealth. This system was promoted largely by Senator John Grant, a follower of Henry George, who had visited Australia in 1890. The ACT's system was overhauled in the 1970s, however. Land rents were abolished, allowing leases to begin selling at market rates. This essentially gutted the model of land value recapture that Grant and his colleagues had put in place (Fitzgerald 2008). On the other hand, the basic structure of title to land separated from title to improvements remains intact. The legal and functional foundation for CLT development would seem, therefore, to still exist.

Another analogue to the CLT can be found in various Aboriginal communities. Most states in Australia have developed variations on a model in which the state owns lands that are conveyed to Aboriginal communities via leasehold. Typically, the head lease to the land is held by a Local Aboriginal Land Council, with individual houses then rented to residents. The 2006 Aboriginal Land Rights (Northern Territory)

This chapter was written for this volume.

Amendment Bill proposed individual ownership of houses on land sublet to individuals from land councils. In this, land councils perform an analogous role to CLTs, holding head lease title to the land and leasing land to residents who can buy the home on that land. This form of home ownership is being supported through the Home Ownership on Indigenous Land Program, which is cosponsored by the federal Department of Families, Housing, Community Services and Indigenous Affairs and Indigenous Business Australia, with the latter providing specialist loan packages. Review of the guidelines of the federal Home Purchase Incentive Scheme is also intended to support this form of home ownership.

A report by the Senate Community Affairs Legislation Committee in 2006 outlined the core concerns raised in response to the Aboriginal Land Rights Amendment, most of which focused on the devolution of rights away from land councils and a perceived lack of use controls in any proposed leases, even though these would be bound by the same terms and conditions of the original head leases held by the land councils. That amendment had the primary aim of boosting economic activity in remote Aboriginal communities, however, so was mainly concerned with the rights of the individual to access imputed land value. It would appear that this proposed form of home ownership could represent a structural analogue of, or precursor to, a more thoroughly articulated CLT model. Ideally, such a model would help to resolve some of the disputes regarding governance, participation, economic development, valuation, and accountability that have arisen between Aboriginal communities that want to retain control over traditional lands and government agencies that are pushing for individual title.

Opportunities for CLT Development

There are three areas in the current political, social, and economic landscape of Australia where the potential for developing CLTs seems especially fertile: affordable home ownership, housing for indigenous Australians (Aboriginal housing), and the retention or recovery of agricultural lands proximate to urban areas.

Affordability and Tenure

Australia's housing is overwhelmingly privately owned and market priced, with 68 percent of all housing in private home ownership. Roughly half of these homes are owned outright, and half are under mortgage. Private rental housing constitutes a further 30 percent of the country's housing, with public housing, community housing, and other tenures making up the remaining 2 percent. Cooperative housing—whether in zero equity or market-rate co-ops—currently exists in minuscule numbers of only several hundred units per state.

In Australia, public housing, which is owned by state agencies, is rented to low-income households with rents set as a percentage of household income. Currently, public housing suffers allocation and maintenance backlogs of about 10 years.

What is known in Australia as "community housing" is owned and managed by private nonprofit organizations. As in public housing, low-income renters are the principal beneficiaries of community housing, with rents geared to household income. Community housing providers have more recently been able to expand their clientele into moderate and median income brackets, however. Some nonprofit organizations are now housing households earning up to AU$75,000 a year, roughly 140 percent of national median income, adjusted for household size. While the primary clientele of community housing providers is still lower-income households, they are now able to achieve a degree of income mix and internal cross-subsidization within their residential projects.

A 2008 report by the Senate Select Committee on Housing Affordability found that, by a number of measures, housing affordability in Australia is now at a record low.[1] Among its findings, the report (Senate Select Committee on Housing Affordability in Australia, 2008) stated:

- The average house price in the capital cities is now equivalent to over seven years of average earnings; up from three in the 1950s to the early 1980s.
- Only a third of transacted dwellings would have been accessible to the median young household in 2006–2007, compared to a long-run average of almost a half.
- Around two-thirds of households in the lowest 40 percent of the income distribution with a mortgage or renting were spending over 30 percent of their income on housing, the established benchmark for "housing stress."

Current attempts to address Australia's housing affordability problem have been many and varied, but have overwhelmingly favored and promoted private home ownership. In the 20 most heavily subscribed postcodes in New South Wales alone, over AU$1.1 billion have been spent on aiding just under 56,000 first-time homeowners via the first homeowner grant (FHOG) program over the past 12 months (Office of State Revenue 2009).[2] This program, which combines federal and state monies, has been criticized for driving up housing prices. There was, in fact, a degree of market frenzy and rapid price rises that occurred as the deadline approached for the recent release of FHOG assistance. In many instances, these price increases outstripped the grant money on offer; indeed, recent surveys of first-home buyers have revealed that these buyers are now waiting until *after* the deadline, as the market heat that has been generated by the program has made the subsidies redundant. Further, such assistance is not tied to the supply of a physical housing stock, so while this can be used to access existing or new stock, it does not necessarily stimulate the expansion of an affordable housing pool. Further, it carries no conditions or requirements for restricting future income eligibility or future resale prices, so does not maintain any affordability gained. This funding stream is poured exclusively into market-rate housing.

Additional federal investment to address the affordability crisis comes through the recently adopted National Affordable Housing Agreement (NAHA), the Housing Affordability Fund (HAF), and the National Rental Affordability Scheme (NRAS). NAHA is the nationwide funding mechanism for both public housing and community housing, with a total budget of $6.2 billion over its first five years, including a growth fund of $200 million for the social housing sector (public and community housing) for each of the years 2008–2009 and 2009–2010. This represents a significant increase over the previous federal administration's history of decreasing funds for social housing in real terms on an annual basis.

The HAF makes $512 million available over five years to local governments that show that the money will be passed on as savings to home buyers, through reduced development approval times and/or reduced infrastructure costs. Again, however, this carries no terms or conditions regarding eligibility or resale, so may not engender affordability beyond the first buyer. NRAS aims to build 50,000 rental homes by 2012, with another 50,000 after that date, subject to demand. NRAS provides an AU$6,000 per-unit subsidy from the federal government (as a tax credit) and a AU$2,000 per-unit subsidy from state government over a period of 10 years, on the condition these assisted units are rented at 20 percent below market rent.[3]

In addition, several states are now experimenting with shared-equity financing schemes. These are essentially dual mortgages, in which the state holds a mortgage alongside the homeowner. At the point of resale, the state can buy out the private share and make the home available for purchase by another eligible buyer. Alternatively, the owner has the option to buy the state out and assume full ownership.

More recently, the federal government has announced funding for housing as part of its Nation Building Economic Stimulus Plan, a response to the global financial crisis. This includes a historic AU$6 billion to be spent in building at least 20,000 new units of social (public and community) housing across the country. Moreover, the state of New South Wales recently announced that it will transfer title to all community housing stock from the state housing departments to the community housing providers (CHPs), allowing them to borrow against their asset base for the first time, for the purpose of expanding this sector.

There is a clear opportunity here for partnerships between CHPs and CLTs. Such a partnership could address the impediment faced by CHPs in gaining access to land on which to build affordable rental housing. Further, some CHPs have become interested in diversifying their tenure models, moving beyond rentals alone. This could open up the possibility of CLTs being started as affiliates or programs within CHPs. Another opportunity for CLT development would seem to lie in correcting the flaw in current dual-mortgage schemes. CLTs could serve as successors or stewards, serving to lock subsidies in place and to retain the affordability created by public subsidization of a shared-equity scheme.

Aboriginal Housing

Australia's Aboriginal housing system is currently fraught with problems of over-crowding, undersupply, and maintenance backlogs. Under this system, Aboriginal tenants typically rent their houses, with the land held by a Local Aboriginal Land Council. There is currently a lot of interest among indigenous communities and government in converting a portion of this Aboriginal housing to home ownership, allowing the occupants to gain title to both their houses and the underlying land. Recent surveys undertaken by Moran et al. (2002) in remote Aboriginal communities have revealed, in fact, a high level of interest in home ownership and awareness of the responsibilities that accompany owning a home. These discussions of Aboriginal home ownership have raised three issues.

First, the basic form of tenure for this owner-occupied housing has yet to be determined. A "mainstream" model of unrestricted, market-rate ownership of both the house and the land was seen as most appealing by respondents to the survey conducted by Moran et al., but this model jars with the Aboriginal understanding of land as a shared and living heritage. Second, Moran et al.'s work suggests that controls need to be put in place to prevent speculation and predatory landlordism by "outside" parties. Third, there is an issue of determining and maintaining property value. Much Aboriginal housing does not hold value, especially in remote areas. This raises two issues. The first is that owners do not want to risk losing money in a closed market of devaluing properties. The second, related, issue is that it may be useful to train local communities in maintenance to prevent deterioration of properties.[4] Moran's surveys also revealed that many potential homeowners wanted an ongoing relationship with an agency throughout their tenure, to assist with financial and maintenance issues.

Early discussions about the CLT model, sparked by a visit to Australia in March 2009 by John Emmeus Davis, a CLT expert from the United States, suggest there may be much potential for applying the CLT model to Aboriginal housing renewal and development. The common ownership of land through a CLT would seem to be more compatible with the Aboriginal tradition of treating land as a common heritage than would individual ownership. The discomfort that Aboriginal tenants expressed to Moran et al. about not owning land can be attributed largely to a perceived lack of clarity in the model put to indigenous communities regarding use controls and the rights and obligations of homeowners and any landholding body. The homeowner protections embedded in a CLT's ground lease, combined with a CLT board structure that includes leaseholder representatives, could offset these concerns about not owning the land. Recent discussions with Aboriginal elders and housing companies in Sydney suggest, in fact, that the CLT model might be welcome.

CLTs have a long history of successfully preventing both speculation and predatory landlordism. Furthermore, a core part of a CLT's function is to provide postpurchase services and supports for new homeowners, helping with maintenance and preventing foreclosures. These CLT activities would mesh well with those of both Healthhabitat and Habitat for Humanity Australia, which similarly focus on building houses and local skills capacity.

Any engagement with the CLT model that is based on Aboriginal perceptions of land and ownership may reveal insightful and nuanced interpretations of the model and require refinements to it. However the model is adopted, in this context, it will be imperative that Aboriginal needs and issues set the core priorities and that Aboriginal stakeholders be the primary drivers of the model's adoption and adaptation.[5]

Agricultural Lands

Australia's agricultural system is facing a number of challenges. Many large nonurban landholdings in semiarid regions are folding under pressure from banks as droughts persist, salinity spikes, and crops fail. Older generations of rural populations are experiencing rising suicide rates, which are frequently avoided or disguised in public discussion. Younger generations see no future in the system and are migrating to cities in search of livelihoods. Meanwhile, peri-urban agriculture—agriculture on the fringe of Australia's cities, which generally receive higher rainfalls and have better soils—is under constant threat from encroaching suburban development, often bringing unsympathetic neighbors and the temptation to sell land to developers for windfall capital gains.[6]

More adept producers in the Sydney Basin have witnessed the emerging desire for locally produced, organic food and have been able to reinvent themselves as food providers or as food tourism operators. This requires and has relied on the producers' personal ownership of land. In contrast, market gardening of more mundane staples is dominated by recent migrants, frequently working on rented land. These migrants often have poor English and, hence, a degree of vulnerability to labor exploitation. Some may have access to low-cost housing nearby; however, increases in property prices are increasingly forcing growers to move farther from the land they lease and work. The significance of farming to peri-urban farmers varies immensely, however, with some very keen to pass the business down through the family and others determined that their children not have to toil in the same way.

Local governments with agriculture in their jurisdictions have made policy moves to support and promote peri-urban agriculture, recognizing this as a valid, substantial, and unique aspect of local economies and landscapes. None of these address fundamental issues of the development pressures facing landholders, however, or the insecurity of rental properties—nor can they, as these are driven primarily by property market and state planning forces.

This would seem like fertile ground for the establishment of a CLT sector, perhaps combining peri-urban agricultural lands and low-cost housing. The potential of CLTs in combination with alternative food distribution systems such as community supported agriculture (CSA) schemes is also worth exploring, as this may help reverse some of the collapse of the agricultural system through the provision of regular and stable income streams to farmers implementing sustainable farming practices. Given the harsh realities of the Australian environment and climate, it may be that such systems can survive only on the better lands adjacent and within cities, highlighting the need to secure land and housing in these regions on a perpetually affordable basis—the forte of a CLT.

Why CLTs? And Why Now? Opportunities and Challenges

As Australia begins experimenting with new financing schemes like dual mortgages and expands the scale of homebuyer assistance under HAF and the FHOG, all of these approaches to expanding home ownership allow a subsidy leak. Federal and state money leave this assisted housing at the point of resale. Even in the rare instances when these funds are recaptured by a public agency, the U.S. experience suggests that further subsidization will be required to provide a similar level of affordability to subsequent buyers due to market heating that has occurred since purchase (see Jacobus and Cohen, *forthcoming*).

Politically, housing affordability has become a burning issue in Australia, with older generations realizing that their children may not be able to afford a standard of housing similar to that of the homes they grew up in. Land prices, in particular, are a large part of the problem of housing *un*affordability. Land release constraints, land taxes, and infrastructure charges mean that land is expensive to bring to market for the purpose of building new housing.

It is in this context of leaking subsidies and increasingly expensive land that CLTs can potentially make a significant contribution to the creation and retention of affordable housing. A percentage of the current federal and state money targeting home ownership and rentals could be used to create a CLT sector to underpin and steward affordable ownership and rental units, whether managed by community housing providers, housing cooperatives, or newly formed CLTs. While requiring an initial outlay of public funds, the retention of that subsidy on an ongoing basis would appear fiscally attractive. The historic scale of the funds available under the present Economic Stimulus Plan would seem an ideal opportunity to broaden the very limited tenure options currently operating in the Australian housing market. Further, CLTs would appeal to the persistent Australian desire for home ownership, offering the potential to develop a stock of permanently affordable homes and grow the pool of individuals to whom ownership is available, without exposing them to risk or directly subsidizing the private market. The substantial funding and new thinking occurring at all levels of government would appear to provide fertile ground to plant some seeds.

With all that said, there are numerous challenges to be faced in implementing a CLT model in Australia. First, Australians are deeply committed to the idea of free-market individual wealth creation through home ownership. The construction, sale, and resale of market-rate housing has been a primary economic driver since World

War II. Second, while analogues of the model do exist in Australia, they are not widely known or understood. The CLT represents an unfamiliar and, possibly, legally difficult model. Implementation and acceptance of the model in Australia will require that existing Australian, U.S., and UK leases, bylaws, and other legal mechanisms be analyzed and translated into a coherent and replicable set of legal templates. Finally, much Australian third-sector housing (i.e., community housing in its various forms) is still in its infancy. The sector has a limited, although growing, capacity as regards its systems, assets, skills, and capital.

None of these obstacles is insurmountable, however. The scale and persistence of the current affordability problem, in particular, may help to unseat private, market-rate home ownership from its primacy in the Australian economy and psyche, opening space for alternative forms of tenure. Preliminary work in Australia is already under way to translate existing legal documents from Australia, the United States, and the UK into a workable set of CLT templates that can be made available to the embryonic, but rapidly growing, Australian CLT network. As of late-2009, several groups are in the process of formation, and one, the Mount Alexander Community Land Limited in Castlemaine, Victoria, has incorporated, held its first board meetings, identified prospective sites, and begun attracting donations. CLTs are being investigated by state and church bodies as a potential mechanism to steward public or church lands for affordable housing and community development. Finally, third-sector housing is now being recognized by federal, state, and local governments as a key player in the expansion of affordable housing. Expanded governmental support is being used to develop the capacity and skills of community housing providers—who are potential partners or sponsors of CLTs and who are presently showing great interest in the model.

Issues are emerging relating to the exact form the CLT will take in Australian environs. Discussions are under way regarding board structures, membership, financing mechanisms, land rents, and resale formulae, drawing not only on the CLT model, but also on housing cooperatives, land banks, caravan parks, and mutual housing associations. Early investigation suggests that under Australian property law, even use of the word "trust" in a CLT's name may be problematic, as this traditionally implies that there is a trustee for whom the property is held. As with that unique Australian animal oddity, the platypus—seemingly part duck, part beaver, and part reptile—the CLT in Australia may well take on a peculiarly antipodean shape.

Resilience and CLTs

CLTs may also offer a unique opportunity for fostering sustainability and resilience in human settlements, a timely issue in Australia. Recent environmental theory and practice have taken a fresh look at the types of systems that are best able to manage social and environmental resources—so-called socioecological systems. That work has found that the most effective structures for *sustainably* managing socioecological systems are those that display resilience—that is, the ability to respond to stress or surprise without losing the ability to perform core functions. Such managerial systems share a number of core traits, as summarized by Olsson, Folke, and Hahn (2004, 75):

> These include the following: vision, leadership, and trust; enabling legislation that creates social space for ecosystem management; funds for responding to environmental change and for remedial action; capacity for monitoring and responding to environmental feedback; information flow through social networks; the combination of various sources of information and knowledge; and sensemaking and arenas of collaborative learning for ecosystem management.

If the focus is changed from environmental systems to social or socioecological systems, the traits described by Olsson and his colleagues sound a lot like those displayed by most CLTs. In other words, the CLT may represent a mechanism not just for developing and maintaining affordable housing, but for developing and maintaining empowered and flexible institutions and communities that can respond to locally specific challenges in more creative and innovative ways than more traditional centralized structures.

That is not an argument for abandoning centralized support for housing and community development, leaving communities to sink or swim on their own. Just the opposite: Research on resilience has found that the most successful mechanisms combine agents, knowledge, and resources from multiple levels on an ongoing basis. What seems to work best is centralized funding of locally based and locally accountable mechanisms that keep these various stakeholders in ongoing communication and negotiation.

Emerging challenges such as climate change, energy prices, food security, and global economic instability have thrown harsh light on the varying resilience of our communities. To date, CLTs in the United States have shown interesting, innovative, and diverse responses not only to core concerns such as housing affordability and loss of agricultural and conservation lands, but also to issues subsequently identified by CLT members and boards, such as unemployment and food insecurity. These are often combined in a multifaceted program, moreover, where affordable home ownership, youth leadership training, commercial development, and even sustainable food production on urban lands are all undertaken by the same CLT.[7] The CLT's potential in Australia as an appropriate and sustainable mechanism for stewarding land, building community, and fostering resilience is substantial. There is fertile ground Down Under for this new model of tenure.

NOTES

1. That report also stated that more renters than homeowners were in housing stress and that up to 100,000 Australians are homeless (out of a population of just under 22 million).

2. A postcode may correspond to a suburb, or a larger area if nonmetropolitan.

3. Queries have been raised, though, regarding the insensitivity of the grant to local market dynamics or unit size; hence, a three-bedroom unit in the middle of an overheated suburb gets the same $8,000 per unit subsidy as a one-bedroom unit in a less sought-after area. This makes the latter viable but not the former, which will affect the types and locations of housing that gets built. Queries have also been raised as to whether 80 percent of market rent is affordable.

4. Such training is already core work of Healthhabitat, an Australian nonprofit organization that focuses on intensive, hands-on training of Aboriginal communities to perform housing repair and maintenance work, with the dual aims of performing as much critical repair as possible while on site and leaving in place a core team of skilled residents able to carry out such work on an ongoing basis.

5. In a recent visit to Australia, Professor Michael E. Stone of the University of Massachusetts proposed a "resident-saver" model that may be particularly useful in indigenous areas and could mesh well with an underlying CLT (see Stone 1993 for full illustration of the model). In this, capital finance is used to build homes; ideally debt-free. Residents then pay a deposit and regular payments to cover the operating costs of the CLT (or a variation of a CHP or mutual housing association located on a CLT's land), cover any debt, and generate a maintenance fund. In addition, residents agree and are required to make regular savings payments into an investment vehicle associated with the housing organization, which invests in the broader economy. When selling, residents receive their deposit, plus their savings with earned interest. This decouples wealth creation from the physical housing stock and offers a vehicle for broader (ideally, ethical and community-oriented) investment—a promising model which would seem particularly appropriate for remote communities where housing stock might not hold value.

6. The exact extent and productivity of these landholdings are unknown—estimates for productivity in the Sydney catchment area (the Sydney Basin) range up to 100 percent of the city's leafy greens and $1 billion annual value—and many feel that suburban Australia may be rapidly expanding over the few remaining viable regions available for growing the food it needs in the face of a variable and volatile climate regime.

7. The CLT developed by the Dudley Street Neighborhood Initiative in Boston, Massachusetts is a prime example of such a multifaceted program.

REFERENCES

Fitzgerald, K. 2008. Canberra's Leasehold Land System. http://www.prosper.org.au/2008/01/16/canberra.

Jacobus, R., and A. Cohen. *Forthcoming*. Creating permanently affordable homeownership through community land trusts. In *California affordable housing deskbook*. Rob Weiner and Neal Richman (eds.). Point Arena, CA: Solano Press. http://www.rjacobus.com/Portfolio/docs/CLTChapter9–03.pdf.

Moran, M., P. Memmott, S. Long, R. Stacy, and J. Holt. 2002. Indigenous home ownership and community title land: A preliminary household survey. *Urban Policy and Research* 20 (4):357–370.

Office of State Revenue. 2009. First Home Benefits: Top 20 Postcodes by Value—NSW, 1 July 2008 to 30 June 2009. http://www.osr.nsw.gov.au/lib/doc/stats/fhb_top20.pdf.

Olsson, P., C. Folke, and T. Hahn. 2004. Adaptive comanagement for building resilience in social-ecological systems. *Environmental Management* 34 (1):75–90.

Senate Community Affairs Legislation Committee. 2006. Aboriginal Land Rights (Northern Territory) Amendment Bill 2006. August 2006. http://www.aph.gov.au/Senate/committee/clac_ctte/completed_inquiries/2004-07/aborig_land_rights/report/c01.htm.

Senate Select Committee on Housing Affordability in Australia. 2008. Executive Summary: The housing affordability problem. http://www.aph.gov.au/Senate/committee/hsaf_ctte/report/b01.htm.

Stone, M. 1993. *Shelter Poverty: New Ideas on Housing Affordability.* Philadelphia: Temple University Press.

Yates, J. 2003. "The more things change?" An overview of Australia's recent home ownership policies. *European Journal of Housing Policy* 3 (1):1–33.

Community-Based Land Reform

Lessons from Scotland and Reflections on Stewardship

John Bryden and Charles Geisler
(2009)

Interest in land reform appears to be rekindling. In the past, land reform promised many things, most of which were technical, legal, and economic in nature. Dovring's (1987:394) description of land reform offers textbook language: "Land reform is one of the classical instances of attempts to correct market failures by institutional reform enacted by or induced by the public powers. Land reform means systematic change in property distribution, farm size, and land tenure conditions." What is missing here is the community component of land reform. Relatively self-sufficient, secure, and sustainable communities, so essential to enduring social infrastructure, are typically taken for granted or not an explicit goal of land reform. This may be explained by the ideological aversion of western land reformers to the various "communal" formulations of socialist land reforms (Sobhan, 1993), by the influence of Hardin's "tragedy of the commons" (wherein "community" signified land tenure in common, the victim of utility-maximizing individuals [Brox, 1990]), or by the perception that community-based moral economies in Europe and elsewhere are vestigial and nonessential to contemporary political economy (Polanyi, 1944). In this paper, we explore certain connections between land ownership and community in an attempt to diversify and enrich future land reform discourse.

The neglect of community in land reform planning is of much interest, given the widespread rush to incorporate "community" in natural resource decision making and local development (c.f., Bryden, 1994) by government and nongovernment managers. Given the intimate relationship between land, property, "development" and the environment (c.f., Richards, 2002), they qualify as *de facto* land reformers. This drive to decentralize control of resources of every description stems in part from reactions to globalization (Griffin, 1999; Dorner, 1999), from normative views that "local is better" (Pimbert and Pretty, 1997; Western and Wright, 1994), and from a range of interests who see political advantage in identifying with "local" (Barrett et al. 2001; Wittman and Geisler, 2005). Yet the florescence of interest in local has not pervaded the core thinking of land reformers. Here the tendency persists to view land reform as a

This is an updated and revised version of John Bryden and Charles Geisler, "Land Reform and Community—A 'New Wave' Land Reform?" *Land Use Policy* 24:1 (2007): 24–34. It is reprinted by permission of Elsevier. Original note numbers have been changed.

state-based managerial challenge freighted with technical and tenure complexities. With notable exceptions (e.g., Li, 1996; Agrawal and Gibson, 1999), community is equated with resettlements which often do little more than warehouse rural people in culturally-neutered spaces.

Our interest here is in community-based land reform, a melding of land reform, community-based natural resource management and local development. This interest is constrained by the difficulty to which we just alluded: for many land reformers, "community development" is a rhetorical objective. Our empirical referent springs from an unlikely quarter—the peripheral zones of Scotland—where momentum has recently gathered for The Land Reform (Scotland) Act 2003 (Reid, 2003). Central to this statute is a "community right to buy" provision which puts communities in the foreground of the country's land reform. If, as we suggest, the precedents for tight coupling between land reform and community are increasingly problematic, the focal research question becomes: What might we expect from community-centric land reform where the state has empowered communities to purchase and manage lands to which they have historically had neither ownership nor much control? And how have the issues of postacquisition stewardship regarding long-term affordability and tenure security, so significant in the case of community land trusts in the United States (Davis, 2008), been dealt with so far?

Before examining the Scottish case, we offer a fuller argument for why community matters to successful land reforms and land reform to successful communities. In the course of this clarification, we expand upon reasons for why this neglected relationship persists. In the second section we ground the case for community-centric land reform in actual experiences, past and present. This becomes an exercise in "seeing" the counterfactual. Land reform is viewed as a community tool for managing land and resources rather than a state intervention to attain greater outputs, placate rural unrest, resettle landless laborers or those displaced by public works, or achieve narrow "land regularization." We then turn our attention to Scotland's recent land reform. We suggest that its explicit approval of state-assisted community appropriation of land has far-reaching implications for standard land reform thinking. The community's right to buy is fundamentally a right "to be" and to secure a place-based arena of common identity and interests, protected by title. This said, what is to keep community-centric land reform from succumbing to reconcentration of ownership, unaffordable and degraded housing stock, and other counter-reform revenge effects known to plague more traditional land reforms?

Theorizing Community-Centric Land Reform

Readers tracing the literature on community are well aware that the task of finding community—let alone "bringing it back in" to land reform—is fraught with definitional and operational problems. Many have noted that communities are dynamic and internally diverse (Bell and Newby, 1971; Bryden and Hart, 2000) and that place-based community has been widely eclipsed by other noncommunity forms of organization (for a summary, see Barton, 2002; Barrow and Murphree, 2001). Resurgent interest in community of late is heavily attributable to research on social capital. Despite certain limitations, this scholarship drives home one seemingly irrefutable conclusion: places lacking in solidarity, trust, and association are likely to have lower levels of well-being and general welfare than those endowed with these qualities (Pretty, 1999). These qualities can be frustratingly subjective, illusive, and underspecified. But they can neither be dismissed nor taken for granted. It is thus conceptually frustrating to see the World Bank, in advocating both land reform and social capital, use "devolution" narrowly to mean the shift to private ownership (e.g., Deininger, 2003:169–71).

Since at least the 1980s, conservationists have embraced devolution in many forms in a quest for socially sensitive and culturally acceptable protection of nature. According to Hulme and Murphree (2001:2), this approach became so popular in the 1990s that at times it appeared to be a new orthodoxy, seeking to displace the conventional wisdom of state-enforced environmental protection. The new paradigm came to be known as "community conservation" or community-based natural resource management (IIED, 1994). Its motivations were multiple. Some embraced community conservation for humanitarian and environmental justice reasons (Zerner, 2000; Brechin et al., 2003). Others, reviewing the common property record (Ostrom, 1990; Bromley, 1991)[1] as well as accounts of sustainable resource management among indigenous and settler communities, advocated comanagement or full transfer of management to local communities (Western and Pearl, 1989; Borrini-Feyerabend, 1996; Eghenter, 2002; Buck et al., 2001). The newest argument for educating and empowering communities to share responsibility for local conservation comes from the realization that vast amounts of biodiversity and ecological services lie outside of protected areas, that is, in place-based communities of many descriptions (Cary and Webb, 2000; O'Riordan and Stoll-Kleeman, 2002; McNeeley and Scherr, 2003). Community-centric conservation has gained allies from above and below.

There was an almost parallel movement for community involvement in rural development issues, started around the 1970s mainly as an "alternative development" paradigm (Bassand et al., 1985; Stohr, 1990; Bryden, 1994). Once again there were multiple rationales and motives—the failure of "top down" development; the "downsizing" of the state; the need to capture local knowledge and resources; the development of democratic practice; a move towards more holistic development, and so on. In the European Union this movement resulted in the creation of the EU's "Leader programme" in 1991—an official program to stimulate holistic, bottom-up development in rural areas suffering from decline and marginalization.

Land reformers are forewarned, however, that these decentralist impulses are not uncontested. Implacable adherents of the state-based models remain skeptical about the capacities of "parochial" local citizens (Terborgh, 1999), and there are social scientists who assert that devolution to local communities is based on unproven assumptions about local people (Wells, 1994–95; Eghenter and Sellato, 1999) and about community development (Brandon, Redford, and Sanderson, 1998). Hard questions have come to the fore regarding issues of "community for whom" and about "which local community" among many (Shortall and Shucksmith, 1998; Belsky, 2003). For purposes of the present paper, the most trenchant concern lies elsewhere, however. It has to do with the hollowness of community participation if devoid of property rights, a key form of empowerment. Barrow and Murphree (2001:31) raise these concerns in the African case, stating:

> Tenure . . . [is] a key variable in determining the performance of community conservation initiatives. . . . As inhabitants of what is technically state land, the residents of most communal lands in Africa do not have strong property rights. Their tenure is uncertain and their decisions on the use of resources subject to a plethora of conditionalities. As in colonial times, communal lands continue to be in various degrees the fiefdoms of state bureaucracies, political elites and their private sector partners. The persistence of this condition in the modern post-colonial state is an indication that the devolution of strong property rights to the peoples of communal land is a fundamental allocative and political issue and that power structures at the political and economic center are unlikely to surrender their present position easily.

There are, then, valuable lessons to be learned from the community-centric logic circulating among conservation and other practitioners. First, communities are a cornerstone of social existence and time-honored arenas of cultural reproduction and collective action. To mobilize reform affecting place and bypass community is to imperil primary social structure and identity. Second, the logic used by community conservationists applies to land as a productive resource every bit as much as it does to land as a consumptive resource. If land and resources targeted for conservation are fit for community devolution and people-centered management, the same shoe fits land reformers charged with a broad array of social objectives. Third, devolution of responsibility and stewardship without entitlement is a contradiction. It is symbolic devolution at best, and likely to be dysfunctional when the political cache of land redistribution fades. And, as we suggest below, the devolution of entitlement without responsibility to community is similarly ill-conceived. Wightman (1996:205) knowingly states with reference to Scotland's land reform that devolution needs to go beyond property rights to tackle other social, economic and institutional issues—laws on taxation and inheritance, services, community development, equitable representation, and the like. We return to this insight about what must follow the initial stage of reform—successful land acquisition—later.

"Seeing" Community-Centric Land Reform

To this point we have made the case that land reformers have generally accorded low priority to community. We have suggested assorted reasons why this is so and is not easily overcome. But this was not always so. As with community-based conservation, some strains of past land reform revolved around community but have been forgotten. The challenge at hand is not only to find analogs in other policy domains but to recall the community priorities in past land reforms that, for reasons already mentioned, have fallen into obscurity. As Rose (1994) reminds us, we must learn to "see" property forms that are uncommon and unconventional and, by extension, to see relationships between property and community that are largely erased from recent memory.

Historically, property questions were deeply embedded in the social relations of community and were mutually constituted. The annals of prefeudal and feudal society attest to this. Max Weber (1947) saw the spread of quasifreehold society arise on the frontiers of the late Roman Empire, a policy intended to enlist loyalty among subdued tribal communities. Ferdinand Tonnies' (1963) widely read treatise on *Gemeinschaft and Gesellschaft* (Community and Society), took pains to identify *gemeinschaft* with feudal property arrangements and *gesellschaft* with their postfeudal counterparts. Colonial settlements were often experimental sites for proprietary models infused with community rights and obligations. In colonial America, quasicorporations ("town proprietors") were established and given land allotments by the Crown (Woodward, 1936; Sakolski, 1957; Clark, 1983). Shareholders served as town fathers and elders. They drew lots, divided the Crown allotment lands among themselves, and enjoyed franchise rights not accorded to those without land. Land title and political entitlement went hand in hand. Freeholders selling land were compelled to offer it first to the town—an early form of "community right-to-buy." Though antithetical in some ways to current "land reform," these settler experiments were significant departures from the unreformed feudal tenures still practiced in seventeenth century Europe.

A more familiar "land reform" came to North America in the form of the Homestead Act of 1862. This legislation culminated a vision set forth by Jefferson early in the nineteenth century upon his return to the United States from his ambassadorship in France (1784–87). Jefferson was enthralled with what Roman colonizers had accomplished to the north (Kennedy, 2003). He presented Congress with a township system that would undergird his agrarian republic—a concept incorporated in the Northwest Ordinance of the 1780s and the Homestead Act of 1862 (Dovring, 1987). Land allocations east of the 100th Meridian would be of equal size (160 acres per household); to the west, larger accommodations were made to offset climate constraints. In both, one or more sections of each township were set aside as school lands to educate farming communities in the new republic (Souder and Fairfax, 1996) Though the Homestead Act suffered setbacks and perversions (Kennedy, 2003), it was a self-avowed blueprint for a community-centric land reform.

Land reform with unambiguous community content was popular among English land reformers as well (Girardet, 1976; Bronstein, 1999). At the same time free soilers and would-be homesteaders were agitating in the United States, Chartists were calling for parish-based land reform in rural England. Between 1710 and 1850, 7 million acres of commons land had been legally enclosed by landlords and perhaps an equal acreage illegally appropriated (Spowers, 2002). Land reform manifestos proliferated in kind. Building on the writings of Paine, Godwin and Spense,[2] the Chartists proposed an agricultural utopia for commoners-turned-laborers caught in urban squalor. Spense's early notion of parish-based communities in rural England captured public imagination and assuaged public conscience. Herein, parishes would be subdivided into 4-acre farms, with parishioners themselves as "landlords." A "commonwealth" of parishes was foreseen similar to Jefferson's new republic. At its height, the Chartist plan had 70,000 subscribers, organized 600 branches in England, and was institutionalized as the Chartist Co-operative Land Society (later, the National Land Company). At core, Chartists advocated a new vision of community secured by a tenure model replacing the disrupted commons culture (Tod and Wheeler, 1978).

Still more community-centric land reforms were prompted by the appearance of the "second Domesday Book" of 1872. Its revelations of persistent land concentration (Bateman 1883)[3] prompted cries for land nationalization by distinguished intellectuals, including Alfred Wallace, Herbert Spencer, Joseph Chamberlain, J. S. Mill (senior and junior), H. M. Hyndmann, Alfred Marshall, and Ebenezer Howard. During the economic crisis of 1892, the Liberal government empowered county councils to buy large farms and divide them into smaller units of 1–50 acres for lease to individuals or cooperatives. Soon afterwards, Ebenezer Howard (who in 1871 had farmed in Nebraska under the Homestead Act) unveiled his garden cities concept to relieve urban overcrowding. The core concept was marriage between town and countryside, to which some 2 million people responded (Hall, Hardy, and Ward, 2003). In 1913 England passed land reform legislation (Astor and Rowntree, 1938), and by 1914 some 15,000 smallholdings were situated on 200,000 acres. After the First World War and during the Great Depression, additional smallholdings were created for ex-servicemen and unemployed factory workers in England and Scotland with both community and tenure concerns foremost in mind.[4] In the 1940s the Garden Cities Movement gained new momentum and set the stage for both the Town and Country Planning Act of 1947 and the Community Land Act of 1975. The latter, along with the Development Land Tax Act of 1976, was a self-conscious effort to empower communities to capture socially created land value (Huntsman, 1976/77).[5]

Other land reforms have made innovative connections between tenure and community as well. As in Japan and Taiwan, land reform was an urgent priority in post–World War II Italy. Feudal land tenure traditions there originated with Norman colonization a millennium before. Due to success of the fee communes in Lombardy and elsewhere (Medici, 1952), Italy's feudal estates prevailed in the South but bore the brunt of the ten-year (1950–1960) reform following the war (Lopreato, 1967). In that decade, some 673,000 hectares were expropriated and another 94,000 hectares purchased, leading to the creation of 44,000 new farms and the distribution of 70,000 parcels to supplement existing smallholdings. Perhaps most relevant, some 900 new cooperatives were created, as were 180 rural service centers to serve as surrogate communities (McEntire, 1970; Cesarini, 1978).

In India, the Gramdan movement, inspired by Gandhi and initiated by his close friend and colleague Vinoba Bhave, required land titles to be vested in the village community as organized in the Gram-Sabha or village assembly, itself a democratic and autonomous body (Prasad, 1970). Gramdans were gifted by large landowners as part of the nonviolent movement to resolve inequalities of access to land and related poverty. By 1969, there were 95,835 Gramdans in India spread through 17 States. National and international foundations (e.g., Gram+Dhan, Gramdhan India Foundation and Association of Sarva Seva Farms or ASSEFA) have thrown their support behind Gramdan efforts, as have numerous nongovernmental organizations (e.g., Gandhi Smaraka Grama Seva Kendram and Anchalik Gramdhan Sangh, among others).

More recently, Brazil's Movimento dos Trabalhadores Rurais Sem-Terra (MST) has distinguished itself as a major land reform movement dedicated to broad-based ownership encased in new rural communities and ideas of agrarian citizenship. MST has attracted landless people from all regions of the country, urban and rural, often with little prior contact or familiarity, and sought to settle them together in sustainable fashion (Wright and Wolford, 2003). Organizers now devote as much effort to implanting sustainable settlement programs as they do to mapping land recovery strategies and new member recruitment. MST boasts between 1 and 2 million members (making it the largest social movement in Latin America) in a country where 3 percent of the population owns two-thirds of the arable land and communities are routinely displaced by public works, land grabs, and failed public-sector land reforms. When the dangers associated with land invasion subside, questions of community become paramount and are given full attention (Wolford, 2003). MST failures, where they occur, are not for lack of resources, courage, or ranks of militant followers, but for stinting on the postinvasion challenges of civil society and postinvasion title security. Community education and capacity building are issues that will make or break MST, issues in which its leaders—schooled in political tactics, land rights, and Brazil's new constitution—must learn to excel (Wittman, 2009).

This short overview of community-centric land reforms is conspicuously incomplete. To it might be added land reforms in societies which periodically equate community with collectivization, for example, China, Tanzania, Ethiopia and the Balkan states (e.g., Sobhan, 1993; Lapping, 1993). Mexico's 80-year experiment with *ejidos* and Israel's evolving *moshavim* initiate community and land reform in their own culturally specific fashions. And in myriad cases the community nexus to land reform is present but indirect, from Canada's Prince Edward Island (Lapping and Forster, 1984) to parts of the global South. Widespread tenancy reforms in West Bengal in the 1970s and 1980s led to a dramatic increase in agricultural output that increased local incomes, land values, and tax potential for community infrastructure and services (World Bank, 2000/2001). Urban land reforms such as Ian McHarg's proposals for cluster-housing developments aim to create new commons-centered communities (Arendt et al., 1994). Similarly, community land trusts (Davis, 1984; Abromowitz, 2000; Williamson, Imbroscio, and Alperovitz, 2002) and modern proprietary towns (Nelson, 2004) are "land reform" experiments that privilege community, as are the many expressions of the so-called new urbanism (Nolan, 2002). Community land trusts are unlike most other *de facto* land reforms listed in that they go well beyond land acquisition for nonaffluent populations and attend to matters of postreform security and affordability—a topic to which we will be attentive in the case of Scotland.

Scotland's Community-Centric Land Reform

Scotland's land ownership concentration had been the focus of research for several generations (e.g., Bateman, 1883; MacKenzie, 2004; Millman, 1970; Bryden and Houston, 1976; MacEwen, 1977; Cramb, 1996; and Wightman, 1996), along with numerous testimonials on the need for land reform. Just over 1200 landowners hold two-thirds of Scotland's land, a level of concentration unrivaled anywhere else in Europe (Bryden, 1996; Wightman, 1999a). The consequences of such concentration and the feudal "burdens" to which tenants in Scotland were subject until 2000 were and are far-ranging. Absentee landlords can legally counteract proposals for community and regional development through active opposition or mere indifference (MacGregor, 1988; Bird, 1982; Mather, 1988–1989). They can allocate vast acreages to sport hunting at the expense of crop production (Gray, 1981) and have done so for generations. They can claim the foreshore and kelp washing onto it, severing an important source of green manure for local fields and thus the food chain (Macaskill, 2005). They can and do degrade the environment which, if managed for biodiversity and community owned, could be a renewable source of local income (Cramb, 1996). These and other impacts were summarized by Bryan McGregor in the first John MacEwen Memorial Lecture in 1993:

> The impact of the land tenure system goes far beyond land use. It influences the size and distribution of an area's population; the labour skills and the entrepreneurial experiences of the population; access to employment and thus migration; access to housing; access to land to build new houses; the social structure; and the distribution of power and influence. In many areas of rural Scotland, large landowners play a crucial role in local development; *they are the rural planners.* (Emphasis added; cited in Wightman, 1996:15)

A sea change was triggered in 1997, however, by the election of a New Labour Party committed to Devolution for Scotland, Wales and Northern Ireland. The new government quickly set about fulfilling a campaign pledge to establish a Land Reform Policy Group (LRPG) under the chairmanship of the then Scottish Office Minister of State, Lord Sewel. Sewel was responsible for steering legislation for Scottish Devolution from England through the House of Lords. The LRPG developed a set of proposals with extensive public consultation and published its final report early in 1999, the same year Scotland elected its own Parliament for the first time in nearly 300 years. The prospects for land reform advanced swiftly as well. In 2000, Scottish Feudal Law originating in the 11th Century was officially repealed. In February of 2001, the new Scottish Executive in Edinburgh issued the Consultation Paper on Land Reform that led to a Draft Land Reform Bill. Two years later, the Scottish Parliament passed land reform legislation with important community components. For the first time in centuries, it was possible for Scottish communities to attain tenure and livelihood options experienced by the rest of Europe.

At the heart of the 2003 land reform statute was a provision granting communities a first option to purchase the feudal estates of which they were a part—and the basis for viewing the land reform as community-centric. Community interests historically restricted to vassal or (more often) tenant status were now empowered to become full owners of the land. In fact, this empowerment was the final phase in an ownership shift dating back more than a century and having three recognizable periods. The first came on the heels of the infamous clearances in northwest Scotland and of the "new" Domesday survey of 1872–1873 referred to above. The clearances were largely the result of expanding sheep farming and recreational land uses by landed elites and accomplished through rack rents and crofter evictions (Bryden and Houston, 1976).[6] The Crofters Holdings (Scotland) Act of 1886 curtailed landlord prerogatives to a degree. Crofters were guaranteed fair rents, the right to assign their crofts, and other measures of tenure security (Hunter, 1976). In 1892 a Royal Commission targeted over 300,000 ha of private hunting land for redistribution to new crofts and another 225,000 ha for enlarging existing crofts (Mather, 1988–1989). Though not implemented, the Commission's work and later legislation (e.g., an 1897 Act, which established new croft townships, and the 1911 and 1916 Land Settlement Acts) made strong connections between land insecurity and economic destitution in the northern half of Scotland (Leneman, 1989).

Notwithstanding these commissions and legislative acts, little changed in the structure of landownership in Scotland's Crofting Counties until well into the twentieth century (Wightman, 1996). This second period of community empowerment was fueled by a spreading awareness that land tenure was an issue everywhere in Scotland, not just in the northwest, and by the land resettlement predicament posed by World War I. To encourage enlistment in the army, the British Government promised homesteads to soldiers upon their return from the war. The appeal was immense, given Scotland's land concentration and the vivid memory of the Victorian-era clearances. Giving it teeth, the Land Settlement (Scotland) Act of 1919 contained powers of compulsory purchase of private estates (Mather, 1978). Returning soldiers found the government to be equivocating, however. Protests and land invasions ensued, peaking in 1922. These were carefully covered in the media because, unlike the crofters' "war" of the past, these "raids" were by war veterans trained in the use of arms. Against this backdrop, Lord Leverhulme gave his sizeable estate on the Isle of Lewis to the local community, and Scotland's historic Stornoway Trust was born in 1923 (Boyd, 1999).

Between World War I and II roughly 2000 new holdings were created in the Highlands and Islands; resettlement projects spread to lower Scotland to relieve the traumas of the Depression and rural blight after World War II (Mather, 1978).[7] Another significant development after the war was a series of planning acts that further legitimated the nationalization of development rights and public ownership. Private ownership in Scotland in fact decreased as lands were purchased by the Forestry Commission, the Agricultural Department, the National Coal Board, and the Ministry of Defense (Wightman, 1996). Thus, the second period was marked by expanding public ownership across Scotland, increasing set-asides of conservation lands by nonprofit groups (Cramb, 1996), and a growing sentiment that small, privately owned farms were problematic (and in any case had little support in the House of Lords in London).[8] Scotland's feudal land law continued to protect the sanctity of large holdings, and would not expire for several decades.

The third phase in Scotland's community-centric land reform dates from roughly 1970. Two years previously, the Crofters Commission proposed state acquisition and transfer of croft land to crofting communities. In 1969 the White Paper on Land Tenure in Scotland appeared, calling for full abolition of feudal land law. Five years later, the Land Tenure Reform (Scotland) Act passed, prohibiting new duties to feudal superiors and allowing the redemption of others (Wightman, 1996). In 1977 John MacEwen reminded the public that ownership concentration was a chronic blight on rural Scotland, an indictment with many echoes. In the same year the HIDB developed amendments to its land powers and, following public consultation, published these in 1979. By the 1990s few Scots dismissed the Scottish "land question" as irrelevant or hopeless. Indeed, hope rekindled in proportion to the success of community claims. In February of 1990, the government offered its own crofting estates to local communities, and the Arkleton Trust Report on "The Future of the DAFS Estates in Skye and Raasay" appeared. It supported the transfer of land and related assets to local crofting trusts set up as nonprofit companies ("limited by guarantee") with democratic constitutions (Bryden, Fraser, Houston and Robertson, 1990).[9]

Thanks to the prior momentum of crofting communities intent on regaining their collective land rights, community-based land reform permeated Scotland's political climate well before the 2003 land reform act. The Assynt Crofters Trust was created through a large scale community buyout in 1992 (MacKenzie, 2004; Macaskill, 1999), followed by the Borve and Melness Crofting Trusts (Chenevix-Trench and Philip, 2001). Country-wide momentum was now mounting. The Highlands and Islands Forum (HIF) sponsored an important conference in 1994 under the banner "The People and the Land" which in turn spawned country-wide workshops on community-based forestry. This culminated in full community ownership of forest lands in Treslaig, purchased from the Forestry Commission (Ritchie and Haggith, 2005). In 1995 Secretary of State Michael Forsyth proposed that the Scottish Office transfer ownership of 250,000 acres of crofting land to community trusts. In 1996, three other communities (Cairnhead, Culag, and Abriachan) bought or leased forest lands from the government to expand their economic base. In 1997, the Eigg estate (coterminous with the Island of Eigg) was purchased by its residents with assistance from a nongovernmental organization (The Scottish Wildlife Trust) and a private donor. Recapping the momentum of this period, Ritchie and Haggith (2005:10) state:

> Throughout this process, grassroots gatherings such as HIF and Community Woodlands conferences helped the community movement to develop a shared vision, spreading ideas and building confidence. Grassroots networks such as the Scottish Crofters Union, Reforesting Scotland, the Scottish Community Woodland Association . . . and the former Rural Forum helped by sharing information and lobbying.

The Scottish Land Fund

In a prescient move, the Highlands and Islands Development Board had proposed changes to its powers of land acquisition in the 1970s, thereby laying groundwork for noncrofting local communities to trigger buyouts.[10] Several things would happen to fuel such buyouts. In the same year as the Assynt Crofter Trust was formed, residents from the Isles of Eigg and Knoydart initiated legal actions to gain control of their land and forests. On the day of the Eigg estate purchase in 1997, Highlands and Islands Enterprise was asked by the Scottish Office to set up a Community Land Unit to assist communities in the purchase and management of land, a sign of active promotion and financial assistance for acquisition (Chenevix-Trench and Philip, 2001). The Land Reform Policy Group, established in 1997, issued a report in 1999 recommending a fund to support community land purchases and the community right to buy. The following year, the Scottish Land Fund (SLF) was established and capitalized by UK Lottery money (through the New Opportunities Fund's "Green Spaces and Sustainable Communities" program). This created an initial fund of £10m (later increased to £15m) to assist rural communities acquire and develop land and buildings on a voluntary basis.

Although this fund was absorbed into a larger fund operated by the Big Lotteries Fund in 2006, and was later "poached" to support investment for the London Olympics and Glasgow Commonwealth Games, its role was highly significant in the period to 2006. By June 2005 the SLF had assisted roughly 200 communities and committed some £12 million for a wide range of eligible projects, including community purchase of two large estates—the island of Gigha and the North Harris estate, both in the Scottish Highlands and Islands. Two more large crofting estates, South Uist and Galson, both in the Western Isles, were also acquired by the residents between 2003 and 2006. In fact, two thirds of SLF grants have been in the Highlands and Islands, reflecting the fact that people of this region led the land reform campaign.[11] SLF-funded community purchases have been vital tools for community empowerment and enterprise in rural areas of Scotland.[12] For example, since the Gigha acquisition, three second-hand wind generators were purchased which now provide a net profit to the community of £156,000 (in 2008), new enterprises have started and attracted new families, and the population has increased from 97 (and falling) to 150 (and rising). A small local housing enterprise was started, and housing improvements in the existing housing stock have been completed. The school roll has increased for the first time in many years. In Eigg, the installation of new water driven turbines serving small communities has been part of a sustainable energy drive managed by the community, and a new grid serving the whole island has been completed. A new pier has been built, thereby preserving the ferry service to the Island. In Harris, a small but significant wind turbine project received the go-ahead after long delays caused by Scottish Natural Heritage and the planning system. In many other cases, wind turbines are being evaluated for their economic potential.

SLF funding was only available to communities of 3000 or less for most of its life (although this barrier was later raised to reflect higher limits in the new Land Reform legislation, and during the shift to the Big Lotteries Fund [BLF]); all funded projects had to demonstrate economic, social, and environmental benefits and address any minority issues that might arise. Communities have to have, and establish, a democratic and locally controlled body (commonly a company limited by guarantee or "nonprofit," often known as a "Community Trust") to acquire and manage the land and other assets, as well as majority support for the acquisition from community residents. There have already been a significant number of new inquiries for assistance to purchase whole estates and common grazing lands since 2006, when upwards of 163,000 ha of rural land had come under ownership and control of local communities in Scotland, at least a fourth of this with substantial SLF or BLF assistance.

In sum, community buyouts and upgrades became synonymous with Scotland's land reform in this period. However, it is noteworthy that, so far, the land reform legislation was not used—except as a threat—by the communities involved. In all cases, including the contested case of Galson, a negotiated outcome proved possible in the end. Although interest in community purchase remains strong, the shortage of BLF funding since 2006 has meant little action in the past three years, and interest has shifted somewhat to the acquisition of unused or marginal lands from the State, especially the Forestry Commission. However, this has also been held up by the Treasury rules that State owned land must be sold at "market value," and by the unwillingness of the SLF and later the BLF to fund purchases from the State where inflated market values were involved. More recently, funds for this purpose have been altogether lacking.

Discussion

Land reform is returning to the center stage of rural policy but in a context quite different from the past. This context is community-centric, inspired in part by community-based natural resource management and other decentralist tendencies bolstering local autonomy, ownership, and control. Scotland is of particular interest because formal Devolution from the UK Westminster Government coincides with a long overdue land reform with explicit provisions for community-based acquisition of the land. The Scottish case is in many ways unique. A stronghold of feudal land tenure, Scotland's land holdings are not only concentrated but subject to layered tenures and related interdependencies. Though feudalism was formally abolished in 2000, it has remained relatively stable for hundreds of years and its imprint will fade slowly. Even if community buyouts now proceed aggressively according to the 2003 legislation, local owners must contend with a slowly changing ownership structure embedded in an enduring power structure. Equally as challenging, they must confront postreform threats to affordability and tenure security which most land reformers, riveted on initial transfer of land to the landless, have tended to ignore. One must ask if Scotland's land reformers, preoccupied with finding remedies for past tenure inequalities, are somehow the exception.

We framed this research around several issues, one of which was postreform stewardship, a subject to which we now return. In Davis' (2008) case for postacquisition stewardship, he poses several arguments that apply equally well to North America's housing crisis and to the transition to a postfeudal Scotland. First, renting is the common choice of people of limited means in either society, despite their powerful ownership aspirations. Second, reformers in both settings have honed skills of land acquisition through assorted means. The emphasis in both has been on leveraging public subsidies for front-end development and broader entitlement, particularly among the most needy. Even if successful, according to Davis, failure to incorporate the "back-end" (postacquisition) costs of stewardship means that ownership gains can easily slip away. Unless long-term provisions are made, housing stock will be lost outright or deteriorate in quality after the blush of initial reform passes and old problems return. This is one reason why finding other sources of income, such as sales of renewable energy, has been so important in the Scottish case.

Thirdly, there are working examples of stewardship that apply across national boundaries. Davis advances the claim that stewardship rests on organizational partnerships with legal standing that share the risks and rewards of ownership innovations. These partnerships between owners and larger organizations run critical interference for the former who, though entitled, face on-going economic whip-lash—gentrification pressures, soaring utility costs, predatory lending, escalating taxes, income uncertainties, and an unfounded faith that land markets will always be secure investments. Scotland's 2003 land reform leverages community formation with its buyout assistance. But has it animated an equivalent commitment to sustaining these communities and their members well into the future through sober stewardship?

In our judgment, stewardship as prescribed by Davis is a potential weak link in the Scottish land reform and, for that matter, in most land reforms focused primarily on redistributive solutions to the classical "land question." The prospects for stewardship incorporation in the buyout communities of Scotland are far from remote, however. For one thing, stewardship thus defined has been dealt with so far by a mixture of national legislation (e.g., security of tenure for farmers, crofters, and house tenants and rent controls) and conditions of financial aid as laid down by the Scottish Land Fund. The SLF was (together with HIE) the main source of external funding for the Reform. The cases examined, for example Eigg and Gigha, indeed addressed the issues of housing supply, quality, and affordability as a top priority. The 2008 Final Report of the Committee of Inquiry on Crofting offers another potent endorsement for housing affordability (Donnelley, 2008). Moreover, to the extent that the land reform legislation insists on democratic local governance through a board elected by local residents, issues of long-term affordability and tenure protections are unlikely to be sidelined. By itself, community-centric land reform is a necessary—though insufficient—condition for stewardship. But it should not be underestimated as a form of democratic partnership that brings such issues to the fore.

Another reason to be cautiously optimistic about stewardship concerns spreading in buyout communities is the existence of roughly parallel housing models in Scotland, such as the Highlands Small Communities Housing Trust (HSCHT). This Trust was established in 1998 to meet the challenges of housing affordability head-on by a coalition of interests committed to innovative housing solutions. Some of the solutions share the equity limitation mechanisms of community land trusts and their kin in the United States. Several community buyout groups (e.g., Isle of Eigg Trust and Assynt Crofters Trust) are member organizations of HSCHT and conduits for stewardship ideas; so is a broad network of rural Community Councils in the Highland area where the 2003 Reform is concentrated. HSCHT works effectively on both front-end agendas (identifying and buying sites for affordable housing, liaising with critical outside institutions and government agencies, needs assessments and consultations with Community Councils) and back-end agendas (land-banking to withhold critical properties from markets, community education about tenure options, administering preemption rights ["burdens"] giving the Trust first options to buy, and other cost-capping protections for new buyers).[13] It provides subsidized "stepping stone" housing for new arrivals to rebuild depopulated regions and performs other "social surgeries" to avert set-backs to tenure and affordability.[14]

There is no explicit provision in the 2003 Land Reform Scotland Act for long-term affordability and tenure security. These, along with housing quality, are goals left to local ingenuity rather than law. For community-centric land reform to succeed—and succeed across generations—the stewardship insights of resident populations (croft and noncroft), land reform practitioners, and scholars will need to be elevated in importance. The 2003 legislation has undoubtedly been a powerful lever to voluntary sales and land assembly; the longer term challenge will be to keep it in the hands of the communities that have benefited from it to date.

Conclusion

Some will assert that Scotland's land reform and its willing-seller underpinnings are radically conservative. They will portray "buyouts" as a tame response to an antiquated and unjust landownership system with funds which might better serve other public ends. The powers of the state to acquire properties that are inefficiently used, absently owned, and badly distributed are hardly contemplated. Moreover, the community right-to-buy is compromised by exemptions for offshore owners, heirship transfers, beneficial ownerships, and daunting legal complexity. Others will counter that Scotland's new Parliament was astute in finding a nonconfiscatory tool for transferring title, one that largely requires willing sellers and buyers and a commitment to fair compensation. It is a model with appeal in other societies and at the World Bank.[15] Oddly enough, it also saves possible confrontation with the European legislation on Human Rights. Scotland is the home of great land reformers but also the cradle of classical, market-based economics and pragmatism.

This paper draws particular attention to an attribute of Scotland's land reform which has both conservative and progressive qualities—the foregrounding of community. It would seem that Scotland's land reform is simultaneously top-down (state authorized and assisted) and bottom-up (privileging communities). "Community" is both place-based, as in the resulting right-to-purchase section of the law, and functional. Just as important, the current law must be seen as the result of the multistage historical process in which vast numbers of communities and community advocates have had a stake and made important sacrifices. No one believes that this process is complete. There is every reason to think that it will continue and that Scotland's land reform law will be amended and improved as community rights and responsibilities are better understood in practice. Stewardship that protects the advances made to date for generations yet to be born—and securely housed in quality homes—seems like a self-evident direction for community-based land reform to take next.

NOTES

The authors acknowledge the assistance and input of Matthew Hoffman in preparing this chapter, a revision of Bryden and Geisler (2007), and thank the editors of *Land Use Policy*, where the earlier version appeared.

1. Common property is not necessarily property held by a community (see Barrow and Murphree, 2001).

2. Britain has had a wide spectrum of land reformers old and new (e.g., the Land Tenure Reform Association and the bioregionalists). Some, like William Ogilvie (see his Rights Of Property), focus on ownership rights with fixed rents and services. Others, like Bright, Fawcett, Arnold, Thornton, Kinnear, Brodrick and Kay, have advocated a market-driven "private" reform. Still others have pressed for outright nationalization or state ownership of the fee (Astor and Rowntree, 1938).

3. The Survey, which included landownership in Scotland, was conducted in 1872–1873, and revealed that half of Scotland was owned by a mere 118 people (Wightman, 1996).

4. In Scotland, the Congested Districts Board set up in 1897 following the Royal Commission on Crofters and Cottars (The Napier Commission) established 640 new holdings and 1138 enlargements between 1897 and 1912. Its activities were taken over by the Board of Agriculture which implemented the Land Settlement Acts in Scotland, under which 6000 new smallholdings were created after World War I (Leneman, 1989). In 1934 the Land Settlements Association was established with Government sponsorship so that, by 1947, nearly 30,000 smallholders were cultivating over 450,000 acres of agricultural land owned by local authorities and other government bodies. In that same year, new laws encouraged cooperatives (the recommendation of the Scott Committee on Land Utilization in the Rural Areas [1942]), but the industrial boom drew farmers to cities and the 30,000 fell to 22,000 (Girardet, 1976:108–109). Nevertheless, there has been a strong demand for home-production allotments in recent years (Daniels, 2009). Pretty (1998) estimated a decade ago that there were more allotment units than the number of "significant" farms.

5. A land tax was proposed twenty years later in the context of Scottish Land reform, but the Land Reform Policy Group considered this too risky a subject to broach in the light of the constraints on tax raising powers of the Scottish Government agreed in the Scottish Devolution Act implemented in 1999.

6. Crofting tenancies were (and are) organized into "townships" throughout much of the Highlands and Islands region. Most crofters held a legal interest in a commons (a "common grazing") managed by elected committees of crofters. Today, some 17,000 crofting tenancies occupy 800,000 ha or 20 percent of the Highlands and Islands (Ritchie and Haggith, 2005). For commentary on the complexity of "commons" in Scotland, see Callander (1987).

7. Mather (1978) states that this was part of a larger resettlement impulse across Europe intended, at least in part, to head off Bolshevism.

8. In 1964 the Highlands and Islands Development Act was passed. In 1970, according to Mather (1988–1989), the Highlands and Islands Development Board rejected the idea of creating new smallholdings as nonviable.

9. The Solicitor of the Team, Simon Fraser, subsequently became the principle legal advisor to many community land purchases from Assynt to Gigha and North Harris, thereby having a major effect on land reform thinking in this period.

10. These proposals were accepted by the Labour Government in 1979, shortly before the elections which were won by a Conservative party not in favour of land reform. Nevertheless, the HIDB's proposals were advanced as a private Members Bill in 1980 by Robert MacLennan, then Labour MP for Caithness and Sutherland. The Bill unsurprisingly failed to gain sufficient support in the Commons.

11. Measuring the "interest" in land reform by the number of respondents in relation to the population of each region in Scotland, we note that of the 338 responses to the first Consultation Paper, 38 percent came from the Highlands and Islands, which has 7 percent of Scotland's population—by far the highest rate of response of any region (Bryden and Hart, 2000).

12. More detailed information summarizing community land acquisitions in Scotland between 1908 and 2005 appears in Bryden and Geisler (2007).

13. These burdens put conditions on sales. In 2007 the HSCHT introduced its "rural housing burden" (shared equity and preemption rights) on the titles of home plots it sells. This gives the Trust a way to keep such properties below market value and within reach of the next buyers on an on-going basis (see http://www.communityland.org.uk/, accessed on July 16, 2009).

14. An overview of the Highlands Small Communities Housing Trust can be found at http://www.hscht.co.uk/old_site/what_we_do/overview.html (accessed on July 9, 2009).

15. Powelson and Stock (1987) maintains that when the Shah of Iran came to power he asserted ownership over some 2000 villages in that country; villages and individuals were allowed to buy back their land titles, a source of considerable revenue for the Shah. Of late, Indian villages in Highland Guatemala have raised funds among international NGOs to buyout the holders of their village titles, including wealthy foreigners. Bangladesh's largest NGO is currently using its resources to acquire land for low income and landless families, with the potential for communities to acquire it as well. The World Bank is currently promoting a Land Fund intended to help individuals and organizations buy land essential to their livelihood.

REFERENCES

Abercrombie, K. 1981. *Rural Development in Lewis and Harris*. The Arkleton Trust, Oxford.

Abromowitz, D. M. 2000. "An Essay on Community Land Trusts." In C. Geisler and G. Daneker (Eds.), *Property and Values: Alternatives to Public and Private Ownership*. Island Press: Washington, DC, pp. 213–232.

Agrawal, A., Gibson, C. C. 1999. Enchantment and disenchantment The role of community in natural resource conservation. *World Development* 27, 629–649.

Arendt, R., et al. 1994. *Rural by Design: Maintaining Small Town Character*. American Planning Assn. Press, Chicago.

Astor, V., Rowntree, B. S. 1938. *British Agriculture: Principles for Future Policy*. Longmans Green, London.

Barrett, C., Brandon, K., Gibson, C., Gjertsen, H. 2001. Conserving tropical biodiversity amid weak institutions. *BioScience* 51, 497–502.

Barrow, E., Murphree, M. 2001. Community conservation: From concept to practice. In D. Hulme and M. Murphree (Eds.), *African Wildlife and Livelihoods: The Promise and Performance of Community Conservation*. James Currey, Oxford, pp. 24–37.

Barton, H. 2002. *Sustainable Communities*. Earthscan, London.

Bassand, M., Brugger, E., Bryden, J., Friedmann, J., Stuckey, B. (Eds.) 1985. *Self-Reliant Development for a New Europe: Theory, Practice, Conflicts*. Gower Press, Aldershot.

Bateman, J. 1883. *The Great Landowners of Great Britain and Ireland*. 4th Edition. First published in 1876 as *The Acre-Ocracy of England*. The Victorian Library at Leicester University Press first published the 4th Edition 1883 text in 1971.

Bell, C., Newby, H. 1971. *Community Studies: An Introduction to the Sociology of the Local Community*. George Allen & Unwin Ltd., London.

Belsky, J. 2003. Unmasking the "local": Gender, community, and the politics of community-based rural ecotourism in Belize. In S. R. Brechin, P. R. Wilshusen, C. L. Fortwangler, and P. C. West (Eds.), *Contested Nature: Promoting International Biodiversity with Social Justice in the Twenty-first Century.* SUNY Press, Albany, NY, pp. 89–102.

Bird, S. 1982. The impact of estate ownership on social development in a Scottish rural community. *Sociologia Ruralis* 22, 36–48.

Borrini-Feyerabend, G. 1996. *Collaborative Management of Protected Areas: Tailoring the Approach to the Context.* World Conservation Union, Gland, Switzerland.

Boyd, G. 1999. To restore the land to the people and the people to the land. In G. Boyd and J. Reid (Eds.), *Social Land Ownership: Eight Case Studies from the Highlands and Islands.* Not-for-Profit Landowners Group, Inverness, pp. 13–22.

Brandon, K., Redford, K. H., Sanderson, S. E. (Eds.). 1998. *Parks in Peril: People, Politics, and Protected Areas.* Island Press, Washington, DC.

Brechin, S., Wilschusen, P. R., Fortwangler, C. L., West P. C. (Eds.). 2003. *Contested Nature: Promoting International Biodiversity with Social Justice in the Twenty-First Century.* SUNY Press, Albany, NY.

Bromley, D. W. 1991. *Environment and Economy: Property Rights and Public Policy.* Blackwell, Oxford.

Bronstein, J. L. 1999. *Land Reform and Working-Class Experience in Britain and the United States, 1800–1862.* Stanford University Press, Stanford.

Brox, O. 1990. The common property theory: Epistemology status and analytics utility. *Human Organization* 49, 13–26.

Bryden, J. 1994. *Towards Sustainable Rural Communities.* University of Guelph, Canada.

———. 1996. *Land Tenure and Rural Development in Scotland.* The 1996 John McEwen Lecture. A. K. Bell Library, Perth.

Bryden, J., Fraser, S., Houston, G., Robertson, I. 1990. *The Future of the DAFS Estates in Skye and Raasay.* Ullinish, Scotland.

Bryden, J., Geisler, C. 2007. Community-based land reform: Lessons from Scotland. *Land Use Policy* 24, 24–34.

Bryden, J., Hart, K. 2000. Land Reform, Planning and People: An Issue of Stewardship? RSE/SNH Millennium Conference Paper (March). Published as Chapter 7 in G. Holmes and R. Crofts (Eds.), *Scotland's Environment: Resetting the Agenda?* Tuckwell Press, Edinburgh.

Bryden, J., Houston, G. 1976. Agrarian Change in the Scottish Highlands. *Glasgow Social & Economic Research Studies* 4. Martin Robertson in association with Highlands & Islands Development Board, London.

Buck, L., Geisler, C., Shelhaus, J., Wollenberg, E. 2001. *Biological Diversity: Balancing Interests Through Adaptive Collaborative Management.* CRC Press, Boca Raton, Florida.

Callander, R. F. 1987. *A Pattern of Landownership in Scotland.* Haughend Publications, Finzean, Aberdeenshire.

Cary, J., Webb, T. 2000. *Community Landcare, the National Landcare Program and the Landcare Movement: The Social Dimensions of Landcare.* Social Services Centre, Bureau of Rural Sciences, Mimeo, Canberra.

Cesarini, G. 1978. *Agricultural Cooperatives in the Mezzogiorno.* The Arkleton Trust, Enstone, Oxford.

Chenevix-Trench, H., Philip, L. J. 2001. Community and conservation land ownership in Highland Scotland: A common focus in a changing context. *Scottish Geography* 117, 139–56.

Clark, C. E. 1983. *The Eastern Frontier, the Settlement of Northern New England, 1610–1763.* University Press of New England, Hanover, NH.

Cramb, A. 1996. *Who Owns Scotland Now?: The Use and Abuse of Private Land*. Mainstream Publishing, London.

Daniels, I. 2009. Join the allotment community. Available on line: http://www.dobbies .co.uk/blog/allotment-community (accessed on December 30, 2009).

Davis, J. E. 1984. Reallocating Equity: A Land Trust Model of Land Reform. In C. Geisler and F. Popper (Eds.), *Land Reform, American Style*. Totowa, NJ, Rowman and Littlefield, pp. 209–232.

———. 2008. Homes That Last: The Case for Counter-cyclical Stewardship. *Shelterforce* 156 (Winter), 18–25.

Deininger, K. 2003. *Land Policies for Growth and Poverty Reduction*. Oxford University Press, New York.

Dewar, D. 1998. *Land Reform for the 21st Century*. 5th John MacEwen Memorial Lecture. AK Bell Library, Aviemore, Perth.

Donnelley, R. R. 2008. *Final Report of the Committee of Inquiry on Crofting*. Crown Copyright, Edinburgh.

Dorner, P. 1999. Technology and Globalization: Modern-Era constraints on Local Initiatives for Land Reform. UNRISD Discussion Paper No. 100 (June). U.N. Research Institute for Social Development, Geneva.

Dovring, F. 1987. *Land Economics*. Breton Publishers, Boston.

Eghenter, C., Sellato, B. 1999. *Kebudayaan dan pelestarian alam: penelitian interdisipliner di pedalaman Kalimantan*. PHPA, Ford Foundation and World Wildlife Fund, Jakarta.

Eghenter, C. 2002. Planning for Community-based Management Conservation Areas. In D. Chatty and M. Colchester (Eds.), *Conservation and Mobile Indigenous Peoples. Studies in Forced Migration* Vol. 10. Berghahn Books, Oxford, pp. 329–346.

Girardet, H. 1976. *Land for the People*. Crescent Books, London.

Gray, M. 1981. The Regions and Their Issues: Scotland. In G. E. Mingay (Ed.), *The Victorian Countryside*. Routledge & Kegan Paul, London, pp. 81–93.

Griffin, K. 1999. *Alternative Strategies for Rural Development*. St. Martin's, New York.

Hall, P., Hardy, D., Ward, C. 2003. Commentator's Introduction: *To-Morrow: A Peaceful Path to Real Reform* by E. Howard. Facsimile. Routledge, London.

Hulme, D., Murphree, M. 2001. *African Wildlife and Livelihoods: The Promise and Performance of Community Conservation*. James Curry, Oxford.

Hunter, J. 1976. *The Making of the Crofting Community*. John Donald, Edinburgh.

Huntsman, P. W. 1976/77. The Community Land Act of 1975, *Farm Management* 3, 174–183.

IIED. 1994. *Whose Eden? An Overview of Community Approaches to Wildlife Management*. International Institute for Environmental and Development, London.

Kennedy, R. G. 2003. *Mr. Jefferson's Lost Cause*. Oxford, New York.

Lapping, M. B. 1993. The Land Reform in Independent Estonia: Memory as Precedent—Toward the Reconstruction of Agriculture in Eastern Europe. *Agriculture and Human Values* X (Winter), 52–59.

Lapping, M. B., Forster, V. D. 1984. From Insurgency to Policy: Land Reform in Prince Edward Island. In C. Geisler and F. Popper (Eds.), *Land Reform, American Style*, Rowman & Allanheld, Totowa, NJ, pp. 245–272.

Leneman, L. 1989. *Fit for Heroes? Land Settlement in Scotland after World War I*. Aberdeen University Press, Aberdeen.

Li, T. M. 1996. Images of community: Discourse and strategy in property relations. *Development and Change* 27, 501–527.

Lopreato, J. 1967. *Peasants No More*. Chandler Publishing Co., San Francisco.

Macaskill, J. 1999. *We Have Won the Land: The Story of the Purchase of the Assynt Crofters' Trust of the North Lochinver Estate*. Island of Lewis, Acair.

———. 2005. The Scottish Foreshore, the Crofting Community and Land Reform: An Opportunity Missed? Paper presented at the 2004 Annual Meetings of the International Rural Sociological Assn., Trondheim, Norway, July. Based on the author's PhD thesis at the University of Aberdeen [2003].

MacEwen, J. 1977. *Who Owns Scotland?* EUSPB, Edinburgh.

MacGregor, B. D. 1988. Owner motivation and land use on landed estates in north-west Highlands of Scotland. *Journal of Rural Studies* 4, 389–404.

Mackenzie, A. F. D. 2004. Re-imagining the land, North Sutherland, Scotland. *Journal of Rural Studies* 20 (3), 273–287.

Mather, A. S. 1978. *State-Aided Land Settlement in Scotland.* University of Aberdeen Press, Aberdeen.

———. 1988–1989. Government agencies and land development in the Scottish Highlands: a centenary survey. *Northern Scotland* 8, 39–50.

McEntire, D. 1970. Land Reform in Italy. AID Spring Review Country Paper.

McNeely, J. A., Scherr, S. J. 2003. *Ecoagriculture: Strategies to Feed the World and Save Wild Biodiversity.* Island Press, Washington, DC.

Medici, G. 1952. *Land Property and Land Tenure in Italy.* Edizioni Agricole, Bologna.

Millman, R. 1970. The landed estates of Northern Scotland. *Scottish Geographical Magazine* 86, 186–203.

Nelson, R. 2004. Local Government as Private Property. In H. M. Jacobs (Ed.), *Private Property in the 21st Century: The Future of an American Ideal.* Edward Elgar, Cheltenham, pp. 66–78.

Nolan, J. 2002. In praise of parochialism: The advent of local environmental law. *Harvard Environmental Law Review* 2 (26), 482–528.

O'Riordan, T., Stoll-Kleeman, S. (Eds.). 2002. *Biodiversity, Sustainability, and Human Communities: Protecting Beyond the Protected.* Cambridge University Press, Cambridge, UK.

Ostrom, E. 1990. *Governing the Commons: The Evolution of Institutions for Collective Action.* Cambridge University Press, New York.

Pimbert, M., Pretty, J. 1997. Diversity and Sustainability in Community Based Conservation. Paper presented to UNESCO-IIPA regional workshop on Community-based Conservation (online at http://www.iucn.org/themes/ceesp/Publications/TILCEPA/MPimbert-UNESCOCommunityDiversity.pdf).

Polanyi, K. 1944. *The Great Transformation: The Political and Economic Origins of Our Time.* Beacon Press, Boston.

Powelson, J. P., Stock, R., 1987. *The Peasant Betrayed: Agriculture and Land Reform in the Third World.* Oelgeschlager, Gunn, and Hain, Boston.

Prasad, D. (Ed.). 1970. *Gramdhan: The Land Revolution of India.* War Resisters International, London.

Pretty, J. 1998. *The Living Land: Agriculture, Food, and Community Regeneration in Rural Europe.* Earthscan Publications, London.

Putnam, R. 2000. *Bowling Alone: The Collapse and Revival of American Community.* Simon and Schuster, New York.

Reid, K. 2003. *Abolition of Feudal Tenure in Scotland.* Butterworths Law, London.

Richards, J. F. (Ed.), 2002. *Land, Property, and the Environment.* Institute for Contemporary Studies, Oakland, CA.

Ritchie, B., Haggith, M. 2005. Push-Me, Pull-You of Forest Devolution in Scotland. In C. Colfer and D. Capistrano (Eds.), *The Politics of Decentralization: Forests, People and Power.* Earthscan, London, Chapter 12.

Rose, C. M. 1994. *Property and Persuasion: Essays on the History, Theory, and Rhetoric of Ownership.* Westview Press, Boulder.

Sakolski, A. 1957. *Land Tenure and Land Taxation in America*. The Robert Schalkenbach Foundation, New York.

Selman, P. 2002. Multi-function landscape plans: A missing link in sustainability planning? *Local Environment*, 7, 283–294.

Shortall, S., Shucksmith, M. 1998. Integrated rural development: Issues arising from the Scottish experience. *European Planning Studies* 6.1, 73–88.

Sobhan, R. 1993. *Agrarian Reform and Social Transformation: Preconditions for Development*. ZED Books, London.

Souder, J., Fairfax, S. 1996. *State Land Trusts: History, Management, and Sustainable Use*. University of Kansas Press, Lawrence.

Spence, T. 1782. *A Supplement to the History of Robinson Crusoe, Being the History of Crusonia on Robinson Crusoe's Island, Down to the Present Time*. New Edition. T. Saint, New Castle upon Tyne.

Spowers, R. 2002. *Rising Tides: The History and Future of the Environmental Movement*. Canongate, Edinburgh.

Stohr, W. B. (Ed.). 1990. *Global Challenge and Local Response: Initiatives for Economic Regeneration in Contemporary Europe*. The United Nations University and Mansell Press, New York.

Terborgh, J. 1999. *Requiem for Nature*. Island Press, Washington, DC.

Tod, I., Wheeler, M. 1978. *Utopia*. Harmony Books, New York.

Tonnies, F. 1963. *Community and Society*. Translated by C. P. Loomis. Harper, New York.

Weber, M. 1947. *The Theory of Social and Economic Organization*. Oxford, New York.

Wells, M. 1994–1995. Biodiversity Conservation and Local Peoples' Development Aspirations: New Priorities for the 1990s. Rural Development Forestry Network Paper 18a: 1–24.

Western, D., Pearl, M. C. (Eds.). 1989. *Conservation for the Twenty-First Century*. Oxford, New York.

Western, D., and Wright, R. M. (Eds.). 1994. *Natural Connections: Perspectives on Community-based Conservation*. Island Press, Washington DC.

Wightman, A. 1996. *Who Owns Scotland?* Canongate, Edinburgh.

———. 1999a. *Scotland: Land & Power. The Agenda for Land Reform*. Luath Press, Edinburgh.

———. 1999b. The Scottish Executive Land Reform White Paper of July 1999: An Analysis. Briefing Paper No. 1 of the Land Programme of the Caledonia Centre for Social Development (online at http://www.caledonia.org.uk/land/brief01.htm).

Williamson, R., Imbroscio, D., Alperovitz, G. 2002. *Making a Place for Community: Local Democracy in a Global Era*. Routledge, New York.

Wittman, H. J. 2005. The Landscape of Agrarian Reform: Ecological Countermovements and Agrarian Citizenship in Mato Grosso, Brazil. Unpublished PhD Dissertation, Dept. of Development Sociology, Cornell University, Ithaca, NY.

———. 2009. Reframing agrarian citizenship: Land, life and power in Brazil. *Journal of Rural Studies* 25, 120–130.

Wittman, H. J., Geisler, C. 2005. Negotiating locality: Decentralization and communal forest management in the Guatemalan Highlands. *Human Organization* 64 (1), 62–74.

Wolford, W. 2003. Producing community: The MST and land reform settlements in Brazil. *Journal of Agrarian Change* 3(4), 500–520.

Woodward, F. M. 1936. *The Town Proprietors of Vermont: The New England Town Proprietorship in Decline*. Columbia University Press, New York.

World Bank. 2000/2001. *World Development Report*. New York.

Wright, A., Wolford, W. 2003. *To Inherit the Earth*. Food First Books, Oakland, CA.

Zerner, C. 2000. *People, Plants, and Justice: The Politics of Nature Conservation*. Columbia University Press, New York.

PART SEVEN

BEYOND THE HORIZON

Low-Income Homeownership

American Dream or Delusion?

Anne B. Shlay

(2006)

Introduction

Since the Great Depression, the hallmark of U.S. housing policy, *sine qua non,* has been homeownership (Wright, 1983; Hayden, 1985; Jackson, 1985). Historical accounts of the initial motivations behind the push to create a nation of homeowners cite industrialists' interest in homeownership because they feared communism and labor unrest (Hayden, 1981, p. 283) and the belief that stable housing was intrinsically linked to the maintenance of a loyal citizenry (Wright, 1983). But the federal government's push for homeownership, its subsequent intervention in housing markets and its revolutionizing of the housing finance industry occurred in the wake of the failed U.S. economy in the late 1920s (Jackson, 1985). Homeownership became a tool to stimulate consumption and increase production while improving Americans' housing conditions (Carliner, 1998). While World War II created a temporary hiatus in the homeownership push, when the troops came home, they were welcomed with federally insured long-term amortization loans—a central ingredient to the success of a homeownership strategy (Wright, 1983).

It is not clear who pegged homeownership as the American Dream. Homeownership policy, however, has not been about imagining the unattainable but about creating the expectation of owning one's own home. Ideologically, homeownership has been portrayed as a political right seemingly more popular than voting (Shlay, 1985, 1986).[1] Indeed, anthropologist Constance Perin argues that homeownership is symbolically equivalent to citizenship—a status conveyed to the homebuyer through establishing a debt relationship with a bank (Perin, 1977).

Yet homeownership is also valued as the lynch pin for the maintenance and growth of a huge housing infrastructure that includes developers, the financial services industry, the real estate industry, planners, road builders and the like. Homeownership is politically popular, in part, because it has a myriad of constituencies (Buchholz, 2002).

To be sure, homeownership is criticized for escalating suburbanization, fostering central-city decay, promoting neighborhood racial change and segregation, and intensifying environmental damage, pollution and waste (Squires, 1994; Wright, 1983;

Hayden, 1985; Jackson, 1985; Bradford, 1979). But even its critics fail to come up with good, feasible alternatives given homeownership's enormous popularity. In 2002, 67.9 percent of U.S. households owned their own homes (U.S. Census, 2002b).

Within the U.S., desires for homeownership have been longstanding. The colonising British, notes historian Kenneth Jackson (1985), quickly organized land into parcels for private consumption. This earliest version of the American dream was not about owning a home *per se* but about owning land. Owning land, however, was not a value indigenous to Americans; Native American Indians did not believe that natural resources such as land could be owned (Jackson, 1985). Detached housing development was enabled by appropriated land from the Indians and fuelled by a strong antiurban bias imported from England.

The post–World War II growth in homeownership has largely stemmed from housing finance innovations directed at making the purchase of a home possible through a range of guarantees, instruments and incentives as well as increasing the supply of credit through the secondary mortgage market (Lea, 1996; Monroe, 2001). But the beneficiaries of homeownership have historically been working- and middle-class White households, rather than poor households and households of colour (Denton, 2001). In recent years, this has changed. Low-income families represent a new target of homeownership policy. Nationwide, low-income homeownership is now a policy goal for government at the local, state and federal levels, is claimed as an accomplishment by both the Clinton and Bush presidencies, and is featured in television and radio advertisements.

This paper provides a critical analysis of the recent policy shift to promote low-income homeownership. It examines the ideology and assumptions buttressing this policy, evaluates evidence on the effects of low-income homeownership and assesses the viability of homeownership as a strategy for low-income families.

This paper has several parts. Parts one and two review the rationale for low-income homeownership and the genesis of low-income homeownership policy. Part three examines trends in low-income homeownership and the potential for growth in this market. The fourth part looks at research on the effects of low-income homeownership. The fifth part examines characteristics of metropolitan housing markets that may prevent low-income families from benefiting from homeownership. The final part presents a set of possible policy alternatives to explore for strengthening homeownership and other housing opportunities for low-income families.

The Rationale for Low-Income Homeownership

Within the housing field, there is a longstanding tradition of viewing housing as a source of social problems (Dean, 1949; Hartman, 1975; Wright, 1983). Public interventions in the housing market, including housing codes, zoning, urban renewal and slum clearance, and public housing, were based on a set of beliefs that poor housing caused social, psychological and behavioral problems (Glazer, 1980; Rainwater, 1980; Bellush and Hausknecht, 1967; Gans, 1977; Babcock, 1966). Ideologically, this was rooted, in part, in an antiurban bias suggested by leaders of the Chicago School of Urban Sociology who worried about the effects of urban size, density and heterogeneity on the breakdown of social norms and community (Bassett and Short, 1980; Fischer, 1982; Baldassare, 1979; Wirth, 1969). To be sure, urbanization and massive immigration brought with them unhealthy and unsanitary housing conditions. But the rationale for public intervention in housing was linked to the alleged social conditions and social pathologies associated with bad housing. Critics called these unsubstantiated links between housing and behavior the "myths of housing reform" (Dean, 1949).

Promoting homeownership, and particularly low-income homeownership, is firmly rooted in this deterministic tradition. Low-income homeownership is expected to bring with it a wide range of social, behavioral, political, economic and neighborhood changes, many due to behaviors expected with the economic investment that homeownership represents. The goals associated with low-income homeownership are shown in Table 1.

The economic goals associated with low-income homeownership are the most intuitive. As with higher-income households, proponents view low-income homeownership

TABLE 1: Low-Income Homeownership Rationales/Goals			
Family Economic	**Family Social**	**Political**	**Neighborhood**
Asset-building	>Social stability	<Criminal activity	>Property values
Substitute investment for 401Ks, stocks, trust funds, etc.	>Family functioning	>Political (voting) participation	>Care of property
Enforced savings	>Satisfaction	>Commitment to employment	>Stability
Created "fixed" housing costs	>Voluntary/civic participation	>Tax base	<Abandonment
	Children's outcomes (cognitive and behavioral)	>Population growth	<Graffiti, litter and other signs of decline
	<Juvenile delinquency		
	>School attendance		
	>Physical and mental health		

as an asset-building strategy for owners to build up equity in their homes (Retsinas and Belsky, 2002b). In addition, low-income homeownership is viewed as a substitute investment for other types, including 401Ks, stocks and mutual funds. It is also viewed as a type of forced savings where making a monthly mortgage payment is similar to putting money in a bank, unlike with making a rental payment. With a fixed-rate mortgage, low-income homeownership is expected to keep housing costs more predictable.

Anticipated social changes are those that affect family well-being because home-ownership is believed to give people more control over their housing and, therefore, their lives (Rohe et al., 2002b; Rohe and Stegman, 1994a, 1994b). It is also expected to provide families with more opportunities (Rohe et al., 2002a). For adults, expected social changes include greater life satisfaction, increased participation in voluntary civic organizations and improved physical and psychological health (Dietz and Haurin, 2003). Through homeownership, low-income families are expected to become healthier, happier and more involved in community. For children, homeownership is expected to produce both positive cognitive and behavioral changes resulting in less juvenile delinquency and better school performance (Haurin et al., 2002).

Through a more definitive commitment toward place, low-income homeownership is expected to bring with it changes in political behavior as well as changes in the local political climate (Gilderbloom and Markham, 1995; Rossi and Weber, 1996; Rohe and Basalo, 1997; Heskin, 1983; Blum and Kingston, 1984; Saunders, 1990). Low-income homeowners are expected to vote more than renters and to be more politically engaged and aware. Low-income homeownership is projected to affect positively the local tax base and to spur local population growth (Rohe et al., 2002a).

At the level of the neighborhood, low-income homeownership is expected to strengthen local housing markets (Rohe and Stewart, 1996). These homeowners are expected to take better care of their property than renters and therefore create positive neighborhood spillovers. Presumably, property values will then rise and abandonment and other forms of blight will decrease (Haurin et al., 2003).

The Genesis of Low-Income Homeownership Policy

Homeownership and, in particular, suburbanized homeownership, have deep roots in the activities of the federal government (Jackson, 1985). Yet homeownership has become so entangled with American ideas of social status that it is not entirely evident whether federal policy came to reflect prevailing popular culture or whether desires for homeownership became the ideological manifestation of these political forces. Clearly, public policy and housing preferences have been "in sync," leading to home-ownership's enormous popularity in the U.S.

The roots of low-income homeownership policy lie in the creation of the Federal Home Administration (FHA) in 1934 and the subsequent establishment of Fannie

Mae (Jackson, 1985; van Order, 2000). FHA made homeownership possible for many U.S. households by guaranteeing payment in the event of default. Fannie Mae, Freddie Mac and the evolving Government Sponsored Enterprise (GSE) infrastructure created a secondary market for these loans. These federal interventions in the mortgage market pioneered innovation in mortgage instruments and products, expanded homeownership to the middle class, fuelled suburbanization and created what economist Michael Lea (1996) calls "a wonderful life" in mortgage finance where government propelled innovation by sharing risk with the private sector.

But the government also defined risk by developing lending guidelines that made it difficult, if not impossible, to make FHA-insured loans in minority neighborhoods, racially changing neighborhoods and older neighborhoods more generally. By classifying many urban neighborhoods as poor risks, FHA guidelines effectively redlined cities (Jackson, 1985; Bradford, 1979; Stuart, 2003).

The civil rights movement highlighted FHA's racial and antiurban bias. Agitation brought about important reforms in the late 1960s. These reforms, largely through the now-infamous 235 program, increased the availability of FHA finance to minority households. Mortgage brokers heavily marketed FHA loans to inner-city communities using relaxed credit standards for minority homebuyers and massively inflated appraisals (Hays, 1993). Home improvement companies, often in partnership with mortgage companies, bought older homes from the exiting Whites moving to the suburbs and sold them to minorities (a practice known as flipping). Many of these new minority homebuyers could not afford to maintain the homes that they purchased (Bradford, 1979; Squires, 1994). FHA reforms with flawed underwriting, inflated appraisals, scandalous lending practices and massive foreclosures led to wholesale neighborhood devastation in many city neighborhoods, particularly in Midwestern and Northeastern cities. The alleged wonderful life in mortgage innovation became a death sentence for many central-city minority neighborhoods.

With the recognition that lenders were redlining communities, a practice with roots in the neighborhood underwriting guidelines perpetrated by FHA, came the impetus for another innovation in lending—community reinvestment. The logic behind community reinvestment was that mortgage originators, typically savings and loans institutions, had responsibilities to invest in communities that were the source of local deposits (Squires, 1992). Lenders who failed to invest in communities from which they derived deposits were *disinvesting* from communities by taking their deposits and investing them in someone and somewhere else. An important contribution of the community reinvestment movement was the recognition of the role of private investment decisions in promoting urban decay and inequality (Shlay, 1993).

Sophisticated organizing led to the establishment of two federal policies in response to disinvestment, the Home Mortgage Disclosure Act of 1975 (HMDA) and the Community Reinvestment Act of 1977 (CRA). HMDA mandated lenders to report the location of their residential lending, permitting people to document where lenders were making loans. CRA made reinvestment a federal requirement for lenders under federal regulatory oversight (Squires, 1992).

The community reinvestment movement, however, did not advocate for low-income homeownership. But this movement, as it changed form in the last part of the late twentieth century, was highly influential in the evolution of low-income homeownership as a desired policy goal.

How did this happen? A variety of forces converged, providing the impetus to move on the low-income homeownership frontier. These included the community reinvestment movement, the collapse of the savings and loan industry, a new political administration in Washington and technological changes in underwriting.

The merger mania and financial restructuring of the "go-go" 1980s created opportunities for Community Reinvestment Act (CRA) challenges—a regulatory moment when local community groups and others could protest a merger or acquisition based on a lender's lack of compliance with CRA mandates. This led to the negotiation of a host of CRA agreements where lenders committed large amounts of money targeted for urban, minority and low-income lending (National Housing Conference, 2001; Squires, 1992, 2003; Shlay, 1999).

During this same time-period, the collapse of many institutions within the savings and loan industry suggested that prevailing definitions of risk were not firmly grounded in realistic underwriting standards. The understanding that loans to low-income families did not cause savings and loans to fail was accompanied by a growing recognition that low-income loans were profitable and good insurance against loss (Listokin et al., 2002). This perceptual shift fostered a new look at the potential low-income homebuyer.

Lenders were also seeking new markets. Changes in homeownership rates remained flat during the late 1980s and early 1990s, hovering at around 64 per cent (Masnick, 2001). Low-income homebuyers represented a new and untapped market.

Other federal policy initiatives intensified their focus on low-income homeownership. The Federal Housing Enterprises Financial Safety and Soundness Act of 1992 established performance standards for Government Sponsored Enterprises (GSEs Fannie Mae and Freddie Mac) to make homeownership available to a wider variety of households (Case et al., 2002; Fishbein, 2003). The Department of Housing and Urban Development then established target goals for the purchase of loans made to low- and moderate-income homebuyers (less than or equal to the MSA median income) in central cities and to specifically targeted lower households.[2] The GSEs were required to target the "underserved" markets. Both Fannie Mae and Freddie Mac increased activities around innovating loan products that would help them to meet these goals.

President Clinton also made low-income homeownership part of his housing agenda. He established a policy goal of increasing homeownership to 67.5 percent (Masnick, 2001; Bratt, 2002). As George Masnick notes, the Clinton administration set this goal and achieved it without either new funding initiatives or momentum from earlier trends. The strategy to accomplish the goal depended heavily on boosting home-ownership among groups with low homeownership rates and involved vigorously enforcing fair housing and banking laws already on the books. By partnering with over two dozen public and private organizations that serve as national housing advocates, the Clinton administration developed a far-reaching program to help minorities and others who have been historically underserved by housing markets (Masnick, 2001, pp. 7–8). In other words, low-income homeownership would be facilitated by eliminating the barriers preventing it, many already against the law but never enforced under previous administrations (Bostic and Surette, 2000). Clinton's homeownership agenda was not new policy per se although it gave increased emphasis to low-income homebuyers.

Technological changes also converged as financial and political institutions began to focus on low-income homeownership. Both the computerization of the mortgage-lending industry along with automated underwriting cut the time and therefore the cost in underwriting, making home mortgages more accessible to lower-income borrowers (Lea, 1996).

Trends and Potential in Low-Income Homeownership

During the late 1990s, low-income homeownership grew to such an extent that it was labelled a boom (Belsky and Duda, 2002a). From 1993 to 2000, the number of home purchase loans to low-income families grew by 79 percent (Retsinas and Belsky, 2002a). Home purchases to low-income families and minorities increased more sharply than for other groups (Bostic and Surette, 2000).

The number of low-income minority households increased by more than 800,000, representing 11 percent of the net increase in homeowners (Belsky and Duda, 2002a). Belsky and Duda (2002a) note that homeownership rates for low-income and minority households grew more rapidly than for other groups. Therefore, a surge in low-income homeownership, particularly among minority households, constituted a significant proportion of the net growth in homeownership more generally (Retsinas and Belsky, 2002a).

Where have low-income buyers been purchasing homes? Analysis of the spatial patterns associated with these purchases shows that low-income buyers have been moving to neighborhoods in both suburbs and central cities (Belsky and Duda, 2002a). Some research shows that increases in low-income homeownership have not been accompanied by a reduction in racial and ethnic segregation (Immergluck, 1998). Other research shows that, although Black homeownership increased in neighborhoods within more racially diverse communities, minority composition in these neighborhoods was much higher than the national average (Herbert and Kaul, 2005).

What are the prospects for sustaining this growth? This article reports on research that looks at both the demand- and supply-side potential for low-income homeownership.

On the demand side, Eggers and Burke (1996) examined how reducing race- and income-based disparities would affect homeownership rates. Using simulation techniques, they suggested that policy changes to reduce gaps created by race and income could increase low-income and minority homeownership by the year 2000. This research effectively outlined the market's responses to policy changes around fair lending and housing affordability introduced during the Clinton years.

More recent research on the demand side suggests that the market for low-income homeownership has a limit. Looking at mortgage instruments available to serve the low- to moderate-income market, Listokin et al. (2002) examined how many renters could qualify for loans given their income and assets. Using simulation techniques, this research estimated the share of the rental population that could potentially reap the benefits of these mortgage products.

They found that homeownership remained unaffordable for about 80 percent of renters. This represents 21 million renter families that cannot be served by the low-income mortgage market given the most liberal underwriting standards. Underscoring renters' lack of assets the researchers note that

> with such a trace level of assets, even a 100 percent LTV (loan to value) mortgage will not facilitate homeownership because of the resources required to meet substantial closing costs. (Listokin et al., 2002, p. 493)

They suggest that additional income and asset supplements are needed to address the renters financial barriers to homeownership. This includes assistance with housing downpayments (Herbert and Tsen, 2005; Herbert et al., 2005).

Some policy analysts suggest that increasing low-income homeownership solely through credit liberalization and mortgage lending product innovation may have already reached its limit (Carasso et al., 2005). They speculate that greater emphasis should be placed on low-income homeowners' housing retention and equity accumulation.

Research shows that a large Black–White gap in homeownership remains. This continued gap, argue some researchers, is due not to credit barriers per se but to other household characteristics, indicating a limit on how much mortgage finance innovation can increase minority homeownership rates (Gabriel and Rosenthal, 2005). Importantly, some researchers now argue that credit barriers based on discrimination or lack of information may no longer explain gaps in homeownership rates, by income, race and ethnicity (Herbert et al., 2005). Rather, they believe that wealth, income, human capital and employment remain obstacles to homeownership. This does not necessarily absolve discrimination as an explanation in racial and ethnic gaps in homeownership rates. Rather, obstacles to homeownership may be tied more to the legacy of past discrimination that results in racial and ethnic disparities in education, employment and human capital (Masnick, 2004).

At the same time, there are supply-side constraints on homeownership. Research finds that there is a lack of adequate housing units at affordable prices and that affordable homes are being swallowed up by housing price inflation and vacancies (Collins et al., 2002). Few nonmobile housing units are being added to the affordable housing stock. According to Collins et al.,

> Policymakers need to recognize the failure of filtering as a mechanism to expand the supply of affordable homes. (Collins et al., 2002, p. 198)

With the recognition that filtering may not produce affordable homeownership opportunities for low-income families, research is now examining whether manufactured housing (modular homes built in factories) is a reasonable homeownership option. It suggests that manufactured housing, under the right conditions, would be a beneficial investment (Boehm and Schlottmann, 2004c).

The Effects of Low-Income Homeownership

What does social science tell us about the impact of low-income homeownership? The literature focuses on three areas of concern: the social and behavioral effects of homeownership; the economic returns to low-income homeownership; and, the impact of low-income homeownership on children.

Social and Behavioral Effects of Homeownership

Most research on the effects of homeownership, however, is not on low-income homeowners but on middle- and high-income homeowners. The research focus on homeowners at the higher end of the economic spectrum reflects that, by definition, the market for homeownership has been largely the domain of higher income families (Rohe and Stegman, 1994b).

Research on these largely middle-class homeowners shows positive effects of homeownership. Homeowners, compared with renters, have longer tenure in their housing and comparably less residential mobility. They are more likely to maintain their property and experience greater property value appreciation (Rohe and Stewart, 1996). Homeowners are also more likely than renters to be satisfied and to participate in political and voluntary activities (Rohe et al., 2002; Blum and Kingston, 1984; DiPasquale and Glaeser, 1999).

Coulson and Fisher (2002) address the relationship between homeownership and mobility directly by examining the impact of homeownership on labor market outcomes. Theorizing that homeowners would be constrained in their search for employment because of the costs of relocation, they examined employment differences in renters and owners. If homeowners are constrained, they would be more likely to be unemployed, have longer spells of unemployment and have lower wages than renters. To the contrary, they found just the opposite—that owners experienced less and shorter unemployment and received higher wages compared with renters.

Rossi and Weber (1996) address the effects of homeownership on social characteristics. They examined a wide range of characteristics including household composition, well-being, sociability, marriage and the family, confidence in major American institutions, attitudes toward neighborhoods, levels of political engagement and views on various public issues. Weak although consistent differences were found between renters and homeowners along dimensions of life satisfaction, self-esteem and participation in community organizations. Yet for the bulk of their analyses, they found no consistent differences between renters and owners and conclude that "tenure status is not a line of ideological cleavage in American society" (Rossi and Weber, 1996, p. 29).

These effects of homeownership, however, may be confounded by the simultaneous effects of income, education, length of residence and family life cycle (Rossi and Weber, 1996; Rohe and Stegman, 1994b; Blum and Kingston, 1984; DiPasquale and Glaeser, 1999). This is because homeownership may coincide with, or be a product of, being at the stage in the family life cycle when owning one's home is feasible and/or desirable.

Homeowners may become homeowners because they are ready, willing and able to stay in one housing situation for a considerable amount of time. Therefore, these effects of homeownership may be an artifact of a homeowners' self-selection process into this form of housing tenure (Rohe et al., 2002). Blum and Kingston note in an early study of homeownership that they

> prefer to see homeownership as part of a cluster of reinforcing statuses and outlooks that both sustains and creates social attachment. (Blum and Kinston, 1984, p. 176)

In addition, Rossi and Weber (1996) found that, even when accounting for age and income, there were many family and economic differences between renters and owners. Correlates of homeownership are not necessarily caused by homeownership (DiPasquale and Glaeser, 1999).

Certain behavioral and social characteristics that appear due to homeownership may actually be due to unobserved individual or household characteristics (Dietz and Haurin, 2003). Dietz and Haurin (2003) discuss household planning activities or labor force behavior associated with the goal of homeownership as being an antecedent, not a consequence of homeownership.

In addition, it may not be appropriate to generalize findings about middle-income households to behaviors of low-income households. As noted by Rohe and Stegman (1994b, p. 155), "Social class, ecological conditions, or other factors may result in a very different pattern of involvement among lower-income homeowners." The effects of homeownership may not be uniform across classes. A report from the National Housing Conference states that

> whether the assumed social benefits of homeownership are really caused by homeownership or rather are so strongly associated with the types of families that become homeowners, that one cannot truly tease them apart. And this is for all homeowners; arguably, many of the potential benefits of homeownership ought to be lower for very low-income families than for higher-income families. (National Housing Conference, 2004, p. 4)

An important study that focused directly on the effects of homeownership on low-income families incorporated a quasiexperimental design to compare social, attitudinal and behavioral changes for a sample of recent low-income homebuyers with a sample of low-income Section 8 renters (Rohe and Stegman, 1994a, 1994b, 1996). They interviewed households at three points in time separated by 18-month intervals. Using multivariate techniques that controlled for family, economic, social and housing characteristics, they examined the effects of homeownership on changes in self-esteem and perceived control, life satisfaction, neighboring, extent of organizational involvement and the intensity of organizational involvement. They found limited although positive effects of homeownership. Compared with low-income renters, homeowners were more likely to increase their involvement in neighborhood organizations but not in other types of organizations. Homeowners became more satisfied with their lives compared with renters (Rohe and Stegman, 1996). This may potentially indicate the positive influence of homeownership, but also the problems occurring with living in neighborhoods of low-income, rental housing.

The Economic Returns to Low-Income Homeownership

Homeownership is expected to bring economic benefits to low-income families. But, as noted by Nicolas Retsinas and Eric Belsky (2002a), there is not clear evidence that homeownership delivers economic gains to low-income households. The question is whether homeownership is a good asset-building strategy for low-income families compared with renting. And the answer is, we do not know.

It is difficult to generalize about homeownership as an investment because the rate of return depends both on the timing and place of purchase (Belsky and Duda, 2002b). The amount of time the property is held and the size of transactions costs are also crucial variables. Whether homeownership brings economic gains to households depends on the timing and location of purchases.

Moreover, the pay-off from homeownership may not result from the sale of one's first home but from re-entering the market and purchasing another house for a significant amount of time (Belsky and Duda, 2002b). As a good investment strategy that pays dividends to homeowners, homeownership may require a long-term, sustained investment in multiple houses. While the potential risk for low-income homeowners rests on timing as to when they enter or exit the housing market, it also rests on whether they can afford to continue to stay in the market for a considerable amount of time. According to Belsky and Duda,

> for those who are unable to buy again or whose timing once again triggers a loss, homeownership can turn out to be less than its idealized billing. (Belsky and Duda, 2002b, p. 219)

When one enters the market is critical (Case and Marynchenko, 2002). Entering the market at the end of a cycle of appreciation may result in buying high, but selling low—obviously not a good situation for any income homebuyer. For low-income homebuyers with fewer assets, the incurred loss may be much more deeply felt than by households with more resources to fall back on.

How long someone owns the house and stays in the market is also a crucial variable. Belsky and Duda (2002b) found that many low-income homeowners sell their homes for less than what they paid for them without experiencing appreciation levels large enough to cover the associated transaction costs.

Once becoming homeowners, low-income households do not stay homeowners like their higher-income counterparts (Boehm and Schlottmann, 2004a). One study found that low-income homebuyers returned to renting at extremely high rates, suggesting that these households need more support after they purchase their homes (Reid, 2004). Incorporating a longitudinal design that followed household housing decisions over time, Boehm and Schlottmann (2004a) found that low-income homeowners, particularly minority ones, were more likely to revert back to renting without ever purchasing a home again. They suggest that for low-income and minority families, homeownership "may be less beneficial than it otherwise might be" (Boehm and Schlottmann, 2004a, p. 129).

Although many low-income and minority homebuyers transition back from owning to renting, Boehm and Schlottmann (2004b) also find that those who remained homeowners accumulated wealth that their rental counterparts did not. Moreover, the wealth accumulated from homeownership represented the sole net worth of these households who otherwise would be bereft of assets. These low-income and minority homeowners who managed to buck the trend to transition back to renting experienced significant wealth benefits from homeownership.

The strength of the regional economy and low housing market conditions are additional critical variables affecting the profitability of low-income homeownership (Case and Marynchenko, 2002). It may be good to buy in the lower-priced market in Philadelphia in the late 1980s, but not in Los Angeles in the mid 1990s. Where, when and how long represent the big "ifs" associated with whether low-income homeowners will come out ahead of renting.

In addition, a question is whether homeownership is a good investment compared with others. Goetzmann and Spiegel (2002) argue that homeownership may be a relatively poor asset to invest the bulk of a household's net worth because of its low performance compared with other investments. Of course, the concept of an investment portfolio may seem a bit unrealistic in the context of discussing the financial well-being of low-income households. Given, however, the precarious financial situation of many low-income households and the significance of financial loss for them, the opportunity costs of their capital should be scrutinized like those of households with more economic resources. Examined along these lines, the conclusions reached by economists Goetzman and Spiegel in their analysis of housing's economic performance are severe.

> Overinvestment in housing by families with modest savings means underinvestment in financial assets that will grow and provide income for retirement. In fact, *encouraging homeownership among low-income families will only increase the wealth gap in the United States.* (Goetzman and Spiegel, 2002, p. 272; emphasis added)

The problem of overrelying on housing as an investment compared with others is compounded by tax issues as well. Mortgage interest deductions are worth more to higher-income people than to low-income households (Collins et al., 1999; Carasso et al., 2005). The economic benefits from mortgage interest deductions to higher-income households mean that lower-income families may be better off renting from higher-income landlords.

The continued high level of racial segregation in most U.S. cities also means that returns to investments may be affected by what has long been regarded as a dual housing market (Denton, 2001). Neighborhoods of Black homeowners, on average, have been found to be better than those housing Black renters. But the differences between neighborhoods of White owners and White renters were much larger. Therefore, benefits accrued to White low-income homebuyers may be greater than those accrued to Black low-income homebuyers. Both place, race and neighborhood are vital parts of the equation when assessing economic benefits to low-income homeownership.

Is homeownership a quality economic investment for low-income families? The answer is complex. The diverse nature of housing markets, the leveraged nature of home purchases, the costs of entering and leaving the homeownership market, the rate of return from housing compared with other investments and differential effects of tax policy on higher- versus lower-income families present questions as to whether low-income homeownership is a uniformly positive economic investment strategy.

The Effects of Low-Income Homeownership on Children

A significant body of research demonstrates positive benefits of homeownership for children. Children in families of homeowners are more likely to have fewer emotional and behavioral problems (Boyle, 2002), graduate from and perform better in school, have fewer teenage pregnancies (Green and White, 1997) and acquire more education and income (Boehm and Schlottmann, 1999). Moreover, homeowners' children are more likely to become homeowners as adults, therefore continuing this cycle of increased benefits accrued to children who live in homes their parents own (Boehm and Schlottmann, 1999). Boehm and Schlottmann (2002) show that home-owners' children accumulate more wealth because they are more likely to own their homes and acquire greater educational credentials. Regarding children, Green and White (1997) find that homeownership benefits lower-income families more than higher-income families.

Homeownership also has been found to influence the cognitive and behavioral outcomes of young children (Haurin et al., 2002). Children living with homeowning parents tested higher on math and reading tests. The home environments of home-owners were rated higher in terms of providing cognitive stimulation and emotional support for children.

Finding that homeownership influences child outcomes leads to more questions. How does homeownership affect children? Developmental psychologist Michael Boyle suggests that becoming a homeowner may be as much a process as an outcome with the implication that going through this process may select families more likely to raise children with lower risks of emotional or behavioral problems (Boyle, 2002). Economists Boehm and Schlottmann ask "which components of owned housing make the biggest difference for children?" (Boehm and Schlottman, 2002, p. 231). Are homeowning parents more vigilant in watching out for their children because they have an investment in the neighborhood or do better child outcomes reflect the personal traits of homebuying parents (Green and White, 1997)? Are the skills sets associated with becoming and remaining homeowners similar to those associated with being good parents (Dietz and Haurin, 2003)? Does the effect of homeowner-ship operate through neighborhoods, the physical characteristics of housing or what? In other words, are outcomes the direct effects of homeownership or indirect effects that are mediated through other variables?[3] What are the unobserved variables that might explain why homeownership has positive effects on children?

In a major effort to control for some of the previously unobserved variables that may mediate the effects of homeownership, preliminary research has replicated and ex-tended some of the prior research on homeownership and children (Barker and Miller, 2005). It looked at a range of child outcomes including high school drop-out rates, cognitive ability, behavioral problems and ratings of the home environment. Added control variables included residential mobility, wealth, housing type and automobile ownership; the researchers also incorporated some additional methodological tech-niques. The inclusion of these different measures and methods substantially reduced or eliminated previously found effects of homeownership, indicating the importance of mediating and unobserved factors that operate coincident with homeownership.

Focusing specifically on low-income homeowners, one study separated the effects of neighborhood from homeownership per se and examined the net effects of tenure and neighborhood conditions on adult outcomes for children who lived with homeowning low-income parents (Harkness and Newman, 2002). They found that homeownership influenced positive outcomes later in life including less idleness, higher wages and lower levels of welfare receipt.

Neighborhood conditions affected the magnitude of this effect. Problematic neighborhood conditions like high rates of poverty and residential instability reduced the effects of homeownership and, in some situations, bad neighborhoods could produce worse outcomes for children with homeowning families. Better neighborhood conditions increased the positive effects of homeownership. The impact of renting was less affected by neighborhood conditions. Therefore, this research suggests that homeownership produces positive outcomes but produces the largest effects in combination with being in better neighborhoods.

Expanding the analysis to compare the effects of homeownership on children living in high- and low-income families, Harkness and Newman (2003) found that homeownership benefits lower-income children more than higher-income children. For higher-income children, positive outcomes were influenced by parent characteristics such as education and income, not homeownership. For lower-income children, homeownership brought with it benefits over and above family characteristics. The difference in homeownership effects for high- versus low-income homeowners stemmed from *a priori* differences between high- and low-income homebuyers. For higher-income homeowners, the alleged effects of homeownership operated through, and are attributed to, parent characteristics.

But it is also not clear how homeownership affects the children within lower-income homeowning families. Harkness and Newman (2003) ask whether the positive effects of homeownership are outcomes of the owned status of housing and its function as an asset or because they increase the residential stability of households?

Research finds consistently positive effects of homeownership on children that operate through adulthood, particularly for low-income children. How homeownership works to deliver these benefits (for example, through family characteristics or residential stability), however, remains undetermined. As noted by Boehm and Schlottmann,

> if effective housing policies are to be developed, which are also cost-efficient to implement, the intricacies of the process by which children raised in owner-occupied housing benefit from their environment must be better understood. (Boehm and Schlottmann, 2002, p. 424)

Metropolitan Housing Markets and Low-Income Homeownership

Within the housing literature, housing is conceptualized as a multidimensional phenomenon that comprises a bundle of characteristics (Shlay, 1995). The housing bundle includes features of the housing unit, neighborhood composition (family, racial and ethnic and economic), neighborhood conditions, location, housing type, housing quality and access to schools, services and employment. Housing tenure (renting or owning) is one feature of the overall housing bundle.

But tenure is highly correlated with other housing bundle characteristics (Shlay, 1985, 1986). Owner-occupancy often coincides with better neighborhood conditions and locations. Are the desired outcomes or alleged effects of homeownership due to ownership per se (direct effects of homeownership) or do they stem from other aspects of housing such as location or access to amenities?

A major question is what is being delivered through homeownership? There are no "pure" tenure effects because of the high correspondence between tenure and other characteristics. In addition, the concept of ownership per se is messy in that few households, particularly low-income ones, own their units outright. Ownership is mediated by financial institutions that underwrite the purchase of the home.

Two major housing market characteristics are central variables to homeownership's ability to deliver for low-income families. These include residential location (a home's relationship with space) and financial intermediaries (a household's relationship with sources of housing finance). These two factors can either undermine or support a household's opportunities for success in the low-income housing market.

Location and Low-income Homeownership

Low-income homeownership is billed as a mechanism for helping neighborhoods. But what are the risks to low-income families, compared with higher-income families, when buying into this market? Low-income housing is typically more available in neighborhoods with poor-quality housing (Listokin and Wyly, 2000; Shlay, 1993) although many low-income homebuyers are buying homes outside low-income neighborhoods (Belsky and Duda, 2002a). Low-income homebuyers face greater risks in terms of costly home repairs, lower rates of appreciation and lower-quality neighborhood amenities (Retsinas, 1999; Louie et al., 1998). Therefore, low-income homeownership as a policy goal may move already-at-risk households to take on even more risk under conditions of great uncertainty. It is unclear whether policy directed at helping low-income families should encourage people with the least amount of assets to take on more risk.

Low-income homeownership is also promoted as a tool for central-city revitalization. Like low-income neighborhoods, central cities, however, may not be good locations for investment, particularly for low-income families. Central cities typically have poorer quality schools and services than suburban locations. Therefore, buying homes in central-city neighborhoods may not be the best mechanism for providing low-income families with greater access to economic opportunities and upward social mobility (Rohe et al., 2002a). A study of first-time, low-income homebuyers within two heavily subsidized Nehemiah complexes indicated that, although families gained better housing conditions, their new neighborhoods had poorer schools and higher crime rates than their previous ones (Cummings et al., 2002). It may not be good policy to encourage low-income families to invest in communities with the least resources.

The Financial Services Industry and Low-Income Homeownership

The community reinvestment movement combined with heightened enforcement of the Fair Housing Act has helped to eliminate some credit barriers for prospective low-income homeowners (Squires, 2003) although several significant ones remain (Rosenthal, 2002; Brakova et al., 2003). Low-income homebuyers' recognition by the financial services industry, however, as a potential market for lending has been accompanied by the growth of a new segment of the industry—the subprime lending market. The growth of the subprime lending market represents a major shift in the housing finance industry in the U.S.

Subprime loans carry higher interest rates and fees to cover the additional risk incurred from making loans to borrowers with problematic credit ratings (Squires, 2004). During the 1990s, the number of subprime loans made in the U.S. grew by 900 percent (Hurd and Kest, 2003).

A subset of loans made within the subprime lending industry is termed predatory lending (Renuart, 2004). Predatory loans contain excessive terms including points and fees, poor underwriting, high and extended prepayment penalties, flipping and repeated financing, inflated house appraisals and other illegal and deceptive practices (Hurd and Kest, 2003). These loans are considered predatory because lenders use deception, unfairly making these high-priced loans to vulnerable populations (White, 2004). In particular, predatory loans, and subprime loans more generally, are marketed to elderly, low-income and minority families (Stein, 2001). Subprime loans have been disproportionately concentrated in minority communities (Immergluck and Smith, 2004; Calem et al., 2004).

Predatory lending is a process that strips equity from people's homes. While conventional mortgage instruments are used by households to build equity in their property, predatory lending takes equity out of property in the form of excessive fees to lenders—estimated to have reached $2.1 billion annually (Stein, 2001; Renuart, 2004). The estimated total cost of subprime lending is $9.1 billion annually. This does not include the costs of excessive foreclosures (Stein, 2001). Research shows that subprime lending increases the number of foreclosures in communities (Immergluck and Smith, 2004).

Subprime lending in its predatory form has devastating consequences for households and communities, particularly minority, low-income and elderly ones (White, 2004). By increasing the number of low-income and minority homebuyers, policy is increasing the number of households at risk of being preyed upon by predatory lenders. That is, policy designed to promote savings and asset accumulation by low-income families may be serving up potential customers for the subprime lending industry. A reasonable question is whether low-income homeownership places low-income homebuyers at risk of having would-be equity in their homes stripped away by predatory lenders.

Housing Policy Alternatives for Low-Income Families

Low-income homeownership has been elevated to flagship housing policy status with the goal of providing a myriad of benefits that include asset accumulation, social and behavioral changes for adults and children; increased political involvement, less criminal and deviant behavior, and neighborhood improvements that contribute to urban revitalization. Low-income homeownership is portrayed as a policy that will help to solve complex social and political problems associated with being low-income and as a launching-pad for family socioeconomic mobility.

Yet meeting these goals for low-income families is confounded by many factors including the financial constraints on low-income families that preclude homeownership as an option, low-income families' rapid movement from owning back to renting, risks of overrelying on housing as an investment, negative externalities associated with the location of homes affordable to low-income households and opportunistic and exploitative behavior by financial intermediaries. Low-income homeownership's ability to deliver is limited precisely by the financially perilous situation of low-income families. With homeownership, potential low-income homebuyers are more at risk because they are low-income.

To address fully the housing needs of low-income families and to provide policy that will enhance their opportunities in ways that will permit social and economic advancement, policy needs to account for the multifaceted nature of the housing bundle. Policy should not solely work at getting families into a homeownership situation without ensuring that it is a viable investment and is in a quality location. Housing policy should not increase risks for families already at risk of a host of problems. It should work at eliminating them or at least minimizing their probability of occurring.

With these conditions in mind, this paper offers three general policy directions for low-income housing policy as related to housing tenure: improve access to quality homeownership opportunities through providing households with increased financial supports and incorporating a place-based strategy; increase supports for rental housing; and, initiate support for housing that incorporates alternative tenure forms to conventional renting or owning.

Improve Access to Quality Homeownership Opportunities

Solely facilitating low-income families' access to homeownership without altering other aspects of the housing market is unlikely to provide many of the economic, political and social benefits suggested by proponents of low-income homeownership. A successful homeownership strategy will require a more comprehensive approach that works simultaneously at improving local social and physical infrastructure including schools and neighborhood conditions, protecting families against the exploitation of predatory lenders and breaking down barriers to the inclusion of low-income housing within suburban communities. Delivering on low-income homeownership means delivering on the full set of life-sustaining housing bundle characteristics.

Increasing access to quality homeownership opportunities may mean enlarging direct public subsidy of low-income households (Hockett et al., 2005). Deeper public subsidies of low-income homeownership may mitigate against some of the potential risks of investment in the low-income housing market while increasing opportunities to families who, without subsidy, would not be able to participate (Herbert et al., 2005; Carasso et al., 2005).

Increase Supports for Rental Housing

Tenure relationships exist within the social and political context that defines them. Federal policy supports homeownership and this is part of the reason why homeownership is a desirable housing tenure situation. Policy, in part, makes homeownership a preferred housing option.

The opposite exists for renting. Fewer policies support the production of rental housing or the inclusion of rental units within local communities. To be sure, the Low Income Housing Tax Credit (LIHTC) program and Section 8 subsidies make renting more affordable. But Section 8 funds continue to be cut while complex syndication deals required by the LIHTC do not meet massive unmet needs for affordable units (Orlebeke, 2000) and are inefficient tools for producing low-income housing (Stegman, 1990).

The incentives that exist to encourage landlords to invest in and improve rental housing pale when compared with the array of institutions and supports underlying homeownership. There are no special pools of capital for rental housing. There are few, if any, programs designed to help renters save for their security deposits or become better consumers except in the context of encouraging them to escape from renting (Sherraden, 1991; Shapiro and Wolff, 2001). Zoning laws often explicitly exclude rental housing from suburbs or relegate it to undesirable locations (Shlay, 1993; Pendall, 2000; Fischel, 2004). While policy helps to make homeownership a positive housing situation, policy helps to make renting a negative housing situation.

Since most low-income families cannot qualify for homeownership without deep subsidies, an important area of exploration is determining how policy can support rental housing as a viable housing option for low-income families. Housing policy has, in part, produced a rental housing market in which the available housing is often undesirable. But rental housing in the abstract is not negative *a priori* but reflects how rental units are packaged as housing bundles.

If housing policy can render rental housing an unattractive housing option, it can also be used to make this type of housing option more desirable. This includes modifying financial incentives for investment and maintenance, enhancing alternative opportunities for household tax benefits and savings, revitalizing communities in which rental housing is located, altering the size and physical layout of units, providing tenants with more control over their housing situations and breaking down land use barriers to including rental housing within more well-off communities. We also need to determine how housing subsidies can be delivered to low-income families in a manner that neither stigmatizes them nor isolates them within undesirable communities.

Providing attractive and affordable rental housing has been accomplished in small but significant ways within the nonprofit sector and community development corporations (Dreier and Hulchanski, 1993; Keyes et al., 1996). Some advocate for supporting the growth of this organizational infrastructure around affordable housing through public-private partnerships and housing trust funds (Walker, 1993; Brooks, 1996; Davis, 1994).

Initiate Support for Alternative Tenure Forms

Conceptually, alternative tenure forms do not treat tenure as encapsulating discrete categories (owning or renting) but as a variable that can indicate different forms and degrees of ownership and control (Geisler and Daneker, 2000). Alternative tenure forms tend to socialize ownership so that it is shared among a community. Within typical conventional housing situations, a family unit either owns the property or someone who does not live there owns it. Alternative tenure forms involve ownership among groups of households or residential users. These alterative forms include limited equity cooperatives and land trusts (Miceli et al., 1994; White and Saegert, 1996).

The focus of limited equity cooperatives and land trusts is on collective asset accumulation and social equity. Individual households acquire many of the rights associated with ownership including tax benefits and secure housing. With housing collectively owned, risk is shared and the economic exposure of individual households is held to a minimum.

Low-Income Homeownership: Reasonable Expectations

Low-income homeownership has been promoted with the expectation that it will engender significant changes for families, neighborhoods and local housing markets. Yet we lack definitive evidence to substantiate these claims.

It is unclear how many low-income families will be able to become homeowners. Much of the recent increase in low-income and minority homeownership has been the result of increased enforcement within the regulatory environment (for example, CRA, Fair Housing Act) as well as lower interest rates, indicating pent-up demand for homeownership within low-income and minority families. But whether this demand can be sustained is questionable. On the demand side, the vast majority of renters cannot be served by the most lenient available underwriting standards because of economic problems. On the supply side, the affordable housing stock for the low-income homeownership market is not readily available.

Research examining the economic returns from low-income homeownership suggests that a myriad of factors interfere with low-income households' ability to reap material gains from homeownership. Timing, location, finance terms, length of owner-ship and other factors wreak havoc with whether low-income families will come out ahead or not after becoming homebuyers. Of course, homeownership may have positive outcomes for families even if it is not always a money-making venture. But advocating homeownership for families who already have fewer economic resources seems problematic, particularly if homebuyer families' economic circumstances deteriorate more than they would have if they had been renting. This is a crucial area for continued research.

Limited evidence exists on whether low-income homeowners experience social and behavioral changes as a result of their changed housing circumstances. In part, our dearth of knowledge about how homeownership benefits low-income families is for methodological reasons; most research that looks at the effects of homeownership cannot disentangle the impact of family life cycle and class from homeownership on outcomes. It is unclear if homeownership is a cause or consequence of these families' life cycle or economic circumstances.

A growing body of research shows that homeownership has positive educational, social and psychological outcomes for children. Importantly, some studies show higher benefits for lower-income children than for higher-income children. Yet these studies also question how homeownership becomes manifested as a critical variable in children's lives. It is unclear what features of the housing bundle produce positive and therefore also, negative consequences for children. There are many observed variables that may more clearly produce the outcomes attributed to homeownership. Clearly, this is an area where substantially more work is needed.

What homeownership does and why is not well understood because it is difficult to disentangle what homeownership means. Given the multidimensional nature of the housing bundle and the inherent inevitability of predictable housing bundle packaging (by race, class, location, housing type, etc.), what constitutes the homeownership "treatment" is not clear. Is homeownership secure housing, more space, greater psychological well-being, better neighborhoods, better communities, the ability to be stable residentially, the accumulation of economic assets or what? Delineating the critical variables associated with homeownership that produce particular outcomes is another crucial area for research.

But determining how homeownership works on family well-being is also important for developing alternative housing policies that support low-income families. Are there features of homeownership that provide positive benefits that could be configured within a redefined tenure arrangement that approximates renting or some other alternative tenure form to owning? That is, are there features of homeownership that could become a reconstituted tenure form that would eliminate some of the problematic aspects of either renting or owning—for example, by limiting family economic exposure and vulnerability? Can we configure the bundle of housing characteristics with known beneficial consequences for low-income families as a policy tool for supporting these families?

The elevation of low-income homeownership to its current status has deflected political attention away from other policies for affordable housing. As noted over 30 years ago by planner Peter Marcuse,

> the stance that public policy should take towards homeownership for low-income families lies in the possibilities of institutional changes in existing tenure arrangements, and in the social or political, not the financial characteristics of homeownership. (Marcuse, 1972, p. 143)

While low-income homeownership has been the predominant focus of housing policy for low-income families, policies supporting public housing, housing vouchers and low-income housing tax credits have been cut, battered and denigrated. By holding center stage in the low-income housing policy debate, low-income homeownership has crowded out ideas about affordable housing policy alternatives ranging from subsidies to cooperatives.

Many of the policy goals surrounding low-income homeownership are framed by ideological statements about homeownership as the American Dream. But what if these dreams are delusions? Should housing policy be the stuff of dreams or hard-nosed analysis of what works for families, communities and local economies?

NOTES

1. In the 2000 presidential election, the voting turnout rate represented 60 percent of registered and unregistered voters (U.S. Census, 2002a). In 2000, the homeownership rate was 67.4 percent (U.S. Census, 2002b).

2. Special targeted households were those either making less than 60 percent of the area median income or less than 80 percent of the area median income and located within low-income neighborhoods (Case et al., 2002).

3. Haurin et al. (2002) report that they controlled for community factors in their analyses of the effects of homeownership on child outcomes. The control variables that they use (income, race, ethnicity, unemployment, poverty, crime and education), however, are aggregated at the county level—a level too large to be a meaningful control for community characteristics. They also report that these variables were too highly correlated to determine separate effects of each variable, not surprising given their level of aggregation. Therefore, their analysis cannot address the issue of the effects of homeownership net of neighborhood or community factors.

REFERENCES

Babcock, R. F. (1966) *The Zoning Game.* Madison, WI: University of Wisconsin Press.
Baldassare, M. (1979) *Residential Crowding in Urban America.* Berkeley, CA: University of California Press.

Barker, D. and Miller, E. (2005) *Homeownership and child welfare. Paper presented at Mid Year Meetings of the American Real Estate and Urban Economic Association*, May–June. Washington, DC.

Barkova, I. A., Bostic, R. W., Calem, P. S. and Wachter, S. M. (2003) Does credit quality matter for homeownership?, *Journal of Housing Economics*, 12(2), pp. 318–336.

Bassett, K. and Short, J. (1980) *Housing and Residential Structure: Alternative Approaches.* New York: Routledge.

Bellush, J. and Hausknecht, M. (1967) *Urban Renewal: People, Politics and Planning.* Garden City, NY: Anchor.

Belsky, E. S. and Duda, M. (2002a) Anatomy of the low income homeownership boom in the 1990s. In N. P. Retsinas and E. S. Belsky (Eds) *Low-income Homeownership: Examining the Unexamined Goal*, pp. 15–63. Washington, DC: The Brookings Institution.

Belsky, E. S. and Duda, M. (2002b) Asset appreciation, timing of purchases, and sales, and returns to low-income homeownership. In N. P. Retsinas and E. S. Belsky (Eds) *Low-income Homeownership: Examining the Unexamined Goal*, pp. 208–238. Washington, DC: The Brookings Institution.

Blum, T. C. and Kingston, P. W. (1984) Homeownership and social attachment, *Sociological Perspective*, 27(2), pp. 159–180.

Boehm, T. and Schlottman, A. M. (1999) Does home ownership by parents have an economic impact on their children?, *Journal of Housing Economics*, 8, pp. 217–232.

Boehm, T. P. and Schlottman, A. M. (2002) Housing and wealth accumulation: intergenerational impacts. In N. P. Retsinas and E. S. Belsky (Eds) *Low-income Homeownership: Examining the Unexamined Goal*, pp. 407–426. Washington, DC: The Brookings Institution.

Boehm, T. P. and Schlottmann, A. M. (2004a) The dynamics of race, income and homeownership, *Journal of Urban Economics*, 55(1), pp. 113–130.

Boehm, T. P. and Schlottmann, A. M. (2004b) *Wealth Accumulation and Homeownership: Evidence for Low-income Households.* Washington, DC: Office of Policy Development and Research, US Department of Housing and Urban Development.

Boehm, T. P. and Schlottmann, A. M. (2004c) *Is Manufacturing Housing a Good Alternative for Low-income Families? Evidence from the American Housing Survey.* Washington, DC: Office of Policy Development and Research, US Department of Housing and Urban Development.

Bostic, R. W. and Surette, B. J. (2000) *Have the doors opened wider? Trends in homeownership rates by race and income.* Working Paper, April. Board of Governors of the Federal Research System, Washington, DC.

Boyle, M. (2002) Home ownership and the emotional and behavioral problems of children and youth, *Child Development*, 73(3), pp. 883–892.

Bradford, C. (1979) Financing home ownership: the federal role in neighborhood decline, *Urban Affairs Quarterly*, 14(3), pp. 313–335.

Bratt, R. G. (2002) *Housing for very low-income households: the record of President Clinton, 1993–2000.* Working Paper W02-8, Joint Center for Housing Studies, Harvard University, Cambridge, MA.

Brooks, M. E. (1996) Housing trust funds: a new approach to funding affordable housing. In W. van Vliet (Ed.) *Affordable Housing and Urban Redevelopment in the United States: Learning from Failure and Success*, pp. 270–286. Thousand Oaks, CA: Sage.

Buchholz, T. G. (2002) *Safe at Home: The New Role of Housing in the U.S. Economy.* Washington, DC: Home Ownership Alliance.

Calem, P. S., Hershaff, J. E. and Wachter, S. M. (2004) Neighborhood patterns of subprime lending: evidence from disparate cities, *Housing Policy Debate*, 15(3), pp. 603–622.

Carasso, A., Bell, E., Olsen, E. O. and Steuerle, C. E. (2005) *Improving Homeownership among Poor and Moderate-income Households.* Washington, DC: The Urban Institute (available at http://www.urban.org/url.cfm?ID=311184).

Carliner, M. (1998) Development of federal homeownership "policy," *Housing Policy Debate,* 9(2), pp. 299–321

Case, B. D., Gillen, K. and Wachter, S. M. (2002) Spatial variation in GSE mortgage purchase activity, *Cityscape,* 6(1), pp. 9–35.

Case, K. and Marynchenko, M. (2002) Home price appreciation in low- and moderate-income markets. In N. P. Retsinas and E. S. Belsky (Eds) *Low-income Homeownership: Examining the Unexamined Goal,* pp. 239–256. Washington, DC: The Brookings Institution.

Collins, J. M., Belsky, E. S. and Retsinas, N. P. (1999) *Toward a targeted homeownership tax credit.* Working Paper, Brookings Institution Center on Urban and Metropolitan Policy, Washington, DC.

Collins, M., Crowe, D. and Carliner, M. (2002) Supply-side constraints on low-income homeownership. In N. P. Retsinas and E. S. Belsky (Eds) *Low-income Homeownership: Examining the Unexamined Goal,* pp. 175–200. Washington, DC: The Brookings Institution.

Coulson, N. E. and Fisher, L. M. (2002) Tenure choice and labour market outcomes, *Housing Studies,* 17(1), pp. 35–49.

Cummings, J. L., diPasquale, D. and Kahn, M. E. (2002) Measuring the consequences of promoting inner city homeownership, *Journal of Housing Economics,* 11(3), pp. 330–359.

Davis, J. E. (1994) *The Affordable City: Toward a Third Sector Housing Policy.* Philadelphia, PA: Temple University Press.

Dean, J. P. (1949) The myths of housing reform, *American Sociological Review,* 14(2), pp. 281–288.

Denton, N. A. (2001) Housing as a means of asset accumulation: a good strategy for the poor? In T. M. Shapiro and E. N. Wolff (Eds) *Assets for the Poor: The Benefits of Spreading Asset Ownership,* pp. 232–268. New York: Russell Sage.

Dietz, R. D. and Haurin, D. R. (2003) The social and private micro-level consequences of homeownership, *Journal of Urban Economics,* 54(4), pp. 401–450.

diPasquale, D. and Glaeser, E. L. (1999) Incentives and social capital: are homeowners better citizens?, *Journal of Urban Economics,* 45(2), pp. 354–384.

Dreier, P. (1982) The status of tenants in the United States, *Social Problems,* 30(2), pp. 179–198.

Dreier, P. and Hulchanski, J. D. (1993) The role of nonprofit housing in Canada and the United States: some comparisons, *Housing Policy Debate,* 4(1), pp. 43–80.

Eggers, F. J. and Burke, P. E. (1996) Can the national homeownership rate be significantly improved by reaching underserved markets?, *Housing Policy Debate,* 7(1), pp. 83–101.

Fischel, W. A. (2004) An economic history of zoning and a cure for its exclusionary effects, *Urban Studies,* 41(2), pp. 317–340.

Fischer, C. S. (1982) *To Dwell among Friends: Personal Networks in Town and City.* Chicago, IL: University of Chicago Press.

Fishbein, A. (2003) Filling the half-empty glass: the role of community advocacy in redefining the public responsibilities of government sponsored housing enterprises. In G. D. Squires (Ed.) *Organizing Access to Capital: Advocacy and the Democratization of Financial Institutions,* pp. 102–118. Philadelphia, PA: Temple University Press.

Gabriel, S. A. and Rosenthal, S. S. (2005) Homeownership in the 1980s and 1990s: aggregate trends and racial gaps, *Journal of Urban Economics,* 57(1), pp. 101–127.

Gans, H. (1977) Planning for people, not buildings. In M. Stewart (Ed.) *The City,* pp. 363–386. New York: Penguin.

Geisler, C. D. and Daneker, G. (2000) *Property and Values: Alternatives to Public and Private Ownership.* Washington, DC: Island Press.

Gilderbloom, J. L. and Markham, J. P. (1995) The impact of homeownership on political beliefs, *Social Forces*, 73(4), pp. 1589–1607.

Glazer, N. (1980) The effects of poor housing. In J. Pynoos, R. Schafer and C. Hartman (Eds) *Housing Urban America*, pp. 164–171. Hawthorne, NY: Aldine.

Goetzmann, W. N. and Spiegel, M. (2002) Policy implications of portfolio choice in underserved mortgage markets. In N. P. Retsinas and E. S. Belsky (Eds) *Low-income Homeownership: Examining the Unexamined Goal*, pp. 257–274. Washington, DC: The Brookings Institution.

Green, R. K. and White, M. J. (1997) Measuring the benefits of homeowning: effects on children, *Journal of Urban Economics*, 41, pp. 441–461.

Harkness, J. and Newman, S. J. (2002) Homeownership for the poor in distressed neighborhoods: does this make sense?, *Housing Policy Debate*, 13(3), pp. 597–630.

Harkness, J. and Newman, S. J. (2003) Differential effects of homeownership on children from higher- and lower-income families, *Journal of Housing Research*, 14(1), pp. 1–19.

Hartman, C. (1975) *Housing and Social Policy.* Englewood, NJ: Prentice-Hall.

Haurin, D. R., Dietz, R. D. and Weinberg, B. A. (2003) The impact of neighborhood homeownership rates: a review of the theoretical and empirical literature, *Housing Policy Debate*, 13(2), pp. 119–151.

Haurin, D. R., Parcel, T. L. and Haurin, R. J. (2002) Impact of homeownership on child outcomes. In N. P. Retsinas and E. S. Belsky (Eds) *Low-income Homeownership: Examining the Unexamined Goal*, pp. 427–446. Washington, DC: The Brookings Institution.

Hayden, D. (1981) *The Grand Domestic Revolution: A History of Feminist Designs for American Homes, Neighborhoods and Cities.* Cambridge, MA: MIT Press.

Hayden, D. (1985) *Redesigning the American Dream: The Future of Housing, Work, and Family Life.* New York: W. W. Norton.

Hays, R. A. (1993) *Ownership, Control, and the Future of Housing Policy.* Westport, CT: Greenwood.

Herbert, C. E. and Kaul, B. (2005) *The Distribution of Homeownership Gains during the 1990s across Neighborhoods.* Washington, DC: Office of Policy Development and Research, U.S. Department of Housing and Urban Development.

Herbert, C. E. and Tsen, W. (2005) *The Potential of Downpayment Assistance for Increasing Homeownership among Minority and Low-income Households.* Washington, DC: Office of Policy Development and Research, U.S. Department of Housing and Urban Development.

Herbert, C. E., Haurin, D. R., Rosenthal, S. S. and Duda, M. (2005) *Homeownership Gaps among Low-income and Minority Borrowers and Neighborhoods.* Washington, DC: Office of Policy Development and Research, U.S. Department of Housing and Urban Development.

Heskin, A. D. (1983) *Tenants and the American Dream: Ideology and the Tenant Movement.* New York: Praeger.

Hockett, D. W., McElwee, P., Pelletier, D. and Schwartz, D. (2005) *The Crisis in America's Housing: Confronting Myths and Promoting a Balanced Housing Policy.* Washington, DC: National Low Income Housing Coalition.

Hurd, M. and Kest, S. (2003) Fighting predatory lending from the ground up: an issue of economic justice. In G. D. Squires (Ed.) *Organizing Access to Capital: Advocacy and the Democratization of Financial Institutions*, pp. 119–134. Philadelphia, PA: Temple University Press.

Immergluck, D. (1998) Progress confined: increases in black homebuying and the persistence of racial barriers, *Journal of Urban Affairs*, 20(4), pp. 443–457.

Immergluck, D. and Smith, G. (2004) *Risky Business: An Econometric Analysis of the Relationship between Subprime Lending and Neighborhood Foreclosures.* Chicago, IL: Woodstock Institute.

Jackson, K. T. (1985) *Crabgrass Frontier: The Suburbanization of the United States.* New York: Oxford University Press.

Keyes, L. C., Schwart, A., Vida, A. and Bratt, R. G. (1996) Networks and nonprofits: opportunities and challenges in an era of federal devolution, *Housing Policy Debate*, 7(2), 201–229.

Lea, M. J. (1996) Innovation and the cost of mortgage credit: a historical perspective, *Housing Policy Debate*, 7(1), pp. 147–174.

Listokin, D. and Wyly, E. K. (2000) Making new mortgage markets: case studies of institutions, home buyers and communities, *Housing Policy Debate*, 11(3), pp. 575–644.

Listokin, D. D., Wyly, E., Schmitt, B. and Voicu, I. (2002) *The Potential and Limitation of Mortgage Innovation in Fostering Homeownership in the United States.* Washington, DC: The Fannie Mae Foundation.

Louie, J., Belsky, E. S. and McArdle, N. (1998) *The housing needs of lower-income home-owners.* Working Paper W98-9, Joint Center for Housing Studies, Harvard University, Cambridge, MA.

Marcuse, P. (1972) Homeownership for low income families: financial implications, *Land Economics*, 48(2), pp. 134–143.

Masnick, G. S. (2001) *Home ownership trends and racial inequality in the United States in the 20th century.* Working Paper W01-4. Joint Center for Housing Studies, Harvard University, Cambridge, MA.

Masnick, G. S. (2004) Homeownership and social inequality in the United States. In K. Kurz and H.-P. Blossfeld (Eds) *Homeownership and Social Inequality in Comparative Perspective*, pp. 304–337. Stanford, CA: Stanford University Press.

Miceli, T. J., Sazama, G. W. and Sirmans, C. F. (1994) The role of limited-equity cooperatives in providing affordable housing, *Housing Policy Debate*, 5(4), pp. 469–490.

Monroe, A. (2001) *How the Federal Housing Administration affects homeownership.* Unpublished paper, Department of Economics, Harvard University.

National Housing Conference (2001) Expanding the dream of homeownership, *NHC Affordable Housing Policy Review*, 1(1), pp. 1–51.

National Housing Conference (2004) *Strengthening the ladder to homeownership for very low-income renters and homeownership retention among very low-income homeowners.* Policy paper prepared for the Annie E. Casey Foundation, June.

Order, R. van (2000) The U.S. mortgage market: a model of dueling charters, *Journal of Housing Research*, 11(2), pp. 233–255.

Orlebeke, C. J. (2000) The evolution of low-income housing policy, 1949–1999, *Housing Policy Debate*, 11(2), pp. 489–520.

Pendall, R. (2000) Local land use regulation and the chain of exclusion, *Journal of the American Planning Association*, 6(2), pp. 125–142.

Perin, C. (1977) *Everything in Its Place: Social Order and Land Use in America.* Princeton, NJ: Princeton University Press.

Rainwater, L. (1980) Fear and the house-as-haven in the lower class. In J. Pynoos, R. Schafer and C. Hartman (Eds) *Housing Urban America*, pp. 187–196. Hawthorne, NY: Aldine.

Reid, C. K. (2004) *Achieving the American Dream? A longitudinal analysis of the homeownership experiences of low-income households.* Working Paper No. 04-04, Center for Studies in Demography and Ecology, University of Washington, Seattle, WA.

Renuart, E. (2004) An overview of the predatory lending process, *Housing Policy Debate*, 15(3), pp. 467–502.

Retsinas, N. P. (1999) Lower-income homeowners: struggling to keep the dream alive, *Housing Facts and Findings*, 1(3), pp. 1–2.

Retsinas, N. P. and Belsky, E. S. (2002a) Examining the unexamined goal. In N. P. Retsinas and E. S. Belsky (Eds) *Low-income Homeownership: Examining the Unexamined Goal*, pp. 1–14. Washington, DC: The Brookings Institution.

Retsinas, N. P. and Belsky, E. S. (Eds) (2002b) *Low-income Homeownership: Examining the Unexamined Goal*. Washington, DC: The Brookings Institution.

Rohe, W. M. and Basolo, V. (1997) Long-term effects of homeownership on the self-perceptions and social interactions of low-income persons, *Environment and Behavior*, 29(6), pp. 793–819.

Rohe, W. M. and Stegman, M. A. (1994a) The effects of homeownership on the self-esteem, perceived control and satisfaction of low-income people, *Journal of the American Planning Association*, 60(2), pp. 173–184.

Rohe, W. and Stegman, M. A. (1994b) The impact of home ownership on the social and political involvement of low-income people, *Urban Affairs Quarterly*, 30(1), pp. 152–172.

Rohe, W. M. and Stewart, L. S. (1996) Homeownership and neighborhood stability, *Housing Policy Debate*, 7(1), pp. 27–78.

Rohe, W. M., Zandt, S. van and McCarthy, G. (2002a) Homeownership and access to opportunity, *Housing Studies*, 17(1), pp. 51–61.

Rohe, W, M., Zandt, S. van and McCarthy, G. (2002b) Social benefits and costs of homeownership. In N. P. Retsinas and E. S. Belsky (Eds) *Low-income Homeownership: Examining the Unexamined Goal*, pp. 381–407. Washington, DC: The Brookings Institution.

Rosenthal, S. S. (2002) Eliminating credit barriers: how far can we go? In N. P. Retsinas and E. S. Belsky (Eds) *Low-income Homeownership: Examining the Unexamined Goal*, pp. 111–145. Washington, DC: The Brookings Institution.

Rossi, P. H. and Weber, E. (1996) The social benefits of homeownership: empirical evidence from national surveys, *Housing Policy Debate*, 7(1), pp. 1–35.

Saunders, P. (1990) *A Nation of Homeowners*. London: Unwin Hyman.

Shapiro, T. M. and Wolff, E. N. (2001) *Assets for the Poor: The Benefits of Spreading Asset Ownership*. New York, NY: Russell Sage.

Sherraden, M. (1991) *Assets and the Poor: A New American Welfare Policy*. Armonk, NY: M. E. Sharpe, Inc.

Shlay, A. B. (1985) Castles in the sky: measuring housing and neighborhood ideology, *Environment and Behavior*, 17(5), pp. 593–626.

Shlay, A. B. (1986) Taking apart the American Dream: the influence of income and family composition on residential preferences, *Urban Studies*, (23)4, pp. 253–270.

Shlay, A. B. (1993) Shaping place: institutions and metropolitan development patterns, *Journal of Urban Affairs*, 15(5), pp. 387–404.

Shlay, A. B. (1995) Housing in the broader context in the United States, *Housing Policy Debate*, 6(3), pp. 695–720.

Shlay, A. B. (1999) Influencing the agents of urban structure: evaluating the effects of community reinvestment organizing on bank lending practices, *Urban Affairs Annual Review*, 35(1), pp. 247–278.

Squires, G. D. (1992) *From Redlining to Reinvestment: Community Responses to Urban Disinvestment*. Philadelphia, PA: Temple University Press.

Squires, G. D. (1994) *Capital and Communities in Black and White: The Intersections of Race, Class and Uneven Development*. Albany, NY: State University of New York Press.

Squires, G. D. (2003) *Organizing Access to Capital: Advocacy and the Democratization of Financial Institutions*. Philadelphia, PA: Temple University Press.

Squires, G. D. (2004) *Why the Poor Pay More: How to Stop Predatory Lending*. Westport, CT: Praeger.

Stegman, M. A. (1990) The excessive costs of creative finance: growing inefficiencies in the production of low-income housing, *Housing Policy Debate*, 2(2), pp. 357–372.

Stein, E. (2001) *Quantifying the Economic Cost of Predatory Lending*. Durham, NC: Coalition for Responsible Lending (http://www.responsiblelending.org; accessed 10 May 2004).

Stuart, G. (2003) *Discriminating Risk: The U.S. Mortgage Lending Industry in the Twentieth Century*. Ithaca, NY: Cornell University Press.

U.S. Census (2002a) *Registered voter turnout improved in 2000 presidential election*. Press release (http://www.census.gov/Press-Release/www/2002/cb02-31.html).

U.S. Census (2002b) *Moving to America: Moving to Homeownership: 1993–2002* (http://www.census.gov/prod/2003pubs/h121-03-1.pdf).

Walker, C. (1993) Nonprofit housing development: status, trends, and prospects, *Housing Policy Debate*, 4(3), pp. 369–414.

White, A. M. (2002) Risk-based mortgage pricing: present and future research, *Housing Policy Debate*, 15(3), pp. 503–532.

White, A. and Saegert, S. (1996) The tenant interim lease program and the development of low-income cooperatives in New York City's most neglected neighborhoods. In W. van Vliet (Ed.) *Affordable Housing and Urban Redevelopment in the United States: Learning from Failure and Success*, pp. 205–220. Thousand Oaks, CA: Sage.

Wirth, L. (1969) Urbanism as a way of life. In R. Sennett (Ed.) *Classic Essays on the Culture of Cities*, pp. 143–165. New York: Appleton-Century-Crofts.

Wright, G. (1983) *Building the Dream: A Social History of Housing in America*. Cambridge, MA: MIT Press.

The Case for Plan B

Tim McKenzie
(2007)

Since their inception, most subsidized affordable-ownership housing programs administered by federal, state, and municipal agencies have used a single strategy for increasing homeownership among U.S. households. Let's call this strategy Plan A. Focused on creating affordable-ownership housing payments to make an otherwise unattainable home attainable, this national homeownership strategy of choice has yet to produce a single unit of affordable-ownership housing.

Ownership housing is affordable if the price is right. However, public funders and private lenders alike have embraced affordable *payments* as the strategic outcome of choice, making Plan A virtually the only way nonprofit housing advocates and developers can get funding. Thus, those of us in the nonprofit housing field have had little choice but to get on board.

In fact, Plan A is so firmly entrenched, most of us can't grasp any other affordability paradigm. Yet a better strategic response to a shortage of affordable-ownership housing does exist. Let's call this strategy Plan B.

Grounded in a more equitable assessment of what constitutes a viable and vibrant community, Plan B is a response that better balances the dual goals of secure, affordably priced homeownership opportunities and meaningful wealth-accumulation. It's time to go to Plan B. Here's why.

The Case Against Plan A

"Affordable Payments!"—the heart of Plan A—is an effective marketing gimmick on a used-car lot. But a simple cost/benefit analysis—billions of tax dollars expended without producing a single unit of affordable-ownership housing—shows that Plan A fails the straight-face test as our nation's primary and dominant subsidized affordable ownership housing strategy.

Plan A's strategy is to subsidize the purchase of an unaffordable home. The lion's share of the required subsidy comes from federal taxpayers and is funneled to homebuyers through a vast national network of downpayment or homebuyer-assistance programs administered by state and local governments. A relatively small portion of

---

the required subsidy comes from tax-deductible contributions to private, nonprofit foundations and community-based affordable-housing organizations. Subsidy is delivered to the homebuyer in the form of a low- or no-cost loan. Monthly payments on the loan are not required; thus, the total monthly cost of ownership is made affordable. The loans are typically "due-on-sale," but repayment requirements vary from place to place at the discretion of the local governing body and its program administrators. Some loans are repaid. Most loans are partially forgiven. Some are forgiven entirely.

If subsidy is recovered from an outgoing homeowner when the home sells—again at an unaffordable price—it is generally recycled back into the assistance program to be combined with an infusion of new subsidy and loaned to another eligible household. The required infusion of new subsidy steadily increases from one sale transaction (or resale) to the next, because homes keep getting more expensive and incomes don't keep up. The only outcome possible from this plan is a plentiful supply of unaffordable ownership housing. Just look around.

Plan A's goal is to increase homeownership, but the percentage of U.S. households that own their homes has been hovering between 65 percent and 70 percent for the past several decades. After discounting for temporary increases attributable to the tsunami of predatory lenders preying on the unsuspecting, the misinformed, and the overeager, the stagnant homeownership stats constitute an indictment of Plan A.

Decades of uncritical acceptance have lent Plan A an aura of institutional permanence, impervious to direct challenge or question. Critical assessment is not only necessary, however, but possible and long overdue.

I recently completed a comparative analysis of forecasted Plan A and Plan B outcomes over a 25-year period in a hypothetical jurisdiction using typical transaction details for each plan based on standard housing-development and affordability factors faced by communities everywhere. A few of the outcomes from this analysis are summarized in Table 1. The outcomes were measured against the following key objectives: number of affordable units produced, effective use of available subsidy, number of households served, and wealth accumulation among households served.

An analysis of these projected outcomes shows that Plan A is an inefficient and costly response to the affordable-ownership housing problem. Worse, given identical allocations of program subsidy, Plan A can be expected to serve fewer households at a higher cost per assisted household. This is because Plan A is essentially an exercise in treading water. Each of Plan A's affordable payment homes eventually returns to the market for sale at an unaffordable price. In the sample analysis, 85.57 percent of the transactions occurring over the program period merely replace or re-subsidize previously "affordable" homes while requiring ever-increasing allocations of per-transaction subsidy to do so.

TABLE 1: Projected Program Outcomes (25-year program)		
	Plan A Affordable Payments	Plan B Affordable Prices
Number of units of affordable-ownership housing created	0	46
Number of affordable transactions	97	182
Number of transactions where subject property returns to market at unaffordable price	83	0
Total cash subsidy allocation over program period	$2,655,000	$2,655,000
Average annual allocation	$106,200	$106,200
Average cost per assisted household	$27,371	$14,588
Wealth creation:		
cash in (required to close–1st buyer; trend typical)	$2,301	$1,995
cash out (net sale proceeds–1st buyer; trend typical)	$57,323	$37,532
annual rate of return* on cash in	70.90%	63.08%

Note: Actual amounts are jurisdiction-specific; comparative trends are typical.
*Compound interest over 6 years of subsidized tenure

The Case for Plan B

Limited-equity housing cooperatives, some community land trusts, some deed-restricted housing programs, and some inclusionary-zoning ordinances are examples of programs that for decades now have been using Plan B to develop and steward an inventory of homes in their communities that continuously sell and resell at *prices* that eligible households can actually afford.

Plan B's strategy is to subsidize the development of affordably priced homes by non-profit, community-based organizations. This enables the community-based organization to sell homes for less than they cost to develop (or acquire from another developer).

Plan B's housing organizations don't just build and run. They think allocating ever-increasing amounts of public and private subsidy to combat a plentiful and growing supply of *un*affordable housing doesn't constitute much of a plan. In exchange for subsidy that supports its housing development activity, the community-based organization—as part of its mission—stays connected to each home it develops to ensure that every sale, not just the first one, occurs at an affordable price.

As for Plan B's homebuyers, they agree to pass the same deal they get—i.e., an affordable purchase price, opportunity to begin building wealth, and facilitated access to mortgage financing on favorable terms—on to other eligible homebuyers.

What a concept! Imagine simple purchase options from homeowners to nonprofit, community-based organizations that are managing waiting lists of credit-worthy, mortgage-ready households eager to stop renting. That pretty much cuts through the Gordian knot of legal, marketing, financing, policy, and program administration issues faced by affordable-ownership housing professionals every day.

In the best Plan B programs, eligible households are invited to participate in the development (and periodically review the performance) of the formula that determines the price at which homes in their price-stabilized marketplace will sell. It's not surprising, then, that such formula-determined prices are not only reliably affordable (if *you* were able to set the price, would you make it *un*affordable?) but also provide eligible households with a real opportunity to accumulate wealth (would you set yourself up to lose money?).

Table 1 shows that counting units is not a good or even useful element of comparison when measuring the effectiveness of these strategies against the affordable-ownership housing objective. Counting the number of affordable *transactions,* however, effectively quantifies the number of households benefiting under either plan. The affordable-transaction totals for both plans will always include any newly developed homeownership opportunities, but Plan B's totals will also include resales of the price-stabilized homes in its existing inventory. For the same money, the typical Plan B transaction will always serve more households (85 more in this instance) than the typical Plan A transaction.

If Plan B Is So Much Better, Why Isn't It Plan A?

Perhaps the biggest barrier to a clear-eyed assessment of Plan A vs. Plan B among housing professionals is our failure to connect with the priorities of typical American households. Ask 100 of your affordable-ownership housing colleagues what "affordable housing" means, and you will likely get 75 responses that go something like this: "Housing is affordable if it consumes no more than a certain percentage (typically 30 percent) of the gross monthly income of a household of a certain size earning a certain percentage (typically 80 percent) of the median income that is earned by households of the same size living in the standard metropolitan statistical area or the standard nonmetropolitan statistical area or, if neither, then the county in which the dwelling unit is situated." The other 25 responses you get are likely to be more complicated, start with "It depends," include a probing look . . . and have something to do with the IRS tax code.

Ask the person on the street what "affordable housing" means, and most of the time you are likely to hear something like this: "Housing is affordable if it sells for a price I can afford." The rest of the time you will be listening to someone who has been duped by us and our colleagues in the for-profit housing industry into believing that "affordable housing" and "affordable housing payments" *are* the same thing.

Because an affordable-payment mindset dominates the nation's affordable-housing policies and programs (not to mention its car lots), the policy underpinnings and programmatic tools of Plan A are routinely superimposed on virtually every effort to even *imagine* Plan B at scale—let alone implement it. For Plan B to thrive, we need the ability to think outside the Plan A toolbox. Plan B programs require a different set of tools altogether—think metric vs. standard.

Under the rubric of "shared-equity homeownership," several Plan B programs and projects were featured in the Spring 2007 issue of *Shelterforce*. John Emmeus Davis, research fellow at the National Housing Institute, offered some insightful and powerfully important observations about these alternative approaches to affordable homeownership. Davis notes how similar the featured alternative ownership housing models are at the micro (i.e., transactional) level, with their emphasis on affordable purchase and sale *prices*. He stresses the common barriers and strategic disadvantage that advocates and practitioners of these models face for lack of better communication among themselves about their shared emphasis on affordable *prices*. He argues that there is a persistent and "deep-seated bias against shared-equity homeownership" among those who design and administer first-time homebuyer programs that receive state or federal subsidies. Most important, Davis says that for these alternative homeownership models to thrive, "a deeper understanding of what works and what does not" is needed.

First, there should be no confusion about what does *not* work: that would be Plan A.

Second, it is instructive to ponder the fact that most housing advocates, policymakers, and funders still regard Plan B programs, their projects, and the ownership structures they use as "models." Models sit on shelves and are usually most meaningful to the builder. Eventually they end up in the closet, out of sight. If they are particularly elegant, they may end up in a museum for others to admire.

Just as fee-simple ownership and the condominium way of achieving it are not models, shared-equity homeownership and the community land trust way of achieving it (or the housing cooperative way, or the deed-restricted housing way, etc.) are not models. Airplanes and helicopters don't look the same on the ground, but they are both airworthy. Fee-simple ownership and shared-equity homeownership don't look the same on paper, but from the front yard they both look and feel the same—they are groundworthy.

The programs and projects featured in the spring issue of *Shelterforce* are examples of Plan B up and running in hundreds of communities nationwide, as Davis points out. Some have been operating for 30+ years.

In each case, the underlying purchase-and-sale transaction makes homes initially and continuously affordable to a succession of buyers with only a fraction of the subsidy required to administer the development of a like number of Plan A's affordable-ownership housing opportunities. For example, without changing any other of the specified program variables in the comparative analysis summarized in Table 1, Plan B requires only $1,444,320 over the 25-year period (as compared to $2,655,000 for Plan A) in order to produce the same 97 affordable transactions.

Let's be honest. The principal barrier to bringing Plan B to scale *is* a deep-seated bias against affordable prices. Those who design and administer state and/or federally funded first-time homebuyer programs are loath to consider changes to "the way we do it here"; seasoned bureaucrats point to the effort required to "turn the ship." And let's not forget the flat-out political and/or philosophical opposition from a large number of real estate industry professionals (whether operating for profit or against it) whose livelihood depends on the status quo.

Plan A advocates, administrators, and practitioners routinely tolerate the allocation of scores, even hundreds of thousands of per-transaction subsidy dollars in order to close the ever-widening gap between the price that eligible households can afford and what it costs to build new or buy (and perhaps refurbish) existing homes. But the mere prospect that a Plan B, formula-determined resale price may result (and on occasion has resulted) in a housing payment that is not affordable—even by only a few dollars—is reason enough for hidebound Plan A advocates (or bureaucrats) to characterize Plan B as intrinsically flawed.

On first pass, this doesn't seem entirely unreasonable. But on reflection, this conclusion not only fails to consider that only a small amount of additional subsidy may be all that is occasionally required to further reduce an already deeply discounted resale price in order to hit a specified affordability target; it fails to consider that most of the time no additional subsidy is required at all.

It is Plan A that is intrinsically flawed. In fact, measured against the "effective use of subsidy" objective, Plan A's emphasis on affordable payments—to the exclusion of affordable prices—is flat-out absurd. Plain and simple.

Nothing is plain or simple, however, about the wealth-accumulation objective. Very little substantive discussion occurs regarding what constitutes enough, too much, or too little wealth-accumulation for eligible households. Nonetheless, many affordable-ownership housing advocates argue that wealth-accumulation—especially among minority households—is such an important objective that it should not only trump assurances of affordable-ownership housing for future households (including minority households) but also any concerns that program donors or taxpayers (including all eligible households) may have about effective use of subsidy.

Plan A's elaborately constructed subordinate lien documents and loan transactions (the administrative burden of which is not reflected in the per-transaction costs reported in the data in Table 1) require that loans be repaid in order that the recovered subsidy can be used to lower the total monthly payment associated with the purchase of unaffordable homes by subsequent borrowers. Yet many of those Plan A documents provide for a portion (if not all) of the loan to be forgiven to boost the borrower's net sale proceeds when the home is sold—once again—at an unaffordable price. Such a plan fails to balance the importance of competing social goods in the name of privileging one above all others.

Under Plan A, not only are large allocations of subsidy routinely tolerated, but unaffordable prices are presumed necessary to produce the aforementioned "acceptable" but unspecified level of wealth accumulation.

There is no denying that most Plan A transactions will result in greater economic "betterment" for an eligible household, especially when net sale proceeds are considered. The outcomes summarized in the table have it $57,323 vs. $37,532 for the Plan A and Plan B homeowners, respectively. And when the compounded annual rate of return on cash down payment is considered, the Plan A homeowner also does better.

But look at these projected outcomes more closely. The Plan B homeowner can hardly be characterized as having made a *poor* investment for earning a compounded annual rate of return of 63.08 percent. And it turns out that bad matters are made worse for eligible households overall when affordable-housing professionals choose Plan A over Plan B. The table illustrates that choosing Plan A effectively denies 182 households an opportunity to choose between net sale proceeds of $37,532 and $0 (the net they will enjoy for continuing to rent) in order that 97 households can choose between net sale proceeds of $57,323 and $37,532.

Who benefits from this? This is a tough question, which housing professionals in most communities circumvent by deciding to operate both plans concurrently. As a result, the Plan B program ends up either struggling on the margins or dead in the water.

Another barrier to bringing Plan B to scale is worry that an adequate supply of homes trading in a publicly and/or privately subsidized price-stabilized housing marketplace might lower property values in an open, unrestricted marketplace. But Plan B transactions are not done at arm's length. Affordable prices are transparently offered in exchange for use, occupancy, income, and resale restrictions that benefit current and future homebuyers alike. Because of this quid-pro-quo arrangement, they cannot be used as comparables to establish the value of homes trading in the unrestricted, open marketplace. Accordingly, a price-stabilized ownership-housing marketplace exerts *no* influence on the prices at which property trades in an unrestricted marketplace.

In other words, price-stabilized marketplaces and open marketplaces are mutually exclusive. Access is denied to the one if income is too high (and/or the restrictions are not acceptable); access is denied to the other if income is too low.

Hundreds of thousands of households nationwide aspire to homeownership but must continue to rent for lack of homes selling at prices they can afford. Many affordable-housing professionals, however, presume that these households share a value system that views housing primarily as a wealth-creating opportunity and only secondarily as a secure, safe, and sound place to live and establish a legacy.

For those aspiring households, a lack of homes selling at affordable prices is a big problem. It's also a big problem that professional affordable-ownership housing program administrators, practitioners, opinion leaders, and policymakers are not asked (let alone expected) to pursue a strategy that actually produces affordable-ownership housing. It is a breach of public trust for us to promote affordable-ownership housing *payment* programs as affordable-ownership *housing* programs when they are not. Ownership housing is affordable when the price is right.

I was thrilled to read the Spring 2007 issue of *Shelterforce* and see that, once again, Plan B may be poised to become the "next big thing" in the subsidized affordable-ownership housing industry. But I worry that the emerging momentum for Plan B will, once again, be stalled at the "model" stage, as the object of more study.

Let's study this: No matter how simple, clever, unique, complex, or innovative the housing development project, the project financing scheme, or the purchase-and-sale transaction, Plan A does not produce affordable-ownership housing. No matter how many affordable-ownership housing programs use it and no matter how much money is spent on it, the only outcome possible from a strategy that seeks to make the payments affordable, but not the housing, is a plentiful supply of unaffordable ownership housing. Just look around.

It's time to go to Plan B.

Note: A complete copy of the comparative analysis discussed in this article can be obtained by sending an email to TMcKenzie@TimMcK.com with the words "comparative analysis" in the subject line.

FROM *The City–CLT Partnership*
Municipal Support for Community Land Trusts

John Emmeus Davis and Rick Jacobus
(2008)

Trends in City–CLT Partnerships

Over the past decade, the relationship between municipalities and community land trusts has shifted from adversarial to collaborative as the two have joined in partnerships to achieve their common goals. In the years ahead, their working relationship may evolve even more significantly as cities play a more dominant role in the startup and operation of CLTs, and as CLTs become more focused on stewardship than on development. While holding special promise for bringing CLTs to scale, these trends challenge the ways in which the model has been structured, championed, and applied for most of its history (see Table 1).

From City-as-Supporter to City-as-Instigator

In the past, the initiative for organizing a CLT nearly always came from individuals or organizations outside of local government. If municipal officials participated at all, they were drawn into the process after local community members had made most of the key organizational decisions for setting up the CLT.

Today, a municipality is just as likely to be the driving force behind a CLT as it is to be an impartial lender or grantmaker. Municipal officials in Highland Park, Irvine, and Chicago, for example, took the lead in evaluating the feasibility of a new CLT, introducing this unfamiliar model to the public and providing staff to plan and organize the startup process.

Municipal leadership clearly brings several advantages to the new organization. In particular, local government sponsorship often provides direct access to both federal and local subsidies to acquire land and build housing. Municipal employees may staff the new CLT, further speeding development of the CLT's first projects. Moreover, municipal sponsorship often results in the CLT becoming a favored beneficiary of inclusionary zoning, density bonuses, or other regulatory measures that require private developers to provide affordable units.

This selection was originally published in *The City–CLT Partnership: Municipal Support for Community Land Trusts* (Cambridge, MA: Lincoln Institute of Land Policy, 2008), 33–38. It is reprinted by permission. Original box numbers have been changed.

TABLE 1: Major Trends in Affordable Housing Policy and City–CLT Partnerships, 1980–2008		
Federal Housing Policy	**State and Local Housing Policy**	**City–CLT Partnerships**
• Reduction in federal funding for affordable housing and community development.	• Creation of state and local housing trust funds, capitalized through nonfederal funding sources.	• Expanded number of CLTs working in partnership with local government instead of in opposition to municipal policies and plans.
• Devolution of authority and responsibility for housing and community development programs from the federal government to state and local governments.	• Expanded use of regulatory *mandates* such as inclusionary zoning and growth management controls that require developers to produce affordable housing.	• Expanded number of cities playing a lead role in starting CLTs instead of waiting for new CLTs to emerge from the community.
• Expanded use of tax credits instead of grants in subsidizing production of affordable housing.	• Expanded use of regulatory *incentives* such as streamlining, density bonuses, and fee waivers that reward developers for producing affordable housing.	• Expanded number of cities playing a more dominant role in governing CLTs.
• Expansion of capacity funding and technical assistance for Community Housing Development Organizations (including CLTs).	• Wider commitment to preserving the affordability of owner-occupied housing created through the investment of public funds or the exercise of public powers.	• Expanded number of CLTs focusing on stewardship, acting on a city's behalf to monitor and enforce long-term controls over affordability.

CLTs formed by local government face a special set of challenges, however. Winning popular acceptance for a new CLT may be difficult when a municipal sponsor has neither the staff to run a participatory planning process nor the street-level credibility to attract grassroots leaders. Especially in neighborhoods scarred by urban renewal or municipal neglect, residents may regard a CLT started by local government with suspicion and leave the program with little support in the larger community.

Municipally sponsored CLTs also tend to focus only on housing, ignoring the model's potential for holding lands, developing projects, and mobilizing constituencies for nonresidential activities. Particularly when a local government starts a CLT expressly to enhance the effectiveness and longevity of its affordable housing investments, it is unlikely to take a more comprehensive approach to community development and community empowerment.

From City-as-Participant to City-as-Governor

A more serious challenge for municipally sponsored CLTs is getting government to let go. Having controlled the startup process, some in city hall may want to remain involved by governing the organization as well.

From the earliest days of the CLT movement, most land trusts included at least one local government employee or elected official within the one-third of board members designated as public representatives. These officials were usually nominated and appointed by the rest of the CLT's directors, who were themselves elected by CLT members. Municipal representatives were seldom appointed by a mayor or city council, and were not authorized to speak on the municipality's behalf. Their role was simply to serve as an informal conduit for the flow of information between the CLT and the city.

In recent years, the number of seats reserved for municipal representatives has increased and the power to decide who fills the seats has passed to municipal authorities outside of the CLT. In a growing number of CLTs, all of the public representatives on the board are both affiliated with and appointed by a local government. Even so, more public representative seats on a CLT's board does not necessarily translate into municipal control, especially if the seats are split among several municipalities or among multiple departments within the same municipality. In the cases of the Champlain Housing Trust and the Orange Community Housing and Land Trust, for example, municipal officials occupy a third of the seats on the governing boards, but the representatives come from four different towns in those regions.

In a few recent cases, however, the municipality plays a more dominant role. The City of Irvine, for instance, appointed every member of the initial board of the Irvine Community Land Trust and has retained the right to appoint a third of the seats on all future boards. The Chicago CLT, an initiative of the City of Chicago, has a classic three-part governing board, but the mayor and city council appoint every member. As an even more extreme example of municipal control, the City of Flagstaff operates a CLT as an internal program with no separate identity from local government.

In some places, greater municipal involvement in governance may be a practical and productive strategy, either as a temporary arrangement until the CLT is firmly established or as a permanent alternative to the classic community-based structure. However, the consensus among most practitioners who staff, assist, or fund CLTs is that community land trusts are more successful when they are structured and perceived as somewhat independent of their municipal sponsors. Too close an affiliation with local government may create trouble for the CLT in marketing its homes, diversifying its funding, and retaining its community base.

How much separation a CLT should have from its supporting municipality and how accountable a CLT should be to local residents relative to local government are open questions. The classic CLT provides a very specific organizational recipe: (1) a corporate membership open to any adult resident of the CLT's service area; (2) a governing board composed of equal numbers of lessees, corporate members who are not lessees, and any other category of persons described in the CLT's bylaws; and (3) direct election of a majority of the board by the CLT's members. This structure reflects both the federal definition of a community land trust adopted by Congress in 1992 and the definition of the classic CLT model approved by the National CLT Network in 2006.

Many of today's CLTs do not match this definition. Recognizing this reality, the National CLT Network has opened its membership to land trusts that are variants of the classic model. For example, an organization is eligible to join the network even if it lacks a voting membership, "as long as some structure exists to ensure the board's accountability to the residents of its service area." In addition, there is no barrier to membership in the National CLT Network if the CLT is sponsored by local government—even if more than a third of the seats are taken by municipal appointees or employees.

This signals a shift in the company that older CLTs have been willing to keep, as well as a major change in what it means to be a CLT. Is there some point between being completely independent of or completely controlled by local government where a CLT can no longer be considered a *community* land trust? More practically, is there some point where the ability to succeed as a CLT is undermined by too tight a municipal rein over its assets and operations, or too dominant a municipal presence on the CLT's board? These are questions that the CLT Network, CLT practitioners, and municipal officials will wrestle with for years to come.

From CLT-as-Developer to CLT-as-Steward

Most CLTs play the role and perform the tasks of a real estate developer, using their own employees to initiate, manage, and market newly constructed or rehabilitated housing. Some CLTs have spearheaded nonresidential projects as well, including development of commercial buildings, nonprofit incubators, and community centers.

Development is not the CLT's forté, however. Nothing in the model's distinctive approach to ownership, organization, and operation makes real estate development easier or cheaper to do. Indeed, nothing makes a CLT a better developer than any other nonprofit or for-profit entity that has municipal support to produce affordable housing or other community facilities. Instead, the model's real strength lies in protecting a municipality's investment and a community's assets, and in preserving access to land and housing for people of modest means. It is in the period *after* a project is developed that a CLT makes its most durable and distinctive contribution to a community's well-being (see Box 1).

BOX 1. Another Strength of CLTs: Preventing Foreclosures

The municipal rationale for supporting CLTs has long focused on permanent affordability—the model's effectiveness in ensuring that homes made affordable today will remain affordable tomorrow. Until recently, much less attention has been paid to permanent responsibility i.e., the CLT's durable commitment to back-stop the security and success of its first-time homeowners.

The mounting crisis in the U.S. mortgage market has turned the spotlight toward the latter aspect of stewardship. In December 2007, the National Community Land Trust Network surveyed 49 CLTs (nearly a quarter of the nation's total), evaluating the number of mortgage defaults and foreclosures in their portfolios from the time of their founding to the present. Within this small but typical subpopulation of 3,115 residential mortgages, CLTs had intervened 108 times to cure a default before it could result in foreclosure. Nationally, there were only 19 reported cases of foreclosure or transfer of a deed in lieu of foreclosure, a foreclosure rate of 0.6 percent over the entire organizational lifetime of the CLTs. In only 12 of these foreclosures did a lower-income homeowner actually lose his or her home, and in just three cases was a foreclosed property eventually lost from a CLT's portfolio.

This is not to say that CLTs have wrongly become developers. The organizers of local CLTs eagerly and reasonably took on the developer's role when offered, for example, a once-in-a-lifetime chance to develop a sizable parcel of city-owned land (as in Albuquerque); or priority access to municipal or state funding for the construction of affordable housing (as in Burlington, VT); or millions of dollars from local employers to build starter homes for working families (as in Rochester, MN).

In other situations, CLT organizers only reluctantly became housing developers after concluding they had no other choice. In Gloucester, MA, Albany, NY, and Cincinnati, for example, private developers were not building anything that residents could afford and nonprofit developers were doing little to fill the gap. The CLTs saw no other way to serve their communities than to be developers of last resort.

In several other cities, including Portland, OR, Cleveland, and Boston, CLTs had originally intended to confine their activities to stewardship. Existing community development corporations were supposed to be responsible for development, and the CLTs were to preserve the long-term affordability of whatever housing was created. In reality, this seldom happened and the CLTs had to do more development than they had intended.

Whether by choice or by default, real estate development is likely to remain a CLT activity. Nevertheless, a countertrend is emerging as a number of newer CLTs confine their activities to managing land and the affordable housing stock. The CLT-as-steward is slowly becoming a more prominent part of the national landscape.

Indeed, CLTs are being pushed in this direction by the need to distinguish themselves from other nonprofit developers of affordable housing in what has become, in some jurisdictions, a very crowded field. Instead of competing for project subsidies, some CLTs have found a more sustainable niche by specializing in stewardship, an activity that other nonprofits are less willing or less suited to do.

In other jurisdictions, CLTs are being pulled toward stewardship by the vacuum created by a seismic shift in public policy. Municipal funding for affordable housing—and municipal mandates or incentives for inclusionary housing—once focused almost exclusively on the front end of the development process. It seemed achievement enough to expand the supply of affordably priced or affordably financed housing, with little concern for what happened to the occupancy, condition, and affordability of the homes after they were purchased.

This is no longer the prevailing attitude. Municipal officials have increasingly come to accept the policy prescription that, when public assets or public powers are used to create affordably priced, owner-occupied housing, something must be done to preserve those units for lower-income people for years to come. A growing number of local governments have also recognized that the CLT is one of the most effective and sustainable options for monitoring and enforcing long-term controls over the use and resale of publicly assisted owner-occupied housing.

Of course, serving as a municipality's designated steward is not without challenges. As CLTs discovered in the past when they agreed to leave development entirely in the hands of local community development corporations, allowing others to control the property pipeline can sometimes result in the CLT receiving only a trickle of land and housing—or only those assets no one else wants. Furthermore, when CLTs are not involved in the process of designing and developing the homes, they can find themselves marketing, managing, and stewarding a product no one wants to buy.

Getting government to pay for stewardship can be an even more serious obstacle. Public officials at all levels tend to be more receptive to covering the costs of constructing and financing owner-occupied housing than to covering the costs of monitoring the occupancy, maintaining the condition, and managing the resale of the units once they are built. If CLTs are to forego the fees they now receive from developing housing, they must find other sources of revenue to cover their stewardship costs—either operating subsidies provided by local government or internal fees generated by their own portfolios.

Concentrating on stewardship requires no recasting of the classic CLT. In fact, it might be argued that stewardship, not development, is what the CLT model was always about. The evolving municipal roles in instigating and governing CLTs stretch the model beyond the boundaries within which it was initially conceived and structured. But the role of steward draws the CLT back to its original mission of shepherding resources that a community invests and of capturing value that a community creates. Making stewardship its principal activity brings the model full circle, refocusing the CLT on what it does best.

Sharing the Wealth of the Commons

Peter Barnes
(2004)

We're all familiar with private wealth, even if we don't have much. Economists and the media celebrate it every day. But there's another trove of wealth we barely notice: our common wealth.

Each of us is the beneficiary of a vast inheritance. This common wealth includes our air and water, habitats and ecosystems, languages and cultures, science and technologies, political and monetary systems, and quite a bit more. To say we share this inheritance doesn't mean we can call a broker and sell our shares tomorrow. It *does* mean we're responsible for the commons and entitled to any income it generates. Both the responsibility and the entitlement are ours by birth. They're part of the obligation each generation owes to the next, and each living human owes to other beings.

At present, however, our economic system scarcely recognizes the commons. This omission causes two major tragedies: ceaseless destruction of nature and widening inequality among humans. Nature gets destroyed because no one's unequivocally responsible for protecting it. Inequality widens because private wealth concentrates while common wealth shrinks.

The great challenges for the twenty-first century are, first of all, to make the commons visible; second, to give it proper reverence; and third, to translate that reverence into property rights and legal institutions that are on a par with those supporting private property. If we do this, we can avert the twin tragedies currently built into our market-driven system.

Defining the Commons

What exactly is the commons? Here is a workable definition: *The commons includes all the assets we inherit together and are morally obligated to pass on, undiminished, to future generations.*

This definition is a practical one. It designates a set of assets that have three specific characteristics: they're (1) inherited; (2) shared; and (3) worthy of long-term preservation. Usually it's obvious whether an asset has these characteristics or not.

At the same time, the definition is broad. It encompasses assets that are natural as well as social, intangible as well as tangible, small as well as large. It also introduces a

This selection was originally published in *Dollars & Sense* 256 (2004). It is reprinted by permission of *Dollars & Sense*, a progressive economics magazine based in Boston, MA. www.dollarsandsense.org.

moral factor that is absent from other economic definitions: it requires us to consider whether an asset is worthy of long-term preservation. At present, capitalism has no interest in this question. If an asset is likely to yield a competitive return to capital, it's kept alive; if not, it's destroyed or allowed to run down. Assets in the commons, by contrast, are meant to be preserved regardless of their return.

This definition sorts all economic assets into two baskets, the market and the commons. In the market basket are those assets we want to own privately and manage for profit. In the commons basket are the assets we want to hold in common and manage for long-term preservation. These baskets then are, or ought to be, the yin and yang of economic activity; each should enhance and contain the other. The role of the state should be to maintain a healthy balance between them.

The Value of the Commons

For most of human existence, the commons supplied everyone's food, water, fuel, and medicines. People hunted, fished, gathered fruits and herbs, collected firewood and building materials, and grazed their animals in common lands and waters. In other words, the commons was the source of basic sustenance. This is still true today in many parts of the world, and even in San Francisco, where I live, cash-poor people fish in the bay not for sport, but for food.

Though sustenance in the industrialized world now flows mostly through markets, the commons remains hugely valuable. It's the source of all natural resources and nature's many replenishing services. Water, air, DNA, seeds, topsoil, minerals, the protective ozone layer, the atmosphere's climate regulation, and much more, are gifts of nature to us all.

Just as crucially, the commons is our ultimate waste sink. It recycles water, oxygen, carbon, and everything else we excrete, exhale, or throw away. It's the place we store, or try to store, the residues of our industrial system.

The commons also holds humanity's vast accumulation of knowledge, art, and thought. As Isaac Newton said, "If I have seen further it is by standing on the shoulders of giants." So, too, the legal, political, and economic institutions we inherit—even the market itself—were built by the efforts of millions. Without these gifts we'd be hugely poorer than we are today.

To be sure, thinking of these natural and social inheritances primarily as economic assets is a limited way of viewing them. I deeply believe they are much more than that. But if treating portions of the commons as economic assets can help us conserve them, it's surely worth doing so.

How much might the commons be worth in monetary terms? It's relatively easy to put a dollar value on private assets. Accountants and appraisers do it every day, aided by the fact that private assets are regularly traded for money.

This isn't the case with most shared assets. How much is clean air, an intact wetlands, or Darwin's theory of evolution worth in dollar terms? Clearly, many shared inheritances are simply priceless. Others are potentially quantifiable, but there's no current market for them. Fortunately, economists have developed methods to quantify the value of things that aren't traded, so it's possible to estimate the value of the "priceable" part of the commons within an order of magnitude. The surprising conclusion that emerges from numerous studies is that *the wealth we share is worth more than the wealth we own privately.*

This fact bears repeating. Even though much of the commons can't be valued in monetary terms, the parts that *can* be valued are worth more than all private assets combined.

It's worth noting that these estimates understate the gap between common and private assets because a significant portion of the value attributed to private wealth is in fact an appropriation of common wealth. If this mislabeled portion was subtracted from private wealth and added to common wealth, the gap between the two would widen further.

Two examples will make this point clear. Suppose you buy a house for $200,000 and, without improving it, sell it a few years later for $300,000. You pay off the mortgage and walk away with a pile of cash. But what caused the house to rise in value? It wasn't anything you did. Rather, it was the fact that your neighborhood became more popular, likely a result of the efforts of community members, improvements in public services, and similar factors.

Or consider another fount of private wealth, the social invention and public expansion of the stock market. Suppose you start a business that goes "public" through an offering of stock. Within a few years, you're able to sell your stock for a spectacular capital gain.

Much of this gain is a social creation, the result of centuries of monetary-system evolution, laws and regulations, and whole industries devoted to accounting, sharing information, and trading stocks. What's more, there's a direct correlation between the scale and quality of the stock market as an institution and the size of the private gain. You'll fetch a higher price if you sell into a market of millions than into a market of two. Similarly, you'll gain more if transaction costs are low and trust in public information is high. Thus, stock that's traded on a regulated exchange sells for a higher multiple of earnings than unlisted stock. This socially created premium can account for 30 percent of the stock's value. If you're the lucky seller, you'll reap that extra cash—in no way thanks to anything you did as an individual.

Real estate gains and the stock market's social premium are just two instances of common assets contributing to private gain. Still, most rich people would like us to think it's their extraordinary talent, hard work, and risk-taking that create their well-deserved wealth. That's like saying a flower's beauty is due solely to its own efforts, owing nothing to nutrients in the soil, energy from the sun, water from the aquifer, or the activity of bees.

The Great Commons Giveaway

That we inherit a trove of common wealth is the good news. The bad news, alas, is that our inheritance is being grossly mismanaged. As a recent report by the advocacy group Friends of the Commons concludes, "Maintenance of the commons is terrible, theft is rampant, and rents often aren't collected. To put it bluntly, our common wealth—and our children's—is being squandered. We are all poorer as a result."

Examples of commons mismanagement include the handout of broadcast spectrum to media conglomerates, the giveaway of pollution rights to polluters, the extension of copyrights to entertainment companies, the patenting of seeds and genes, the privatization of water, and the relentless destruction of habitat, wildlife, and ecosystems.

This mismanagement, though currently extreme, is not new. For over 200 years, the market has been devouring the commons in two ways. With one hand, the market takes valuable stuff from the commons and privatizes it. This is called "enclosure." With the other hand, the market dumps bad stuff into the commons and says, "It's your problem." This is called "externalizing." Much that is called economic growth today is actually a form of cannibalization in which the market diminishes the commons that ultimately sustains it.

Enclosure—the taking of good stuff from the commons—at first meant privatization of land by the gentry. Today it means privatization of many common assets by corporations. Either way, it means that what once belonged to everyone now belongs to a few.

Enclosure is usually justified in the name of efficiency. And sometimes, though not always, it does result in efficiency gains. But what also results from enclosure is the impoverishment of those who lose access to the commons, and the enrichment of those who take title to it. In other words, enclosure widens the gap between those with income-producing property and those without.

Externalizing—the dumping of bad stuff into the commons—is an automatic behavior pattern of profit-maximizing corporations: if they can avoid any out-of-pocket costs, they will. If workers, taxpayers, anyone downwind, future generations, or nature have to absorb added costs, so be it.

For decades, economists have agreed we'd be better served if businesses "internalized" their externalities—that is, paid in real time the costs they now shift to the commons. The reason this doesn't happen is that there's no one to set prices and collect them. Unlike private wealth, the commons lacks property rights and institutions to represent it in the marketplace.

The seeds of such institutions, however, are starting to emerge. Consider one of the environmental protection tools the U.S. currently uses, pollution trading. So-called cap-and-trade programs put a cap on total pollution, then grant portions of the total, via permits, to each polluting firm. Companies may buy other firms' permits if they want to pollute more than their allotment allows, or sell unused permits if they manage to pollute less. Such programs are generally supported by business because they allow polluters to find the cheapest ways to reduce pollution.

Public discussion of cap-and-trade programs has focused exclusively on their trading features. What's been overlooked is how they give away common wealth to polluters.

To date, all cap-and-trade programs have begun by giving pollution rights to existing polluters for free. This treats polluters as if they own our sky and rivers. It means that future polluters will have to pay old polluters for the scarce—hence valuable—right to dump wastes into nature. Imagine that: because a corporation polluted in the past, it gets free income forever! And, because ultimately we'll all pay for limited pollution via higher prices, this amounts to an enormous transfer of wealth—trillions of dollars—to shareholders of historically polluting corporations.

In theory, though, there is no reason that the initial pollution rights should not reside with the public. Clean air and the atmosphere's capacity to absorb pollutants are "wealth" that belongs to everyone. Hence, when polluters use up these parts of the commons, they should pay the public—not the other way around.

Taking the Commons Back

How can we correct the system omission that permits, and indeed promotes, destruction of nature and ever-widening inequality among humans? The answer lies in building a new sector of the economy whose clear legal mission is to preserve shared inheritances for everyone. Just as the market is populated by profit-maximizing corporations, so this new sector would be populated by asset-preserving trusts.

Here a brief description of trusts may be helpful. The trust is a private institution that's even older than the corporation. The essence of a trust is a fiduciary relationship. A trust holds and manages property for another person or for many other people. A simple example is a trust set up by a grandparent to pay for a grandchild's education. Other trusts include pension funds, charitable foundations, and university endowments. There are also hundreds of trusts in America, like the Nature Conservancy and the Trust for Public Land, that own land or conservation easements in perpetuity.

If we were to design an institution to protect pieces of the commons, we couldn't do much better than a trust. The goal of commons management, after all, is to preserve assets and deliver benefits to broad classes of beneficiaries. That's what trusts do, and it's not rocket science.

Over centuries, several principles of trust management have evolved. These include:

- Trustees have a fiduciary responsibility to beneficiaries. If a trustee fails in this obligation, he or she can be removed and penalized.
- Trustees must preserve the original asset. It's okay to spend income, but don't invade the principal.

- Trustees must assure transparency. Information about money flows should be readily available to beneficiaries.

Trusts in the new commons sector would be endowed with rights comparable to those of corporations. Their trustees would take binding oaths of office and, like judges, serve long terms. Though protecting common assets would be their primary job, they would also distribute income from those assets to beneficiaries. These beneficiaries would include all citizens within a jurisdiction, large classes of citizens (children, the elderly), and/or agencies serving common purposes such as public transit or ecological restoration. When distributing income to individuals, the allocation formula would be one person, one share. The right to receive commons income would be a nontransferable birthright, not a property right that could be traded.

Fortuitously, a working model of such a trust already exists: the Alaska Permanent Fund. When oil drilling on the North Slope began in the 1970s, Gov. Jay Hammond, a Republican, proposed that 25 percent of the state's royalties be placed in a mutual fund to be invested on behalf of Alaska's citizens. Voters approved in a referendum. Since then, the Alaska Permanent Fund has grown to over $28 billion, and Alaskans have received roughly $22,000 apiece in dividends. In 2003 the per capita dividend was $1,107; a family of four received $4,428.

What Alaska did with its oil can be replicated for other gifts of nature. For example, we could create a nationwide Sky Trust to stabilize the climate for future generations. The trust would restrict emissions of heat-trapping gases and sell a declining number of emission permits to polluters. The income would be returned to U.S. residents in equal yearly dividends, thus reversing the wealth transfer built into current cap-and-trade programs. Instead of everyone paying historic polluters, polluters would pay all of us.

Just as a Sky Trust could represent our equity in the natural commons, a Public Stock Trust could embody our equity in the social commons. Such a trust would capture some of the socially created stock-market premium that currently flows only to shareholders and their investment bankers. As noted earlier, this premium is sizeable—roughly 30 percent of the value of publicly traded stock. A simple way to share it would be to create a giant mutual fund—call it the American Permanent Fund—that would hold, say, 10 percent of the shares of publicly traded companies. This mutual fund, in turn, would be owned by all Americans on a one share per person basis (perhaps linked to their Social Security accounts).

To build up the fund without precipitating a fall in share prices, companies would contribute shares at the rate of, say, 1 percent per year. The contributions would be the price companies pay for the benefits they derive from a commons asset, the large, trusted market for stock—a small price, indeed, for the hefty benefits. Over time, the mutual fund would assure that when the economy grows, everyone benefits. The top 5 percent would still own more than the bottom 90 percent, but at least every American would have *some* property income, and a slightly larger slice of our economic pie.

Sharing the Wealth

The perpetuation of inequality is built into the current design of capitalism. Because of the skewed distribution of private wealth, a small self-perpetuating minority receives a disproportionate share of America's nonlabor income.

Tom Paine had something to say about this. In his essay "Agrarian Justice," written in 1790, he argued that, because enclosure of the commons had separated so many people from their primary source of sustenance, it was necessary to create a functional equivalent of the commons in the form of a National Fund. Here is how he put it:

> There are two kinds of property. Firstly, natural property, or that which comes to us from the Creator of the universe—such as the earth, air, water. Secondly, artificial or acquired property—the invention of men. In the latter, equality is impossible; for to distribute it equally, it would be necessary that all should have contributed in the same proportion, which can never be the case. . . . Equality of natural property is different. Every individual in the world is born with legitimate claims on this property, or its equivalent.

Enclosure of the commons, he went on, was necessary to improve the efficiency of cultivation. But

> the landed monopoly that began with [enclosure] has produced the greatest evil. It has dispossessed more than half the inhabitants of every nation of their natural inheritance, without providing for them, as ought to have been done, an indemnification for that loss, and has thereby created a species of poverty and wretchedness that did not exist before.

The appropriate compensation for loss of the commons, Paine said, was a national fund financed by rents paid by land owners. Out of this fund, every person reaching age 21 would get 15 pounds a year, and every person over 50 would receive an additional 10 pounds. (Think of Social Security, financed by commons rents instead of payroll taxes.)

A Progressive Offensive

Paine's vision, allowing for inflation and new forms of enclosure, could not be more timely today. Surely from our vast common inheritance—not just the land, but the atmosphere, the broadcast spectrum, our mineral resources, our threatened habitats and water supplies—enough rent can be collected to pay every American over age 21 a modest annual dividend, and every person reaching 21 a small start-up inheritance.

Such a proposal may seem utopian. In today's political climate, perhaps it is. But consider this. About 20 years ago, right-wing think tanks laid out a bold agenda. They called for lowering taxes on private wealth, privatizing much of government, and deregulating industry. Amazingly, this radical agenda has largely been achieved.

It's time for progressives to mount an equally bold offensive. The old shibboleths—let's gin up the economy, create jobs, and expand government programs—no longer excite. We need to talk about *fixing* the economy, not just growing it; about *income* for everyone, not just jobs; about nurturing *ecosystems, cultures,* and *communities,* not just our individual selves. More broadly, we need to celebrate the commons as an essential counterpoise to the market.

Unfortunately, many progressives have viewed the state as the only possible counterpoise to the market. The trouble is, the state has been captured by corporations. This capture isn't accidental or temporary; it's structural and long-term.

This doesn't mean progressives can't occasionally recapture the state. We've done so before and will do so again. It does mean that progressive control of the state is the exception, not the norm; in due course, corporate capture will resume. It follows that if we want lasting fixes to capitalism's tragic flaws, we must use our brief moments of political ascendancy to build institutions that endure.

Programs that rely on taxes, appropriations, or regulations are inherently transitory; they get weakened or repealed when political power shifts. By contrast, institutions that are self-perpetuating and have broad constituencies are likely to last. (It also helps if they mail out checks periodically.) This was the genius of Social Security, which has survived—indeed grown—through numerous Republican administrations.

If progressives are smart, we'll use our next New Deal to create common property trusts that include all Americans as beneficiaries. These trusts will then be to the twenty-first century what social insurance was to the twentieth: sturdy pillars of shared responsibility and entitlement. Through them, the commons will be a source of sustenance for all, as it was before enclosure. Life-long income will be linked to generations-long ecological health. Isn't that a future most Americans would welcome?

Givings
The Flip Side of Takings

David Morris
(2005)

Last November, by a resounding margin (61–39 percent) Oregon voters approved Measure 37. The ballot measure requires public entities to compensate property owners for any decline in the value of their property due to a public regulation.

The initiative's passage may have marked the sweetest victory to date for the 25-year-old "takings movement," a private property rights advocacy effort that seeks to "justly compensate" owners for any government action that reduced the value of their land. I hope it also marks the end of the defensive way we oppose such measures (e.g., arguing that compensating the victims of government action will cost us too much).

It is time we took the offense in the takings debate and launched a "givings movement." If the public must pay private property owners whenever a public action diminishes the value of their property, then property owners should compensate the public whenever public actions increase the value of the property.

The fact of the matter is that the vast majority of public actions elevate land and property values. If the public were compensated for the increase in land value that results from public actions, a number of public services, such as transit, could become self-financing.

The takings movement gets its traction from 12 words in the Fifth Amendment to the U.S. Constitution: ". . . nor shall private property be taken for public use without just compensation." For almost 200 years after the Constitution was ratified, the courts interpreted those words to mean that compensation was due only if the government physically confiscated or occupied the property, or issued a regulation that stripped the property of virtually all its economic value.

For example, in 1978 the U.S. Supreme Court decided a case involving Penn Central, the owner of the Grand Central Station in mid-town Manhattan. Penn Central wanted to build a 50-story building above the station. The New York City Landmarks Commission rejected its application. The Supreme Court ruled that no taking had occurred because the property retained its economic use as a railroad and transit station.

In 1980, Ronald Reagan won the presidency and the takings clause quickly became one of the conservative movement's principal levers for restricting the public sector. University of Chicago law professor Richard Epstein's 1985 book, *Takings,*

This selection was originally published online on April 19, 2005 at www.alternet.org. It is printed by permission of the author. David Morris is director of the New Rules Project at the Institute for Local Self-Reliance. www.newrules.org.

became the movement's bible. Epstein asserted that a compensable taking occurs even when there is only a minor and even hypothetical economic impact on the affected land. Moreover, he declared that the takings clause could and should be extended to hobble many government actions.

He boldly maintained that the clause renders "constitutionally infirm or suspect many of the heralded reforms and institutions of the 20th century: zoning, rent control, workers' compensation laws, transfer payments [and] progressive taxation."

In March 1988, Reagan adopted Epstein's thesis as federal policy when he signed Executive Order 12630: "(e)xecutive departments and agencies should review their actions carefully to prevent unnecessary takings. . . ."

In his memoir, Reagan administration Solicitor General Charles Fried recalls that era. "Attorney General Meese and his young advisers—many drawn from the ranks of the then fledgling Federalist Societies and often devotees of the extreme libertarian views of Chicago professor Richard Epstein—had a specific, aggressive, and it seemed to me, quite radical project in mind: to use the Takings Clause of the Fifth Amendment as a severe brake upon federal and state regulation of business and property."

By the mid 1990s, takings bills had been enacted in 14 states and had been debated in many others. In the 1990s the U.S. Supreme Court began to broaden the use of the takings clause to inhibit local land use regulations. We can expect equivalent initiatives to Measure 37 to gain ballot status in other states.

We need a "givings" initiative. We need to make the concept of "givings" as well known as "takings." In most people's minds, giving signifies something one does voluntarily while taking is done to one against one's will. But in the real world of land values, both givings and takings are involuntary.

Real estate and economic developer Donovan Rypkema of Place Economics has explained that real estate is a unique form of property, for two reasons. First, the way one uses one's land affects the value of surrounding land. Second, the primary source of value in real estate is largely external to the property lines.

As to the first point, if I owned two residential lots and built a 20-story apartment building, it would reduce the value of my neighbors' lands. Installing a car repair shop on my property would cause an even greater reduction. Which is why local governments require me to ask for a variance or change in zoning before undertaking such constructions.

As to the second point, the old real estate cliché, "The three most important things in real estate are location, location, location," is entirely valid. "Public decisions affect the value of real estate in both directions," notes Rypkema, "it is one of the risks and potential rewards of ownership."

Land values are largely determined by actions taken outside the plot's boundaries. A nearby good public school raises values. So does a park. So does access to transportation.

Gaining a zoning change is the pot of gold at the end of any developer's rainbow. A change in zoning can increase the value of a piece of land tenfold. That is giving on a majestic scale. Why not tax the publicly generated increased value of their land 100 percent? That would be consistent with giving just compensation to property owners who lose out when government acts.

More than a century ago economist Henry George led a powerful movement based on the idea that, by taxing the increase in the value of land resulting from public actions, most other taxes could be eliminated.

Given the much higher level of public services and public demands these days, a land tax cannot eliminate the need for all other taxes. But it might allow us to finance some desperately needed services.

Consider the transportation sector. When government builds a train or bus stop, it is increasing the value of land within walking distance of that access point. Nobel laureate in economics William Vickrey has proposed that government finance transportation improvements by taxing this increased value of land near the improvements.

The concept has been successfully applied in Hong Kong. Its rail transit system receives no subsidy. All costs, including interest on bond indebtedness, are paid from land rents derived from development in station areas. A study of the added land values resulting from the development of Washington, DC's metro found that it exceeded the entire cost of building the metro.

Indeed, in the past, private developers often built transit systems to urban fringe neighborhoods and recouped the capital costs from the sales of developed sites.

What would a givings ballot initiative look like? Italics mark the changes from the original wording in the first two paragraphs of Measure 37:

(1) If a public entity enacts or enforces a new land use regulation or enforces a land use regulation enacted prior to the effective date of this amendment that *expands* the use of private real property or any interest therein and has the effect of *increasing* the fair market value of the property, or any interest therein, then the *public entity* shall be paid *the increased value.*

(2) *The amount owed the public entity* shall be equal to the *increase* in the fair market value of the affected property interest resulting from enactment or enforcement of the land use regulation as of the date the *public entity* makes written demand for compensation under this act.

We could rely on none other than Adam Smith as a support witness for a givings initiative. "As soon as the land of any country has all become private property," Smith observed, "the landlords, like all others, love to reap where they never sowed."

The Challenge of Perpetuity

James M. Libby, Jr.
(2010)

All people shall have the right to live where they choose, to be decently housed, and to bring up their families in comfort and security.
—Freedom Charter, African National Congress

In Vermont, community-based nonprofits developing affordable homes and conserving land receive financial assistance from a unique public body created in 1987, the Vermont Housing and Conservation Board ("VHCB").[1] Housing and conservation projects funded by VHCB must include an organizational commitment and a contractual mechanism for assuring a permanent benefit to the people and communities of Vermont. Conservation lands and historic buildings are protected by perpetual easements held by qualified stewards.[2] Assisted housing must remain perpetually affordable to lower income Vermonters under housing subsidy covenants held by community groups or public agencies.[3] Such covenants ensure that homes will remain affordable to future generations and the value and effectiveness of the public's investment will continue forever.

When the Legislature first appropriated state funds for VHCB for affordable housing and land conservation,[4] VHCB's enabling act dictated that permanence would be a feature of such investments. Using different methods of subsidy retention, VHCB-funded homes must provide Vermonters with decent, safe, and affordable housing for generations to come. If Vermont had based its housing policy on subsidy recapture instead, requiring funds to be repaid to the state at the time of resale, homes would have left the affordable housing portfolio and new and larger public subsidies would have been needed to replace them. Permanence has remained the cornerstone of Vermont's affordable housing delivery system for over 20 years, providing VHCB staff with decades of practical experience promoting and enforcing the stewardship of publicly subsidized, privately owned housing. This chapter will discuss some of the lessons we have learned as a public agency in confronting both the promise and the challenge of perpetuity.

This selection has been adapted from James Libby and Darby Bradley's discussion of the problem of perpetuity that appeared in the chapter "Vermont Housing and Conservation Board: A Conspiracy of Good Will Among Land Trusts and Housing Trusts," in *Property and Values: Alternatives to Public and Private Ownership,* by Charles Geisler and Gail Daneker, eds. Copyright © 2000 Island Press. It is used by permission.

Commitment to Permanent Affordability and Stewardship

Since 1987, VHCB has helped community-based nonprofits develop 9400 permanently affordable homes. Permanent affordability means that homes will continue to be occupied by lower income households at a cost they can afford. Tenants rent homes that are owned and operated by nonprofit corporations that agree to hold this real estate to provide affordable shelter. The buyers of owner-occupied homes assisted by VHCB sign housing subsidy covenants or ground leases held by a community land trust ("CLT") or public agency. These recorded legal documents ensure that resale prices are kept affordable for a targeted class of future owners, typically households whose income is below 80 percent of area median income. In their stewardship of these homes, CLTs provide resources, training, and support to buyers so that they will be successful as homeowners. Later, at resale, CLTs assist these owners in selling their homes to the next income-eligible buyers.

Rationale for Preserving Affordability

Vermont's policy of permanent affordability is based on subsidy retention, reflecting a policy decision that public investment in affordable housing should neither be lost nor used to displace people.[5] The policy applies to single family homes, condominiums, cooperatives, rentals, transitional housing, and emergency shelters so that today's investment will provide a long-term social and financial return. Accepted by Vermont legislatures and governors for 25 years, the rationale is simply that it is a prudent public investment to provide grant funds once and to earn an ongoing, permanent social return by locking in affordability. Community-based nonprofits are deserving of state support, within this rationale, because they serve as the long-term stewards of this investment. Also, if publicly funded housing is built within city, town, and village centers, it should result in a measurable community gain. Housing construction is a catalyst for economic development, community reinvestment, revitalization, responsible growth, and energy conservation. By directing new housing away from farm and forest land, VHCB also furthers the state's commitment to conservation, protecting the rural landscape and natural world for agriculture, forestry, recreation, tourism, historic preservation, health, and bio-diversity.

An investment in permanently affordable homes also illustrates that a one-time expenditure will ensure their availability to future occupants for a long time. This is also a very efficient use of public funds. When the Housing and Conservation Coalition first proposed permanent protection for homes and conservation lands to the Legislature, fiscal conservatives were impressed by the promise of investing in a CLT home and watching that investment help future generations of homeowners, without additional subsidies. And though development of multifamily housing may be more expensive and less understood, legislators also understood that rental units would be owned and managed by nonprofits and agreed that this was an important and efficient use of public funds.

Mechanisms Used to Preserve Affordability

To create initial affordability, VHCB and its community partners use a financing package that maximizes grants (equity), minimizes loan repayment (debt), and mandates reserve funds for operating cost increases and anticipated capital needs. To maintain continuing affordability, the homes are restricted by recorded housing subsidy covenants and by ground leases that tie rents to project costs in tenant-occupied housing and place resale price restrictions on owner-occupied homes. In theory and practice, these legal restrictions perpetuate housing affordability for a targeted class of income-eligible occupants for years to come. For resale-restricted, owner-occupied homes in Vermont, ground leases and housing subsidy covenants, both of which limit the homes' resale price, are equally valid and enforceable.[6] Even with clear and enforceable legal documents, however, there is recognition in Vermont that effective and sustainable stewardship is the key to success. An adequately staffed entity must stand behind the housing long after it is first rented or sold, performing the duties of stewardship.

The Problem of Perpetuity

Woody Allen is reputed to have said, "Perpetuity is a long time, especially near the end." The stewardship of permanently affordable homes is a big responsibility. It presents three challenges: affordability, durability, and sustainability. Though separate, these challenges are interconnected; they are based upon a common goal of sustaining people and communities. My colleague at VHCB, Gus Seelig, calls this work a "Conspiracy of Good Will,"[7] saying that the greatest value of these homes is the people they shelter and the events that will define their lives while residing within these walls. Affordability, durability, and sustainability are like a three-leaf red clover: separate parts, joined as a whole, sustaining people, communities, and land.

The Challenge of Affordability

Given the need to maintain affordability controls over a long period of time, two different enforcing entities, VHCB and its nonprofit partners, must be prepared for regular, meaningful communication about the financial and structural vitality of the homes. Each nonprofit and VHCB must collaborate to find solutions that balance the financial health of the project with the need for rents and resale prices to be as low as possible. So, the relationship between VHCB and a nonprofit's staff needs to be both professional and supportive. This may be a new role for some public funders to play but, given the realities of affordable housing development and property management, it is essential. Specifically, a public or quasipublic agency like VHCB is not only a funder and regulator. It is also a collaborative problem solver, bringing its own resources and expertise to bear on problems that threaten the affordability, safety, or viability of the housing which the agency has helped to create.

Here is an example of VHCB behaving in precisely this way. In Summer 2008, nonprofit owners of multifamily rental housing faced a huge increase in the cost of heating fuel oil for the coming winter.[8] They were entitled to add an oil surcharge to their tenant rents under the terms of VHCB's housing subsidy covenant, but rent increases would have threatened some tenants with displacement, especially during a period of economic recession. So, given the volatility and unpredictability of fuel oil prices and the negative impact of rent increases on thousands of tenants, VHCB began collaborating with the nonprofits to solve the problem together: conducting a comprehensive analysis of the fuel oil problem and developing a set of proposals to address it. Such collaboration is made possible by VHCB's positive relationship with the nonprofit housing delivery system, established over many years. It is necessary because of VHCB's duty to monitor rents, to improve housing conditions, to maintain affordability and to protect people from displacement.

The Challenge of Durability

Buildings experience ordinary wear and tear. They deteriorate without regular repair and periodic replacement of major systems. We need to care for these structural assets by prudent management, maintenance, and capital investment. Given the need to replace roofs, to upgrade heating and cooling systems, and to repair and replace floors, walls, fixtures, and appliances, managers need not only to pay annual operating costs; they must also complete needs assessments and set aside funds for current maintenance and future capital expenditures. Even for single-family homes, the homeownership centers operated by Vermont's nonprofits need to educate first-time buyers that ownership is much more than principle, interest, taxes, and insurance. Yes, you *do* need to pay the mortgage! But you must also maintain the structure you call "home" in order to keep it safe, sanitary, and warm. For rental properties and single-family homes alike, we need to plan for future capital investment.

Economic recession, volatile energy prices, and a new awareness of the importance of residential energy efficiency investments present a rare opportunity for CLTs and other nonprofit housing developers to provide a real service for their homeowners. If CLTs take this opportunity to reduce the carbon footprint and annual operating cost of CLT homes, it will enhance permanent affordability and provide dramatic, long-term benefits for the residents. Now is the time to embrace green building and rehabilitation standards, to encourage mortgage lenders to use energy-efficient mortgages, and to urge policymakers to invest in permanent affordability by improving the energy efficiency and environmental health of our residential buildings. As part of the CLT homeowner education process, moreover, prospective buyers should be educated about ways to reduce their carbon footprint, cut energy costs, and increase the health and safety of their homes. Such action will protect the public's investment while promoting healthy people, buildings, and communities through education and stewardship.

We have learned in Vermont that a comprehensive evaluation of every building's energy and capital needs is critical to the long-term success of publicly funded rentals, cooperatives, and condominiums. This evaluation allows the nonprofit's management team to estimate the annual operating expenses and to accumulate reserve accounts large enough to cover future capital expenditures. Since most projects cannot afford to fully capitalize reserve accounts at the time of initial acquisition or rehabilitation, reserves must be built up month by month. Without these reserves, future capital needs may push rents and condominium association fees beyond affordability. Planning for capital needs is also critical to the comfort, security, and energy efficiency of housing. To assist in this latter effort, VHCB's AmeriCorps program[9] has hired a member to work with tenants all over the state to develop and to implement energy saving measures so that rent increases can be held to a minimum and tenants can use less energy to stay warm this winter. For homeowners, successful planning for a house's energy and capital needs is a team effort. It starts at the homebuyer education workshops, continues through the mortgage qualification process, and continues postclosing. It is necessary for all parties (homeowner, nonprofit sponsor, and mortgage lender) to contribute to this effort but much is gained from careful planning at the time of purchase. When helping homebuyers to make the transition from renter to borrower, the nonprofit sponsor must help newly minted homeowners to understand the business and maintenance side of homeownership. This will help the nonprofit to perform its own duties as steward of the public's investment, assuring the comfort, safety, privacy, and affordability of the homes under its care.[10]

The Challenge of Sustainability

One lesson that proponents of permanent housing affordability could learn from their colleagues in the land conservation movement is the need to establish effective stewardship of perpetual legal obligations when we purchase or conserve the asset.[11] This means developing a financially viable residential project and ensuring that professional, nonprofit stewardship activities can be sustained over time as an independent and self-sustaining business activity. Where easements and covenants are coheld by governmental entities, the long-term success of a stewardship program depends on having a dependable, local nonprofit partner with professional staff and access to community resources. In fact, given valid concerns about the ability of public agencies to monitor and enforce easements or covenants in perpetuity, states would be well advised to consider investment in nonprofit or community-based stewardship. Vermont has taken this approach in providing for the stewardship of thousands of homes created through VHCB.

In order to protect our investment in affordable housing, VHCB has long accepted the fact that we need to support and enhance the organizational capacity of nonprofits to work with residents, to provide high quality property management, to promote sound maintenance and capital investment, and to maintain affordability. Regardless of the contractual mechanism chosen, the lights must be on in the stewardship office and qualified staff must be paid to complete this work.[12] When states promote permanently affordable housing, states must also provide the resources required to ensure that nonprofit stewards are financially viable, fiscally responsible, and programmatically responsive to human needs. Again, if the responsibilities of stewardship are viewed and treated as a *partnership* between public agencies and private nonprofits with shared but realistic goals, then ongoing technical and financial support from the state for the nonprofit's operations must be seen as an integral component of success.

Addressing the Problem of Perpetuity in Vermont

We have been gaining valuable experience addressing all three of these challenges in Vermont, where permanent affordability has long been a benchmark of the state's housing policy. Vermont has been a leader in promoting permanent affordability and in establishing the legal basis for housing subsidy covenants and ground leases. Affordability restrictions are never "self-enforcing." Instead, community-based, nonprofit stewards are tapped to enforce and monitor resale controls, in collaboration with VHCB's staff. The main job of monitoring and enforcing affordability provisions is done by people working at the community level. Vermont's former governor, Howard Dean, often said that VHCB represented the ideal role that state government should play: ask a community to identify its most important affordable housing and community development projects and then provide the resources to the community to achieve success.

Stewardship and Enforcement of Covenants
Since its inception, the CLT movement in the United States has taken very seriously the potential for legal challenges to perpetual affordability. CLTs have been fortunate to have creative and skilled lawyers drafting legal documents that might withstand any such challenge. In Vermont, the longevity or enforceability of the CLT's resale restrictions have not been challenged.[13] There have been no court decisions on CLT ground leases or covenants. There are now about 900 permanently affordable, owner-occupied homes in Vermont, most of them under the stewardship of a local CLT. A recent review by VHCB found that, between 1988 and 2007, only 32 homes had been released from a CLT's resale restrictions. These homes were sold at market value because of financial problems following mortgage default, structural problems, serious property damage, or fire. They were removed from a CLT's portfolio only after the CLT consulted with VHCB and VHCB decided not to invest additional public funds to rehabilitate them. It is very important to use good clear and enforceable legal documents, therefore, but it is equally important to complete thorough building inspections, to select buyers and renters carefully, to help residents solve financial problems, and to be an active community-based steward standing behind the deal.

CLT Training, Capital Needs, and Recapitalization of Assisted Buildings

All buildings have a useful life that is shorter than perpetuity. So, when nonprofits construct or buy and rehabilitate rental property, financing should include adequate revenue to cover immediate operating costs as well as long-term capital needs. When CLTs help first-time buyers to purchase a home, CLTs in Vermont now underwrite both the buyers and the building to assure payment of the mortgage, taxes, and insurance. They also invest in meeting the long-term capital needs and energy costs of the home. This is one of the most important lessons that Vermonters have learned since the Burlington Community Land Trust launched the first resale-restricted homeownership program with city funds in 1984. CLTs now plan for future capital needs and energy efficiency when designing and constructing owner-occupied homes.

Fair and Equitable Property Taxation

Across the country, many CLT homeowners are receiving property tax bills which are based on the fair market value of their homes, with no consideration for the resale restrictions that encumber their homes. In 2005, VHCB and its CLT partners identified property taxation of owner-occupied single-family homes with resale restrictions as an issue that needed to be addressed, either by the Tax Department or by the State Legislature. After Burlington changed its method of valuing resale-restricted homes in 2006, CLTs proposed to the state's Tax Department that it form a committee to find an administrative solution to the disparity in methods used by Vermont towns to calculate listed value for owner-occupied homes with resale restrictions. The committee met a number of times in the Spring 2007 and provided valuable input to the Department, during multiple drafts of an Advisory Bulletin. In November 2008, the Vermont Tax Department finally issued its Memorandum. Municipalities were advised that (1) they must use a uniform approach to establish the listed value of owner-occupied, single family homes that are subject to resale restrictions contained in a housing subsidy covenant or ground lease; and (2) the listed value of these homes must be based on their *restricted* value. This means that all CLT homeowners in Vermont may eventually have their homes assessed in a fair fashion that is consistent across the state. This new approach took effect on April 1, 2009.

Stewardship and Sustainability Are Good Investments

VHCB has helped to create a statewide delivery system for the conservation of land and the development of affordable housing.[14] With respect to housing, VHCB helped bring into being a statewide system of nonprofit, community-based organizations with the capacity to develop, manage, and steward homes along a continuum from emergency shelters to resale-restricted homeownership units. Many of these nonprofits are CLTs. By providing annual organizational grants to nonprofits, VHCB also helps to sustain this delivery system. As a companion to these capacity grants, VHCB provides support and training for its nonprofit partners on board training, leadership development, fundraising, community relations, financial systems, and Executive Director transitions. VHCB also stands behind its nonprofit partners, especially in times of Executive Director turnover or organizational difficulties. In a worst-case scenario, should a nonprofit no longer be able to perform its duties (or entirely disappears), the covenant recorded against assisted properties would allow VHCB to assume control of these assets. So far, this has not been necessary.

VHCB understands that stewardship is worth paying for, protecting the investment that Vermonters have made in every permanently affordably priced home built or rehabilitated with public dollars, and that the success of its housing program depends on having healthy nonprofit partners. Stewardship has costs that the state should be willing to cover. Neglecting stewardship is a recipe for allowing the housing gains made by public policy and public investment to erode over time, costing the public far more in the long run.

Conclusion

With the passage of the Housing and Conservation Trust Fund Act in 1987, Vermont embarked upon a challenging journey of investing public funds in creating permanently affordable homes and sustaining a statewide nonprofit housing delivery system. Twenty-three years later, there continues to be strong support for the VHCB's mission among Vermonters.[15] The promise of perpetuity continues to burn brightly among housing advocates and providers of affordable housing, as well as land conservationists. And fiscal conservatives have been impressed by the promise and performance of investing in affordably priced homes and watching that state investment continue to help successive generations of homeowners, without the need for additional subsidies.

As Vermont now struggles with the worst economic recession in decades, new revenues for affordable housing and land conservation are in short supply. Nevertheless, the Vermont Housing and Conservation Board and Vermont's two-decade experiment with perpetuity still garner wide support. Vermonters have come to accept that permanent affordability and the stewardship of publicly funded, privately owned housing are essential to maintaining the health, vitality, diversity, and affordability of their communities.[16] Similarly, conserving farmland and forest land, preserving the working landscape, and protecting historic buildings and cultural resources are seen as essential to maintaining much of what makes Vermont beautiful, livable, and unique. A key to VHCB's success has been a strong, harmonious marriage among all of these interests, joining those organizations and individuals who advocate for affordable housing and those who advocate for land conservation, farm preservation, and historic preservation. This marriage has already weathered many years of an overheated economy, where building homes and buying lands with public funds were sometimes challenged for "costing too much." It will surely weather the current economic downturn, where public investment in housing and conservation are sometimes challenged for "being unnecessary" now that speculative pressures have eased.

Having survived the boom, Vermont's longtime commitment to perpetuity will survive the bust as well.

NOTES

1. Vermont Housing and Conservation Trust Fund Act, 10 VSA 301-325a (June 11, 1987) ("Act"). For more information about VHCB, visit www.vhcb.org.

2. Conservation and historic preservation easements are filed in the land records and require the owner to limit development on farmland or maintain historic features of a building forever. Easements are held and enforced by nonprofit stewardship partners with monitoring and enforcement costs funded by stewardship endowment funds and charitable donations.

3. In Vermont, public and private funders may use deed restrictions called "housing subsidy covenants." Authorized under state law (27 VSA 610), these covenants may be perpetual in duration.

4. In 1987, the Legislature created VHCB and appropriated $3,000,000 for housing and conservation projects. In 1988, the Legislature created a dedicated funding source so that 50 percent of the revenues generated by the real estate transfer tax are provided to VHCB annually. And, on a one-time basis, VHCB received $20,000,000 of a general fund surplus.

5. Section 322(a)(5) of the Act prohibits displacement of lower income Vermonters.

6. If CLTs decide to use deed restrictions rather than ground leases to control resale of homes, it is important that they be consistent with state law to overcome common law rules that discouraged long term ownership of land. Some states, including Vermont and Massachusetts, have passed laws which permit CLTs to use deed restrictions to ensure permanent affordability.

7. Also the title that Darby Bradley and I chose when we wrote a short history of VHCB. See Libby & Bradley, "VHCB, A Conspiracy of Good Will Among Land Trusts and Housing Trusts," *Property and Values,* Island Press, 2000. http://www.vhcb.org/pdfs/propertyvalues.pdf ("Libby/Bradley Chapter")

8. In August 2008, industry analysts were predicting that fuel oil would sell for $4.50 a gallon in the winter of 2008–2009 while many owners had paid $2.35 a gallon in the previous two winters.

9. The Vermont Community Stewardship Program (VCSP) is a statewide AmeriCorps project of VHCB. VCSP places AmeriCorps members in sponsoring nonprofit affordable housing and land conservation organizations around the state. http://www.vhcb.org/vcsp.html.

10. Given the dramatic increase in heating oil costs, all potential buyers should consider hiring a qualified professional to conduct an energy audit of the home. Such an audit yields important information about the heating, plumbing, and ventilation systems—all of which may need to be replaced or repaired, making the house safer and more comfortable.

11. Established conservation organizations comply with national standards on land stewardship established by the Land Trust Alliance. See 2004 Revisions of LTA Standards and Practices, Land Trust Alliance, Washington, DC. Standard 11 requires conservation easement stewards to fund monitoring and enforcement at the time of conservation and most do so by contributing to stewardship endowment accounts at the time of purchase.

12. Some conservation groups like the Upper Valley Land Trust in NH & VT rely heavily on volunteer land stewards. However, the training and organization of volunteers requires paid staff to assure that the organization is fulfilling its legal responsibilities.

Furthermore, though volunteers may be good at monitoring conservation easements, they may not be effective in affordable multifamily housing management, maintenance, and stewardship.

13. A few homeowners have claimed that they did not receive good information about the resale restrictions and asked to be allowed to sell for market value; only in one case did the CLT agree and releasing the condominium in return for repayment of the subsidy.

14. The Housing and Conservation Trust Fund Act provides, "In the best interests of all of its citizens and in order to improve the quality of life for Vermonters and to maintain for the benefit of future generations the essential characteristics of the Vermont countryside, Vermont should encourage and assist in creating affordable housing and in preserving the state's agricultural land, historic properties, important natural areas and recreational lands."

15. For more on the Vermont Housing and Conservation Coalition, see James Libby & Darby Bradley, "VHCB, A Conspiracy of Good Will Among Land Trusts and Housing Trusts," pp. 259–281 in Charles Geisler and Gail Daneker (eds.), *Property and Values*. Washington, DC: Island Press, 2000. http://www.vhcb.org/pdfs/propertyvalues.pdf.

16. In 2007, VHCB was awarded the U.S. Environmental Protection Agency's National Award for Smart Growth Achievement. The citation read in part:

> The State of Vermont promotes compact settlements surrounded by rural countryside. VHCB supports this goal by funding affordable housing development in existing population centers and by preserving historic resources, farmland, forests and public access to recreational lands. The agency pursues affordable housing, land conservation and historic preservation initiatives under a single, unique, synergistic program, which balances priorities. . . . These investments have created pedestrian-friendly, walkable communities while limiting the impacts on valuable open spaces.

Homes That Last

The Case for Counter-Cyclical Stewardship

John Emmeus Davis
(2008)

Until this year's mortgage meltdown, the preservation of affordable housing was defined mostly in terms of rentals. How do we preserve the affordability and quality of an aging rental stock? How do we prevent the displacement of low-income renters when the real estate market is hot? How do we discourage deferred maintenance when the market is cold? How do we save millions of units of federally subsidized rental housing as the contractual controls over how they are priced and who they may serve begin to lapse?

These remain serious concerns. The pressing problems of renters do not go away simply because public attention is suddenly focused on the frightening spike in foreclosures now occurring among homeowners. This latest housing crisis is a stunning reminder, however, that policies and programs to preserve affordability cannot be aimed at rental housing alone. Rentals are not the only homes that can be lost.

Affordability can slip away, housing quality can erode, and security of tenure can tragically disappear in owner-occupied housing as well, especially at the top and bottom of the business cycle. That is when persons of modest means are endangered the most, both those who are striving to *become* homeowners and those who are struggling to *remain* homeowners. That is when stewardship is needed the most: moderating prices that push housing out of reach; promoting repairs that keep housing sound; and managing risks that pry housing out of the tenuous grasp of less affluent homeowners in times of crisis.

Most of our nation's efforts to boost lower-income households into the ranks of first-time homeowners have stubbornly ignored these dangers and risks. Policymakers have continued to design homeownership programs for the sunny middle of the business cycle, assuming that affordability, quality, and security would take care of themselves. Of the storms that rage among the peaks and valleys of a real-world economy more prone to fluctuation than stability, there has been little acknowledgement—and even less accommodation.

That has been a glaring failure of public policy. Whenever public dollars or public powers are used to expand the supply of affordably priced, owner-occupied housing, more must be done to preserve these homes, especially when the economy is at its hottest—or coldest. More must be done to ensure that the public's investment remains in these homes, neither immediately removed at resale nor gradually depleted through deferred maintenance. More must be done to ensure that lower-income families can stay in their homes, neither nudged out by rising costs nor forced out by foreclosure. Counter-cyclical stewardship is how this is done. It is the only way to create homes that last.

Homes at Loss: The Cyclical Threats to Affordable Housing

Since the early 1980s, affordable housing in the United States has been buffeted by one crisis after another, roughly tracking the ups and downs of the business cycle. During periods of rapid economic growth, the price of renting or buying a home has usually risen far faster than the annual earnings of low-income and moderate-income households, producing a *crisis of housing affordability,* where persons of modest means are pushed out of the market or forced to skimp on other necessities to house themselves.

The downside of the business cycle has regularly and predictably brought a different set of problems. During periods of rapid economic decline, low- and moderate-income households are often hit with a *crisis of housing quality.* Less money flows into the construction of new housing and the rehabilitation and repair of existing housing. Builders break ground or break plaster on fewer units. They make less of an investment in the units on which they do work, since there is little incentive during lean economic times to employ more durable materials or to install more efficient or longer-lasting systems. As for lower-income homeowners who already occupy an aging house, townhouse, or condominium, the highest incentive in a bad economy is to invest nothing at all, reducing routine maintenance, foregoing major repairs, and putting off the replacement of major systems.

A *crisis of housing security,* by contrast, can happen at either end of the business cycle. Economic downturns are usually accompanied by rising unemployment, stagnant wages, and falling financial security for households on the bottom half of the income ladder. Until recently, this has seldom been accompanied by falling prices for housing. Real estate has historically been the exception to the rule that big-ticket items decline in price during a recession. Housing prices have often continued to climb even during downturns, although more slowly than during booms. When wages fall but prices do not, lower-income people have a harder time paying their rents or meeting their mortgage payments. This can loosen their hold on the housing that is theirs.

When prices fall along with wages, as they have during the current foreclosure crisis, the housing security of many more homeowners is put at risk. The profligate use of adjustable-rate mortgages, shared appreciation mortgages, and other creative schemes for financing high-priced homes gave many more households a personal stake in what

President Bush was fond of calling the "ownership society." But when creative financing (or predatory lending) collided with a sudden deflation in housing values, millions of homeowners were left owing more on their mortgages than their homes were worth. With no safety net to catch them as a faltering economy sent their real estate fortunes into free fall, many homeowners have faced individually a no-win choice between continuing to make payments on devalued homes or to default on overpriced mortgages. They have come belatedly to realize that the "ownership society," in a time of crisis, actually means "if you own it, you are on your own."

On the other side of the business cycle, the security of lower-income homeowners can also be undermined by economic prosperity. If homeowners are locked into an adjustable-rate mortgage that is tied to an economic indicator like the CPI, if they live in a state with no property tax protections for elderly and lower-income homeowners on fixed incomes, or if their utility costs soar far beyond their ability to pay, their homes can steadily become less and less affordable during good economic times. Tenure can become less secure.

Taking precautions to cope with such cyclical crises, public policy began long ago making corrections in the way that rental housing is structured and operated. As a result, we have gradually created an expanding stock of publicly assisted, privately owned rental housing with three protective features:

- affordability is perpetuated for many years, either through the nonprofit ownership of rental housing or through long-term regulatory agreements between public agencies and private landlords by which rent increases are moderated and income-eligibility is maintained;
- the safety, soundness, and condition of rental housing is preserved through the imposition of housing quality standards and through mandated maintenance and replacement reserves; and
- security of tenure is enhanced by careful screening of prospective tenants, by requirements for just cause eviction, by vacancy reserves that insulate owners against financial hazard if tenants default, and by periodic, third-party review of the records and practices of private landlords receiving public money to provide affordably priced rentals for lower-income people.

While protections like these have become standard practice in the rental sector, homeownership programs have been slow to follow suit. We have continued to lavish public resources on helping lower-income households to attain homeownership with little regard for what happens to these homes *after* they are purchased. This hands-off approach may be appropriate in places with stable real estate markets and in periods of gradual economic growth. Such places and periods are hardly the norm, however, even though most of our homeownership assistance programs have been designed as if they were. A better design is needed, one that weaves into the programs and tenures of publicly assisted homeownership some of the same protections for housing affordability, quality, and security that have long been a part of publicly assisted rentals. Homes that last are those that are wrapped in the durable garment of stewardship.

Homes That Last: The Stewardship of Homeownership

Although rarely a component of conventional programs for helping lower-income households gain access to market-priced homes, stewardship has long been a standard feature of shared-equity homeownership, a sector that includes community land trusts (CLTs), limited-equity cooperatives (LECs), and resale-restricted houses and condominiums with affordability covenants lasting many years. Because many of the rights, responsibilities, risks, and rewards of homeownership are shared between the occupants and sponsors of this housing, homeowners are not forced to go it alone. There is an organizational entity that stands behind these homes long after they are sold, performing various duties of stewardship.

What are these duties? They are defined, in large measure, by the cyclical dangers already described. Stewardship preserves the affordability of owner-occupied housing at the top of the business cycle. It promotes the durability and maintains the condition of owner-occupied housing at the bottom of the business cycle. It manages risks, protecting security of tenure at both ends of the business cycle. Any organization that would serve as the long-term steward for shared-equity homes must have the commitment and capacity to perform all of these duties (Table 1).

Responsibility for stewardship is sometimes retained by the governmental agency that provided funding for the housing's initial development or that required inclusion of affordably priced homes as a condition of the municipality's permission to build. The agency serves, in effect, as the long-term steward for the resale-restricted, owner-occupied housing it helped to create. Increasingly, this responsibility is being delegated to a nonprofit organization that performs these duties on the public's behalf. This may be a community development corporation that has been building or rehabilitating affordably priced homes for many years, which is now asked to assume the duties and to master the details of stewardship. Alternatively, it may be a community land trust or a limited-equity cooperative that has espoused and practiced the stewardship of owner-occupied housing from the very beginning. Indeed, in these models, stewardship is intrinsic to the way their housing is owned and operated. It is what they do best.

Regardless of whether the duties of stewardship are assigned to an external entity or are embedded in an organization's internal structure, they must be performed by *someone* over a long period. These duties are not self-enforcing. They do not get done unless someone is always present and adequately staffed to carry them out—and gets paid to do so.

There must be a dependable way to cover the steward's costs. The question is: Who should pay? The obvious answer would seem to be that whoever benefits the most

TABLE 1: The Stewardship of Homeownership	
Major Goals of Stewardship	**Minimal Duties of Stewardship**
Preserving housing affordability	• Maintain a waiting list of prospective buyers for the purchase of resale-restricted homes that are offered for sale • Certify the income-eligibility of prospective homebuyers • Regulate subletting • Inspect homes at time of resale • Calculate the formula-determined price at time of resale • Educate prospective buyers about special conditions on the use and resale of these homes • Oversee the transfer of homes, ensuring their resale to income-eligible buyers at affordable prices
Promoting housing quality	• Promote the installation of more durable materials and energy efficient systems • Prepare homebuyers for the maintenance responsibilities of homeownership • Inspect periodically the condition and repair of homes • Review proposed capital improvements • Oversee necessary rehabilitation before transfer • Maintain reserves for unexpected repairs and necessary replacements
Protecting housing security	• Screen and approve mortgages, preventing predatory lending • Review and approve refinancing of resale-restricted homes • Restrict the attachment of liens • Ensure adequate insurance coverage • Monitor the payment of property taxes • Secure equitable taxation of resale-restricted homes, preventing the displacement of homeowners too poor to pay taxes on real-estate profits they cannot claim as their own • Intervene to cure defaults and prevent foreclosures

from stewardship should pay most of its costs. This is not as simple as it seems, however, for the beneficiaries are multiple, including the private lenders, present homeowners, future homebuyers, and public funders of shared-equity housing. A case can be made for tapping any one of them to cover the costs of stewardship. In practice, the burden seldom falls solely upon a single beneficiary. Nor should it. All should pay their fair share, commensurate with the benefits received.

Private Lenders

The first beneficiaries of stewardship are the private, for-profit lenders who provide mortgage financing for owner-occupied housing. Stewardship is a credit enhancement that preserves the collateral, protects the investment, and reduces the risk of a for-profit financial institution. With stewardship in place, there is a third party standing behind the borrower, backstopping the deal: someone the mortgage lender can notify should a homeowner default; someone who can act swiftly to cure a default and prevent foreclosure. These are valuable services for which a private lender should arguably be expected to pay.

Long before the current mortgage crisis, there were in fact a number of private lenders that began treating stewardship as a credit enhancement—and began subsidizing part of its on-going costs. Some lenders, for example, have helped to subsidize the prepurchase costs of homebuyer counseling. Some have paid a per-capita fee to a nonprofit organization for every mortgage-ready household that is brought through their doors. In places where a CLT or other form of shared-equity homeownership is well established, there are also many examples of a mortgage lender offering a reduction in closing costs or a discount in mortgage rates in recognition of the enhanced security that a steward brings to the deal.

Although private lenders have so far not been asked to subsidize the postpurchase costs of stewardship, this is worth considering. A lender could make a front-end contribution to a maintenance or replacement reserve when closing on the mortgage for a shared-equity home. Alternatively, a steward could collect a back-end fee from lenders for every mortgage default it prevents from proceeding to foreclosure. With a foreclosure rate for its resale-restricted, owner-occupied homes that is many times *lower* than the current foreclosure rate in market-rate homes, CLTs in particular have begun making a compelling case for the cost-effectiveness of stewardship in helping a lender to avoid the losses that accompany most foreclosures. When a lender benefits so obviously from a steward's intervention, it is fair to ask the lender to cover a portion of the steward's costs.

Future Homebuyers

Another beneficiary of any stewardship regime that preserves the financial affordability and structural condition of owner-occupied housing is the next generation of homebuyers who are able to purchase these affordably priced, well-maintained homes. It is primarily for them, it may be argued, that stewardship is put in place. Because they reap most of stewardship's benefits, it is fair to charge them for much of its costs.

This is how a growing number of CLTs, LECs, and deed-restricted houses and condominiums cover a portion of their operating costs. At the time of resale, the steward repurchases the shared-equity home for a below-market price, determined by a formula embedded in the home's ground lease, share certificate, or deed covenant. Depending on the spread between the formula price for which the home is repurchased by the steward and the resale price that another lower-income homebuyer could afford, the steward may be able to add a "transfer fee" to the price charged to the next buyer without compromising the home's affordability. These fees are either used to cover a portion of the steward's direct costs of monitoring and managing its portfolio of shared-equity homes or they are deposited into a "stewardship fund" and used for repairs and replacements as necessary. By paying a slightly higher purchase price, the next generation of homebuyers covers some of the costs that have made their homes affordable and kept their homes in good repair.

Present Homeowners

The present generation of homeowners is also a beneficiary of stewardship. Aside from the obvious boon of being able to acquire a high-value home for a reduced price because of public and private subsidies the steward has brought to the deal, the owner-occupants of shared-equity homes are typically recipients of other services before and after the home's purchase. Most stewards provide homebuyer counseling, referrals to favorable financing, screening against predatory lenders, and training and support for on-going repairs. Nearly all stewards regulate capital improvements, require insurance coverage, and control the refinancing of shared-equity homes. Some operate revolving loan funds that lower-income homeowners can access for repairs, system replacements, or rehabilitation. Most intervene to cure defaults and prevent foreclosures in times of crisis.

Quite often, homeowners help to pay for these services, directly or indirectly. After purchasing a shared-equity home, they may be charged a monthly "stewardship fee," whether as an add-on to their ground rent (in a CLT), as a component of their carrying charge (in an LEC), or as part of their homeowner association fee (in a deed-restricted house or condo), that pays a portion of the steward's operating costs or capitalizes a reserve for maintenance and replacement. Alternately, at the time of purchasing a shared-equity home, these new homeowners may be required to take out a mortgage for slightly more than the home's initial purchase price in order to capitalize a maintenance and replacement reserve for their new home. Some stewards collect back-end fees when shared-equity homes resell, charging the seller for any extraordinary costs the steward has incurred in intervening to prevent a foreclosure or in refurbishing a poorly maintained home before it is resold to another lower-income household.

Public Funders

Finally, it may be argued that the benefits of stewardship accrue most abundantly to the public at large. Covering its costs, therefore, should come largely from public coffers. Just as government pays for the construction and maintenance of roads, schools, and other essential infrastructure and services—including the cost of developing affordable housing—government should pay the cost of stewarding affordable housing as a *public* good.

Some state and local governments have, in fact, begun making contributions to stewardship, using three different strategies.

First, governmental agencies have either paid their employees to perform the duties of stewardship or they have assigned that task to a community land trust, a community development corporation, or some other nonprofit, paying them an annual fee to monitor and manage resale-restricted homes.

Second, as a hedge against the possibility of deferred maintenance in the future, there have been instances of a governmental agency endowing a maintenance or replacement reserve at closing for each resale-restricted, owner-occupied home assisted with public funds.

Third, to reduce the threat of lower-income households being displaced from their resale-restricted homes as a result of rising property taxes, a number of state and local governments have adopted a more equitable approach to valuing shared-equity homes. They are assessed and taxed on the basis of the contractual cap that is placed on their resale prices, not on their "highest and best" market value. The ongoing affordability of these resale-restricted homes is protected because lower-income homeowners are not forced to pay taxes on real estate profits they can never reap.

Beyond these few helpful examples, however, public funders have usually been far more willing to subsidize the front-end costs of development than the back-end costs of stewardship. Their reluctance may melt away in the next few years, however, as the bills come due for the government's bailout of Fannie Mae, Freddie Mac, and other troubled financial institutions that are saddled with millions of nonperforming mortgages. Paying for stewardship is going to look increasingly like a bargain, when seen in light of the public's cost of repairing the damage that more attention to stewardship might have helped to avert.

A New Way Home: Toward a Policy of Counter-Cyclical Stewardship

Although stewardship has been slow in coming to programs designed to expand homeownership for persons of modest means, there are signs this may be changing. Faced with soaring real estate prices in some markets and collapsing real estate values in others, policymakers have begun to embrace new models of tenure that protect the affordability, quality, and security of owner-occupied housing *after* its sale. The stewardship of homeownership has been gaining ground as a policy priority.

Stewardship means different things to different people, however. The principal policy and programmatic divide has been between those who focus on preserving the *money* that is poured into subsidizing homeownership versus those who focus on preserving the *housing* such public largess has helped to create. "Dollars that last" or "homes that last" becomes the fundamental choice once stewardship moves to the fore.

Only the latter is fully capable of countering the triple threat that looms most ominously when real estate markets are very hot or very cold. Dollars that last, implemented through various mechanisms for recapturing the public's investment in owner-occupied housing when homes resell, do nothing to preserve the affordability of homes at the top of the business cycle. These homes return to the market at resale, moving beyond the reach of lower-income homebuyers as housing prices rise at a faster rate than household earnings. Mixed-income projects gradually shed their lower-priced units. Mixed-income neighborhoods eventually lose their lower-income homeowners.

At the bottom of the business cycle, affordably priced homes and lower-income homeowners may fare even worse. Recapture programs make no provision for protecting either the quality of owner-occupied housing or the security of lower-income homeowners. Government gets back the dollars it invested, but nothing is done to promote good maintenance when times are bad. Nor is anything done to prevent foreclosures when financially stressed homeowners can no longer make mortgage payments on properties that may have dropped in value.

On the steeper slope of economic expansion and on the slippery slope of economic decline, a higher standard of stewardship is needed. It is not enough to recapture public dollars when assisted homes are resold. It is not enough to reinvest recaptured dollars in helping lower-income households to enter the homeownership market. The homes themselves must be preserved. It is poor public policy when dollars are saved but homes are lost.

A better policy is needed: one that anticipates dangers that predictably lurk in an economic climate less prone to sun than to rain; one that takes precautions that prudently back the owner-occupied housing that public agencies and their private partners have worked so hard to create. Homes can be made to last, but they must be designed for days that are stormy, not only for days that are fair.

SELECTED BIBLIOGRAPHY

Abromowitz, David M. 1991. An essay on community land trusts: Towards permanently affordable housing. *Mississippi Law Journal* 61:663–682.

———. 1992. Long-term affordability, community land trusts and ground leases. *ABA Journal of Affordable Housing & Community Development Law* 1(2):5–6, 17.

———. 2000. An essay on community land trusts: Toward permanently affordable housing. In *Property and values*, ed. Charles Geisler and Gail Daneker, 213–231. Washington, DC: Island Press.

———. 2008. *Addressing foreclosures: A great American dream neighborhood stabilization plan*. Washington, DC: Center for American Progress.

Abromowitz, David M., and Rick Jacobus. 2010. *A path to homeownership: building a more sustainable strategy for expanding homeownership*. Washington, DC: Center for American Progress.

Abromowitz, David, and Roz Greenstein. 2008. A foreclosure-free option. *Boston Globe*, January 23.

Abromowitz, David, and Kirby White. 2006. Deed restrictions and community land trust ground leases: Two methods of establishing affordable homeownership restrictions. *Housing News Network, Journal of the Florida Housing Coalition* 22 (May):7–10, 24.

Angotti, Thomas. 2007. Community land trusts and low-income multifamily rental housing. Working paper. Cambridge, MA: Lincoln Institute of Land Policy.

Apgar, William. 2004. Rethinking rental housing: Expanding the ability of rental housing to serve as a pathway to economic and social opportunity. Working Paper Series, WO4–11. Cambridge, MA: Joint Center for Housing Studies, Harvard University.

Baker, A. 1992. This land is not for sale. *Social Policy* 22(4):24–35.

Baldassari, Carol. 1988. *A catalogue of methods for preserving affordable housing*. Boston: Metropolitan Planning Council.

———. 1989. *Limited equity homeownership: Programs that create and protect affordable housing*. Boston: Metropolitan Planning Council.

Barnes, Peter. 2004. Sharing the wealth of the commons. *Dollars & Sense*, no. 256.

———. 2006. Trusteeship of creation. In *Capitalism 3.0: A guide to reclaiming the commons*, chapter 6. San Francisco: Berrett-Koehler Publishers.

Bassett, Ellen M. 2005. Tinkering with tenure: The planning implications of the community land trust experiment in Voi, Kenya. *Habitat International* 29:375–398.

Bassett, Ellen M., and Harvey M. Jacobs. 1997. Community-based tenure reform in urban Africa: The community land trust experiment in Voi, Kenya. *Land Use Policy* 14(3):215–229.

Bergeron, Emily. 2006. Community land trusts: Using historic preservation for affordable housing in the Florida Keys. In *Contributions of historic preservation to the quality of life in Florida*, ed. Timothy McLendon et al., chapter 7. Gainesville: Florida Department of State, Division of Historical Resources, Bureau of Historic Preservation.

Blackmore, John. 1978. Community trusts offer a hopeful way back to the land. *Smithsonian* 9 (June).

Borsodi, Ralph. 1968. The possessional problem. In *Seventeen problems of man and society*. Anand, India: Charotar Book Stall. Repr. in *Green Revolution*, 1978; ed. and rev. by Gordon Lameyer and Lydia Ratcliff.

———. 1974. Plowboy interview: Dr. Ralph Borsodi. *Mother Earth News*, no. 26 (March/April).

Boucher, Norman. 1990. The death and life of Dudley: A lesson in urban economics. *Boston Globe Magazine,* April 18.

Bourassa, Steven C. 2006. The community land trust as a highway environmental impact mitigation tool. *Journal of Urban Affairs* 28. Available as Working paper WP05SB1, Lincoln Institute of Land Policy, http://www.lincolninst.edu/pubs/pub-detail.asp?id=1072.

———. 2006. Community land trusts and housing affordability. In *Land policies and their outcomes*, ed. Gregory K. Ingram and Yu-Hung Hong, 331–366. Cambridge, MA: Lincoln Institute of Land Policy.

Briechle, Kendra J. 2006. OPAL Commons and Bonnie Brae. In *Conservation-based affordable housing*, 79–81. Arlington, VA: Conservation Fund.

Burns, Heather. 2007. Retention or recapture: A comparison of two Seattle first-time homebuyer subsidy programs. Unpublished MPA thesis, Evans School of Public Affairs, University of Washington.

Campbell, Marcia Caton, and Danielle A. Salus. 2003. Community and conservation land trusts as unlikely partners? The case of Troy Gardens, Madison, Wisconsin. *Land Use Policy* 20:169–180.

Chasnoff, Deborah, and Helen S. Cohen. 1998. *Homes & hands: Community land trusts in action.* Video produced for the Institute for Community Economics by Women's Educational Media, distributed by New Day Films, Hohokus, NJ.

Cirillo, Marie. 2001. Stories from an Appalachian community. Twentieth Annual E. F. Schumacher Lecture, presented at Salisbury, CT, October 2000.

Citizens' Housing and Planning Association. 1990. *Looking to the future: A report on mechanisms for preserving the long-term affordability of privately owned, publicly assisted housing in Massachusetts.* Boston: Citizens' Housing and Planning Association.

———. 2002. Alternative development and ownership models. In *Taking the initiative: A guidebook on creating local affordable housing strategies*, chapter 8. Boston: Citizens' Housing and Planning Association.

Cohen, Helen S. 1994. Diminishing returns: A critical look at subsidy recapture. In *The affordable city: Toward a third sector housing policy*, ed. J. E. Davis, 107–121. Philadelphia: Temple University Press.

Collins, Chuck, and Kirby White. 1994. Boston in the 1980s: Toward a social housing policy. In *The affordable city: Toward a third sector housing policy*, ed. J. E. Davis, 201–225. Philadelphia: Temple University Press.

Community Finance Solutions. 2008. *Placeshaping: A toolkit for urban community land trusts*. Salford, England: Community Finance Solutions at the University of Salford.

———. 2008. Ready to take over the land: Sponsored briefing on community land trusts. *New Start* (November 14):22–25.

———. 2008. *Then we'll do it ourselves: A report on the rural community land trusts part of the community land trust national demonstration programme*. Salford, England: University of Salford and Wessex Reinvestment Trust.

———. 2009. *Lessons from the first 150 homes: Evaluation of the national community land trust demonstration programme 2006–2008*. Salford, England: University of Salford.

Community Finance Solutions & New Economic Foundation. 2005. *Capturing value for rural communities: Community land trusts and sustainable rural communities*. Wetherby, England: Countryside Agency Publications.

Community Legal Resources. 2005. *Community land trusts: A primer for local officials*. Detroit, MI: Community Legal Resources, Community Land Trust Project. http://www.community-wealth.org/_pdfs/articles-publications/clts/paper-community.pdf.

Conaty, Pat, Johnston Birchall, Steve Bendle, and Rosemary Foggitt. 2003. *Common ground—for mutual home ownership: Community land trusts and shared-equity co-operatives to secure permanently affordable homes for key workers*. London: New Economics Foundation and CDS Co-operatives.

Corey, Jeff. 2009. Community land trust: A model for all markets? *Shelterforce* 31(3&4): 50–53.

Crabtree, Louise. 2008. *Models of perpetually affordable homeownership: Report and case studies from the United States of America*. Sydney, Australia: Urban Research Centre, University of Western Sydney.

———. 2008. The role of tenure, work and cooperativism in sustainable urban livelihoods. *ACME: An International E-Journal for Critical Geographies* 7(2):260–282.

Cramer, Reid. 2009. In pursuit of a responsible homeownership policy. *Shelterforce* 31(2): 22–25.

Crowe, Daniel. 2004. *Community land trusts & mutual housing models: A research report for the mayor of London*. London: GLA Housing and Homelessness Unit, Greater London Authority.

Curtin, Julie Farrell, and Lance Bocarsly. 2008. CLTs: A growing trend in affordable home ownership. *Journal of Affordable Housing and Community Development Law* 17(4):367–394.

Davis, John Emmeus. 1983. CLTs and the politics of ownership. *Community Economics* 2 (Fall).

————. 1984. Reallocating equity: A land trust model of land reform. In *Land reform, American style*, ed. Charles C. Geisler and Frank J. Popper, 209–232. Totowa, NJ: Rowman & Littlefield.

————. 1990. An interview with John Davis. *Community Economics* 21 (Fall).

————. 1991. *Contested ground: Collective action and the urban neighborhood.* Ithaca, NY: Cornell University Press.

————. 1994. *The affordable city: Toward a third sector housing policy.* Philadelphia: Temple University Press.

————. 2000. Homemaking: The pragmatic politics of third sector housing. In *Property and values*, ed. Charles Geisler and Gail Daneker, 233–258. Washington, DC: Island Press.

————. 2005. A primer on membership development for community land trusts. CLT Resource Center, www.burlingtonassociates.com.

————. 2006. Between devolution and the deep blue sea: What's a city or state to do? In *A Right to Housing*, ed. Rachael Bratt, Michael Stone, and Chester Hartman. Philadelphia: Temple University Press.

————. 2006. *Shared equity homeownership: The changing landscape of resale-restricted, owner-occupied housing.* Montclair, NJ: National Housing Institute.

————. 2006. Starting a community land trust: Organizational and operational choices. CLT Resource Center, www.burlingtonassociates.com.

————. 2007. Toward a common agenda: Growing shared equity housing. *Shelterforce* 29(1):26–27.

————. 2008. Homes that last: The case for counter-cyclical stewardship. *Shelterforce* 30(4):18–25.

————. 2009. Community land trusts: The developer that doesn't go away. *Around the House* 77 (June):7–9.

————. 2009. Shared equity homeownership: Designed to last. *Communities and Banking* 20(4).

————. 2010. More than money: What is shared in shared equity homeownership? *ABA Journal of Affordable Housing & Community Development Law* 19:2 (forthcoming).

Davis, John Emmeus, and Amy Demetrowitz. 2003. *Permanently affordable homeownership: Does the community land trust deliver on its promises?* Burlington, VT: Burlington Community Land Trust.

Davis, John Emmeus, and Charles C. Geisler. 1983. The role of alternative land institutions in employment and local economic development. Paper presented at the Annual Meeting of the Rural Sociological Society, Lexington, KY.

Davis, John Emmeus, and Rick Jacobus. 2008. *The city–CLT partnership: Municipal support for community land trusts.* Policy Focus Report. Cambridge, MA: Lincoln Institute of Land Policy.

Davis, John Emmeus, Tim McKenzie, and Diana Carminati. 1993. *Designing a home equity living plan for Madison, Wisconsin: A pre-feasibility study.* Madison, WI: Madison Area Community Land Trust and Independent Living, Inc.

Davis, John Emmeus, and Alice Stokes. 2009. *Lands in trust, homes that last: A performance evaluation of the Champlain Housing Trust.* Burlington, VT: Champlain Housing Trust.

Dayson Karl, Steve Bendle, and Bob Paterson. 2007. *Community land trusts: A practitioner's guide.* Salford, England: Community Finance Solutions.

DeFilippis, James. 2001. The myth of social capital in community development. *Housing Policy Debate* 12(4):781–806.

———. 2002. Equity vs. equity: Community control of land and housing in the United States. *Local Economy* 17(2):149–153.

———. 2004. *Unmaking Goliath: Community control in the face of global capital.* New York: Routledge.

Diacon, Richard Clarke, and Silvia Guimaraes. 2005. *Redefining the commons: Locking in value through community land trusts.* Coalville, Leicestershire, UK: Building and Social Housing Foundation.

Dwyer-Voss, Ron. 1997. Community land trusts: A flexible form of homeownership. *Pacific Mountain Review* 15(1):1–8.

Equity Trust. 2005. *Farmland and farmers for the future: Beyond conservation easements.* Video. Turners Falls, VT: Equity Trust, Inc.

Finkel, Ed. 2005. Affordable forever. *Planning* 71 (November):24–27.

Fireside, Daniel. 2005. Burlington busts the affordable housing debate. *Dollars & Sense* 258 (March/April):19–21, 28–29.

———. 2008. Community land trust keeps prices affordable—For now and forever. *Yes! Magazine*, no. 47 (Fall):28–32.

Foldy, Erica, and Jonathan Walters. 2004. *The power of balance: Lessons from Burlington community land trust.* New York: NY Research Center for Leadership in Action, Leadership for a Changing World, Wagner School, New York University.

Gauger, William R. 2006. *Is the community land trust the best model for achieving your organization's goals? Community land trust performance in different housing markets.* Report prepared for Community Legal Services, Detroit.

Geisler, Charles C. 1980. In land we trust. *Cornell Journal of Social Relations* 15(1):98–115.

Gent, Cathleen, William Sawyer, John Emmeus Davis, and Alison Weber. 2005. *Evaluating the benefits of living in the Burlington community land trust's rental housing and cooperative housing.* Burlington: Center for Rural Studies, University of Vermont.

Gottschalk, Shimon, and Robert S. Swann. 1970. Planning a rural new town in southwest Georgia. *Arete* (Journal of the Graduate School of Social Work, University of South Carolina) 2(1).

Gray, Jim. 2008. Shared equity gains acceptance in affordable multifamily development. *Commercial Mortgage Insight* (May).

Gray, Karen. 2008. Community land trusts in the United States. *Journal of Community Practice* 16(1):65–78.

Greenstein, Rosalind. 2007. Henry George and community land trusts. *The Housing Journal* (Delaware Housing Coalition, Winter/Spring):6.

Greenstein, Rosalind, and Yesim Sungu-Eryilmaz. 2005. Community land trusts: Leasing land for affordable housing. *Land Lines* 17(2):8–10.

———. 2007. Community land trusts: A solution for permanently affordable housing. *Land Lines* 19(1):8–13.

Gura, Jeanne Goldie. 2001. Preserving affordable homeownership opportunities in rapidly escalating real estate markets. *Journal of Affordable Housing and Community Development Law* 78 (Fall).

Harmon, Tasha R. 1992. *Affordable housing: The Vermont model.* Amherst: Center for Rural Massachusetts, University of Massachusetts.

———. 1998. Who pays the price for regional planning? How to link growth management and affordable housing. *Planners Network* 128 (March/April).

———. 2003. *Integrating social equity and growth management: Linking community land trusts and smart growth.* Springfield, MA: Institute for Community Economics.

Harper, David. 2007. Community land trusts: Saving the land to which we belong. *Exchange* (Newsletter of the National Land Trust Alliance, Summer):9–13.

Heartt, Sarah. 1980. Improving our use of the land: Thoughts of the Institute for Community Economics. *Living Alternatives Magazine* (February):43–46.

Herman, Kim. 2006. Community land trusts come of age. *Washington State Housing Finance Commission Executive Director's Newsletter* (April). www.wshfc.org/newsletter/.

Hetherington, Peter. 2009. Common ground. *The Guardian* (April 8).

Hicks, George L. 2001. *Experimental Americans: Celo and utopian community in the twentieth century.* Urbana: University of Illinois Press.

Institute for Community Economics. 1982. *The community land trust handbook.* Emmaus, PA: Rodale Press.

———. 1993. *Profiles of community land trusts.* Springfield, MA: Institute for Community Economics.

———. 2002. *Community land trust legal manual.* Springfield, MA: Institute for Community Economics.

International Independence Institute. 1972. *The community land trust: A guide to a new model for land tenure in America.* Cambridge, MA: Center for Community Economic Development.

Jacobus, Rick. 2001. Understanding subsidy retention. Flash animation available on line at: www.burlingtonassociates.com.

————. 2007. Resale formula comparison tool. Interactive spreadsheet available on line at CLT Resource Center: www.burlingtonassociates.com.

————. 2007. Shared equity, transformative wealth. Washington, DC: National Housing Council. www.nhc.org/pdf/chp_se_transwealth_0407.pdf.

————. 2007. Stewardship for lasting affordability: Administration and monitoring of shared equity homeownership. Paper presented at the NeighborWorks symposium Taking Shared Equity to Scale, Portland, OR, December 12.

Jacobus, Rick, and Michael Brown. 2007. City hall steps in. *Shelterforce* 24(1):12–15.

Jacobus, Rick, and Amy Cohen. Forthcoming. Creating permanently affordable homeownership through community land trusts. In *California affordable housing deskbook,* ed. Rob Weiner and Neal Richman. Point Arena, CA: Solano Press. Available on line at: http://www.rjacobus.com/resources/archives/homeownership/000049.html.

Jacobus, Rick, and Jeffrey Lubell. 2007. Shared equity homeownership: An effective strategy for balancing affordability and asset-building objectives. Policy brief prepared for the Center for Housing Policy, Washington, DC.

Jacobus, Rick, and Ryan Sherriff. 2009. *Balancing durable affordability and wealth creation: Responding to concerns about shared equity homeownership.* Prepared for the Annie E. Casey Foundation. Washington, DC: Center for Housing Policy.

Jacobus, Rick and John Emmeus Davis. 2010. *The asset building potential of shared equity homeownership.* Washington, DC: New America Foundation.

Jaffer, Murtaza. 2000. Expanding equity by limiting equity. In *Property and values,* ed. Charles Geisler and Gail Daneker, 175–188. Washington, DC: Island Press.

Keeley, Michael F., and Peter B. Manzo. 1992. Resale restrictions and leverage controls. *Journal of Affordable Housing & Community Development Law* 1(2):9–11.

Kelly, James J. Forthcoming. Homes affordable for good: Covenants and ground leases as long-term resale-restriction devices.

————. Forthcoming. Land trusts that conserve communities.

Krinsky, John, and Sarah Hovde. 1996. *Balancing acts: The experience of mutual housing associations and community land trusts in urban neighborhoods.* New York: Community Service Society of New York.

Kunz, Jonathan D. 1991. Forever housing: State support for community based permanently affordable housing in Connecticut. Unpublished MCP thesis, Department of Urban Studies and Planning, Massachusetts Institute of Technology.

Lauria, Mickey, and Erin Comstock. 2007. The effectiveness of community land trusts: An affordable homeownership comparison. Working paper WP07ML2. Cambridge, MA: Lincoln Institute of Land Policy.

Lederman, Jess. 1995. Pioneering new affordable strategies. *Mortgage Banking* (September):1–4.

Lehavi, Amnon. 2008. Mixing property. *Seton Hall Law Review* 38:137–212.

Lesser, Robert Charles, & Company. 2007. Measuring the market for shared equity housing. Paper prepared for the NeighborWorks symposium Taking Shared Equity to Scale, Portland, OR, December 12. www.nw.org/Network/training/documents/SymposiumTab2-MarketFULL.pdf.

Levinger, George. 2001. *Owning a community land trust home: A survey report on homeowner satisfaction.* Springfield, MA: Institute for Community Economics.

Libby, James M. 1990. The Vermont housing and conservation trust fund: A unique approach to affordable housing. *Clearinghouse Review* 23(10):1275–1284.

Libby, James M., and Darby Bradley. 2000. Vermont housing and conservation board: A conspiracy of good will among land trusts and housing trusts. In *Property and values,* ed. Charles Geisler and Gail Daneker, 261–281. Washington, DC: Island Press.

Lindsay, Vicki. 2001. Roots of the community land trust movement. www.burlingtonassociates.com.

Loomis, Mildred J. 1978. Ralph Borsodi's principles for homesteaders. *Land & Liberty* (November-December).

———. 2005. *Decentralism: Where it came from—Where is it going?* Black Rose Books, Ltd.

Lubell, Jeffrey M. 2005. *Strengthening the ladder for sustainable homeownership.* Washington, DC: National Housing Conference and Annie E. Casey Foundation.

———. 2007. Developing a policy framework for taking shared equity to scale. Paper presented at the NeighborWorks symposium Taking Shared Equity to Scale, Portland, OR, December 12.

Mahan, Leah, and Mark Lipman. 1996. *Holding ground: The rebirth of Dudley Street.* Video distributed by New Day Films, Hohokus, NJ, www.newday.com.

Mallach, Alan. 2005. *Building a better urban future: New directions for housing policies in weak market cities.* Montclair, NJ: National Housing Institute, Community Development Partners' Network, The Enterprise Foundation, and Local Initiatives Support Corporation.

———. 2008. How to spend $3.92 billion: Stabilizing neighborhoods by addressing foreclosed and abandoned properties. Discussion paper. Community Affairs Department, Federal Reserve Bank of Philadelphia, October.

Marcus, Beth Elyce. 1986. Resale restrictions: Designing an alternative pricing mechanism for below-market homeownership programs. Unpublished MCP thesis, Department of Urban Studies and Planning, Massachusetts Institute of Technology.

Marshall, Polly V., and Barbara E. Kautz. 2006. *Ensuring continued affordability in homeownership programs.* Sacramento, CA: Institute for Local Government.

Matthei, Chuck. 1981. Community land trusts as a resource for community economic development. In *Financing community economic development,* ed. Richard Schramm. Ithaca, NY: Program in Urban and Regional Studies, Cornell University.

————. 1992. U.S. land reform movements: The theory behind the practice. *Social Policy* (Spring):36–45.

————. 1993. The value of land in economics. *Sojourners* (November).

McClaughry, John. 1976. Farmers, freedom, and feudalism. *South Dakota Law Review* 21 (Summer).

McCulloch, Heather. 2001. *Sharing the wealth: Resident ownership mechanisms.* Oakland, CA: PolicyLink.

McKenzie, Tim. 2007. The case for plan B. *Shelterforce* 29(151):36–41.

Medoff, Peter, and Holly Sklar. 1994. *Streets of hope: The fall and rise of an urban neighborhood.* Boston: South End Press.

Meehan, James. 1996. Reinventing real estate: The community land trust and the social market in land. Unpublished PhD thesis, Graduate School of Arts and Sciences, Boston College.

Merkley, J. 1996. Discussion of issues associated with bringing housing into a land trust. Unpublished report of the Community Housing Land Trust Foundation of British Columbia, Vancouver.

Meyer, Diana, Jenifer Blake, Henrique Caine, and Beth Williams Pryor. 2000. Program profile: Dudley Street Neighborhood Initiative, Roxbury, Massachusetts. In *On the ground with comprehensive community initiatives*, 151–171. Columbia, MD: Enterprise Foundation.

Mintz-Roth, Jesse. 2008. *Long-term affordable housing strategies in hot housing markets.* Cambridge, MA: Joint Center for Housing Studies at Harvard University.

Morgan, Arthur E. 1942. *The small community.* Yellow Springs OH: Community Services.

NCB Capital Impact and NeighborWorks America. 2007. *A new way home: Sharing equity to build wealth.* Video. Hare in the Gate Productions. http://www.ncbcapitalimpact.org/default.aspx?id=534&terms=SHARING+EQUITY.

Newman, Judy. 2008. Balancing: Shared equity home ownership addresses affordable housing needs. *On Common Ground* (Winter):10–15.

Newport, Gus. 2005. The CLT model: A tool for permanently affordable housing and wealth generation. *Poverty & Race* (January/February). www.prrac.org/full_text.php?text_id=1022&item_id=9348&newsletter_id=79&header=Housing.

Nozick, Marcia. 1992. Attaining Community Control. In *No place like home: Building sustainable communities*, chapter 5. Ottawa: Canadian Council on Social Development.

OPAL Community Land Trust. 1999. *Of people and land: Telling our stories, building homes, creating community.* Eastsound, WA: Author.

Packnett, Dwan. 2005. The first homes community land trust. Working paper WP05DP. Cambridge, MA: Lincoln Institute of Land Policy.

Pastel, S. J. 1991. Community land trusts: A promising alternative for affordable housing. *Journal of Land Use and Environmental Law* 6:293–320.

Peterson, Tom. 1996. Community land trusts: An introduction. *Planning Commissioners Journal* 23 (Summer).

Pitcoff, Winton. 2002. Affordable forever: Land trusts keep housing within reach. *Shelterforce* 24(1):12–15.

Putnam, Robert D., Lewis M. Feldstein, and Don Cohen. 2003. Dudley Street Neighborhood Initiative. In *Better together: Restoring the American community,* 75–97. New York: Simon and Schuster.

Rioux, Gerald L., Rick Jacobus, and Steve Wertheim. 2005. *CLT financing in California: California housing finance agency.* Working paper #1. Springfield, MA: Institute for Community Economics.

Rioux, Gerald L., and Rick Jacobus. 2005. *CLT financing in California: California redevelopment law.* Working paper #2. Springfield, MA: Institute for Community Economics.

Rioux, Gerald L., and Rick Jacobus. 2005. *CLT financing in California: Inclusionary housing.* Working paper #3. Springfield, MA: Institute for Community Economics.

Robinson, Carla J. 2008. *Valuation and taxation of resale-restricted, owner-occupied housing.* Working paper (May). Cambridge, MA: Lincoln Institute of Land Policy.

Rose, Kalima. 2001. Beyond gentrification: Tools for equitable development. *Shelterforce* 23 (May/June):10–11.

Rose, Kalima, and Julie Silas. 2001. *Achieving equity through smart growth: Perspectives from philanthropy.* Oakland, CA: PolicyLink and the Funders' Network for Smart Growth and Livable Communities.

Roseland, Mark. 1992. Linking affordable housing and environmental protection: The community land trust as a sustainable urban development institution. *Canadian Journal of Urban Research* 1 (December):162–180.

Rosenberg, Greg. *Troy Gardens case study.* Madison, WI: Madison Area Community Land Trust. http://www.troygardens.net/.

Sacon, Neil. 1996. *Study of alternatives for preserving homeownership subsidies.* Report prepared for the Bureau of Housing and Community and Development, City of Portland. Portland, OR: Deloitte & Touche.

Salman, Nancy. 1987. *Resale strategies.* Report prepared for the Neighborhood Reinvestment Corporation, New England District. Boston: NRC.

Salsich, Peter W. 2000. Toward a property ethic of stewardship: A religious perspective. In *Property and values,* ed. Charles Geisler and Gail Daneker, 21–40. Washington, DC: Island Press.

Seeger, C. A. 1989. Note, the fixed price preemptive right in the community land trust lease: A valid response to the housing crisis or an invalid restraint on alienation? *Cardozo Law Review* 11:471–502.

Sherriff, Ryan. 2009. Affordable homeownership. *Urban Land* (September), 128–131.

Shlay, Anne B. 2006. Low-income homeownership: American dream or delusion? *Urban Studies* 43(3):511–531.

Shook, Jill Suzanne. 2007. HOME: Introduction to community land trusts. In *Making housing happen: Faith-based housing models*, 185–195. St. Louis, MO: Chalice Press.

Sklar, Holly. 2009. No foreclosures here. *Yes! Magazine* (Winter).

Soifer, Steven D. 1990. The Burlington community land trust: A socialist approach to affordable housing? *Journal of Urban Affairs* 12(3):237–252.

Stern, Jeff. 2007. Financing shared equity housing: An overview of tools, affordable stewardship entities, and lenders. Paper presented at the NeighborWorks symposium Taking Shared Equity to Scale, Portland, OR, December 12.

StipeMaas, Skipper G. 2005. Realizing the promise of manufactured homes in Georgia: A community land trust model. *Housing Facts and Findings* 7(4):5.

Stone, Michael. 1986. Homeownership without speculation. *Shelterforce* 9(4):12–14.

———. 1993. *Shelter poverty: New ideas on housing affordability.* Philadelphia: Temple University Press.

———. 2006. Social ownership. In *A right to housing*, ed. Rachael Bratt, Michael Stone, and Chester Hartman. Philadelphia: Temple University Press.

Swann, Robert. 1972. *Land, land trusts, and employment.* Great Barrington, MA: E. F. Schumacher Society. www.smallisbeautiful.org/clts/land_trusts_and_employment.htm.

———. 1973. Lifestyle interview: Bob Swann. *Lifestyle! A Magazine of Alternatives*, no. 5 (Summer).

———. 1978. *Land trusts as part of a threefold economic strategy for regional integration.* Great Barrington, MA: E. F. Schumacher Society. www.smallisbeautiful.org/clts/threefold_strategy.htm.

———. 1978. Ralph Borsodi (1886–1977): Prophet of decentralism. *Catholic Worker* (January).

———. 1992. Bob Swann: An interview. *Community Economics* 25 (Summer).

———. 2001. *Peace, civil rights, and the search for community: An autobiography*, esp. chapters 18–20. Great Barrington, MA: E. F. Schumacher Society. www.smallisbeautiful.org/about/biographies/swann_autobiography/swann_toc.html.

Tax Credit Advisor. 2006. Community land trusts may be source of housing deals for developers. October.

Topelson, Sara. 2009. Exitoso esquema de crédito para la vivienda. *El Economista* (October).

Tulloss, Janice K. 1998. Transforming urban regimes—A grassroots approach to comprehensive community development: The Dudley Street neighborhood initiative. http://comm-org.wisc.edu/papers98/tulloss.htm#landtrust. A previous version of this unpublished paper was delivered at the Annual Meeting of the American Political Science Association, San Francisco, August 31, 1996.

Turnbull, Shann. 2007. Affordable housing policy: Not identifiable with orthodox economic analysis. Working paper. Sydney, Australia: International Institute for Self-Governance.

U.S. Department of Housing and Urban Development. 1992. Community land trusts and the HOME Program. Notice from Community Planning and Development to CPD Regional and Field Office Directors (HUD 21B).

———. 1999. *Homeownership options under the HOME program: A model for publicly held properties and land trusts.* Washington, DC: Office of Affordable Housing Programs, Community Planning and Development.

Von Hassell, M. 1996. *Homesteading in New York City, 1978–1993: The divided heart of Loisaida.* Westport, CT: Bergin & Garvey.

Watson, Greg. 1997. The wisdom that builds community. Seventeenth Annual E. F. Schumacher Lecture, Williams College, Williamstown, MA.

Webster, Harriet. 2000. From hopeless to home run: How a community land trust transformed a neighborhood. *Planning* (December).

Weiss, Kelly. 2005. *The community land trust report: Creating permanent affordable homeownership opportunities in Austin, Texas.* Prepared for the Austin City Council by the Department of Neighborhood Housing and Community Development, Austin Housing Finance Corporation. www.community-wealth.org/_pdfs/articles-publications/clts/report-weiss.pdf.

White, Kirby, Jill Lemke, and Michael Lehman. 1999. Community land trusts and rural housing. In *Housing in rural America,* ed. Joseph N. Belden and Robert J. Wiener, 185–194. Thousand Oaks, CA: Sage Publications.

White, Kirby, and Charles Matthei. 1987. Community land trusts. In *Beyond the market and the state: New directions in community development,* ed. Severyn T. Bruyn and James Meehan, 41–64. Philadelphia: Temple University Press.

Williamson, Thad, David Imbroscio, and Gar Alperovitz. 2002. Community land trusts and community agriculture. In *Making a place for community,* 249–262. New York: Routledge.

Witt, Susan. 1985. Regional responsibility for farm land. *Newsletter of the E. F. Schumacher Society* (Spring).

Witt, Susan, and Jay Rossier. 2000. *A new lease on farmland: Assuring a future for farming in the Northeast,* rev. ed. Great Barrington, MA: E. F. Schumacher Society.

Witt, Susan, and Robert Swann. 2005. *Land: The challenge and the opportunity.* Great Barrington, MA: E. F. Schumacher Society.

ABOUT THE AUTHORS

David Abromowitz is a partner in the Boston law firm of Goulston & Storrs and a senior fellow at the Center for American Progress. He is a leading authority in the area of housing law and a former chair of the American Bar Association Forum on Affordable Housing and Community Development. He was the principal attorney for the Dudley Street Neighborhood Initiative, as it created its CLT subsidiary (Dudley Neighbors Inc.) and developed its first projects. He was the main legal advisor to the Institute for Community Economics in preparing both editions of *The CLT Legal Manual.* He has served on the board of Equity Trust since 1994.

Jennifer Aird is a research assistant at Community Finance Solutions, based at the University of Salford near Manchester, England. She has contributed to several CFS publications and is the author of "Lessons from the First 150 Homes: Evaluation of the National Community Land Trust Demonstration Programme 2006–2008." She maintains an online networking forum for CLTs in the UK and has coproduced a film on rural CLT projects.

Peter Barnes has started and run several socially responsible businesses, including Working Assets Long Distance, Working Assets Money Fund, and the Solar Center. He has served on the boards of the National Cooperative Bank and Greenpeace International. He has written for *Newsweek, The New Republic,* the *New York Times,* and other publications.

Lance Bocarsly is a partner in the Los Angeles office of Bocarsly, Emden, Cowan, Esmail & Arndt LLP. He is a real estate attorney specializing in affordable housing and community and economic development transactions. Bocarsly was on the Governing Committee of the American Bar Association's Forum on Affordable Housing and Community Development Law from 1994 through 2003 and served as the chair of the forum in 2001–2002.

Ralph Borsodi (1886–1977) was a writer, teacher, homesteader, and social philosopher. He published the first of his 13 books in 1928, decrying land speculation along lines similar to those of Henry George. He went further than George, however, in saying that land should never be individually owned. In 1936, he founded an intentional community on leased land in Suffern, New York, named the School of Living. He spent five years in India, teaching economics, examining the Gramdan Movement's village title to land, and writing *A Decentralist Manifesto.* In 1967 he founded the International Independence Institute, precursor to the Institute for Community Economics.

Michael Brown has worked with CLTs for nearly 30 years, getting his start with the Woodland Community Land Trust in Clairfield, Tennessee, where he served for five years as WCLT's executive director. He later became administrative director of the Institute for Community Economics (1985–1987). He joined Burlington Associates in Community Development as a partner in 1997, assisting with the development of new and mature CLTs across the United States. He is on the faculty of the National CLT Academy.

John Bryden is a research professor at the Norwegian Agricultural Economics Research Institute in Oslo, Norway. He is also an emeritus professor at the University of Aberdeen and former joint director of the Arkleton Institute for Rural Development Research and director of the Arkleton Trust. He was an external advisor to the Land Reform Policy Group in the Scottish office from 1997 to 1999.

Marcia Caton Campbell is Milwaukee program director at the Center for Resilient Cities. Prior to joining Resilient Cities, she was an assistant professor of urban and regional planning at the University of Wisconsin–Madison. She was a member of the board of the Madison Area Community Land Trust from 2004 to 2008, serving as the board's president from December 2006 to May 2008. She also served on the board of directors of Friends of Troy Gardens from 2001 through 2007.

Marie Cirillo is a community organizer in the coalfields of East Tennessee. She moved to Appalachia from Chicago in 1967, after she and 43 other women left the Glenmary Home Mission Sisters of America and formed the Federation of Communities in Service (FOCIS). In 1978, she started one of the first CLTs in the United States, the Woodland Community Land Trust. She was a contributing author to *The Community Land Trust Handbook* (1982) and has been on the board of the National CLT Network since its founding in 2006.

Helen S. Cohen is an award-winning filmmaker and working artist based in San Francisco. She coproduced with Debra Chasnoff the video *Homes & Hands: Community Land Trusts in Action*. Until the end of 2004, when she became an independent producer, Cohen was codirector of Women's Educational Media, now called Groundspark. She is a long-standing member of New Day Films, a national cooperative of independent filmmakers.

Louise Crabtree is the research program coordinator and a research fellow at the Urban Research Centre, University of Western Sydney. She has been studying CLTs since 1999 and is now spearheading an effort to establish the model Down Under. In 2008, after visiting CLTs in the United States, she reported her findings to the Australian Federal Senate. In 2009, she organized briefings for local, state, and federal officials and trainings for Australian housing professionals, introducing the CLT. She is helping to build a national network of individuals and organizations in Australia who are interested in the CLT.

Julie Farrell Curtin is an associate in the Bethesda, Maryland, office of Bocarsly, Emden, Cowan, Esmail & Arndt LLP. She practices general real estate law with an emphasis on affordable housing. She was formerly an Equal Justice Works fellow with the Community Economic Development Unit of the Legal Aid Foundation of Los Angeles and represented community-based groups implementing innovative housing models like the community land trust.

John Emmeus Davis has been involved with the CLT movement since 1980, when he joined the writing team for *The Community Land Trust Handbook* (1982). As a member of the technical assistance staff of the Institute for Community Economics from 1981 to 1985, he worked with many of the first urban CLTs in the United States, including those in Cincinnati and Burlington, Vermont. He was later employed for ten years as the City of Burlington's housing director. He coauthored the CLT definition that was enacted into U.S. federal law in 1992 and cofounded Burlington Associates in Community Development in 1993, a consulting cooperative that has assisted over 90 CLTs. An original member of the faculty and board of the National CLT Academy, he presently serves as the Academy's dean.

Daniel Fireside is the book editor for *Dollars & Sense* and a frequent contributor to the magazine. He has written recently about the impact of the foreclosure crisis on renters. He is a coauthor of several readers on the "real world" of microeconomics, macroeconomics, world banking and finance, and current economic and environmental issues.

Henry George (1839–1897) was a writer, lecturer, politician, land reformer, and political economist. His most famous work was *Progress and Poverty*, published in 1879. He proposed a "single tax," whereby the state would capture all gains in economic value accruing to land, but remove taxes on structural improvements and abolish all other taxes. He made six trips outside the United States between 1881 and 1890, lecturing in Ireland, England, Australia, and New Zealand. He was twice a candidate for the mayor of New York City.

Charles Geisler is a professor of development sociology at Cornell University. His writing and teaching focus on land tenure, property theory, social equity issues in conservation and protected areas, and innovative forms of land reform in the United States and abroad. He was a contributing author to *The Community Land Trust Handbook* (1982) and coeditor of *Land Reform, American Style* and *Property and Values*. He served on the boards of the Institute for Community Economics in the 1980s and Equity Trust in the 1990s.

Dennis Hardy is an historian and urban planner with previous experience in local government. He is Emeritus Professor of Urban Planning at Middlesex University, UK and is currently completing a book on Mediterranean cities.

Ebenezer Howard (1850–1928) wrote *Garden Cities of To-Morrow,* a seminal text in city planning. The sweeping solution that Howard proposed for the crowding and chaos of urban areas was the creation of planned communities of 32,000 people, ringing major cities and combining the best features of town and country. Inspired by Henry George, he wanted these Garden Cities to be developed on land that was leased from a municipal corporation in order to capture land gains for public improvement, instead of private enrichment. Eventually, 32 Garden Cities were developed in England, beginning with Letchworth in 1903.

Rick Jacobus joined Burlington Associates in Community Development as a partner in 2004, assisting in the development of CLTs and inclusionary housing programs on the West Coast. He was previously employed as a senior program officer for the Local Initiatives Support Corporation and as director of neighborhood economic development for the East Bay Asian Local Development Corporation in Oakland, California. He is currently leading a national initiative by NCB Capital Impact to bring shared equity homeownership to scale. He is a member of the faculty of the National CLT Academy.

James M. Libby, Jr. is general counsel for the Vermont Housing and Conservation Board. Formerly, he was the director of the Vermont Legal Housing and Community Development Law Project. An incorporator and former trustee of the Central Vermont Community Land Trust and the Vermont Community Loan Fund, he specializes in legal, organizational, and policy issues related to nonprofit development of affordable housing.

Mildred Loomis (1905–2000) was an author, educator, and social activist who was sometimes called the "grandmother of the counter culture." She settled at the School of Living in Suffern, New York, soon after this leased-land community was started by Ralph Borsodi. After teaching there for several years, she moved with her husband, John Loomis, to Brookville, Ohio. The School of Living was relocated to the Loomis homestead in 1945. Mildred Loomis became editor of the school's newsletter, *The Interpreter,* and was later made the school's dean. A collection of her essays, first published in 1980, was reprinted in 2005 under the title *Decentralism: Where It Came From—Where Is It Going?*

Chuck Matthei (1948–2002) was executive director of the Institute for Community Economics from 1980 to 1990. He crisscrossed the United States lecturing and consulting on community land trusts, socially responsible investment, land stewardship, affordable housing, and other economic issues. He convened the teams that produced *The Community Land Trust Handbook* (1982), the *Common Ground* slide show (1985), and the first edition of *The CLT Legal Manual* (1991). He also guided the development of many community loan funds and chaired the National Association of Community Development Loan Funds, an organization he helped to create. In 1991, he founded Equity Trust, Inc., and served as its executive director until his death.

Tim McKenzie was a cofounder and first executive director of the Burlington Community Land Trust, a position he held from 1984 to 1991. He later served short stints as executive director of the Jackson Hole Community Land Trust in Jackson, Wyoming, and as interim director of the Sawmill Community Land Trust in Albuquerque, New Mexico. He was a cofounder of Burlington Associates in Community Development, remaining a partner from 1993 to 2005.

Arthur E. Morgan (1878–1975) was an engineer, educator, author, and social philosopher. For 15 years, he served as president of Antioch College in Yellow Springs, Ohio. In 1933, he was appointed by President Franklin D. Roosevelt as one of three cochairmen of the Tennessee Valley Authority. After returning to Yellow Springs, he founded Community Service, Inc., in 1940, creating correspondence courses and publishing a national newsletter focused on revitalizing America's small communities. He helped to create planned communities on leased land in Tennessee and North Carolina, forerunners of the modern-day CLT.

David Morris is vice president and cofounder of the Institute for Local Self-Reliance, a nonprofit organization based in Minneapolis and Washington, DC, that promotes humanly scaled, environmentally sound economies and institutions. An economist by training, Morris is a syndicated columnist and author of numerous books and articles on rural communities, energy, and sustainability.

Greg Rosenberg served as executive director of the Madison Area Community Land Trust in Madison, Wisconsin from 2001 to 2010, where he initiated and managed all housing development, including MACLT's award-winning project, Troy Gardens. He was a member of the founding boards of both the National CLT Network and the National CLT Academy. He became the Academy's director in 2010.

Peter W. Salsich, Jr. is the McDonnell Professor of Justice in American Society at Saint Louis University School of Law. He has served as the editor of the *ABA Journal of Affordable Housing and Community Development Law* and was past chair of the ABA Commission on Homelessness and Poverty.

Danielle A. Salus is vice president of development at the Community Housing Development Corporation (CHDC) in Minneapolis. CHDC owns and operates over 3000 units of affordable rental housing in Minnesota, primarily in the Twin Cities Metro area.

Mark Shepard is a journalist specializing in Mahatma Gandhi and nonviolence. He is also a musician who plays flute, drums, and other instruments. After becoming involved in storytelling and theater around 1985, he began writing for children. He changed his name to Aaron Shepard and became an award-winning children's author. His work has been honored by the American Library Association, the National Council for the Social Studies, the American Folklore Society, the New York Public Library, and the Bank Street College of Education.

Charles Sherrod was a cofounder of New Communities, Inc., and served as president of its board from 1969 to 1985. He first came to Albany, Georgia, in 1961 as an organizer for the Student Nonviolent Coordinating Committee (SNCC). Soon after moving to Albany, he became part of the Albany Movement and helped to start the Southwest Georgia Project for Community Education. He led the latter organization for 26 years, agitating and organizing against segregated schools and other vestiges of Jim Crow. He has also served as chaplain at Georgia State Prison in Homerville, Georgia.

Anne B. Shlay is a professor of sociology, geography, and urban studies at Temple University. Her teaching and research are focused on urban domestic problems such as child care, housing, poverty and welfare reform, and discriminatory practices in the banking industry. She was formerly on the editorial board of *Housing Policy Debate* and served as the book review editor for *City and Community*.

Holly Sklar is the director of Business for Shared Prosperity, a network of business owners, executives, and investors who support public policies and business practices that expand economic opportunity, reduce inequality, and rebuild the nation's infrastructure. She is the author or coauthor of many magazine articles and several books, including *Streets of Hope: The Fall and Rise of an Urban Neighborhood,* describing the early years of the Dudley Street Neighborhood Initiative.

Robert Swann (1918–2003) was a pacifist, house designer, and land reformer. Exposed to the writings of Ralph Borsodi and Arthur Morgan while in prison for resisting induction into the armed forces during World War II, he developed a lifelong interest in rebuilding community through alternative models of local currency and land tenure. He was hired by Borsodi in 1967 as field director for the International Independence Institute. When Borsodi retired, Swann became the institute's executive director, later changing its name to the Institute for Community Economics. With three colleagues at the Institute, he coauthored *The Community Land Trust: Guide to a New Model for Land Tenure in America* (1972), drawing upon his experience in helping to plan New Communities, Inc., in southwest Georgia. He founded the E. F. Schumacher Society in 1980 and served as the organization's president until shortly before his death.

Kirby White has been involved with CLTs since the early 1980s, when he served as the editor of *The Community Land Trust Handbook* (1982) for the Institute for Community Economics. He went on to supervise the production of most of ICE's educational materials, including both editions of *The CLT Legal Manual,* the *Homes & Hands* video, and *Community Economics,* the periodical published by ICE from 1983 to 1996. He served two terms as ICE's director of technical assistance and later played the same role at Equity Trust. In 2002, he joined his wife, Nola White, and others in forming the Honduras Community Support Corporation to help mountain communities along the northern coast of Honduras near the Guatemalan border to acquire and steward lands surrounding local watersheds.

Henry Wiencek is an American historian who has written and edited more than a dozen books about architecture, the founding fathers, and various topics relating to slavery. His 1999 book, *The Hairstons: An American Family in Black and White,* won the National Book Critics Circle Award for Biography. In 2008, he was named the first Patrick Henry Fellow at Washington College.

INDEX

COMMENTARIES

We've recently seen an immensely damaging housing bubble that was built on speculation suddenly burst, with disastrous results not just for our national economy, but for individual homeowners and renters. Homes that are needed by working families are too often priced beyond their reach—or pried from their grasp—by dramatic rises and falls in real estate prices. *The Community Land Trust Reader* shows us there is a more equitable way of keeping land-based resources available, affordable, and secure for people who need them the most.

—Bernie Sanders
United States Senator
Washington, DC

Forty years ago, the Civil Rights movement in the South gave birth to the community land trust. The nation's first CLT, New Communities Inc., was created to help African American farmers and their families gain economic independence in a turbulent time. CLTs of today are still engaged in making land available for rural homesteads, but many more CLTs are now working in cities and suburbs, serving families in need of affordable housing and neighborhoods in need of revitalization. Having been a part of New Communities at the beginning, I always hoped for the day when CLTs might be implemented nationally. From what I see in *The Community Land Trust Reader,* it would seem that day has finally arrived.

—Mtamanika Youngblood
President/CEO
Sustainable Neighborhood Development Strategies, Inc.
Atlanta, Georgia

The community land trust is a practical, innovative model for affordable housing and community engagement with a potential applicability, as this book suggests, that is *worldwide*. An exemplary CLT in the United States, the Champlain Housing Trust, was selected as a 2008 winner of the World Habitat Award, receiving the Award at the United Nations global celebration of World Habitat Day. Global interest in the model has begun to grow.

—Diane Diacon
Director
Building and Social Housing Foundation
Leicestershire, United Kingdom

ABOUT THE LINCOLN INSTITUTE OF LAND POLICY

The Lincoln Institute of Land Policy is an independent, nonpartisan organization whose mission is to help solve global economic, social, and environmental challenges to improve the quality of life through creative approaches to the use, taxation, and stewardship of land. As a private operating foundation whose origins date to 1946, the Lincoln Institute seeks to inform public dialogue and decisions about land policy through research, training, and effective communication. By bringing together scholars, practitioners, public officials, policy makers, journalists, and involved citizens, the Lincoln Institute integrates theory and practice and provides a forum for multi-disciplinary perspectives on public policy concerning land, both in the United States and internationally.

LINCOLN INSTITUTE
OF LAND POLICY

113 Brattle Street
Cambridge, MA 02138-3400 USA

Phone: 1-617-661-3016 x127 or 1-800-526-3873
Fax: 1-617-661-7235 or 1-800-526-3944
E-mail: help@lincolninst.edu
Web: www.lincolninst.edu